World Literature in Theory

World Literature in Theory

Edited by

David Damrosch

WILEY Blackwell

This edition first published 2014
© 2014 John Wiley & Sons, Ltd

Registered Office
John Wiley & Sons, Ltd, The Atrium, Southern Gate, Chichester, West Sussex, PO19 8SQ, UK

Editorial Offices
350 Main Street, Malden, MA 02148-5020, USA
9600 Garsington Road, Oxford, OX4 2DQ, UK
The Atrium, Southern Gate, Chichester, West Sussex, PO19 8SQ, UK

For details of our global editorial offices, for customer services, and for information about how to apply for permission to reuse the copyright material in this book please see our website at www.wiley.com/wiley-blackwell.

Library of Congress Cataloging-in-Publication Data

World Literature in Theory / edited by David Damrosch.
    pages cm
  Includes bibliographical references and index.
  ISBN 978-1-118-40768-4 (hardback) – ISBN 978-1-118-40769-1 (paper)   1. Damrosch, David, editor of compilation.   2. Literature–Philosophy.
  PN45.W69 2014
  801–dc23
                                        2013033150
A catalogue record for this book is available from the British Library.

Cover design by Richard Boxall Design Associates

Set in 10.5/13pt Minion by SPi Publisher Services, Pondicherry, India

Printed in Malaysia by Ho Printing (M) Sdn Bhd

1   2014

Contents

Introduction: World Literature in Theory and Practice   1

Part One: Origins   13

1   Conversations with Eckermann on *Weltliteratur* (1827)   15
    Johann Wolfgang von Goethe

2   The Emergence of *Weltliteratur*: Goethe and
    the Romantic School (2006)   22
    John Pizer

3   Present Tasks of Comparative Literature (1877)   35
    Hugo Meltzl

4   What Is World Literature? (1886)   42
    Hutcheson Macaulay Posnett

5   World Literature (1907)   47
    Rabindranath Tagore

6   A View on the Unification of Literature (1922)   58
    Zheng Zhenduo

Part Two: World Literature in the Age of Globalization   69

7   Reflections on Yiddish World Literature (1938–1939)   71
    Melekh Ravitsh and Borekh Rivkin

8   Should We Rethink the Notion of World Literature? (1974)   85
    René Etiemble

9   Constructing Comparables (2000)   99
    Marcel Detienne

10 Traveling Theory (1982)   114
    Edward W. Said

11 Toward World Literary Knowledges: Theory in the Age
    of Globalization (2010)   134
    Revathi Krishnaswamy

12 Conjectures on World Literature (2000) *and* More
    Conjectures (2003)   159
    Franco Moretti

13 World Literature without a Hyphen: Towards a Typology
    of Literary Systems (2008)   180
    Alexander Beecroft

14 Literature as a World (2005)   192
    Pascale Casanova

15 Globalization and Cultural Diversity in the Book Market: The Case
    of Literary Translations in the US and in France (2010)   209
    Gisèle Sapiro

16 From Cultural Turn to Translational Turn: A Transnational
    Journey (2011)   234
    Susan Bassnett

Part Three: Debating World Literature   **247**

17 Stepping Forward and Back: Issues and Possibilities for
    "World" Poetry (2004)   249
    Stephen Owen

18 To World, to Globalize: World Literature's Crossroads (2004)   264
    Djelal Kadir

19 For a World-Literature in French (2007)   271
    Michel Le Bris et al.

20 For a Living and Popular Francophonie (2007)   276
    Nicolas Sarkozy

21 Francophonie and Universality: The Ideological Challenges
    of *Littérature-monde* (2009)   279
    Jacqueline Dutton

22 Universalisms and Francophonies (2009)   293
    Françoise Lionnet

23 Orientalism and the Institution of World Literatures (2010)   313
    Aamir R. Mufti

24 Against World Literature (2013)   345
    Emily Apter

25 Comparative Literature/World Literature: A Discussion (2011)   363
    Gayatri Chakravorty Spivak and David Damrosch

Part Four: World Literature in the World   **389**

26 The Argentine Writer and Tradition (1943)   391
    Jorge Luis Borges

27 Cultures and Contexts (2001)   398
    Tania Franco Carvalhal

28 An Idea of Literature: South Africa, India, the West (2001)   405
    Michael Chapman

29 The Deterritorialization of American Literature (2007)   416
    Paul Giles

30 Islamic Literary Networks in South and Southeast Asia (2010)   437
    Ronit Ricci

31 Rethinking the World in World Literature: East Asia
    and Literary Contact Nebulae (2009)   460
    Karen Laura Thornber

32 Global Cinema, World Cinema (2010)   480
    Denilson Lopes

33 The Strategy of Digital Modernism: Young-hae Chang
    Heavy Industries' *Dakota* (2008)   493
    Jessica Pressman

Epilogue: The Changing Concept of World Literature   513
Zhang Longxi

Index   524

Introduction

World Literature
in Theory and Practice

"The age of world literature is at hand," the 77-year-old Johann Wolfgang von Goethe proclaimed to his young disciple Eckermann in 1827, "and everyone must strive to hasten its approach." Were he to survey the scene today, Goethe would likely feel that his prophecy has come true, but he might wonder whether he'd gotten more than he'd bargained for. Goethe hoped that the age of world literature would be an era of international exchange and mutual refinement, a cosmopolitan process in which Germany would assume a central role as a translator and mediator among cultures, leading an international elite to champion lasting literary values against the vanities of narrow nationalism and the vagaries of popular taste. It is hard to imagine that he would have been pleased with the books recently on offer at the gift shop of Ho Chi Minh's Residence in Hanoi. There wasn't a copy of *Faust* or even Confucius's *Analects* in sight; in their place, a guide to the Residence in Chinese was sandwiched between two volumes in Vietnamese: a cartoon life of Abraham Lincoln, and a collection of children's stories, whose glossy cover boasted a leering Tigger and a roly-poly Pooh, taken from the Disney film. The Disneyfication of the globe was not exactly the future toward which Goethe wanted everyone to strive.

What are we to make of world literature today? The cultural and political realignments of the past two decades have opened the field of world literature to an unprecedented, even vertiginous variety of authors and countries. At once exhilarating and unsettling, the range and variety of literatures now in view raise serious questions of scale, of translation and comprehension, and of persisting imbalances of economic and cultural power. At the same time, the shifting landscape of world literature offers new opportunities for readers to encounter writers located well beyond the select few Western European countries whose works long dominated worldwide attention. Whereas in past eras works usually spread from imperial centers to peripheral

World Literature in Theory, First Edition. Edited by David Damrosch.
© 2014 John Wiley & Sons, Ltd. Published 2014 by John Wiley & Sons, Ltd.

regions (from China to Vietnam, from London to Australia and Kenya, from Paris to almost everywhere), an increasingly multipolar literary landscape allows writers from smaller countries to achieve rapid worldwide fame. While still in his fifties, Orhan Pamuk became the second-youngest recipient of the Nobel Prize for Literature and was translated into 56 languages, Vietnamese included; he has many more readers abroad than in his native Turkey. Increasingly complex patterns of travel, emigration, and publication make "national" languages and literatures more and more international in character. The winner of the Nobel Prize in 2000, Gao Xingjian, has long lived in France and has become a French citizen, yet he continues to write in Chinese. Cultural hybridity is also found within the borders of China itself, as in the stories of the Sino-Tibetan writer Tashi Dawa, who has blended elements drawn from Tibetan folklore and international magical realism for his writings in Chinese; in a very real sense, his works were participating in world literature even before they began to be translated and read abroad.

From China and Vietnam to Turkey and Brazil, scholars and teachers are thinking in new ways about how to explore and present the relations of the world's literatures. The gathering momentum of globalization has furthered both the contacts and the conflicts among peoples across the globe, and courses in world literature are rapidly expanding their purview beyond their traditional focus on Western Europe or on relations of a former colony and its onetime colonizer. Often relegated in the past to lower-level undergraduate curricula, world literature surveys and debates on world literature are now becoming an integral part of comparative literature curricula at all levels of undergraduate study and at the graduate level as well.

These developments raise serious theoretical and methodological questions. Considerable perplexities attend the rapid expansion of the purview of world literature, which encounters resistance today from two quite different perspectives: that a global study of world literature is impossible, and that it is all too easy. Scholars, teachers, and students of world literature must wrestle with problems of method, approach, and perspective. How can we gain an adequate grounding in more than one or two cultures? How do we make intelligent choices of what to read in those traditions? Once we have made our selection, how can we do more than skim the surface of complex works that we may need to read mostly in translation? How do we avoid projecting our home-culture values onto the wider world? How do we negotiate the uneven cultural, political, and economic landscape in which our texts circulate and in which we ourselves take part? Goethe's *Weltliteratur* has never managed to become a stable term (what literatures does it include? What views of the world?); how can we make sense of its multiplying avatars as *vishwa sahitya* in Bengali, *mirovaia literatura* in Russian, *dünya edebiyatı* in Turkish, and *shijie de wenxue* in Chinese?

The widened scope of world literature has important theoretical and methodological implications for the study of individual national traditions as well, and specialists in individual literatures are increasingly aware of the importance of considering their authors within frameworks and networks that often extend far beyond their homeland. These questions arise as much with the literature of earlier periods as with modern and contemporary writing, as world literature existed as a practice long before anyone thought of developing a theory or even a name for it. Historically, very few literatures have arisen in splendid isolation from the creative activity of people in the world beyond their home language and culture. The world's earliest writing systems, developed five thousand years ago by the Sumerians and the Egyptians, evolved in tandem and with relations of mutual influence, carried by traders back and forth between Babylonia and Egypt. Babylonia itself, home to the oldest body of poetic texts, was the site of a congeries of intersecting and competing languages, ethnicities, and cultures. The world's first known patron of literature, King Šulgi of Ur (r. 2094–2047 BCE), boasted of his fluency in five languages, asserting that, "In my palace no one in conversation switches to another language as quickly as I do."[1] Centuries later, newly arrived in Rome from North Africa via Athens, the satirist Apuleius of Madauros would compare his facility in switching from Greek to Latin to the skill of a circus rider jumping from one galloping horse to another. He promises his readers delight if they will attend to "a Greekish tale" (*fabulam Graecanicam*), "if only you will not begrudge looking at Egyptian papyrus inscribed with the sharpness of a reed from the Nile."[2]

Well before Apuleius's time, literary works had became commodities that could be carried in saddlebags and ships' holds, bought, sold, and traded; an international market was born, long before Goethe or Marx and Engels began to develop their theories about it. Similarities among Babylonian, Egyptian, and Hebrew wisdom traditions reflect ongoing literary exchanges between these disparate regions of the ancient Near East, and substantial poetic parallels extend from Mesopotamia eastward through Iran and into India and westward into Greece and Rome. The world's literatures have long been in contact through multiple routes of transmission and influence. Trade routes such as the Silk Road and the sea lanes of the Indian Ocean and the Mediterranean formed networks of transmission, powerfully seconded by the spread of Buddhism, Christianity, and Islam. These world religions brought a great deal of literary material in their wake, often introducing literacy itself to formerly oral cultures. The waxing and waning of empires gave further impetus to cross-cultural literary relations, sometimes suppressing local literary traditions and at other times stimulating them in new and creative ways.

The phenomenon of world literature is thus many centuries older than the national literatures that became the basis for most literary study during the past two centuries. Paradoxically, though, it was the rise of the modern nation-state that led to the elaboration of world literature as a concept – and as a problem. With literary production increasingly seen in national terms, scholars and creative writers began thinking directly about international literary relations, and this subject became central to the new discipline of Comparative Literature. Often such comparative study involved a discussion of two or three national traditions seen as relatively self-contained entities, rooted in a "national language" and engaged only in a modest degree of literary foreign trade, but other thinkers sought to move beyond the often nationalistic approach of such comparatists and began to elaborate ideas of "universal," "general," or world literature.

Moving beyond the nation, however, raised serious problems of language, since the emphasis on national literatures was closely linked to the uniqueness of "the national language" – usually just one per nation – and a widely shared belief that the national language was a privileged bearer of the national spirit. Thus the great philologist Jacob Grimm declared in his *Geschichte der deutschen Sprache* (1848):

> Since the close of the first century the weakness of the Roman Empire had become manifest (even though its flame still flickered from time to time), and among the unconquerable Germans the awareness of their unstoppable advance into every region of Europe had grown ever stronger. ... How else could it be, but that so forceful a mobilization of the people would stir up their language as well, shaking it out of its accustomed pathways and exalting it? Do not a certain courage and pride lie in the strengthening of voiced stop into voiceless stop, and voiceless stop into fricative?[3]

If language was the bearer of the unquenchable spirit of the nation, this spirit was most fully expressed in its literature, both in the refined language of great writers and also in the earthy wisdom of the people. Jacob Grimm is best known today for the collections of folktales that he assembled together with his brother Wilhelm, and language and literature together provided the basis for their fervent hope that the divided German territories could finally be united into a true nation. In the preface to his history of the German language, published in the revolutionary year 1848, Jacob waxed eloquent in evoking "the people's freedom, which nothing can hinder any longer, of which the very birds twitter on the rooftop. ... O, that it would come soon and never withdraw from us!" (1:iv–v).

The very intensity of hope placed upon language and literature raised new problems for the understanding of literature beyond the boundaries of the nation, even as it stimulated an ever-growing volume of translations from a growing number of countries. Goethe, who popularized the term "*Weltliteratur*" in German, was led to reflect on this concept while reading a Chinese novel in a week when he was also reading Persian and Serbian poetry, all in French or German translations, together with poems by Pierre Jean de Béranger in the original; he also took great pleasure in reading his own works in translation. Yet translation was also perceived as newly problematic by many, who doubted that the essence of a work, so intimately bound to race, nation, milieu, and above all to language, could ever be adequately conveyed in a foreign tongue. As Goethe's contemporary, J.G. Herder, remarked, even the tongue itself is subject to continual change:

> Poetry is a Proteus among the peoples; it changes form according to the peoples' language, customs, habits, according to their temperament, the climate, even according to their accent. As nations migrate, as languages mingle und change, as new matters stir men, as their inclinations take another direction and their endeavours another aim, as new models influence their composition of images and concepts, even as the tongue, this little limb, moves differently and the ear gets used to different sounds: thus the art of poetry changes not only among different nations, but also within one people.[4]

Both in Europe and beyond, the early theorists of world literature confronted the central issues still involved in today's debates. How should one conceive of the relations between national literatures and the broader frameworks of regional and world literature? To what extent were national and local literatures revivified, or threatened, by the influx of works flowing "downstream" from major metropolitan centers to smaller or peripheral cultures, and from world languages to local languages? Should the study of world literature seek to discover unities across the world's traditions, or are such cosmopolitan unities little more than projections of great-power values upon politically and economically subordinated cultures? Could literature legitimately live, and be studied, in translation, or only in the original languages? And what should be the purview of the overall concept of *Weltliteratur*, *littérature mondiale*, or *vishwa sahitya*: The sum of all the world's literatures? The smaller set of works that had achieved a readership abroad? Or a further subset of works, the few great classics of each culture? Or perhaps only the classics of ancient Greece and Rome and the major modern Western European powers? How far should oral and folk traditions be brought into the picture? What of popular literature in the nascent world of the bestseller? The 34 essays collected here, several translated for the first time into English, offer a wide range of classic essays and recent reflections on the theory and practice of world literature.

The first part of this volume, "Origins," brings together important statements on world literature from the 1820s through the 1920s, beginning with Goethe's seminal reflections on *Weltliteratur* in his conversations with Johann Peter Eckermann in the late 1820s. Goethe never devoted an extended exposition to his views, but his conversations with Eckermann give a vivid picture of the possibilities and the parameters of world literature as seen by a leading practitioner. This selection is followed by a selection from John Pizer's 2006 book *The Idea of World Literature*, which situates Goethe's idea in the context of eighteenth-century German Romanticism and traces its afterlife in Germany and beyond, including its appearance in the *Communist Manifesto*, where Marx and Engels cite world literature as an example of the growth of international exchange and the obsolescence of merely national markets.

A pair of essays follows giving prime examples of theoretical and methodological reflection by two pioneers of the academic study of comparative and world literature. Founder of the first scholarly journal in the field, the Transylvanian philologist Hugo Meltzl faced squarely the linguistic challenge of discussing literatures from around the world. Having assembled an editorial board of global reach, he established no fewer than ten "official languages" for his *Acta Comparationis Litterarum Universarum*, promoting "polyglottism" as the best check on a cosmopolitan leveling of the world's literatures under the aegis of a few hegemonic languages. Meltzl may well have been the first thinker ever to compare less commonly spoken languages to endangered species, threatened with extinction by nationalists and imperialists intent on promoting their national language in place of local or colonial languages.

A very different approach is pursued by Hutcheson Macaulay Posnett in the next selection, a chapter on world literature from his pioneering book *Comparative Literature* (1886). An Irish scholar who completed his book as he was about to leave

Dublin to take up a professorship in Auckland, New Zealand, Posnett gave extensive attention to work in translation from China, Japan, India, and the Middle East. Whereas Goethe thought of world literature as the product of a quintessentially modern mode of international exchange, Posnett argued that world literature first originated in the Hellenistic world, long predating the modern nation. Unlike Goethe, Posnett saw the emergence of world literature as a decidedly mixed blessing. Anticipating current critiques of "airport novels," Posnett argued that writers such as Apuleius had reached an empire-wide audience at the expense of a deep connection to their own culture, resulting in a deracinated mode of writing more suited to satire than to sincerity, though with Hellenistic writers showing a new appreciation both for the individual and for the wider natural world beyond their city walls.

Ideas of world literature spread far beyond Europe in the early decades of the twentieth century. "Origins" concludes with two path-breaking statements on world literature from very different locations. In his 1907 essay on *vishwa sahitya* or "world literature," Rabindranath Tagore speaks of the universal values that world literature can embody – an argument that served a strategic local purpose of its own, offering a counter to England's strategy of ruling its colonial possessions in India by dividing and conquering. Tagore's universalism had an outward as well as an inward-looking use; a few years after delivering his lecture, Tagore undertook the step of translating his book-length poem *Gitanjali* into English, a self-translation that led to his becoming the first Asian winner of the Nobel Prize in Literature in 1913.

Chinese intellectuals began discussing the idea as well in the years leading up to the New Culture Movement of 1915–21, in an outgrowth of their concern to modernize Chinese culture and strengthen the nation against the military, economic, and cultural incursions of the Western powers and of imperial Japan alike. Appropriately, the term "world literature" (*shijie de wenxue*) made an early appearance in Chinese in the first modern history of Chinese literature, the *History of Chinese Literature* by Huang Ren (1907). In that same year, the concept also appeared in the Chinese translation – from Japanese – of Marx and Engels' *Communist Manifesto*, in the form "*literature of the world*," adapted from the Japanese translation of *Weltliteratur*.[5] Seeking alternatives to classical literary forms inherited from the feudal era, reformists such as Lu Xun and Hu Shih increased the internationalization of Chinese literature, both through their own periods of travel and study abroad and through extensive projects of translation from Japanese and from several European languages. Given here is an important essay reflecting this ambitious cultural project, "A View on the Unification of Literature," by Zheng Zhenduo, who emphasizes the need to study literature beyond national and regional boundaries. For Zheng, the unification of literature becomes a means of strengthening the nation to resist less desirable modes of unification.

The second section of the volume takes up the status of world literature in the age of globalization. Though this process has accelerated in recent decades, it was already fully underway in the early decades of the twentieth century, when the growth of worldwide literary networks gave new impetus to reflection on the possibilities and the challenges for literary circulation on a worldwide scale. Globalization is often associated with the hegemony of a few major powers, but cultural production has never simply reflected great-power politics or economics, and widely dispersed communities and literary movements can share works around the world. Thus in the 1930s, writers in Yiddish journals both in Europe and in the United States discussed Yiddish writing as *velt-literatur*, composed by writers from Argentina and Mexico to Poland, Palestine, and China. This section begins with a pair of essays from the late 1930s reflecting on the worldwide spread of a diasporic literature whose writers sought to create a "quasi-territory" for their people in the absence of a physical nation.

The ensuing essays in this section reflect the full-blown globalization that took hold in the 1960s with the rapid growth of multinational corporations and the increasing internationalization of many forms of cultural production, including the book trade. Writing in 1974, René Etiemble urged his colleagues to look beyond the borders of national literature departments and area studies programs, and to reconceive of world literary studies in light of the realignments of the postwar world, and in particular the growing economic power and cultural influence of East Asia. Etiemble argued that a global approach is needed to keep us from projecting our own cultural values as false universals; genuine "invariants" across cultures can be discerned by direct study of the world's literatures. Very differently, in the 1980s the classicist Marcel Detienne began a two-decade-long collaborative project of studying ancient cultures, finding illuminating differences rather than universals; his essay reflects on the experience of "comparing the incomparable" – a salutary perspective for the study of contemporary literatures as well, as cultural differences have proven to persist and can even be heightened in the process of global contact and contestation.

The next two essays carry the discussion into the realm of literary theory. Edward Said's influential essay "Traveling Theory" extends reconsideration to the sphere of theory itself, considering the ways in which theories developed in a given historical and cultural context can't simply be "applied" elsewhere but need to be critically adapted to new contexts. While Said's concern was principally with the foreign travels of Western theory in a postcolonial world, Revathi Krishnaswamy proposes a decolonization of theory itself, through a new attention to local knowledges and the theories derivable from different literary traditions.

A series of essays follow that consider world literature from systemic perspectives. First comes a pair of widely debated essays by Franco Moretti, who draws both on Darwinian evolutionary theory and on the world systems theory of Immanuel Wallerstein to explore the global circulation and reinvention of the novel. Moretti's project is at once political – studying a global system that he sees as "one, but unequal" – and methodological: the vast scale of world literature, he argues, can't be comprehended through the close reading of a minute fraction of the world's literary production, but requires data-driven practices of "distant reading." Building on and revising the work of Moretti and of Wallerstein, Alexander Beecroft's "World Literature without a Hyphen" proposes a multilayered "typology of literary systems" that would open out the singular quality of a world literature seen as a unified (even if unequal) system; Beecroft outlines six different systemic modes that collectively can encompass literary relations from antiquity to the present.

The next two essays, by Pascale Casanova and Gisèle Sapiro, build on the influential work of Pierre Bourdieu in the field of cultural production, extending his discussion from France to a global scale. Like Moretti, Casanova sees world literature as a space of cultural contestation, marked by inequalities between dominant and dominated cultures, but she argues as well for the need to combine intrinsic as well as extrinsic criticism, moving in this way beyond the strongly structural emphasis of Bourdieu to find a place for close textual analysis. Where Casanova concentrates on writers' struggles to make their place in the international literary field, Sapiro turns to a further stage of the process, the circulation of works in translation, proposing a variety of strategies for analyzing the internationalization of the literary market.

In this section's concluding essay, the leading translation theorist Susan Bassnett discusses the literary market from the point of view of the translator, understood less as an isolated practitioner than as the participant in a market over which the translator has limited but still significant influence. She extends her discussion methodologically as well, calling for translation studies as a field to engage more fully with global frameworks and processes.

If the spread of globalization in the postwar decades gave new impetus to studying world literature, the new developments in the field have also stirred up heightened debate over the problems that attend any attempt to study literature beyond a given nation, language, or region. The third part of this collection features examples of the lively and sometimes sharp critiques that world literary studies have provoked since the turn of the millennium. First is a 2004 essay on the contested subject of "world poetry" by the Sinologist and comparatist Stephen Owen, itself a nuanced response to critiques of a prior essay, "What Is World Poetry?" (1990), which took a generally negative view of poetry written for worldwide circulation. In his newer essay, Owen discusses the challenges of understanding and assessing works once they circulate beyond the institutional networks that canonize works within a national tradition, and he argues for a greater awareness of the varieties of poetry both within and beyond the ambit of world literature. Bringing the institutional critique of world literature home to the critic, Djelal Kadir cautions students and scholars of world literature to be attentive to their own positionality, especially when bringing non-Western works into the realm of a hegemonic power such as the United States, as even progressive scholars can end up participating in a neo-imperial process of assimilation and self-legitimation.

The legacy of imperialism in world literary studies has nowhere been more directly debated than in France, the longtime center of its own empire and also a prime arbiter of cultural value more generally, whether as "the capital of the nineteenth century," in Walter Benjamin's famous phrase, or, more recently, as home to an influential network of publishing houses, translators, and literary reviews. Presented here is a controversial manifesto, "For a World-Literature in French," published in 2007 in the Paris journal *Le Monde* by a group of writers predominantly from France's former colonies, who argued that a distinction could no longer be maintained between "French" literature (often used only for the literature produced within France itself) and the "francophone" literature of France's former colonies. Next comes a pointed response in favor of maintaining the concept of francophonie, written by the conservative politician Nicolas Sarkozy, then running for election as President of the Republic – surely the first time in which debates over world literature have figured in a national political campaign. Two discussions of this debate follow: first, an essay by Jacqueline Dutton contextualizing the manifesto and arguing that it was less radical than its signers supposed, still bound up with the neocolonial hegemony of French; second, an essay by Françoise Lionnet, who argues for an opening up of a pluralized idea of "francophonies" better integrated with the variety of the world's cultures and literatures.

The final three selections in "Debating World Literature" discuss the politics of world literary studies in the United States, where world literature can become the province of a well-meaning but culturally ungrounded liberal multiculturalism, often taught in English departments with little reference to source languages and giving little attention to the cultural politics of translation and assimilation. Aamir Mufti's "Orientalism and the Institution of World Literatures" argues that American world literary studies too often presuppose a transparent world of free communication and international exchange, while Emily Apter's "Against World Literature" presses the question of language, arguing that world literary studies usually assume a linguistic transparency and easy translatability; building on the work of Jacques Derrida, she advocates a world literature fully alive to the irreducible alterity of language. Finally, a debate between Gayatri Spivak and the present editor at the 2011 annual meeting of the American Comparative Literature Association seeks to clarify common ground and to assess persisting differences between current views on the politics of language and culture in world literary studies today.

Theorists of world literature from Meltzl and Posnett to Lionnet and Apter have emphasized the multiplicity of the phenomena grouped under the overall rubric of world literature. It can be said that world literature and national literature display a kind of figure-ground reversal: while in one sense world literature is the broad framework within which individual literatures are formed, it is equally true that for any given reader, world literature exists first and foremost *within* a national or local context. In this sense, world literature is experienced less as an ideal order than as what is translated and published, assigned in schools, and sold in a country's bookstores. The fourth and final section of this collection presents a series of studies of world literature in some of its various manifestations around the world.

The section begins with Jorge Luis Borges's assessment of "The Argentine Writer and Tradition," which opposed provincialism (and the jingoistic Argentine nationalism of his day) by arguing that a writer becomes most authentic, even most authentically regional, when participating in the broader tradition of world literature. The Brazilian comparatist Tania Carvalhal's "Cultures and Contexts" gives a case in point, looking at ways in which Brazilian modernists creatively adapted transnational works of the European avant-garde for very local purposes. Two works follow on aspects of global English, often seen today as the leading edge of a leveling Americanization of culture. In these essays, however, South African comparatist Michael Chapman sees a far more recursive relation between metropolitan and peripheral Englishes and literatures, while the British Americanist Paul Giles builds on the work of Gilles Deleuze and Félix Guattari to reread American literary history in worldly terms, finding it already deterritorialized as early as the heyday of nationalism in the mid-nineteenth century.

Two essays then situate world literature in different Asian locations. Looking at early translations of an Arabic conversation narrative, Ronit Ricci unfolds the presence of early Islamic networks in South and Southeast Asia – a literary network of global reach a thousand years ago. Turning to the twentieth century, Karen Thornber discusses the complex circulation of literature in "contact nebulae" (more shifting and varied than "contact zones") formed between Japan, Korea, mainland China, and Taiwan.

The final essays in the section move from printed literature to newer media. Denilson Lopes looks at world cinema in relation to current theories of world literature, with particular attention to Brazil, while Jessica Pressman studies the heritage of Euro-American modernism in the Internet narratives of the Korean/American duo known as Young-hae Chang Heavy Industries. Whereas Moretti and others have debated close versus distant reading, Pressman compares the slow reading required by poets such as Ezra Pound with the very different intensity of rapid reading demanded by Young-hae Chang Heavy Industries' sped-up, flickering Internet texts. The volume concludes with an epilogue by Zhang Longxi, of City University, Hong Kong, who reflects on the preceding essays from what might be called a post-postcolonial perspective, arguing for the importance of adapting older and newer ideas of world literature to a multipolar literary world today.

In many ways, today's debates on world literature come full circle back to the terms inaugurated by Goethe and the other early exponents of world literature presented in the opening section of this volume. To return for a moment to the beginning of this introduction, some further words may be in order about the book display in the Ho Chi Minh Residence's gift shop. Though one of the books nestled next to Uncle Ho featured an image of Tigger and Pooh, it was actually a collection of Vietnamese folktales. Far from representing a suppression of local content, the Disney image was simply being used to draw young Vietnamese readers into a collection of their own culture's productions. The biography of Lincoln was appropriate in its own way. Ho Chi Minh was an admirer of America's struggles for freedom from British colonial domination, and, during the Vietnam War, various North Vietnamese commentators compared their north–south conflict to the American Civil War; thus the American example aided Ho in resisting French imperialism and then the incursions of America itself. Moreover, the Lincoln bio-comic in the bookshop wasn't an American product at all, but instead illustrates the regional circulation of literature throughout East Asia: it was a Vietnamese translation of a Korean life of Lincoln, composed in the form of a Japanese manga.

Ho Chi Minh's presence at the center of this grouping is a logical outcome of the globalizing literary processes in which Ho actively participated during his lifetime.

The book about him was a guide for Chinese visitors to the site; its cover showed him writing away, not working indoors in his austere office but sitting in a bamboo chair out in his garden, much as a classical Chinese poet might have done. He might, indeed, have been writing a poem at that very moment. Living on the cusp of a shift from the older East Asian literary world to the new global stage of his revolutionary activism, Ho composed poetry in classical Chinese when he wasn't writing speeches in Vietnamese for local consumption and essays in French for dissemination in the anti-imperial struggle in Europe. Appropriately, this book was published by the Gioi Xuat Ban Xa, the "World Publishing House."

The essays in this volume offer many approaches to the study of world literature in theory and in practice. Together, they can help us make sense of the full sweep of world literature from Weimar to Hanoi, from *Faust* to Hollywood films, and from the Babylonian court of Šulgi in the twenty-first century BCE to the global Babel of our own twenty-first century today.

Notes

1 "Šulgi B," line 220. Available online at the Electronic Text Corpus of Sumerian Literature: http://etcsl.orinst.ox.ac.uk/.
2 Apuleius, *Metamorphoses*, ed. and tr. J. Arthur Hanson. Loeb Classical Library 44 (Cambridge, MA and London: Harvard University Press. 2 vols., 1989); 1:3–5.
3 Jacob Grimm, *Geschichte der deutschen Sprache* (Leipzig, 4th ed., 2 vols., 1880), 1:306–7.
4 J.G. Herder, *Briefe zu Beförderung der Humanität*, ed. Hans Dietrich Irmscher. In *Werke*, ed. Martin Bollacher *et al.* (Frankfurt am Main: Deutscher Klassiker Verlag, 1991), 7:572.
5 See Jing Tsu, "Getting Ideas about World Literature in China," *Comparative Literature Studies* 47.3 (2010), 290–317.

Part One
Origins

1

Conversations with Eckermann on *Weltliteratur* (1827)

Johann Wolfgang von Goethe

Though the term "Weltliteratur" had been coined some decades before Goethe took it up in the 1820s, it was his embrace of the concept that first brought it into general currency. Although he never developed a full-scale theoretical essay on the topic, he highlighted the idea in several essays during the decade, and he had himself long participated in the practice of literature on a world scale, both as a reader of several languages and as a writer. His multifaceted personality was described by his secretary and disciple Johann Peter Eckermann as "a many-sided diamond, which in each direction shines with a different hue," and his personal capacious variability informed his views on literature's ability to cross genres, cultures, and political borders. Writing in a Germany still divided into small principalities, Goethe cast his net far more widely. He moved from Roman models for his early erotic poetry (*Römische Elegien*, 1798) to the Persian poetry of Hafiz (*West-östlicher Divan*, 1819), while his admiration both for Greek tragedy and for classical Sanskrit theater helped make *Faust* one of the major works of world literature. To Goethe, Kalidasa's play *Shakuntala* held the world itself in a nutshell and was seminal for literatures abroad: "Would you grasp the earth and heaven itself in one sole name? / I name you, O Shakuntala! and everything is said."

Goethe's ideas of a world literature have come down to us first and foremost through Eckermann's posthumous portrait of his master, first published in 1837 under the title *Gespräche mit Goethe in den letzten Jahren seines Lebens* (Conversations with Goethe in the Final Years of His Life). In the selections included here, Goethe discusses Chinese, French, Greek, Serbian, and Persian literature in

Johann Wolfgang von Goethe, Conversations with Eckermann on *Weltliteratur* (1827). Reprinted (with some alterations) from Johann Wolfgang von Goethe, *Conversations with Eckermann 1823–1832*, trans. John Oxenford (1850) (London: Everyman, 1930).

World Literature in Theory, First Edition. Edited by David Damrosch.

world circulation through translation, emphasizing the authors' similarities and affinities rather than their disjunctions and asymmetries. Goethe could thus assert in a prophetic tone that "the epoch of world literature is at hand, and each of us must work to hasten its approach."

Thursday, January 25, 1827.

At seven o'clock I went with the manuscript of the novel and a copy of Béranger to Goethe. I found M. Soret in conversation with him upon modern French literature. I listened with interest, and it was observed that the modern writers had learned a great deal from De Lille, as far as good versification was concerned. Since M. Soret, a native of Geneva, did not speak German fluently, while Goethe talks French tolerably well, the conversation was carried on in French, and only became German when I put in a word. I took my Béranger[1] out of my pocket, and gave it to Goethe, who wished to read his admirable songs again. M. Soret thought the portrait prefixed to the poems was not a good likeness. Goethe was much pleased to have this beautiful copy in his hands.

"These songs," said he, "may be looked upon as perfect, the best things in their kind – especially when you observe the refrain; without which they would be almost too earnest, too pointed, and too epigrammatic, for songs. Béranger reminds me ever of Horace and Hafiz; who stood in the same way above their times, satirically and playfully setting forth the corruption of manners. Béranger has the same relation to his contemporaries; but, as he belongs to the lower class, the licentious and vulgar are not very hateful to him, and he treats them with a sort of partiality."

Many similar remarks were made upon Béranger and other modern French writers; till M. Soret went to court, and I remained alone with Goethe.

A sealed packet lay upon the table. Goethe laid his hand upon it. "This," said he, "is *Helena*,[2] which is going to Cotta to be printed."

I felt the importance of the moment. For, as it is with a newly-built vessel on its first going to sea, whose destiny is hid from us, so is it with the intellectual creation of a great master, going forth into the world.

"I have till now," said Goethe, "been always finding little things to add or to touch up; but I must finish, and I am glad it is going to the post, so that I can turn to something else. Let it meet its fate. My comfort is, the general culture of Germany stands at an incredibly high point; so I need not fear such a production will long remain misunderstood and without effect."

"There is a whole antiquity in it," said I.

"Yes," said Goethe, "the philologists will find work."

"I have no fear," said I, "about the antique part; for there we have the most minute detail, the most thorough development of individuals, and each personage says just what he should. But the modern romantic part is very difficult, for half the history of the world lies behind it; the material is so rich that it can only be lightly indicated, and heavy demands are made upon the reader."

"Yet," said Goethe, "it all appeals to the senses, and on the stage would satisfy the eye: more I did not intend. Let the crowd of spectators take pleasure in the spectacle; the higher import will not escape the initiated – as with the *Magic Flute* and other things."

"It will produce a most unusual effect on the stage," said I, "that a piece should begin as a tragedy and end as an opera. But something is required to represent the grandeur of these persons, and to speak the sublime language and verse."

"The first part," said Goethe, "requires the best tragic artists; and the operatic part must be sustained by the best vocalists, male and female. That of Helena ought to be played, not by one, but by two great female artists; for we seldom find that a fine vocalist has sufficient talent as a tragic actress."

"The whole," said I, "will furnish an occasion for great splendour of scenery and costume. I look forward to its representation. If we could only get a good composer."

"It should be one," said Goethe, "who, like Meyerbeer, has lived long in Italy, so that he combines his German nature with the Italian style and manner. However, that will be found somehow or other; I only rejoice that I am rid of it. Of the notion that the chorus does not descend into the lower world, but instead disperses itself among the elements on the cheerful surface of the earth, I am not a little proud."

"It is a new sort of immortality," said I.

"Now," continued Goethe, "how do you go on with the novel?"

"I have brought it with me," said I. "After reading it again, I find that your excellency must not make the intended alteration. It produces a good effect that the people first appear by the slain tiger as completely new beings, with their outlandish costume and manners, and announce themselves as the owners of the beasts. If you made them first appear in the introduction, this effect would be completely weakened, if not destroyed."

"You are right," said Goethe; "I must leave it as it is. It must have been my design, when first I planned the tale, not to bring the people in sooner. The intended alteration was a requisition on the part of the understanding, which would certainly have led me into a fault. This is a remarkable case in aesthetics, that a rule must be departed from if faults are to be avoided."

We talked over the naming of the novel. Many titles were proposed; some suited the beginning, others the end – but none seemed exactly suitable to the whole.

"I'll tell you what," said Goethe, "we will call it *The Novel* [Die Novelle]; for what is a novel but a peculiar and as yet unheard-of event? This is the proper meaning of this name; and many a thing that in Germany passes as a novel is no novel at all, but a mere narrative or whatever else you like to call it. In that original sense of an unheard-of event, even the *Wahlverwandtschaften*[3] may be called a 'novel.'"

"A poem," said I, "has always originated without a title, and is that which it is without a title; so the title is not really essential to the matter."

"It is not," said Goethe; "the ancient poems had no titles; but this is a custom of the moderns, from whom also the poems of the ancients obtained titles at a later period. This custom is the result of a necessity to name things and to distinguish them from each other, when a literature becomes extensive. Here you have something new; – read it."

He handed to me a translation by Herr Gerhard of a Serbian poem. It was very beautiful, and the translation so simple and clear that there was no disturbance in the contemplation of the object. It was entitled *The Prison-Key*. I say nothing of the course of the action, except that the conclusion seemed to me abrupt and rather unsatisfactory.

"That," said Goethe, "is the beauty of it; for it thus leaves a sting in the heart, and the imagination of the reader is excited to devise every possible case that can follow. The conclusion leaves untold the material for a whole tragedy, but of a kind that has often been done already. On the contrary, that which is set forth in the poem is really new and beautiful; and the poet acted very wisely in delineating this alone and leaving the rest to the reader. I would willingly insert the poem in *Kunst und Alterthum*,[4] but it is too long: on the other hand, I have asked Herr Gerhard to give me these three in rhyme, which I shall print in the next number. What do you say to this? Only listen."

Goethe read first the song of the old man who loves a young maiden, then the women's drinking song, and finally that animated one beginning "Dance for us, Theodore." He read them admirably, each in a different tone and manner.

We praised Herr Gerhard for having in each instance chosen the most appropriate versification and refrain, and for having executed all in such an easy and perfect manner. "There you see," said Goethe, "what technical practice does for such a talent as Gerhard's; and it is fortunate for him that he has no actual literary profession, but one that daily takes him into practical life. He has, moreover, travelled much in England and other countries; and thus, with his sense for the actual, he has many advantages over our learned young poets.

"If he confines himself to making good translations, he is not likely to produce anything bad; but original inventions demand a great deal, and are difficult matters."

Some reflections were here made upon the productions of our newest young poets, and it was remarked that scarce one of them had come out with good prose. "That is very easily explained," said Goethe: "to write prose, one must have something to say; but he who has nothing to say can still make verses and rhymes, where one word suggests the other, and at last something comes out which in fact is nothing but looks as if it were something."

Wednesday, January 31, 1827.

Dined with Goethe. "Within the last few days, since I saw you," said he, "I have read many things; especially a Chinese novel, which occupies me still and seems to me very remarkable."

"Chinese novel!" said I; "that must look strange enough."

"Not so much as you might think," said Goethe; "the Chinese think, act, and feel almost exactly like us; and we soon find that we are perfectly like them, except that all they do is more clear, pure, and decorous, than with us.

"With them all is orderly, citizen-like, without great passion or poetic flight; and there is a strong resemblance to my *Hermann and Dorothea*, as well as to the English novels of Richardson. They likewise differ from us in that with them external nature is always associated with the human figures. You always hear the goldfish splashing in the pond, the birds are always singing on the bough; the day is always serene and sunny, the night is always clear. There is much talk about the moon; but it does not alter the landscape, its light is conceived to be as bright as day itself; and the interior of the houses is as neat and elegant as their pictures. For instance, 'I heard the lovely girls laughing, and when I got sight of them they were sitting on cane chairs.' There you have, at once, the prettiest situation; for cane chairs are necessarily associated with the greatest lightness and elegance. Then there is an infinite number of legends which are constantly introduced into the narrative and are applied almost like proverbs: as, for instance, one of a girl who was so light and graceful in the feet that she could balance herself on a flower without breaking it; and then another, of a young man so virtuous and brave that in his thirtieth year he had the honour to talk with the Emperor; then there is another of two lovers who showed such great purity during a long acquaintance that, when they were on one occasion obliged to pass the night in the same chamber, they occupied the time with conversation and did not approach one another.

"There are innumerable other legends, all turning upon what is moral and proper. It is by this severe moderation in everything that the Chinese Empire has sustained itself for thousands of years, and will endure hereafter.

"I find a highly remarkable contrast to this Chinese novel in the *Chansons de Béranger*, which have, almost every one, some immoral licentious subject for their foundation, and which would be extremely odious to me if managed by a genius inferior to Béranger; he, however, has made them not only tolerable, but pleasing. Tell me yourself, is it not remarkable that the subjects of the Chinese poet should be so thoroughly moral, and those of the first French poet of the present day be exactly the contrary?"

"Such a talent as Béranger's," said I, "would find no field in moral subjects."

"You are right," said Goethe: "the very perversions of his time have revealed and developed his better nature."

"But," said I, "is this Chinese romance one of their best?"

"By no means," said Goethe; "the Chinese have thousands of them, and had when our forefathers were still living in the woods.

"I am more and more convinced," he continued, "that poetry is the universal possession of mankind, revealing itself everywhere and at all times in hundreds and hundreds of men. One makes it a little better than another, and swims on the surface a little longer than another – that is all. Herr von Matthisson[5] must not think he is the man, nor must I think that I am the man; but each must say to himself, that the gift of poetry is by no means so very rare, and that nobody need think very much of himself because he has written a good poem.

"But, really, we Germans are very likely to fall too easily into this pedantic conceit, when we do not look beyond the narrow circle that surrounds us. I therefore like to look about me in foreign nations, and advise everyone to do the same. National literature is now rather an unmeaning term; the epoch of World-literature is at hand,

and everyone must strive to hasten its approach. But, while we thus value what is foreign, we must not bind ourselves to some particular thing, and regard it as a model. We must not give this value to the Chinese, or the Serbian, or Calderon, or the *Nibelungen*; but, if we really want a pattern, we must always return to the ancient Greeks, in whose works the beauty of mankind is constantly represented. All the rest we must look at only historically; appropriating to ourselves what is good, so far as it goes."

The bells of passing sledges allured us to the window, as we expected that the long procession which went out to Belvidere this morning would return about this time.

We talked of Alexander Manzoni[6]; and Goethe told me that Count Reinhard not long since saw Manzoni at Paris – where, as a young author of celebrity, he had been well received in society – and that he was now living happily on his estate in the neighbourhood of Milan, with a young family and his mother.

"Manzoni," continued he, "lacks nothing except to know what a good poet he is, and what rights belong to him as such. He has too much respect for history, and on this account is always adding notes to his pieces, in which he shows how faithful he has been to detail. Now, though his facts may be historical, his characters are not so – any more than my Thais and Iphigenia. No poet has ever known the historical characters he has painted; if he had, he could scarcely have made use of them. The poet must know what effects he wishes to produce, and regulate the nature of his characters accordingly. If I had tried to make Egmont[7] as history represents him, the father of a dozen children, his light-minded proceedings would have appeared very absurd. I needed an Egmont more in harmony with his own actions and my poetic views; and this is, as Clara says, *my* Egmont.

"What would be the use of poets, if they only repeated the record of the historian? The poet must go further, and give us if possible something higher and better. All the characters of Sophocles bear something of that great poet's lofty soul; and it is the same with the characters of Shakespeare. This is as it ought to be. Nay, Shakespeare goes further, and makes his Romans Englishmen; and there too he is right; for otherwise his nation would not have understood him.

"Here, again," continued Goethe, "the Greeks were so great that they regarded fidelity to historic facts less than the treatment of them by the poet. We have fortunately a fine example in Philoctetes; which subject has been treated by all three of the great tragedians, and lastly and best by Sophocles. This poet's excellent play has luckily come down to us entire; while of the *Philoctetes* of Aeschylus and Euripides only fragments have been found, although sufficient to show how they have managed the subject. If time permitted, I would restore these pieces, as I did the *Phaethon* of Euripides; it would be to me no unpleasant or useless task.

"In this subject the problem was very simple: namely, to bring Philoctetes with his bow from the island of Lemnos. But the manner of doing this was the business of the poet; and here each could show the power of his invention, and one could excel another. Ulysses must fetch him; but shall he be known by Philoctetes or not? and if not, how shall he be disguised? Shall Ulysses go alone, or shall he have companions, and who shall they be? In Aeschylus, there is no companion; in Euripides, it is Diomedes; in Sophocles, the son of Achilles. Then, in what situation is Philoctetes to be found? Shall the island be inhabited or not? and, if inhabited, shall any sympathetic soul have taken compassion on him or not? And so with a hundred other things; which are all at the discretion of the poet, and in the selection and omission of which one may show his superiority to another in wisdom. Here is the grand point, and our present poets should do like the ancients. They should not be always asking whether a subject has been used before, and look to south and north for unheard-of adventures; which are often barbarous enough, and merely make an impression as incidents. To make something of a simple subject by a masterly treatment requires intellect and great talent, and these we do not find."

Some passing sledges again allured us to the window; but it was not the expected train from Belvidere. We laughed and talked about trivial matters, and then I asked Goethe how the novel was going on.

"I have not touched it of late," said he; "but one incident more must take place in the introduction. The lion must roar as the princess passes the booth; upon which some good remarks may be made on the formidable nature of this mighty beast."

"That is a very happy thought," said I; "for thus you gain an introduction that is not only good and essential in its place but also gives a greater effect to all that follows. Hitherto the lion has appeared almost too gentle, shown no trace of ferocity; but by roaring he at least makes us suspect how formidable he is, and the effect when he gently follows the boy's flute is heightened."

"This mode of altering and improving," said Goethe, "where by continued invention the imperfect is heightened to the perfect, is the right one. But the remaking and carrying further what is already complete – as, for instance, Walter Scott has done with my 'Mignon,' whom, in addition to her other qualities, he makes deaf and dumb – this mode of altering I cannot commend."

Notes

1 Pierre-Jean de Béranger (1780–1857) wrote popular poems, many set in taverns or brothels, often with a progressive political message.
2 A drama that Goethe had just completed, which begins as a classical tragedy and ends as a modern opera.
3 Goethe's epistolary novel *Elective Affinities* (1809).
4 *Art and Antiquity*, a journal that Goethe founded and then edited from 1816 to 1832.
5 Friedrich von Matthisson, a poet whose collected works were published in eight volumes in the period 1825–1829.
6 The poet and novelist Alessandro Manzoni had recently published his masterpiece, the historical novel *I promessi sposi* (*The Bethrothed*, 1827).
7 Hero of Goethe's play *Egmont* (1788), set in the sixteenth century.

2

The Emergence of *Weltliteratur*
Goethe and the Romantic School (2006)

John Pizer

A scholar of nineteenth- and twentieth-century European literature and literary theory, John Pizer was educated at the University of Washington and completed his doctoral research in Tübingen on German and French literature; he has written books on genre theory, aesthetics, and German literary history seen in comparative perspective. He is a professor of Foreign Languages and Literatures at Louisiana State University, where he has been a leader in developing a program in world literature. Pizer's pedagogical and methodological focus complements his research interests, as he both theorizes the study of world literature and practices it in the classroom. Both aspects of his work come together in his book *The Idea of World Literature* (2006). In this book Pizer unfolds a historical perspective on the concept of "world literature," tracing its origins to the late eighteenth century and the development of the idea of *Weltliteratur* from Goethe and the German Romantics to the *Communist Manifesto* and beyond. He traces as well the importation of the concept in the 1830s in the United States and its development through teaching in the first decades of twentieth century.

For Pizer, the study of world literature should be focused on the dialectic between the transnational and the subnational, both in theoretical approaches and in pedagogical practice. This dialectic lies at the core of what Pizer calls "Goethe's *Weltliteratur* paradigm." In the selection given here, Pizer emphasizes the value of going back to Goethe's concept today to elaborate a methodology for teaching world literature in the twenty-first century. Goethe's concept is described by Pizer as recognizing alterity and encouraging openness, seeking to open pathways for "the movement of the self *toward* the Other."

John Pizer, "The Emergence of *Weltliteratur*. Goethe and the Romantic School" (2006). From John Pizer, *The Idea of World Literature* (Baton Rouge: University of Louisiana Press), pp. 18–40. © Louisiana State University Press.

World Literature in Theory, First Edition. Edited by David Damrosch.
© 2014 John Wiley & Sons, Ltd. Published 2014 by John Wiley & Sons, Ltd.

When Goethe began to issue his pronouncements on Weltliteratur in the 1820s, the dreams of a united Germany which had helped stoke the fires of resistance to Napoleon earlier in the nineteenth century were but a distant memory. Germany was not one unified country at this time; unification did not occur until 1871. Instead, it was a loose confederation of largely independent entities, called "Kleinstaaten," or small states. The early German Romantics, referred to by Heine as "The Romantic School," had lost much of their idealism. The Congress of Vienna, convened in 1815 after Napoleon had been conclusively vanquished, resolved to maintain a divided, fragmented Central Europe. Only by preserving the extreme diffusion of political power in this region, it was believed, could European stability be restored. Naturally, German nationalists objected. The fiery Friedrich Ludwig Jahn, better known under his pseudonym "Turnvater Jahn," caused quite a stir in the Austrian capital when he showed up to press the cause of a united German state. However, astonishment at his antics turned into bemused contempt, and nationalist fervor was effectively held in check until the 1830s, when the Young Germany movement arose. The absence of political unity in Goethe's homeland occurred in concert with a renewed spirit of cosmopolitanism in Europe and advances in communicative media and transportation infrastructures, as well as increased translation activity.

During the Restoration age, there was a fascination among intellectuals and journalists that the written word could be transmitted to all corners of Western Europe with relative immediacy. Censorship became strict during this politically repressive period, but censors themselves were frequently incompetent. They often were unable to decipher thinly veiled dissent, and not infrequently lacked the capacity to contend with technological advances enabling the rapid spread of the printed word. Perhaps this is why Prince Clemens von Metternich himself, primary author of the restoration measures at the Congress of Vienna, was rather pessimistic about the long-term sustainability of the Restoration regimes. The improvements in publishing technologies and transportation conditions led to expanded international dialogue and literary reception on the continent. Such circumstances provided the perfect intellectual atmosphere for the emergence of Weltliteratur. As Goethe himself noted in 1830, the validity of speaking of a universal "Weltliteratur" was enabled by the fact that all (European) nations, shaken by war and then left to their own devices, realized that they had already adopted foreign influences. This led to a desire for greater contact with one's neighbors, for a free exchange of ideas (*Sämtliche Werke* [Zurich, 1977], 14:934).

Nationalist passions and ethnic enmities did not much concern the worthies who assembled at the Congress of Vienna. The term "Restoration" to describe this epoch from 1815 to the 1830s is apt. Those convened in Austria's capital essentially wanted to return to prerevolutionary political stability, to a monarchic system of checks and balances where popular sentiments held little significance. Hagen Schulze characterizes this epoch as "the last time in the history of Europe that statesmen were in a position to pursue a rational policy that balanced the interests of all the parties and kept the peace without taking account of the emotions of the masses and the hatred of one people for another."[1] Though nothing equivalent in scale to the Congress of Vienna took place when the Soviet Empire collapsed in the late 1980s and early 1990s and what was then termed a "new world order" emerged, European and American politicians also believed that they could make rational assumptions concerning post-Soviet behavior in Europe, assumptions which also failed to take ethnic sentiments into account. As we now know, these surmises that popular feelings would be governed by economic self-interest rather than ethnic pride were far more disastrous, and far more *immediately* disastrous, than the geopolitical calculations made in 1815. In the twenty-first century, globalized culture and globalized economics intersect with tribal solidarities to which the world's peoples seem to be clinging with ever greater tenacity, at least partly *in reaction* to globalization and a concomitant loss of distinct identity.[2] This is why the subnational-transnational dialectic adumbrated in the introduction, a dialectic which grounds Goethe's Weltliteratur paradigm, is relevant in considering the state of world literature today, as well as in dealing with how world literature and Weltliteratur should be addressed in the World Literature classroom.

Of course, there are dangers in exaggerating the parallels between the political/cultural milieu of the *Goethezeit* and that of our own age. In considering the potential of a universal idea of the social, which he makes the central element in his analysis of contemporary globalization, Martin Albrow has reflected on Goethe's Weltliteratur concept. He stresses Goethe's optimism that the tension between universalist and nationalist tendencies in his day could be productively and creatively harnessed. Albrow sees two central ideas at work in Weltliteratur as Goethe conceived it. One is that the diverse forms of human existence evident in national literatures could be made reciprocally beneficial through a world literary dialogue. This dialogue would bring to life the second central Weltliteratur ideal, a universal striving toward mutual goals. Albrow does not perceive such optimism in the current global age. While Goethe associated Weltliteratur with the unlimited potential of human interaction, the contemporary concept of globalization underscores the circumstance that globalism *limits* our actions. The other major difference between globalization today and how Goethe envisioned it in his Weltliteratur paradigm is one of dimensions. While Goethe stressed the interaction of social groups, whether nationally or internationally oriented, globalization in the current age constitutes the frame for *all* social relationships, in Albrow's view.[3] Naturally, this circumstance inevitably lessens our awareness of, and appreciation for, social and cultural alterity. The circumstance that Goethe and his age were unencumbered by this problem makes the adroit consideration of Weltliteratur all the more potentially efficacious today.

Goethe's Weltliteratur concept attained popularity in Europe in the early nineteenth century not simply because a cosmopolitan political climate and technological improvements at that time created a fertile ground. Goethe's own enormous political stature was equally important in establishing a receptive audience. Goethe first gained fame in Europe with the epistolary novel *Die Leiden des jungen Werther* (*The Sorrows of Young Werther*, 1774). Chafing under the perceived cold rationality equated by many with the dominant Enlightenment philosophy in the late eighteenth century, young people in Western Europe were enthralled by this tale of star-crossed passion leading to the title hero's suicide. Indeed, many young men followed Werther's fatal example, and Napoleon always kept a copy of the novel with him on his travels. Though none of his subsequent works matched this early popularity, Goethe enjoyed even greater prestige among Europe's artists, intellectuals, and nobility later in life, when he resided in Weimar. British travelers sought an audience with Goethe there in particularly large numbers, and this personal intercourse was quite beneficial for the furtherance of Weltliteratur as a mode of cosmopolitan interchange.[4] Though Goethe's remarks on Weltliteratur are scattered throughout his correspondence, essays, and in the published conversations with Eckermann, a core motivating factor links them all: the desire for a productive and peaceful coexistence among the nations of Europe after the divisive and destructive Napoleonic Wars. Such fraternal yearning reached beyond Europe, and helped spur the composition of the *West-östlicher Divan*, though Goethe's embrace of the foreign informed his entire poetic career. Todd Kontje has summarized the link between Weltliteratur and Goethe's own creative endeavors as follows: "Goethe's scattered comments about *Weltliteratur* in the late 1820s provide a theoretical justification for his lifelong poetic practice. From the beginning Goethe had demonstrated his ability to feel his way into foreign literary forms; his pseudo-Persian poetry of the *Divan* is only one phase of a career that included Shakespearean drama, Pindaric odes, and Roman elegies."[5] Goethe's receptivity to the foreign, in turn, enhanced his prestige among foreign journalists and intellectuals, further aiding the reception of Weltliteratur during his lifetime as a transnational ideal.

To be sure, Goethe's generous aesthetic outlook did not encompass all nations or cultures. Kontje calls Goethe "the outspoken enemy of everything Indian,"[6] and it is indeed the case that he loathed Indian statuary for its polytheistic representations, which Goethe associated with idolatry. He deplored Indian depictions of gods as variegated animals (1:615, 618), and even praised the zeal of a Muslim in the Middle Ages, Mahmud of Gasna, for destroying such religious art (3:438–439). As privy counselor to Duke Carl August in Weimar, Goethe strongly supported the suppression of democratic ideals linked to the French Revolution. He helped formulate policies designed to crush enthusiasm for such ideals among peasants, students, and professors in the Duchy of Saxony-Weimar-Eisenach. Thus, his cosmopolitanism was not all-encompassing, and his politics showed a strongly intolerant streak.[7] This is why National Socialist propagandists, embarrassed by Goethe's cosmopolitanism, focused on his loyal, unquestioning service to an absolutist German state. This circumstance also explains why the Young Germany author Ludwig Börne famously called him a "princes' lackey" three years after Goethe's death.[8] However, these realities do not diminish the contribution Goethe made to transcultural understanding through his Weltliteratur paradigm, a contribution that can be harnessed in the praxis of the World Literature classroom.

In a letter to Sulpiz Boisserée dated 12 October 1827, Goethe noted that Weltliteratur would come into existence when national particularities were balanced and resolved through international interchange.[9] While Goethe disapproved of the sort of global cultural uniformity he called "sansculottisme,"[10] scholars who have wrestled with Goethe's Weltliteratur concept have increasingly articulated its relevance within the globalized literary context implicit in the term "cultural transnationalism." Goethe introduced the term Weltliteratur in 1827, in the context of a response to discussions of his oeuvre in French newspapers, in the journal *Über Kunst und Altertum* (On Art and Antiquity). After translating a passage from a favorable review of a French adaptation of his drama *Torquato Tasso* (1790) in the Paris *Globe*, Goethe notes his extensive quotation is not merely intended to remind readers of his own work:

> ich bezwecke ein Höheres, worauf ich vorläufig hindeuten will. Überall hört und liest man von dem Vorschreiten des Menschengeschlechtes, von den weiteren Aussichten der Welt- und Menschenverhältnisse. Wie es auch im Ganzen hiemit beschaffen sein mag, welches zu untersuchen und näher zu bestimmen nicht meines Amtes ist, will ich doch von meiner Seite meine Freunde aufmerksam machen, daß ich überzeugt sei, es bilde sich eine allgemeine Weltliteratur, worin uns Deutschen eine ehrenvolle Rolle vorbehalten ist. (14:908)

> [I have something higher in mind, which I want to indicate provisionally. Everywhere one hears and reads about the progress of the human race, about the further prospects for world and human relationships. However that may be on the whole, which it is not my office to investigate and more closely determine, I nevertheless would personally like to make my friends aware that I am convinced a universal world literature is in the process of being constituted, in which an honorable role is reserved for us Germans.]

Goethe's vision of a new literary modality emerging from the progress generated by the increasingly international nature of discursive interchange reflects the holistic perspective that guided his forays into the natural sciences.[11] However, while Goethe's personal authoritativeness is strongly projected into much of his scientific writing, he deliberately masks the discrete, subjective component of his announcement concerning Weltliteratur through the use of the subjunctive case and through the impersonal pronouns "es" and "man." Goethe *as an individual* does not perceive what he describes. Rather, *one* sees and hears of progressive globalization, and one experiences this trend everywhere. Even when Goethe expresses in the first-person a conviction that a universal Weltliteratur is in the process of forming, he uses the indirect discourse subjunctive "sei" to note this belief. It is as though Goethe wishes to disappear into the background so that the impersonal, universal essence of a world literary scene can, conversely, be foregrounded. This is an initial, subtle hint at the death of the author as an independent literary "agent" in both senses of that term, Goethe's perhaps unintended way of announcing that world media (and, by extension, world markets) will weave a writer's products into a transindividual, indeed transnational grid, a grid Goethe terms Weltliteratur.

To be sure, Goethe's discovery of an emerging Weltliteratur is not intended to be read as announcing the demise of discrete national literatures. Indeed, he conveys in the same sentence which carries the newly enunciated discourse a belief in the positive role the Germans will play in its formation. However, he goes on to note that German literature is constituted from so many heterogeneous and contradictory elements that only a common language makes it a coherent field (14:909). This view of German literature as marked by disunity and a lack of cohesion is consistent with remarks Goethe set down in a much earlier essay, "Literarischer Sansculottismus" (1795), where he makes Germany's fragmentary political construction, its *Kleinstaaterei*, responsible for the nation's lack of "classical" authors. A truly classical author must be infused by a national spirit, and both internal factiousness and a concomitant overabundance of foreign influences makes such an infusion impossible in Germany. However, Goethe does not wish for the political upheavals which would make such classicism possible, and only bemoans the lack of a political-cultural center where German authors would be freed from subjection to the highly variegated whims and influences of their individual homelands (14:179–185). Given Germany's own lack of a strong, immanent, infrangible national identity in his time, it is not surprising that Goethe was particularly aware of and open to the possibility of a super- or transnational literary modality. Perhaps Goethe's insights into the contemporary impossibility of creating a "classical" (national) German literature made the formulation of a Weltliteratur desirable as the only possible alternative to cultural fragmentation.[12]

Another obvious political factor in Goethe's enunciation of a Weltliteratur concept was his experience of the Napoleonic Wars. As René Wellek has noted, Goethe believed the desire for greater literary traffic was rooted "in the weariness of strife" after these wars.[13] To be sure, in Goethe's age as in our own, strident nationalism resulted from globalist tendencies, and Goethe's battle against political and cultural xenophobia in Germany is evident in his engagement with Weltliteratur.[14] Nevertheless, in the wake of the Congress of Vienna and prior to new nationalistic outbursts in the 1830s, Europeans could reasonably sense a decline in the significance and autonomy of the individual nation-state, much as the "new world order" which emerged in the wake of Soviet Communism's collapse has led to a globalization of economics, politics, and culture. Thus, if Goethe's Weltliteratur concept anticipates current cultural transnationalism, a certain parallel between the geopolitics of the last phase of the Goethezeit and those of the contemporary age is, in some measure, responsible, though such trends in Goethe's age were restricted to Europe. Indeed, Goethe specifically equated Weltliteratur with "European literature" (14:907). Nevertheless, he also commented that Weltliteratur was a domain being constituted by the ever increasing rapidity of (transnational) interchange and traffic ("Verkehr"). He further noted that what is popular among the masses would spread out into all zones and regions, a tendency serious-minded thinkers ("Die Ernsten") would strive in vain to resist. Such individuals must therefore form their own modest "church" (14:914–915), presumably in order to attain the sort of "aesthetic autonomy" Martha Woodmansee has shown was constructed precisely as a site of critical resistance to nascent literary mass marketing strategies in the age of Goethe.[15] Again, Goethe's remarks anticipate both the postmodern mass global marketing of culture and conservative reaction against this trend, though here too Goethe's thinking is primarily informed by European rather than truly universal tendencies.

When Goethe prefaces a schematic list of some European nations and their strengths and weaknesses in the emerging world-literary age with the cryptic subtitle "European, which is to say World-Literature" (14:907), our instinctive reaction would be to assume a Eurocentric perspective. Gail Finney has noted that "for Goethe, world literature meant only European literature, a fact that significantly differentiates his enterprise from the discipline of comparative literature today."[16] [...] Finney's remark might make us question the relevance of Goethean Weltliteratur for the contemporary World Literature classroom, where such narrow transnational cultural geography appears decidedly anachronistic. Two essays written in the 1980s by the Moroccan-born Germanist Fawzi Boubia establish the genuinely global dimensions of Goethe's Weltliteratur postulations and foreground their seminal and precocious embrace of alterity in the hermeneutic dialogue among the world's literatures. In Boubia's view, Goethe attempted in his formulations to arrive at a means by which one could highlight what is genuinely "other" in works of foreign literature and by which one could approach this alterity with genuine respect and open-mindedness. [...]

[...]

Boubia's essay "Universal Literature and Otherness" (1988) repeated and simply translated some of the salient points found in "Goethes Theorie der Alterität," but broke new ground in establishing the antichauvinist, dialogic purport of Weltliteratur as Goethe defined it. Citing Goethe's view, expressed in the journal *Über Kunst und Altertum*, that one must guard against any tendency toward leading nations to think in a uniform manner, Boubia emphasized that Goethean Weltliteratur is "a conception that is not confined within a blind Eurocentrism. On the contrary, it takes otherness into account and, consequently, the particularity and identity of peoples."[17] If students studying Goethe's paradigm in a World Literature classroom can be brought to understand and appreciate precisely this point – admittedly, no easy task – then their experience of the course will have lifetime value. Boubia's essay further grounds the dialogic element in Weltliteratur; the paradigm can be defined, in part, as a dialogue that will, ideally, lead to greater tolerance. Citing Goethe's tripartite translation scheme discussed in the introduction, and to which we will return at the conclusion of this chapter, Boubia noted that Weltliteratur is "other" directed. That is to say, Goethe's belief that translation in its highest, third, stage must approximate the rhythmic and grammatical nuances of the original language demonstrates that Goethe's paradigm sets as its highest ideal the movement of the self *toward* the Other, not a dominion over the Other or a leveling of the Other. This embrace of alterity, grounded in a unique principle of estrangement that forces the self to become foreign to itself, serves the twin causes of intercultural dialogue and respect for the foreign.[18] Boubia's insights in this regard demonstrate once again the importance of elucidating translation theory in the World Literature classroom if the appreciation of alterity is to be cultivated there.

Despite Goethe's somewhat antipathetic response to the mass aspect of Weltliteratur, his attitude toward what he articulated as an unavoidably emerging paradigm was generally positive. In 1828, after noting the friendly foreign reception of his Weltliteratur notion, a discursive formation he hoped would soon emerge through improved ease of communication in the turbulent present, Goethe eluci-dated the benefits to be gleaned through such inter-national literary interchange: "Eine jede Literatur ennuyiert sich zuletzt in sich selbst, wenn sie nicht durch fremde Teilnahme wieder aufgefrischt wird. Welcher Naturforscher erfreut sich nicht der Wunderdinge, die er durch Spiegelung hervorgebracht sieht?" (14:896) (Every literature dissipates within itself when it is not reinvigorated through foreign participation. What researcher into nature does not rejoice at the marvelous things which he sees brought forth through refraction?). In addition to confirming the tendency of Goethe's scientific perspective to permeate his Weltliteratur articulations, this passage adduces a dynamic quality inherent in the Weltliteratur paradigm, without the aid of which individual (national) literatures would simply dissipate. Referring to this commentary, Wellek defines Weltliteratur as "an ideal of the unification of all literatures into one literature where each nation would play its part in a universal concert."[19] This description captures the cosmopolitan spirit of the Weimar Classical milieu in which Goethe coined the term Weltliteratur while emphasizing its status as, in part, a teleological projection, a future goal. Certainly, Goethe was not in a position in the early nineteenth century to foresee the potential effects of the vigorous commingling taking place in the current age of multicultural exchange on a global scale. However, the "foreign participation" within and among the discrete nation-states he articulated must inevitably multiply on an infinite scale the "hybrid cultural space" Homi Bhabha sees inscribed in postcolonial literature.[20] This is one reason why, as we will see, Bhabha finds Goethe's Weltliteratur formulation a particularly valuable paradigm.

The geopolitical homogenization that emerged in the wake of the Congress of Vienna occurred in concert with a beginning internationalization of literary texts through a dawning mass market system, increased translation activity, and cross-national media coverage. While these circumstances allowed Goethe to sense the onset of Weltliteratur, he of course recognized that the constellation of a truly transnational literature, marked by thematic, stylistic, and even linguistic features drawn from the world and not anchored primarily in the traditions of individual nation-states, was at best, as Wellek puts it, "a distant ideal."[21] In spite of his conflation of "World-Literature" with "European literature," and in spite of a belief that early works of Egyptian, Indian, and Chinese literature could only be viewed as "curiosities," lacking the potential to enhance the modern European's ethical and aesthetic acculturation ("Bildung") (9:602),[22] Goethe's own poetic effort to approximate the ideal of hybridity in world literature is most evident in the *West-östlicher Divan*, inspired by his reading of the medieval Persian poet Hafiz. Drawing on both topical and structural features in the Persian's poetry and striving to appropriate even certain features in his language, the *Divan* represents Goethe's attempt at the "completion and confirmation" of the poetic self, a self enacted through a "return" to the Orient as a locus of both difference and origin, as Edward Said notes in *Orientalism*.[23] Thus, one can recognize another reason Weltliteratur as transnational interchange appealed to Goethe: it allows the development of the poetic self to the fullest possible degree, enabling it to approach the personal totality which finds its objective corollary in the ideal of a universalized poetic framework.

Aside from his antipathy toward the globalized mass marketing aspect of Weltliteratur, what accounts for Goethe's ambivalent attitude toward the world literary epoch? Why would he tell his secretary, Johann Peter Eckermann, in 1827 that Germans will slip into "pedantic darkness" if they do not attempt to look beyond their narrow geographic confines as he proclaims the need to move beyond "national literature" and to hasten the impending arrival of the epoch of Weltliteratur (24:229) and then, two years later, argue that Germans have the most to lose from this dawning age?[24] When he made his original pronouncement concerning Weltliteratur in 1827, Goethe assumed the Germans were assured of an "honorable role" in its formation due to current universal (that is, European) fascination with German literature (14:908–9). Gerhard Kaiser has cogently analyzed Goethe's ambiguous position; while the remarkable achievements of German writers in Goethe's age created the possibility that German arts and letters could play a substantive role in the nascent formation of a Weltliteratur, the particularisms that imbued German literature throughout its history, in contrast to the French, made it doubtful that German literature would be able to retain its unique, specific character as it became constellated within a world literary process.[25] When we consider the increasing globalization of commerce and culture at the present time, a trend that is beginning to render the notion of national literature obsolete and to create a transnational body of work on a truly universal scale, Goethe's concern about German national literature's ability to retain its specificity seems likely to become a worldwide issue in the coming years. Nevertheless, as I will argue, a heightened foregrounding of subnational cultural particularities in much current literature tends to obviate this danger.

Contemplating the problematic of subjective identity in the postcolonial age, Bhabha has posed, on a universal scale, the question of national spiritual fragmentation in the face of all-encompassing cultural border crossings, which Goethe had perceived as a purely domestic difficulty for his people:

> How do we conceive of the "splitting" of the national subject? How do we articulate cultural differences within this vacillation of ideology in which the national discourse also participates, sliding ambivalently from one enunciatory position to another? What are the forms of life struggling to be represented in that unruly "time" of national culture, which Bakhtin surmounts in his reading of Goethe. ... What might be the cultural and political effects of the liminality of the nation, the margins of modernity, which come to be signified in the narrative temporalities of splitting, ambivalence and vacillation?[26]

Such issues troubled Goethe as he wrestled with the concept of Weltliteratur because of the "liminality" of Germany within Europe, a liminality caused by

Germany's political fragmentation, by the regionalism and particularism that made its national culture "unruly" through creating a lack of intellectual cohesion. Goethe recognized the concomitant impossibility of even *arriving* at a truly "national discourse" through which a somewhat unified response to the trends generating a Weltliteratur paradigm could be brought to bear. [...]

[...]

As we noted, when Goethe first coined the term Weltliteratur in 1827, he believed that the Germans would have an honorable role in this process. The world's nations appear to Goethe to cast their gaze at Germany, praising and criticizing, imitating and rejecting its output. Germany's national literature is derived from quite heterogeneous elements, unified only through its composition in a language which is gradually bringing to light the immanent quality of the German people. Goethe tacitly assumes Germany, in his age, lacks both military-physical and ethical-aesthetic cohesion (14:908–9). There was an external element to the political dimension of this initial Weltliteratur formulation. In suggesting Germany's lack of moral and physical unity, Goethe was reflecting on his country's psychological ambience in the wake of the Napoleonic Wars. During these wars, not only populists like Jahn but also German intellectuals such as the Romantic philosopher Johann Gottlieb Fichte were sustained by the hope that a liberated fatherland would emerge from French occupation not only spiritually but politically coadunated. However, Metternich's reactionary measures at the Congress of Vienna, which thwarted the ambitions of those seeking a unified Germany, dashed this optimism. While Goethe's prefatory Weltliteratur formulation evinces an implicit recognition of this circumstance, of a return by Germany to a prewar status quo which (before the 1830s) triggered widespread despair, it points to the positive side of non-nationhood, to an anti-nationalist cosmopolitanism culturally attractive to the world at large. Indeed, as Hartmut Steinecke has noted, the retardation of nationality in eighteenth-century Germany led to a relatively unimpeded view, in Goethe's estimation, of transnational, universally human contexts in his native land.[27]

This perspective is evident in the essay "Literarischer Sansculottismus," which therefore bears a brief reexamination. On the one hand, Goethe bemoans here Germany's lack of national cohesion, for political fragmentation renders impossible the development of "a classical national author." Such a fortunate being only emerges when he is able to find himself the son of a unified country that has enjoyed a history filled with events of great magnitude and a present populated by a resolute, purposeful citizenry (14:181). However, a worthy philosophy and an invisible school ("unsichtbare Schule") have evolved in Germany, helping the talented young poet to represent external objects with clarity and grace (14:184). Particularly compelling in Goethe's metaphoric language is the articulation of the invisible school, a school invisible, presumably, because Germany lacks a physically manifest sociocultural center ("Mittelpunkt gesellschaftlicher Lebensbildung") where young writers could undergo a cohesive, mutually supportive period of aesthetic maturation (14:182). Ironically, the invisible school allows Germany's contemporary writers to enter into a circle now more fully illuminated than in the past (14:184), as though a physical invisibility rendered necessary by Germany's fragmented political status has ultimately led to transcendent enlightenment in the literary domain. Bhabha has noted Bakhtin's foregrounding of optic, ocular tropes in Goethe's oeuvre when the Russian critic putatively attempts to underscore Goethe's rhetorical nation building: "The recurrent metaphor of landscape as the inscape of national identity emphasizes the quality of light, the question of social visibility, the power of the eye to naturalize the rhetoric of national affiliation and its forms of collective expression."[28] However, "Literarischer Sansculottismus" attempts to bring opacity at the geographic national level into a dialectic relationship with luminescence in the aesthetic-pedagogical sphere in order to underscore politically fragmented Germany's ability to sustain a vibrant literary culture. The continued impediments to Germany's political cohesion in 1830 constitute, perhaps, another reason Goethe envisioned the globe as but an expanded fatherland when he discussed the role of improved, accelerated, expanded traffic/communication infrastructures in the development of Weltliteratur (14:914).

This is not to say that Goethe regarded transnationalism and sub-nationalism as simply two sides of one dialectically productive coin. Goethe realized that the average German's lifetime confinement within the narrow boundaries of one of its multitude of petty states tended to result in pedantic narrow-mindedness among the citizenry. However, precisely this circumstance led him to issue his famous proclamation to Eckermann in 1827 that his fellow Germans should follow his lead in observing the culture of foreign lands, and that "national literature now does not signify a great deal, the epoch of world literature has arrived, and everyone must help to accelerate this epoch" (24:229). Only Germany's fractured political status permits Goethe to formulate a transnational cultural ideal through his Weltliteratur concept. […]

[…]

At the conclusion to *Writing Outside the Nation*, Seyhan issues the following precaution with respect to how transnational literature should be taught: "We need to bear in mind, however, that if our reception of transnational, emergent, diasporic literatures is mediated only through English, not only linguistic but also cultural differences and specificities will be lost in translation. And our newly developed transnational, postcolonial literature courses will not be very different from the traditional World Literature in English Translation course."[29] Seyhan is, of course, correct, but the complex linguistic and cultural nuances of bi- and transnational literature can only be approached after the discrete, chronotopic elements in literary works are elucidated. To paraphrase Seyhan, we might call this a pedagogy focused on a writing *below* the nation. Ironically, perhaps, a metatheoretical introduction of Weltliteratur as Goethe understood it will be a prerequisite for such research and the teaching, *in particular*, of World Literature in English Translation courses. This Bakhtinian approach will not only complement the transnational method of postcolonial literary pedagogy, but will micrologically promote the questioning of fixed perspectives advocated by Lawall in elucidating world literature, a calling into question that transnational literary study accomplishes on the macrological level. Chronotopic concretization as critical praxis will also help sustain cultural memory, which is threatened by the antithesis of this praxis, a tacit acceptance of cultural globalization as a *fait accompli*, an acceptance that inevitably distorts our examination of past cultures.

If, as Bhabha correctly suggests in spite of somewhat misunderstanding the significance of the "nation" in the "*Bildungsroman*" essay, Bakhtin was able to overcome the flux and indeterminacy of national culture when viewed from a diachronic perspective through his analysis of Goethe, it seems equally plausible to suggest Goethe's *own* telos in striving toward the evocation of a comprehensive and stable geographic matrix rooted in the local was triggered by the desire to imaginatively compensate for the genuine instability, fragmentation, and lack of cohesiveness that characterized German politics and letters in his time. If Germans had the most to lose in the dawning age of Weltliteratur because of the country's geopolitical and cultural particularisms, then Goethe must configure the world and conjure stability and plenitude within the regional and the particular in his narratives. If we believe Bakhtin's elegant argument that Goethe succeeded in doing just that, then Goethe might be plausibly suggested as a role model not only for those who teach World Literature, but also for authors who seek to come to grips with the demise of their national identity in a transnational, multicultural age.

[...]

Notes

1　Hagen Schulze, *States, Nations and Nationalism: From the Middle Ages to the Present*, trans. William E. Yuill (Oxford: Blackwell, 1996), 198. For Schulze's description of "Turnvater Jahn" in Vienna, see 199.

2　The interdependent antagonism between the poles of globalization and tribalism has been analyzed by Benjamin R. Barber in *Jihad vs. McWorld* (New York: Times Books, 1995).

3　Martin Albrow, "Auf dem Weg zu einer globalen Gesellschaft?" trans. Ilse Utz, in *Perspektiven der Weltgesellschaft*, ed. Ulrich Beck (Frankfurt: Suhrkamp, 1998), 428–32.

4　See Karl S. Guthke, "Destination Goethe: Travelling Englishmen in Weimar," in *Goethe and the English-Speaking World: Essays from the Cambridge Symposium for His 250th Anniversary*, ed. Nicholas Boyle and John Guthrie (Rochester: Camden House, 2002), 111–42, esp. 117–20.

5　Todd Kontje, *German Orientalisms* (Ann Arbor: Univ. of Michigan Press, 2004), 132.

6　*Ibid.*, 123. Kontje exaggerates here; Goethe greatly admired Kalidāsā's celebrated Sanskrit drama *Śākuntala*. See Dorothy Matilda Figueira, *Translating the Orient: The Reception of* Śākuntala *in Nineteenth-Century Europe* (Albany: State Univ. of New York Press, 1991), 12–13.

7　See esp. W. Daniel Wilson, *Das Goethe-Tabu: Protest und Menschenrechte im klassischen Weimar* (Munich: dtv, 1999).

8　See W. Daniel Wilson, "Goethe and the Political World," in *The Cambridge Companion to Goethe*, ed. Lesley Sharpe (Cambridge: Cambridge Univ. Press, 2002), 217.

9　Goethe, cited in Strich, *Goethe und die Weltliteratur*, 398.

10 On Goethe's rejection of this trend, and on its putative spread through the mass media in the present age, see Ulrich Weisstein, *Comparative Literature and Literary Theory: Survey and Introduction*, trans. William Riggan and Ulrich Weisstein (Bloomington: Indiana Univ. Press, 1973), 19.

11 The interconnection between Goethe's Weltliteratur concept and his natural scientific principles is adumbrated by A.R. Hohlfeld, "Goethe's Conception of World Literature," *Fifty Years with Goethe, 1901–1951* (Madison: Univ. of Wisconsin Press, 1953), 343.

12 According to Peter Weber, "Funktionsverständnis in Goethes Auffassung von Weltliteratur," in *Funktion der Literatur: Aspekte, Probleme, Aufgaben*, eds. Dieter Schlenstedt *et al.* (Berlin: Akademie, 1975), Goethe developed his Weltliteratur concept specifically in *opposition* to a program of national literature. Goethe, in Weber's view, saw national particularities as just a "cover" for the "universally human" ("allgemein Menschliches") configurations he would call forth (133–35).

13 René Wellek, *A History of Modern Criticism: 1750–1950*, vol. 1. (New Haven: Yale Univ. Press, 1955), 221.

14 See Strich, *Goethe und die Weltliteratur*, 46–48.

15 See particularly Martha Woodmansee's chapter "Aesthetic Autonomy as a Weapon in Cultural Politics: Rereading Schiller's *Aesthetic Letters*" in *The Author, Art, and the Market: Rereading the History of Aesthetics* (New York: Columbia Univ. Press, 1994), 57–86. On Goethe's prophetic fear that the age of Weltliteratur presupposed the dawning predominance of "mass culture" on a worldwide scale, see also Bollacher, "Goethes Konzeption der Weltliteratur," 183–85.

16 Gail Finney, "Of Walls and Windows: What German Studies and Comparative Literature Can Offer Each Other," *Comparative Literature* 49 (1997): 261.

17 Boubia, "Universal Literature and Otherness," trans. Jeanne Ferguson, *Diogenes* 141 (1988): 81.

18 *Ibid.*, 89–101.

19 Wellek, *A History of Modern Criticism*, 221.

20 Homi K. Bhabha, *The Location of Culture* (London: Routledge, 1994), 7. Bhabha uses this term specifically in connection with the work of Pepon Osorio (7–8).

21 Wellek, *A History of Modern Criticism*, 221.

22 Goethe somewhat contradicted this perspective in one of his conversations with Eckermann (on 31 January 1827) when he expressed the belief that in Chinese novels characters act, think, and feel like those of European authors, except that the Chinese protagonists act in a manner marked by greater clarity, purity, and ethicalness (24:227).

23 Edward Said, *Orientalism* (New York: Vintage Books, 1979), 167–68.

24 Goethe, cited in Strich, *Goethe und die Weltliteratur*, 399.

25 Gerhard R. Kaiser, *Einführung in die vergleichende Literaturwissenschaft: Forschungsstand, Kritik, Aufgaben* (Darmstadt: Wissenschaftliche Buchgesellschaft, 1980), 12.

26 Bhabha, *The Location of Culture*, 147.

27 Hartmut Steinecke, "'Weltliteratur' – Zur Diskussion der Goetheschen 'Idee' im Jungen Deutschland," in *Das Junge Deutschland: Kolloquium zum 150. Jahrestag des Verbots vom 10. Dezember 1835*, ed. Joseph A. Kruse and Bernd Kortländer (Hamburg: Hoffmann and Campe, 1987), 162.

28 Bhabha, *The Location of Culture*, 143.

29 Azade Seyhan, *Writing Outside the Nation* (Princeton: Princeton University Press, 2000), 157.

3

Present Tasks of Comparative Literature (1877)

Hugo Meltzl

Defining the domain of comparative literature at the crossroads of philosophy, aesthetics, ethnology, and anthropology, Hugo Meltzl (1846–1908) is a key figure in the history of the discipline. One of the pioneering theorists of world literature, he was also among the first to institutionalize it, by cofounding and editing the first journal of comparative literature, *Acta Comparationis Litterarum Universarum* (1877–1888). Born in a German family in Transylvania, in the Hungarian wing of the Austro-Hungarian Empire, Meltzl studied Hungarian, Romanian, Greek, and Latin in Cluj (Hungarian Kolosvár and German Klausenburg), now part of Romania. He completed his scholarly training in Leipzig and then at Heidelberg, where he wrote a dissertation on the philosophy of Schopenhauer. In 1873, he returned to Cluj at age 27 to take up the chair in German Language and Literature at the new Franz-Joseph-Universität. Named for the Habsburg emperor, the university had been founded to spread the influence of German culture in the eastern territories of the empire and at the same time to promote Hungarian over Romanian language and culture in this ethnically mixed region. It is in this context that a locally born, Heidelberg-trained scholar could become a welcome candidate for a professorship despite his youth and lack of prior experience.

Both a Hungarian patriot and a resolute internationalist, the young Meltzl found a kindred soul in the oldest member of the faculty, the Hungarian philologist and polymath Samuel Brassai (1800–1897), with whom he founded his journal. "Present Tasks of Comparative Literature" is the journal's programmatic inaugural essay, in which Meltzl states the principles of comparative literature and the tasks of the new

Hugo Meltzl, "Present Tasks of Comparative Literature" (1877), trans. Hans-Joachim Schulz and Phillip H. Rhein. From David Damrosch *et al.*, eds., *The Princeton Sourcebook in Comparative Literature* (Princeton: Princeton University Press, 2009), pp. 42–49. A few notes by Meltzl on contemporary scholarly works are omitted here.

publication. Though recognizing that the discipline of comparative literature was still in its infancy both in theory and practice, Meltzl and Brassai set the ambitious goal that the new discipline should come to embody Goethe's dream of "world literature." To this end, the editors assembled a truly global editorial board, including scholars not only from Europe but from India, Australia, Japan, and the USA. The journal was based upon "the principle of polyglottism," and itself had no fewer than 10 "official languages."

In his essay, emphasizing both multilingualism and translation, Meltzl is concerned, like Goethe, with the international circulation of literary products and, at the same time, with understanding their cultural and linguistic specificity. Meltzl views parallel translations and a comparative literary history as necessary tools to move comparative literature toward its higher goal, a nationally based but not jingoistic internationalism. Impossibly ambitious in its aspirations and its editorial multilingualism, the *Acta* nonetheless pioneered a genuinely global perspective in the very heyday of nineteenth-century nationalism. Though Meltzl himself describes "true 'world literature'" as an unattainable ideal, his journal represents an important first step toward the realization of that ideal.

I

Since our polyglot journal has been mistaken for a philological one by some philologists, it may not be superfluous to discuss briefly once more the tasks of our journal, which – being the very first such effort in this area – cannot rely on achievements of predecessors or other convenient advantages.

Comparative Literature – for which to our knowledge only the Germans, French and Italians already have an established designation – is nevertheless by no means a fully defined and established academic discipline. As a matter of fact, it is still far from that goal. The task, therefore, of an organ of this slowly emerging discipline of the future should not so much consist in definitely comparing the vast (though still insufficient) material at hand as in adding to it from all sides and in intensifying the effort, directly as well as indirectly. A journal like ours, then, must be devoted at the same time to the art of translation and to the Goethean *Weltliteratur* (a term which German literary historians, particularly Gervinus,[1] have thoroughly misunderstood). Literature and language are closely related; the latter being substantially subservient to the former, without which the servant would have not only no autonomy but no existence at all. Therefore it should be understood that linguistic problems will also be touched upon now and then (though not methodically discussed), particularly with regard to exotic peoples. For similar reasons Comparative Literature touches upon the fields of philosophy, aesthetics, even ethnology and anthropology. Without ethnological considerations, for instance, the literatures of remote regions could not be fully understood.[2]

To these tasks we have to add the *reform of literary history*, a reform long awaited and long overdue, which is possible only through an extensive application of the *comparative principle*. As every unbiased man of letters knows, modern literary history, as generally practiced today, is nothing but an *ancilla historiae politicae*, or even an *ancilla nationis*,[3] at best an *ancilla philologiae* (in the modern sense of the latter term). Literary historians have gone so far as to base their divisions into literary epochs on political events, sometimes on the death-years of – kings! For these and similar reasons, even the best and best-known presentations of the literary history of all languages are thoroughly unacceptable to the mature taste and are quite unprofitable for serious literary (not political and philological) purposes. Only extensive work in the comparative fields, particularly translation, can eliminate gradually many preconceptions. Of those many preconceptions, we may mention one in the field of modern German literary history. In Koberstein's monumental work,[4] which is on the whole justly famous (5th ed., by the conscientious Bartsch, Leipzig, 1872, Vol. I, p. 218, footnote 7), there is a lengthy discussion of the question whether the aubade was invented by Wolfram von Eschenbach or by the Provençal poets. Finally the author agrees with the "thorough and cautious" Lachmann that Wolfram is the inventor of this genre. With all their thoroughness and caution they do not consider the fact that Lieder of this type were sung eighteen centuries ago in China (as those contained in the *Shih Ching*) and are frequently found among the folksongs of modern peoples, for instance, the Hungarians.

There is no area of literary study today as overworked, unattractive and, in spite of this, frequented as that of literary history; and there is none that promises less. Lichtenberg already came to that conclusion before the writing of literary histories had properly begun. This is only confirmed by such rare exceptions as Scherr's and Minckwitz's historical works, which – in spite of occasionally fitting literary phenomena into conventional schemes derived from certain preconceptions of liberalism – at least compensate for it by a fresh, intelligent, and universal approach. There is no space here for an extensive discussion of these important questions.[5] Let us conclude by repeating what has been said earlier in this journal: our journal intends to be a meeting place of authors, translators and philosophers of all nations. The established disciplines are excluded, particularly since they serve, openly or not, only practical purposes. Besides, these disciplines have their share of scholarly journals. Only one discipline does not have its journal yet, the one we intend to cultivate: the art of translation as it has been accepted, in its full significance, only since Goethe – whose consequence is nothing less than the emerging discipline of the future: Comparative Literature. The scruple that a discipline still in the process of consolidation should not have its own journal would raise violent objections if directed at our older sister, Comparative Philology, which is also still consolidating itself, although it is already well-structured in many of its vast areas. Besides, comparative literary history is already practiced directly, even in the classrooms of German universities (e.g., Carriere in Munich). Among its indirect representatives belongs the impressive group of German translators of literature (and I am not talking about the mass of second and third rate translators).

II: The Principle of Polyglottism

Our journal has changed its motto with the second volume. Instead of the beautiful one taken from Eötvös which is, after all, limited to the principle of true translation, we have found in Schiller's dictum a more precise and at the same time more universal expression of the tasks of this journal.[6] This seemingly unimportant change of mottoes alone may justify our returning to, or rather, our continuing the above discussion. Besides, much that is important had to be left unsaid on the last occasion for lack of space. We hope that nobody misunderstands our beautiful motto from Schiller.

The art of translation is, and will remain, one of the most important and attractive tools for the realization of our high comparative aims. But the means should not be mistaken for the end. Goethe was still able to conceive of his "Weltliteratur" as basically – or even exclusively? – (German) translation, which for him was an end in itself.[7] To us today it can only be the means to a higher end.

True comparison is possible only when we have before us the objects of our comparison in their original form. Although translations facilitate the international traffic or distribution of literary products immensely (particularly in the German language, which is poetically more adaptable than any other modern language), nobody will dispute Schopenhauer's opinion that even the best translation leaves something to be desired and can never replace the original. Therefore, the *principle of translation* has to be not replaced but accompanied by a considerably more important comparative tool, the *principle of polyglottism*. The limited space of our journal, of course, permits us only a limited realization of this principle. But this modern principle has to be realized above all if literary comparison is to do more than scratch the surface. (Incidentally, polyglottism is not something entirely modern since we are indebted to it for two quite modern disciplines which both deal with the antiquity of human culture: Egyptology and Assyriology. Without the polyglottism of the tablets of Rashid and Nineveh our knowledge would be considerably poorer.)

The principle of translation is confined to the *indirect* commerce of literature in contrast to the principle of polyglottism which is the *direct* commerce itself. This already indicates the great importance of polyglottism, which can be applied in several ways. The most desirable and at the same time most practical way would be, for the time being, if the critical articles of a comparative journal would appear in that language with which they are principally concerned, so that, for instance, a Hungarian contribution to Camões scholarship would be written in Portuguese and a German contribution to Cervantes criticism would appear in Spanish. It should be obvious that in most cases this aim will remain an ideal and unattainable one for the time being. We on our part feel that we should strictly realize it at least with regard to Hungarian and German literature. (This is our reason for giving preference to German and Hungarian literature, which, besides, corresponds to our geographic and cultural situation; therefore the diglottism of the section *Revue*.) Also, a proper use of the principle of polyglottism should not exclude polyglot original production entirely.

It should be obvious, however, that these polyglot efforts have nothing in common with any kind of universal fraternization or similar international *nephelokokkugia*.[8] The ideals of Comparative Literature have nothing to do with foggy, "cosmopolitanizing" theories; the high aims (not to say tendencies) of a journal like ours would be gravely misunderstood or intentionally misrepresented if anybody expected us to infringe upon the national uniqueness of a people. To attempt that would be, for more than one reason, a ludicrous undertaking which even an association of internationally famous scholars would have to consider doomed from the start – supposing such an association would be foolish enough to get together for such a purpose. It can safely be assumed that the purposes of Comparative Literature are more solid than that. It is, on the contrary, the *purely national of all nations* that Comparative Literature means to cultivate lovingly – here within the narrow framework of a journal where every nation is made to institute healthy (or just attractive) comparisons, which would not result from other approaches. Our secret motto is: nationality as individuality of a people should be regarded as sacred and inviolable. Therefore, a people, be it ever so insignificant politically, is and will remain, from the standpoint of Comparative Literature, as important as the largest nation. The most unsophisticated language may offer us most precious and informative subjects for comparative philology. The same is true for the spiritual life of "literatureless peoples," as we might call them, whose ethnic individuality should not be impinged upon by the wrong kind of missionary zeal; rather, it is our duty to protect it honestly and preserve it, if possible, in its purity. (From this comparative-polyglot standpoint should be considered the *ukaz* of the Censorship Office of the Russian Ministry of the Interior of May 16, 1876 [...] which prohibits the literary use of the Ukrainian language. It would appear as the greatest sin against the Holy Spirit even if it were directed only against the folksongs of an obscure horde of Kirghizes instead of a people of fifteen million.) To impede the folk literature of a people would mean to destroy arbitrarily an important expression of the human spirit. In a time when certain animal species such as the mountain goat and the European bison are protected against extinction by elaborate and strict laws, the willful extinction of a human species (or its literature, which amounts to the same thing) should be impossible.

In this sense we want understood the term "world literature" which, along with the art of translation, we intend to cultivate, particularly since the latter has not yet had a journal to itself, while the former has been well represented for some time now by such good, fully recognized and elaborate journals as the *Magazin für die Litteratur des Auslands* and Herrig's *Archiv für das Studium der neueren Sprachen* in Berlin. In England and France, too, it has always been cultivated by all major journals with praiseworthy zeal and good success. However, it cannot be denied that the so-called "world literature" is generally misunderstood, as has been indicated above. For today every nation demands its own "world literature" without quite knowing what is meant by it. By now, every nation considers itself, for one good reason or another, superior to all other nations, and this hypothesis, worked out into a complete theory of *suffisance*,[9] is even the basis of much of modern pedagogy, which today practically everywhere strives to be "national." This unhealthy "national principle" therefore constitutes the fundamental premise of the entire spiritual life of modern Europe – which may take such peculiar forms as the "national ethic" of a Viennese high school teacher who exhibits no little satisfaction with his achievement. In this way, all sound conceptions are undermined from the start, even with regard to the highest spiritual concerns which could otherwise have immeasurably rich consequences considering today's wonderfully intensified commerce of ideas in the world. Instead of giving free rein to polyglottism and reaping the fruits in the future (fruits that it would certainly bring), every nation today insists on the strictest monoglottism, by considering its own language superior or even destined to rule supreme. This is a childish competition whose result will finally be that all of them remain – inferior. The brilliant Dora d'Istria, in the foreword to her fine book *La Poésie des Ottomans* [the second edition appeared quite recently] confirms our opinion by exclaiming impatiently:

> Nous vivons en effet dans une époque fort peu littéraire, et l'Europe livrée aux haines des partis, aux luttes des races, aux querelles des sectes, aux rivalités des classes, n'attache qu'une médiocre importance aux questions qui semblaient, il y a quelques années, capables d'occuper tous les esprits cultivés. Trop de pays chrétiens ressemblent maintenant à la Turquie du XVIIIe siècle.[10]

True "world literature," therefore, in our opinion, can only remain an unattainable ideal in the direction of which, nevertheless, all independent literatures, i.e., all nations, should strive. They should use, however, only those means which we have called the two most important comparative principles, translation and polyglottism, never acts of violence or barbaric hypotheses which will be profitable for nobody but which unfortunately appear occasionally even in the great European journals. It is therefore particularly satisfying to hear a voice from Ultima Thule which I may be permitted to quote here. Our collaborator in Iceland writes us in German (July 29):

> I have always considered it desirable that there would be a journal which would bring together the writers, or all thinkers, of various nations; or, better still, that they would form an international society against the barbaric powers of our time. An important step in this direction seems to be this journal, as a focal point for writers and thinkers, or, to put it humorously, an exhibition of the spirit.

This noble voice of the Icelandic translator of Shakespeare, Steingrimur Thorsteinsson, moves us to submit the following proposal to our collaborators: For a small journal like ours to bring together at least a small number of "writers and thinkers of various nations" effectively, we intend to begin, starting with our next number, a small polyglot parliament on various problems of Comparative Literature, including practical ones. After all, it is necessary to assemble stone by stone the edifice of the future which may be of profit only to future generations.[11]

Notes

1 Georg Gottfried Gervinus (1805–1871), author of a five-volume history of German literature. He used the idea of *Weltliteratur* to celebrate Germany's literary influence abroad and German writers' ability to make creative use of foreign material.

2 Philosophy, particularly modern inductive philosophy, is even the most natural point of departure of literary history, and it is difficult to imagine that it has so far remained *terra incognita* for literary historians. History in the widest sense, especially the so-called universal history, political science, theology, philology, all have the privilege to lead to literary history; but how long will a philosophy with a sound scientific-ethnological basis continue to be dictated by their literary history and their "car tel est notre plaisir"? [Author's note]

3 A handmaiden to political history or even to the nation.

4 August Koberstein, *Grundriss der Geschichte der deutschen national Literatur* (1827).

5 However, I have already discussed, in 1874, the reform of literary history in a lecture delivered at Klausenburg University, which was later published under the title *A kritikai irodalomtörtenelem fogalmarol (On the Concept of a Critical Literary History)*, Vienna: Faesy and Frick, Budapest: Rosenberg, 1875. [Au.]

6 The Eötvös motto is from *Gondolatok* (*Thoughts*) and may be translated as follows: "Let us study but not imitate the great authors of other ages and nations. The seed which grew into a tree elsewhere may sprout in our soil also, but the full-grown tree, if transplanted, would wither and perish the sooner and the more certainly the greater and more splendid it was in its original place." The Schiller motto is from a letter to Gottfried Körner, October 13, 1789: "It would be a pitiful, petty ideal to write for one nation only; for a philosophical spirit this limitation would be unbearable. He could not confine himself to such a changeable, accidental, and arbitrary form of humanity, a fragment – what is the greatest nation but a fragment?" [Translators' note.]

7 In the light of this fact, the "patriotic" misunderstanding of Goethe's "world literature" in Gervinus, Koberstein and their successors is all the more absurd. [Au.]

8 "Cloud-Cuckoo-Land," the ethereal dwelling-place of philosophers in Aristophanes' satiric play *The Clouds*.

9 Self-sufficiency.

10 "We live in effect in an epoch that is hardly literary at all, and Europe – given over to party hatreds, to the battles of races, to sectarian quarrels, to class conflict – attaches little importance to questions that only a few years ago had seemed capable of occupying every cultivated spirit. Too many Christian countries today resemble the Turkey of the 18th century."

11 In the third part of his essay, entitled "The Decaglottism," Meltzl proposes to reduce the number of working languages of his journal to ten: German, French, English, Italian, Spanish, Portuguese, Dutch, Swedish, Icelandic and Hungarian. His criterion for designating these as languages that have genuinely contributed to the literature of an international *niveau* is that in these literatures "classicism" has been achieved. (The term is not defined in the essay.) Portuguese achieved this standard with Camões, Dutch with *Reinaert de Vos*, Swedish with Tegnér, Icelandic with the *Edda*, Hungarian with Eötvös and Petöfi. Meltzl denies Russian literature any importance comparable to Russia's political role, although he admits Pushkin to be an "isolated phenomenon of praiseworthy independence." The inclusion of non-Western languages in the future Meltzl considers possible only when "Asian literatures will finally come around to accepting our alphabet." [Tr.]

4

What Is World Literature? (1886)

Hutcheson Macaulay Posnett

Born in Dublin in 1855, Hutcheson Macaulay Posnett became a barrister in his home town, and began writing on law and on political economy before turning to comparative literary studies. He prided himself on having invented the term "comparative literature" in English for his book *Comparative Literature* (1886), the result of 10 years' work. That same year, Posnett sailed to New Zealand to take up a position as professor of Classics and English at the University of Auckland, thus moving from the inner to the outer margins of the British Empire. Posnett developed an evolutionary theory of literary production, encompassing Western European literature, the Greek and Roman classics, Arabic, Hebrew, Sanskrit, Persian, Chinese, Japanese, Russian, and Eastern European literatures. In the positivist spirit of his era, Posnett focuses on the interdependency between literature and social life as he elaborates a methodology drawing on Herbert Spencer's economic and political theory and Darwin's belief in the existence of evolutionary patterns in social life. Appropriately, his book was published in a British "International Science Series," together with volumes on steam engines, international law, volcanoes, socialism, and jellyfish.

Departing from Goethe's conception of *Weltliteratur* as a future ideal, Posnett sees world literature as occurring at a middle stage in the evolution of literature, in parallel with social evolution from the tribe to the city to the empire and finally the modern nation. In the chapter given here, he describes world literature as arising in imperial settings such as the Hellenistic world. While noting world literature's potential for universality and a new understanding of humanity's relation to nature, Posnett also probes the loss of organic links to particular communities and social

Hutcheson Macaulay Posnett, "What Is World Literature?" (1886). From Hutcheson Macaulay Posnett, *Comparative Literature* (London: Kegan Paul, Trench & Co.), pp. 235–241.

World Literature in Theory, First Edition. Edited by David Damrosch.

experience. Already in 1886, Posnett sets the terms for debate a century later on world-systems theory, literary evolution, and the gains of losses of literature written for a global audience.

What Is World-Literature?

The fundamental facts in literary evolution are the extent of the social group and the characters of the individual units of which it is composed. So long as social and individual life moves within the narrow associations of the clan, or of the city commonwealth, the ideal range of human sympathy is proportionately restricted. It is true that the clan life of the Hebrews supplied in its *Berîth* or League, in its communal associations of property and descent, the central conceptions of a national ideal. It is true that the city of the Greeks supplied the ideal of Greek centralism as of Greek local patriotism. But before the larger destinies of humanity as a whole could come home to either Hebrew or Greek minds, the associations of the clan and the city commonwealth alike required to be widened by enlarged spheres of social action. This expansion among tribal communities like the Hebrews and Arabs leads to religious cosmopolitanism, to an ideal of human unity deeply social in its character, and strictly confined within the circle of a common creed. A similar expansion in municipal communities like Athens and Rome leads to political cosmopolitanism, to an ideal of human unity within a circle of common culture whose peace is secured by centralised force and whose character is intensely individual. Between the world-religions of Israel and Islâm and the world-cultures of Alexandria and Rome there are, no doubt, very wide differences. Yet, though the former reach universality through social bonds of creed and the latter reach universality through the unsocial idea of personal culture, the outcome of both is to rise above old restrictions of place and time, and to render possible a literature which, whether based on Moses or Homer, may best be termed a "world-literature."

What, then, is world-literature? What are the marks by which it may be known? What is its proper place in the evolution of literature?

The leading mark of world-literature has been already stated; it is the severance of literature from defined social groups – the universalising of literature, if we may use such an expression. Such a process may be observed in the Alexandrian and Roman, the later Hebrew and Arab, the Indian and Chinese, literatures; and this universalism, though differing profoundly in its Eastern and Western conceptions of personality, is alike in the East and West accompanied by the imitation of literary work wrought out in days when the current of social life was broken up into many narrow channels foaming down uplands of rock and tree. Closely connected with this imitation of early models is the reflective and critical spirit, which is another striking characteristic of world-literature. Language now becomes the primary study of the literary artist, and the causes of his devotion to words are not difficult to discover. Just as the language of Hebrew life, in its struggle with Northern and

Southern invasion, and in its own internal break-up, underwent a gradual change which necessitated the production of Targûms, or Paraphrases of the Law, Prophets, and Writings, and thus led to a scrupulously exact study of the sacred texts; just as the Sanskrit, in the course of likewise becoming a dead language, roused that spirit of grammatical criticism for which India from early times has been famous; so among Greeks, Romans, and Arabs deterioration in language was met by the rise of verbal criticism. The triumph of Islâm occasioned the corruption of Arabic by making it the official tongue of the conquered, and turned later Arab literature into a pedantic study of classical words which exactly reproduces the Alexandrian spirit. Magdâni, a contemporary of the famous Harîri, collected and explained Arab proverbs precisely in the manner of Suidas; and Harîri's *Makâmât*, in their forced display of erudition, deserve comparison with the Cassandra of Lycophron. This development of linguistic criticism, among the Arabs, as a consequence of their world-wide conquests, illustrates the need of Alexandrian criticism, when the conquests of Alexander had made the Greek a world-language and proportionately increased the danger of its being corrupted into barbarous jargons. The corruption of Arabic in foreign lands also illustrates the necessity which Roman writers experienced of setting up a refined standard of speech, opposed at once to plebeian coarseness and to provincial barbarism. The need and value of grammatical studies at Rome may be estimated by the deterioration of language which set in after the Augustan age. "In the first century of the Imperial period," says Professor Teuffel, "prose begins already to decay by being mixed with poetical diction, and becoming estranged from natural expression. The decay of accidence and syntax begins also about this time. Later on the plebeian element found admission; and when the influence of provincial writers, who were not guided by a native sense of the language, and who mixed up the diction and style of all periods, became prevalent in literature, the confusion became still greater." It can be easily understood how the classical language of India, likewise, in its conflict with a great variety of local dialects, came to depend more on the verbal criticism of grammarians than on that creative originality which in our days of national languages, stereotyped by the aid of printing and widely diffused education, is rightly accounted so much more valuable than the study of words.

But, besides the universal idea of humanity and the critical study of language as the medium of sacred books or models of literary art, there is a third characteristic of world-literature which to our modern European minds is perhaps the most interesting. This is the rise of new æsthetic appreciations of physical nature and its relations to man. Among the Hebrews and Arabs, it is true, we cannot observe this characteristic of world-literature so distinctly as elsewhere. For the Hebrews the idea of Yâhveh was so closely connected with physical conceptions – sunshine, storm, rain, lightning, thunder – that the sights and sounds of Nature were scarcely realisable save through the creator-god of his peculiar people. The Allâh of the Arabs is even a closer approach to that One Unhuman Power which modern science tends to reduce into an Impersonal Force; moreover, the Arabs, while, like the Hebrews, prevented from treating Nature as distinct from the Deity, found the proper subjects of their literature within the limits of the Qur'ân's language and ideas. But in India, China, Greece, and Italy it was otherwise. Indian poetry, for example, through the medium of its polytheistic religion, could deify physical nature without offending religious feelings. The myths of early Greece had been closely connected with physical nature; and, though the city commonwealth tended to humanise and rationalise these myths, they remained, even in the days of Greek world-literature, a treasure-house from which Theocritus, Moschus, and Bion could bring forth things new and old for those who were tired of the crowded and dusty thoroughfares of Alexandria. Italy, indeed, had no real mythology of her own, and the purely practical value attached to agricultural life by the old Romans was fatal to any poetical sentiment of Nature; yet in the world-empire of Rome also we find the poet turning away from man to physical nature, and, though the inspiration of Lucretius may smack too much of the *savant*, and that of Vergil too much of manuals *de re rusticâ* [of country matters], we are justified in regarding the world-literature of Rome, like that of India or Greece, as a witness to the sentiment of Nature in man.

But here we must draw a distinction between some of the world-literatures known to history and others. No doubt the habit of realising humanity as a whole accustoms the mind to the contrast between man and physical nature, and sets it the difficult task of reconciling the claims of each; but the social conception of humanity is connected with physical nature in a different manner from the individual conception. Wherever the idea of personality as distinct from all social ties has been reached, the aspects of the physical world are and must be altered. Hence the great differences between the sentiment of Nature as manifested in the Græco-Latin literature of Alexandria and Rome, and the same sentiment as manifested in the literatures of India and China. In the latter no separate relation between each individual and the physical world is observed; all is social, and differences of human personality do not obtrude themselves between the world of Man and the world of Nature. But in the former the isolated feelings of individuals, their personal loves, their personal pains and pleasures, are brought into constant contrast or comparison with Nature's life. The Western idyll is a "picture-poem" of dramatic and descriptive character curiously differing from such abstract, social, and impersonal poetry as India offers in abundance; and, whatever the origin of the idyll may have been, its essential features – dramatic perception of individual character and picturesque description of physical nature – show how differently the individualism of the West looks upon Nature, compared with the monotheistic social view of Hebrews and Arabs and the polytheistic social view of Indians and Chinese.[1]

But, though it may be readily admitted that in the history of the world there have been certain social stages sufficiently similar in the literature they produced and the conditions of their literary production to warrant our use of the word "world-literature," it may be said that our order of treatment – after the literatures of the city commonwealth and before those of the nation – is not in harmony with prevailing ideas of literary development. Why not pass, it may be asked, from the city commonwealth to the nation, and from national literatures reach the universalism of world-literature? No doubt much might be said for this arrangement if the philosophy of ancient Greece, if the language, law, and religion of ancient Rome, were not so closely intertwined with the growth of our European nationalities; if their social and political progress had not been so profoundly affected by the world-wide ideas of Roman law and the Christian religion. But, since it is clearly impossible to treat of national progress in Europe without allowing great weight to these powerful influences, it would be highly inconvenient to pass from the city commonwealth to those national groups whose internal and external developments have owed so much to days of world-empire and world-literature. We shall, accordingly, examine the literary characteristics of the latter before we approach the national groups.

Note

1   M. Victor de Laprade (*Le Sentiment de la Nature chez les Modernes*, [Paris: Didier, 1868], p. 216) notes the vastness and profundity of the Indian sentiment of Nature and contrasts it in these respects with the Greek. The source of the difference is plainly to be found in the individualism of Greek contrasted with the socialism of Indian life.

5

World Literature (1907)

Rabindranath Tagore

A humanist with universalistic dreams, Rabindranath Tagore (1861–1941) was the leading modern Bengali poet, as well as a noted novelist, playwright, painter, and essayist. Widely known throughout Europe and the United States from the early twentieth century thanks to translations in English, Dutch, German, and Spanish, Tagore achieved worldwide fame with his poetic volume *Gitanjali* (published in English in 1912 with an introduction by W.B. Yeats), which won him the Nobel Prize in 1913, and for his novel *The Home and the World* (*Ghare-Baire*, 1919). Brought up in a home which hosted a dialogue of Indian and Western cultures, Tagore advocated India's cultural as well as political independence from Britain. A leader of the Bengali Renaissance movement, he founded the Visva-Bharati University, a school to which he dedicated half of his life, trying to turn its campus into a bridge between India and the world. Seeing the British regime in India as a "political symptom of our social disease," Tagore promoted humanist education over a "blind revolution" to reunite India to the world.

In his 1907 essay "World Literature," Tagore advocates searching for "the eternal and universal man" in literature. To some extent following Goethe's notion of *Weltliteratur*, Tagore turns it to new purposes in colonial India, opposing both a narrow-minded nationalism and the British policy of dividing and conquering India's many regions and cultures. His "world literature" is a means to move beyond national boundaries to integrate humanity within a universal spirit of culture through the power of imagination. "The nations must serve each other as guides. … Every country would do well, then, to welcome foreign thoughts; for in such matters hospitality makes the fortune of the host."

Rabindranath Tagore, "World Literature" (1907). Trans. Swapan Chakravorty. From Rabindranath Tagore, *Selected Writings on Literature and Language,* ed. Sukanta Chaudhuri (New Delhi: Oxford University Press, 2001), pp. 138–150.

World Literature in Theory, First Edition. Edited by David Damrosch.

Whatever faculties we have within us exist for the sole purpose of forging bonds with others. We are true and we achieve truth only through such bonds. Otherwise, there is no sense in saying 'I am' or 'something is'.

Our bonds with truth in this world are of three kinds – the bonds of reason, of necessity, and of joy.

Of these, the bond of reason may be described as a kind of contest. It is like the bond between the hunter and his prey. Reason builds a dock, makes truth stand in it like a defendant, and cross-examines it till it is forced to yield its secrets bit by bit. That is why reason cannot help feeling a self-conceit with respect to truth. It senses its own power in proportion to its knowledge of truth.

Next comes the bond of necessity. The bond of necessity, that is of work, engenders a collaboration between human power and truth. Enforced by need, this bond draws truth closer to us. Yet there remains a distance. Just as the English trader had once secured his aims by bowing to the Nawab and offering him gifts, but, his mission accomplished, eventually ascended the throne himself, so also we think we have gained the empery of the world when we have used truth to material advantage to achieve our purpose. We then boast that nature is our waiting woman; water, air, and fire, our unpaid servants.

Finally, the bond of joy. The bond of beauty or joy erases all distance: there is no more self-conceit; we do not hesitate to surrender ourselves to the small and the weak. The king of Mathura then has to do all he can to hide his royal dignity from the milkmaid of Vrindavan.[1] Where we are linked by the bond of joy, we feel the power of neither reason nor work: we feel exclusively our own selves; no concealment or calculation comes in the way.

In sum, the bond between truth and human reason is our school, the bond of necessity our workplace, and the bond of joy our home. We do not carry our entire selves to school, nor do we yield ourselves entirely to the workplace; it is at home that we are relieved to let go of our whole selves without restraint. The school is unembellished, the workplace unfurnished, but the home is variously adorned.

What is this bond of joy? It is nothing but knowing others as our own, and our selves as other. Once that knowledge is achieved, we have no more questions. We never ask, 'Why do I love myself?' The very sense of my own being gives me joy. When we feel the same sense of being about someone else, there is no need to ask why I like that person.

Yajnavalkya had told Gargi:[2]

Na va are putrasya kamaya putrah priyo bhavati atmanastu kamaya putrah priyo bhavati.

Na va are vittasya kamaya vittam priyam bhavati atmanastu kamaya vittam priyam bhavati.

I love my son not because I desire him, but because I desire the Self. I love wealth not because I covet it, but because I desire the Self. (And so on.)

It means that I desire that in which I realise my own self more comprehensively. The son fills a certain lack in me, that is, I find myself in greater measure in my son.

It is as if in him 'I' becomes 'more than I'. That is why he is *atmiya* to my self: he makes my *atman*[3] true even outside of me. The truth that I apprehend in myself with immense certainty, and that thereby begets love in me, is the same truth that I apprehend with equal certainty in my son, thereby enhancing the same love. Hence if you want to know what a man is, you must know what he loves. It shows in which objects of the universe he finds his own self, how far he has been able to disperse his own being. Where I do not feel love, my soul has reached its limits.

A child is thrilled when it sees light or spots a moving object: it laughs, it gurgles. In this light and movement, it finds its own consciousness in greater measure – that is the reason for its delight.

But when its consciousness reaches beyond sensory apprehension to the various levels of the heart and the mind, that mild stir is no longer enough to cause delight. Not that it feels no joy at all, but it feels less of it.

Likewise, as a human soul develops, it desires to feel the truth of its own being in a larger way.

To begin with, one can apprehend one's innermost spirit in the outside world most readily and comprehensively in other human beings. It is natural that through sight, hearing, and thought, through the play of the imagination and the attachments of the heart, one should be able to recoup oneself roundly in humanity. That is why one's being is filled to the brim by knowing, befriending, and serving fellow humans. That is why, in every land and age, one is considered great in proportion to the number of souls in which one has merged one's own in order to realise and express oneself. Such a person is indeed a *mahatman*, a great soul. My soul finds fulfilment in all humanity – one who has not realised this even a little, by some means or other, has been deprived of a fair share of human nature. To know the soul as confined to itself is to know it only in a depleted sense.

The human soul has a natural disposition to know itself among others. Self-interest is a great obstacle to this end and so is vanity. Many such worldly impediments break up our souls' natural drift, preventing an unimpeded view of the consummate beauty of human nature.

I know that some will argue, why should the human soul's natural inclinations suffer such ill-use in the world? Why should you not regard self-interest and vanity, things you dismiss as impediments, as part of our natural disposition?

As a matter of fact, many do say such things. That is because the impediments to human nature strike our eyes more than the nature itself. When a man first learns to ride a bicycle, he is destined to fall more often than to move. If someone then says that the man is rehearsing the fall rather than the ride, it is pointless arguing with him. Vanity and self-interest jostle us at every step. But if we fail to see the human effort to preserve our deepest disposition – that is, the effort to unite with all others – if we insist that the fall is the more natural function, that would merely be cavilling.

In fact, the impediments are necessary to learn that what is natural for us is indeed our nature and to make that nature exert itself to the full. That is how our nature knows itself with heightened self-awareness: the fuller the awareness, the deeper its joy. It is thus with every other thing.

Take, for instance, our reason. To determine causal relations is part of its nature. As long as it does so easily among self-evident things, it cannot fully perceive itself. But the causal links of the universe are buried in such obscurity that reason has to labour incessantly to unearth them. This effort to overcome obstacles makes reason apprehend itself most intensely in science and philosophy, and it is this effort that enhances its glory. In fact, if we consider it well, science and philosophy are nothing but the self-realisation of reason in the object. Wherever it perceives its distinctive rationale, it sees that object and itself together. This is what we call understanding. Reason finds joy in this way of seeing. Otherwise, human beings need not have been so happy on discovering that the apple falls to the ground for the same cause as makes the sun attract the earth. If the sun pulls the earth, what is in it for me? This, that I can comprehend the universal phenomenon within my reason, I can apprehend my reason in all things. From the speck of dust to the sun, the moon, and the stars – everything can thus unite with my reason. In this way, the inexhaustible mystery of the universe is drawing human reason into the open to reveal it more fully to human beings and returning it to them after uniting it with all creation. Knowledge is this union of reason with the universe, and it is in this union that our rationality finds joy.

Likewise, it is the nature of the human soul to seek a union of its particular humanness with all humanity: in this lies its true joy. It has constantly to battle hostility and obstruction both outside and within in order to realise this nature with total awareness. That is why self-interest is so potent, vanity so stubborn, the way of the world so difficult. There is great joy when human nature shines in full splendour through these obstacles to express itself forcefully. It is our own enhanced selves that we then discover.

It is for this reason that we wish to read the biographies of great men. In their characters we see our own impeded and obscured nature freed and extended. When reading history, we enjoy descrying our own natures in various people in varying shapes and measures in different countries, periods, and events. Whether I clearly understand it or not, my mind begins to recognise that I am one by embracing all humanity. The more I apprehend that unity, the greater my good and my joy.

In biography and history, however, we do not have a clear view of the whole picture. That too reaches us dimmed by many impediments and doubts. The image of humanity we glimpse even then is certainly a lofty one; but our minds strive to refashion that image after our heart's desire and capture it in language for all time. It is as if that alone can make the image exclusively mine. It becomes the possession of the human heart when I can express my love in it through graceful language and formal skill. It is no longer lost in the world's ebb and flow.

In this manner, all that is exquisitely expressed in the outside world, be it the glow of sunrise or a noble soul's radiance or my own heart's passions – everything that excites the heart from moment to moment – the heart entwines with one of its own creations and clings to it as its own. Every such occasion is a means for it to express itself in a distinctive way.

Human self-expression in the world follows two broad courses. One is work, the other literature. The two courses run parallel. Human beings have poured themselves into the compositions of their work and their thoughts. These two streams complement each other. We must read history and literature to know humanity as revealed in these two currents.

In the field of work, human beings have built homes, societies, political and religious communities with all the strength and experience of body, mind, and heart. All they have known, achieved and desired is expressed in these constructions. Human nature, thus intertwined with the world, has taken various forms and installed itself in the midst of all things. What was inchoate in the realm of ideas assumes concrete form in the world; what was feeble within the one assumes a larger, organic unity among the many. It is increasingly impossible for an individual to achieve clear and full expression except through the home, society, polity, and religious community fashioned by many people through many years. All this has become the means for humanity to reveal itself to itself. Otherwise, we would not call it civilisation, that is, total humanness. Whether in the polity or in society, we are uncivilised in respects where each of us is totally autonomous, where the one is isolated from the rest. For this reason, when society or the polity is hurt, the blow is felt by the extended body of each individual; if a society grows parochial in any respect, the development of each individual self is impeded. One can express one's humanness unreservedly in so far as these structures set up by human beings are open and free. The more the inhibition, the more one lacks expression and remains impoverished, because the world exists to express what is human by means of work, and expression alone brings joy.

But although human beings express themselves through work, such expression is not, in this case, the primary goal: it is an offshoot. The housewife expresses herself in household work, but that is not the purpose uppermost in her mind. Through domestic chores she fulfils various intentions: those intentions reflect off her work and reveal her nature.

But there are times when one wishes primarily to express onself. For instance, when there is a wedding in the house, people are busy making sure that all the work is done well, but, at the same time, they feel the need to proclaim their feelings. On that day, the members of the family cannot help declaring the well-being and happiness of their home to everyone. How do they declare it? The flute is played, lamps are lit, the house is decorated with garlands. Through the beauty of sound, fragrance, and spectacle, through all the radiance, the heart spreads itself like a fountain in a hundred streams in all directions. Thus, by various suggestions, it arouses its own joy in other hearts so as to make that joy true amidst them all.

The mother cannot help caring for the infant in her arms. But that is not all: mother love seeks expression surpassing the demands of care and without apparent cause. It wells up from within in various kinds of play, endearments, and words. Decking the child in many colours and ornaments, such love cannot help spreading wealth through extravagance and sweetness through beauty, quite without need.

It is clear from all this that such is the nature of one's heart. It seeks to join its own emotions to the world outside. Incomplete in itself, it is relieved if it can somehow turn its inner truth into the truth of the world. To the heart, its abode is never just a fabric of brick and timber; it paints its dwelling in its own colours and makes it a home. To the heart, the land that it inhabits is not made up simply of earth, water, and sky. It is happy only when that land unveils for it the maternal, life-fostering aspect of the divine: otherwise the heart cannot view itself in the outside world. Failing this, it becomes indifferent; and for the heart, indifference is death.

By such means, the heart continually establishes affective bonds with truth. Where there are affective ties, there is an exchange. The mistress of one's heart's abode is a proud housewife: her pride is hurt when she cannot send back a gift to match the one her kin, the world, sends her. To express good kinship, she has to create with such ingredients as word and sound, the brush and the chisel, and thus embellish her gift-basket. If some need of her own is served in the process, well and good; but often she is willing to express herself at the expense of her needs. She is eager to proclaim herself even if that makes her bankrupt. Expression is the prodigal wing of human nature: it drives reason, the parsimonious steward, to strike its forehead in repeated despair.

The heart asks, 'How can I be as true outside as I am within? Where in the world will I find the right resource and scope?' It continually wails, 'I cannot reveal my own self, I cannot install myself in the outside world.' When the rich man feels his own wealth in his heart, he can exhaust Kuber's[4] riches in trying to express it to the world. When the lover feels true love in his heart, he can sacrifice wealth, honour, and life in an instant to express that love, that is to make it true in the outside world. The heart never loses its intense eagerness to make the inward into the outward and the outward into the inward in this way. There is a lyric by Balaram Das[5] which says:

You were in my heart, who has brought you out in the open?

It is as if the beloved object were an object within the lover's heart. Someone has drawn it out of doors, so the lover is longing to fetch it back inside again. There is the opposite situation as well. When the heart fails to perceive its desires and passions in the external world, it tries hard to fashion their image with its own hands out of various ingredients. In this way, the heart's longing to make the world its own and itself the world's is constantly at work. To express oneself in the outside world is part of this process. That is why when it comes to expression, the heart makes one agree to lose everything one has.

When a barbarian army marches to battle, victory over the enemy is not its sole concern. It manifests its inner violence in external guise by putting on warpaint, sounding drums and war cries, and dancing a wild war dance. It is as though its belligerence is not complete without all this. Violence secures its practical goal through battle, and slakes its desire for self-expression through such superfluous claptrap.

Western warfare of the present day has not rid itself totally of drums and music, or of dress and trappings, as expressions of bellicose passion. However, strategic wisdom is more crucial in modern battles: they are progressively moving away from the human heart's habitual nature. The band of dervishes who attacked the British army in Egypt[6] did not lay down their lives just to win a battle. They died to the last man to express the fiery zeal of their hearts. Those who fight only to win will never act in such an uncalled-for manner. The human heart expresses itself even at the cost of suicide: can one imagine a greater waste?

Take the instance of worship. It is different for the devout and the clever. The clever one thinks, 'My worship will obtain my salvation.' The devout says, 'My devotion is imperfect without worship; whether it profits me or not, worship brings my heart's devotion out into the world where it finds its full and secure dwelling.' In this way, devotion achieves its own fulfilment by expressing itself in worship. To the clever, worship is laying out money at interest; to the devout, it is idle expense. For when the heart expresses itself, it cares nothing for loss.

One's heart is a willing captive to whatever in the universe displays this quality, which is also its own: it does not then raise a single question. This thriftless excess in the world constitutes beauty. We glimpse the presence of the heart's creed in the wide world when the flower shows no hurry to turn into seed, but surpasses necessity and blooms in beauty; when the cloud does not rush through its chore and dissolve into rain, but tarries to hold our eyes in thrall with uncalled-for bursts of colour; when the trees do not stretch scrawny branches like gaunt beggars for the sun and rain, but shower a wealth of green splendour on the brides of the heavens;[7] when the sea is not just a giant clearing-house for dispersing water around the globe in the form of clouds, but is awesome with the unfathomed dread of its liquid blue; when the mountain is not content merely to supply the earth with water from its rivers but keeps the force of the terrific motionless across the skies, like destruction's lord stilled in meditation. Reason, that is forever old, shakes its head and asks, 'Why such a waste of needless effort all over the world?' The heart, that is forever young, answers, 'Only to beguile me: I see no other reason.' The heart knows that all through the world there is one heart that continually expresses itself. Otherwise why should there be so much beauty and music, so many gestures, shadows, and hints, and such adornments throughout creation? The heart is not blandished by the trafficker's thrift; that is why in water, earth, and sky, there is such superfluous effort to hide necessity at every step. If the world were not replete with rasa,[8] we would have remained small and demeaned: the heart would perpetually have complained that it was uninvited to the festival of the world. But the whole world, brimful of rasa despite its countless chores, gives the heart this honeyed message, 'I want you. I want you in various forms. I want you in laughter and tears, in fear and faith, in sorrow and strength.'

In the world itself, we see two processes at work: the expression of function and the expression of idea. It is beyond our powers to observe and comprehend fully that which is expressed through functions. Our learning cannot encompass the immeasurable potency of knowledge that it contains.

But the expression of idea is unmediated expression. A thing of beauty is simply beautiful. The great has greatness. The fearsome inspires dread. The world's rasa enters one's heart directly and draws the rasa within it out into the world. Whatever hide-and-seek, whatever the hindrance in this meeting, ultimately there is nothing in it other than expression and union.

We thus see a likeness between the universe and the human world. The divine as truth and knowledge is expressed through the world's functioning, and its joyous form is perceived through its various rasas. It is hard to acquaint oneself thoroughly with the divine-as-knowledge through the world's functions; but there is no difficulty in apprehending the divine-as-joy through rasa, because through rasa He directly manifests Himself.

In the human world too, the power of knowledge is busy at work, and the power of joy is creating rasa. In work lies our faculty of self-preservation; in rasa, our faculty for self-expression. Self-preservation is necessary, but self-expression surpasses necessity.

Necessity impedes expression and expression impedes necessity: we have already seen that in the instance of warfare. Self-interest dislikes extravagance, whereas joy declares itself in prodigality. Hence, in the world of self-interest, such as at the office, the less we express ourselves the more we are esteemed; while at a joyous celebration, the festivities shine brighter the more we forget self-interest.

That is why self-expression finds no hindrance in literature. It dwells far from self-interest. There sorrow draws a film of tears over our hearts, but does not invade our homes; fear sways our minds, but does not hurt our bodies; pleasure makes our hearts quiver at its touch, but does not provoke and inflame our lust. Human beings continue to fashion a necessity-free realm of literature right alongside their world of necessity. In the former they can, without doing themselves any material damage, delight in apprehending their own nature variously through various rasas; they can view an unimpeded expression of their selves. In that realm there is no obligation – there is only joy; no beadle and bailiff, only the great king himself.

So what does literature acquaint us with? With humanity's wealth and abundance, which overflows all its material needs and is not exhausted within its mundane limits.

Hence I wrote in an earlier essay[9] that although eating involves a universal rasa, equally familiar to young and old, it is a minor presence in literature outside farcical comedy, because it never exceeds the satisfaction of the meal. Once the stomach is full, we dismiss it with the spot-fee of a resounding 'ah'; we do not invite it to the portals of literature for an honorarium. But the rasas that overspill the pots in our pantry course through literature in a purling flood. Since practical work cannot exhaust them, the human heart, impelled by that flood-tide, finds relief when it can express them in literature.

In such abundance lies the real expression of humanity. It is true that human beings are fond of eating, but true above all that they are heroic. Who can contain the powerful impulse of this truth? Like the Bhagirathi,[10] it flows right into the sea – crushing rocks, sweeping away Airavat,[11] slaking the thirst of town, country, and farmland. Human heroism rises above the world after finishing all the world's work.

In this way, whatever in human life is noble and timeless, whatever transcends human need and work, yields itself naturally to literature and automatically fashions humanity's greater image.

There is one other factor. What we see in the world we see dispersed – a glimpse now and a glimpse then, a little here and a little there; we see an object mingled with ten others. These gaps and admixtures disappear in literature. There all the light is focused on what is being expressed, we are allowed to see nothing else for the moment. Various devices are employed to create a space where that object alone may shine.

Naturally, we will not put something there that would not accord with such intense individuality, such sharp light. That would merely embarrass the unworthy. The glutton is not so visible under the cover of the world's ways; he becomes ridiculous when viewed in focused light on the literary stage. Hence it is natural for human beings to establish in literature the expression that is not trite, that the heart accepts without demur as truly representing its compassion and courage, its fury or calm – that can stand within the pale of proficient art yet withstand, with head held high, the unblinking gaze of abiding time; with any other kind of material, the incongruity jars on us. Our minds rebel at the sight of anyone but the king on the throne.

But not everyone is capable of high-minded discernment, and not every society is great. There are times when petty, passing infatuations diminish human beings. The distorted mirror of such times magnifies the trivial; their literature exalts human pettiness and brazenly highlights its own blemishes. Then virtuosity displaces art, vanity passes for glory, and Kipling takes Tennyson's seat.

But great time[12] lies in wait, and it sifts everything. Whatever is small and worn-out slips through the sieve to blend with the dust. Among different ages and people, only those things survive in which all human beings can discover themselves. The things that pass this test are the permanent and universal human treasures.

Through this process of making and breaking, a timeless ideal of human nature and expression gathers of itself in literature. That ideal stays at the helm to guide the literature of a new age. To judge literature by that ideal is to draw on the support of humankind's collective wisdom.

It is now time to make my main point. It is that literature is not viewed in its true light if we see it confined to a particular space and time. If we realise that universal humanity expresses itself in literature, we shall be able to discern what is worth viewing in the latter. No literary work has succeeded unless its author has become the mere means of composition. A work is admitted to the ranks of literature only when the author has realised the ideas of the human race in his own thoughts and expressed humanity's pain in his writing. We have to regard literature as a temple being built by the master mason, universal man; writers from various countries and periods are working under him as labourers. None of us has the *plan* of the entire building; but the defective parts are dismantled again and again, and every worker has to conform to that invisible *plan* by exercising his natural talent and blending his composition with the total design. This is what brings out his artistic prowess; this is why no one pays him a common labourer's wages but honours him as a master builder.

Comparative Literature is the English title you have given to the subject I have been asked to discuss. In Bengali, I shall call it World Literature.

If we are to understand what people are saying through their work, or what their purpose and endeavour are, we have to follow the course of human intention through all history. The reign of Akbar, the history of Gujarat, the character of Elizabeth – viewing history in such isolated fragments merely satisfies our curiosity about facts. But he who knows that Akbar and Elizabeth are mere vehicles, that throughout history humankind continually tries to fulfil its deepest desire through diverse endeavours, errors, and restitutions; that it strives to emancipate itself by joining in expansive ties with all others in every direction; that the ideal of self-government struggles to realise itself in monarchies and thereafter in democracies; that human beings make and unmake themselves to seek expression and to realise their individual beings in and through the collective being of humankind – such a person seeks in history not an individual but the ever-active intention of the timelessly human. Such a one returns home after viewing not just the pilgrims but the very deity they come to worship from all parts of the world.

Likewise, the thing truly worth seeing in world literature is the way human beings express their joy in literature and the abiding form in which the human soul wishes to reveal itself through the diversity of this expression. We need to enter the world of literature to learn whether the human soul is best pleased to declare itself as sufferer or epicure or ascetic, and how far human kinship has been rendered true in the world – that is how far truth has become a human possession. It will not do to know of literature as artifice: it is an organic world. Its mystery is not any individual's private possession. Its creation is a continuous process like the material world's; and yet in the heart of this unfinished creation, an ideal conclusion dwells immovably.

The mass of matter at the sun's core is forming itself in many ways, both solid and liquid. We cannot see the process, but the surrounding ring of light ceaselessly expresses the sun to the world. It is thus that the sun gifts itself to the world and links itself to all else. If we could make humanity the object of such an integral view, we would see it like the sun. We would see that the mass of matter was gradually forming itself into layers, and around it, perpetually, a luminous ring of expression spreading itself joyously in every direction. Look at literature as this ring of light, made of language, encircling humanity. Here there are storms of light, the wellsprings of radiance, the collision of radiant vapours.

As you walk through human habitations, you see that people have no leisure – the grocer minds his shop, the blacksmith hammers iron, the labourer carries loads, the trader checks his ledger. At the same time, something remains invisible. See it in your mind's eye: on either side of this road, among the houses, shops, and alleyways, the flood of rasa is spreading itself in so many streams and furrows over so much that is bleak, straitened, and impoverished; the *Ramayana* and the *Mahabharata*, stories and fables, kirtan and panchali[13] are portioning out the nectar of the universal human soul to each man and woman day and night; Rama and Lakshmana are drawing up to stand behind the trivial labours of humble folk; the compassionate breeze of Panchavati[14] is blowing through dark tenements; the human heart's creations and expressions are enclasping the privations and stringencies of the labouring world with hands decked in bracelets of beauty and benediction. This is how we must see the whole of literature surrounding the whole of humanity. We need to see that the material being of the human race has extended itself far in every direction through the agency of its conceptual being. The rain that falls upon humankind is girt by many showers of verse and music, many *Meghadutams*[15] and Vidyapatis;[16] the joys and sorrows of its small abode swell with the joys and sorrows of the Chandra and Surya kings.[17] The sorrows of the Mountain King's daughter[18] float around the daughter of a humble home; the poor man's suffering is enlarged in the glory of the poor god on Mount Kailas.[19] By this continuous diffusion of the self, humankind seems to exceed and enhance its being continually in the outside world. Although constricted by its situation, humankind is extending itself through the creation of feelings and ideas. Literature is this second world around the material one.

Do not so much as imagine that I would guide your way through world literature. We must all cut our paths through it as best we can. I simply wished to say that just as the world is not my ploughland added to yours and to someone else's – to see the world in this light is to take a rustic view – so also, literature is not my writing added to yours and to someone else's. We usually regard literature in this rustic light. It is time we pledged that our goal is to view universal humanity in universal literature by freeing ourselves from rustic uncatholicity; that we shall recognise a totality in each particular author's work, and that in this totality we shall perceive the interrelations among all human efforts at expression.

Notes

1   In Hindu tradition, the god Krishna was born in the city of Mathura in northern India; before becoming king of Mathura, he was a cowherd in the forest of Vrindavan outside the city.
2   Tagore is quoting from memory a passage in the Upanishads, in which the sage Yajnavalkya remarks to his wife that people love their son not for his own sake but for the sake of their own self. Tagore here interprets *atman*, "self," as the Supreme Self, transcending the individual.
3   *Atmiya* (usually meaning "a relative") is derived from *atman*, "self."
4   In Hindu mythology, Kuber is the god of wealth.
5   A leading sixteenth-century devotional poet.
6   Sufi Muslims who fought against the growth of British power in the 1880s.
7   Celestial nymphs.
8   Literally meaning "juice" or "taste," *rasa* was used in Sanskrit aesthetics to denote the basic poetic emotion or mood of a work; traditionally, a work of poetry or drama would express one of eight rasas, including love, compassion, fury, and heroism.
9   "A Literary Convention," published in the journal *Bangadarshan* in 1907.
10 A name for the Ganges.
11 A giant elephant that tried to draw up the Ganges into its trunk.
12 An epithet of the destroyer god Shiva.
13 *kirtan*: chants; *panchali*: folksongs.
14 *Panchavati*: In the *Ramayana*, the forest where Rama and Sita lived in exile.
15 The *Meghaduta* or "Cloud Messenger," a narrative poem by Kalidasa (*c*. 5th century), in which a cloud is instructed to carry a message between lovers.
16 Vidyapati (*c.*1352–1448), a poet known for his devotional and love poetry.
17 The divine royal families at the heart of the epic *Mahabharata* and *Ramayana*.
18 Parvati, consort of the god Shiva.
19 Shiva, in his aspect of a solitary ascetic.

6

A View on the Unification
of Literature (1922)

Zheng Zhenduo

Writer, translator, and editor Zheng Zhenduo (1898–1958) was one of the leading intellectuals of the May Fourth Movement, which promoted the ideals of a new and modern Chinese literature. The movement began with a major rally on May 4, 1919, protesting the government's acceptance of the terms of the Versailles Treaty ending World War I, in particular the agreement that Japan should retain territory on mainland China. The movement soon developed into a searching examination of the need for China to modernize as successfully as Japan had been doing since the start of the Meiji Era in 1868. The May Fourth intellectuals criticized traditional values as a major reason for China's belatedness. They advocated a turn to the Western world to find new ideas to revitalize Chinese culture, emphasizing literature as a key arena of social reflection and reform, in addition to economic and scientific advances. Their approach toward traditional Chinese literature was iconoclastic, and they sought to modernize the Chinese language and its literature by drawing on Western models without falling into mere imitation of the foreign.

In 1921 Zheng became a founding member of the Literary Research Society, an organization that dismissed the "art for art's sake" position in favor of realism, turned into "art for life's sake." A leading voice in promoting modern Chinese literature through journals such as *Fiction Monthly*, Zheng emphasized the need for an authentic fiction of "blood and tears" to oppose the mix of Confucian didacticism and popular entertainment offered by the traditional "Butterfly literature." Zheng taught at Fudan and other leading Chinese universities during the 1930s; after the Communist revolution in 1949 he became director of the Literary Research Institute of the Chinese Academy of Social Sciences, and deputy minister of culture. An intellectual of global interests, Zheng died in a plane crash in the Soviet Union in 1958 while leading a cultural delegation en route to the Middle East.

Zheng Zhenduo, "A View on the Unification of Literature" (1922). Trans. Guangchen Chen. First published in *Fiction Monthly* 13:8 (1922).

   Throughout his life, Zheng took an active interest in reassessing classical Chinese literature and in studying world myth and folktales, writing books on Greek and Roman mythology and on Indian tales as well as a history of Chinese literature. He also edited an early world literature series, *Shijie wenku* (The World's Library), and translated widely from Russian, Latin, and Greek; he was the first Chinese translator of Homer's *Iliad*. Zheng was also a leading translator of Indian literatures, including many works by Tagore. Zheng's broad outlook is typified by his 1922 essay "A View on the Unification of Literature," translated for this volume, in which Zheng stresses the need to study literature beyond national and regional boundaries through the creative work of translation and through opening up to foreign literatures, as a means to the renewal of Chinese literary culture on a worldly basis.

I

Nowadays, there are people everywhere studying literature; but no one approaches it as a whole, or as an independent subject of study.[1] There are people specializing in literature of a certain period, for example Georg Brandes with his *Main Currents in the Literature of the Nineteenth Century*, or Joel Elias Spingarn with *A History of Literary Criticism in the Renaissance*, etc. There are those specializing in literature of a certain nation, like Peter Kropotkin with *Ideals and Realities in Russian Literature*, or H.A. Taine with *Histoire de la littérature anglaise*, etc. There are those specializing in a certain genre, like George Saintsbury with *A History of Criticism*, or Ludwig Lewisohn with *The Modern Drama*. There are those specializing in a certain writer, like Richard Moulton with *Shakespeare as a Dramatic Artist*, or *Shakespeare as a Dramatic Thinker*, etc. And there are those specializing in a certain literary movement, a literary issue, or a literary notion, like Arthur Symons with *The Symbolist Movement in Literature*, Henry A. Peers with *A History of English Romanticism in the Nineteenth Century*, Leo Berg with *Der Übermensch in der neueren Literatur* (*The Superman in Modern Literature*), etc. But none of them – absolutely none – takes literature as a whole or an independent subject, unifying time, place, people and genre to pursue a thorough and encompassing study.

   This is not only the case with individual scholars, but also with the way literature is institutionalized in universities: we only see departments of English literature, French literature, German literature, Greek literature, Latin literature, but no – absolutely no – department of *literature* that approaches it as a whole or an independent subject, unifying time, place, people and genre to pursue a thorough and encompassing study.

   When someone mentions the study of philosophy, we instantly understand that this so-called study of philosophy is not the result of someone's interest in Greek philosophy, or in German philosophy. Instead, we admit that there exists something called philosophy, which is independent of all these particular philosophies; it has its own goal and history; it constitutes a unity of its own, rather than the sum of all particularities. In other words, we admit that philosophy is a unity, an independent subject of study. We know that we should unify time, place, people and genre to pursue a thorough and encompassing study of philosophy. It is the same with regard to history, art, biology, sociology, and economics. Just as with philosophy, we approach them as unities; we admit that they are unified and independent subjects; we unify time, place, people and genre to pursue a thorough and encompassing study.

Why then should literature alone be an exception? Why are there only specific studies of authors, times, places, and genres, but no universal and unified study? Why are there only departments of English literature, French literature, German literature, Greek literature, Latin literature, but no independent department of *literature*? It is true that philosophy, history, economics, and biology all have specific branches, like the study of Greek philosophy, or the study of Indian political history, etc., but they also pursue universal and unified studies that transcend these partial concerns. Why then should literature alone be an exception?

This is really a strange and incomprehensible situation.

Someone might argue: don't we have a subject called "comparative literature" in universities? Don't we also have a term called "the philosophy of literature"? Are they not unified and universal studies of literature?

This is not true. Comparative literature indeed approaches but is definitely not the unified study of literature, because it only takes fragments of literature as objects of comparison. This is not universal study. Also, its name is strange: does anyone hear terms like "comparative philosophy," "comparative economics," or "comparative biology"? By the same token, one cannot take the philosophy of literature as the universal study of literature, because it is but one element in the whole study of literature. To take it that way is like taking economics itself as a good businessman.

Alas, literary universalism draws so little attention from today's literary scholars.

We do not understand the reason; we can only say that the study of literature has not yet approached an advanced stage. Richard Moulton thinks that the study of literature has just begun – this is really a correct observation.

II

Why is literary universalism necessary? First, it is because the study of literature itself indeed requires a unified approach.

The study of literature in the past was fragmentary and partial. It recognized an author's literature, but not the author's place in literary history; it knew a period's literature, but not its sources and outcomes; it knew a country's literature, but not its relationship to other countries' literatures, nor those who influenced it, nor those who were influenced by it; it knew one literature well, but not the details of other literatures. Consequently, literary scholars could not form a comprehensive and unified concept of literature. They cannot even succeed in their specialized fields, let alone gain a solid understanding of literature in itself. Let's take the origin of literature as an example: without studying all types of early literatures, how can we decide which one is the origin? Or the evolution of literature: without studying the development of the world's literatures, how can we understand the way literature evolves? As to the theory and art of literature, the most precise concepts can never be reached without putting all the world's literatures side by side to study. In one word, without a unified and universal study of literature, we can never form a precise and comprehensive knowledge.

Let's take English literature as another example: if we are unaware of the specifics of French, German, Greek, or Latin literatures, how can we know their influences on English literature? We know that Dante's *Divina Commedia*, Homer's *Iliad* and *Odyssey*, and Goethe's *Faust* each exerted a great influence on English literature. But what is Dante's status in Italian literary history, and what is the content of the *Divina Commedia*? How about the status of Homer and Goethe in their respective countries' literary histories? Considering all these issues, it is impossible to study English literature without knowledge of Greek, German, and other literatures. Similarly, there are English, German, Greek and other influences in French literature. Specializing in English or French literature alone would not allow one to fully understand either. Or in the case of Renaissance literature: without knowledge of Greek and Hebrew literatures, how can we understand its origin and cause? Without knowledge of European literatures after the Renaissance, how can we understand the result and influence of the latter? Examples are innumerable. In short: time, place, people, and genre are all interrelated in literature. Without a unified and comprehensive study of all literatures, a precise and comprehensive view of even a specialized field is unattainable.

There is an even more important reason beyond literary study itself that makes literary universalism indispensible for both scholars and laymen.

As Moulton says, "national literature, it is generally recognized, is a reflection of national history. Literature is much more than the product of an individual."[2] But I would rather think that the world's literatures are exactly a reflection of the spirit and sentiments of its people. Although geographical difference affects relations among schools and multiplies the number of styles, such difference is after all secondary compared to similarity. This is because, despite geographical distance and racial difference, human beings' spirit and sentiments have much in common. People share many similarities, regardless of differences in cultural development; even peoples of the highest cultural level share the same emotions, and the same primitive instincts such as the need for food and dwelling. As Gorky says,

> We do not have a "Universal Literature" because there is not yet a genuine *lingua franca*. But all literary works, be they essays or poetry, are filled with common emotions, thoughts, ideals, sacred longings for happiness derived from spiritual freedom, disdain for suffering, hope for a better life, and the mysterious thing we call "beauty" that could not be defined by language and thought, nor comprehended through emotion. They will return as an eternal, brighter and happier flower to this world, to our hearts.

He continues:

> It tells us that there is something in common between the frustrated and unrequited love of the Chinese Hen-Toy and of the Spaniard Don Juan; the Abyssinians sing the same love song of joy and sorrow as the French; a Japanese Geisha's love is as

passionate as Manon Lescaut's. Man longs for woman; the fire dispatched from the soul and its desire can be found in all places at all times. Hatred towards a murderer is the same in Asia and Europe. The Russian Plushkin attracts as much sympathy as the French Grandet. Hypocrites of all countries are like Tartuffes. Misanthropes are the same everywhere. Everyone in every place takes pleasure in the self-proclaimed knight Don Quixote's funny delusion. It should be noted that, regardless of which language people speak, they often talk about the same things about themselves and the same things in their fates. (See my translation of "Literature and Today's Russia," in *La Jeunesse*, Vol. 8, No. 2.)[3]

Proceeding from this universalism of human instincts, we come to the conclusion that the literature representing such common instincts, spirits and sentiments must be universalized as well; no separation by country or people should be allowed.

Countless people in England have been moved by Shakespeare's works; so have countless people in Germany, regardless of the fact that he is English. Countless people in Russia have been moved by Leonid Andreyev's "The Red Laugh"; so have countless people in Japan, regardless of the fact that Russia is their enemy. Similarly, though Vladimir Korolenko's *Makar's Dream* tells Siberian stories, we Chinese readers find in it as much suspense. Even the Germans and the Austrians would shed tears when they read *Le feu* (*Under Fire*) and *Clarté* (*Light*), both written by the French Henri Barbusse during the Great War.

Thus we know that literature is a reflection of the human condition, of the universal spirit and sentiment of mankind. We should not be limited by the frames of space or time, but should treat literature as a whole, a mirror reflecting the worry, frustration, pain, joy and mirth of mankind.

Mankind, which has been engulfed and separated by the many circles of different colors, can now be reunited through the unifying power of literature.

Mankind is an inseparable whole. If people see in literature their own sentiments, their crying and painful sentiments, how can they still torture each other?

III

At this point, perhaps many readers might ask: literary universalism is indeed necessary, but is a universalized study of literature possible? This question raises two major issues.

1. There is special difficulty in a universalized study of literature. Although literature contains universal human spirits and sentiments, a universal language – written or spoken – is still lacking. Each country creates its literature with its own language. In such circumstances, how could a universalized study of literature be possible? No one is omniscient; no one can learn every language, and be able to read and study literatures all over the world. Needless to say, it is absolutely impossible for laymen to understand all the world's literatures. They can understand nothing other than their own language. How, then, could a universalized study of literature be possible?

It is true that scholars and even common readers can use translations, but how faithful is a translation to the original? The value and enjoyment of the original may be lost through translation. In the end, how can literature be translated? Literature is the manifestation of the author's emotions and inspirations. At the moment of emotional intensity or epiphany, the work naturally flows under the author's hand. Once the moment passes, the natural flowing of writing can never be repeated, let alone reproduced through translation in someone else's hand. What is more, literature almost always has a local color. Such color is most vivid and lively in the eyes of the local people, but means nothing to others. A deliberate representation is a concession after all. Also, moods, imaginations, and even thoughts in literature are so closely related to words that once the latter change, the former change as well.

There is yet another problem: even if literature can be translated, can the amount of translations satisfy the need of scholars or even readers with a global interest? No country, not even Britain and Germany where foreign literatures are widely translated, can produce a comprehensive catalogue of the world's literatures. Under such circumstances, how can literary universalism be possible?

2. Literature is different from philosophy or other disciplines in that it is an art. The unit of language is either a word or a phrase. The unit of literature is a poem or a short story. In philosophy, biology, economics, or history, what we record are mere facts, reports or a taxonomy of reports. But one cannot do the same with literature. Reports of literature like that would be most boring. What the studies of literature need most are imagination, as well as the ability to perceive resonances and effects in taste, in artistic and spiritual transformations. On the basis of such complex, profound and unpredictable appreciation, how can literary studies be inclusive enough to be universal?

IV

My answers to these two questions are as follows.

1. Since we do not yet have a *lingua franca*, it is indeed not easy to establish literary universalism. But this cannot prevent us from doing so, because we can make use of translations. Even someone who knows no foreign languages can comprehensively study literature, or read the world's literatures for pleasure.

As to whether a translation is a worthy substitute for the original, or whether the value and enjoyment of a work would get lost in the course of the shift of languages, we need to consider the question whether literature is translatable at all. I discussed this problem in my essay "Three issues concerning the translation of literature," published in the vol. 12, no. 3 issue of the present journal. In the vol. 12, no. 5 issue, Mr. Shen Zemin expressed his opinions on this topic in "Discussion on the three issues concerning the translation of literature." I intended to publish a response to Mr. Shen. Now that I come across the same problem again, let me give my answer here instead.

I still hold to the opinion that literature is translatable. I think that if a book is well translated, it can have the same value as the original; the enjoyment of the latter would not be lost. Even an ordinary, conservative translator can transfer the original's value and sense of enjoyment to the translation.

It is true that the author's inspirations and emotions are constantly in flux and as transitory as a flash; the creation of many works could not be repeated at another time. But to translate them is different from repeating them. When the translator reads the original, the author's inspirations and emotions are summoned back to life in the mind of the translator through the medium of words. If the translator's inspirations and sentiments are not too far away from the author's, the translation might be able to transmit the inspirations and sentiments of the original. After all, these elements are stored in the original's words; if the words are faithfully and completely translated, these elements can be transplanted as well. Thus even an ordinary and conservative translator can achieve this.

As to the problem of local color, I think it is the same as inspirations and sentiments. In the hands of Mr. Zhou Zuoren, the local color described in Korolenko's *Makar's Dream* is very well translated.[4] If *Water Margin* is translated into other languages, I believe the tones and accents of characters like Lu Zhishen and Li Kui can also be transmitted. Non-Chinese readers might have no idea about Li Kui or other popular characters, but this doesn't matter. They are so distinctively represented in the novel that their characters would be deeply imprinted on the readers' minds. This is not to mention that the translator surely knows something about the novel's local background. (This of course does not include those translators not working from the original.) Since the translator knows the local life, it is very easy for him or her to transmit its colors.

Although literature expresses sentiments, imaginings, and even thoughts through language, they are not inseparable from the latter. This is a point I have made clear in "Three issues concerning the translation of literature": "In *The Elements of Style*, [David W.] Rannie proves that most 'expressions' are determined by individuals, therefore separated from thoughts. If we compare thoughts to water, then expression is the container; no matter how the container's form changes, the essence and amount of water remain the same. Since the author can use different 'expressions' or 'styles' to represent the same idea, we have no reason to doubt that thoughts can be represented in more than one language." Although this passage discusses thoughts only, the separation of sentiments and imaginings from words can be explained in the same way. Thus we know that even though the language changes, the sentiments, imaginings and thoughts of the original do not necessarily change.

Therefore, the idea that literature is untranslatable proves to be untrue. Thus those who study the universality of literature and are interested in the world's literatures can use translations as much as possible without any restraint.

It is true that for people studying literary universalism, there are too few translations available in China as well as other countries nowadays. This is indeed an obstacle. But it is not a reason for doubts about the validity of literary universalism. It is because literary scholars paid so little attention to literary universalism in the past that they did not care to introduce the world's literatures. Once we accept the concept of literary universalism, translations will naturally flourish. "Provision comes after need rather than the other way round."

However, literary translation is after all a difficult and unappreciated affair. Too much effort has to be made to draw readers' attention; this would be a waste of energy. The lack of a *lingua franca* is to blame. Were there a *lingua franca*, why would we still need the unpleasing work of translation at all? Poor folks! How much labor from our comrades has been sacrificed only because of the curse of Babel!

2. I am talking about this problem from the viewpoint of literary scholarship. On the one hand, literature is different from philosophy, biology, or any other discipline; on the other hand, "literary scholarship" is also different from literature itself. Like philosophy, it is a science rather than an art. Although its subjects are not exactly of the same type as other sciences, the situations are alike. The subjects of botany are all kinds of plants; those of anthropology are human beings or their relics; those of literary scholarship are poems, novels, and dramas, etc. A synthetic study is not impossible even when its subjects are complicated and hybrid.

Literary scholarship sometimes needs the ability to imagine; it needs to consider the effects that imagination and literariness cause on the reader's taste and spiritual development. But it must transcend the level of mere "appreciation." The mission of literary scholarship is not just to point out the value of a novel, the influence of a poem on its time and place, or the everlasting idea represented in a certain book. These are indeed missions of literary scholarship, but its more important purpose is to synthesize all literatures to find out their *raison d'être*, their traces of evolution as well as the ideas and emotions contained therein.

Let's say "appreciation," for example. Its basis is varied from person to person, from place to place, from time to time; but it certainly has something universal: this cannot be incomprehensible. Anyone adhering to literary universalism would take the world's literatures as his or her perspective; if the perspectives are the same, the basis of appreciation cannot be too different. From this point of view, one can again conclude that a unified study of literature must be feasible!

V

At this point, another issue should be mentioned as well: Moulton is also a promoter of literary universalism; he is probably the first in the world to propose this theory. So what is his literary universalism like? Is it the same as the ideas mentioned above? Moulton's urge for literary universalism is the same as mine; or I should say my idea was initially inspired by his; I am especially grateful to him. But his universalism is different from mine in that it is not thorough; this is what I cannot agree with.

A passage in his *World Literature and Its Place in General Culture* clearly demonstrates his ideas:

> It must be admitted that the term "world literature" may legitimately be used in more than one sense; I am throughout attaching to it a fixed and special significance. I make a distinction between Universal Literature and World Literature. Universal Literature can only mean the sum total of all literatures. World Literature, as I use the term, is this

Universal Literature seen in perspective from a given point of view, presumably the national standpoint of the observer. The difference between the two may be illustrated by the different ways in which the science of Geography and the art of Landscape might deal with the same physical particulars. We have to do with a mountain ten thousand feet high, a tree-fringed pond not a quarter of an acre in extent, a sloping meadow rising perhaps by a hundred feet, a lake some four hundred miles in length. So far as Geography would take cognizance of these physical features, they must be taken all in their exact dimensions. But Landscape would begin by fixing a point of view: from that point the elements of the landscape would be seen to modify their relative proportions. The distant mountain would diminish to a snow-covered peak; the pond would become the prominent centre, every tree distinct; the meadow would have some softening of remoteness; on the other side the huge lake would appear a silver streak upon the horizon. By a similar kind of perspective, World Literature will be a different thing to the Englishman and to the Japanese: the Shakespeare who bulks so large to the Englishman will be a small detail to the Japanese, while the Chinese literature which makes the foreground in the one literary landscape may be hardly discernible in the other. World Literature will be a different thing even to the Englishman and the Frenchman; only in this case the similar history of the two peoples will make the constituent elements of the two landscapes much the same, and the difference will be mainly in distribution of the parts. More than this, World Literature may be different for different individuals of the same nation: obviously, one man will have a wider outlook, taking in more of universal literature; or it may be that the individuality of the student, or of some teacher who has influenced him, has served as a lens focusing the multiplex particulars of the whole in its own individual arrangement. In each case the World Literature is a real unity; and it is a unity which is a reflection of the unity of all literature. (*Ibid.*, 6–7)

Moulton's view is indeed inadequate: if he admits the necessity of a unified study of literature, why does he take individual countries rather than human beings as his starting point? To do the former is like painting a landscape: one has to paint a huge mountain as small as a dot, a big lake as a line, but enlarge a little pond as its main theme. This is still partial rather than overarching, unified study. How can one say that such a method treats literature as an organic whole and an independent subject of study? Therefore, in my opinion, although Moulton's literary universalism is more advanced than other methods focusing on a country, an epoch, a genre or a writer, it is still very inadequate.

To study literature, one should take literature – general literature – as the basic position. Any boundary or obstacle that prevents a unified study of literature should be abolished!

Perhaps someone would make objections like this: following your idea, wouldn't literary study become an inorganic accumulation of materials? Moulton starts from the basis of a country; anything related to the country's literary evolution is included; what is less related is mentioned briefly; what is unrelated is not mentioned at all. Only in this way can one demonstrate the organic development of literature, the parts of which are all closely related. Your proposition would end up putting all historically unrelated literary systems together. It is fair to call this the statistics of literatures. But is it appropriate to call it unified literary study?

Such questions arise from a lack of understanding of unified literary study, by which I mean a unified study synthesizing the entire world's literatures and making literariness its main focus. There is no need to heed national boundaries in history. Since we treat the entire world's literatures as our subject, no matter how complicated literary systems are, they can be taken as an organic whole. Just like geology: though it is different from landscape painting, though it studies all kinds of terrain, it is after all a single, comprehensive discipline. No one can say that geology is not a unified and organic whole. Literary scholarship is even more so.

VI

This is more or less what I have in mind. I intended to elaborate on my ideas, but the scale of this essay prevents me from going on. Initially I wanted to attach a "list of world literature" at the end, so as to indicate the contents of world literature. But the same reason requires that I omit it. Therefore, this essay is only a suggestion, but a necessary one, for the unified study of literature. It takes a long time for people to become enlightened. Historiography has had a history of thousands of years; but only now has H.G. Wells' *The Whole Story of Man* appeared as the groundbreaking general human history. Right now the call for universalization of literature has just been heard. When, then, will a general history of literature be published?

I hope for nothing other than the appearance of the first general history of literature.

Notes

1 First published in *Fiction Monthly* 13:8 (1922), with a note by the author: "This is an old piece from a year ago. As I am really busy now, I don't have time to revise it. I quote a lot from *World Literature* by Moulton, to whom I am very grateful."

2 Richard G. Moulton, *World Literature and Its Place in General Culture* (New York: Macmillan, 1916), 429.

3 Founded in 1915 in Shanghai, *La Jeunesse* or *New Youth* magazine became a major venue for writers such as Lu Xun and Hu Shih advocating literary and cultural reform. In the 1920s it promoted Marxism and emphasized Soviet cultural approaches as well as support of the Chinese Communist party.

4 Zhou Zuoren (1895–1967) was a leading figure in the reformist May Fourth Movement, known especially for his essays and his many translations from English, classical Greek, and Japanese. *Makar's Dream* (1885), by the anti-tsarist writer Vladimir Korolenko, tells of a peasant's dream of heaven. The fourteenth-century novel *Water Margin* (also known in English as *All Men Are Brothers*) is one of the four major classical Chinese novels.

Part Two

World Literature in the Age of Globalization

7

Reflections on Yiddish World Literature (1938–1939)

Melekh Ravitsh and Borekh Rivkin

Over the course of the twentieth century, a prime characteristic of globalization has been the worldwide spread of diasporic communities, increasingly linked by ever swifter modes of transportation and spreading networks of communication and exchange. Today's internet sites and budget airfares are only the latest versions of the transatlantic telegraph lines and the steamship steerage berths of a century and more ago. In the 1880s, a flourishing book trade along the pathways of imperial trade routes allowed Rudyard Kipling to reach audiences on six continents while still in his twenties, and by the first decades of the twentieth century new networks were growing up outside the purview of the major powers and their hegemonic languages. Yiddish provides a particularly interesting case in point, as a variety of journal editors, writers, and anthologists in the 1930s promoted the circulation of Yiddish literature on a worldwide scale.

Given here are two essays, translated for this volume, that discuss the spreading network of Yiddish writing and reflect on the nature and goals of this minority mode of *velt-literatur*. Melekh Ravitsh (pen name of Zekharye-Khone Bergner, 1893–1976) was a modernist poet and essayist. Born in Galicia, he established himself as a writer in Warsaw, and later led a peripatetic existence, living in Australia, Argentina, and Mexico before settling in Montreal, a global experience reflected in poems that he collected under such titles as *Di fir zaytn fun mayn velt* (The Four Sides of My World, 1929) and *Kontinentn un okeanen* (Continents and Oceans, 1937). He discusses the decentered ubiquity of Yiddish writing in his 1939 essay "Where is the Center of Yiddish Literature Today? The Source and the Branches," published in

Melekh Ravitsh, "Where is the Center of Yiddish Literature Today? The Stem and the Branches" (1939). Trans. William Gertz Runyan from "Vu itst iz der tsenter fun der yidisher literatur? Der shtam un di tsvaygn," in *Di Tsukunft* 44:2 (February 1939), pp. 109–112. Used by permission.

World Literature in Theory, First Edition. Edited by David Damrosch.
© 2014 John Wiley & Sons, Ltd. Published 2014 by John Wiley & Sons, Ltd.

the socialist journal *Di Tsukunft* ("The Future"). This selection is followed by "The 'Quasi-territorialism' of Yiddish Literature" by Borekh Rivkin (pen name of Borekh Avrom Vaynrib, 1883-1945). Born in Latvia, then part of the Russian Empire, Rivkin emigrated to London and then New York, where he made his career as a literary and cultural essayist. In the essay given here, published in the Warsaw journal *Literarishe bleter*, Rivkin defines Yiddish writing as creating a *"kmoy-teritoriye-literatur"* or "literary quasi-territory" – a world literature for a diasporic nation without a land to call its own.

Where Is the Center of Yiddish Literature Today? The Stem and the Branches

Melekh Ravitsh

Question and Answer

I'll keep the question to the point:

Do we still have a single Jewish literature in Yiddish? (The word "still" would have been absurd 20 years ago – today it is perfectly apt.)

And I'll answer to the point (and if I've ever answered otherwise, it only means I strayed en route to the same end). To the point:

We have a single Jewish literature in Yiddish. At once quarrelsome and harmonious. A literature that, looking head on at the most difficult hurdles to its survival, is at the same time living through a golden age.

I'll go even further: not only do we have a single Jewish literature in the Yiddish language, but we can include with it the Hebrew language as well. Estranged brothers, so estranged that they will perhaps never again understand one another, and will never again draw near. But the fact of brotherhood itself cannot be disputed. A large proportion of Yiddish literary society today no longer understands Hebrew – something that 40 years ago was utterly unthinkable. And a small proportion of Hebrew literary society no longer understands Yiddish. But the fact of brotherhood itself cannot be disputed.

And I'll go another step further: not only do we have a single literature in these two literature-producing Jewish languages, Yiddish and Hebrew, but if the other Jewish languages, Judezmo or Ladino and Judeo-Arabic, were actively literary, one would also need to include those languages. Once four of us were sitting in a cafe in Hong Kong, Jews speaking English. And over the course of our discussion, it came out that our mother tongues were the four aforementioned Jewish languages. It's true that we were unable to find a common Jewish language of conversation, but we all displayed a common Jewish literary interest. We exchanged folk songs, stories, sayings. Yiddish played first fiddle, not so much because of my talkativeness as because Yiddish really does play first fiddle. Facts cannot be disputed. And prophecy should not be toyed with.

But to the point. I'll go one more – and the final – step further: not only do we have one Jewish literature in all Jewish languages, but all Jewish men of letters who have created works, in any language, that have an express Jewish interest should be and are included in the sphere of interest of Jewish literature. We do not thereby advocate the racial point of view, which we reject from its disgraceful "A" to the final "Z." Let us employ a straightforward image:

Jewish literature is a suspended lamp, a light in the house of our life. A lamp with a shade. Beneath the lamp is a table. The table is headed by contemporary Yiddish literature. Its face is the most clearly visible. In the second place comes contemporary Hebrew literature. At the table sit other Jewish languages. Their faces are somewhat visible, but they are silent. In the house many people move about. From time to time one of them comes nearer to the table, to the light, stands beneath the lampshade, and his face is clearly visible. Faces come out from the shadows into the Jewish circle of light. Some stay just a short time, others longer.

Four times we have answered affirmatively the question: do we still have a single literature in Yiddish? But now we must significantly modify the question itself, because we asked about literature in Yiddish and answered about Jewish literature. We did this intentionally, in order to clearly emphasize the difference between these words.

We wanted, in a manner of speaking, to first lay out the question in its full global breadth and offer a principled answer according to our limited abilities. And now we can turn fully to Jewish literature in Yiddish, whose face is today the most clearly visible in the light of Jewish literature.

Quality and Quantity

Immense is the quality of Yiddish literature (from here on we are discussing literature in our mother tongue), perhaps – don't begrudge my saying so – even greater than in the age of Peretz.[1]

But the quantity is also great. Greater than you think. And that is truly surprising, because quantity is tied to the great devotion of individuals. Of course one can say: why the devil do we need quantity? Why the hell do we need so many Yiddish books that it isn't humanly possible to plod through them all? And if Yiddish literature were centralized and regulated according to the laws of a market, according to the laws of supply and demand, perhaps there wouldn't be such quantity. But the market of our literature, if there is such a thing, is a mad market. A wild market, without any stock exchange.

And quantity is necessary; without quantity there is no quality. The worst thing is really that our "stock" is never fully inventoried (if you'll forgive the analogy). Our literature is so completely decentralized that often quality works go unnoticed for years, decades. They are continually thrown from one pile onto the next, one after the other, just a quantity of works. But they are expressive, quality works: works that carry in themselves pieces of the world.

But in this respect nothing can be done. This must be so for an expressive world literature that has no market or, partly, any communication (the Soviet world). To be clear: as long as the works of general Yiddish literature cannot be read in the Soviet Union as easily as the majority of their works can be read by us, we will stubbornly maintain that these groups are without communication.

Blessed be the quality of our literature. But blessed also be its colossal quantity – its great army, which already contains so many heroes, even though today they are no more than unknown soldiers, and many will also die that way.

On Stem, Axis, Pillar of Cloud and Pillar of Fire

If our literature had a clear stem, the question of quality and quantity would not be so vexed. But it does not, and for the time being cannot, have a stem. Is one necessary? Of course. Branches must have a stem. Children – a father. But only those children who want to stick with the family, and we have to and want to stick with the family in our Yiddish literature. That is our great and beautiful strength. Otherwise, we are like the severed limbs of a tree, which can live a while longer off the tree's fluids, but only a while longer. And we desire a long life, no less than do all the peoples of the world.

Having a stem is nothing novel in our literature, although we haven't been spoiled in this regard. Only once have we had a stem in the course our secular existence. That was during the time of the Peretz Kingdom in Warsaw. That is plain and clear, although it is also plain and clear that our king, like all kings, plainly didn't know what he wanted. But he had a kingdom and reigned well and admirably, with kingly dignity.

Since then the crown of our literature has passed from head to head and has remained upon no one head. (This has no relation to the measure of talent, to writerly genius.) "Heavy is the Monomakh's cap"; the crown was quickly thrown off and more often slipped off on its own.[2] Today second-hand goods won't be put up with. Oh, but we truly need that old crown – on whom does it belong? We don't need a dictatorial authority; we need a mild, fatherly authority.

And because the crown passed from head to head, the stem also picked up and began to wander. For a time there was tumult and a global discussion was conducted in our literature on the theme "Warsaw – New York – Moscow." It is no accident that these discussions suddenly fell under the table and that no one recovered them. This is no accident.

For a while the question of the stem was dropped, and attention shifted to the ideational axis around which Yiddish literature turned, and this discussion also turned to dust. And this was a terrible detriment. Because a world literature without an axis is like a whirlwind on the sea, or in the desert … I have seen them on the sea and on dry land. And just as when I observed the whirlwinds, so now do I feel unhinged when I see the ideational axis of Yiddish literature spinning and spinning like a whirlwind across the entire world …

It's true that lately one direction can be felt throughout our entire Yiddish literature (I mean only those parts that can be created without terror). I would say that this direction is the direction of the Pillar of Cloud, the direction of the tearful fog of worldly Jewish suffering. And with an ailing heart I long for the direction marked by the fiery pillar of a clear idea, a clear idea that illuminates, that cleaves the darkness as clearly as the Pillar of Fire does the night. The darker the night, the clearer becomes the light.

Geography and Statistics

I'll say it with flair, I can't help myself.

I've put my heels to the dust of all five parts of the world, 40 countries. I breathed in every climate, was seasick on every ocean, encountered all the races of the world and all the Jewish races too. And everywhere I have managed to speak and read Yiddish and to create abundantly in Yiddish. Jewish world geography is fascinating, like a kaleidoscope in your hand. The same pair of tinted lenses between little mirrors. You don't change a thing. You just give the kaleidoscope a turn of the finger and the image changes and changes without end.

And our statistics too call for a poet. Are our 17 million really *our* 17 million? Just take the word of a witness of time and world that this is far from the case.

To comprehend and to truly grasp Jewish statistics one would need a fair dose of poetic talent, and to thoroughly grasp our poetry one would need to rely on the help of statistics …

On my right hand a map of the world and on my left a statistical table. I hardly need to look at them; I know them both nearly by heart. Quiz me as much as you like. But it is quite true that in large measure Jewish world statistics and geography today correspond to Yiddish literature. They keep pace. Just take the five Jewish communities in the world numbering over a million. (I'm including the British Empire here as a single unit – in this case I'm taking *licentia poetica* with my statistics.) All of these Jewish communities produce Yiddish literature; they are still producing it today. In other words: the better part of the Jewish people today still produces Yiddish literature. As regards its consumption, things are worse. In a bad market situation it is always the case that demand declines first and is followed by production. An awful thing to say, but I won't let it go in silence.

Where Is the Stem?

Where is the stem? That's the question, and the answer is to the point and acutely painful.

Today there is no stem. Or at least it isn't visible to the eye. It is abstract. Abstract, but it can be clearly and simply imagined, like the point, the line, the triangle and the circle in geometry.

The stem is the idea of the unity of Yiddish literature. We all carry the substance of this idea within us, because otherwise Yiddish literature is reduced to ragged and solitary works, good as they may be. And if there is no stem, then the value of average works in our literature is nearly reduced to nil, and works of genius are reduced to literary curiosities, like the works of Joseph Conrad. Then our entire literature is transformed into a wild stretch of sky with nothing but stray comets … And that, we do not want. In the present night of the world, we surely don't want our worthy bearers of light to turn into stray comets …

No stem, but the idea of the stem remains. This is an unusual situation. But so it is, and we must grow accustomed to it, acclimate ourselves to this situation.

And woe will be unto us if we concede that not only is there no stem today, but that its idea has also been lost; then we too are lost.

One would need to search for the stem with the help of geography and statistics. But this is a pure technicality, a method difficult to apply in such a complex matter.

But in our hearts and minds and souls – yes, souls – we carry the idea of the world-wide stem of Yiddish literature, like a Pillar of Fire, and why not, also like a Pillar of Cloud. We carry it across all borders and fences. From Alaska to New Zealand – from Tierra del Fuego to Kamchatka – up, down, and around the earth. Take my word for it. Even if some members of Yiddish literary society are today imprisoned. All prisons are ephemeral and freedom is eternal. And if some members of Yiddish literary society have temporarily clouded their own vision – clouds are ephemeral and light, eternal.

Wherever I have encountered Yiddish poets in the world, they don't live with scraps of Yiddish literature. They live and breathe its entirety. In my world travels I was often a bearer of greetings from one region of Yiddish literature to another, and always the bearer of one region's keen interest in the other.

Where is the stem? I don't know where it is today. But I know that it is there today just as it was in Peretz's time. It's everywhere. We will answer as Spinozists: the stem is substance for Yiddish literature. Its attributes are infinite extension and infinite intellect.[3] And its finite modes, its forms: America, Poland, the Soviet Union, Romania, Argentina, England, France, and where else can't they be found?

The Lost Branches

And since it's already come to talk of stem and branches, I would like to advocate for the forlorn, neglected branches of Yiddish literature. Perhaps it would be more correct to say: orphaned branches. Our literature is a world literature. There are those who maintain that the worldwide reach of our people is its misfortune. And there is the opposing camp. Well, I belong to that opposing camp. (Here I'm not speaking about the economic perspective.) And insofar as the worldwide reach of our people is its fortune, or misfortune, so too is the worldwide reach of our literature either its misfortune or its fortune. I maintain the latter; I'll clarify why that is. Consider, for example, that each literature sends its poets and writers throughout the world in order to take in the world before them, and later to enrich their literature with it. Well, sometimes such writer-travelers remain in a foreign country for a year or two. And we, the poorest of all literatures in the world, are permitted the luxury of having whole contingents of our writing community in the farthest regions of the world. This is a colossal benefit. In this, no literature can outdo us: before our eyes and in our hearts is the very world.

But we ignore this benefit when those branches go unattended, neglected; they grow wild, often creeping over onto other stems.

These branches are scattered and lost, forsaken and forgotten. I encountered them in Argentina and Chile, in South Africa and in Brazil, in Australia and where didn't I find them? We must cultivate in Yiddish literature its global embranchment. Just as every literature cultivates provincial local patriotism, so should we cultivate a worldwide patriotism in the best sense of the word: because it is necessary and because we – the poorest of poor literatures materially – can permit ourselves this luxury.

American Conclusion of a Jewish World Traveler

I was standing on the deck of my ship when it came into New York and passed by the Statue of Liberty. A sharp December sea-breeze was blowing. This wasn't my first time in America, and I had already climbed the steps of the Statue of Liberty a couple of years ago. I know it from the inside out. And when you know something from the inside out, it no longer makes a strong impression. Some little ship approached us, and I caught sight of the American flag. I removed my hat, stepped away from other people, and tears fell from my eyes. I'm no refugee. I've lived for the past few years in free countries; I'm not a victim and these were not personal tears, so to speak. What cried in me was the sentimental heart of a soldier of Yiddish literature, who fights a spiritual fight against a world of inward and outward enemies. One must listen to the silent voice of instinct – and my instinct tells me that over New York today soars Yiddish literature's Pillar of Fire, that it has been there for some years.

A crown roams across the five continents of God's earth.

The crown of Yiddish literature.

Raise it up, Yiddish America! It is the time of the "far West" – your time. The third era in the history of the Jewish world people has begun, the far Western era. And the task of literature is to stand always on the front line.

My words are spent. I can write no more. Deep down surges the heart of a Jewish world traveler who has seen the branches of Yiddish literature, and it seems to him that he can once more discern the stem …

Notes

1   The classic Yiddish writer I.L. Peretz (1852–1915) was a leading figure in Jewish literary circles in Warsaw.
2   "Tiazhela shapka Monomakha" – paraphrase in Russian of a line from Pushkin's play *Boris Godunov.* "Monomakh": monarch.
3   The Jewish-Dutch philosopher Baruch Spinoza (1632–1677) defined a depersonalized God as the substance underlying and extended through the universe.

The *"Quasi-Territorialism"* of Yiddish Literature

Borekh Rivkin

[…]

The basic premise of my approach to Yiddish literature is that it is the literature of a people without territory, which despite its lack of territory has striven to conceive of itself as a people and to remain a people.[1] It follows therefore that the existence of Yiddish literature is abnormal, as abnormal as the people's existence itself. But for literature it is even worse. While the people's existence had some measure of support in the special intermediary function that Jews served among the nations – a fully sufficient support according to certain Marxist historians – this special function is wholly insufficient to support the existence of a normal literature; and it is no support at all when that function begins to vanish.

A national-economic unity obtains its full organic character, in which the function of one class is augmented and strengthened by the function of another class, when it covers the area of an independent territory. We can observe how well this situation, normal for nations, suits the production of literature in the example of the Scandinavian peoples, who in a relatively short time have succeeded in raising their literatures to world significance. Taken individually, each of these peoples is smaller in number than the sum of Yiddish speakers. So do we naturally lag behind them in creativity? It is clear that their advantage over us is their national-territorial economy.

Borekh Rivkin, "'The Quasi-Territorialism' of Yiddish Literature" (1938). Trans. and ed. William Gertz Runyan from "Der 'kmoy-teritorializm' fun der yidisher literatur"; "Kmoy teritorye bimkem religye"; and "Kinstlerisher ekvivalent fun religye", in *Literarishe bleter: Ilustrirte vokhnshrift far literatur, teater un kunst.* Vol. 15, No. 26–29. Warsaw: June 24, July 1, July 8, July 15, 1938.

This abnormal condition has remained the same from the birth of modern Yiddish literature until the present day. How, then, did an apparently normal literature grow out of this abnormality? How could literature become the highest institution of a people without its own fully functioning economy to hold together all its sectors and classes? If we were to take the plain sense of Marxism – and the interpretation of plain-sense Marxists – that literature is a direct reflection of the economic fact, then all that could have precipitated out from the basic fact of Jewish economic isolation and groundlessness, with a bit of help from the Jewish pauper's bitter cry of pain, is the *luftmentsh*.[2] But a literature of full breadth, which speaks for the whole people in all its circumstances throughout the world, a national literature: how could it have come to be?

And yet it did come to be. How so? Yiddish literature raced ahead of Jewish social life, anticipating the conclusions of territorialists of all sorts who came later on – from Lev Pinsker to the most recent territorialists, the Birobidzhanists[3] – and established itself as a quasi-territory for the Jewish people. And thus it became a national literature.

Dr. Khaim Zhitlovsky[4] rendered a great service in coupling his territorialism with Yiddishism, which takes Yiddish literature as its centerpiece; and it is thus thanks to Dr. Zhitlovsky that Yiddish literature was officially introduced into the territorialist schema that is to heal, to normalize the Jewish social economy. That Jews should have a literature, he says, belongs to the plan of Jewish development: so long as it's a literature; so long as it's in Yiddish. Let us conduct ourselves, he says, like the French in France, who have their linguistic sphere, their cultural sphere, in French. But for Yiddish literature a logical place in the Jewish plan of development is not sufficient. In its very essence it must respond to the abnormal Jewish condition with development and healing, with protection and salvation.

Literature – that is to say, the creator of literature – cannot forget that for now we do not have any "France," that with a "French" schema we cannot issue a decree to the Poliakovs and Guggenheims, to the "upper crust" – the Günzburgs and Warburgs[5] – or to those who flock to their balconies, that they must have their linguistic and cultural sphere in Yiddish. Literature itself must be a "France"; it must serve the masses as a quasi-territory.

From the very beginning – from Mendele onward – Yiddish literature knew that it must be a quasi-territory. How did it know? The Jewish condition clued it in, first of all. Secondly, there was a model right before its eyes – its predecessor the Jewish religion, which responded to the same condition in this way: it raised itself up as a quasi-territory in the air, by which the People of Israel could orient itself, while its body, the physical community, barely had a material ground beneath its feet for even one class of Jews – the writer-middlemen – and quite often not even that much ground. A quasi-territory in the air: that was the outspread coattail of the One, who gave the People of Israel a covenant inscribed with "Thou hast chosen us" to carry until the time of the messiah. And thus the People of Israel has held on and remained grounded until the present day, until the free winds of civilization blew the air out from under the quasi-territory in the air, such that nothing remained for even the One to breathe. The whole celestial territory began to shake and could have gone asunder. And how would the People of Israel orient itself then! In this time of trouble appeared literature, which has the virtue of both communicating with civilization and sustaining the national soul. A foreign, secular function, not in the Jewish taste: borrowed from "licentious" civilization, which presumes that man is the full master and that his free play of fantasy is the true world-creating "logos." A mode of creation that was in complete contradiction with the customary Jewish religious mode of creation, closely tied to the One, holding fast to his celestial territory: a habit that for Jews had become a psychological law, pressed by necessity, compelled by ever-present mortal danger. Jews created in a religious mode, under the severe imperative of the One, in order to counteract the imperatives of economic reality, which by nature is severely "Marxist" and has so often mandated Jews to fall as a people.

You may ask: is secular literature then not a natural product of the life of a people? – Yes, but taken by itself, secular literary creation out of free fantasy among Jews barely reached the level of the folk song, the folk tale, and lingered there. What little additional secular work was created was a blind, verbatim copying of non-Jewish examples – precisely because it did not respond to the Jewish condition as religion had done. It was only in the 1860s in Russia that Jewish society with its "classes," with the intelligentsia that served them, began moving into the newly permeable Russian civil society. With its "classes," but without the "masses." The "masses" remained exposed, without a spiritual roof over their heads.

Individual Jews possessed of refined souls resolved, in a time of need, to swallow the contradiction between free literary creation and tightly controlled religious creation, in instinctive certainty that this contradiction would even out in the course of creative digestion. And they made a contract with literature – again instinctively, intuitively – that it would function as religion, responding to the Jewish condition as a "quasi-territory in place of religion."

And under this contract modern Yiddish literature was born; and this contract formed and figured it and spurred on its growth.

II. "Quasi-Territory in Place of Religion"

"Quasi-territory" – "religion replacement" – these are one and the same thing: two sides of one principle. This was the task bestowed on Yiddish literature at its dawn by the Jewish condition: to take the place of religion, to follow religion, which established itself as celestial territory to serve the Jewish community as a support over its head, because it lacked earthly territory, a material ground beneath its feet. And thus the physical community was elevated as the People of Israel. (The People of Israel is the religiously woven national consciousness of the Jewish people, which provided for all of its classes, although the people's existence rested upon the intermediary function of one of its classes.) And Yiddish literature through its three pioneers obeyed the command; it filled with more and more signs of the People of Israel; it began to translate the People of Israel into contemporary celestial territory. Therein lies the originality, the distinction of this innovative literature: the People of

Israel shimmers through each higher innovation. In this way it became a national literature, although the normal socio-economic conditions for this were lacking.

And it was Mendele's great fortune and service that, with the spark of his refined soul, with brilliant intuition, he was the first to see that the only way to establish Yiddish literature as a living organism capable of self-perpetuation – was to bind it to the People of Israel, which is suspended from celestial quasi-territory. And so he was destined to become the originator of a modern Yiddish literature.

"Quasi-territory – religion replacement" gives the most concise, most direct, most unified line of development of Yiddish literature from Mendele until after Peretz.[6] It was a climb, step by step, up to the quasi-territory in the air. Mendele ascends the first few steps. His allegorical method stems from just that – from his climbing fatigue. His allegory aims to capture the community, at first in its situation of physical need, as in "Kabtsansk,"[7] then to raise it to the level of the People of Israel. *The Nag* [1873] is the community in transition to the People of Israel. Riding on *The Nag* Mendele gallops toward higher and higher achievements, until he arrives at his highest achievement: *The Brief Travels of Benjamin the Third* [1878]. Benjamin is not only the prototype for every subsequent *luftmentsh*, but also the first artistic representative of the Yiddish territory in the air: pitted against the wide world and included in it, whereas previously, in its ghetto-like insularity, it was set apart from the world. Benjamin mirrors back a figure from world literature – Don Quixote – in similarity and impossibility: and thus initiates the revision through literature of the great Jewish reckoning with the world, which was previously conducted through religion.

Was that Mendele's conscious aim? No, this cannot be said. The aim came to him in the form of a question: For what? Why do I labor? What purpose does Yiddish literature serve? First of all could have come the simple question: Where is the reader? It could also have been a question borrowed from Russian literature, which then was oriented toward social ends. Just as he had borrowed the allegorical method from Hebrew didacticism, and the form of his narrative – the biography that follows the protagonist from childhood onward – let's say, from Dickens' *David Copperfield*: with Mendele all these "borrowings," harnessed in the service of the community, adapted into the frame of the People of Israel, seized by the Quasi-Territorial drive, underwent a radical transformation. And with Mendele the question of basic utility was elevated to the question of grand purpose, which the Jew, pragmatic even in his idealism, always asks without permitting himself to indulge in "trifles," amusement and diversion. And when Mendele approached literature with the question of purpose, it is clear from his own answer that this question was secondary to that of whether literature would be willing to enlist in quasi-religious, quasi-territorial service.

III. "Artistic Equivalent to Religion"

Peretz began to activate the celestial territory, to draw use for the present from the People-of-Israel model of Yiddish literature. He would not and could not be satisfied with Mendele's pledge through Benjamin: "Just wait now, we'll yet have something to show to the world!" and not even with Sholem Aleichem's stronger pledge through Menachem Mendl and Tevye, that we'll yet have something to give to the world.[8] Peretz actually wanted to make the pledge a reality – to demonstrate and pronounce just what we have to offer and what we have to do in the world.

The problem turned out to be much more difficult than it first appeared; not only were the existing means of Yiddish literature too limited for Peretz, but for him it became a question of the whole of literature in the form in which we borrowed it from the nations – whether it was a suitable instrument for molding the strength of the old Jewish faith into modern moral energy. The contradiction that Mendele anticipated between the Jewish religious and free literary creative methods – which came to him in the form of a question: What is the purpose of Yiddish literature? – stood out so sharply in Peretz's consciousness that it nearly invalidated the whole matter of literature for him. This contradiction occupied him in a series of critical essays about Yiddish literature. He vacillated between poet and artist, between prophetic severity and licentiously enjoying himself with art. His pen constantly leaves traces of something of a special Jewish reconciliation.

Behind all of this was the cardinal question of whether literature would be capable of taking on the quasi-territorial function of the Jewish religion. The religious quasi-territory had held firmly together because it was congealed around an all-constricting center – the One – and could serve to preserve the people's existence. But literature is changeable, mobile, playful, diffuse, without a center – how can it, without resting upon a real territory, remain firmly balanced as a quasi-territory in the air, for the people to base its existence upon it?

Peretz completed the opening up of the Quasi-Territorial tendency. And this is the primary innovation of his *Folktales* [1904–1915]: a form that, without any contradiction, at once produces religiosity and narration. Narration moralizes; morality narrates. The narration is woven from the stuff of pure morality, but without any sermon or didactic moral. It is a fable of faith that is carried into free artistic motion. At the same time, with *Folktales*, which is freed from the religious tendency by its artistic force, Peretz, perhaps unknowingly, solved the problem of how a delicately woven literature could be fortified into a quasi-territory for the people without territory. Literature's general disadvantage – its changeability, its mobility – can be made altogether into its strength. Such that it becomes more active, more intense; such that it moves swiftly from triumph to triumph, overtaking itself – it will reach the heights by its own momentum.

Thus Peretz is a multifaceted innovator. And moreover, a literary critic who arrived at his discoveries through critical analysis. He first researched the methods that he subsequently practiced. He was a literary critic in the grand sense of the word – the creative literary critic: the kind who creates the conditions that create literature. Of the same stature as Lessing and Herder in Germany, Coleridge and Wordsworth in England, Sainte-Beuve and Taine in France. The first and perhaps the only creative critic we have had; most of our critics are appraisers and announcers of prizes.

Thus such prosperity surrounded Peretz. And in a flash came the illusion that quasi-territory was suddenly true territory – one sat and created Yiddish literature as if right at home, as does a people with its own state. This is the illusion for which the quasi-territorial tendency strives: that a literature without territory may feel like and conduct itself as a territorial literature. Literature becomes normalized: thin air becomes swollen with fruitfulness, which infects the writers who are called forth in droves.

The quasi-territorial illusion that ignited around Peretz fostered a literary abundance that, in turn, produced a great number of writers, who spread over all parts of the Jewish world.[9] And of the three pioneers Peretz serves even today as a vital inspiration – even for those who struggle against his influence.

It should already be clear that these tendencies are not merely tendencies in the conventional sense of the word, but laws of Yiddish literature's existence. Because for Jews there cannot be literature otherwise than raised up as a quasi-territory. It hangs there by a thread, and at any moment could evaporate into thin air. Therefore all of the tendencies that obtain from the position of quasi-territory, such as grand purposiveness, transfiguration, heritage-transformation, and yet others that will appear later, which may or may not be present in other literatures – in Yiddish literature are necessities, commandments not to be transgressed.

Hence the particular role, the particular responsibility of the Yiddish writer. He must always be vigilant, maintain the meaning of literature. And there is always a spiritual danger for the people, from which literature must protect it. And quasi-territory, with its daughter tendencies, is the fundamental means for safeguarding the integrity of the people's soul.

Notes

1 Translated and edited by William Gertz Runyan. This selection is excerpted from a longer essay, "Der 'kmoy-teritorializm' fun der yidisher literatur," published in four installments in the weekly Warsaw literary journal *Literarishe bleter* in June–July 1938. The full essay narrates the development of Yiddish literature in Eastern Europe through the key works of its three classic exponents: S.Y. Abramovitsh (popularly known as Mendele), Sholem Aleichem, and I.L. Peretz. Each figure is presented as endowing Yiddish literature with one of the "basic tendencies" that allow it to function as a "quasi-territory," paving the way for Yiddish literature's subsequent expansion across the world. The prefix "quasi-" translates the Yiddish *kmoy* (from Hebrew *kmo*, "like" or "as") and invokes likeness and virtuality.

2 A dreamer with no business sense; literally: person of the air. However, Rivkin also valorizes the *luftmentsh* as the denizen of the "territory in the sky."

3 Lev Pinsker (1821–1891) was a physician who was a central figure in the Russian Hibbat-Zion movement, which organized Jewish settlement in Palestine. Birobidzhan is the Jewish Autonomous Region in far eastern Russia, designated under Stalin in 1928 as the Soviet Jewish homeland. Rivkin thus invokes diverse forms of Jewish territorial ambition, from pre-Zionist to anti-Zionist.

4 Khaim Zhitlovsky (1865–1943) was a Russian-Jewish philosopher and the principal theorist of Diaspora nationalism, predicated on socialism, territorialism, and Yiddish language and culture.

5 Prominent philanthropic Jewish families in Eastern and Western Europe.
6 Abramovitsh (Mendele) published his first work in 1864, and Peretz wrote until his death in 1915.
7 "Beggarsville," one of Abramovitsh's fictional settings.
8 Menachem Mendl and Tevye the Dairyman are Sholem Aleichem's most iconic characters, the protagonists of extended story cycles.
9 In his major study, *Basic Tendencies of Yiddish Literature in America*, Rivkin argues that the distance between Eastern Europe and America has allowed literary quasi-territory to take on global dimensions. He writes: "the striving toward worldwide territoriality originates in America. From there came the initial stimulus. In the American Jew the sense of quasi-territory broadened in scope until it reached the intuition of a worldwide Jewish territory – by virtue of the simple physical fact that the land of America is across the ocean, and on the other side of the ocean remained a large number of Jewish countries, and from each of those countries there was a diaspora community in America – and this intuition called and wished for a work that would give it substance." B. Rivkin, *Grunt-tendentsn fun der yidisher literatur in Amerike*, ed. Mina Bordo-Rivkin (New York: IKUF, 1948), 167–168.

8

Should We Rethink the Notion of World Literature? (1974)

René Etiemble

A lively and polemical scholar with an endlessly inquisitive spirit, René Etiemble (1909–2002) was one of the leading figures in comparative literature in the twentieth century. His combative views on the need to move comparative literary studies beyond their predominant focus on Western Europe informed both his theoretical studies and his own practice as a novelist. In his important book *Comparaison n'est pas raison* (best translated, perhaps, as "What's the point of comparing?"), Etiemble argued for pushing the boundaries of comparative literature even as he ironically pointed out the unreasonableness around which the idea of comparison spins. Etiemble fought preconceptions circulated by literary historians, in such works as his three-volume study of Arthur Rimbaud, *Le Mythe de Rimbaud*, and he intervened in public discourse in his best-selling *Parlez-vous franglais?* (1964), in which he vehemently rejected the casual importation of words from America in postwar France.

A linguistic purist, Etiemble was anything but a narrow nationalist. His advocacy of the expansion of literary studies beyond Europe was the result of his years of training at Paris's École Normale Supérieure, where he studied Chinese literature and culture. His internationalist spirit was furthered by teaching in Alexandria, Egypt, during World War II. While there, he published the literary journal *Valeurs* in collaboration with the Egyptian writer Taha Hussein. In 1955 he returned to France to become professor of Comparative Literature at the Sorbonne, where he remained until his retirement in 1978. During his years at the Sorbonne, in addition to his comparative studies Etiemble wrote books on Confucius, on Taoism, and on the Jesuits in China, and he published

René Etiemble, "Should We Rethink the Notion of World Literature?" (1974). Trans. Theo D'haen from "Faut-il réviser la notion de Weltliteratur?" in *Essais de littérature (vraiment) générale* (Paris: Gallimard, 1974), pp. 15–34. Translation first published as "Do We Have to Revise the Notion of World Literature?" in Theo D'haen, César Domínguez, and Mads Rosendahl Thomsen, eds., *World Literature: A Reader* (Abingdon: Routledge, 2013), pp. 94–103.

a 50-volume collection of Asian and Middle Eastern literatures under the title "Connaissance de l'Orient." Drawing on these works, Etiemble argued for a "planetary comparatism" in his 1988 book *Ouverture(s) sur un comparatisme plané-taire*. In his essay "Should We Rethink the Notion of World Literature?," from his 1974 collection *Essais de littérature (vraiment) générale* (Essays on (Truly) General Literature), Etiemble proposes rethinking Goethe's concept of world literature on a global scale.

How can we avoid being struck by the criticisms formulated these days against the concept of world literature [*Weltliteratur*]? Mr. Árpád Berczik compares it to a concerto grosso and suspects that it is only an intellectual form of internationalism, guilty after all of serving an eternal idea of the beautiful.[1] The reservations of this Hungarian are echoed by a Czech, Mr. Jan Mukařovský, who relates *Weltliteratur* to the rise of the bourgeoisie, and therefore sees it as something that needs to be overcome, because "for the first time in the history of human culture, we now witness the birth of a truly universal literature," born from the October Revolution, a literature that finally con-demns "the subordination of the overwhelming majority of national literatures to that of some (so-called) *great literatures*, the privileged source of all creative initiative."[2]

It is not because these arguments have been put forward by academics from the socialist world that we should spurn them.

In fact, when I reread the two passages from [Eckermann's] *Conversations* [with Goethe] where there is talk of *Weltliteratur*, I can approve of the passage in which Goethe rejoices that world literature offers us the opportunity to mutually correct ourselves: "*In den Fall kommen uns einander zu korrigieren*," and in which he praises Carlyle to have judged Schiller so aptly as would not have been possible for a German. But I am astonished that his idea of *Weltliteratur* came to him on the basis of some superficial judgments on a few mediocre Chinese novels and on a couple of songs of Béranger: the Chinese novels being so utterly moralistic [*so sittlich*] and the works of the French poet being so little moralistic [*so unsittlich*]. With Mr. Árpád Berczik, I would also object to an altogether too naïve interpretation of poetry on the part of Goethe that it is the common good of mankind: "I see ever more clearly that poetry is the common property of all humanity" [*Ich sehe immer mehr dass die Poesie ein Gemeingut der Menschheit ist*]. Of course, I am happy that Goethe com-posed his *Diwan*; but in order for poetry to be common to all humanity it suffices to consider that the poetic sensibility is in fact equitably distributed throughout the human species. The poem, on the other hand, only belongs to those that know and that are able to savor perfectly the language in which it was written. The most universal linguistic art is the least poetic prose.[3]

All this does not prevent me from supporting Goethe when he is looking for the invariable features of all literary beauty in *Weltliteratur*.

Still, how could I forget that this *Weltliteratur* that may well have been the product of a bourgeois conscience during the period of free-trade liberalism has illiberally participated in the denigration or even the systematic destruction of the African,

Indian, Amerindian, Madagascan, Indonesian, Vietnamese and other literatures? Like free-trade liberalism, colonialist imperialism constitutes one moment of bourgeois consciousness. The European priests, soldiers, and merchants have in effect replaced Goethe's generous conception with one in which literature is divided between that of the masters and that of the slaves. In this sense our socialist colleagues are right. But if their conception of world literature [*littérature universelle*] may seem to be more open, I still have to conclude that not one word of Goethe on *Weltliteratur* allows us to see in him a conscious or unconscious agent of imperialism. On the contrary, his elevated idea of world literature implicitly condemns German nationalism and along with it all nationalism. Let us therefore simply admit that Goethe is no more guilty of the destruction of the Amerindian literatures than is the Jew Karl Marx, the theoretician of socialism, guilty of the anti-Semitic and anti-Yiddish excesses of Stalin.

Renouncing, then, all political perspectives as too exclusionary, let us return to language, as our disagreements are always in the first place linguistic. Because the concept of *Weltliteratur* was coined in German (and by what a German!) it has always retained, at least for certain people, the taint of a germanocentrism. Some have proposed alternative terms such as universal literature [*littérature universelle*], or general literature [*littérature générale*], or *World literature*, or мировая литература. There is even at least one Spaniard, Guillermo de Torre, who conflates world literature and comparative literature when he wonders "whether the only field close to that envisaged by *Weltliteratur* is not comparative literature." For M. Hankiss, on the contrary, comparative literature does not deal with overall literary production, but restricts itself to "research involving more than one national literature."[4] As if things were not complicated enough yet, Mrs. Nieoupokoyeva, of the Academy of Sciences of the Soviet Union, conflates general literature and мировая литература, something that more than one proponent of general literature would contest.

Rather than trip over the adjectives clinging to the notion of literature and so in the last analysis turn out just as ridiculous as the various supporters of "proximate power" in the first [of Blaise Pascal's] *Provincial Letters*, may we candidly admit that the totality of all national literatures simply makes up *literature*, without adjective? In so far as I have understood the program and the projects of the Gorky Institute for world literature as they have been explained to me by our colleague Anissimov, who at the time was the director of that Institute, the literature in question, мировая литература, to me seems closer to universal literature [*littérature universelle*], or world literature, than to *littérature générale* or general literature. Let me add that in order to study this literature without adjective we have at our disposal – independent of works of literary history, sociology or criticism on separate literatures – the comparatist method, which can be subdivided into several sub-disciplines: comparative literary history, comparative sociology of literatures, genre theory, general aesthetics, and general literature [by which Étiemble means something that in our day we would probably call "theory of literature"]. If comparative literature, then, can be considered in relation to world literature, this is not because it is identical with the latter, but only in so far as it allows us to gain access to it.

If we agree on this we could also now serenely move on to more serious things and ask ourselves if in the twentieth century we should not revise that notion of world literature that we have inherited from our predecessors.

The Soviet Orientalist N.I. Conrad thinks that indeed we should enlarge the historical and geographical scope of comparative literature, that is to say of the method that opens up world literature for us, and the Harvard sinologist James Hightower concurs. Fine! I think I have found out that to understand the genesis of *The Chanson de Roland*, and to properly evaluate the *Légendes épiques* of Bédier, it is at least very useful to have some knowledge of the works of Jirmounsky on the epic in Central Asia, of Rolf A. Stein on the Tibetan *Gesar de Ling*, the ballads of the Oranian bard Mest'fa ben Brahim, even if the latter lived in the nineteenth century, the Armenian epic *David de Sassoun*, and, why not, half a dozen African epics?[5]

We no longer live in a time such as that of the Hungarian scholar Hugo von Meltzl, a follower of Goethe and a supporter of *Weltliteratur*, who could still preach a *Dekaglottismus* of civilized languages: German, English, Spanish, Dutch, Icelandic, Italian, Portuguese, Swedish and French – to which he added Latin. Literatures in all other languages for him amounted to no more than folk literatures or, if they were artistic literatures, they were of too recent origin. For anyone with any idea of the wealth, the age, and the quality of the Sanskrit, Chinese, Tamil, Japanese, Bengali, Iranian, Arab or Marathi literatures, all, or at least some, of which had already produced their master works at a time when the majority of the *Dekaglottismus* literatures did not yet exist, or were still in their infancy, this stingy idea of world literature definitely seems to have had its day. Observe, moreover, that even Greek literature plays no part in this concert, to say nothing about Pharaonic literature (still little known in the time of Metzl, but without which it would now be impossible to understand anything at all about the history of the theater or of the novella in the Mediterranean world!)

Following Conrad, the Soviet scholar, and Hightower, the American scholar, let us proclaim that literature from now on can only mean the totality of all literatures, whether alive or dead, of which there remain written, or even only oral, traces, without further discrimination as to language, politics or religion.

Thus replacing the world literature of *Dekaglottismus* with literature *tout court* I am immediately seized by a kind of panic terror, which reminds me of the proverb "grasp all, lose all." What would such theoretical openness of spirit to all literatures, whether present or past, bring us given that any human mind, however capacious we may imagine it, is limited by the average length of our lives? Fortunately, another German, Hermann Hesse, has already come up with the basic reply to this question in his *A Library of World Literature*:[6] on the one hand nobody can effectively get to know even the totality of one literature, let alone that of all literatures; on the other hand each of us, in order to become a fully rounded human being, can and hence must construct his own personal library of world literature. In short, for us and even more so for those whom we educate, one route only lies open to world literature, that of our affinities, of love: "He [the reader] must travel the road of love, not that of duty".[7]

I see more proof that we have arrived at a point in history where what occupies us is a question that faces every thinking man in the inquiry that Raymond Queneau conducted on the *Bibliothèque idéale* or ideal library. He asked several dozen writers to pick from a list of approximately 3500 works their ideal library of one hundred titles. Some authors refused to reply and explained their decision. Yvon Belaval, for instance, replies in the spirit of Hermann Hesse: "the ideal library for me is that which I am reading at the moment."[8] Gaston Bachelard replied: "my ideal library remains essentially open."[9] We do not even mention those who, like Hervé Bazin, reject the very idea: "there is no such thing as an ideal library. The times, nationality, taste, temperament, the specialization that culture imposes make impossible any common denominator."[10]

After having sorted through the 61 replies he received, Queneau drew up a table of one hundred titles. At the top of the list figured Shakespeare and the Bible, in this order, followed by Marcel Proust. What worries me from the beginning is that there are 60 French titles and 39 foreign titles. And what worries me even more is that of these 39 foreign titles 9 are of English or American authors, 8 belong to Greek literature, 6 to German literature, 6 are Russian, 4 are Latin authors, 3 Spanish; while Arab, Danish, Hebrew and Italian literature all can boast one title. You can easily guess that 58 of the 61 writers who replied were French: Henry Miller, Marion Moore and Frederick Prokosch represent foreign opinion.

As Apollinaire's *Alcools* is inadvertently cited twice, as numbers 25 and 85 respectively, may I take the liberty to suggest that instead of one of these two *Alcools* we should insert the [Japanese] *Genji monogatari* [*Tale of Genji*], the [Chinese] *Hong leou mong* [*The Dream of the Red Chamber*, also called *The Story of the Stone*], the [Sanskrit] *Pançatantra* [*Five Principles*], the [Sanskrit] *Jataka*, the [Japanese] *Tzurezuregusa* [*Essays in Idleness*, also called *The Harvest of Leisure*], the *Zhuangzi*, Wang Chong, the *Prolegomenon* [*Muqaddimah*] of Ibn Khaldoun, or one or other of the thousands of titles that are worth more or at least as much as *Alcools*? The great merit of this inquiry surely is to demonstrate how far removed French writers are from acceding to the wish of Goethe, or to answering the hopes of Karl Marx.[11] Werner Kraus would undoubtedly be more indulgent than I am for the French men of letters, as he is of the opinion that until the 19th century French literature was in fact the model for all other literatures: "serving as example to all other literatures" [*für alle andern Literaturen beispielgebend gewesen*]. To which I would respond, with the frankness of friendship, admiration even, that another literature has enjoyed, and continues to enjoy, and this since millennia, a situation that is as privileged as ours has been for eight centuries: the Chinese, which is not represented, not even with one title, in the *Bibliothèque idéale*.

Maybe someone will object that one hundred titles, one hundred names, imposes impossible restrictions? Give us one thousand titles, ten thousand titles, and you will see something else. Well then, let's see! Let us first have a look at Adolf Spemann's *Vergleichende Zeittafel der Weltliteratur, von Mittelalter bis zur Neuzeit 1150–1939*, published in 1951, after the defeat of Nazism. Let us leave aside that, given this work's chronological limitations, three quarters at least of all literature is excluded, and let us probe the little we are presented with. We do not find Lu Hsun, Kouo Mojo, Hou Zhe, Premchand, Taha Hussein, Tawfiq al-Hakim, Jorge Luis

Borges, Octavio Paz, Haldor Laxness, Rafael Alberti, Federico García Lorca, Miguel
Hernández. Eugène Brieux, on the contrary, is included. No mention of Henry
Miller or Arthur Miller, but a listing for the eighteenth-century Johann von Müller.
As if aware of all that is missing, the author confesses that the war prevented him
from seriously occupying himself with the literatures of Asia. This really is a pitiful
excuse, because Murasaki Shikibu, Sei Shonagon, Kenkô, Zeami, Saikaku and
Jippensha Ikku, to name only six of the masters of Japanese prose accessible in
translation, were not unknown before 1939: in Europe, I mean. Or let us suppose
that, putting together a world literature following his own judgment, a Japanese
scholar would overlook Goethe, Schiller, Nietzsche, Jean Paul, Hölderlin and
Thomas Mann, how would this go over this side of Eurasia? If on a list of eleven
thousand titles one assigns twenty to Mr Joséphin Péladan but one ignores, or
neglects, the [Japanese Jippensha Ikku's] *Hizakurige* [*Shank's Mare*], the [Vietnamese
Nguyen Du's] *Kim-Vân-Kiêu*, the [Japanese Ueda Akinari's] *Ugetsu Monogatari*
[*Tales of Moonlight and Rain*] and the oeuvre of [the Indian-Pakistani] Muhammad
Iqbal, is one qualified – I allow myself to ask – to compose the list of honor of world
literature? Finally, if French writers give to France two thirds of world literature,
Mr. Spemann gives to German literature of the twentieth century exactly the same
role that some of us claim (who at least have the excuse of being writers only, and
not scholars). Should we be more content with the three fat volumes of *Die
Weltliteratur* published in Austria in the same year 1951 by a group of specialists,
serious ones this time? Some ten thousand names here too. Doumic, Estaunié,
Péladan are there in honor of France, but I look in vain for Cavafy, Rastko Petrovich,
Mao Dun, Jean Paulhan, Dai Wangshu (one of the three or four leading Chinese
poets of the twentieth century), Mulk Raj Anand, whose Indian novels have more
strength and beauty than those of our Octave Feuillet, who is included. Again,
there is a scandalous disproportion between Europe's part, from which the worst
are highlighted, and that of Asia, where even the best are excluded from the paradise of world literature; that is to say from a biased [*orientée*] world literature: see
what part Islam, Buddhism, and atheism play in this world literature, and you will
see that it is very small, justifying the criticisms of our colleagues from the socialist
world. Presented thus, world literature is nothing but a celebration of bourgeois
and Christian values.[12]

I have much the same to say with regard to the work of a French scholar who is
the zealous, and more unfortunate even than zealous, author of a universal literature
with a comprehensive list from the Middle Ages until the present: Alice Berthet.[13]
On her list we find the inevitable Brieux, we also encounter Blasco Ibáñez and Victor
Cherbuliez, and three hundred more individuals of this kind, all of them coming
from our part of the world: Western Europe. As far as the romantic lyric in Russia is
concerned you are entitled to just the following three words: "Pushkin, lyrical poet."
Asia is represented by Tagore, along with Okakura Kakuzo "who studied – as did
Tagore – in England."[14] The reader might conclude that an Asian writer is only
acceptable when he has studied at a British public school. If this is not a case of a
colonialist spirit I really do not know what these words might mean.

Let us finally take a look at *Les Écrivains célèbres*, a volume edited by Raymond Queneau and Pierre Josserand. About ten thousand names. A pleasant surprise: here we find Mao Dun and Kouo Mojo, Cao Yu and Lao Tse, Ai Qing and Lu Hsun, Hou Zhe and Liu E for China past and present, which is a good thing, a very good thing even; for Greece we see Cavafy, Sikelianos, Kazantzakis, Seferis and even Engonopoulos, which is not bad either. For Japan, next to Tanizaki, I notice Shiga Naoya, Mori Ogai, Natsume Soseki, Ueda Bin, which always gives pleasure; for Iran, Sadegh Hedayat, with his admirable *Blind Owl*, is not overlooked. With just a little bit of competence and courage it is thus possible from now on to draw up a fair list of literature, and even of the literature of the first 30 or 40 years of the twentieth century, and this, let us reassure ourselves, without sacrificing Estaunié or Brieux, who continue to figure on our list, or anything else.[15]

That it is possible to present a more or less correct idea of world literature in the form of a manual is proved abundantly (literally so) by the *Histoire universelle synchronoptique* of Arno Peters, especially so in the French edition here mentioned as revised and enlarged under the editorship of M. Minder.

I fear, however, that we will have to wait a long time still before the spirit of the *Écrivains célèbres*, which overall is also that of this synchronoptic history, triumphs over the idols of the different tribes. On our side of the world an insidious Eurocentrism continues to throw a false light on everything, while on the other side of the world for a while yet one will continue to celebrate well-meaning mediocrities for the sole reason that they celebrate the revolution, or atheism. Let us for instance have a look at the recent and, I agree on this, very useful work of Elizabeth Frenzel: *Stoffe der Weltliteratur*.[16] Three examples will do. In the article on *Cäsar* (pp. 94–98) I looked in vain for any reference to the Tibetan *Gesar*, an epic on which a lot of work had been done even before Stein's dissertation on it. And yet this is an exciting theme: a Roman Emperor who dominates the great epic of Tibet! The article on *Buddha* refers me to *Balaam and Josaphat*. Nothing more. Now as far as I know Buddha has not been less of an inspiration for world literature, that is to say for literature *tout court*, than has Jesus. He has even inspired many a literary craftsman in Western Europe. Final example: *Ann Boleyn* and even *Die Schöne Iren* receive the accolade of being considered "themes," but I look in vain for Yang Kwei-fei, who certainly can hold the candle to them in this respect, and who has found literary echoes in Europe, and even in the United States, up to our days.[17]

What other way is there to improve future repertories of names, those bio-bibliographies to which unfortunately until now most works on world literature limit themselves, than to confide them to a truly international association of comparative literature in which all adherents to our discipline, whether they work in the socialist or in the capitalist world, can collaborate without too much difficulty when it comes to ascertaining facts. In this way, for instance, I have during my first stay in Japan discovered a list of one hundred titles, selected by qualified Japanese – namely the Rector of the University of Tokyo, Mr. Watanabe Kazuo, and Mr. Nakano, Professor of English Literature and a well-known Marxist sympathizer, a counterpart to Raymond Queneau's ideal library. Mr. Araki Toru has been so good as to translate this document, which is published as an appendix to all volumes in the collection Iwanami, the best world literature or *literature* collection one can find in Tokyo, recommended to all students from fifteen to twenty-five years of age. This is an encouraging list in the sense that, notwithstanding the riches and variety of Japanese literature itself, two thirds of the hundred titles are taken from foreign literatures: China, Germany, England, France, Russia, Denmark, Norway, and the United States. That is to say that in spite of their Chikamatsu and Zeami, the Japanese also know about Shakespeare, Corneille, Molière, *Faust*, *The Cherry Orchard*, and *A Doll's House*, while with us Shakespeare or Molière keep us away from Chikamatsu, *Cyrano* from the nô theatre, and the *Hamburgische Dramaturgie* from the *Treatises* of Zeami.[18] Still, two lacunae come as a surprise, and suggest that the Japanese themselves, as cosmopolitan as they may be in the best sense of this word, have still some way to go in this respect: India is absent from the list, and so is the Arab world. *The Arabian Nights* apparently do not merit mention, while *Tonio Kröger* and *Quo Vadis?* do. It is evident that it would profit the Japanese to acquire a better knowledge of these two literary worlds. I've also asked Mr. Attia Naboul Naga to forward me the program of a forthcoming Egyptian collection called *Deux mille chefs-d'oeuvre, patrimoine de l'humanité*, or Two Thousand Masterpieces, The Heritage of Mankind. That the *Odyssey* does not figure in this repertory does not worry me too much, because even if it is also absent from Queneau's ideal library (where it is replaced by its modern subversion, James Joyce's *Ulysses*), it does figure among the hundred Japanese titles. Moreover, one cannot judge an undertaking of this kind by one isolated title. Let us rather rejoice that next to Ibn Rouchid [Averroes], Ibn Sinna [Avicenna], Ben Arabi, Ibn Hazm, Al Farabi, Al Ghazali and the Brethern of Purity, the list also contains the names of Aristotle, Hegel, Heidegger, Hume, Husserl, Kant, Leibniz, Nietzsche, Plato, Plotinus, Schopenhauer and – as the only French philosopher – Sartre, with *Being and Nothingness*. Let us not be surprised if, with names to choose from such as the *Mu'allaqat*, Abul 'Ala al Ma'arri, El Moutannabi, Abou Nuwas for literature in Arabic, and the *Shahnameh,* the *Rubaiyat*, Hafiz and Saadi for the Persian, the Egyptians retain only a few poems by Blake, Burns, Byron, Shelley, Lamartine and Musset. If poets, as I believe at variance with what Goethe says, belong only to those knowing their language, this choice seems judicious. Let us rather express our appreciation that while among the two thousand masterpieces figure the *Seances* of Hariri, the novels of Tara Hussein, Tawfiq al-Hakim and Mahmoud Taymour – all of which I looked for in vain in most of our works on *Weltliteratur* – *Gil Blas, Zadig, Werther*, and twenty other European novels are not forgotten. Still, how could we not notice some omissions here too? Latin literature, the literatures of India, China and Japan have no place among these two thousand masterpieces. Another case of faulty procedures, you say? Not even. Simply that, victims of their own particularisms, of the idols of their tribe, we still have a long way to go before we are ready to shoulder the task that Goethe assigned to us a century and a half ago: to hasten the dawn of world literature.

Of course it makes sense that a German should know his own literature much better than that of the Persians or Japanese, and vice versa; but could we not agree that henceforth nobody has the right to meddle with world literature, or better with *literature*, if he or she has not done his or her best to escape the determinism of his or her birth? One day at the Sorbonne I overheard a number of sociologists discuss which authors should be part of a program on the origins of their discipline. None of them mentioned Ibn Khaldoun. Having admired, in French translation, the *Prolegomenon* and the *History of the Berbers*, and having read, amongst other things, the thesis of Taha Hussein on *La Pensée sociale d'Ibn Khaldoun*, I, a layman here, allowed myself to suggest that the founding father of sociology, and this several centuries before Montesquieu, was the Arab-speaking Berber from Tunisia. They pitilessly told me that I spoke of what I did not know, that my intervention was only a pose, or even an imposture; and they refused to take it into consideration. Well then, I maintain that it is inadmissible to talk of sociology without knowing the *Prolegomenon*, and I think that from now on nobody will be able to talk seriously about the theater if he has not read the *Treatises* of Zeami, or if he has not taken cognizance of the nô drama, or of the Peking opera.

In one sense, this amounts to saying that the world literature of the future, that is to say *literature*, will merit, even more than does the *Weltliteratur* of which Goethe dreamed, Mr. Árpád Berczik's reproach that it largely depends upon translations.[19] In fact, the good use to which each of us will put literature will depend on the progress made in an art usually looked down upon. This also means that whoever wants to really educate himself in literature will have to read Saikaku in translation rather than Péladan in the original, Ilango Idagal in translation rather than Françoise Sagan in the original, Hallaj in translation rather than Géraldy in the original, Kabir in translation rather than Anna de Noailles in the original. Indeed, do the sum yourself: give yourself fifty years of life without one day of illness or rest, or altogether 18,262 days. Rigorously taking into account periods of sleep, meals, the obligations and the pleasures of life and of your profession, estimate the time left to you for reading masterpieces with the sole purpose of finding out what precisely is literature. As I'm extremely generous, I will grant you the privilege of reading every day – good ones as well as bad ones – one very beautiful book of all those that are accessible to you in your own language and in the foreign languages you have mastered, in the original, or in translation. You know that it will take you more than one day to read *The Magic Mountain* or the *Arabian Nights*; but I also take into account that with a little bit of luck and zeal you might read in one day the *Hojoki*, the *Romancero gitano*, the *Menexenos* and *The Spirit of Conquest* of Benjamin Constant. This will give you the couple of days extra that you will need to read *And Quiet Flows the Don*, which for the longest time was thought to have been written by Sholokhov, but which is not any less good for actually being mostly the work of Krioukov. In any case better than *Cleared Land* by the same Sholokhov. Now, when measured against the total number of very beautiful books that exist in the world, what are 18,262 titles? Sheer poverty.

And yet no one will be able to get it out of my head that, if there is a future for man, it is that in which our students will know how to read, and will want to read, Jippensha Ikku and Rabelais, Wang Chong and Hobbes, the *Risalat ul ghufran* and the *Li Sao*, the *Vita* of Cellini and the *Confessions* of St. Augustine and that, the world of men being what it is, it is to this ideal that we have to dedicate what in a previous century was world literature. This means that instead of wasting one's time with reading a thousand bad books of which the whole world talks, one will be able to choose from the tens of thousands of great works that are only awaiting our good-will. Maybe this also means that, while we may continue to educate specialists in the Romance languages, the Germanic languages, or the Slavic languages, or Dravidian, or Sino-Tibetan, or Turkish-Mongolian, or Finno-Ugrian, or Semitic, and many Africanists, we will also educate another type of scholar: people who will know well a Semitic language, a Dravidian language, a Sino-Tibetan language, and a Malay language. These are the people who would be particularly apt to enrich and define more precisely the notion of literature. And let no one object that I am dreaming, that I am wallowing in utopia. In Paris I know a few very gifted students who are beginning to acquire this kind of education. It is they who one day might write this history of literature, and of literatures, that we unfortunately still lack. They are the ones who one day might elaborate a history and theory of literary genres. Our traditional teachings should therefore be complemented with those offered by institutes of literature conceived in such a spirit. They are the people who, building on the work done by scholars of Slavic, Germanic, Chinese, Romance, and Semitic literatures, might try to put together those syntheses of literary history, criticism and aesthetics that still continue to elude us because, owing to a lack of means but also to a lack of foresight and imagination, we continue in our usual groove.

But I sense that I risk falling afoul of the complaint that a famous comparatist, Arturo Farinelli, formulated in a review of a book by Richard M. Meyer, *Die Weltliteratur der Gegenwart von Deutschland aus überblickt*. "Let us not be envious of the luster of faraway meteors and let us not yearn to roam the tempting meadows of the loud world, looking for bliss, and forgetting our own quiet and green home" [*Beneiden wir den Glanz der Fernleuchtenden Meteore nicht und trachten wir nicht danach, wonnesuchend, der stillen grünen Heimat vergessend, die lockenden Fluren der lärmenden Welt zu durchschweifen*].[20] After which, and by way of conclusion, he cites a few lines of verse by Theodor Fontane, among them the following two lines:

> *Das Haus, die Heimat, die Beschränkung,*
> *Die sind das Glück und sind die Welt.*
> [House, home, limitation,
> In these lie happiness and the world.]

One word above all strikes me, and worries me while it yet also reassures me: limitation [*Beschränkung*], because it reminds me that it is precisely the champion of world literature who is responsible for putting into my head the following precept which I find at the same time so judicious and so difficult to respect:

> *In der Beschränkung zeigt sich erst der Meister.*
> [The true master knows what to limit himself to.]

Goethe himself, then, at one and the same time calls upon us to contribute with all our might to the dawn of *Weltliteratur* and to know how to limit ourselves or otherwise never to excel at anything. This is where I see eye to eye with Hermann Hesse, who refuses to back any preconceived program of world literature; and yet I propose to organize our studies via a truly international association of comparatists that might even serve to distribute the great tasks that face us.

Do I contradict myself? Am I caught in full aporia? Not at all, it seems to me. On the one hand I think that it is to be wished, that it is necessary even, that from now on an educated person should be able to take whatever suits him or her from anywhere: even though neither of them knows Chinese, Cyril Connolly in England and Jean Grenier in France have understood and assimilated part of Taoism. Of course, we have to be wary of the traps of exoticism. The present fashion for a *Zen* little understood ill serves the cause of world literature. World literature should not be allowed to become mere pap. But if I'm allowed to draw on my own experience, I owe as much to Confucius and Zhuangzi as to Montaigne, almost as much to Sun Tzu as to Kant, and much more to Wang Chong than to Hegel. Without this detour by way of China I would probably never have encountered my own truth, my own moral universe and my happiness. Hallaj, the crucified, the Indian mystics Toukaram and Kabir, have helped me to better appreciate St. John of the Cross and Teresa of Avila. One can put literature to humanist purposes, then: as amateur (in the favorable sense of *he who loves*, like Hermann Hesse). In this case, following the precept of Goethe, everyone limits his choice according to his own taste, his preferences, his moral or intellectual stature. But let us not confound this *usage*, this *enjoyment*, this *assimilation* of world literature with the *knowledge* it behooves us to compile about it in the form of lists, treatises, histories, dictionaries. In that case our only limits should be comprehensiveness and truth. A true history of literature and of literatures will have to be as truthful as possible, acceptable for all peoples involved. If it does not satisfy these criteria, it is worth nothing. In order to bring such an enterprise to a fruitful end, there will be need of teams of men who have an extraordinary capacity, indefatigable scholars, men of a totally different affective and intellectual caliber than Jean Grenier or Cyril Connolly. Perhaps we will be able to reconcile these two requirements. Because after all, as since 1929 I have never ceased to work on Rimbaud and his myth, from Mexico to Russia, from Turkey to China, and I've only succeeded in coming to understand what maybe there is to be understood in [Rimbaud's sonnet] "*Voyelles,*" I know that the pleasure that the [Malagasy] *Hain-tenys* or the *Tzurezuregusa* give me can never be more than that of an amateur;[21] but why should I deprive myself of that? This is one of the contradictions of the world in which we live, in which our students will live: we are at one and the same time filled with information and overwhelmed by its excess. To the point even that at precisely the moment at which world literature finally becomes possible it becomes at the same time almost impossible. Of course, I hope that everyone of us feels under obligation to the impossible.

Notes

1 "Goethe's concept of world literature can be compared to a concerto grosso, in which singular phrases sound the voices of the various nations and the whole yet fuses into one superb symphony. All this is to say that the Goethean world literature idea constituted an internationalism of the mind. As such it does not absorb into itself the separate literatures, as these become participants in world literature precisely because of their specific national characteristics, and the separate nations make what is really of value in their literatures into the common property of mankind through well-crafted translations and adaptations." "A Hungarian Conception of World Literature," in *Comparative Literature in Eastern Europe*, Budapest Conference, 26–29 October 1962, edited by I. Söter, of the Hungarian Academy of Sciences and K. Bor, T. Klaniczay Gy. M. Vajda (Budapest, Akadémiai Kiadó, 1963), p. 289.

2 "With the emergence of the bourgeoisie, the relations between the national literatures have even intensified, and become more varied, with literary contacts being facilitated by improved means of transport and becoming at the same time profitable from the point of view of economic exchanges too, etc. One even arrives at positing the idea of a set of literary values common to all humanity – the world literature of Goethe. But what is coming into being before our very eyes is deeply and fundamentally different from anything that ever went before. For the first time in the history of human culture we witness, etc." "What literary scholarship owes to contemporary world-literature," *ibid.*, p. 184.

3 Johann Peter Eckermann, *Gespräche mit Goethe....,* [*Conversations with Goethe ....*], herausgegeben von Prof. Dr. H.H. Hausman (Wiesbaden, F. Brockhaus, 1959). See entries for 31 January 1827, pp. 172–174 and 15 July 1827, p. 199.

4 Jean Hankiss, "Littérature universelle?," *Helicon* (Debreczen, 1938), nos 1–2, p. 159.

5 *Mest'fa Ben Brahim et Turoldus, Gesar et Roland*, Paper given at the Congress of the French Comparative Literature Association in Rennes, 1963, and "Une épopée tibétaine," *Nouvelle Revue Française*, Septembre 1963.

6 *Eine Bibliothek der Weltliteratur.* Zürich, Werner Classen Verlag, 1946.

7 "Nobody could even then completely study the entire literature of even one single cultured nation, and get to know it, let alone that of all of humanity," p. 12, the quotation from the text is on p. 15. See also p. 17: "Education without heart is one of the worst sins against the spirit," in which we recognize the German equivalent ["Bildung ohne Herz ist eine der schlimmsten Sünden gegen den Geist"] to our French *science without conscience only leads to the ruin of the soul* [*science sans conscience n'est que ruine de l'âme*].

8 *Pour une bibliothèque idéale, enquête présentée par Raymond Queneau*, de l'académie Goncourt (Paris, Gallimard, 1946), p. 40.

9 *Ibid.*, p. 28.

10 *Ibid.*, p. 38.

11 "The age of Weltliteratur has begun; and everyone should further its course," Goethe, *loc. cit.*, p. 174.

12 See *Vergleichende Zeittafel ....* (Stuttgart, Engelman Verlag Adolf Spemann, 1951), *passim*. In 1906, over against 34 German and 6 Austrian titles, Spemann mentions 8 English titles, 8 American, 1 Irish, 10 French, 1 Flemish, 1 Dutch, 3 Danish, 2 Norwegian, 2 Swedish, 1 Belgian, 1 Italian, 3 Spanish, 1 Hungarian, 1 Polish, 1 Japanese, 1 Russian. In 1915, while I find 31 German and 7 Austrian titles, I find 1 Swiss, 2 Danish, 1 Icelandic, 2 Norwegian, 1 Swedish, 14 English, 1 Irish, 7 American, 3 Australian, 4 French, 1 Italian,

1 Romanian, 1 Guatemalan, 1 Hungarian, 1 Polish, 2 Russian, 1 Japanese, 2 Indian. For 1939, the Germans are entitled to 70 titles, Austria to 11, and German Switzerland to 8; Flemish counts for 1, like Dutch, Danish, Swedish, Scottish, Irish, Finnish; English gets 10, American 11, French 15. And so on for each year. – In *Die Weltliteratur*, herausgegeben von E. Frauwallner, H. Giebisch, E. Heinzel (Wien, Verlag Brüder Hollinek, 1951), three fat volumes (2118 pages with double columns), one does not have the excuse that there is not enough space.

13　*Tout ce qu'il faut savoir de la littérature universelle*, par Alice Berthet (Paris, édition du Fauconnier, s.d.).

14　*Loc. cit.*, p. 67.

15　*Les écrivains célèbres*, [*The Famous Authors*], in three volumes, appeared with the publisher Lucien Mazenod, 1951–1952. Occasionally one here confuses, in Japanese, name and first name, because our first name in Japanese becomes an *after name*.

16　Elizabeth Frenzel, *Stoffe der Weltliteratur, Ein Lexikon dichtunggeschichtlicher Längsschnitte* [*Themes of World Literature, A Literary-Historical Lexicon*], (Stuttgart, Alfred Kröner Verlag, 1962), xv + 670 very dense pages. In her preface the author clarifies what method she used: "The various articles in my lexicon base themselves in the numerous researches into literary themes (Ger. Stoff), that in the course of the last hundred years have been published in the form of books, articles, and above all dissertations, and that already feature in bibliographies, the German by K. Bauerhorst (1932) and its continuation by F.A. Schmitt (1959) as well as the international one by F. Baldensperger/W.P Friederich (1950) and the 'Yearbook of Comparative and General Literature' meant as the latter's continuation." This implicitly also indicates the limitations of Frenzel's sources.

17　I have briefly dealt with this theme in my article "Yang Kwei-fei" in the encyclopedia *Les Femmes célèbres* [*Famous Women*], in two volumes, published with Lucien Mazenod, 1960–1961.

18　One should do a study on the affinities between *Cyrano de Bergerac* and the Japanese *kabuki* theatre. I outline such a study in "Shirano Benjuro et le nô," *Nouvelle Revue Française*, July and October 1964.

19　"Is primarily fed by translations, indeed, it is almost identical with translation." *loc. cit.*, p. 288.

20　"Contemporary World Literature seen from Germany," in *Aufsätze, Reden und Charakteristiken zur Weltliteratur* [*Essays, Speeches and Definitions on World Literature*] (Bonn and Leipzig, Kurt Schroeder Verlag, 1925), p. 421. – The author of the book that serves as pretext for this review: Richard M. Meyer, to whom we owe *Die Weltliteratur im zwanzigsten Jahrhundert. Vom deutschen Standpunkt aus betrachtet* [*World Literature in the Twentieth Century: Seen from a German Perspective*] (Stuttgart and Berlin, Deutsche Verlagsanstalt, 1913), in the very terms he uses goes against the idea that Goethe had formed himself about this discipline, and abuses the term *Weltliteratur*. *Weltliteratur* is pressed into the service of Prussian imperialism: "there is being formed a universal world literature, in which an honorable role is reserved for us Germans [...]", French literature, on the contrary, is "the most unmodern," and this in 1913. As Farinelli says, we stand "before the tribunal of a Berlin judge," a judge that deplores that "contemporary world literature is still less imbued with German spirit than it is with the French one," which is just a pitiful argument if one compares it to the requirements of Weltliteratur according to Goethe: "correcting each other's errors."

　　By giving over one volume to *German Literature*, and another to *World Literature*, the Dalp collection (Bern, A. Francke A.G. Verlag, 1946) commits the reverse error of that of the *History of Literatures* of [the French series] the Pléiade: one volume for literatures in French, and two volumes for all other literatures. If I do not refer to the great work of Fritz Strich, *Goethe and World Literature* (Bern, A. Francke A.G. Verlag, 1946) it is because I intend to deal with the following question: *"Should we revise the notion of world literature?"*, Not *Goethe and World Literature*.

21   Kenkô's work, *Les Heures oisives* [*Essays in Idleness*], is now available in French, in *Connaissance de l'Orient* [*Knowledge of the Orient*], Unesco collection of representative works, no. 27, Gallimard, 1968, together with the *Hôjô-ki, Notes de ma cabane de moine* [*Hôjô-ki, Notes from my monk's cabin*], by Kamo no Chômei.

9

Constructing Comparables (2000)

Marcel Detienne

A prominent figure in the study of classical antiquity, Marcel Detienne is a Belgian historian and emeritus professor of Classics at Johns Hopkins University, where he has taught since 1992, having previously taught at the École Pratique des Hautes Études in Paris. Trained in classics, philosophy, and the history of religion, Detienne early on developed a comparatist view of ancient societies, drawing on Claude Lévi-Strauss's structural anthropology. Detienne has written extensively on Greek mythology and religion, on the social and cultural history of Archaic and Classical Greece, and on anthropological and comparative approaches to classical civilization. His more than 20 books include *The Gardens of Adonis* (1977), *Dionysos Slain* (1979), *The Creation of Mythology* (1986), *Dionysos at Large* (1989), and *The Masters of Truth in Archaic Greece* (1996). He edited and co-edited several volumes of essays, including *Les savoirs de l'écriture en Grèce ancienne* (1992), *Transcrire les mythologies: tradition, écriture, historicité* (1994), and *Destins de Meurtriers* (1996).

For two decades, Detienne directed an ambitious collaborative program of comparatist study of ancient societies through the *Centre de recherches comparées sur les sociétés anciennes*, which he founded in Paris. The essay given here reflects on the theoretical and methodological challenges of this work. Detienne describes his method as "constructive, experimental comparativism," taking the example of one of his group's research projects, a comparative study of foundational cultural sites in four widely dispersed early cultures. Detienne argues for the value of juxtaposing "incomparable" societies so as to learn from differences and dissonances instead of privileging direct cultural relations and comparisons. As he

Marcel Detienne, "Constructing Comparables" (2000). From Marcel Detienne, *Comparing the Incomparable*, trans. Janet Lloyd (Stanford, CA: Stanford University Press, 2008), pp. 22–39. English translation © 2008 Board of Trustees of Leland Stanford Junior University. All rights reserved.

World Literature in Theory, First Edition. Edited by David Damrosch.
© 2014 John Wiley & Sons, Ltd. Published 2014 by John Wiley & Sons, Ltd.

says, "The incomparable ... disturbs the initial comparatist's approach, facing him with a first resistance, forcing him to ask himself how and why this category doesn't exist or doesn't seem to make sense in one of the societies studied." Derived from his work with historians and anthropologists, Detienne's argument can be applied equally to literary studies, not only of earlier periods but also of the many literary cultures that continue to resist, or to exist outside of, the unifying forces of globalization.

Historians and anthropologists working together: What, on the face of it, could be more simple? During the past two or three decades historical-research centres have been attracting historians of all kinds. And anthropologists, for their part, have at their disposition laboratories that are wide open to many windswept cultural areas and continents. Indianists, Africanists, and Americanists can engage together in comparative investigations into systems of thought assuredly more ambitious than that of scholars specializing in the seventeenth century. Meanwhile, historians not drawn to national matters and all their competitiveness can choose to engage in a comparativism that tends to be more socioeconomic than cultural, although there should be no harm in that so long as it is generally recognized that on the whole there is nothing to separate those studying exotic places from those studying other times. The only stumbling block lies in that 'on the whole', as I realize when I note that, apart from myself, only Bernard Cohen, far away in Chicago, has explicitly said as much in his sketch of 'An anthropologist among the historians' (1980).[1] Everywhere else, those 'useful prejudices', so beloved whenever identity comes under threat, rise to the surface like so many bobbing figurines.

   To be sure, there will always be historians ready to leap to the defence of the diehard thesis that only that which is comparable can be compared. Likewise, even among ethnologists, who are in principle more accustomed to comparativism, often enough one comes across references to a 'my place' when it is a matter of asserting the specificity of some abutting area or the total originality of some culture. But never mind. The main thing, when it comes to working together, is to shake free from what is close at hand, what one is born to or native to, and recognize as soon as possible that we need to learn about *all* human societies, every community possible or imaginable, for as far as the eye can see, with historians and anthropologists all intermingling. Forget the lavish advice of those who for half a century have been repeating endlessly that the best thing to do is to set up comparisons between neighbouring societies, bordering one another, that have progressed, hand in hand, in the same direction, or between human groups that have reached the same level of civilization and at a first glance present enough similarities for one to proceed safely. In the 1930s, linguists in Prague set up a laboratory in which languages that were unrelated and with dissimilar structures were deliberately chosen for comparative study. They certainly did not wait for epistemologists to grant them a license to experiment. One of the products of that laboratory was to be phonology.

Singular and Plural

The advantages of anthropologists and historians working together are well known. With a contrastive approach, one can discover cognitive dissonances; or, to put that more simply, one may bring out some detail or feature that had escaped the notice of other interpreters and observers. One can radically question the status of the economies of ancient societies, ancient civilizations, and our own, as Karl Polanyi did not so long ago at Columbia University, when he persuaded ethnologists and historians to think together. Or it may be a matter of observing from the vantage point of India how salt was administered in the Ottoman Empire or the kingdom of France;[2] or else how, from what angles, in what aspects of a more restricted configuration, a philosopher in Greece differed from a sage in China.[3]

The constructive comparativism whose aims and procedures I intend to defend must start by adopting as its field of exercise and experimentation the entire gamut of cultural representations among the most distant societies of the past as well as those closest to hand, and groups of living human beings observed on our planet both yesterday and today. A comparativist seeking to construct his subjects must be able to move, without a passport, between the members of the Constituent Assembly of the French Revolution, the inhabitants of the high plateau of southern Ethiopia, the European Commission in Brussels, and the earliest tiny cities of Greece, stopping off, if he decides to, in Siena or Verona to see, for example, how assemblies functioned between the twelfth and thirteenth centuries.[4] I have been speaking of 'a' comparativist, but in truth, he or she must be at once singular and plural. In some cases, the polymathy or encyclopaedism of one person suffices to tackle a domain such as the Indo-European civilization, which Georges Dumézil studied on his own. But once a project encompasses the entire gamut of human societies, it does not make sense for a single person to work alone. So what kind of a comparativist do I have in mind? One who emerges from an intellectual network of three or four historian-anthropologists or anthropologist-historians, all convinced that it is just as important for each of them to feed on the knowledge and questions of the others as it is to set out to produce an in-depth analysis of the civilization or society whose 'professional' interpreter each of them began by being. For 'a' comparativist to become plural, it is necessary to form a microgroup of ethnologists and historians who are colleagues or even accomplices and who are prepared to think aloud, together. A regular meeting place is more important than a big research grant, for in that shared space, a comparativist can acquire the competence of a historico-anthropological microcommunity. The project may begin with no more than two members, the one a historian, the other an anthropologist, just so long as each partakes of the intellectual curiosity and competence of the other.

How does this 'we-I' proceed in practical terms? On the strength of having worked over a ten-year period with a group of researchers that has to date published four comparativist volumes[5] and has recently completed one more, I am in a position to make a retrospective analysis of some of the procedures that make it possible to produce a comparative work aiming to construct comparables between historians and anthropologists. The enquiry that I reckon to provide the best example was published in 1990, with the title *Tracés de fondation* (Paths leading to foundations). It started off with a collaboration between, on the one hand, a Hellenist interested in the enquiries of Africanists into ways of constructing a territory that involve certain rituals and collections of representations, and, on the other, an ethnologist fascinated by a Hellenist historian's research into the actions ascribed to a god that, in the course of four centuries, carved out a territory of a political nature involving scores of tiny cities. The collaboration that led to raising or readdressing the question 'What is a site?' may have been prompted by a playful comparison between two configurations: one had been studied by an Africanist and showed that in order to create the space for a village it was necessary to clear an area of bush. The other, some distance away, had been studied by an Indianist and showed that in Brahmin India it was the village that determined its own boundaries, not the boundaries that determined the village. The bush, boundaries, and villages all began to look uncertain against a still unclear horizon of territorialization, or rather, of the remarkably different ways, in different places, of establishing a territory.

The Shock of the Incomparable

In order to access the teeming variety of modes of territorialization we needed to select a category, making sure that it was generic enough to allow the beginnings of a comparison but neither too general nor too specific to any particular culture. The category we chose was that of 'founding, foundations, founders'. From the reactions of the various members of the group – Africanists, Japanese specialists, Americanists, and Hellenists – it became clear that, although this category was complex, it was useful in that it prompted a whole series of questions. It was neither too strong nor too weak. Had it been too strong, too powerfully classificatory, it would have impeded the work of comparison; if too weak, it would have produced nothing to think about as a group, whatever the sites and forms of beginning and inauguration that seemed to be covered by the common meaning of 'to found'.

It seemed easy enough to slip from 'hard-edged' founding, complete with a founder, into a study of a whole series of journeys, processes, and ritual gestures that were involved in territorialization quite apart from or even before the actual act of founding. But we experienced a salutary heuristic shock when we discovered what appeared to be an instance of incomparability. One day, two Japanese specialists who had long remained silent as we fumbled our way forward, came to confess, to their chagrin, that, according to the most ancient texts, in Japan there simply was no founding, no founder. I thanked them most warmly and told them that now we could at last begin to think about what 'to found, to establish lastingly' really meant. Thanks to the provocation caused by that incomparability, a familiar category such as 'founding' was about to become cloudy, to fracture and disintegrate.[6]

Certain societies that awaited us seemed stubbornly resistant to the idea of founding: in the first place Japan, next Vedic India.[7] Japan, in its insularity, cultivated the idea of an interrupted continuity ever since primordial days. The gods had engineered it all, celestial gods and autochthonous ones, of which there were two varieties: on the one hand, autochthonous masters of the land, the civilizers who would serve as matrimonial partners for the celestial gods; on the other, wild autochthonous beings, relegated to the underworld or the depths of the sea. The masters of the land and the celestial gods, between them, engendered the royal lineage, which then developed without a break. From the very start right down to the present day, the power of the emperor was directly associated with cosmogony. This was a model of 'continuous creation', but it was subject to entropy. It therefore became necessary to regenerate the world and restore it through contact with the live forces of the Beyond. At regular intervals, temples were rebuilt, domestic sanctuaries were remade, and boundaries were redefined. There was no refounding, for the very good reason that there never had been any founding. Vedic India provided another example of not thinking in terms of foundation, refusing to localize or create sites. Of course, villages were inhabited and the Indians had towns and fortresses. However, although they were thus sedentary, these people set a high value on nomadism and held localization in horror. The notion of a fixed place revolted them. Vedic India presented an open space with no individualized temples or sites. One and the same space was everywhere. The intense module that a sacrificial precinct represented was never founded; rather, it materialized around the fires lit by nomads and disappeared when the sacrificers moved on. It was a perfect nonplace.

What are the elements that we introduce into the act of founding that seem to us central to 'the creation of a territory'? Probably the uniqueness of this particular space, designated by a particular name, with particular characteristics and a boundary drawn within a vaster space; certainly a beginning in time, in a history, in a chronology, and some kind of an initial, isolated, recognized, remarkable, or even solemn event. Founding seems to need a significant beginning that leads to a historical process. Lastly, when we think of founding, we refer to some action, gestures, ritual, or ceremonial, inseparable from a particular individual (Romulus, say, or … Clovis) who links us with or even roots us in this particular unique place, right from the start.[8]

Proceeding in this way, plural comparativism throws up many questions around the misleading transparency of 'founding'. It undertakes a conceptual analysis of what 'creating a territory' might mean as it moves from one society to another, all of which actively engage in establishing a territory, some of them resorting to the idea of 'founding', others calling only minimally upon that notion, and yet others simply doing without it.

The Art of Coining Something New

Having become a 'we/I', a comparativist moves among communities that differ increasingly from one another the more fragile the bridges between them become, always carrying with him or her a little bunch of questions, as if to sweep over as extensive as possible a field of investigation that is as yet without limits. For how could any limits possibly be fixed? Daoist China has taught him or her that what one founds is never a town, but rather a holy place, and that founding a holy place involves gestures to purify an altar along with its sacrificial precinct; the Africa of walled cities glimpsed in the Cameroon area seems to have undermined the comparativist's primordial image of Rome, with its founders whose power feeds on the blood of close neighbours that drenches the earth and sustains the city's crown of battlements. How many more societies and cultures so far unknown or misunderstood should he or she include in the field of comparison under construction? Actually, that does not really matter, given that this is a comparativist who is not concerned with exhaustiveness; his or her aim is not to construct an abstract model of founding, nor to devise the most delicate classification possible of cultural forms of 'creating a territory'. Aiming to fashion the notion of 'founding' in order 'to create a territory' as accurately as possible, our singular-plural comparativist constantly ponders such questions as 'What makes a place? What is a boundary? What does beginning something involve?', secure in the knowledge that he or she is seeking to discover not an essential quality but rather the multiple and shifting forms that a place may take. Some places speak to one, others signal; some are wombs to impregnate, mouths to feed, eyes that weep. Does this place have a name? Is it fixed? What does it mean to live in a place? Does living there lead inevitably to making alterations and putting up new constructions? Some places are declared to be vacant, purged, there for the taking. Some societies, such as China and Africa, develop a science of places, a learned knowledge of sites: this is known as geomancy. A Greek philosopher in his village in Attica, which he turns into an Academy, may reveal to a comparativist how strange a place can be in relation to movement and to the body: for example, that a place is an infinite succession of borders that come into being, then vanish as the body moves along; that a place always remains behind since it is a trace left behind as the body moves on, a wake that follows the moving body like a shining shadow. Such an idea is enough to blur the clear-cut image of an altar either rectangular or round and fixed forever in the same spot. And what about limits or boundaries? What is a boundary? Where does it come from? From the bush, from the village, from the earth's skin, from its very silence? One must be prepared for anything: Is a boundary fixed, shifting, porous, inviolable, or transparently passable? Must it always be marked out, inspected, circumscribed? If, by some miracle, it is clearly marked, what means were used to make it so? Who enforces its observance? A boundary is a fascinating thing. It may consist in a window, in a set of hinges, in bolts; it may well lie at the centre or even in a hearth.

Let us continue this process of coining something new, spurred on by any instance of incomparability that lays bare the strangeness of founding gestures and initial beginnings. How does each culture think, as a community, separately, or in configurations never before beheld? How does a culture make things, produce, create, procreate, and invent them? What is an origin, as opposed to a becoming or a beginning? How can cosmogony exist alongside starting, founding, and inaugurating? The Upper Volta, contemporary India, Romulus' Rome, and the first Greek cities are all characterized by concrete or metaphorical gestures:

incising with a knife, encircling with a string, constructing a basis, rooting in the earth, setting down an infant. Some objects are more prone to territorialize than others: holy places, the oldest houses, architectural altars, sacrificial precincts, temples. … Certain constructions operate as matrixes: in India, a temple can be a whole kingdom, a whole inhabited land. Where did founding originate? In the heavens, as the people of the Gourmantche believe? In the earth from which it arose, as in Hinduism today? From the coming together of something already there and something from elsewhere that hails from a foreign land, a distant country? For some foundations are as solid as bronze or brass: in the colonies that China, Rome, and Greece all, in their own ways, founded, there is a fusing of different elements. What do founders bring with them? A jar containing fragments of their ancestors? A sacrificial knife and a calabash half-full of soupy honey? A cooking pot and a few embers from the common Hearth? And what do they do about lineages, ancestors, the dead? Can ancestrality not be fabricated on the spot? (At this point Nationalism no doubt pricks up its ears!)

And we must not forget the founders themselves, the figures that they cut, the masks that they don, the configurations to which they belong and on which they stamp their gestures and leave their mark. Some come from the heavens, others from the earth: in Mesopotamia it was a god who took the initiative after which the king, who founded the temples and towns, scrupulously followed the plan that had been drawn up on high. In Africa, India, and Greece, the founder would be a mortal, maybe a hunter led to a particular site by his prey, maybe a Hindu renouncer who found his way to some forest, maybe an exiled murderer following a path indicated by the Delphic oracle. Depending on the nature of his relations with the earth and his representations of this, he would enjoy a greater or lesser measure of initiative. For example, if, as in Burkina Faso, the real power circulates among the Masters of the Earth, a founder will not be able to behave as an authoritarian leader in the manner of a Greek founder, known as an *archegetes*, who marches forward as a conqueror, seizes a space decreed to be empty and deserted, marks it out and assigns its boundaries. Some founders are timid and cautious and set up an initial dwelling that in itself shelters a whole village and a community already provided with ancestors. Some founders are possessed by their doubles or are spurred on by violence and bloodshed that roots them to the place. And some founders are taken over by the foundation itself and become a special ancestor or one ancestor among others or even just some abstract dead figure without a lineage, no more than a political symbol, a mere idealization.

Mechanisms of Thought

As he or she proceeds along 'the paths leading to foundation', a comparativist feels he or she is discovering a whole set of possibilities whose conceptual manipulation enables one to spot certain unique and essential elements organized into a variety of arrangements. By dividing up the 'founding category' into 'the creation of a territory' in the dozen or so cultures selected for this experiment, the comparativist engages in a logical dismantling operation that makes it possible to discern how two or three elements interact and pick out microconfigurations that reveal differences that turn out to be interrelated ever more subtly. The creative comparativist realizes that he or she is analysing mechanisms of thought into patterns that become detectable when approached from a number of unobtrusive and by no means thematic angles. For example, the concepts of 'an inaugural figure from outside', 'a local force in the form of the Earth', or 'a nonbeginning' and what happens after it, when applied to two, three, or four different cultures, offer similar but never exactly identical schemata.

Using these tactics, let us see what transpires. Take 'nonbeginning', which has been represented as incomparable: it can be applied in the cases of Vedic India, Japan, and forest-dwelling Indians of South America (the Guayaki and the Yanomani). In Vedic India, nonbeginning is connected with 'nonplaces' and a rejection of temporal singularity. In Japan, it is cosmogony that makes 'nonbeginning' viable but at the same time calls for continuous regeneration and restoration. The way the Indians of South America cope with 'nonbeginning' is by refusing to create sites, keeping on the move within the same territory but always carrying with them an ephemeral centre every trace of which they efface when they move on, just as they wipe out all signs of the remains of their dead. An approach via 'remains' or 'the dead as an anchor' would immediately allow for a comparison between Vedic India, the Guayaki, and the *archegetes*-founders of Greece.

Now let us consider an approach via 'a local force in the form of the Earth'. Burkina Faso, in the land of the Kasena, features a primeval Earth figure that incorporates troglodytes that are already present and all the scraps of bush known as 'the Earth's skin' beneath which there is no firm basis. The Master of the Earth controls every territorialization that is attempted by a creature known as 'the Filani Stranger', which wanders about in the bush. In Daoist China, a ground god is present in every holy place and can also take the form of a Wall god. In traditions relating to foundation by kings, the Ground god is double, taking the form of a son of the Sky, in the shape of a dancer with a sword, and a son of the First Rebel, in the shape of a victim buried beneath a door so as to anchor the precinct wall in the ground. It is as if the Ground that is a holy place effects a foundation that retains links with both the Sky and the Earth.

So, for historians and anthropologists working together, what is it that is comparable? Not themes, as I said above, but the thought mechanisms that can be observed at work in interrelations between elements arranged in accordance with whatever entry point is adopted: the concepts of 'an inaugural figure from outside', 'nonbeginnings' and so on. These mechanisms serve as 'localized plates of quasi-causal connections' (*des plaques localisées d'enchaînement quasi causal*), to quote Gérard Lenclud. Let me explain. Once a significant feature or mental attitude is detected (choice or rejection, for instance), that feature becomes part of a particular configuration, and the manner in which that feature or attitude (arbitrary or conventional) is linked to the configuration as a whole is not random. In one way or another, 'the configuration must be somehow systematic'. We are thus led to postulate some kind of relative coherence, 'plates of coherence'. The hypothesis that accompanies such dismantling operations, that is to say, this coining of new concepts (of which we have provided many examples), is that the distribution of the elements that make up a microconfiguration is not random. With Lenclud reading over my shoulder, I have come to realize that there is an interrelation between the various elements. Every microconfiguration displays, so to speak, a particular orientation.

The comparables that we were setting up on the basis of a sequence of intuitions could thus be said to be orientations, interlinked choices: choices made in preference to other possibilities. When a society (not a global one, but a local one committed to such microconfigurations as it has retained) adopts a particular element of thought, it makes a particular choice that might have been different. The job of a singular/plural analyst is to discern the constraints that affect the configurations that he or she is studying. It is a matter of understanding that a microsystem of thought is constrained to organize its essential elements so as to fit in with the kind of angles considered above: 'nonbeginnings', 'local forces such as the Earth', and so on. In this kind of comparativism which – as can be seen – is definitely constructive, what are 'comparable' are not types that may be used to establish a typology (which would feature, for example, founders who are specifically hunters or wanderers, cautious or impetuous, and so on); nor are they forms that make it possible to construct the morphology of either a territory or a household. Rather, they are interconnecting plates determined by some initial choice. Historians and anthropologists who have learned how to work together are particularly interested in groupings that result from logical choices that may be similar but are actually all different.

Passing from Autochthony to Refoundation

An example taken from the Greek community will reveal more clearly still to what extent a comparison between logical solutions radically differs from one devoted to noting the incidental resemblances or contrasts between an ascetic founder of Hinduism, a Filani hunter charging into a Gourmantche region, and an *archegetes* setting foot on the shores of an unknown land. However, I shall at this point be concentrating on various Greek communities, so as to dispel any idea that we are always bound to set up comparisons between Greeks and Chinese or Greeks and Indians. On Greek terrain, rich in twelve centuries of history and seven hundred or so cities, historian-anthropologists sense from the start that they will find numerous possible and observable microconfigurations. Given that these are remarkably clearly defined, they will at once pick out two modes in which founding may proceed: that of the *archegetes*, already several times mentioned above, and that of autochthony, a concept certainly familiar to French nationalists. In a whole series of small cities, an *archegetes* of the archaic period took the form of an inaugural figure from elsewhere. In my *Apollon, le couteau à la main* (Apollo, the butcher),[9]

I concentrated on the relations between paths trodden, feet firmly placed, thresholds, doors, and precincts circumscribed by a line incised with a knife. An *archegetes* with a sacrificial knife carves out a section of land that is declared to be empty and deserted. He then circumscribes a space to contain the first altar, on which his knife will slit the throat of an animal victim that he will then cut up and distribute between the members of the new community, each of whom will receive a portion of equal weight. An *archegetes*-founder – an inaugural figure from elsewhere – marches firmly toward a 'political' model of territorialization. What he institutes is neither a temple nor simply a house: it is a city, one that appears to find nothing 'already there' or any local power in the form of the Earth. The ancient figure of Earth, the Gaia of Hesiod's *Theogony*, who founded herself, called herself Self-Founded. Through the way that this first type of configuration operates in the sanctuary from which the inaugural figure of the *archegetes* sets out, it establishes a link between the actor from elsewhere and some power who is lastingly established (in Delphi, the latter is Themis) and who, via the oracle constructs paths of words that lead to the virtues of creating and making things. And at the heart of the *archegetes*-deity's dwelling, that link leads to recognition of the internal relations between Poseidon, the god of bases, and Hestia, the power of the Hearth that is at once a centre and a sacrificial fire with a primordial purpose.

The features of autochthony stand in contrast to the model of 'a founder who arrives from elsewhere, while the Earth remains silent', and an anthropologist-historian studying Greek communities has no difficulty in distinguishing them.[10] Autochthony was the configuration that the Athenians arrogantly brandished in the faces of all the rest of the Greeks. It may seem a minor aberration, but it was one that became dominant in a century that 'armchair historians' tend to label as a 'Golden Age', whether they are thinking of Spain or Greece. In Greece, this means the fifth century BC, the one that certain academicians, both female and male, claim as their own preserve. Now, please pay attention: the people of Athens of that time proclaimed themselves to be the very sons of the Earth, not mere common *Gegeneis* who, even in Arcadia, emerged from the ground like so many muddy-arsed yokels, but sons born from the timeless Earth of Attica itself, with an identity all their own that was so perfect that it led to Isocrates, Plato (in pastiche mode), and Euripides (but ironically, of course) to point a scornful finger at the city's impure elements that sullied the purity of pedigree Athenians, that is to say all the *perioikoi* and resident aliens whose very presence there was an insult to Erechtheus, the great-hearted child of the black Earth, nurtured by Athena herself on the soil of Attica:[11] Attica in its finest essence, just as the Past was later to be essentialized. The sons of admirable Athens could claim to be purely Greek, since they were quintessential pure-blooded Athenians. In 451 they passed a law (with what majority we do not know) decreeing (and about time too …) that Athenians had to be Athenian on both sides, not just in the paternal line, but in the maternal one too. (Hooray for Athenian women, for they were in the avant-garde of feminism!) Why ever had all these citizens had to wait for Pericles before they could at last feel themselves to be authentic, pure Athenians? Here was obviously an example of a quite different orientation, whose brilliance could not fail to strike any 'we/I' seeking to identify choices and elements that might throw an oblique light on another microconfiguration to be found close by, in Thebes, the Thebes of Oedipus, or rather the Thebes prior to Oedipus and all those swarms of interpreters that later fell on him.[12] Far from the region of great nocturnal hunts stood the city of Thebes, which had foundation stories of its own. Thebes was founded by Cadmus, but before he came across Harmonia, Cadmus, an 'inaugural figure from elsewhere' and perhaps the least fortunate of those *archegetes*, followed a path prescribed by the oracle of Apollo, along which he was guided by a heifer with a dappled hide that gleamed with white spots as round as a full moon. Impossible to miss her. At the spot where this lunar heifer collapsed of exhaustion, Cadmus was to sacrifice her and found a city. The first remarkable feature of the future Thebes was that, here, something *was* 'already there', in the form of a snake, the progeny of Ares, the god of warfare of attrition, and the Erinys Tilphussa, the goddess of bloodthirsty vengeance. Ares, who was 'already there', as was Earth, an accomplice of the Erinys, was sometimes known as the 'Old Man of the Earth', Palaichton, a close cousin of those who were autochthonous. All the elements of the plot were now in place. Needing water for his sacrifice of the heifer, Cadmus went off to the nearest spring, where he slew the serpent that kept watch over it, thereby incurring the anger of Ares, who told him that, if he wished to found the town as Delphi had foretold, he must sow this dragon's teeth in the earth. From those murderous teeth that Cadmus sowed fully armed warriors sprang up. These were the *Spartoi*, born from the earth, and they immediately set about slaughtering one another. Only five survived the carnage to become the first citizens of Thebes. Even at a first glance, the Theban model manifests a series of interconnected approaches, all with divergent orientations but ones that require to be analysed from the angle of refounding. Impossible to do this in Thebes, for it is off-limits. However, a number of other cities present this configuration as a recurring choice that may prove more significant than it seems. As we turn away from Thebes, it is the configuration at Athens that looks the most promising, for it is so unusual that autochthony experts have long since dismissed it. Many aspects of 'being born from oneself' are certainly far from transparent: those slight discontinuities between Erechtheus and Cecrops, the first snake-tailed man, and the discrepancies between Erechtheus and Erichthoneus (born from the seed-sowing, or at least the ejaculation of Hephaestus, which Athena, with a twist of the hips, managed to dodge, but which spurted straight into the Earth). But these are mere trifles, for the prime element is Poseidon's return in force. The whole business had appeared to be settled, with the jury unanimous and the worst of the anger forgotten. But suddenly, right in the middle of the Golden Age, Poseidon, at the head of the Thracian cavalry, charged to the assistance of the Sweet Singer, Eumolpus, the master of Eleusis and its Mysteries. Now a serious war raged between Poseidon's clan and Athena's. The people of Athens were haunted by rumours of an oracle that declared that, if the city was to be saved, the blood of Erechtheus must be shed. One of his daughters had to be slaughtered on the altar of the mournful Persephone or on the parched Earth. And even that was not enough: Erechtheus himself was violently thrust down into *his* earth on the Acropolis, where the imperturbable Athena apparently reigned supreme. There, deep in the ground, together with Poseidon, who, as Poseidon-Erechtheus, proudly bore the name of his victim, he – or rather they, the two of them together – were to become the very basis and foundation of Athens. Thanks to all of them – Erechtheus' slaughtered daughter and Erechtheus himself, now forced to merge with Poseidon – the foundations of the city were 'restored'. From then on, autochthony, so deeply rooted, seemed protected from all upheavals. Founding and refounding was a theme familiar to Solon. Long before the Golden Age, *he* had spoken of founding the city on its laws, *thesmoi*, words firmly set down in lasting fashion or – he hoped – at the very least for a hundred years,[13] for he was well aware that he was not the first founder nor would he be the last. It does not take a great comparativist to see how an enquiry aiming to construct comparables might blow away the cobwebs in all those historian heads bent over Athens, its imaginary representations, and the dazzling events that took place there between 451 and 404.

What Is the Use of Comparison?

A good question? It is one that certainly cannot be avoided, for it springs up like a weed again and again in the gloomy halls of the Sorbonne, in Johns Hopkins University, in Pisa, in Berkeley, and even in Chicago, but always on the pursed lips of a 'classicist'. Let us look him calmly in the eye. He is still thinking 'whatever is the use of it?', but we must not let this get us down. We must try to understand. I can imagine a young historian sitting in the metro or on a bench in the Jardin du Luxembourg. For the price of a couple of sandwiches, he has just purchased *L'Identité de France* (The identity of France). Ravenously, he devours the introduction penned by Braudel, recently made an Academician, in which the author confesses his nostalgia for France, a retrospective France, infinitely rich in its past experiences: a heaven-sent terrain for comparative history. As he chews this over, the young man hastens to read on, wondering 'What kind of comparative history?' 'A history in search of similarities, the real condition of any social science'.[14] Let us hope that this unfortunate young man does not, that very day, also dip into a late little work by Sir Moses I. Finley, in which the great Ancient Historian expresses his view of what should be thought about the relations between anthropology and classical Antiquity.[15] It is a perfect high-table topic for Cambridge scholars. And, over dinner, Finley addresses it squarely, seeking a vote of confidence. He asks, 'In what way is anthropology *of use* to ancient history?' Was he really so bankrupt of ideas? (I shall be coming back to that.) However, in passing, Finley scrutinizes Radcliffe-Brown and explains to his public, the audience of the Jane Harrison Memorial Lecture, that the purpose of anthropology is obviously to establish 'its own general laws' and trample differences underfoot. A chorus of historians takes up the cry: contexts are neglected; what we should compare is that which is comparable .... I tell you, it's like weeds: however much you root out prejudices, some always remain.

A straight question deserves a straight answer, so here goes. What is the use of comparison? Quite simply, I have joined the camp of those who prefer a history that is open to all human societies across both space and time. I prefer this to the rabbit hutch of parochial history or that of the national history of the exclusive territory of France. On the basis of that choice, I maintain that anthropology leads the way in nurturing a great project that is inspired by the strongest comparative urge. Certainly, let us compare. But not in order to find and impose general laws that may at last account for the variability of the cultural inventions of the human species, the how and the wherefore of variables and constants. Rather, let historians and anthropologists, working together, construct comparables and analyse microsystems of thought that all stem from a single initial choice, a choice that we are free to set alongside other choices, those that are made by societies that, for the most part, have no knowledge of one another. In what follows, I shall be providing more examples of that kind of comparativism, for it seems to me that it eludes the shortcomings of those who declare comparative activities to be 'useless', alleging that to engage in comparison is to sink ineptly into analogy and all its attendant naive findings. It is, alas, as though it were inevitably a matter of stepping aside from what we know simply to hurry to annex whatever more or less resembles it;[16] as if we pathetic human beings were bound to take some object already complete and well defined and to compare it, compulsively, to another object said to be similar from the vantage point of the other side of the Rhine or some other, mountain, frontier.

The comparativism of comparables that I am championing cannot be accused of a 'transfer of objects' or of what Durkheim regarded as a capital sin, namely, typology or even morphology. An objector might continue to ask, 'In what way is it useful to detect and analyse mechanisms of thought?' But that is an objection that could be addressed to anybody seeking to explain or argue in order to establish some relation of causality or some connection between elements of sets of relations within any cultural, economic, or social system. If we choose to prioritize intellectual understanding, understanding of others either elsewhere or in the past, we hope we can rely on not being summoned in the early hours to appear before some Grand Jury, abruptly aroused from its somnolence in order to interrogate us as to the utility of our activities. What is its use, you ask? I will answer you. I have already mentioned how great an obstacle to the comparativist endeavour the phenomenon of nationalism represents, 'the thick consistency of the national phenomenon', as François Furet, who has so lastingly separated history from ethnology, has put it. Even if nationalists go every year, on the same grey date, to lay increasingly ostentatious flowers and wreathes on the tomb of Marc Bloch, the Resistance member and martyr of comparative history, they show no interest *at all* in the comparative adventure. For they have been born and bred and have aged in the bosom of Incommensurability and the holy, Incomparable Nation of which they, once chosen, become the guardians, vouched for by their academic qualifications and the mission that they have been handed by the teachers.

I should like to defend an ethical virtue possessed by comparative activity: namely, that it encourages one to set in perspective the values and choices of the society to which one belongs, whether, by God's grace, one has been born into it or one has chosen it as a result of one's personal history or one has been led to live in it and become resident within it, a resident more or less assimilated, accepted, and acculturated. It is surely not too presumptuous to suggest that, by constructing more or less sturdy comparables within a group of historians and anthropologists working together, one learns how to distance oneself from one's baser instincts and to bring a critical eye to bear on one's own traditions so as to see, or at least glimpse, that in all likelihood they represent but one choice among others. Of course everyone, at his or her own risk, is free to cultivate and deepen that choice, whether it be for a particular landscape or for a particular nation. However, understanding a number of cultures as well as they have understood themselves, and then coming to understand these in relation to others and to recognize the differences that they have constructed by comparing them to one another, all this makes for a good, even an excellent way to learn to live with other people, whoever they may be. As Tzvetan Todorov has said, this is a way to come closer to a necessary detachment from oneself and a true understanding of social factors.[17] And that, assuredly, must be a practical aim.

Notes

1   Bernard S. Cohn, *An Anthropologist Among the Historians and Other Essays* (Oxford: Oxford University Press, 1987), chap. 2, 'History and Anthropology: The State of Play' (1980), p. 19.

2   See Lucette Valensi, 'Retour d'Orient. De quelques usages du comparatisme en histoire', in *Marc Bloch aujourd'hui. Histoire comparée et sciences sociales*, ed. Hartmut Atsma and André Burguière (Paris: EHESS, 1990), pp. 307–316. True enough, on one's return from the East, one sees more clearly even what is going on in the *Annales* periodical and can note objectively that it certainly did not encourage 'comparative history', let alone any comparativism between anthropologists and historians. Other writers tend either not to care in the slightest or to heap academic praise on the historical practices that have so profoundly transformed the 'national memory': for example, Krzysztof Pomian, 'L'heure des *Annales*', in *Les Lieux de mémoire, II, La Nation*, 1, ed. Pierre Nora (Paris: Gallimard, 1986), pp. 378–429.

3   I am thinking of the work of François Jullien. The work of Geoffrey Lloyd, who also chooses to compare aspects of Greece and China, has virtues of its own.

4   These happen to be the societies studied in our project on 'assembly practices'.

5   As these are so widely dispersed and hard to find even in good bookshops, here is a list of them:
    –*Tracés de fondation*, ed. M. Detienne (Louvain and Paris: Bibliothèque de l'Ecole pratique des hautes études, Sciences religieuses, vol. CXIII, Peeters, 1990).
    –*Transcrire les mythologies. Tradition, écriture, historicité*, ed. M. Detienne (Paris: Albin Michel, 1994).
    –*La Déesse Parole. Quatre figures de la langue des dieux (Inde, Célèbes-Sud, Géorgie, Cuna du Panama)*, ed. M. Detienne and G. Hamonic (Paris: Flammarion, 1994).
    –*Destins de meurtriers*, ed. M. Cartry and M. Detienne (*Systèmes de pensée en Afrique noire*, no. 14) (Paris: Ecole pratique des hautes études, 1996).

6   I chose the title 'What is a site?' for my efforts to think about comparative work. The following year, Gérard Lenclud produced his thoughts on the problem of comparison, in connection with the publication of *Tracés de fondation* (Approaches to founding). His comments are most illuminating for a study of ways to construct comparables, as I have assured him and as can be seen from the following pages.

7   All the civilizations mentioned below are the subjects of chapters of *Tracés de fondation*.

8   Charles Malamoud has pursued just such a conceptual search and has also drawn attention to the shock of one instance of incomparability, presented expressly to raise a whole collection of questions and tentative approaches. See 'Sans lieu ni date. Note sur l'absence de fondation dans l'Inde védique', in *Tracés de fondation*, pp. 183–191.

9   Marcel Detienne, *Apollon, le couteau à la main* (Paris: Gallimard, 1998).

10   Explored in particular by Nicole Loraux, *The Children of Athena: Athenian Ideas About Citizenship and the Division Between the Sexes*, translated by C. Levine (Princeton, NJ: Princeton University Press, 1993).

11   The time for a demonstration is not yet ripe. For the time being, see the following two essays: 'Qu'est-ce qu'un site?', in Detienne, *Tracés de fondation*, pp. 13–15; 'La force des femmes, Héra, Athéna et les siennes', in *The Daily Life of the Greek Gods*, by Giulia Sissa and Marcel Detienne, trans. Janet Lloyd (Stanford, CA: Stanford University Press, 2000), pp. 208–229.

12   See François Vian, *Les Origines de Thèbes. Cadmos et les Spartiates* (Paris: Klincksieck, 1963).

13   F. Blaise, 'Solon, Fragment 36 West. Pratique et fondation des normes politiques', *Revue des études grecques*, 108 (1995): 24–37.

14   Fernand Braudel, *L'Identité de France* (Paris: Flammarion, 1986), p. 16.

15   Moses I. Finley, *The Use and Abuse of History* (London: Chatto & Windus, 1975), 'Anthropology and the Classics', p. 113.

16   See the reflections of J. Dakhlya, 'La question des lieux communs', in *Les Formes de l'expérience*, ed. Bernard Lepetit (Paris: Albin Michel, 1995), pp. 39–61.

17   Tzvetan Todorov, *Nous et les autres. La réflexion française sur la diversité humaine* (Paris: Editions du Seuil, 1989), pp. 85–109.

10

Traveling Theory (1982)

Edward W. Said

A leading name in postcolonialist theory, the Palestinian-American literary theorist and cultural critic Edward Wadie Said (1935–2003) paved the way for today's postcolonial studies and the reformation of Middle Eastern Studies. Born in a Palestinian Christian family in Jerusalem, attending school in Egypt and then moving to the United States to complete his education, Said experienced a feeling of deracination throughout his lifetime, which would inform his theoretical stands. Said studied at Princeton University and got his doctoral degree in English from Harvard, and then taught for four decades as a professor of English and Comparative Literature at Columbia University. Translated into more than two dozen languages, his 20 books probe the relations between literature, culture, knowledge, and power. Said is best known for his path-breaking book *Orientalism* (1978), which argued that Orientalist scholarship from the nineteenth century to the present had constructed "the Orient" as a discursive field that implicitly or explicitly aided Europe's imperial and neocolonial domination of an alien, exotic Other. Highly influential for the contemporary development of Middle Eastern studies, Said's book also met with sharp criticism from Western Orientalists, who accused him in turn of creating a stereotypical view of the West, undergirded by his own political interests. Said was a member of the Palestinian National Council from 1977 to 1991 and supported the creation of a Palestinian state alongside Israel and equal rights for Palestinians in Israel itself. His political views can be found in his books *The Question of Palestine* (1979), *Covering Islam* (1981), *The Politics of Dispossession* (1994), and *The End of the Peace Process* (2000).

"Traveling Theory" is taken from Said's influential collection *The World, the Text, and the Critic* (1983), and looks into the circulation of ideas and theories in the world

Edward W. Said, "Traveling Theory" (1982). From Edward W. Said, *The World, the Text, and the Critic* (Cambridge, MA: Harvard University Press, 1983), pp. 226–247.

market. Said calls into question the appropriation and transplantation of ideas and theories from one space and time to another, a process that raises issues of representation and institutionalization specific to the host culture. Skeptical of Goethe's ideal of a harmonized world literature, Said argues that "the history of ideas and comparative literature ... do not routinely authorize in their practitioners quite the same Goethean sense of a concert of all literatures and ideas." Instead, the world is full of irregularities and inequalities, which have to be attended to when tracing the worldly fortunes of literary theory.

Like people and schools of criticism, ideas and theories travel from person to person, from situation to situation, from one period to another. Cultural and intellectual life are usually nourished and often sustained by this circulation of ideas, and whether it takes the form of acknowledged or unconscious influence, creative borrowing, or wholesale appropriation, the movement of ideas and theories from one place to another is both a fact of life and a usefully enabling condition of intellectual activity. Having said that, however, one should go on to specify the kinds of movement that are possible, in order to ask whether by virtue of having moved from one place and time to another an idea or a theory gains or loses in strength, and whether a theory in one historical period and national culture becomes altogether different for another period or situation. There are particularly interesting cases of ideas and theories that move from one culture to another, as when so-called Eastern ideas about transcendence were imported into Europe during the early nineteenth century, or when certain European ideas about society were translated into traditional Eastern societies during the later nineteenth century. Such movement into a new environment is never unimpeded. It necessarily involves processes of representation and institutionalization different from those at the point of origin. This complicates any account of the transplantation, transference, circulation, and commerce of theories and ideas.

There is, however, a discernible and recurrent pattern to the movement itself, three or four stages common to the way any theory or idea travels.

First, there is a point of origin, or what seems like one, a set of initial circumstances in which the idea came to birth or entered discourse. Second, there is a distance transversed, a passage through the pressure of various contexts as the idea moves from an earlier point to another time and place where it will come into a new prominence. Third, there is a set of conditions – call them conditions of acceptance or, as an inevitable part of acceptance, resistances – which then confronts the transplanted theory or idea, making possible its introduction or toleration, however alien it might appear to be. Fourth, the now fully (or partly) accommodated (or incorporated) idea is to some extent transformed by its new uses, its new position in a new time and place.

It is obvious that any satisfactorily full account of these stages would be an enormous task. But though I have neither the intention nor the capacity to undertake it, it seemed worthwhile to describe the problem in a sketchy and general way so that I might at length and in detail address a particularly topical, highly

limited aspect of it. Of course the discrepancy between the general problem and
any particular analysis is itself deserving of comment. To prefer a local, detailed
analysis of how one theory travels from one situation to another is also to betray
some fundamental uncertainty about specifying or delimiting the field to which
any one theory or idea might belong. Notice, for example, that when professional
students of literature now use words like "theory" and "criticism" it is not assumed
that they must or should confine their interests to literary theory or literary
criticism. The distinction between one discipline and another has been blurred
precisely because fields like literature and literary study are no longer considered
to be as all-encompassing or as synoptic as, until recently, they once were. Although
some polemical scholars of literature can still, nonetheless, attack others for not
being literary enough, or for not understanding (as who should not?) that literature,
unlike other forms of writing, is essentially mimetic, essentially moral, and
essentially humanistic, the resultant controversies are themselves evidence of the
fact that no consensus exists on how the outer limits of the word "literature" or the
word "criticism" are to be determined. Several decades ago, literary history and
systematic theory, of the kind pioneered by Northrop Frye, promised an orderly,
inhabitable, and hospitable structure in which, for instance, it might be demonstrated
that the mythos of summer could be transformed definably into the mythos of
autumn. "The primal human act in Frye's system," writes Frank Lentricchia in *After
the New Criticism*, quoting Frye's *The Educated Imagination*, "and a model for all
human acts, is an 'informative,' creative act which transforms a world that is merely
objective, set over against us, in which we 'feel lonely and frightened and unwanted'
into a home."[1] But most literary scholars find themselves now, once again, out in the
cold. Similarly, the history of ideas and comparative literature, two disciplines
closely associated with the study of literature and literary criticism, do not routinely
authorize in their practitioners quite the same Goethean sense of a concert of all
literatures and ideas.

   In all these instances the specific situation or locality of a particular intellectual
task seems uneasily distant from, and only rhetorically assisted by, the legendary
wholeness, coherence, and integrity of the general field to which one professionally
belongs. There seem to be too many interruptions, too many distractions, too
many irregularities interfering with the homogeneous space supposedly holding
scholars together. The division of intellectual labor, which has meant increasing
specialization, further erodes any direct apprehension one might have of a whole
field of literature and literary study; conversely, the invasion of literary discourse by
the *outré* jargons of semiotics, post-structuralism, and Lacanian psychoanalysis has
distended the literary critical universe almost beyond recognition. In short, there
seems nothing inherently literary about the study of what have traditionally been
considered literary texts, no literariness that might prevent a contemporary literary
critic from having recourse to psychoanalysis, sociology, or linguistics. Convention,
historical custom, and appeals to the protocols of humanism and traditional
scholarship are of course regularly introduced as evidence of the field's enduring

integrity, but more and more these seem to be rhetorical strategies in a debate about what literature and literary criticism ought to be rather than convincing definitions of what in fact they are.

Geoffrey Hartman has nicely dramatized the predicament by analyzing the tensions and vacillations governing contemporary critical activity. Today's criticism, he says, is radically revisionist. "Freed from a neoclassical decorum that, over the space of three centuries, created an enlightened but also over-accommodated prose," criticism is undergoing what he calls "an *extraordinary language* movement."[2] At times this language movement is so eccentric as to approach, even challenge, literature itself; at others it obsesses the critics who are borne along its currents toward the ideal of a completely "pure" language. At still others, the critic discovers that "writing is a labyrinth, a topological puzzle and textual crossword; the reader, for his part, must lose himself for a while in a hermeneutic 'infinitizing' that makes all rules of closure appear arbitrary."[3] Whether these alternatives for critical discourse are called terrorist or "a new type of sublimity or an emerging transcendentalism,"[4] there remains the need for the humanist critic both to define more clearly "the special province of the humanities" and to materialize (rather than spiritualize) the culture in which we live.[5] Nevertheless, Hartman concludes, we are in transition, which is perhaps another way of saying (as he does in his title *Criticism in the Wilderness*) that criticism today is alone, at loose ends, unlucky, pathetic, and playful because its realm defies closure and certainty.

Hartman's exuberance – for his attitude is at bottom exuberant – ought to be qualified by Richard Ohmann's devastating observation in *English in America* that English departments represent "a moderately successful effort by professors to obtain some benefits of capitalism while avoiding its risks and, yet, a reluctance to acknowledge any link between how we do our work and the way the larger society is run."[6] This is not to say that literary academics present a united ideological front, even though Ohmann is right *grosso modo*. The divisions within cannot be reduced simply to a conflict between old and new critics or to a monolithically dominant antimimetic ideology, as Gerald Graff very misleadingly argues. Consider that, if we restrict the number of debated issues to four, many of those in the vanguard on one issue are very conservative on another:

(1) Criticism as scholarship, humanism, a "servant" to the text, mimetic in its bias, versus criticism as revisionism and as itself a form of literature.

(2) The role of critic as teacher and good reader: safeguarding the canon versus subverting it or creating a new one. Most Yale critics are revisionist with respect to (1), conservative with respect to (2).

(3) Criticism as detached from the political/social world versus criticism as a form of philosophical metaphysics, psychoanalysis, linguistics, or any of these, versus criticism as actually having to do with such "contaminated" fields of history, the media, and economic systems. Here the distributional spread is much wider than in (1) or (2).

(4)   Criticism as a criticism of language (language as negative theology, as private
      dogma, as ahistorical metaphysics) versus criticism as an analysis of the language
      of institutions versus criticism as a study of relationships between language and
      nonlinguistic things.

In the absence of an enclosing domain called literature, with clear outer
boundaries, there is no longer an authorized or official position for the literary
critic. But neither is there some new sovereign method, some new critical
technology compelling allegiance and intellectual loyalty. Instead there is a babel of
arguments for the limitlessness of all interpretation; of ideologies that proclaim the
eternal yet determinate value of literature or "the humanities"; for all systems that
in asserting their capacity to perform essentially self-confirming tasks allow for no
counterfactual evidence. You can call such a situation pluralistic if you like or, if you
have a taste for the melodramatic, you can call it desperate. For my part, I prefer to
see it as an opportunity for remaining skeptical and critical, succumbing neither
to dogmatism nor to sulky gloom.

Hence the specific problem of what happens to a theory when it moves from one
place to another proposes itself as an interesting topic of investigation. For if fields
like literature or the history of ideas have no intrinsically enclosing limits, and if,
conversely, no one methodology is imposable upon what is an essentially
heterogeneous and open area of activity – the writing and interpretation of texts – it
is wise to raise the questions of theory and of criticism in ways suitable to the
situation in which we find ourselves. At the outset, this means an historical approach.
Assume therefore that, as a result of specific historical circumstances, a theory
or idea pertaining to those circumstances arises. What happens to it when, in
different circumstances and for new reasons, it is used again and, in still more
different circumstances, again? What can this tell us about theory itself – its limits,
its possibilities, its inherent problems – and what can it suggest to us about the
relationship between theory and criticism, on the one hand, and society and culture
on the other? The pertinence of these questions will be apparent at a time when
theoretical activity seems both intense and eclectic, when the relationship between
social reality and a dominant yet hermetic critical discourse seems hard to determine,
and when, for all of these reasons and some of the ones I have just referred to, it is
futile to prescribe theoretical programs for contemporary criticism.

Lukacs' *History and Class Consciousness* (1923) is justly famous for its analysis
of the phenomenon of reification, a universal fate afflicting all aspects of life in an
era dominated by commodity fetishism. Since, as Lukacs argues, capitalism is the
most articulated and quantitatively detailed of all economic systems, what it
imposes upon human life and labor under its rule has the consequence of radically
transforming everything human, flowing, processual, organic, and connected into
disconnected and "alienated" objects, items, lifeless atoms. In such a situation,
then, time sheds its qualitative, variable, flowing nature; it freezes into an exactly
delimited, quantifiable continuum filled with quantifiable "things" (the reified,
mechanically objectified "performance" of the worker, wholly separated from his

total human personality): in short, it becomes space. In this environment where time is transformed into abstract, exactly measurable, physical space, an environment at once the cause and effect of the scientifically and mechanically fragmented and specialised production of the object of labour, the subjects of labour must likewise be rationally fragmented. On the one hand, the objectification of their labor-power into something opposed to their total personality (a process already accomplished with the sale of that labour-power as a commodity) is now made into the permanent ineluctable reality of their daily life. Here, too, the personality can do no more than look on helplessly while its own existence is reduced to an isolated particle and fed into an alien system. On the other hand, the mechanical disintegration of the process of production into its components also destroys those bonds that had bound individuals to a community in the days when production was still "organic." In this respect, too, mechanization makes of them isolated abstract atoms whose work no longer brings them together directly and organically; it becomes mediated to an increasing extent exclusively by the abstract laws of the mechanism which imprisons them.[7] If this picture of the public world is bleak, it is matched by Lukacs' description of what happens to intellect, "the subject" as he calls it. After an astonishingly brilliant account of the antinomies of classical philosophy from Descartes to Kant to Fichte, Hegel, and Marx, in which he shows the increasing retreat of the subject into passive, privatized contemplation, gradually more and more divorced from the overwhelmingly fragmented realities of modern industrial life, Lukacs then depicts modern bourgeois thought as being at an impasse, transfixed and paralyzed into terminal passivity. The science that it produces is based on mere fact gathering; the rational forms of understanding therefore cannot cope with the irrationality of physical *données*, and when efforts are made to compel "the facts" to submit to "system," their fragmentation and endlessly atomized *thereness* either destroy the system or turn the mind into a passive register of discrete objects.

There is, however, one form of experience that concretely represents the essence of reification as well as its limitation: crisis. If capitalism is the embodiment in economic terms of reification, then everything, including human beings, ought to be quantified and given a market value. This of course is what Lukacs means when he speaks of articulation under capitalism, which he sometimes characterizes as if it were a gigantic itemized list. In principle nothing – no object, person, place, or time – is left out, since everything can be calculated. But there are moments when "the qualitative existence of the 'things' that lead their lives beyond the purview of economics as misunderstood and neglected things-in-themselves, as use-values [Lukacs here refers to such "irrational" things as sentiment, passion, chance] suddenly becomes the decisive factor (suddenly, that is, for reified, rational thought). Or rather: these 'laws' fail to function and the reified mind is unable to perceive a pattern in this 'chaos.'"[8] At such a moment, then, mind or "subject" has its one opportunity to escape reification: by thinking through what it is that causes reality to appear to be only a collection of objects and economic *données*. And the very act of looking for process behind what appears to be eternally given and objectified, makes it possible for the mind to know itself as subject and not as a lifeless object, then to go beyond empirical reality into a putative realm of possibility. When instead of inexplicable shortage of bread you can imagine the human work and, subsequently, the human beings who produced the bread but are no longer doing so because there is a bakers' strike, you are well on your way to knowing that crisis is comprehensible because process is comprehensible; and if process is comprehensible, so too is some sense of the social whole created by human labor. Crisis, in short, is converted into criticism of the status quo: the bakers are on strike for a reason, the crisis can be explained, the system does not work infallibly, the subject has just demonstrated its victory over ossified objective forms.

Lukacs puts all of this in terms of the subject-object relationship, and proper justice to his argument requires that it be followed to the point where he shows that reconciliation between subject and object will be possible. Yet even he admits that such an eventuality is very far into the future. Nevertheless, he is certain that no such future is attainable without the transformation of passive, contemplative consciousness into active, critical consciousness. In positing a world of human agency outside the reach of reification, the critical consciousness (the consciousness that is given rise to by crisis) becomes genuinely aware of its power "unceasingly to overthrow the objective forms that shape the life of man."[9] Consciousness goes beyond empirical givens and comprehends, without actually experiencing, history, totality, and society as a whole – precisely those unities that reification had both concealed and denied. At bottom, class consciousness is thought thinking its way through fragmentation to unity; it is also thought aware of its own subjectivity as something active, energetic, and, in a profound sense, poetic. (Here we should note that several years before *History and Class Consciousness* Lukacs had argued that only in the realm of the aesthetic could the limitations of pure theory and of pure ethics be overcome; by the former he meant a scientific theory whose very objectivity symbolized its own reification, its thralldom to objects, by the latter a Kantian subjectivity out of touch with everything except its own selfhood. Only the Aesthetic rendered the meaning of experience as lived experience – *der Sinn des Erlebnisses* – in an autonomous form: subject and object are thereby made one.[10])

Now because it rises above objects, consciousness enters a realm of potentiality, that is, of theoretical possibility. The special urgency of Lukacs' account of this is that he is describing something rather far from a mere escape into fantasy. Consciousness attaining self-consciousness is no Emma Bovary pretending to be a lady in Yonville. The direct pressures of capitalist quantification, that relentless cataloguing of everything on earth, continue to be felt, according to Lukacs; the only thing that changes is that the mind recognizes a class of beings like itself who have the power to think generally, to take in facts but to organize them in groups, to recognize processes and tendencies where reification only allows evidence of lifeless atoms. Class consciousness therefore begins in critical consciousness. Classes are not real the way trees and houses are real; they are imputable by consciousness, using its powers to posit ideal types in which with other beings it finds itself. Classes are the result of an insurrectionary act by which consciousness refuses to be confined to the world of objects, which is where it had been confined in the capitalist scheme of things.

Consciousness has moved from the world of objects into the world of theory. Although Lukacs describes it as only a young German philosopher could describe it – in language bristling with more metaphysics and abstractions than even I have been using – we must not forget that he is performing an act of political insurgency. To attain to theory is to threaten reification, as well as the entire bourgeois system on which reification depends, with destruction. But, he assures his readers, this destruction "is no single unrepeatable tearing of the veil that masks the process [of reification] but the unbroken alternation of ossification, contradiction and movement."[11] Theory, in fine, is won as the result of a process that begins when consciousness first experiences its own terrible ossification in the general reification of all things under capitalism; then when consciousness generalizes (or classes) itself as something opposed to other objects, and feels itself as a contradiction to (or crisis within) objectification, there emerges a consciousness of change in the status quo; finally, moving toward freedom and fulfillment, consciousness looks ahead to complete self-realization, which is of course the revolutionary process stretching forward in time, perceivable now only as theory or projection.

This is very heady stuff indeed. I have summarized it in order to set down some small indication of how powerfully responsive Lukacs' ideas about theory were to the political order he described with such formidable gravity and dread. Theory for him was what consciousness produced, not as an avoidance of reality but as a revolutionary will completely committed to worldliness and change. According to Lukacs, the proletariat's consciousness represented the theoretical antithesis to capitalism; as Merleau-Ponty and others have said, Lukacs' proletariat can by no means be identified with a ragged collection of grimy-faced Hungarian laborers. The proletariat was his figure for consciousness defying reification, mind asserting its powers over mere matter, consciousness claiming its theoretical right to posit a better world outside the world of simple objects. And since class consciousness derives from workers working and being aware of themselves that way, theory must never lose touch with its origins in politics, society, and economics.

This, then, is Lukacs describing his ideas about theory – and of course his theory of sociohistorical change – in the early twenties. Consider now Lukacs' disciple and student, Lucien Goldmann, whose *Le Dieu caché* (1955) was one of the first and certainly among the most impressive attempts to put Lukacs' theories to practical scholarly use. In Goldmann's study of Pascal and Racine, class consciousness has been changed to "vision du monde," something that is not an immediate, but a collective consciousness expressed in the work of certain highly gifted writers.[12] But this is not all. Goldmann says that these writers derive their world vision from determinate political and economic circumstances common to members of their group; yet the world vision itself is premised not so much on empirical detail as on a human faith that a reality exists "which goes beyond them as individuals and finds its expression in their work."[13] Writing as a politically committed scholar (and not like Lukacs as a directly involved militant), Goldmann then argues that because Pascal and Racine were privileged writers, their work can be constituted into a significant whole by a process of dialectical theorizing, in which part is related to assumed whole, assumed whole verified empirically by empirical evidence. Thus individual texts are seen to express a world vision; second, the world vision constitutes the whole intellectual and social life of the group (the Port-Royal Jansenists); third, the thoughts and feelings of the group are an expression of their economic and social life.[14] In all this – and Goldmann argues with exemplary brilliance and subtlety – the theoretical enterprise, an interpretive circle, is a demonstration of coherence: between part and whole, between world vision and texts in their smallest detail, between a determinate social reality and the writings of particularly gifted members of a group. In other words, theory is the researcher's domain, the place in which disparate, apparently disconnected things are brought together in perfect correspondence: economics, political process, the individual writer, a series of texts.

Goldmann's indebtedness to Lukacs is clear, although it has not been noted that what in Lukacs is an ironic discrepancy between theoretical consciousness and reified reality is transformed and localized by Goldmann into a tragic correspondence between world vision and the unfortunate class situation of the *noblesse de robe* in late seventeenth-century France. Whereas Lukacs' class consciousness defies, indeed is an insurgent against, the capitalist order, Goldmann's tragic vision is perfectly, absolutely expressed by the works of Pascal and Racine. True, the tragic vision is not directly expressed by those writers, and true also that it requires an extraordinarily complex dialectical style of research for the modern researcher to draw forth the correspondence between world vision and empirical detail; the fact nevertheless is that Goldmann's adaptation of Lukacs removes from theory its insurrectionary role. The sheer existence of class, or theoretical, consciousness for Lukacs is enough to suggest to him the projected overthrow of objective forms. For Goldmann an awareness of class or group consciousness is first of all a scholarly imperative, and then – in the works of highly privileged writers – the expression of a tragically limited social situation. Lukacs' *zugerechnetes Bewusstsein* (imputed consciousness) is an unverifiable, yet absolutely prior theoretical necessity if one is to effect a change in social reality; in Goldmann's version of it, admittedly limited to an acutely circumscribed situation, theory and consciousness are expressed in the Pascalian wager upon an unseen and silent god, the *deus absconditus;* they are also expressed for Goldmann the scientific researcher, as he calls himself, in the theoretical correspondence between text and political reality. Or to put the matter in another way, for Lukacs theory originates as a kind of irreducible dissonance between mind and object, whereas for Goldmann theory is the homological relationship that can be seen to exist between individual part and coherent whole.

The difference between the two versions of Lukacs' theory of theory is evident enough: Lukacs writes as a participant in a struggle (the Hungarian Soviet Republic of 1919), Goldmann as an expatriate historian at the Sorbonne. From one point of view we can say that Goldmann's adaptation of Lukacs degrades theory, lowers it in importance, domesticates it somewhat to the exigencies of a doctoral dissertation in Paris. I do not think, however, that degradation here has a moral implication, but rather (as one of its secondary meanings suggests) that degradation conveys the lowering of color, the greater degree of distance, the loss of immediate force that occurs when Goldmann's notions of consciousness and theory are compared with the meaning and role intended by Lukacs for theory. Nor do I want to suggest that there is something inherently wrong about Goldmann's conversion of insurrectionary, radically adversarial consciousness into an accommodating consciousness of correspondence and homology. It is just that the situation has changed sufficiently for the degradation to have occurred, although there is no doubt that Goldmann's reading of Lukacs mutes the latter's almost apocalyptic version of consciousness.

We have become so accustomed to hearing that all borrowings, readings, and interpretations are misreadings and misinterpretations that we are likely to consider the Lukacs-Goldmann episode as just another bit of evidence that everyone, even Marxists, misreads and misinterprets. I find such a conclusion completely unsatisfying. It implies, first of all, that the only possible alternative to slavish copying is creative misreading and that no intermediate possibility exists. Second, when it is elevated to a general principle, the idea that all reading is misreading is fundamentally an abrogation of the critic's responsibility. It is never enough for a critic taking the idea of criticism seriously simply to say that interpretation is misinterpretation or that borrowings inevitably involve misreadings. Quite the contrary: it seems to me perfectly possible to judge misreadings (as they occur) as part of a historical transfer of ideas and theories from one setting to another. Lukacs wrote *for* as well as *in* a situation that produced ideas about consciousness and theory that are very different from the ideas produced by Goldmann in his situation. To call Goldmann's work a misreading of Lukacs', and then to go on immediately to relate that misreading to a general theory of interpretation as misinterpretation, is to pay no critical attention to history and to situation, both of which play an important determining role in changing Lukacs' ideas into Goldmann's. The Hungary of 1919 and post-World War II Paris are two quite different environments. To the degree that Lukacs and Goldmann are read carefully, then to that precise degree we can understand the critical change – in time and in place – that occurs between one writer and another, both of whom depend on theory to accomplish a particular job of intellectual work. I see no need here to resort to the theory of limitless intertextuality as an Archimedean point outside the two situations. The particular voyage from Hungary to Paris, with all that entails, seems compelling enough, adequate enough for critical scrutiny, unless we want to give up critical consciousness for critical hermeticism.

In measuring Lukacs and Goldmann against each other, then, we are also recognizing the extent to which theory is a response to a specific social and historical situation of which an intellectual occasion is a part. Thus what is insurrectionary consciousness in one instance becomes tragic vision in another, for reasons that are elucidated when the situations in Budapest and Paris are seriously compared. I do not wish to suggest that Budapest and Paris determined the kinds of theories produced by Lukacs and Goldmann. I do mean that "Budapest" and "Paris" are irreducibly first conditions, and they provide limits and apply pressures to which each writer, given his own gifts, predilections, and interests, responds.

Let us now take Lukacs, or rather Lukacs as used by Goldmann, a step further: the use made of Goldmann by Raymond Williams. Brought up in the tradition of Cambridge English studies, trained in the techniques of Leavis and Richards, Williams was formed as a literary scholar who had no use whatever for theory. He speaks rather poignantly of how intellectuals educated as he was could use "a separate and self-defining language" that made a fetish of minute, concrete particulars; this meant that the intellectuals could approach power but speak antiseptically only of microcosm, profess not to understand reification, and to speak instead of the objective correlative, not to know mediation although they knew catharsis.[15] Williams tells us that Goldmann came to Cambridge in 1970 and gave two lectures there. This visit, according to Williams in the moving commemorative essay he wrote about Goldmann after his death, was a major event. It introduced Cambridge to theory, Williams claims, understood and employed as it had been by thinkers trained in the major Continental tradition. Goldmann induced in Williams an appreciation of Lukacs' contribution to our understanding of how, in an era of "the dominance of economic activity over all other forms of human activity," reification was both a false objectivity so far as knowledge was concerned and a deformation thoroughly penetrating life and consciousness more than any other form. Williams continues:

> The idea of totality was then a critical weapon against this precise deformation; indeed, against capitalism itself. And yet this was not idealism – an assertion of the primacy of other values. On the contrary, just as the deformation could be understood, at its roots, only by historical analysis of a particular kind of economy, so the attempt to overcome and surpass it lay not in isolated witness or in separated activity but in practical work to find, assert and to establish more human social ends in more human and political and economic means.[16]

Once again Lukacs' thought – in this instance the avowedly revolutionary idea of totality – has been tamed somewhat. Without wishing in any way to belittle the importance of what Lukacs' ideas (via Goldmann) did for the moribund state of English studies in late twentieth-century Cambridge, I think it needs to be said that those ideas were originally formulated in order to do more than shake up a few professors of literature. This is an obvious, not to say easy, point. What is more interesting, however, is that because Cambridge is not revolutionary Budapest, because Williams is not the militant Lukacs, because Williams is a reflective critic – this is crucial – rather than a committed revolutionary, he can see the limits of a theory that begins as a liberating idea but can become a trap of its own.

> At the most practical level it was easy for me to agree [with Lukacs' theory of totality as a response to reification]. But then the whole point of thinking in terms of a totality

is the realization that we are part of it; that our own consciousness, our work, our methods, are then critically at stake. And in the particular field of literary analysis there was this obvious difficulty: that most of the work we had to look at was the product of just this work of reified consciousness, so that *what looked like the methodological breakthrough might become, quite quickly, the methodological trap.* I cannot yet say this finally about Lukacs, since I still don't have access to all his work; but in some of it, at least, *the major insights of History and Class-Consciousness,* which he has now partly disavowed, *do not get translated into critical practice* [Williams refers here to Lukacs' later, much cruder work on European realism] and certain cruder operations – essentially still those of base and superstructure – keep reappearing. *I still read Goldmann collaboratively and critically asking the same question,* for I am sure the practice of totality is still for any of us, at any time, profoundly and even obviously difficult.[17]

This is an admirable passage. Even though Williams says nothing about the lamentable repetitiveness of Goldmann's later work, it is important that as a critic who has learned from someone else's theory he should be able to see the theory's limitations, especially the fact that a breakthrough can become a trap, if it is used uncritically, repetitively, limitlessly. What he means, I think, is that once an idea gains currency because it is clearly effective and powerful, there is every likelihood that during its peregrinations it will be reduced, codified, and institutionalized. Lukacs' remarkably complex exposition of the phenomenon of reification indeed did turn into a simple reflection theory; to a degree of course, and Williams is too decently elegaic to say it about a recently dead old friend, it did become this sort of idea in Goldmann's hands. Homology is, after all, a refined version of the old Second International base-and-superstructure model.

Beyond the specific reminder of what could happen to a vanguard theory, Williams' ruminations enable us to make another observation about theory as it develops out of a situation, begins to be used, travels, and gains wide acceptance. For if reification-and-totality (to turn Lukacs' theory now into a shorthand phrase for easy reference) can become a reductionist implement, there is no reason why it could not become too inclusive, too ceaselessly active and expanding a habit of mind. That is, if a theory can move down, so to speak, become a dogmatic reduction of its original version, it can also move up into a sort of bad infinity, which – in the case of reification-and-totality – is the direction intended by Lukacs himself. To speak of the unceasing overthrow of objective forms, and to speak as he does in the essay on class consciousness, of how the logical end of overcoming reification is the self-annihilation of the revolutionary class itself, means that Lukacs had pushed his theory farther forward and upward, unacceptably (in my opinion). The contradiction inherent in this theory – and perhaps in most theories that develop as responses to the need for movement and change – is that it risks becoming a theoretical overstatement, a theoretical parody of the situation it was formulated originally to remedy or overcome. To prescribe "an *unbroken* alternation of ossification, contradiction and movement" toward totality as a theoretical remedy for reification is in a sense to substitute one unchanging formula for another. To say of theory and theoretical consciousness, as Lukacs does, that they intervene in reification and introduce process is not carefully enough to calculate, and allow for, the details and the resistances offered by an intransigent, reified reality to theoretical consciousness. For all the brilliance of his account of reification, for all the care he takes with it, Lukacs is unable to see how even under capitalism reification itself cannot be totally dominant – unless, of course, he is prepared to allow something that theoretical totality (his insurrectional instrument for overcoming reification) says is impossible, namely, that totality in the form of totally dominant reification is theoretically possible under capitalism. For if reification is totally dominant, how then can Lukacs explain his own work as an alternative form of thought under the sway of reification?

Perhaps all this is too fussy and hermetic. Nevertheless, it seems to me that however far away in time and place Williams may be from the fiery rebelliousness of the early Lukacs, there is an extraordinary virtue to the distance, even the coldness of his critical reflections on Lukacs and Goldmann, to both of whom he is otherwise so intellectually cordial. He takes from both men a sophisticated theoretical awareness of the issues involved in connecting literature to society, as he puts it in his best single theoretical essay, "Base and Superstructure in Marxist Cultural Theory." The terminology provided by Marxist aesthetic theory for mapping the peculiarly uneven and complicated field lying between base and superstructure is generally inadequate, and then Williams goes on to do work that embodies *his* critical version of the original theory. He puts this version very well, I think, in *Politics and Letters*: "however dominant a social system may be, the very meaning of its domination involves a limitation or selection of the activities it covers, so that by definition it cannot exhaust all social experience, which therefore always potentially contains space for alternative acts and alternative intentions which are not yet articulated as a social institution or even project."[18] *The Country and the City* records both the limits and the reactive alternatives to dominance, as in the case of John Clare, whose work "marks the end of pastoral poetry [as a systematic convention for describing the English countryside] in the very shock of its collision with actual country experience." Clare's very existence as a poet was threatened by the removal of an acceptable social order from the customary landscape idealized by Jonson and Thomson; hence Clare's turning – as an alternative not yet fully realized and not yet completely subdued by the inhuman relationships that obtained under the system of market exploitation – to "the green language of the new Nature," that is, the Nature to be celebrated in a new way by the great Romantics.[19]

There is no minimizing the fact that Williams is an important critic because of his gifts and his insights. But I am convinced it would be wrong to underestimate the role in his mature writings played by what I have been alluding to as borrowed, or traveling, theory. For borrow we certainly must if we are to elude the constraints of our immediate intellectual environment. Theory we certainly need, for all sorts of reasons that would be too tedious to rehearse here. What we also need over and above theory, however, is the critical recognition that there is no theory capable of covering, closing off, predicting all the situations in which it might be useful. This is another way of saying, as Williams does, that no social or intellectual system can be so dominant as to be unlimited in its strength. Williams therefore has the critical recognition, and uses it consciously to qualify, shape, and refine his borrowings from Lukacs and Goldmann, although we should hasten to add that it does not make him infallible or any less liable to exaggeration and error for having it. But unless theory is unanswerable, either through its successes or its failures, to the essential untidiness, the essential unmasterable presence that constitutes a large part of historical and social situations (and this applies equally to theory that derives from somewhere else or theory that is "original"), then theory becomes an ideological trap. It transfixes both its users and what it is used on. Criticism would no longer be possible.

Theory, in short, can never be complete, just as one's interest in everyday life is never exhausted by simulacra, models, or theoretical abstracts of it. Of course one derives pleasure from actually making evidence fit or work in a theoretical scheme, and of course it is ridiculously foolish to argue that "the facts" or "the great texts" do not require any theoretical framework or methodology to be appreciated or read properly. No reading is neutral or innocent, and by the same token every text and every reader is to some extent the product of a theoretical standpoint, however implicit or unconscious such a standpoint may be. I am arguing, however, that we distinguish theory from critical consciousness by saying that the latter is a sort of spatial sense, a sort of measuring faculty for locating or situating theory, and this means that theory has to be grasped in the place and the time out of which it emerges as a part of that time, working in and for it, responding to it; then, consequently, that first place can be measured against subsequent places where the theory turns up for use. The critical consciousness is awareness of the differences between situations, awareness too of the fact that no system or theory exhausts the situation out of which it emerges or to which it is transported. And, above all, critical consciousness is awareness of the resistances to theory, reactions to it elicited by those concrete experiences or interpretations with which it is in conflict. Indeed I would go as far as saying that it is the critic's job to provide resistances to theory, to open it up toward historical reality, toward society, toward human needs and interests, to point up those concrete instances drawn from everyday reality that lie outside or just beyond the interpretive area necessarily designated in advance and thereafter circumscribed by every theory.

Much of this is illustrated if we compare Lukacs and Williams on the one hand with Goldmann on the other. I have already said that Williams is conscious of what he calls a methodological trap. Lukacs, for his part, shows in his career as a theorist (if not in the fully fledged theory itself) a profound awareness of the necessity to move from hermetic aestheticism (*Die Seele und die Formen, Die Theorie des Romans*) toward the actual world of power and institutions. By contrast, Goldmann is enmeshed in the homological finality that his writing, brilliantly and persuasively in the case of *Le Dieu caché*, demonstrates. Theoretical closure, like social convention or cultural dogma, is anathema to critical consciousness, which loses its profession when it loses its active sense of an open world in which its faculties must be exercised. One of the best lessons of that is to be found in Lentricchia's powerful *After the New Criticism*, a wholly persuasive account of what he calls "the currently paralyzed debates" of contemporary literary theory.[20] In instance after instance he demonstrates the impoverishment and rarefication that overtake any theory relatively untested by and unexposed to the complex enfolding of the social world, which is never a merely complaisant context to be used for the enactment of theoretical situations. (As an antidote to the bareness afflicting the American situation, there is in Fredric Jameson's *The Political Unconscious* an extremely useful account of three "semantic horizons" to be figured in dialectically by the interpreter as parts of the decoding process, which he also calls "the cultural mode of production."[21])

Yet we must be aware that the social reality I have been alluding to is no less susceptible to theoretical overtotalization, even when, as I shall be showing in the case of Foucault, extremely powerful historical scholarship moves itself out from the archive toward the world of power and institutions, toward precisely those resistances to theory ignored and elided by most formalistic theory – deconstruction, semiotics, Lacanian psychoanalysis, the Althusserian Marxism attacked by E.P. Thompson.[22] Foucault's work is most challenging because he is rightly considered to be an exemplary opponent of ahistorical, asocial formalism. But he too, I believe, falls victim to the systematic degradation of theory in ways that his newest disciples consider to be evidence that he has not succumbed to hermeticism.

Foucault is a paradox. His career presents his contemporary audience with an extraordinarily compelling trajectory whose culmination, most recently, has been the announcement made by him, and on his behalf by his disciples, that his real theme is the relationship between knowledge and power. Thanks to the brilliance of his theoretical and practical performances, *pouvoir* and *savoir* have provided his readers (it would be churlish not to mention myself; but see also Jacques Donzelot's *La Police des familles*) with a conceptual apparatus for the analysis of instrumental discourses that stands in stark contrast to the fairly arid metaphysics produced habitually by the students of his major philosophical competitors. Yet Foucault's earliest work was in many ways remarkably unconscious of its own theoretical force. Reread *Histoire de la folie* after *Surveiller et punir* and you will be struck with how uncannily prescient the early work is of the later; and yet you will also be struck that even when Foucault deals with *renfermement* (confinement), his obsessive theme, in discussing asylums and hospitals, power is never referred to explicitly. Neither for that matter is *volonté*, will. *Les Mots et les choses* might be excused for the same neglect of power, on the grounds that the subject of Foucault's inquiry was intellectual, not institutional history. In *The Archeology of Knowledge* there are intimations here and there that Foucault is beginning to approach power through a number of abstractions, surrogates for it: thus he refers to such things as acceptability, accumulation, preservation, and formation that are ascribed to the making and the functioning of statements, discourses, and archives; yet he does so without spending any time on what might be the common source of their strength within institutions or fields of knowledge or society itself.

Foucault's theory of power – to which I shall restrict myself here – derives from his attempt to analyze working systems of confinement from the inside, systems whose functioning depends equally on the continuity of institutions as on the proliferation of justifying technical ideologies for the institutions. These ideologies are his discourses and disciplines. In his concrete presentation of local situations in which such power and such knowledge are deployed, Foucault has no peer, and what he has done is remarkably interesting by any standard. As he says in *Surveiller et punir*, for power to work it must be able to manage, control, and even create detail: the more detail, the more real power, management breeding manageable units, which in turn breed a more detailed, a more finely controlling knowledge. Prisons, he says in that memorable passage, are factories for producing delinquency, and delinquency is the raw material for disciplinary discourses.

With descriptions and particularized observations of this sort I have no trouble. It is when Foucault's own language becomes general (when he moves his analyses of power from the detail to society as a whole) that the methodological breakthrough becomes the theoretical trap. Interestingly, this is slightly more evident when Foucault's theory is transported from France and planted in the work of his overseas disciples. Recently, for example, he has been celebrated by Ian Hacking as a kind of hard-headed alternative to the too backward and forward-looking "Romantic" Marxists (which Marxists? all Marxists?), and as a ruthlessly anarchistic opponent of Noam Chomsky, who is described inappropriately as "a marvelously sane liberal reformer."[23] Other writers, who quite rightly see Foucault's discussions of power as a refreshing window opened on to the real world of politics and society, uncritically misread his pronouncements as the latest thing about social reality.[24] There is no doubt that Foucault's work is indeed an important alternative to the ahistorical formalism with which he has been conducting an implicit debate, and there is great merit to his view that as a specialized intellectual (as opposed to a universal intellectual)[25] he and others like him can wage small-scale guerrilla warfare against some repressive institutions, and against "silence" and "secrecy."

But all that is quite another thing from accepting Foucault's view in *History of Sexuality* that "power is everywhere" along with all that such a vastly simplified view entails.[26] For one, as I have said, Foucault's eagerness not to fall into Marxist economism causes him to obliterate the role of classes, the role of economics, the role of insurgency and rebellion in the societies he discusses. Let us suppose that prisons, schools, armies, and factories were, as he says, disciplinary factories in nineteenth-century France (since he talks almost exclusively about France), and that panoptic rule dominated them all. What resistances were there to the disciplinary order and why, as Nicos Poulantzas has so trenchantly argued in *State, Power, Socialism*, does Foucault never discuss the resistances that always end up dominated by the system he describes? The facts are more complicated of course, as any good historian of the rise of the modern state can demonstrate. Moreover, Poulantzas continues, even if we accept the view that power is essentially rational, that it is not held by anyone but is strategic, dispositional, effective, that, as *Discipline and Punish* claims, it invests all areas of society, is it correct to conclude, as Foucault does, that power is exhausted in its use?[27] Is it not simply wrong, Poulantzas asks, to say that power is not *based* anywhere and that struggles and exploitation – both terms left out of Foucault's analyses – do not occur?[28] The problem is that Foucault's use of the term *pouvoir* moves around too much, swallowing up every obstacle in its path (resistances to it, the class and economic bases that refresh and fuel it, the reserves it builds up), obliterating change and mystifying its microphysical sovereignty.[29] A symptom of how overblown Foucault's conception of power can become when it travels too far is Hacking's statement that "nobody knows this knowledge; no one yields this power." Surely this is going to extremes in order to prove that Foucault is not a simple-minded follower of Marx.

In fact, Foucault's theory of power is a Spinozist conception, which has captivated not only Foucault himself but many of his readers who wish to go beyond Left optimism and Right pessimism so as to justify political quietism with sophisticated intellectualism, at the same time wishing to appear realistic, in touch with the world of power and reality, as well as historical and antiformalistic in their bias. The trouble is that Foucault's theory has drawn a circle around itself, constituting a unique territory in which Foucault has imprisoned himself and others with him. It is certainly wrong to say, with Hacking, that hope, optimism, and pessimism are shown by Foucault to be mere satellites of the idea of a transcendental, enduring subject, since empirically we experience and act according to those things daily without reference to any such irrelevant "subject." There is after all a sensible difference between Hope and hope, just as there is between the Logos and words: we must not let Foucault get away with confusing them with each other, nor with letting us forget that history does not get made without work, intention, resistance, effort, or conflict, and that none of these things is silently absorbable into micro-networks of power.

There is a more important criticism to be made of Foucault's theory of power, and it has been made most tellingly by Chomsky. Unfortunately most of Foucault's new readers in the United States seem not to know of the exchange that took place between them several years ago on Dutch television[30], nor of Chomsky's succinct critique of Foucault contained in *Language and Responsibility*. Both men agreed on the necessity of opposing repression, a position Foucault has since found it more difficult to take unequivocally. Yet for Chomsky the sociopolitical battle had to be waged with two tasks in mind: one, "to imagine a future society that conforms to the exigencies of human nature as best we understand them; the other to analyze the nature of power and oppression in our present societies."[31] Foucault assented to the second without in any way accepting the first. According to him, any future societies that we might imagine now "are only the inventions of our civilization and result from our class system." Not only would imagining a future society ruled according to justice be limited by false consciousness, it would also be too utopian to project for anyone like Foucault who believes that "the idea of justice in itself is an idea which in effect has been invented and put to work in different societies as an instrument of a certain political and economic power or as a weapon against that power."[32] This is a perfect instance of Foucault's unwillingness to take seriously his own ideas about resistances to power. If power oppresses and controls and manipulates, then everything that resists it is not morally equal to power, is not neutrally and simply a weapon against that power. Resistance cannot equally be an adversarial alternative to power and a dependent function of it, except in some metaphysical, ultimately trivial sense. Even if the distinction is hard to draw, there is a distinction to be made – as, for example, Chomsky does when he says that he would give his support to an oppressed proletariat if as a class it made justice the goal of its struggle.

The disturbing circularity of Foucault's theory of power is a form of theoretical overtotalization superficially more difficult to resist because, unlike many others, it is formulated, reformulated, and borrowed for use in what seem to be historically documented situations. But note that Foucault's history is ultimately textual, or rather textualized; its mode is one for which Borges would have an affinity. Gramsci, on the other hand, would find it uncongenial. He would certainly appreciate the fineness of Foucault's archeologies, but would find it odd that they make not even a nominal allowance for emergent movements, and none for revolutions, counterhegemony, or historical blocks. In human history there is always something beyond the reach of dominating systems, no matter how deeply they saturate society, and this is obviously what makes change possible, limits power in Foucault's sense, and hobbles the theory of that power. One could not imagine Foucault undertaking a sustained analysis of powerfully contested political issues, nor, like Chomsky himself and writers like John Berger, would Foucault commit himself to descriptions of power and oppression with some intention of alleviating human suffering, pain, or betrayed hope.

It may seem an abrupt conclusion to reach, but the kinds of theory I have been discussing can quite easily become cultural dogma. Appropriated to schools or institutions, they quickly acquire the status of authority within the cultural group, guild, or affiliative family. Though of course they are to be distinguished from grosser forms of cultural dogma like racism and nationalism, they are insidious in that their original provenance – their history of adversarial, oppositional derivation – dulls the critical consciousness, convincing it that a once insurgent theory is still insurgent, lively, responsive to history. Left to its own specialists and acolytes, so to speak, theory tends to have walls erected around itself, but this does not mean that critics should either ignore theory or look despairingly around for newer varieties. To measure the distance between theory then and now, there and here, to record the encounter of theory with resistances to it, to move skeptically in the broader political world where such things as the humanities or the great classics ought to be seen as small provinces of the human venture, to map the territory covered by all the techniques of dissemination, communication, and interpretation, to preserve some modest (perhaps shrinking) belief in noncoercive human community: if these are not imperatives, they do at least seem to be attractive alternatives. And what is critical consciousness at bottom if not an unstoppable predilection for alternatives?

Notes

1   Frank Lentricchia, *After the New Criticism* (Chicago: University of Chicago Press, 1980), p. 24.

2   Geoffrey H. Hartman, *Criticism in the Wilderness: The Study of Literature Today* (New Haven: Yale University Press, 1980), p. 85.

3   *Ibid.*, p. 244.

4   *Ibid.*, p. 151.

5   *Ibid.*, p. 301.

6   Richard Ohmann, *English in America: A Radical View of the Profession* (New York and London: Oxford University Press, 1976), p. 304.

7   Georg Lukacs, *History and Class Consciousness: Studies in Marxist Dialectics*, trans. Rodney Livingstone (London: Merlin Press, 1971), p. 90.

8   *Ibid.*, p. 105.

9   *Ibid.*, p. 186.

10 Lukacs, "Die Subjekt-Objekt-Beziehung in der Ästhetik," originally published in *Logos*, 7 (1917–18), republished in Lukacs, *Heidelberger-Ästhetik, 1916–18* (Darmstadt: Luchterhand, 1974); see pp. 96–97.

11 Lukacs, *History and Class Consciousness*, p. 199.

12 Lucien Goldmann, *The Hidden God: A Study of Tragic Vision in the "Pensées" of Pascal and the Tragedies of Racine*, trans. Philip Thody (London: Routledge and Kegan Paul, 1964), p. 15.

13 *Ibid.*, p. 15.

14 *Ibid.*, p. 99.

15 Raymond Wiliams, *Problems in Materialism and Culture* (London: Verso, 1980), p. 13.

16 *Ibid.*, p. 21.

17 *Ibid.*, p. 21; emphasis added.

18 Williams, *Politics and Letters: Interviews with New Left Review* (London: New Left Books, 1979), p. 252.

19 Williams, *The Country and the City* (1973; rprt. New York: Oxford University Press, 1975), p. 141.

20 Lentricchia, *After the New Criticism*, p. 351.

21 Fredric Jameson, *The Political Unconscious: Narrative as a Socially Symbolic Act* (Ithaca: Cornell University Press, 1981), pp. 74, 102.

22 E.P. Thompson, *The Poverty of Theory and Other Essays* (London: Merlin Press, 1978).

23 Ian Hacking, "The Archaeology of Foucault," *New York Review of Books*, 28 (May 14, 1981), p. 36.

24 There is much evidence of this in the Winter 1980 issue of *Humanities in Society*, vol. 3, entirely devoted to Foucault.

25 The distinction is made by Foucault in *Radical Philosophy*, 17 (Summer 1977).

26 Michel Foucault, *The History of Sexuality, I: An Introduction*, trans. Robert Hurley (New York: Pantheon, 1978), p. 93.

27 Foucault, *Discipline and Punish: The Birth of the Prison*, trans. Alan Sheridan (New York: Pantheon, 1977), pp. 26–27.

28 Nicos Poulantzas, *State, Power, and Socialism*, trans. Patrick Camiller (London: Verso, 1980), p. 148.

29 *Ibid.*, pp. 150ff.

30 A transcript is to be found in *Reflexive Water: The Basic Concerns of Mankind*, ed. Fons Elders (London: Souvenir Press, 1974). The curious thing about this book and the program – "the Basic concerns of mankind" – is that "mankind" is spoken for entirely by white European-American males. No one seems bothered by the claims for universality.

31 Noam Chomsky, *Language and Responsibility* (New York: Pantheon, 1979), p. 80.

32 *Reflexive Water*, pp. 184–185.

11

Toward World Literary Knowledges
Theory in the Age of Globalization (2010)

Revathi Krishnaswamy

Revathi Krishnaswamy is a professor of English at San José State University in California. Her work in postcolonial studies includes her book *Effeminism: The Economy of Colonial Desire* (1999), in which she builds on Edward Said's work to argue that the stereotypical narrative of the Orient as produced by Western studies "effeminized" the colonized other so as to reinforce the dominant power of the West through the embodied metaphor of exoticism. Krishnaswamy analyzes British writers in and on India (Flora Annie Steel, Rudyard Kipling, and E.M. Forster) through the colonizer–colonized relation, drawing on questions of political legitimacy and the power of discourse. Since then, her work has turned to global issues, as in her co-edited volume *The Postcolonial and the Global* (2007). Published in the journal *Comparative Literature* in 2010, her essay "Toward World Literary Knowledges" offers a fresh attempt to consider the role of literary theory in a global context. Krishnaswamy argues that even as a wider range of literatures is being read today, theories and methodologies remain highly Westernized and Eurocentric, and she proposes a re-examination and decolonization of the field of literary theory. Krishnaswamy's alternative to Euro-American literary theory is a body of "world literary knowledges," which she illustrates with pre- and postcolonial examples from the Indian context.

At the 2004 annual MLA convention, I attended a panel on "Comparative Literature in an Age of Globalization" in which the ACLA draft report on the state of the discipline was being discussed. During the Q&A session, I asked Jonathan Culler, who was one of the panelists, why the turn toward the global in literary

Revathi Krishnaswamy, "Toward World Literary Knowledges: Theory in the Age of Globalization" (2010). In *Comparative Literature* 62:4 (2010), pp. 399–419. © 2010 University of Oregon.

World Literature in Theory, First Edition. Edited by David Damrosch.

studies and the enthusiasm over "World Literature" in America had not generated as much interest in "world poetics" or "world literary theory"? Why, I asked, had W.W. Norton, the arbiter of American pedagogy, published an expanded anthology of world literature that included several "great works" of non-Western literature, but not a comparable anthology of world literary theory that included non-Western poetics, criticisms, or commentaries. Culler jokingly suggested that I should perhaps propose such a project to Norton. Meanwhile, someone in the audience brought up East–West studies and comparative poetics, mentioning the names of Earl Miner and Patrick Hogan. Before I could ask why the work of these outliers was not more widely debated, especially as literary productions from elsewhere were being voraciously consumed and rapidly curricularized into alternative canons across American campuses, Hogan himself recounted his experience editing a special issue of *College Literature* that focused on "non-Western literary theory before European colonialism." Whenever he mentioned the project to his colleagues, he recalled, they invariably said, "Oh, you mean Homi Bhabha and Gayatri Spivak." And when he insisted his focus was "non-Western theory *before* colonialism," he was confronted with "looks of blank incomprehension."[1] The "incomprehension" Hogan encountered reflects a widespread assumption that theory is the product of a uniquely Western philosophical tradition. From this perspective, the non-West may be a source of exotic cultural production but cannot be a site of theory. Even the one theory produced by the non-West – postcolonial theory – is, we are told, simply a response to the West. Furthermore, although scholars in comparative poetics and East–West studies have tried to challenge this assumption by drawing attention to pre-colonial textual traditions (Chinese, Japanese, Sanskrit, and Arabic), their work has had little impact on the practice of comparative literature or literary theory.

After returning from the MLA convention that year, I took up Culler's suggestion in earnest. I contacted my Norton representative and wrote to the editors, pointing out the Eurocentric nature of the publisher's current anthology of theory and criticism,[2] giving examples of some Indian and Chinese theories I use in class, and suggesting that Norton might consider doing a multivolume anthology of world poetics. Perhaps the project I proposed didn't seem worthwhile or practical enough. Perhaps my letter wasn't addressed to the right people. Whatever the case, I got no response. My sense of urgency faded and I went back to supplementing the Norton anthology with my own collection of criticism and theories from India and elsewhere.

Meanwhile, obituaries for comparative literature continue to be written apace. Some mourn the discipline's demise while others try to bring it back in a new avatar. In the wake of globalization and the rise of postcolonialism and multiculturalism, a debate has ensued over reinventing Comparative Literature in the form of World Literature (Moretti, Damrosch, Cooppan), World Bank Literature (Kumar), Globalit (Baucom), and Planetary Literature (Dimock, Spivak). As conducted in the pages of the PMLA, the ACLA reports, and other prestigious forums, the discussion is usually well intentioned, at times heated, occasionally xenophobic (Delbanco), shifting rapidly from *whether* to *what* to *how* different literary traditions are to be studied. Not surprisingly, the discussion has centered largely on developments within the United States, and, with a few notable exceptions (Bassnett, Tötösy), commentators have seemed largely unaware that the discipline of comparative literature has a history, albeit problematic, outside Euro-America. The 1993 ACLA report called for comparative literature to move away from the old model of literary study according to author, nation, period, or genre toward a more cultural studies model that would embrace transnational studies of discourse, ideology, race, and gender (Bernheimer 41–42). Prominent American theorists have taken it upon themselves to construct grand sweeping metanarratives theorizing literary productions across the (third) world (Jameson, Moretti), while others have expressed skepticism and apprehension about projects that seemed to consolidate the rest in the name of the West (Ahmad, Baucom, Chow, Kumar, Kadir, Spivak). But few, even among the skeptics, have called for redefining theory itself as a way out of comparative literature's Eurocentrism. The result is what we have today: world lit without world lit crit.

My essay aims to address this gap by proposing a new component to global literary studies called "world literary knowledges." I use the term *knowledges* instead of *theory, poetics, aesthetics,* or *criticism* for reasons elaborated more fully below. Intended as both a critique of and a contribution to the field of comparative poetics, the notion of "world literary knowledges" outlined here aims to go beyond inducting a few token non-Western greats into theory's hall of fame; rather, it asks us radically to re-vision the question of what counts as theory in the first place. The conceptual contributions of diverse cultural traditions across the globe, I contend, cannot properly be recognized or evaluated unless the domain of theory is extended beyond the formal explicit systematic meta-discourses of dominant, prestigious, textual traditions to include regional, subaltern, and popular epistemologies that may be "emergent" (more informally formulated; less fully systematized) or "latent" (embryonic; embedded in praxis).[3] This is not a call to abandon the study of formal poetics; rather, it is a call to expand the definition of theory and to relocate its study in the broader field of world literary knowledges. In my view, such an inclusive approach to theory can (i) promote greater understanding of diverse literary texts/traditions by enlarging the global repertoire of aesthetic epistemologies; (ii) uncover cultural differences as well as common (possibly "universal") features of our shared aesthetic nature by placing different conceptualizations of literature/literariness side by side; and (iii) expose within and across literary traditions new historical networks of influence, antagonism, and affiliation that have been obscured by Eurocentric or nationalistic ideologies of comparison that rely on a Manichean opposition between East and West or colonial and national.

The first half of the essay surveys the disciplines of comparative literature, literary theory, and comparative poetics in order to show that, despite the good intentions of many scholars, all three fields continue to be Eurocentric pedagogical projects that reproduce colonial stereotypes and perpetuate a neocolonial division of labor between the knowing West and the known rest. My discussion also suggests that anticolonial nationalism and postcolonialism, despite their enormous influence, have only dented, not dismantled, Eurocentric practices of knowledge production. The second half of the essay delineates the notion of "world literary knowledges" with the help of three examples drawn from the multilingual terrain of (pre- and postcolonial) India. The first example focuses on how the revival of Sanskrit during the anticolonial nationalist period effectively marginalized and reduced to regional or local knowledge the sophisticated eco-theory of language/literature present in the rival classical tradition of Tamil. The second example identifies certain aesthetic innovations in the popular *bhakti* poetry of medieval India and shows how the poetics latent in *bhakti* subverts the dominant tradition of Sanskrit poetics. My last example showcases Dalit aesthetics as a "not-quite postcolonial" epistemology emerging at the unstable intersection of national, regional, and transnational literary networks in India today. The essay concludes with the claim that "world literary knowledges," as conceived here, can potentially develop into a valuable ethical and epistemological ally of global literary studies.

World Lit without World Lit Crit

Comparative literature

The colonial model of cultural management was premised on a tripartite disciplinary division: comparative literature was the proper method for studying Europe, Orientalism for Asia, and anthropology for Africa. As this model was restructured in the American twentieth century, Area Studies replaced Orientalism to meet the needs of the Cold War. Today, world literature is emerging out of the ashes of comparative literature to meet the needs of an America-in-globalization.[4] But if the model of world literature involves sampling texts from different parts of the world, the epistemologies used to interpret them remain predominantly Western or Westocentric. Assorted texts from the world's literary traditions are not only sorted into genres identified and defined by the Western theoretical tradition, they also are interpreted and judged according to Western literary norms. From this perspective, postcolonial material becomes a reflection of current metropolitan trends – multiculturalism, theories of ethnicity and race, national allegories, magical realism, and the postmodernist aesthetic of the fragment – and there is often little or no awareness of how these materials are conceptualized or contested in their own sites of production.[5]

The very notion of comparison had been Eurocentric by exclusion when applied only to European literature and Eurocentric by discrimination when adapting evolutionary models to place European literature at the forefront of human development. These older forms of comparison may have lost their hold today, but the newer ones that have emerged are still anchored to a Eurocentric, nation-centered formulation of inter-nationalism that Rey Chow has labeled "Europe and Its Others": "In this formulation, the rationale for comparing hinges on the conjunction *and*; the *and* … signals a form of supplementation that authorizes the first term, Europe, as the grid of reference, to which may be added others in subsequent and subordinate fashion" ("The Old/New Question of Comparison" 294). Even models of comparativism propagated by postcolonial studies have not escaped the "Europe and" formulation, for they perpetuate neocolonial geopolitics in the form of linguistic fields such as Anglophone, Francophone, and so on (Apter). Furthermore, postcolonial comparisons also risk "feminizing" the expressive cultures of the periphery in relation to the more "masculine" intellectual capital that broad conceptual categories and universalizing theories tend to acquire within the field of comparative literature (Lionnet 105).

The "Europe and" model of comparative literature, moreover, has also been adopted by many non-Western countries and frequently yoked to nationalist agendas, often with problematic effects. Susan Bassnett correctly points out that in India, China, Japan, and elsewhere, comparative literature arose not in antagonism to nationalism (as was the case in Europe and America) but rather as an expression or assertion of national cultural identity, typically constructed in direct opposition to a putative Western identity (5). Bassnett approvingly notes that just as Euro-American comparativists have often treated "Indian literature" or "African literature" in singular monolithic terms, so others are now deploying "European literature" or "Western literature" as an overarching category within which French, German, and English get reduced to component "sub-national" or "regional" units (Bassnett 37–38). But if such inversions "invite re-examination of the old models that placed component literatures of the Western tradition in a position of international superiority" (Bassnett 38), by merely reversing the old neocolonial equation they nevertheless remain trapped within the "Europe and" model of comparison.

To the extent Bassnett seeks to learn not merely *about* but also *from* the practice of comparative literature in other parts of the world, her study represents a refreshing departure from the navel-gazing lamentations of much Western scholarship on the subject. But, unfortunately, when Bassnett goes beyond the frontiers of Europe to find a cure for the ills plaguing comparative literature, she often ends up uncritically endorsing the practices of anticolonial cultural nationalisms wholesale. "A fundamental task of Indian comparative literature," Bassnett writes, "is the assertion of the importance of tradition and the creation of a literary history constructed upon Indian models" (39). This statement, which takes "tradition" and "Indian models" to be self-evident terms, simply echoes the goals articulated by the Indian Comparative Literature Association (founded in 1981): "to arrive at a conception of Indian literature which will not only modernize our literature departments but also take care of the task of discovering the greatness of our literature and to present a panoramic view of Indian literary activities through the ages" (Bassnett 39). A nationalistic undertaking to the core, the association's project is driven by a desire to distill a quintessential "Indianness" from the country's diverse literary traditions and to consolidate this sense of "Indianness" through contrast with the "West." The agenda articulated in 1968 by the first secretary of the Sahitya Akademi, the premier literary institution of India, similarly states that "the multi-lingual and multi-regional character of modern Indian culture, and the roots of its inspiration lie in two major sources – the national, mainly embodied in the Sanskrit heritage, and the modern, which is imported from the West, derived from its European or American or Soviet varieties" (Kripalani 179). Here, the superiority of the national (equated with Sanskrit), as well as the necessity of the modern (equated with Western) – a paradigmatic feature of Indian nationalist discourse – is made axiomatic to the task of Indian literary studies: to consolidate the national by strategically deploying the modern (see, for example, Das, "Why Comparative Indian Literature" and S. Mukherjee, *Idea*). The goal was to weave India's many diverse linguistic/literary strands into a singular overarching category called "Indian literature" (ironically, in English translation), a category that would reveal the national unity underlying India's multilingual diversity.[6] This dream project came to fruition in the Sahitya Akademi's proposed ten-volume history of Indian literature (inevitably written in English), three of which have been published so far (Das, *A History* 1991; 1995; 2005). But in the wake of globalization and the rise of various social movements in India, such nationalistic literary projects have come under attack for replicating the exclusionary gestures of both colonialist and anticolonial nationalist historiography, as well as for marginalizing or assimilating various regional, linguistic, caste, class, and gender struggles into a nationalist literary agenda.[7] Bassnett, however, seems unaware of these developments, for she reassures her readers that comparative literature, although dead in the West, is alive and well in the non-West:

> The way in which comparative literature is used in places such as China, Brazil, India or many African nations is constructive in that it is employed to explore both indigenous traditions and imported or imposed traditions, throwing open the whole vexed problem of the canon. There is no sense of crisis in this form of comparative literature, no quibbling about the terms from which to start comparing, because those terms are already laid down. What is being studied is the way in which national culture has been affected by importation, and the focus is that national culture. (8)

In treating the category of "national culture" as a given, this optimistic assessment of comparative literature in the non-West obscures the exclusionary gestures through which anticolonial nationalisms have often consolidated themselves in these postcolonial spaces, erasing in the process the myriad subnational, subaltern, and regional cultural formations fighting to assert their own identities there.

The development of comparative literature in China is similarly instructive. Haun Saussy points out that the Chinese discipline of *bijiao wenzue* was created in 1917 to address the following question: "what does modern China need to take from the cultures of the already modernized countries." "The resulting discipline," Saussy notes, "is strongly marked by the need to define what is properly, uniquely Chinese, through contrast with the 'others'" ("Exquisite Cadavers" 29). Indeed, the rise of comparative literature in East Asia led to the emergence of a "Chinese" school of comparative literature (Chen). In opposition to the "French" school of influence studies and the "American" school of parallel studies, the "Chinese" school proposed its own methodology: the application of Western theory to Chinese texts. Although in principle this methodology promised to open up a new way of reading Chinese texts and examining the claim to universality by Western theory, in practice it became a simplistic and mechanical application of imported epistemologies on indigenous material. Sweeping generalizations were frequently made by reductively reifying "the West" and "China" into opposing categories. After the publication of Said's *Orientalism* and the ascent of postcolonial theory, this form of East–West studies was rightly debunked for perpetuating the colonization of Eastern literary traditions by Western theory (Yokota-Murakami; Yu; Zhang). But since no viable alternatives have yet been proposed, the problem of how different literary traditions of the world are to be studied and what epistemologies are to be used to compare them remains an as-yet-unresolved issue both in the East and in the West.

Literary theory

Acknowledging that non-Western texts "present new challenges for teachers and scholars trained in the New Critical or historical schools in the United States," Emory Elliott makes an interesting observation: "So far the solution to this problem seems to have been mainly to wait until scholars with the same cultural heritages can bring their personal knowledge of the cultures together with their *professional training in Western criticism*" (16; emphasis added). What Elliot's statement inadvertently reveals is that "professional training in Western criticism" is still the key element that inserts the native informant into World Literature. Without Western theory, the world, it would seem, cannot be made visible.

A cursory glance at the contents of any standard anthology of literary theory commonly used in college courses across the United States quickly reveals that the field of literary theory is a resolutely Eurocentric high ground relatively untouched by the rising tide of globalization reshaping American academia. *The Norton Anthology of Theory and Criticism* is exemplary in this respect. As presented in this authoritative tome of over 2500 pages, the (his)story of high theory runs from Aristotle through Horace, Longinus, other neoclassical and medieval scholars, representative Renaissance critics, Enlightenment philosophers, English and German Romantics, British Victorians, nineteenth-century Continental thinkers, Modernists, Marxists, Russian Formalists, Structuralists, New Critics, feminists and poststructuralists. This rich and complex story contains interesting detours and invigorating deviations, heated debates and profound disagreements. But because the cast of characters, as diverse and distinctive as it may be, is nevertheless overwhelmingly Western, the narrative presents literary theory as the product of cultural or epistemological changes taking place primarily within Europe.

In fact, out of the nearly 140 theorists on the Norton list, fewer than fifteen are "minority" or non-Western critics: W.E.B. Du Bois, Zora Neale Hurston, Langston

Hughes, Frantz Fanon, Chinua Achebe, Ngugi wa Thiongo (*et al.*), Gloria Anzaldúa, bell hooks, and the postcolonial trio, Edward Said, Gayatri Spivak, and Homi Bhabha.[8] No non-Western critic or literary tradition is mentioned prior to the twentieth century – and this despite the fact that India, China, Japan, and the Arab world developed rigorous systematic theories of literature that produced long traditions of abstract and illuminating thought about the structure, function, effect, and origin of literature, traditions that are comparable, if not superior, in clarity and sophistication to much pre-Romantic European literary theory (see Hogan and Pandit). Instead, every non-Western or minority critic included in the Norton collection falls under the now familiar rubric of East–West studies or race/postcolonial theory.[9] As a result, they become "in-house" critics whose dissentions once again return narcissistically to expand and enrich Western thought. The story of literary theory as told in the Norton can thus be summed up as follows: the West produces theory autogenetically; the rest do so only in response to the West.

The assumption that the non-West cannot produce any independent form of abstract thought is perhaps one of the most enduring legacies of Orientalism. William Jones, the first major British Orientalist and father of the Indo-European hypothesis, believed that his translations from the Sanskrit would infuse new life into Europe's artistic/literary creativity and provide new material for European science/philosophy. But he could not imagine that the Sanskrit tradition might contribute anything of value to contemporary (European) science or philosophy (Jones 107) – a view that the colonial philologists who followed Jones held even more emphatically. The Reverend Robert Caldwell, who is credited with establishing Dravidian as a separate language family, claimed that the learning of "versified enigmas and harmonious platitudes" resulted in Indians developing a great capacity for patient labor and an accurate knowledge of details, but also prevented the development of the "power of generalization and discrimination" (qtd. in Cohn 52). Similarly, the German philologist Max Müller categorically claimed theory for Europe by arguing that Hellenic thought had developed in Europeans a unique capacity for abstraction and generalization, while Indian thinking, lacking the benefit of Hellenic influence, had remained trapped in a particularistic mode (qtd. in Wilson 92).[10] The story is repeated elsewhere with reference to Chinese, Arabic, and other non-European traditions of the world (on China, see, for example, Chow, "Inscrutable Chinese"; Zhang, "What Is Wen"; and Shih).

Why did literary theory become such a highly valued commodity in the Western world, and how did the Western theoretical tradition emerge as the privileged marker of cultural superiority the world over? As regards the English literary tradition, Terry Eagleton has shown that literary criticism came to be recognized as an area of study only after land ceiling acts during the eighteenth century had created sharply divided class structures. As a result, literary criticism emerged as a tool for social protest and acquired the status of a valued class possession in England (Eagleton 26–27). But it was not only class conflict that gave value to English literary criticism. It also acquired significance because in order to educate colonial peoples in the finer points of English literature it became necessary to export a large number of critical commentaries on English writers (on British India, see Viswanathan). In fact, G.N. Devy believes that "the steady decline in the philosophical substance of English criticism" from Shelley's *Defense* to F.R. Leavis's text/author based assessment may be ascribed to "the rising need in the colonies for critical commentaries on authors and texts" (104). And as natives became acculturated through education in English literature and English literary criticism, they came to accept it (and by extension, European/Western theory) as an index of cultural superiority. Even today, it is the Western tradition of literary theory and criticism, frequently filtered through the medium of English, which is widely circulated and studied all over the world. Professional training in Western criticism continues to legitimize non-Western scholars, even when speaking of their own literary texts and traditions.

Comparative poetics

If the dominance of Western theory has been questioned at all, it has been done only within the marginalized and underdeveloped subdiscipline of comparative poetics. Following the pioneering efforts of Horst Frenz, René Etiemble, and René Wellek to draw Arabic, Indian, Chinese, and Japanese, as well as African and other (little-studied) Asian literatures into the orbit of comparative literature, scholars such as C.D. Narasimhaiah, Li Zehou, Karatani Kojin, Earl Miner, Patrick Hogan, Lalita Pandit, Zhang Longxi, Nabil Matar, Ashmita Khasnabish, and others have tried to argue for the inclusion of non-Western traditions of poetics on the basis of both their intrinsic merit and their historical impact on Western thought.

Scholarship in comparative poetics is of two main types: sequential and parallel. Sequential studies, which deal with historically related literary traditions and focus on issues of influence, have explored such topics as the role of the Arab Aristotelians in shaping the ethical concerns of Western literary theory, the influence of Indian philosophies on Romanticism or poststructuralism, and the impact of Chinese thought on Modernist poetry.[11] These kinds of influence studies are valuable in so far as they restore to the historical record the contributions of the non-West in the formation of the West. But in so far as they retain Europe as the central category and deal with the influence of non-Western traditions on the West rather than on one another, they remain tied to a "Europe and" frame of reference. Parallel studies, which focus on similarities/differences between historically unrelated traditions (Hogan, "Ethnocentrism" 5–6), likewise seem to rely on Eurocentric or Orientalist practices and methods. Although Haun Saussy has argued that comparative literature has not imitated comparative philology and mythology in making linguistic diffusion and differentiation the basis of comparison – choosing, instead, "the universality of human experience" as "another basis" for comparison ("Exquisite Cadavers" 13) – when comparative studies venture into the non-Western world, universality inevitably disappears and "omnipotent definitions" make their appearance (Said, *Orientalism* 156). That is, although universal features may be acknowledged, it is difference between the East and the West that often becomes an obsessive and myopic focus of analysis.[12]

There is yet another fundamental limitation inhibiting the growth of comparative poetics. Scholarship in this field has, for the most part, concentrated on expanding the canonical Western tradition by comparing or complementing it with classical non-Western theory – Sanskrit, Arabic, Chinese, and Japanese. While this focus is both understandable and necessary, it nevertheless perpetuates the ideology of "masterpieces" – or "masterpoetics," as one might say in this case. A few prominent Asian and Arabic traditions are admitted as tokens into the exclusive club of theory, while other lesser-known traditions continue to be ignored – marginalized as others to the Other of the "Great" Asian/Arabic civilizations.[13] As a result, alternative conceptualizations of literature and literariness, whether they are latent in literary praxis or emergent in subaltern, popular, and regional notions of literature, are rarely recognized for their conceptual value, and poetics or theory continues to be defined in highly exclusionary terms as consisting only of the sort of explicit systematic, written, and abstract thought that only some cultures have produced and in only some periods. Such a confined and confining conception of theory excludes significant swathes of the globe (Africa, for instance) and sizable populations of the world (women and other minorities) whose epistemologies may not be articulated in formal, explicit, textual, or abstract modes of expression. Perhaps now is the time to move away from this older model of "comparative poetics" toward a more open-ended and inclusive understanding of theory.

World Literary Knowledges

In recent years the term *knowledges* (in the plural) has emerged as a way of notating various local or indigenous epistemologies that have been marginalized by the universal claims of Western high theory (Smith). With the goal of challenging and reversing the "epistemic dependency" of the rest on the West, scholars in different parts of the world are today engaged in the difficult task of recuperating and reactivating diverse indigenous knowledges appropriated by coloniality/modernity (Mignolo 110). In keeping with this trend, I would like to propose as a new component to global literary studies the category "world literary knowledges," the purpose of which is to open up the canon of literary theory and criticism to alternative ways of conceptualizing and analyzing literary production. This means that regional, subaltern, and popular traditions, whether latent or emergent, may be studied, analyzed, and evaluated as epistemologies of literature/literariness alongside the traditions of poetics that currently constitute both the canon (Euro-American) and the counter-canon (Arabic, Sanskrit, Chinese, Japanese) of literary theory. This also means that conceptualizations of literature/literariness may be approached as historically and culturally situated knowledges (or ideologies) – but without foreclosing the possibility that an open-ended, cross-cultural study of literary knowledges from around the world might at some point disclose certain literary or aesthetic features that characterize our shared humanity. What follows is a tentative and modest attempt to initiate such an epistemologically inclusive and methodologically open-ended study of "world literary knowledges." My examples, which come mainly from the multilingual Indian context with which I am familiar, are therefore intended to be more emblematic than exceptional.

Example 1: Alternative explicit literary knowledge

Although the Indian subcontinent represents a rich multilingual literary terrain, only the Sanskrit tradition has commanded substantial scholarly attention (European as well as Indian) and so provided the basis for a pan-Indian poetics. Nourished on the Sanskritocentrism of British Orientalism, nineteenth-century Indian cultural nationalism identified this ancient brahminical language as the primary source and symbol of national identity, effectively rolling back centuries of struggle with other rival languages. In accordance with the linguistic hierarchy of colonial comparative philology, which ranked the Dravidian family of languages to which Tamil belongs below the Indo-European family to which Sanskrit belongs, the Tamil literary tradition came to be regarded as essentially regional in scope despite its antiquity and influence. While concepts from Sanskrit poetics (*rasa, dhvani, vakroti*) were revived and applied to Indian texts, and, on occasion, to Western ones, concepts from Tamil poetics were either rarely studied or applied only to Tamil texts.[14] But in fact, the *Tolkappiyam* (5th century AD), which constitutes the central text of Tamil/Dravidian linguistics and poetics, contains rich possibilities for global literary theory, especially the concept of *tinai* or landscape.

Deeply rooted in an ecological view of language/literature, *tinai* envisions a biome-based social order integrating land, man, and god. There are five basic *tinais* or landscapes recognized in the *Tolkappiyam*: mountain (*kurinji*), forest (*mullai*), riverbelt (*marutham*), seacoast (*neithal*), and desert (*paalai*), each with its indigenous natural and human communities, its appropriate mode of resource use (gathering, hunting, cultivation, trade, and herding), and its appropriate style of cultural expression. Language, culture, customs, behavior, thoughts, and feelings (and hence literature) spring from the habitat or environment, which incorporates not only natural flora and fauna but also sociocultural features, including humans, gods, dance, and music. Since language, in this view, is profoundly conditioned by context, every *tinai* generates its own fables, stories, poetry, and folklore – all of which are influenced by the immediate concerns of the people in the region and partake of this ecological orientation.

Just as Aristotle's *Poetics* is based on Greek drama, so the typology of landscapes set forth in the *Tolkappiyam* (including the term *tinai*) is derived from the practices of ancient Tamil poetry, commonly referred to as *Cankam* literature (200 BC – 250 AD).

As such, it is generally taken to refer to purely conventional landscapes that are connected with certain themes and images internal to Tamil poetry (see, for example, Ramanujan). Although some scholars claim that the landscapes described in *Cankam* literature actually reflect the prehistoric geographical realities of the Tamil region, they also concede that after the *Cankam* period (possibly by the time of *Tolkappiyam*'s composition) these landscapes became "depleted literary devices" that no longer served as "a mirror of life" (Sivathamby 34). Whether understood as allegorical and conventional or mimetic and realistic, the concept of *tinai* has the potential to become a valuable theoretical tool with applications beyond the narrow, specialized field of Dravidian linguistics/literature. Thus, for instance, the Tamil typology of landscapes could be used to isolate different generic conventions through cross-cultural comparison with other traditions (such as the Japanese) that exhibit similar patterns. Furthermore, the Tamil mode of reading literary production in terms of landscape could provide the basis for an alternative (third-world-based) ecologically grounded approach to criticism – one that could conceivably enter into a productive dialog with what is currently a West/North-based ecocriticism.[15]

Example 2: Latent literary knowledge

The (his)story of modern literary theory in India tells of how the great hegemonic tradition of Sanskrit thought was displaced by Western thought under the impact of colonialism. This storyline infused a strong revivalist flavor into modern Indian literary criticism from its inception in the nineteenth century. The long history of exchange and tension between the *marga*, or metropolitan traditions, and the *desi*, or popular regional subcultures, metamorphosed, under the aegis of anticolonial nationalism, into a battle between Indian high culture and the West. As a result, few Indian critics recognized that the heterogeneous regional linguistic/literary subcultures of India might be rich sources of criticism and epistemology. For instance, Sri Aurobindo Ghosh (1872–1950), an important and influential theorist of the Bengal Renaissance, wrote a series of essays (*The Future of Poetry*) in which he employed Sanskrit poetics to implicitly indict English Romantic poetry for lacking the visionary intensity of the Vedas and the Upanishads. He concluded his argument by rejecting the Romantic idea of the poet as creator in favor of the Vedic conception of the poet as seer. But, as G.N. Devy has demonstrated, because the structure of *The Future of Poetry* bears a striking resemblance to Shelley's *A Defense of Poetry*, it ironically reveals the Indian critic's reliance on the very English critical tradition he wished to overcome (112–116).[16] Furthermore, although Sri Aurobindo knew several Indian languages and was well acquainted with some of the sub-continent's regional literatures, he relied mainly on Sanskrit and English literary terms since to him – and others like him – only these two systems of abstract philosophical thought qualified as theory. As a result, Sri Aurobindo and other nationalist scholars who followed in his wake (Narasimhaiah, for instance) remained blind to the epistemological and aesthetic alternatives embedded in the popular multilingual *bhakti* or devotional literatures that had risen up in waves from the medieval period onward to challenge the Sanskritic tradition, question religious beliefs, reform social attitudes, and reshape literary expression all over India (Devy 42–43). Composed by cobblers, weavers, cowherds, shepherds, untouchables, and women (among others), *bhakti* poetry drew on the oral traditions of folksong and epigram to articulate an incandescent iconoclastic vision of spiritual liberation.[17]

Important strands of *bhakti* literature emerged in self-conscious opposition to Sanskrit literature. For example, unlike the Sanskrit religious texts, which are described as *sruti* and *smrti* (what is heard and what is remembered), the Kannada Virasaiva *bhakti* poets of south India called their compositions *vacanas* (what is said). A.K. Ramanujan has pointed out that

> *Vacana*, as an active mode, stands in opposition to both *sruti* and *smrti*: not what is heard, but what is said; not remembered or received, but uttered here and now. To the saints, religion is not a spectator sport, a reception or consumption; it is an experience of Now, a way of being. This distinction is expressed in the language of the *vacanas*, in the forms the *vacanas* take. Though medieval Kannada was rich in native Dravidian meters, and in borrowed Sanskritic forms, no metrical line or stanza is used in the *vacanas* …. The *vacana* is thus a rejection of premeditated art … (37–38)[18]

Vacana involves both a sayer or speaker and a listener, with each supplying half of what is said (V. Narayanaravku, qtd. in Hart 165). Dialogic participation between speaker and listener, writer and reader, is therefore an important component of the praxis of *bhakti*. The *bhakti* lyric is thus, at the most fundamental level, an invitation to the listener to share the speaker's experience. Unlike the disembodied visionary in Vedic poetry, the speaker of the *bhakti* lyric is an embodied figure shackled by the social categories of caste, class, and gender. Indeed, the paradigmatic speaker/ devotee of *bhakti* is feminine and speaks in a feminized voice. For example, Mahadeviakka, a twelfth-century south Indian Virasaiva poet who composed her *vacanas* in the local "substandard" or "vulgar" dialect of Kannada, repeatedly complains of the restrictions placed on women both by the stifling demands of parents, husbands, and in-laws and by the fierce opposition from pundits and priests. In many of her lyrics the speaker finally breaks free of worldly restrictions by means of shocking images of fornication, adultery, and prostitution. Reflecting the late medieval emphasis on bodily or carnal knowledge, Mahadeviakka uses an unabashedly erotic language with many explicit descriptions of sexual union. The conventional structure of love – longing, separation, and union between devotee and divine – set forth in Sanskrit poetics becomes, in effect, nothing more than a flimsy veil for a more subversive message about social transgression and spiritual transformation (Krishnaswamy "Subversive Spirituality").

Moreover, although the structure of the *bhakti* lyrics replicates the gendered hierarchy of patriarchal society – the divine is always masculine and the quintessential *bhakta* or devotee is imagined in feminine or feminized terms[19] – it nevertheless inverts that hierarchy on the psycho-spiritual and literary levels where even male *bhakti* poets must assume or take on femininity in order to experience the divine. Thus Basavanna (1106–1167 CE), one of the greatest (male) Virasaiva poets, often speaks in the voice of a woman and uses feminine alienation in patriarchal society as a metaphor for the saint's sense of spiritual abandonment in the material world: "I went to fornicate / but all I got was counterfeit / I went behind a ruined wall, but scorpions stung me." The speaker then points out that, instead of coming to her aid, "The watchman who heard my screams / just peeled off my clothes." And when she goes home in shame, her husband, instead of comforting her, "raised weals on my back." The final blow is dealt by the king, the ultimate embodiment of worldly masculine authority: "All the rest, O lord of the meeting rivers," the speaker laments in the concluding line, "the king took for his fines" (*Speaking of Siva* 75). The female speaker in a *bhakti* poem, however, is not always so vulnerable, helpless, or conventionally subservient, even in her appeal to or longing for the male deity-lover. In the *padam*, another south Indian genre of *bhakti* poetry, the female-devotee is typically a bold and independent courtesan, who on occasion even withholds her favors from the god-customer if insufficiently compensated. Thus, in a *padam* composed by the male *bhakti* poet Ksetrayya (1600–1680 CE), the female speaker asks the god-customer, "Prince of playboys, you may be/ But is it fair/ To ask me to forget the money?" And she boldly declares, "I earned it, after all/ By spending time with you." So "Put up the gold you owe me," she commands, "and then you can talk" (*When God Is a Customer* 69). In *padams* such as this it is the woman devotee who has the upper hand. Taken together, these lyrics suggest that *bhakti* poets not only conceived of gender as a constructed or performance-based category, but also associated femininity with the experience of *ananda*, the Sanskritic notion of bliss that Ashmita Kashnabish has recently linked to Lacan and Irigaray's conceptions of *jouissance*.

The *bhakti* movement which produced such prodigious poetry did not, however, produce a comparable body of explicit poetics. This is not an accident of literary history; rather, it represents a conscious move from the brahminical text-based philosophical tradition toward a more spontaneous, performance or praxis-centered approach to life and literature. Because *bhakti* literature lacks an explicit poetics, the aesthetic innovations and conceptual contributions latent in it have rarely been elevated to the level of theory. Yet to do so would not only deepen our understanding of the craft of *bhakti* poetry itself, but also provide a basis for comparing different (related and unrelated) mystic traditions based in protest. To do so would also throw light on a form of cultural expression in India that cannot be explained solely in terms of nationalism and postcolonialism,[20] as well as lead to a better understanding of one of the most pressing cultural questions of our times: how does religion become a means for fundamentalists, resistors, and revolutionaries alike to express social, economic, and political conflict?[21]

Example 3: Emergent literary knowledge

Alongside a vibrant multilingual Dalit literature, a new discourse dealing with "Dalit aesthetics" is emerging in India today. "Dalit" is the self-chosen name of the so-called untouchable castes that, following B.R. Ambedkar, reject the Gandhian designation "Harijan" as uppercaste patronizing. The term "Dalit," which means "broken" or "downtrodden," implies militancy and alliance with other disenfranchised groups, including peasants, workers, and women. Drawing on anti-racist movements in the United States and elsewhere, the post-Ambedkarite Dalit movement has sought to link the category of caste to race in an attempt to globalize its dissent against discrimination. Dalit writers aim not only to expose or challenge India's hegemonic literary traditions but also to critique or deconstruct its dominant aesthetic categories.

The growing popularity and prominence of Dalit literature has not been without controversy, however. While the (upper-caste) literary establishment in India has readily acknowledged the social value of Dalit writing, many scholars and critics have questioned its literary merit. Dalit literature, they have argued, is "artless" because it lacks aesthetic qualities. They also contend that literature is not simply another arena of affirmative action in which Dalit writers can demand equal representation even when they do not exhibit equal talent. They further charge Dalit writers with being divisive and sectarian, with using disrespectful and offensive language towards Hindu divinities and revered figures, and with engaging in distortions of pre- and post-independence Indian history. Dalits, in turn, insist that their writing has a particular purpose and audience, both of which have an important bearing on literary/aesthetic decisions, and that their work should not be assessed by "universal" criteria, which in India carry the markers of caste and class. Furthermore, because Hindu religious literature has nourished the unequal caste system, Dalit writers deliberately reject the use of religious symbols except to deconstruct them or infuse them with new meaning and purpose (Limbale 34). The need for an accompanying Dalit aesthetics was first expressed in 1988 by Sharad Patil, who, drawing attention to Dalit reliance on brahmanical poetics, challenged Dalit writers to forge their own theoretical "weapon" (Patil 6; Limbale 113). Taking up this challenge, Omprakash Valmiki, Sharankumar Limbale, Raj Gowthaman, and other Dalit writers are trying to theorize Dalit writing as a distinct and different stream of Indian literature: an "artless art" that offers novel experiences, a new sensitivity, a distinct vocabulary, a different protagonist, and an alternate vision. In his pioneering work on Dalit aesthetics, Sharankumar Limbale asserts that modern Indian literary criticism, which is based primarily on Sanskrit or Western literary theories, cannot do justice to Dalit literature (106). In Limbale's view, Dalit literature does not adhere to classical Sanskrit aesthetics, according to which the purpose of art and literature is to give pleasure by evoking different emotions and feelings (pity, love, joy, fear, and anger, for instance). If pleasure provides the basis of the aesthetics of uppercaste literature, then pain or suffering, Limbale contends, is the basis for the aesthetics of Dalit literature: "it is a literature that is intended to make readers restless or angry" (115). Raj Gowthaman similarly describes Dalit aesthetics as characterized by protest, anger, roughness in language, and an attack on the icons and practices that marginalize Dalits. In its attempt to destabilize hegemonic literary discourse, Dalit literature, he suggests, ruptures both content and craft. It negates literary traditions, violates standardized grammar, and practices an aesthetics of violence – linguistic, generic, and narratalogical (Gowthaman 7–8). And when an artistic creation disturbs in this way, Limbale argues, "either its lack of artifice will become a minor issue or it will have to be acknowledged that this quality of 'artlessness' is, in fact, its artistic value" (108). Limbale also dismisses the efforts of some Indian theorists to accommodate the different experiences and emotions represented in Dalit writing by adding two new *rasas* – "revolt" and "cry" – to the traditional nine in Sanskrit poetics (love, laughter, compassion, fury, valor, horror, disgust, wonder, and tranquility). In his opinion, these efforts are "simply tantamount to proving the incompleteness of the *rasa* theory" in the first place (115).[22]

If classical Indian theory (Sanskrit poetics) cannot deal adequately with the peculiarities and particularities of Dalit writing, postmodern cultural theory, which is preoccupied with the instability of individual identity, seems even less applicable to a literature devoted to claiming and asserting a collective identity (see Krishnaswamy "Globalization"; and Mukherjee). Yet, as Alok Mukherjee notes, Dalit literature's commitment to collective identity also cannot be decoded as simply a "national allegory," because even though its protagonists tend to be representative, the life stories and struggles of these protagonists "do not engage exclusively with colonialism and imperialism but also with Indian society's internal contradictions" (Limbale 17). Theories associated with subaltern studies and postcolonial studies have not fared much better in their attempts to analyze or evaluate Dalit literature, in part because these theoretical models are dominated by the binary colonizer and colonized, and in part because they are overly reliant on a (postmodernist/poststructuralist) terminology of mobility and hybridity. Dalit literature complicates the binary world of colonizers and colonized by focusing on caste divisions within Indian society, exposing how a subjugated society can simultaneously be a subjugating society and how that subjugation can continue in a postcolonial independent India (A. Mukherjee 17). In fact, instead of categorically denouncing westernization and colonialism, Dalits have often selectively embraced modernity and sought colonial intervention. Dalit leaders such as Phule and Ambedkar did not give their support to the anticolonial nationalist movement automatically or unconditionally; instead, they were quite prepared to enter into strategic conversations with the colonial rulers in order to obtain remedies for centuries of caste oppression. As a result, both bourgeois liberal and Marxist nationalists accused them of complicity with the colonial power during and after independence. "Postcolonial thought, of whatever ideological hue," Alok Mukherjee observes, "has found it difficult to come to terms with this two-pronged move" (6). By refusing to abide by the binary of Indian/national vs Western/colonial, Ambedkar and other Dalit leaders were probably seeking the kind of hybridity and mobility that uppercaste nationalists had access to and that postcolonial theory now celebrates as subversive and liberatory. But they were forced to remain within the prison house of caste. So, in drawing attention to the persistence, even proliferation, of binary forms of (caste) identity under conditions of uneven globalization in India, Dalit literature is implicitly questioning the optimistic claims of hybridity and mobility in contemporary cultural theory.

According to leading Dalit theorists, what gives Dalit literature its unique power and force is "Dalit *chetna*" or Dalit consciousness (Limbale 116–117; Valmiki 31). Rooted in Ambdekarite thought, Dalit *chetna* infuses literature with a social purpose and a commitment to justice. As Limbale puts it, "that work of Dalit literature will be recognized as beautiful, and therefore 'good,' which causes the greatest awakening of Dalit consciousness in the reader" (117), a consciousness that, according to Valmiki and Limbale, defines and differentiates Dalit literature from other literatures.[23] Thus, they insist that, despite the revolutionary intent, and the fact that many of the *bhakti* poets were Dalits, *bhakti* literature neither expresses Dalit consciousness nor destroys the caste system. The spiritual terms and otherworldly concerns of *bhakti* poetry, Limbale contends, ultimately undermined its social criticism, gradually diluting its revolutionary message, which could then be domesticated and assimilated into dominant Hindu ideologies (49–51). In contrast, the aesthetics of contemporary Dalit literature, even though it originates in *bhakti*, is materialistic (Limbale 116). A more appropriate parallel to Dalit literature, Limbale believes, can be found in African-American literature: the first expressions of both were spiritual in form (87); both consider literature as an important weapon in the effort to achieve freedom and so give primacy to revolt (98); and because both literatures originate in social inequality, they require a form of criticism that includes sociological perspectives (99). Comments such as these expose new and different literary affiliations that go beyond simplistic oppositions between East and West or colonizer and colonized; indeed, they point us toward a transnational comparative study of trauma and apartheid narratives that may provide the basis for articulating an aesthetics of discrimination and dissent.[24]

New Beginnings

The case for expanding the field of literary theory to non-Western poetics, criticisms, and commentaries, for moving away from the received notion of explicit poetics toward an alternative conception of "world literary knowledges" that includes "latent" and "emergent" epistemologies, obviously goes far beyond the pressing practical problems of pedagogy in world literature classes. After all, critical standards derived from one literary tradition may or may not be applicable to another (even though this has not prevented anyone from applying Western standards to non-Western literatures); criticism of particular writers and texts may or may not be meaningful to those who cannot read them in the original language, and so on. But there can be little doubt that at the level of epistemology the comparative study of different literary traditions can expand our common storehouse of aesthetic concepts and produce important insights about the nature of literature/literariness and the ways in which different societies/cultures view these categories. It also may lead us to discover what aesthetic concepts are universal, what concepts are limited to certain cultural traditions, and what concepts are unique to a particular tradition. We may likewise find that some literary features are common or shared by all languages, that some are limited to literatures written in certain languages, and that some are unique to a particular linguistic or literary tradition. These and other (unforeseen, unforeseeable) discoveries may further enable us to craft a more thoughtful response to the question of universals than the one we have at present (a hasty abandonment of all universals as always already oppressive and an equally hasty embrace of cultural relativism as always already emancipatory).[25] In a new field where basic research and scholarship is yet to be undertaken, it makes good sense to start out with an open mind about methodologies, at least until we are in a position to make more informed choices. As such, we may well have to entertain the possibility that the study of "world literary knowledges" will support projects grounded in positivistic, empirical, materialistic thought, as well as those grounded in more anti-positivitistic, deconstructive, or hermeneutical thinking. When pursued in this open-ended and egalitarian way, the study of world literary knowledges could globalize the field of literary theory in a way that would also make the study of world literatures both intellectually rigorous and ethically grounded.

Notes

1 For Hogan's own account of this experience, see "Ethnocentrism" 1–14.
2 These comments relate to the 2001 (first) edition of the Norton anthology only.
3 My terminology ("dominant," "emergent," "latent") is obviously drawn from Raymond Williams, although I use it more suggestively than systematically. Among the suggestive corollaries left unexplored here are the possibilities that both "emergent" and "latent" epistemologies may be either "alternative" or "oppositional," that "latent" theories could be "residual," and so on.
4 For a helpful analysis of different practices in world literature courses, see Lawall.
5 On the methods by which Rushdie's magical realism is assimilated into Western theories of postmodernism, see Sangari, and Krishnaswamy "Mythologies of Migrancy." On the ways in which Jameson's theory of allegory reductively reads the third world in terms of the first, see Ahmad. Spivak discusses the problem of assimilation in "Can the Subaltern Speak?"
6 For an extended discussion of the vexing problem of "unity in diversity" as it relates to (comparative) Indian literature(s), see Ahmad, and Dev.
7 For a Dalit critique of this project, see Satyanarayana; for a feminist critique, see Tharu, and Tharu and Lalita. Another useful analysis can be found in Trivedi.
8 It is also worth noting that only twenty-five are women, and only two of these appear before the twentieth century. Norton has of course published a separate anthology of feminist theory and criticism, but it is likewise dominated by the West; only toward the second half of the twentieth century do names of minority/third-world critics begin to appear on the list.

9   In the second edition of the Norton anthology (2010), which appeared just after this essay was completed, the editors have tried to expand the non-Western component by adding four more theorists to the modern period: C.D. Narasimhaiah (India), Li Zehou (China), Kojin Karatani (Japan), and Paul Gilroy ("Black Atlantic"). While this is indeed a welcome move, these additions still fall into the predictable (and contemporary) categories of transnational black/race studies, nationalistic revivals of indigenous classical traditions, and East–West studies.

10 Reacting to this kind of thinking, the nineteenth-century Indian Sanskritist R.G. Bhandarkar commented caustically: "there are very important branches of Sanskrit literature which are not understood in Germany and Europe … it appeared to me that works in the narrative or Puranic style and the dramatic plays were alone properly understood in Europe, while those written in the style of discourse or works of philosophy and exegesis were not" (qtd. in Staal 86–87).

11 Examples include Ludescher, Matar, Zhang, Pan, Pandit, and Lehmann, as well as all of the essays in Hogan and Pandit; see also Krishnaswamy, "Nineteenth-century Language Ideology."

12 As Patrick Hogan shows ("Beauty" 6–8), several essays in the Dimock *et al.* collection indulge in this kind of contrastive analysis. Pandit's attempt to link the Sanskrit concept of *dhvani* (suggestion) with Lacanian theory ("Dhvani and the 'Full Word'") and Kashnabish's attempt to synthesize Irigaray's *jouissance* with Sri Aurobindo Ghosh's *ananda* in order to define the "political sublime" stand out as refreshing departures from this trend.

13 Responding to the Bernheimer report, Rey Chow argues that if we "simply substitute India, China, and Japan for England, France, and Germany," the concept of literature is still "strictly subordinated to a social Darwinian understanding of the nation: 'masterpieces' correspond to 'master' nations and 'master' cultures. With India, China, and Japan being held as representative of Asia, cultures of lesser prominence in Western reception such as Korea, Taiwan, Vietnam, Tibet, and others simply fall by the wayside – as marginalized 'others' to the 'other' that is the 'great' Asian civilization" (109). This process is at work not only at the international level but also at the intra-national level, as my discussion of the Indian context here confirms.

14 For the application of Sanskrit poetics to Western texts, see Pandit "Patriarchy and Paranoia" and "Non-Western Literary Theories." For an attempt to compare Sanskrit poetics and New Criticism, see C.D. Narasimhaiah. Ramanujan's application of terms from Tamil poetics (*akam/puram*) to ancient Tamil poetry is an instance of this kind of restricted application (262–269).

15 Indeed, a few Tamil scholars (Pannikar; the essays collected in Selvamony, Nirmal, Nirmaldasan, and Rayson) draw on the concept of *tinai* to theorize the global and the planetary. Linking *tinai* with *oikos* (habitat), Selvamony attempts to develop a form of ecocriticism or "oikopoetics" (see "Oikopoetics" in Selvamony, Nirmal, and Nirmaldasan).

16 For an extended discussion of Sri Aurobindo Ghosh's literary criticism, including his use of Sanskrit poetics, see (in addition to Devy) Narasimhaiah. Whereas Narasimhaiah praises Aurobindo for reviving Sanskrit poetics, Devy argues that Aurobindo is a "colonial critic," whose attempt to synthesize the High Sanskrit tradition with English Romantic aesthetics in order to inaugurate a new system of poetics is motivated by an elitist form of nationalism (112–116).

17   The undifferentiated cultural formation commonly referred to as "bhakti" not only spans centuries but is also ideologically diverse. On the one hand, it includes texts that are composed in Sanskrit and quite conservative on matters of caste and gender (the *Bhagavad Gita*, for example). Aspects of (Ram) *bhakti* have also been co-opted by Hindu fundamentalism in recent years. On the other hand, there are also texts within the larger Sanskrit tradition (Vedantic works like the *Brhadaranyaka Upanishad*; the *Yoga Sutra*) that contest social hierarchies, even though the Sanskrit Ritual School tends to be quite rigid and conservative. In this essay I focus rather selectively on certain oppositional strands of *bhakti* in order to identify their literary practices as latent sources of literary knowledge.

18   Ramanujan also notes that *vacana* means prose, for poetry was associated with the Sanskritic status quo (37).

19   This and other aspects of *bhakti* may be fruitfully compared to other mystic traditions including Islamic and Christian ones.

20   *Bhakti* poetry remains the bedrock of popular cultural consciousness and artistic expression in all the regional languages of India, and no classical Indian musician's or dancer's repertoire is complete without the compositions of the *bhakti* poets. Although important *bhakti* works were composed in the colonial period (the nineteenth-century compositions of Annamayya, Thyagaraja, and others are central to Carnatic music), they cannot simply be explained in terms of colonialism/nationalism.

21   Gita Hariharan retrieves the oppositional literary politics and liberatory erotics of medieval *bhakti* to critique present-day Hindu fundamentalism and its distorted cultural politics in her recent novel *In Times of Siege*.

22   Thatte, Jawdekar, and others, however, contend that there is no reason for *rasa* theory to be discarded when it can be revised and improved to account for Dalit aesthetics.

23   For an extended analysis of the origins of Dalit *chetna*, see Zelliot; for Dalit *chetna* within literary criticism, see Brueck. For a heated debate over whether "Dalit" denotes an essential identity based on birth and the experience of untouchability (i.e., only Dalits can produce Dalit literature and Dalit *chetna*) or represents a critical perspective that even non-Dalits can consciously adopt (like feminism), see Rawat and the essays in Rao.

24   Ashis Nandy has suggested that suffering could serve as the basis for an ethical transnationalism or cosmopolitanism (440–460). Dalit literature, along with other trauma/apartheid texts, could provide a literary archive for such a project.

25   Breaking with the deconstructive mode of much postcolonial criticism, Satya Mohanty draws on the Chomskyan notion of universal grammar to argue that "unless we come up with some common criteria by which to judge or evaluate right and wrong, good and bad, in cultures and literatures, we may avoid ethnocentric errors, but we have also by the same logic precluded … disagreement about the way the world is or about the right course of action in a particular situation" (*Literary Theory* 144). Building on Mohanty's ideas, Esha Niyogi De has suggested that, despite a strong "strain of male nationalist nostalgia," Rabindranath Tagore's concepts of *milan, samanjasya* and *sahit* – concord, harmony, and harmony building – contain the seeds for a universalist poetics (48).

Works Cited

Ahmad, Aijaz. *In Theory: Classes, Nations, Literatures*. London: Verso, 1992.

Apter, Emily. "Je ne crois pas beaucoup a la littérature comparée: Universal Poetics and Postcolonial Comparatism." Saussy 54–62.

Bassnett, Susan. *Comparative Literature: A Critical Introduction* Oxford: Blackwell, 1993.

Baucom, Ian. "Globalit, Inc.: or, The Cultural Logic of Global Literature Studies." Gunn 158–172.

Bernheimer, Charles, ed. *Comparative Literature in the Age of Multiculturalism*. Baltimore: Johns Hopkins University Press, 1993.

Brueck, Laura R. "Dalit Chetna in Dalit Literary Criticism." *Seminar* 558 (February 2006). <http://www.india-seminar.com/2006/558.htm>.

Chakrabarty, Dipesh. *Provincializing Europe: Postcolonial Thought and Historical Difference.* Princeton: Princeton University Press, 2000.

Chatterjee, Partha. *Nationalist Thought and the Colonial World: A Derivative Discourse.* Minneapolis: University of Minnesota Press, 1986.

Chen, Peng-hsiang. "Theory and Practice in the Development of Chinese-Western Comparative Literature." *Asian Culture* 17 (1993): 14–31.

Chow, Rey. "How (the) Inscrutable Chinese Led to Globalized Theory." Gunn 69–74.

Chow, Rey. "In the Name of Comparative Literature." Bernheimer 109.

Chow, Rey. "The Old/New Question of Comparison in Literary Studies: A Post-European Perspective." *ELH* 71.2 (2004): 289–311.

Cohn, Bernard. *Colonialism and Its Forms of Knowledge: The British in India*. Princeton: Princeton University Press, 1966.

Cooppan, Vilashini. "Ghosts in the Disciplinary Machine: The Uncanny Life of World Literature." *Comparative Literature Studies* 41.1 (2004): 10–36.

Cooppan, Vilashini. "World Literature and Global Theory: Comparative Literature for the New Millenium." *Symplokē* (2001): 15–43.

Damrosch, David. "Comparative Literature?" *PMLA* 118 (2003): 326–330.

Damrosch, David. *What Is World Literature?* Princeton: Princeton University Press, 2003.

Damrosch, David. "World Literature in a Postcanonical, Hypercanonical Age." Saussy 43–53.

Damrosch, David. "World Literature, National Contexts." Special Centennial Issue on World Literature. Ed. Richard Maxwell, Joshua Scodel, and Katie Trumpener. *Modern Philology* 100.4 (2003): 512–531.

Das, Sisir Kumar. *A History of Indian Literature 1800–1910, Western Impact, Indian Response.* New Delhi: Sahitya Akademi, 1991.

Das, Sisir Kumar. *A History of Indian Literature: 1911–1956, Struggle for Freedom, Triumph and Tragedy*. New Delhi: Sahitya Akademi, 1995.

Das, Sisir Kumar. *A History of Indian Literature: 500–1399, From the Courtly to the Popular*. New Delhi: Sahitya Akademi, 2005.

Das, Sisir Kumar. "Why Comparative Indian Literature?" *Comparative Literature: Theory and Practice*. Ed. Amiya Dev and Sisir Kumar Das. Shimla: Indian Institute of Advanced Study, 1989. 94–103.

De, Esha Niyogi. "Decolonizing Universality: Postcolonial Theory and the Quandary of Ethical Agency." *Diacritics* 32.2 (2002): 42–59.

Delbanco, Andrew. "The Decline and Fall of Literature." *New York Review of Books* 4 Nov. 1999: 32–38.

Dev, Amiya. "Comparative Literature in India." *Comparative Literature and Comparative Cultural Studies*. Ed. Steven Tötösy de Zepetnek. Purdue: Purdue University Press, 2003. 23–33.

Devy. G. N. *After Amnesia: Tradition and Change in Indian Literary Criticism*. Hyderabad: Orient Longman, 1992.

Dimock, E., E. Gerow, C. Naim, A. Ramanujan, G. Roadarmel, and J. van Buitenen. *The Literatures of India: An Introduction*. Chicago: University of Chicago Press, 1978.

Dimock, Wai Chee. "Literature for the Planet." Gunn 173–188.

Eagleton, Terry. *Literary Theory: An Introduction*. Oxford: Oxford University Press, 1983.

Elliott, Emory. "Cultural Diversity and the Problem of Aesthetics." *Aesthetics in a Multicultural Age*. Ed. Emory Elliott, Louis Freitas Caton, and Jeffrey Rhyne. Oxford University Press, 2002. 3–30.

Ghosh, Sri Aurobindo. *The Future of Poetry*. Pondicherry: Birth Centenary Library, 1972.

Gunn, Giles, ed. *Globalizing Literary Studies*. Spec. issue of *PMLA* 116 (2001): 1–272.

Hariharan, Gita. *In Times of Seige*. New Delhi: Penguin India, 2003.

Hart, George. "Archetypes in Classical Indian Literature and Beyond." *Syllables of Sky*. Ed. David Shulman. Oxford University Press, 1996. 165–77.

Hogan, Patrick Colm. "Beauty, Politics, and Cultural Otherness: The Bias of Literary Difference." *Literary India: Comparative Studies in Aesthetics, Colonialism, and Culture*. Ed. Patrick Hogan and Lalita Pandit. Albany: SUNY Press, 1995. 3–43.

Hogan, Patrick Colm. "Ethnocentrism and the Very Idea of Literary Theory." Hogan and Pandit 1–14.

Hogan, Patrick Colm, and Lalita Pandit, eds. *Comparative Poetics: Non-Western Traditions of Literary Theory*. Spec. issue of *College Literature* 23.1 (1996): 1–237.

Jawdekar, Acharya. "The 10th Rasa." *Yugvani* (April-June 1987): 3–10.

Jones, Sir William. *The Works of Sir William Jones*. Vol. 4. Ed. Anna Maria Jones. London: John Stockdale and John Walker, 1807.

Kadir, Djelal. "Comparative Literature in an Age of Terrorism." Saussy 68–77.

Kadir, Djelal. "To World, To Globalize: Comparative Literature's Crossroads." *Comparative Literature Studies* 41.1 (2001): 1–9.

Khashnabish, Ashmita. *Jouissance as Ananda: Indian Philosophy, Feminist Theory, and Literature*. Lanham: Lexington Books, 2003.

Kripalani, Krishna. "Criteria of Literary Criticism in India." *The Idea of an Indian Literature: A Book of Readings*. Ed. Sujit Mukherjee. Mysore: Central Institute of Indian Languages, 1981.

Krishnaswamy, Revathi. "Globalization and Its Postcolonial (Dis)Contents: Reading Dalit Literature." *Journal of Postcolonial Writing* 41.1 (2005): 69–82.

Krishnaswamy, Revathi. "Mythologies of Migrancy." *Ariel* 26 (1995): 125–46.

Krishnaswamy, Revathi. "Nineteenth-Century Language Ideology: A Postcolonial Perspective." *Interventions* 7 (2005): 43–71.

Krishnaswamy, Revathi. "Subversive Spirituality: Woman as Saint-Poet in Medieval India." *Women's Studies International Forum* 16.2 (1993): 139–147.

Kumar, Amitava, ed. *World Bank Literature*. Minneapolis: University of Minnesota Press, 2003.

Lawall, Sarah. "Shifting Paradigms in World Literature." *ACLA Bulletin* 24 (1993): 11–28.

Limbale, Sharankumar. *Toward an Aesthetics of Dalit Literature*. Trans. Alok Mukherjee. New Delhi: Orient Longman, 2004.

Lionnet, Francoise. "Cultivating Mere Gardens? Comparative Francophonies, Postcolonial Studies, and Transnational Freminisms." Saussy 100–113.

Mignolo, Walter. "Globalization and the Geopolitics of Knowledge." *Neplanta: Views from the South* 4.1 (2003): 97–119.

Mohanty, Satya. "Can Our Values Be Objective? On Ethics, Aesthetics, and Progressive Politics." *Aesthetics in a Multicultural Age*. Ed. Emory Eliott, Louis Freitas Caton, and Jeffrey Rhyne. Oxford: Oxford University Press, 2002. 31–60.

Mohanty, Satya. *Literary Theory and the Claims of History: Postmodernism, Objectivity, and Multicultural Politics*. Ithaca: Cornell University Press, 1997.

Moretti, Franco. "Conjectures on World Literature." *New Left Review* 1 (2000): 54–68.

Moretti, Franco. "The Slaughterhouse of Literature." *Modern Language Quarterly* 61 (2000): 207–227.

Mukherjee, Alok. Translator's Introduction to Sharankumar Limbale's *Toward an Aesthetics of Dalit Literature*. New Delhi: Orient Longman, 2004. 1–17.

Mukherjee, Sujit. *The Idea of Indian Literatures: A Book of Readings*. Mysore: Central Institute of Indian Languages, 1981.

Mukherjee, Sujit. *Toward a Literary History of India*. Simla: Indian Institute of Advanced Study, 1995.

Mukherjee, Sujit, and D.V.K. Raghavacharyulu, eds. *Indian Essays in American Literature*. Bombay: Popular Prakashan, 1968.

Nandy, Ashis. *Bonfire of Creeds: The Essential Ashis Nandy*. New Delhi: Oxford University Press, 2004.

Narasimhaiah, C.D. "New Criticism: An Assessment." Mukherjee and Raghavacharyulu 267–284.

The Norton Anthology of Theory and Criticism. Ed. Vincent Leitch, William Cain, Laurie Finke, Barbara Johnson, John McGowan, and Jeffrey Williams. New York: W.W. Norton, 2001.

Pandit, Lalita. "Dhvani and the 'Full Word': Suggestion and Signification from Abhinavagupta to Jacques Lacan." Hogan and Pandit 142–163.

Pandit, Lalita. "Non-Western Literary Theories and What to Do with Them." Hogan and Pandit 179–190.

Pandit, Lalita. "Patriarchy and Paranoia: Imaginary Infidelity in *Uttararamacharita and The Winter's Tale*." *Literary India: Comparative Studies in Aesthetics, Colonialism, and Culture*. Ed. Patrick Hogan and Lalita Pandit. Albany: SUNY Press, 1995. 103–134.

Panniker, Aiyappa. *Interiorization: Essays on Literary Theory*. Trans. Krishna Rajan. Thiruvanandapuram: ICKS Press, 2000.

Patil, Sharad. *Abrahmani Sahityanche Saundaryashastra*. Pune: Sugawa Prakashan, 1988.

Patil, Sharad. "Like a River Fed by Many a Stream: Reflections on the Confluence of Cultures." 19th Sahitya Akademi Samvatsar lecture. <http://www.ayappapanikar.net/profile/works/samvatsar-lecture.htm>. October 2008.

Ramanujan. A. K. *Interior Landscapes: Love Poems from a Classical Tamil Anthology*. Bloomington: Indiana University Press, 1967.

Rao, Anupama, ed. *Gender and Caste: Issues in Contemporary Indian Feminism*. New Delhi: Kali for Women, 2003.

Rawat, Ramnarayan S. "The Problem." *Seminar* 558 (2006). <http://www.India seminar.com/2006/558.htm>.

Said, Edward. "'East Isn't East': The Impending End of the Age of Orientalism." *Times Literary Supplement* 3 Feb. 1995: 3.

Said, Edward. *Orientalism*. New York: Vintage, 1979.

Sangari, Kumkum. "The Politics of the Possible." *Cultural Critique* 7 (1987): 157–186.

Satyanarayana, K. *Nation, Literary History and the Lens of Caste: Dalit Reconfigurations of Modernity*. Diss. Central Institute of English and Foreign Languages, Hyderabad, India, 2007.

Saussy, Haun, ed. *Comparative Literature in an Age of Globalization*. Baltimore: Johns Hopkins University Press, 2006. 1–261.

Saussy, Haun. "Exquisite Cadavers Stitched from Fresh Nightmares." Saussy 3–42.

Selvamony, Nirmal, and Nirmaldasan (N. Watson Soloman), eds. *Tinai* 1–3. Occasional literary miscellany published by Madras Christian College. http://www.angelfire.com/nd/nirmaldasan/tinai.html. October 2008.

Selvamony, Nirmal, Nirmaldasan (N. Watson Soloman), and Rayson K. Alex, eds. *Essays in Ecocriticism*. Chennai and Delhi: OSLE-India and Swarup and Sons, 2007.

Shih, Shu-mei. "Global Literature and the Technologies of Recognition." *PMLA* 119 (2004): 16–30.

Sivathamby, K. "Early South Indian Society and Economy: The Tinai Concept." *Social Scientist* 3.5 (1974): 20–37.

Smith, Linda Tuhiwai. *Decolonizing Methodologies: Research and Indigenous Peoples*. London: Zed Books, 1999.

Speaking of Siva. Trans. A.K. Ramanujan. Harmondsworth: Penguin Books, 1973.

Spivak, Gayatri. "Can the Subaltern Speak?" *Marxism and the Interpretation of Cultures*. Ed. Cary Nelson and Lawrence Grossberg. Urbana: University of Illinois Press, 1988. 271–313.

Spivak, Gayatri. *Death of a Discipline*. New York: Columbia University Press, 2003.

Spivak, Gayatri. "A New Comparative Literature." New Institutional Forms of Comparison panel, MLA Annual Convention. Philadelphia, 29 Dec. 2004.

Staal, J. F., ed. *A Reader on the Sanskrit Grammarians*. Cambridge: MIT Press, 1972.

Tharu, Susie. "The Arrangement of an Alliance: English and the Making of Indian Literatures." *Rethinking English: Essays in Literature, Language, History*. Ed. Svati Joshi. Bombay: Oxford University Press, 1994. 160–180.

Tharu, Susie, and K. Lalita. "Empire, Nation and the Literary Text." *Interrogating Modernity: Culture and Colonialism in India*. Ed. Tejaswini Niranjana, R. Sudhir, and Vivek Dhareshwar. Calcutta: Seagull, 1993. 199–219.

Thatte, Yadunath. "The 11th Rasa." *Yugvani* (April-June 1990): 2–9.

Tolkappiyam. Trans. V. Murugan. Chennai: Institute of Asian Studies, 2001.

Tötösy de Zepetnek, Steven. *Comparative Literature: Theory, Method, Application*. Amsterdam: Rodopi, 1998.

Trivedi, Harish. "Theorizing the Nation: Constructions of 'India' and 'Indian Literature.'" *Indian Literature* 160 (1994): 31–45.

Valmiki, Omprakash. *Dalit Sahitya ka Saundaryashastra*. Delhi: Radhakrishna, 2001.

Viswanathan, Gauri. *Masks of Conquest: Literary Study and British Rule in India*. New York: Columbia University Press, 1989.

When God Is a Customer: Telugu Courtesan Songs by Ksetrayya and Others. Ed. and trans. A. K. Ramajunan, Velcheru Narayanaravu, and David Shulman. Berkeley: University of California Press, 1994.

Wilson, H. H. *Essays: Analytical, Critical and Philosophical Subjects Connected with Sanskrit Literature*. London: Trubner, 1864.

Yokota-Murakami, Takayuki. *Don Juan East/West: On the Problematics of Comparative Literature*. Albany: SUNY Press, 1998.

Yu, Pauline. "Alienation Effects: Comparative Literature and the Chinese Tradition." *The Comparative Perspective on Literature: Approaches to Theory and Practice*. Ed. Clayton Koelb and Susan Noakes. Ithaca: Cornell University Press, 1988. 162–176.

Zhang Longxi. *Mighty Opposites: From Dichotomies to Differences in the Comparative Study of China*. Stanford: Stanford University Press, 1998.

Zhang Longxi. "Penser d'un dehors: Notes on the 2004 ACLA Report." Saussy 230–236.

Zhang Longxi. "What Is Wen and Why Is It made So Terribly Strange?" Hogan and Pandit 15–35.

Zelliot, Eleanor. "The Roots of Dalit Consciousness." *Seminar* 471 (1998): 28–32.

12

Conjectures on World Literature (2000) *and* More Conjectures (2003)

Franco Moretti

An expert in modern European literature with a special focus on the novel and on narrative and genre theory, Franco Moretti is professor of English and Comparative Literature at Stanford University and founder of Stanford's Center for the Study of the Novel. Educated at the University of Rome, he taught first in Italy and then at Columbia University before moving to Stanford. Following an influential early book on politics and aesthetics, *Signs Taken for Wonders* (1983), Moretti began to study the politics of global aesthetics. He was drawn to the world systems theory of the sociologist Immanuel Wallerstein, and builds on this theoretical approach in *The Modern Epic: The World System from Goethe to García Márquez* (1998). Increasingly, Moretti has combined world-systems theory with a Darwinian perspective, and has sought to understand literary processes on a grand scale.

In the influential pair of essays given here, and in a subsequent book, *Graphs, Maps, Trees: Abstract Models for a Literary History* (2005), Moretti argues that large movements such as the rise and spread of the novel can best be studied by using a method that he calls "distant reading." Unlike its American opposite, the "close reading" of a relatively small number of canonical works, "distant reading" can survey large-scale trends to account for the historical evolution of the world literary system, mapping literary space using statistical data to explain the circulation of literature and literary influences. Moretti sees the world's literary system as "one, but unequal," with powerful literary forms such as the novel moving from the centers of cultural authority outward to peripheral and semi-peripheral regions. Moretti argues that this movement entails "a compromise between foreign form and local materials." In the process, the form of the novel becomes a mirror for the

Franco Moretti, "Conjectures on World Literature" (2000). In *New Left Review* 1 (Jan./Feb. 2000), pp. 1–12.

World Literature in Theory, First Edition. Edited by David Damrosch.

functioning of the world literary system itself; Moretti thus turns his formal analysis into an analysis of symbolic power.

Conjectures on World Literature (2000)

'Nowadays, national literature doesn't mean much: the age of world literature is beginning, and everybody should contribute to hasten its advent.' This was Goethe, of course, talking to Eckermann in 1827; and these are Marx and Engels, twenty years later, in 1848: 'National one-sidedness and narrow-mindedness become more and more impossible, and from the many national and local literatures, a world literature arises.' *Weltliteratur*: this is what Goethe and Marx have in mind. Not 'comparative', but world literature: the Chinese novel that Goethe was reading at the time of that exchange, or the bourgeoisie of the *Manifesto*, which has 'given a cosmopolitan character to production and consumption in every country'. Well, let me put it very simply: comparative literature has not lived up to these beginnings. It's been a much more modest intellectual enterprise, fundamentally limited to Western Europe, and mostly revolving around the river Rhine (German philologists working on French literature). Not much more.

This is my own intellectual formation, and scientific work always has limits. But limits change, and I think it's time we returned to that old ambition of *Weltliteratur*: after all, the literature around us is now unmistakably a planetary system. The question is not really *what* we should do – the question is *how*. What does it mean, studying world literature? How do we do it? I work on West European narrative between 1790 and 1930, and already feel like a charlatan outside of Britain or France. World literature?

Many people have read more and better than I have, of course, but still, we are talking of hundreds of languages and literatures here. Reading 'more' seems hardly to be the solution. Especially because we've just started rediscovering what Margaret Cohen calls the 'great unread'. 'I work on West European narrative, etc.…' Not really, I work on its canonical fraction, which is not even one per cent of published literature. And again, some people have read more, but the point is that there are thirty thousand nineteenth-century British novels out there, forty, fifty, sixty thousand – no one really knows, no one has read them, no one ever will. And then there are French novels, Chinese, Argentinian, American…

Reading 'more' is always a good thing, but not the solution.[1]

Perhaps it's too much, tackling the world and the unread at the same time. But I actually think that it's our greatest chance, because the sheer enormity of the task makes it clear that world literature cannot be literature, bigger; what we are already doing, just more of it. It has to be different. The *categories* have to be different. 'It is not the "actual" interconnection of "things"', Max Weber wrote, 'but the *conceptual* interconnection of *problems* which define the scope of the various sciences. A new "science" emerges where a new problem is pursued by a new method.'[2] That's the point: world literature is not an object, it's a *problem*, and a problem that asks for a new critical method: and no one has ever found a method by just reading more texts. That's not how theories come into being; they need a leap, a wager – a hypothesis, to get started.

World Literature: One and Unequal

I will borrow this initial hypothesis from the world-system school of economic history, for which international capitalism is a system that is simultaneously *one*, and *unequal*: with a core, and a periphery (and a semiperiphery) that are bound together in a relationship of growing inequality. One, and unequal: *one* literature (*Weltliteratur*, singular, as in Goethe and Marx), or perhaps, better, one world literary system (of inter-related literatures); but a system which is different from what Goethe and Marx had hoped for, because it's profoundly unequal. 'Foreign debt is as inevitable in Brazilian letters as in any other field', writes Roberto Schwarz in a splendid essay on 'The Importing of the Novel to Brazil': 'it's not simply an easily dispensable part of the work in which it appears, but a complex feature of it';[3] and Itamar Even-Zohar, reflecting on Hebrew literature: 'Interference [is] a relationship between literatures, whereby a ... source literature may become a source of direct or indirect loans [*Importing* of the novel, direct and indirect loans, foreign debt: see how economic metaphors have been subterraneously at work in literary history] – a source of loans for...a target literature ... *There is no symmetry in literary interference. A target literature is, more often than not, interfered with by a source literature which completely ignores it.*'[4]

This is what one and unequal means: the destiny of a culture (usually a culture of the periphery, as Montserrat Iglesias Santos has specified)[5] is intersected and altered by another culture (from the core) that 'completely ignores it'. A familiar scenario, this asymmetry in international power – and later I will say more about Schwarz's 'foreign debt' as a complex literary feature. Right now, let me spell out the consequences of taking an explanatory matrix from social history and applying it to literary history.

Distant Reading

Writing about comparative social history, Marc Bloch once coined a lovely 'slogan', as he himself called it: 'years of analysis for a day of synthesis';[6] and if you read Braudel or Wallerstein you immediately see what Bloch had in mind. The text which is strictly Wallerstein's, his 'day of synthesis', occupies one third of a page, one fourth, maybe half; the rest are quotations (fourteen hundred, in the first volume of *The Modern World-System*). Years of analysis; other people's analysis, which Wallerstein's page synthesizes into a system.

Now, if we take this model seriously, the study of world literature will somehow have to reproduce this 'page' – which is to say: this relationship between analysis and synthesis – for the literary field. But in that case, literary history will quickly become very different from what it is now: it will become 'second hand': a patchwork of other people's research, *without a single direct textual reading*. Still ambitious, and actually even more so than before (world literature!); but the ambition is now directly proportional *to the distance from the text*: the more ambitious the project, the greater must the distance be.

The United States is the country of close reading, so I don't expect this idea to be particularly popular. But the trouble with close reading (in all of its incarnations, from the new criticism to deconstruction) is that it necessarily depends on an extremely small canon. This may have become an unconscious and invisible premiss by now, but it is an iron one nonetheless: you invest so much in individual texts *only* if you think that very few of them really matter. Otherwise, it doesn't make sense. And if you want to look beyond the canon (and of course, world literature will do so: it would be absurd if it didn't!) close reading will not do it. It's not designed to do it, it's designed to do the opposite. At bottom, it's a theological exercise – very solemn treatment of very few texts taken very seriously – whereas what we really need is a little pact with the devil: we know how to read texts, now let's learn how *not* to read them. Distant reading: where distance, let me repeat it, *is a condition of knowledge*: it allows you to focus on units that are much smaller or much larger than the text: devices, themes, tropes – or genres and systems. And if, between the very small and the very large, the text itself disappears, well, it is one of those cases when one can justifiably say, Less is more. If we want to understand the system in its entirety, we must accept losing something. We always pay a price for theoretical knowledge: reality is infinitely rich; concepts are abstract, are poor. But it's precisely this 'poverty' that makes it possible to handle them, and therefore to know. This is why less is actually more.[7]

The Western European Novel: Rule or Exception?

Let me give you an example of the conjunction of distant reading and world literature. An example, not a model; and of course my example, based on the field I know (elsewhere, things may be very different). A few years ago, introducing Kojin Karatani's *Origins of Modern Japanese Literature*, Fredric Jameson noticed that in the take-off of the modern Japanese novel, 'the raw material of Japanese social experience and the abstract formal patterns of Western novel construction cannot always be welded together seamlessly'; and he referred in this respect to Masao Miyoshi's *Accomplices of Silence*, and Meenakshi Mukherjee's *Realism and Reality* (a study of the early Indian novel).[8] And it's true, these books return quite often to the complicated 'problems' (Mukherjee's term) arising from the encounter of western form and Japanese or Indian reality.

Now, that the same configuration should occur in such different cultures as India and Japan – this was curious; and it became even more curious when I realized that Roberto Schwarz had independently discovered very much the same pattern in Brazil. So, eventually, I started using these pieces of evidence to reflect on the relationship between markets and forms; and then, without really knowing what I was doing, began to treat Jameson's insight as if it were – one should always be cautious with these claims, but there is really no other way to say it – as if it were a *law of literary evolution*: in cultures that belong to the periphery of the literary system (which means: almost all cultures, inside and outside Europe), the modern novel first arises not as an autonomous development but as a compromise between a western formal influence (usually French or English) and local materials.

This first idea expanded into a little cluster of laws,[9] and it was all very interesting, but … it was still just an idea; a conjecture that had to be tested, possibly on a large scale, and so I decided to follow the wave of diffusion of the modern novel (roughly: from 1750 to 1950) in the pages of literary history. Gasperetti and Goscilo on late eighteenth-century Eastern Europe;[10] Toschi and Martí-López on early nineteenth-century Southern Europe;[11] Franco and Sommer on mid-century Latin America;[12] Frieden on the Yiddish novels of the 1860s;[13] Moosa, Said and Allen on the Arabic novels of the 1870s;[14] Evin and Parla on the Turkish novels of the same years;[15] Anderson on the Filipino *Noli Me Tangere*, of 1887; Zhao and Wang on turn-of-the-century Qing fiction;[16] Obiechina, Irele and Quayson on West African novels between the 1920s and the 1950s[17] (plus of course Karatani, Miyoshi, Mukherjee, Even-Zohar and Schwarz). Four continents, two hundred years, over twenty independent critical studies, and they all agreed: when a culture starts moving towards the modern novel, it's *always* as a compromise between foreign form and local materials. Jameson's 'law' had passed the test – the first test, anyway.[18, 19] And actually more than that: it had completely reversed the received historical explanation of these matters: because if the compromise between the foreign and the local is so ubiquitous, then those independent paths that are usually taken to be the rule of the rise of the novel (the Spanish, the French, and especially the British case) – *well, they're not the rule at all, they're the exception*. They come first, yes, but they're not at all typical. The 'typical' rise of the novel is Krasicki, Kemal, Rizal, Maran – not Defoe.

Experiments with History

See the beauty of distant reading plus world literature: they go against the grain of national historiography. And they do so in the form of *an experiment*. You define a unit of analysis (like here, the formal compromise),[20] and then follow its metamorphoses in a variety of environments[21] – until, ideally, *all* of literary history becomes a long chain of related experiments: a 'dialogue between fact and fancy', as Peter Medawar calls it: 'between what could be true, and what is in fact the case'.[22] Apt words for this research, in the course of which, as I was reading my fellow historians, it became clear that the encounter of western forms and local reality did indeed produce everywhere a structural compromise – as the law predicted – but also, that the compromise itself was taking rather different forms. At times, especially in the second half of the nineteenth century and in Asia, it tended to be very unstable:[23] an 'impossible program', as Miyoshi says of Japan.[24] At other times it was not so: at the beginning and at the end of the wave, for instance (Poland, Italy and Spain at one extreme; and West Africa on the other), historians describe novels that had, certainly, their own problems – but not problems arising from the clash of irreconcilable elements.[25]

I hadn't expected such a spectrum of outcomes, so at first I was taken aback, and only later realized that this was probably the most valuable finding of them all, because it showed that world literature was indeed a system – but a system *of variations*. The system was one, not uniform. The pressure from the Anglo-French core *tried* to make it uniform, but it could never fully erase the reality of difference. (See here, by the way, how the study of world literature is – inevitably – a study of the struggle for symbolic hegemony across the world.) The system was one, not uniform. And, retrospectively, of course it had to be like this: if after 1750 the novel arises just about everywhere as a compromise between West European patterns and local reality – well, local reality was different in the various places, just as western influence was also very uneven: much stronger in Southern Europe around 1800, to return to my example, than in West Africa around 1940. The forces in play kept changing, and so did the compromise that resulted from their interaction. And this, incidentally, opens a fantastic field of inquiry for comparative morphology (the systematic study of how forms vary in space and time, which is also the only reason to keep the adjective 'comparative' in comparative literature): but comparative morphology is a complex issue, that deserves its own paper.

Forms as Abstracts of Social Relationships

Let me now add a few words on that term 'compromise' – by which I mean something a little different from what Jameson had in mind in his introduction to Karatani. For him, the relationship is fundamentally a binary one: 'the abstract formal patterns of Western novel construction' and 'the raw material of Japanese social experience': form and content, basically.[26] For me, it's more of a triangle: foreign form, local material – *and local form*. Simplifying somewhat: foreign *plot*; local *characters*; and then, local *narrative voice*: and it's precisely in this third dimension that these novels seem to be most unstable – most uneasy, as Zhao says of the late Qing narrator. Which makes sense: the narrator is the pole of comment, of explanation, of evaluation, and when foreign 'formal patterns' (or actual foreign presence, for that matter) make characters behave in strange ways (like Bunzo, or Ibarra, or Bràs Cubas), then of course comment becomes uneasy – garrulous, erratic, rudderless.

'Interferences', Even-Zohar calls them: powerful literatures making life hard for the others – making *structure* hard. And Schwarz: 'a part of the original historical conditions reappears as a sociological form...In this sense, forms are the abstract of specific social relationships.'[27] Yes, and in our case the historical conditions reappear as a sort of 'crack' in the form; as a faultline running between story and discourse, world and worldview: the world goes in the strange direction dictated by an outside power; the worldview tries to make sense of it, and is thrown off balance all the time. Like Rizal's voice (oscillating between Catholic melodrama and Enlightenment sarcasm),[28] or Futabatei's (caught between Bunzo's 'Russian' behavior, and the Japanese audience inscribed in the text), or Zhao's hypertrophic narrator, who has completely lost control of the plot, but still tries to dominate it at all costs. This is what Schwarz meant with that 'foreign debt' that becomes a 'complex feature' of the text: the foreign presence 'interferes' with the very *utterance* of the novel.[29] The one-and-unequal literary system is not just an external network here, it doesn't remain *outside* the text: it's embedded well into its form.

Trees, Waves and Cultural History

Forms are the abstract of social relationships: so, formal analysis is in its own modest way an analysis of power. (That's why comparative morphology is such a fascinating field: studying how forms vary, you discover how symbolic *power* varies from place to place.) And indeed, sociological formalism has always been my interpretive method, and I think that it's particularly appropriate for world literature...But, unfortunately, at this point I must stop, because my competence stops. Once it became clear that the key variable of the experiment was the narrator's voice, well, a genuine formal analysis was off limits for me, because it required a linguistic competence that I couldn't even dream of (French, English, Spanish, Russian, Japanese, Chinese and Portuguese, just for the core of the argument). And probably, no matter what the object of analysis is, there will always be a point where the study of world literature must yield to the specialist of the national literature, in a sort of cosmic and inevitable division of labour. Inevitable not just for practical reasons, but for theoretical ones. This is a large issue, but let me at least sketch its outline.

When historians have analysed culture on a world scale (or on a large scale anyway), they have tended to use two basic cognitive metaphors: the tree and the wave. The tree, the phylogenetic tree derived from Darwin, was the tool of comparative philology: language families branching off from each other – Slavo-Germanic from Aryan-Greco-Italo-Celtic, then Balto-Slavic from Germanic, then Lithuanian from Slavic. And this kind of tree allowed comparative philology to solve that great puzzle which was also perhaps the first world system of culture: Indo-European: a family of languages spreading from India to Ireland (and perhaps not just languages, a common cultural repertoire, too: but here the evidence is notoriously shakier). The other metaphor, the wave, was also used in historical linguistics (as in Schmidt's 'wave hypothesis', that explained certain overlaps among languages), but it played a role in many other fields as well: the study of technological diffusion, for instance, or the fantastic interdisciplinary theory of the 'wave of advance' by Cavalli-Sforza and Ammerman (a geneticist and an archaeologist), which explains how agriculture spread from the fertile crescent in the Middle East towards the North-West and then throughout Europe.

Now, trees and waves are both metaphors – but except for this, they have absolutely nothing in common. The tree describes the passage from unity to diversity: one tree, with many branches: from Indo-European, to dozens of different languages. The wave is the opposite: it observes uniformity engulfing an initial diversity: Hollywood films conquering one market after another (or English swallowing language after language). Trees need geographical *discontinuity* (in order to branch off from each other, languages must first be separated in space, just like animal species); waves dislike barriers, and thrive on geographical *continuity* (from the viewpoint of a wave, the ideal world is a pond). Trees and branches are what nation-states cling to; waves are what markets do. And so on. Nothing in common, between the two metaphors. But – *they both work*. Cultural history is made of trees *and* waves – the wave of agricultural advance supporting the tree of Indo-European languages, which is then swept by new waves of linguistic and cultural contact... And as world culture oscillates between the two mechanisms, its products are inevitably composite ones. Compromises, as in Jameson's law. That's why the law works: because it intuitively captures the intersection of the two mechanisms. Think of the modern novel: certainly a wave (and I've actually called it a wave a few times) – but a wave that runs into the branches of local traditions,[30] and is always significantly transformed by them.

This, then, is the basis for the division of labour between national and world literature: national literature, for people who see trees; world literature, for people who see waves. Division of labour ... and challenge; because both metaphors work, yes, but that doesn't mean that they work equally well. The products of cultural history are always composite ones: but which is the dominant mechanism in their composition? The internal, or the external one? The nation or the world? The tree or the wave? There is no way to settle this controversy once and for all – fortunately: because comparatists need controversy. They have always been too shy in the presence of national literatures, too diplomatic: as if one had English, American, German literature – and then, next door, a sort of little parallel universe where comparatists studied a second set of literatures, trying not to disturb the first set. No; the universe is the same, the literatures are the same, we just look at them from a different viewpoint; and you become a comparatist for a very simple reason: *because you are convinced that that viewpoint is better*. It has greater explanatory power; it's conceptually more elegant; it avoids that ugly 'one-sidedness and narrow-mindedness'; whatever. The point is that there is no other justification for the study of world literature (and for the existence of departments of comparative literature) but this: to be a thorn in the side, a permanent intellectual challenge to national literatures – especially the local literature. If comparative literature is not this, it's nothing. Nothing. 'Don't delude yourself', writes Stendhal of his favourite character: 'for you, there is no middle road.' The same is true for us.

Notes

1   I address the problem of the great unread in a companion piece to this article, 'The Slaughterhouse of Literature', in a special issue of *Modern Language Quarterly* on 'Formalism and Literary History', (MLQ 61:1 [2000], 207–227).

2   Max Weber, 'Objectivity in Social Science and Social Policy', 1904, in *The Methodology of the Social Sciences*, New York 1949, p. 68.

3   Roberto Schwarz, 'The Importing of the Novel to Brazil and Its Contradictions in the Work of Roberto Alencar', 1977, in *Misplaced Ideas*, London 1992, p. 50.

4   Itamar Even-Zohar, 'Laws of Literary Interference' in *Poetics Today*, 1990, pp. 54, 62.

5   Montserrat Iglesias Santos, 'El sistema literario: teoría empírica y teoría de los polisistemas', in Dario Villanueva (ed.), *Avances en teoría de la literatura*, Santiago de Compostela 1994, p. 339: 'It is important to emphasize that interferences occur most often at the periphery of the system.'

6   Marc Bloch, 'Pour une histoire comparée des sociétés européennes', *Revue de synthèse historique*, 1928.

7   Or to quote Weber again: 'concepts are primarily analytical instruments for the intellectual mastery of empirical data'. ('Objectivity in Social Science and Social Policy', p. 106.) Inevitably, the larger the field one wants to study, the greater the need for abstract 'instruments' capable of mastering empirical reality.

8   Fredric Jameson, 'In the Mirror of Alternate Modernities', in Karatani Kojin, *Origins of Modern Japanese Literature*, Durham–London 1993, p. xiii.

9   I have begun to sketch them out in the last chapter of the *Atlas of the European Novel 1800–1900* (Verso: London 1998), and this is more or less how they sound: second, the formal compromise is usually prepared by a massive wave of West European translations; third, the compromise itself is generally unstable (Miyoshi has a great image for this: the 'impossible programme' of Japanese novels); but fourth, in those rare instances when the impossible programme succeeds, we have genuine formal revolutions.

10   'Given the history of its formative stage, it is no surprise that the early Russian novel contains a host of conventions popularized in French and British literature', writes David Gasperetti in *The Rise of the Russian Novel* (De Kalb 1998, p. 5). And Helena Goscilo, in her 'Introduction' to Krasicki's *Adventures of Mr. Nicholas Wisdom*: 'The Adventures is read most fruitfully in the context of the West European literature on which it drew heavily for inspiration.' (Ignacy Krasicki, *The Adventures of Mr. Nicholas Wisdom*, Evanston 1992, p. xv.)

11   'There was a demand for foreign products, and production had to comply', explains Luca Toschi speaking of the Italian narrative market around 1800 ('Alle origini della narrativa di romanzo in Italia', in Massimo Saltafuso (ed.), *Il viaggio del narrare*, Florence 1989, p. 19). A generation later, in Spain, 'readers are not interested in the originality of the Spanish novel; their only desire is that it would adhere to those foreign models with which they have become familiar': and so, concludes Elisa Martí-López, one may well say that between 1800 and 1850 'the Spanish novel is being written in France' (Elisa Martí-López, 'La orfandad de la novela española: política editorial y creación literaria a mediados del siglo XIX', *Bulletin Hispanique*, 1997).

12   'Obviously, lofty ambitions were not enough. All too often the nineteenth century Spanish-American novel is clumsy and inept, with a plot derived at second hand from the contemporary European Romantic novel.' (Jean Franco, *Spanish-American Literature*, Cambridge 1969, p. 56.) 'If heroes and heroines in mid-nineteenth century Latin American novels were passionately desiring one another across traditional lines... those passions might not have prospered a generation earlier. In fact, modernizing lovers were learning how to dream their erotic fantasies by reading the European romances they hoped to realize.' (Doris Sommer, *Foundational Fictions: The National Romances of Latin America*, Berkeley–Los Angeles 1991, pp. 31–2.)

13 'Yiddish writers parodied – appropriated, incorporated, and modified – diverse elements from European novels and stories.' (Ken Frieden, *Classic Yiddish Fiction*, Albany 1995, p. x.)

14 Matti Moosa quotes the novelist Yahya Haqqi: 'there is no harm in admitting that the modern story came to us from the West. Those who laid down its foundations were persons influenced by European literature, particularly French literature. Although masterpieces of English literature were translated into Arabic, French literature was the fountain of our story.' (Matti Moosa, *The Origins of Modern Arabic Fiction*, 1970, 2nd ed. 1997, p. 93.) For Edward Said, 'at some point writers in Arabic became aware of European novels and began to write works like them' (Edward Said, *Beginnings*, 1975, New York 1985, p. 81). And Roger Allen: 'In more literary terms, increasing contacts with Western literatures led to translations of works of European fiction into Arabic, followed by their adaptation and imitation, and culminating in the appearance of an indigenous tradition of modern fiction in Arabic.' (Roger Allen, *The Arabic Novel*, Syracuse 1995, p. 12.)

15 'The first novels in Turkey were written by members of the new intelligentsia, trained in government service and well-exposed to French literature', writes Ahmet O. Evin (*Origins and Development of the Turkish Novel*, Minneapolis 1983, p. 10); and Jale Parla: 'the early Turkish novelists combined the traditional narrative forms with the examples of the western novel' ('Desiring Tellers, Fugitive Tales: Don Quixote Rides Again, This Time in Istanbul', forthcoming).

16 'The narrative dislocation of the sequential order of events is perhaps the most outstanding impression late Qing writers received when they read or translated Western fiction. At first, they tried to tidy up the sequence of the events back into their prenarrated order. When such tidying was not feasible during translation, an apologetic note would be inserted... Paradoxically, when he alters rather than follows the original, the translator does not feel it necessary to add an apologetic note.' (Henry Y.H. Zhao, *The Uneasy Narrator: Chinese Fiction from the Traditional to the Modern*, Oxford 1995, p. 150.) 'Late Qing writers enthusiastically renewed their heritage with the help of foreign models', writes David Der-wei Wang: 'I see the late Qing as the beginning of the Chinese literary "modern" because writers' pursuit of novelty was no longer contained within indigenously defined barriers but was inextricably defined by the multilingual, crosscultural trafficking of ideas, technologies, and powers in the wake of nineteenth-century Western expansionism.' (*Fin-de-siècle Splendor: Repressed Modernities of Late Qing Fiction*, 1849–1911, Stanford 1997, pp. 5, 19.)

17 'One essential factor shaping West African novels by indigenous writers was the fact that they appeared after the novels on Africa written by non-Africans... the foreign novels embody elements which indigenous writers had to react against when they set out to write.' (Emmanuel Obiechina, *Culture, Tradition and Society in the West African Novel*, Cambridge 1975, p. 17.) 'The first Dahomean novel, *Doguicimi*... is interesting as an experiment in recasting the oral literature of Africa within the form of a French novel.' (Abiola Irele, *The African Experience in Literature and Ideology*, Bloomington 1990, p. 147.) 'It was the rationality of realism that seemed adequate to the task of forging a national identity at the conjuncture of global realities... the rationalism of realism dispersed in texts as varied as newspapers, Onitsha market literature, and in the earliest titles of the African Writers Series that

dominated the discourses of the period.' (Ato Quayson, *Strategic Transformations in Nigerian Writing*, Bloomington 1997, p. 162.)

18   In the seminar where I first presented this 'second-hand' criticism, Sarah Golstein asked a very good, Candide-like question: You decide to rely on another critic. Fine. But what if he's wrong? My reply: If he's wrong, you are wrong too, and you soon know, because you don't find any corroboration – you don't find Goscilo, Martí-López, Sommer, Evin, Zhao, Irele... And it's not just that you don't find positive corroboration; sooner or later you find all sorts of facts you cannot explain, and your hypothesis is falsified, in Popper's famous formulation, and you must throw it away. Fortunately, this hasn't been the case so far, and Jameson's insight still stands.

19   OK, I confess, in order to test the conjecture I actually did read some of these 'first novels' in the end (Krasicki's *Adventures of Mr. Nicholas Wisdom*, Abramowitsch's *Little Man*, Rizal's *Noli Me Tangere*, Futabatei's *Ukigumo*, René Maran's *Batouala*, Paul Hazoumé's *Doguicimi*). This kind of 'reading', however, no longer produces interpretations but merely *tests* them: it's not the beginning of the critical enterprise, but its appendix. And then, here you don't really read the *text* anymore, but rather through the text, looking for your unit of analysis. The task is constrained from the start; it's a reading without freedom.

20   For practical purposes, the larger the geographical space one wants to study, the smaller should the unit of analysis be: a concept (in our case), a device, a trope, a limited narrative unit – something like this. In a follow-up paper, I hope to sketch out the diffusion of stylistic 'seriousness' (Auerbach's keyword in *Mimesis*) in nineteenth and twentieth century novels.

21   How to set up a reliable sample – that is to say, what series of national literatures and individual novels provide a satisfactory test of a theory's predictions – is of course quite a complex issue. In this preliminary sketch, my sample (and its justification) leave much to be desired.

22   Scientific research 'begins as a story about a Possible World', Medawar goes on, 'and ends by being, as nearly as we can make it, a story about real life.' His words are quoted by James Bird in *The Changing World of Geography*, Oxford 1993, p. 5. Bird himself offers a very elegant version of the experimental model.

23   Aside from Miyoshi and Karatani (for Japan), Mukherjee (for India), and Schwarz (for Brazil), the compositional paradoxes and the instability of the formal compromise are often mentioned in the literature on the Turkish, Chinese and Arabic novel. Discussing Namik Kemal's *Intibah*, Ahmet Evin points out how 'the merger of the two themes, one based on the traditional family life and the other on the yearnings of a prostitute, constitute the first attempt in Turkish fiction to achieve a type of psychological dimension observed in European novels within a thematic framework based on Turkish life. *However, due both to the incompatibility of the themes and to the difference in the degree of emphasis placed on each, the unity of the novel is blemished. The structural defects of* Intibah *are symptomatic of the differences between the methodology and concerns of the Turkish literary tradition on the one hand and those of the European novel on the other.*' (Ahmet O. Evin, *Origins and Development of the Turkish Novel*, p. 68; emphasis mine.) Jale Parla's evaluation of the Tanzimat period sounds a similar note: 'behind the inclination towards renovation stood a dominant and dominating Ottoman ideology that recast the new ideas into a mould fit for the Ottoman society. The mould, however, was

supposed to hold two different epistemologies that rested on irreconcilable axioms. *It was inevitable that this mould would crack and literature, in one way or another, reflects the cracks.*' ('Desiring Tellers, Fugitive Tales: Don Quixote Rides Again, This Time in Istanbul', emphasis mine.) In his discussion of the 1913 novel *Zaynab*, by Husayn Haykal, Roger Allen echoes Schwarz and Mukherjee ('*it is all too easy to point to the problems of psychological fallacy here*, as Hamid, the student in Cairo acquainted with Western works on liberty and justice such as those of John Stuart Mill and Herbert Spencer, proceeds to discuss the question of marriage in Egyptian society on such a lofty plane with his parents, who have always lived deep in the Egyptian countryside': *The Arabic Novel*, p. 34; emphasis mine). Henry Zhao emphasizes from his very title – *The Uneasy Narrator*: and see the splendid discussion of uneasiness that opens the book – the complications generated by the encounter of western plots and Chinese narrative: 'A salient feature of late Qing fiction', he writes, 'is the greater frequency of narrative intrusions than in any previous period of Chinese vernacular fiction... The huge amount of directions trying to explain the newly adopted techniques betrays the narrator's uneasiness about the instability of his status... the narrator feels the threat of interpretive diversification... moral commentaries become more tendentious to make the judgments unequivocal', and at times the drift towards narratorial overkill is so overpowering that a writer may sacrifice narrative suspense 'to show that he is morally impeccable' (*The Uneasy Narrator*, pp. 69–71).

24   In some cases, even *translations* of European novels went through all sorts of incredible somersaults. In Japan, in 1880, Tsubouchi's translation of *The Bride of Lammermoor* appeared under the title *Shumpu jowa* [*Spring breeze love story*], and Tsubouchi himself 'was not beyond excising the original text when the material proved inappropriate for his audience, or converting Scott's imagery into expressions corresponding more closely to the language of traditional Japanese literature' (Marleigh Grayer Ryan, 'Commentary' to Futabatei Shimei's *Ukigumo*, New York 1967, pp. 41–42). In the Arabic world, writes Matti Moosa, 'in many instances the translators of Western fiction took extensive and sometimes unwarranted liberties with the original text of a work. Yaqub Sarruf not only changed the title of Scott's *Talisman* to *Qalb al-Asad wa Salah al-Din* (*The Lion Heart and Saladin*), but also admitted that he had taken the liberty of omitting, adding, and changing parts of this romance to suit what he believed to be his audience's taste... Other translators changed the titles and the names of the characters and the contents, in order, they claimed, to make the translated work more acceptable to their readers and more consistent with the native literary tradition.' (*The Origins of Modern Arabic Fiction*, p. 106.) The same general pattern holds for late Qing literature, where 'translations were almost without exception tampered with... the most serious way of tampering was to paraphrase the whole novel to make it a story with Chinese chracters and Chinese background... Almost all of these translations suffered from abridgment... Western novels became sketchy and speedy, and looked more like Chinese traditional fiction.' (Henry Zhao, *The Uneasy Narrator*, p. 229.)

25   Why this difference? Probably, because in Southern Europe the wave of French translations encountered a local reality (and local narrative traditions) that weren't that different after all, and as a consequence, the composition of foreign form and local material proved easy. In West Africa, the opposite situation: although the novelists themselves had been influenced by Western literature, the wave of translations had been much

weaker than elsewhere, and local narrative conventions were for their part extremely different from European ones (just think of orality); as the desire for the 'foreign technology' was relatively bland – and further discouraged, of course, by the anti-colonial politics of the 1950s – local conventions could play their role relatively undisturbed. Obiechina and Quayson emphasize the polemical relationship of early West African novels vis-à-vis European narrative: 'The most noticeable difference between novels by native West Africans and those by non-native using the West African setting, is the important position which the representation of oral tradition is given by the first, and its almost total absence in the second.' (Emmanuel Obiechina, *Culture, Tradition and Society in the West African Novel*, p. 25.) 'Continuity in the literary strategic formation we have identified is best defined in term of the continuing affirmation of mythopeia rather than of realism for the definition of identity ... That this derives from a conceptual opposition to what is perceived as a Western form of realism is difficult to doubt. It is even pertinent to note in this regard that in the work of major African writers such as Achebe, Armah, and Ngugi, the movement of their work has been from protocols of realist representation to those of mythopeic experimentation.' (Ato Quayson, *Strategic Transformations in Nigerian Writing*, p. 164.)

26   The same point is made in a great article by António Cándido: 'We [Latin American literatures] never create original expressive forms or basic expressive techniques, in the sense that we mean by romanticism, on the level of literary movements; the psychological novel, on the level of genres; free indirect style, on that of writing ... the various nativisms never rejected the use of the imported literary *forms* ... what was demanded was the choice of new *themes*, of different *sentiments*. ('Literature and Underdevelopment', in César Fernández Moreno, Julio Ortega, Ivan A. Shulman (eds), *Latin America in Its Literature*, New York 1980, pp. 272–273.)

27   'The Importing of the Novel to Brazil', p. 53.

28   Rizal's solution, or lack thereof, is probably also related to his extraordinarily wide social spectrum (*Noli Me Tangere*, among other things, is the text that inspired Benedict Anderson to link the novel and the nation-state): in a nation with no independence, an ill-defined ruling class, no common language and hundreds of disparate characters, it's hard to speak 'for the whole', and the narrator's voice cracks under the effort.

29   In a few lucky cases, the structural weakness may turn into a strength, as in Schwarz's interpretation of Machado, where the 'volatility' of the narrator becomes 'the stylization of the behaviour of the Brazilian ruling class': not a flaw any longer, but the very point of the novel: 'Everything in Machado de Assis's novels is coloured by the *volatility* – used and abused in different degrees – of their narrators. The critics usually look at it from the point of view of literary technique or of the author's humour. There are great advantages in seeing it as the stylization of the behaviour of the Brazilian ruling class. Instead of seeking disinterestedness, and the confidence provided by impartiality, Machado's narrator shows off his impudence, in a gamut which runs from cheap gibes, to literary exhibitionism, and even to critical acts.' (Roberto Schwarz, 'The Poor Old Woman and Her Portraitist', 1983, in *Misplaced Ideas*, p. 94.)

30   '*Grafting* processes', Miyoshi calls them; Schwarz speaks of 'the *implantation* of the novel, and of its realist *strand* in particular', and Wang of '*transplanting* Western narrative typologies'. And indeed, Belinsky had already described Russian literature as 'a *transplanted* rather than indigenous growth' in 1843.

More Conjectures (2003)

In the past year or so, several articles have addressed the issues raised in 'Conjectures on World Literature': Christopher Prendergast, Francesca Orsini, Efraín Kristal and Jonathan Arac in *New Left Review*, Emily Apter and Jale Parla elsewhere.[1] My thanks to all of them; and as I obviously cannot respond to every point in detail, I will focus here on the three main areas of disagreement among us: the (questionable) paradigmatic status of the novel; the relationship between core and periphery, and its consequences for literary form; and the nature of comparative analysis.

I

One must begin somewhere, and 'Conjectures' tried to sketch how the literary world-system works by focusing on the rise of the modern novel: a phenomenon which is easy to isolate, has been studied all the world over, and thus lends itself well to comparative work. I also added that the novel was 'an example, not a model; and of course my example, based on the field I know (elsewhere, things may be very different)'. Elsewhere things are different indeed: 'If the novel can be seen as heavily freighted with the political, this is not patently the case for other literary genres. Drama seems to travel less anxiously...How might the...construct work with lyric poetry?', asks Prendergast; and Kristal: 'Why doesn't poetry follow the laws of the novel?'[2]

It doesn't? I wonder. What about Petrarchism? Propelled by its formalized lyrical conventions, Petrarchism spread to (at least) Spain, Portugal, France, England, Wales, the Low Countries, the German territories, Poland, Scandinavia, Dalmatia (and, according to Roland Greene, the New World). As for its depth and duration, I am sceptical about the old Italian claim that by the end of the sixteenth century over two hundred *thousand* sonnets had been written in Europe in imitation of Petrarch; still, the main disagreement seems to be, not on the enormity of the facts, but on the enormity of their enormity – ranging from a century (Navarrete, Fucilla), to two (Manero Sorolla, Kennedy), three (Hoffmeister, Kristal himself), or five (Greene). Compared to the wave-like diffusion of this *'lingua franca* for love poets', as Hoffmeister calls it, western novelistic 'realism' looks like a rather ephemeral vogue.[3]

Other things being equal, anyway, I would imagine literary movements to depend on three broad variables – a genre's potential market, its overall formalization

Franco Moretti, "More Conjectures" (2003). In *New Left Review* 20 (Mar./Apr. 2003), pp. 73–81.

and its use of language – and to range from the rapid wave-like diffusion of forms with a large market, rigid formulas and simplified style (say, adventure novels), to the relative stasis of those characterized by a small market, deliberate singularity and linguistic density (say, experimental poetry). Within this matrix, novels would be representative, not of the *entire* system, but of its most mobile strata, and by concentrating only on them we would probably overstate the mobility of world literature. If 'Conjectures' erred in that direction it was a mistake, easily corrected as we learn more about the international diffusion of drama, poetry and so on (here, Donald Sassoon's current work on cultural markets will be invaluable).[4] Truth be told, I would be very disappointed if all of literature turned out to 'follow the laws of the novel': that a single explanation may work *everywhere* is both very implausible and extraordinarily boring. But before indulging in speculations at a more abstract level, we must learn to share the significant facts of literary history across our specialized niches. Without collective work, world literature will always remain a mirage.

II

Is world-system theory, with its strong emphasis on a rigid international division of labour, a good model for the study of world literature? On this, the strongest objection comes from Kristal: 'I am arguing, however, in favour of a view of world literature', he writes, 'in which the West does not have a monopoly over the creation of forms that count; in which themes and forms can move in several directions – from the centre to the periphery, from the periphery to the centre, from one periphery to another, while some original forms of consequence may not move much at all'.[5]

Yes, forms *can* move in several directions. But *do* they? This is the point, and a theory of literary history should reflect on the constraints on their movements, and the reasons behind them. What I know about European novels, for instance, suggests that hardly any forms 'of consequence' don't move at all; that movement from one periphery to another (without passing through the centre) is almost unheard of;[6] that movement from the periphery to the centre is less rare, but still quite unusual, while that from the centre to the periphery is by far the most frequent.[7] Do these facts imply that the West has 'a monopoly over the creation of the forms that count'? Of course not.[8] Cultures from the centre have more resources to pour into innovation (literary and otherwise), and are thus more likely to produce it: but a monopoly over creation is a theological attribute, not an historical judgment.[9] The model proposed in 'Conjectures' does not reserve invention to a few cultures and deny it to the others: it specifies *the conditions under which it is more likely to occur*, and the forms it may take. Theories will never abolish inequality: they can only hope to explain it.

III

Kristal also objects to what he calls the 'postulate of a general homology between the inequalities of the world economic and literary systems': in other words, 'the assumption that literary and economic relationships run parallel may work in some cases, but not in others'.[10] Even-Zohar's argument is a partial response to the objection; but there is another sense in which Kristal is right, and the simplifying euphoria of an article originally conceived as a 30-minute talk is seriously misleading. By reducing the literary world-system to core and periphery, I erased from the picture the transitional area (the semi-periphery) where cultures move in and out of the core; as a consequence, I also understated the fact that in many (and perhaps most) instances, material and intellectual hegemony are indeed very close, but not quite identical.

Let me give some examples. In the 18th and 19th centuries, the long struggle for hegemony between Britain and France ended with Britain's victory on all fronts – except one: in the world of narrative, the verdict was reversed, and French novels were both more successful and formally more significant than British ones. Elsewhere I have tried to explain the reasons for the morphological supremacy of German tragedy from the mid-eighteenth century on; or the key role of semi-peripheral realities in the production of modern epic forms. Petrarchism, which reached its international zenith when its wealthy area of origin had already catastrophically declined (like those stars which are still shining long after their death), is a particularly spooky instance of this state of affairs.

All these examples (and more) have two features in common. First, they arise from cultures which are close to, or inside the core of the system – but are not hegemonic in the economic sphere. France may be the paradigm here, as if being an eternal second in the political and economic arena encouraged investment in culture (as in its feverish post-Napoleonic creativity, compared to the postprandial somnolence of the victorious Victorians). A – limited – discrepancy between material and literary hegemony does therefore exist: wider in the case of innovation *per se* (which does not require a powerful apparatus of production and distribution), and narrower, or absent, in the case of diffusion (which does).[11] Yet, and this is the second feature in common, all these examples *confirm the inequality of the world literary system*: an inequality which does not coincide with economic inequality, true, and allows some mobility – but a mobility *internal* to the unequal system, not alternative to it. At times, even the dialectic between semi-periphery and core may actually widen the overall gap (as in the instances mentioned in note 11, or when Hollywood quickly 'remakes' successful foreign films, effectively strengthening its own position). At any rate, this is clearly another field where progress will only be possible through the good coordination of specific local knowledge.

IV

The central morphological point of 'Conjectures' was the contrast between the rise of the novel in the core as an 'autonomous development', and the rise in the periphery as a 'compromise' between a Western influence and local materials. As

Parla and Arac point out, however, early English novels were written, in Fielding's words, 'after the manner of Cervantes' (or of someone else), thus making clear that a compromise between local and foreign forms occurred there as well.[12] And if this was the case, then there was no 'autonomous development' in western Europe, and the idea that forms have, so to speak, *a different history* at the core and at the periphery crumbles. The world-system model may be useful at other levels, but has no explanatory power at the level of form.

Here things are easy: Parla and Arac are right – and I should have known better. After all, the thesis that literary form is *always* a compromise between opposite forces has been a Leitmotiv of my intellectual formation, from Francesco Orlando's Freudian aesthetics to Gould's 'Panda principle', or Lukács' conception of realism. How on earth could I 'forget' all this? In all likelihood, because the core/periphery opposition made me look (or wish…) for a parallel morphological pattern, which I then couched in the wrong conceptual terms.[13]

So let me try again. 'Probably all systems known to us have emerged and developed with interference playing a prominent role', writes Even-Zohar: 'there is not one single literature which did not emerge through interference with a more established literature: and no literature could manage without interference at one time or another during its history'.[14] No literature without interference…hence, also, no literature without compromises between the local and the foreign. But does this mean that all types of interference and compromise *are the same*? Of course not: the picaresque, captivity narratives, even the *Bildungsroman* could not exert the same pressure over French or British novelists that the historical novel or the *mystères* exerted over European and Latin American writers: and we should find a way to express this difference. To recognize when a compromise occurs as it were *under duress*, and is thus likely to produce more unstable and dissonant results – what Zhao calls the 'uneasiness' of the late Qing narrator.

The key point, here, is this: if there is a strong, systematic constraint exerted by some literatures over the others (and we all seem to agree that there is),[15] then we should be able to recognize its effects *within literary form itself*: because forms are indeed, in Schwarz's words, 'the abstract of specific social relationships'. In 'Conjectures', the diagram of forces was embodied in the sharp qualitative opposition of 'autonomous developments' and 'compromises'; but as that solution has been falsified, we must try something else. And, yes, 'measuring' the extent of foreign pressure on a text, or its structural instability, or a narrator's uneasiness, will be complicated, at times even unfeasible. But a diagram of symbolic power is an ambitious goal, and it makes sense that it would be hard to achieve.

V

Two areas for future discussion emerge from all this. The first concerns the type of knowledge literary history should pursue. 'No science, no laws' is Arac's crisp description of Auerbach's project; and there are similar hints in other articles too.

This is of course the old question of whether the proper object of historical disciplines are individual cases or abstract models; and as I will argue at extravagant length for the latter in a series of forthcoming articles, here I will simply say that we have a lot to learn from the methods of the social and of the natural sciences. Will we then find ourselves, in Apter's words, 'in a city of bits, where micro and macro literary units are awash in a global system with no obvious sorting device'? I hope so...it would be a very interesting universe. So, let's start looking for good sorting devices. 'Formalism without close reading', Arac calls the project of 'Conjectures', and I can't think of a better definition. Hopefully, it will also be a formalism where the 'details' so dear to him and to Prendergast will be highlighted, not erased by models and 'schemas'.[16]

Finally, politics. Several articles mention the political pressure behind Auerbach's *Mimesis*, or Casanova's *République mondiale des lettres*. To them I would add Lukács's two versions of comparative literature: the one which crystallized around World War I, when *The Theory of the Novel*, and its (never completed) companion study on Dostoevsky mused on whether a world beyond capitalism could even still be imagined; and the one which took shape in the Thirties, as a long meditation on the opposite political significance of German and French literature (with Russia again in the background). Lukács' spatio-temporal horizon was narrow (the nineteenth century, and three European literatures, plus Cervantes in *The Theory of the Novel* and Scott in *The Historical Novel*); his answers were often opaque, scholastic, philistine – or worse. But his lesson lies in how the articulation of his comparative scenario (western Europe or Russia; Germany or France) is simultaneously an attempt to understand the great political dilemmas of his day. Or in other words: *the way we imagine comparative literature is a mirror of how we see the world.* 'Conjectures' tried to do so against the background of the unprecedented possibility that the entire world may be subject to a single centre of power – and a centre which has long exerted an equally unprecedented symbolic hegemony. In charting an aspect of the pre-history of our present, and sketching some possible outcomes, the article may well have overstated its case, or taken some wrong turns altogether. But the relationship between project and background stands, and I believe it will give significance and seriousness to our work in the future. Early March 2003, when these pages are being written, is in this respect a wonderfully paradoxical moment, when, after twenty years of unchallenged American hegemony, millions of people everywhere in the world have expressed their enormous distance from American politics. As human beings, this is cause to rejoice. As cultural historians, it is cause to reflect.

Notes

1 'Conjectures on World Literature', NLR 1; Christopher Prendergast, 'Negotiating World Literature', NLR 8; Francesca Orsini, 'Maps of Indian Writing', NLR 13; Efraín Kristal, '"Considering Coldly...": A Response to Franco Moretti', NLR 15; Jonathan Arac,

'Anglo-Globalism?' NLR 16; Emily Apter, 'Global *Translatio*: The "Invention" of Comparative Literature, Istanbul, 1933', *Critical Inquiry*, 29, 2003; Jale Parla's essay ('The object of comparison') will be published in a special issue of *Comparative Literature Studies* edited by Djelal Kadir in January 2004.

2   'Conjectures', p. 58; 'Negotiating World Literature', pp. 120–1; ' "Considering Coldly…" ', p. 62. Orsini makes a similar point for Indian literature: 'Moretti's novel-based theses would seem to have little application to the Subcontinent, where the major nineteenth and twentieth-century forms have been poetry, drama and the short story, whose evolution may show quite different patterns of change': 'Maps', p. 79.

3   See Antero Meozzi, *Il petrarchismo europeo (secolo xvi)*, Pisa 1934; Leonard Forster, *The Icy Fire: Five studies in European Petrarchism*, Cambridge 1969; Joseph Fucilla, *Estudios sobre el petrarquismo en España*, Madrid 1960; Ignacio Navarrete, *Orphans of Petrarch*, California 1994; William Kennedy, *Authorizing Petrarch*, Ithaca 1994; Maria Pilar Manero Sorolla, *Introducción al estudio del petrarquismo en España*, Barcelona 1987; Gerhart Hoffmeister, *Petrarkistische Lyrik*, Stuttgart 1973; Roland Greene, *Post-Petrarchism: Origins and Innovations of the Western Lyric Sequence*, Princeton 1991. Kristal's implicit acknowledgement of the hegemony of Petrarchism over European and Latin American poetry comes where he writes that 'the lyrical conventions of modern Spanish poetry were developed in the 16th century by Boscán and Garcilaso de la Vega … The first signs of a reaction against the strictest conventions of Spanish prosody did not take place in Spain but in Spanish America in the 1830s': ' "Considering Coldly…" ', p. 64.

4   See, for a preliminary account, 'On Cultural Markets', NLR 17.

5   ' "Considering Coldly…" ', pp. 73–4.

6   I mean here the movement between peripheral cultures which do not belong to the same 'region': from, say, Norway to Portugal (or vice versa), not from Norway to Iceland or Sweden, or from Colombia to Guatemala and Peru. Sub-systems made relatively homogeneous by language, religion or politics – of which Latin America is the most interesting and powerful instance – are a great field for comparative study, and may add interesting complications to the larger picture (like Darío's modernism, evoked by Kristal).

7   The reason why literary products flow from the centre to the periphery is spelt out by Even-Zohar in his work on polysystems, extensively quoted at the beginning of 'Conjectures': peripheral (or, as he calls them, 'weak') literatures 'often do not develop the same full range of literary activities … observable in adjacent larger literatures (which in consequence may create a feeling that they are indispensable)'; 'a weak … system is unable to function by confining itself to its home repertoire only', and the ensuing lack 'may be filled, wholly or partly, by translated literature'. Literary weakness, Even-Zohar goes on, 'does not necessarily result from political or economic weakness, although rather often it seems to be correlated with material conditions'; as a consequence, 'since peripheral literatures in the Western hemisphere tend more often than not to be identical with literatures of smaller nations, as unpalatable as this idea may seem to us, we have no choice but to admit that within a group of relatable national literatures, such as the literatures of Europe, hierarchical relations have been established since the very beginnings of these literatures. Within this (macro-)polysystem some literatures have taken peripheral positions, which is only to say that they were often modelled to a large extent upon an exterior literature.' Itamar Even-Zohar, 'Polysystem Studies', in *Poetics Today*, spring 1990, pp. 47, 81, 80, 48.

8   Nor does it have a monopoly over criticism that counts. Of the twenty critics on whose work the argument of 'Conjectures' rests, writes Arac, 'one is quoted in Spanish, one in Italian, and eighteen in English'; so, 'the impressive diversity of surveying some twenty national literatures diminishes into little more than one single means by which they may be known. English in culture, like the dollar in economics, serves as the medium through which knowledge may be translated from the local to the global': 'Anglo-Globalism?', p. 40. True, eighteen critics are quoted in English. But as far as I know only four or five are from the country of the dollar, while the others belong to a dozen different cultures. Is this less significant than the language they use? I doubt it. Sure, global English may end up impoverishing our thinking, as American films do. But for now, the rapid wide public exchanges it makes possible far exceed its potential dangers. Parla puts it well: 'To unmask the hegemony [of imperialism] is an intellectual task. It does no harm to know English as one sets out for the task.'

9   After all, my last two books end on the formal revolutions of Russian and Latin American narrative – a point also made (not 'conceded', as Kristal puts it, suggesting reluctance on my part) in an article on European literature ('an importer of those formal novelties that it is no longer capable of producing'), another one on Hollywood exports ('a counter-force at work within the world literary system') and in 'Conjectures' itself. See 'Modern European Literature: A Geographical Sketch', NLR I/206, July–August 1994, p. 109; 'Planet Hollywood', NLR 9, May–June 2001, p. 101. 'Conjectures' pointed out that 'in those rare instances when the impossible programme succeeds, we have genuine formal revolutions' (note 9), and that 'in a few lucky cases, the structural weakness may turn into a strength, as in Schwarz's interpretation of Machado' (note 29).

10 ' "Considering Coldly…" ', pp. 69, 73.

11 The fact that innovations may arise in the semi-periphery, but then be captured and diffused by the core of the core, emerges from several studies on the early history of the novel (by Armstrong, Resina, Trumpener and others: all written in total independence from world-system theory), which have pointed out how often the culture industry of London and Paris discovers a foreign form, introduces a few improvements, and then retails it as its own throughout Europe (ending in the masterstroke of the 'English' novelist Walter Scott). As the picaresque declines in its native country, Gil Blas and Moll Flanders and Marianne and Tom Jones spread it all over Europe; epistolary novels, first written in Spain and Italy, become a continental craze thanks to Montesquieu and Richardson (and then Goethe); American 'captivity narratives' acquire international currency through *Clarissa* and the Gothic; the Italian 'melodramatic imagination' conquers the world through Parisian *feuilletons*; the German *Bildungsroman* is intercepted by Stendhal, Balzac, Dickens, Brontë, Flaubert, Eliot… This is of course not the only path of literary innovation, perhaps not even the main one; but the mechanism is certainly there – half swindle, half international division of labour – and has an interesting similarity to larger economic constraints.

12 'Anglo-Globalism?', p. 38.

13 This seems a good illustration of the 'Kuhnian' point that theoretical expectations will shape facts according to your wishes – and an even better illustration of the 'Popperian' point that facts (usually gathered by those who disagree with you) will be finally stronger.

14 'Polysystem Studies', p. 59. A page later, in a footnote, Even-Zohar adds: 'This is true of almost all literatures of the Western hemisphere. As for the Eastern hemisphere, admittedly, Chinese is still a riddle as regards its emergence and early development.'

15   Except Orsini: 'Implicit in [Casanova's] view – explicit in Moretti's – is the traditional assumption of a "source" language, or culture – invariably carrying an aura of authenticity – and a "target" one, seen as in some way imitative. In place of this, Lydia Liu much more usefully proposed the concept of "guest" and "host" languages, to focus attention on the translingual practice through which the hosts may appropriate concepts and forms…Cultural influence becomes a study of appropriation, rather than of centres and peripheries': 'Maps', pp. 81–82. The culture industry as a 'guest' invited by a 'host' who 'appropriates' its forms…Are these concepts – or daydreams?

16   'Anglo-Globalism?', pp. 41, 38; 'Global *translatio*', p. 255.

13

World Literature without a Hyphen
Towards a Typology of Literary Systems (2008)

Alexander Beecroft

Alexander Beecroft is a professor of Classics and Comparative Literature at the University of South Carolina. His first book analyzes the birth of authorship in the ancient Greek and Chinese worlds as the texts circulate from local to wider audiences, foregrounding a cosmopolitan world (*Authorship and Cultural Identity in Early Greece and China: Patterns of Literary Circulation*, 2010). Beecroft's next book project, *An Ecology of Verbal Art: Literature and Its Worlds, from Local to Global*, develops his theoretical views on world literature as a literary system based on the relation between literature and its environment. The essay included here builds on the work of Immanuel Wallerstein and Franco Moretti, but moves beyond them to propose "a typology of literary systems" in six modes of manifestation: the epichoric, panchoric, cosmopolitan, vernacular, national, and global. These might be thought of as "a meta-system of literary systems," which Beecroft illustrates with examples from Chinese, Sanskrit, Greek, Arabic, and English literatures.

The rubric of 'world literature' has in recent years come to assume a prominent, perhaps even dominant, role in discussions over the future of Comparative Literature, and of literary studies more generally. While discussions necessarily and automatically begin with Goethe's use of the term *Weltliteratur* in conversation with the young Johann Peter Eckermann in January of 1827,[1] I would argue that a more immediate point of origin is Immanuel Wallerstein and, through him, Fernand Braudel. Wallerstein traces the development of his world-systems theory to the 1970s and to contemporary debates in the social sciences concerning the usefulness of the nation-state as the proper unit of analysis. In place of the

Alexander Beecroft, "World Literature without a Hyphen" (2008). In *New Left Review* 54 (2008), pp. 87–100.

World Literature in Theory, First Edition. Edited by David Damrosch.

nation-state, Wallerstein and the world-systems analysts offered the historical system, and described three kinds of such systems that have existed: the mini-system of the pre-modern world, geographically limited in scope; the world-empire, such as Rome or Han-dynasty China, 'a large bureaucratic structure with a single political centre and an axial division of labour, but multiple cultures'; and a world-economy, such as that in place in modern times, which is 'a large axial division of labour with multiple political centres and multiple cultures'.

Wallerstein traces his use of the phrase 'world-system', and indeed 'world-economy', to Fernand Braudel's work on the *économie-monde* of the sixteenth-century Mediterranean. For Wallerstein, the word 'world' in the phrases 'world-economy' and 'world-system' functions as a noun in apposition to the other noun in the phrase, rather than as an adjective modifying that noun, with a hyphen marking the distinction.[2] This point forms one of the unspoken assumptions most writers on world literature seem to have taken from Wallerstein, namely that world-literature (to restore the hyphen Wallerstein might demand) is not the sum total of the world's literary production, but rather a world-system within which literature is produced and circulates.

The other assumption for which writers on world-literature are indebted to Wallerstein is that of an axial division of labour. This aspect of world-systems theory is one (understandably) less explicitly endorsed by writers on world-literature, given its echoes of imperialism and/or of contemporary global capitalism. Nonetheless, models presented by Pascale Casanova and Franco Moretti both assume some form of an axial division of labour, the former reserving higher-order and higher-value work for core cultures, and the latter for core specialists within the field of literary study (located, naturally, within the academic centres of those same core cultures). In either case, each of these models has the perhaps unintended effect of re-inscribing a hegemonic cultural centre, even as their avowed desire is to globalize literary studies. I examine the models of Casanova and Moretti in turn.

Literature and Power

Pascale Casanova has shown us a *république mondiale des lettres*, for her a decidedly mercantilist republic, in which the global cultural-capital markets in Paris determine the exchange-value of texts. Her model has much explanatory power for the Europe of the past several centuries, and, arguably, for the post-1945 world at large, but by her own admission, can say little about the non-European world before 1945. Casanova goes so far as to date the non-'Western' world's entry into *literature* (not merely 'world literature' or 'world-literature') to the era of decolonization. Her point is perhaps less that literature did not exist in non-European languages before decolonization, than that it could not be recognized as literature until after decolonization, an argument which begs the question: 'recognized by whom?' Casanova is working within a very specific and localized definition of literature, one which is effective enough, perhaps, for the periods, texts and languages which have provided the traditional focus of literary studies, but which cannot account for the full range of literary production across all cultures and times.

Another problematic feature of Casanova's work is her reading of the relationship between literary and politico-economic systems of power. She identifies a parallel between the inequalities of what she calls 'national history' and the inequalities in literary resources between nations, but sees these parallels as analogical, rather than causal.[3] For her, the literary world is an alternative universe, operating under laws different from but analogous to those of the political world. The circulation of power within her republic of letters remains distinct from the circulation of power in the larger world; the currency of her republic cannot, it seems, be exchanged for dollars.

Casanova's model constructs a world-system of literary circulation and exchange centred on Paris, and a given nation's access to 'literature' is a function of its recognition as such by Paris. Forms of literary circulation which predate French literary culture, or which exist outside it today, have no real place in Casanova's world-system. There is a pronounced division of labour within her system, in that the core (Paris) performs the value-added work of evaluating, setting prices for, and admitting to literature the textual production of the periphery (most of the rest of the world, with London and New York as slightly less central components of the core and Germany, perhaps, as what Wallerstein would label the semi-periphery). Peripheral production is only of value once recognized by the centre.

Franco Moretti, who makes explicit use of the world-systems model developed by Immanuel Wallerstein, presents a less innocent vision of the relationship between literary and economic systems. He proposes a theory of the novel in which peripheral cultures – those outside the Anglo-French core of novelistic production – develop the novel, not as an indigenous formation, but as a 'compromise between a Western formal influence (usually French or English) and local materials.'[4] There seems to be a dilemma inherent in the formulation of Moretti's law of the novel: the more rigorously the novel is defined as a 'Western' form, the less explanatory power the law has (since by definition if a Western form is imported into a culture the result will be a mix of that Western form and local materials), while the more inclusive the definition of the 'novel', the less valid the law (since there will then be more 'novels' which don't especially partake of the form of the Western novel).[5]

Although I disagree with the details of the law's formulation, I nonetheless recognize the urgent significance of framing the question of the development of the novel (as we know it) outside its Anglo-French homeland in terms like Moretti's.[6] As with Casanova's *république mondiale*, however, his model has its chronological limitations. Wallerstein himself insists that the world-system is a product of the Columbian Exchange and the Industrial Revolution, and he has resisted attempts by the late Andre Gunder Frank and others to apply his framework to earlier times.[7] Moretti does not altogether share Wallerstein's timidity about projecting his model backwards in time; he has offered, for example, an analysis of

Petrarchism as a poetic phenomenon that suggests that it obeys something like the same law he describes for the modern novel.[8]

The axial distribution of labour in Moretti's theory of the novel is quite clear: core cultures develop new genres for export to the periphery, and the mapping of that distribution of labour onto that of the larger economy is too neat to be accidental.[9] The relationship between the diffusion of Petrarchism and the contemporary centres of political and economic power is nowhere near as clear – which reminds us that to expand the field of inquiry for literary studies beyond the modern West will entail the analysis of systems of literary circulation quite distinct from that experienced by the nineteenth-century Anglo-French novel. Where Casanova's model suggests the autonomy of literary markets from the economic and political spheres, Moretti's may insist on too easy an equivalence between the two. If we wish our model of world literature to extend deeply into the past, then the theories of Casanova and Moretti, useful as they are in their own context, will not suffice.

Six Modes

The model of world literature that I seek is one constructed as a means of understanding and appreciating the multiplicity of strategies used by literatures to relate to their political and economic environments. As such, it should neither innocently claim that literature is exempt from this larger economic and political order, nor engage in *a priori* assumptions about what that order, and literature's relationship with it, look like. It will recognize the multiple centres and systems of cultural power in operation across human history, and in addition will affirm that profound theoretical insights can and must come from the study of diverse literatures, rather than from the study of a core tradition or from the work of a dedicated class of theoreticians exempted from the cultural labour of textual analysis. In sum, it will be a theory of 'world literature' rather than 'world-literature', focused on the production of verbal art and its relationship to its environment as a genuinely universal phenomenon in human culture. As such, the world-literatures of Casanova or Moretti emerge, I would argue, as the current manifestation of the more general problem of the relationship between literature and its environment.[10]

What follows is not a definitive configuration of a discipline-to-be, but rather a suggested organizing principle, together with a set of six modes in which that principle seems to have manifested itself. I suggest that the shifting configuration of the relationship between literatures and environments forms the most useful object of study for a future 'world literature without the hyphen'. None of these six modes (the epichoric, panchoric, cosmopolitan, vernacular, national and global) are my own invention; in each case I draw on considerable existing scholarship and my only contribution is to suggest that these six modes might constitute a meta-system of literary systems.[11] I will present the six in the order of their chronological emergence, but do not suggest that they constitute a teleological history of world literature, or of any one literature. No single literature or language has passed through all six of these modes, and in past periods several of these modes have co-existed. Nor is this list exhaustive; based as it is in scholarship on individual literatures, the list can and should be added to or altered in light of further literary encounters. In what follows, I will briefly sketch the features of each mode, and will suggest examples of texts or literatures which fall under their rubrics.

The *epichoric* is a mode of literary production in which literature is produced within the confines of a local community. It represents the zero-grade of literary circulation, since epichoric literature as such does not circulate beyond the community in which it is produced. I borrow the concept of epichoric literature from the work of Gregory Nagy on archaic Greek poetry. Nagy introduces the term epichoric, in opposition to the Panhellenic, in the context of myth, and identifies the epichoric as that which is produced in a local context and whose meaning depends on that context – local hero-cults, versions of myths and songs which do not travel well. Inasmuch as it is associated with small polities, which may or may not share a language with their neighbours, the epichoric may well have a political dimension in establishing and delimiting that polity or as a form of resistance to a broader cultural and political sphere.[12] I would like to suggest the potential applicability of the concept of the epichoric to contexts other than Archaic Greece: the Chinese *Canon of Poetry*, for example, includes a collection of *Airs* representing epichorically the various states into which Zhou-dynasty China was divided, and the concept may help understand, among other things, pre-Islamic Arabic poetry, the South Slavic oral epic tradition as studied by Milman Parry and Albert Lord, or the cultural practices of many of the First Nations of the Americas.[13]

The traces of epichoric literatures are generally difficult to discern, especially in the written records of past times. Instead, what we most often find are epichoric refractions of what I will call *panchoric* texts, as well as epichoric approaches to reading and interpreting such texts. I extrapolate the term 'panchoric' from 'Panhellenic', and use the term to refer to literary texts and systems of circulation operating across a range of epichoric communities, united to some degree in language and culture, but generally fragmented politically. Panchoric texts such as Homeric epic and the Chinese *Canon of Poetry* often represent themselves as some form of negotiation of epichoric tensions. More speculatively, I would suggest that Sanskrit epic, similarly composed in a culturally-unified but politically fragmented world, likewise contains elements of the panchoric. Epichoric and panchoric impulses are perhaps most frequently encountered in mutual interaction, and the opposition between them is frequently productive. The great Panhellenic epics, the *Iliad*, with its famous Catalogue of Ships, and the *Odyssey*, with its world-spanning journey, project into their narratives the assimilation of epichoric traditions to panchoric cultural agendas.

My notion of the panchoric has some affinities with Wallerstein's 'mini-system', which I take to be an analogue to the world-system on a smaller scale. They represent the first historical contexts in which literatures circulate, and come to be aware of that circulation as a problem. That is, panchoric literatures must adapt themselves to different political niches, and questions of the origins of texts become especially important in this mode. The panchoric and epichoric exist primarily in opposition to each other, and the panchoric in particular frequently represents itself as some sort of negation of the epichoric.[14]

The Sanskrit Example

The term *cosmopolitan*, derived from Stoic philosophy, has seen active service in recent years in a series of debates about the contemporary world.[15] My own use of the term, however, derives instead from the work of the Sanskritist Sheldon Pollock. Pollock has written compellingly about the pervasiveness of inscriptional poetry in Sanskrit, from modern Pakistan to Java, in the years 300–1300 AD. In the regions Pollock discusses (which he identifies as 'the Sanskrit cosmopolis'), Sanskrit inscriptions exist alongside inscriptions in vernacular languages – Prakrits, Kannada, Tamil, Khmer, Old Javanese – throughout much of this period, but with the important distinction that the vernacular languages are used to 'document' the world, whereas Sanskrit is used to 'interpret' the world.[16] In other words, practical matters such as the granting of lands and privileges happen in the vernacular; the idealized and aestheticized self-representation of the ruling order happens in Sanskrit. In contrast to contemporary models of cultural diffusion, the spread of Sanskrit across South and Southeast Asia takes place without military conquest or large-scale colonization; it seems to be a free and voluntary act on the part of dozens of polities.

Not only does Pollock provide one of the most compelling examples of an incongruity between cultural and political power in the pre-modern world, but even more importantly he explicitly identifies this incongruity as one worth studying – a concern that should, I argue, be reflected more broadly in pre-modern studies. Indeed, Sanskrit is far from the only cosmopolitan language whose cultural status does not map neatly onto its political and economic one. The prestige of Akkadian and Greek as literary languages in the eastern Mediterranean so long outlives the conquests of Sargon and Alexander as to undermine the role of political hegemony in establishing that prestige, while the enduring and complex status of Chinese literature in Japan, Korea and Vietnam, like that of Persian literature at the Mughal and Ottoman courts, can again hardly be explained in terms of conquest, colonization or trade alone. The cultural prestige of Latin in the European Middle Ages likewise has little to do with imperial power. Cosmopolitan literary languages, then, may sometimes follow in the wake of a world-empire of the kind discussed by Wallerstein, but the two cannot be elided into a single phenomenon.

The circulation of literature within a cosmopolitan literary system is distinct from that encountered in a panchoric system, partly because cosmopolitan literary languages can be used by groups speaking a variety of mother tongues and partly because cosmopolitan literatures tend to represent themselves as agents of an ideology of universal rule, whether or not that ideology is seen as practiced or practicable. In theorizing the constitution of the ideal state, for example, I would see

Plato as engaging in an incipiently cosmopolitan gesture, while the New Testament's appropriation of the Hebrew Bible, re-reading what I would characterize as the 'panchoric' nature of the tribes of the former as the 'nations' of the world, undeniably has cosmopolitan ambitions. Where a panchoric literary language allows literature to circulate among a set of political entities sharing a native language (but likely not a political regime), a cosmopolitan literary language creates a cross-cultural system, in which speakers of many languages share a common literary idiom. This language may be the cultural expression of a world-empire, or a nostalgic reminiscence of a former empire, or it may constitute a cultural world-empire without political ramifications. Core–periphery relations may be present (as in the Chinese case: Sino-Japanese and Sino-Korean poetries do not circulate within China itself), or the system may be more polycentric (as is the case with Greek in the Hellenistic and Imperial periods, or with Latin in the Middle Ages). However they are configured, cosmopolitan literary languages aim at a universal reach.

Vernacular to National

While in some senses *vernacular* languages resemble panchoric languages, being used for literary purposes over comparatively large territories sharing linguistic but not necessarily political unity, the distinction comes in the kind of cultural difference they are required to negotiate. Where panchoric literatures evolve in relationship to epichoric traditions, vernacular languages react against the hegemony of a cosmopolitan literary language. Just as cosmopolitan literatures need not depend on a political infrastructure for support, so vernacular literatures need not reflect a political declaration of independence from empire. Indeed, as in the case of the emergence of Anglo-Saxon literature and of other European vernaculars, the cosmopolitan language in use may long since have lost its political and economic supports. The programmatic declaration of a new vernacular literature is nonetheless frequently a political and politicized gesture (especially if it involves choices among a variety of dialects), as in the case of Dante's *De Vulgari Eloquentia* or the May Fourth movement in China. Alternatively, literary languages may choose to retain their cosmopolitan status, rather than yield to any one vernacular standard, as has been generally the case with Arabic. Vernacular languages need not map onto the political world; in delimiting the range of dialects he considers 'Italian', Dante sketches very nearly the borders of modern Italy, but his project of nation-building (if we can call it that) remains unrealized for centuries. Furthermore, vernacular literatures can circulate beyond cultural as well as political borders, as, successively, did Occitan, Dante's Italian, and du Bellay's French in medieval and early modern Europe.

Sheldon Pollock's work on the vernacular reminds us of the nearly-simultaneous development of vernacular languages in South India and Western Europe, beginning with Old English and Kannada in the eighth century CE, and spreading across the Latin and Sanskrit ecumenes in the following seven or eight centuries.[17] Pollock sketches these twin phenomena, of the rise of a cosmopolitan idiom in one millennium, followed by the rise of vernacular languages in the next, mainly to suggest that both phenomena, and vernacularization in particular, have histories which remain to be written. Beyond the historical questions, ideas about cosmopolitan and vernacular literatures as developed by Pollock offer a useful framework for understanding the structure of a wide variety of literary systems, past and present, which function in ways analogous to those described by Moretti and Casanova but do not fit their specific parameters.[18] As both the South Asian and European examples illustrate, vernacular literary languages tend to operate within systems, incorporating a cosmopolitan language or languages and a range of vernacular rivals. The continued presence of cosmopolitan languages in many vernacular contexts renders the relationships among vernacular literatures more complex, and complicates the picture of literary rivalry imagined, for example, by Casanova.

It is in the realm of *national* literatures that we enter Morettian and Casanovan territory more explicitly. The boundary between a vernacular literature and a national literature is necessarily a vague one, but I will provisionally suggest that the moment of transition occurs when the history of a given literature, and its contemporary practices, are mapped onto the history and contemporary status of a particular political state. As such, national literatures are, I would argue, a product in part of the nationalisms of the nineteenth century, although certainly with earlier roots in some cases. The phenomenon which Casanova identifies as '*l'effet Herder*', the development of a literature out of a mix of folk traditions and nationalism, is another version of this mode. I would suggest as well that the history of the novel outside its homelands, as sketched by Moretti, constitutes in some measure the construction of explicitly *national* literatures, especially in non-Western cultures – that is, the larger-scale absorption of European ideas of the nation and of national literature mirrors to some extent the absorption of the European literary form of the novel. Wherever a national literature emerges, it will represent itself as a manifestation of the political and/or cultural dimension of a nation-state. Such literatures are characterized by their marginalization of dialectal and minority-language literatures, and the construction of narratives of literary history which prize the autochthonous over the cosmopolitan (i.e. the history of English literature as beginning from *Beowulf*, or of Bengali literature from the *Charyapada*).[19] In other words, they represent a projection of national political goals onto the literary system, and, in spite of obvious difficulties arising from the non-coincidence of linguistic and political borders, this national model retains considerable power, even today, in literary studies.

Regional and Global

The national-literature model is now clearly inadequate, both because a number of languages and their literatures transcend national borders, and because the de-centring of the nation-state brought about by contemporary global capitalism alters literary circulation. As such, we may begin to imagine what might reasonably be termed a *global* literature. This category, still more conjectural than real, consists of literatures whose linguistic reach transcends national, even continental, borders. In some senses, a global literature resembles a cosmopolitan literature, except that (at least at this time) global literatures continue to represent themselves as systems of national literatures to an extent that cosmopolitan literatures do not. They are in that sense inter-national rather than extra-national. The concept of 'global' literature, or verbal art, as it now exists in an age of proliferating media, also raises the question of how broadly 'literature' is to be defined. A definition which focuses on those texts which receive critical esteem in the West will generate a model of global literature looking much like that described by Casanova or Moretti; whereas one which embraces all verbal art, popular as well as 'literary', and including the cinematic, will acknowledge the centrality of otherwise peripheral locations such as Mumbai and Hong Kong. I do not believe we need to (or can) draw firm boundaries around categories of verbal art in this context; indeed, one of the most exciting aspects of a global literature is the extent to which it lends itself to *bricolage*, with texts serving different purposes in different systems of circulation.

In the case of global literatures the legacies of nineteenth-century empires and of contemporary global capitalism wield considerable power. The clearest example of a global literature is English, with its well-developed theoretical infrastructure of postcolonial studies and institutions such as the Booker Prize working to construct the notion that literary production and consumption in English is in principle universal (even if, like contemporary trade in goods, national borders and invisible barriers render the claim of universality and equality of access hollow). The institutional representation of the English global literary system still varies greatly from nation to nation; within the United States, a tripartite division into British, American and 'postcolonial' literature is most common, while in Canada, for example, a quadripartite structure, including Canada as a fourth term, is the norm. Postcolonial literatures are to some extent represented as a distinct system, and to some extent as a series of national or regional literatures; that is, a Nigerian author writing in English might, from different angles, be a participant in a national Nigerian literary system and also in a postcolonial circuit of Global English literature.

French literature has an undeniable claim to a similar status, as reflected in the recent literary manifesto *Pour une littérature-monde*, whose title illustrates its clear debt to Braudel.[20] The relationship between the status of these two literatures and contemporary political and economic systems is obvious, and is reflected in the particular interest that they both hold for Moretti and Casanova. There are few other languages that might rival English and French as global literatures, given the political and economic power, demographic weight and geographic breadth they possess; however, each of their major rivals (Chinese, Spanish, Hindi, Arabic, Russian) participates in a global circulation of some kind, as do a very few other literatures under more limited circumstances. That reality is not a sign of failure or defeat (as, arguably, Casanova's model would suggest); the national, vernacular and cosmopolitan successes of these and other languages can serve to ensure their continued literary vitality, and to warrant an increased attention to their role in the current world-literary system.[21]

This survey of various modes in which literary systems operate has of necessity been generalizing and schematic, and presents problems as severe as those it attempts to address. The status of Spanish or Arabic in the modern world is an obvious case in point; the former's international, but for the most part geographically-constrained circulation, might better be called 'regional' than global, while the latter, with its preservation of a classical written language linked to a universalist religion, is in many ways a cosmopolitan language in a global era. I do not intend, however, for this to be an exhaustive survey, nor do I intend for it to provide a continuous and adequate narrative of world literary history. Rather, I hope to have at least established that the question of the structure and function of literary systems in different environments is a problem worthy of study, and that there might exist typological parallels among these systems whose examination could yield useful results for specialists in a variety of literatures.

Rather than a division of labour in which national-literature specialists produce raw data for processing by world-literature scholars, I propose a sharing of labour by which, say, specialists in Persian literature find useful theoretical and practical insights in the work of Sinologists, or Anglo-Saxonists in the work of specialists of Old Kannada. Such a sharing of labour holds out, I believe, the possibility of world literature, unhyphenated, as a coherent field of study; taking as its object not a world-literary system which maps roughly onto Wallerstein's world-system, but rather, and simply, the literature – the verbal artistic production – of the world.

Notes

1 For an enlightening discussion of Goethe and *Weltliteratur*, see David Damrosch, *What is World Literature?*, Princeton 2003, pp. 1–36.

2 Immanuel Wallerstein, *World-Systems Analysis: An Introduction*, Durham, NC 2004, pp. 15–16 and 98–99.

3 Pascale Casanova, *La République mondiale des lettres*, Paris 1999, pp. 24, 62–63.

4 Franco Moretti, 'Conjectures on World Literature', NLR 1, January–February 2000, reprinted in Christopher Prendergast, ed., *Debating World Literature*, London 2004. Moretti and Prendergast have continued a lively exchange on the subject: see NLR 8, 20, 24, 26, 28, 34 and 41.

5 Jonathan Zwicker uses a methodology owing much to Moretti (including numerical analyses of the numbers of books published per year in different forms, and the numbers held in particular library collections), as well as close readings, to show *inter alia* that pre-Meiji literature – that is, prior to Western influence – continued to have a major impact on Japanese readers and writers into the twentieth century. Zwicker, *Practices of the Sentimental Imagination: Melodrama, the Novel and the Social Imaginary in Nineteenth-Century Japan*, Cambridge, MA 2006.

6 The five volumes of *Il romanzo* edited by Moretti between 2001 and 2003 provide an indispensable foundation for further and ever more nuanced work on these problems.

7 See Janet Abu-Lughod for what she characterizes as a 'thirteenth-century world system' in *Before European Hegemony: The World System AD 1250–1350*, Oxford 1989. Andre Gunder Frank and Barry Gills both attempt to stretch the beginnings of a world-system to much earlier times: Frank and Gills, *The World System: Five Hundred Years or Five Thousand?*, London 1993; Frank, REORIENT: *Global Economy in the Asian Age*, Berkeley 1998.

8 'More Conjectures', NLR 20, March–April 2003, pp. 73–74.

9 Moretti's model of 'distant reading', which involves the reading of scholarship *about* the novel rather than novels themselves, seems another version of the axial division of labour: specialists in national literatures do the resource-extracting work of reading vast numbers of texts, while generalists add surplus value to this work through their theoretical syntheses.

10 I am inspired to make this turn away from economic metaphors towards ecology by Niklas Luhmann's discussion of 'environment' as that which lies outside a particular social subsystem. The notion of literature as such a subsystem, recognizing distinctions within its environment but only selectively interconnected with it, is a useful refining of the discussions of literary and economic systems found, for example, in Casanova. Luhmann, *Ecological Communication*, Chicago 1989, pp. 15–21.

11 I find, in other words, that scholars on Greek and Sanskrit provide not merely the raw data which theories of literature can attempt to explain, but the very theoretical structures which those theories seek to develop.

12 Gregory Nagy notes that Archaic Greek lyric is in fact usually in a dynamic tension between the epichoric and what I call the panchoric. *Pindar's Homer: The Lyric Possession of an Epic Past*, Baltimore 1990, pp. 66–67.

13 Milman Parry, *The Making of Homeric Verse*, Oxford 1971; Albert Bates Lord, *The Singer of Tales*, Cambridge, MA 1960. The appeal to the oral histories of the Gitxsan and Wet'suwet'en nations in the establishment of aboriginal land title in *Delgamuukw v. British Columbia* offers a contemporary example of the use of epichoric literary tradition to define communities and their territories. Richard Daly, *Our Box Was Full: An Ethnography for the Delgamuukw Plaintiffs*, Vancouver 2005, provides an excellent introduction to these issues by an anthropologist involved in the case.

14 Although the reverse can also be true. On the use of Stesichorus's *Palinode* – an epichoric rejection of the Panhellenic myth of the abduction of Helen to Troy – by Plato in the *Phaedrus* as a means of situating Socrates's own work in opposition to rhetoric (which Plato has Socrates align with epic and the Panhellenic), see Alexander Beecroft, ' "This is not a true story": Stesichorus's *Palinode* and the Revenge of the Epichoric', *Transactions of the American Philological Association*, vol. 136 (2006), pp. 47–69.

15 Basic bibliography here would include: Pheng Cheah and Bruce Robbins, eds., *Cosmopolitics: Thinking and Feeling beyond the Nation*, Minneapolis 1998; Carol Breckenridge *et al.*, *Cosmopolitanism*, Durham, NC 2002; Gillian Brock and Harry Brighouse, eds., *The Political Philosophy of Cosmopolitanism*, Cambridge 2005, and Kwame Appiah, *Cosmopolitanism: Ethics in a World of Strangers*, New York 2006.

16 Sheldon Pollock, 'The Sanskrit Cosmopolis, 300–1300: Transculturation, Vernacularization and the Question of Ideology', in Jan Houben, ed., *Ideology and Status of Sanskrit: Contributions to the History of the Sanskrit Language*, Leiden 1996, p. 219.

17 Sheldon Pollock, 'Cosmopolitan and Vernacular in History', in Breckenridge *et al.*, *Cosmopolitanism*. As Pollock himself points out, Tamil occupies a somewhat problematic position

within this schema: 'The Cosmopolitan Vernacular', *Journal of Asian Studies*, vol. 57, no. 1 (1998), p. 20, note 14. If the (disputed) traditional dating of early Sangam literature to the first few centuries CE is accepted, then Tamil becomes a quite disruptive vernacular intrusion on the cosmopolitan millennium. The point need not be to embrace Pollock's model dogmatically, something that the nature of this article would in any event hardly permit. Rather, the value in this exercise lies in identifying a typological similarity, which can inform the study of a variety of literary contexts.

18 In effect Casanova takes the vernacular moment as the birth of her narrative. Prendergast finds in it phases analogous to the vernacular, national and global, although I would prefer to stress their status as a synchronic system of systems rather than as an evolutionary process.

19 Strikingly, both texts, recovered respectively in the early 19th and 20th centuries, have been deployed as the autochthonous origins of multiple literatures: English and (erroneously) Danish for *Beowulf*; Bengali, Assamese and Oriya for the *Charyapada*.

20 Jean Rouaud and Michel Le Bris, eds, *Pour une littérature-monde*, Paris 2007.

21 A productive example is the collection of essays edited by Françoise Lionnet and Shu-mei Shih, which explores in part the connections between the two editors' respective Francophone and Sinophone interests: *Minor Transnationalisms*, Durham, NC 2005.

14

Literature as a World (2005)

Pascale Casanova

A literary critic, journalist, and researcher at the Center for Research in Arts and Language in Paris, Pascale Casanova's main interest is in the politics of literary culture. Best known for her book *La République mondiale des lettres* (*The World Republic of Letters*, 1999), Casanova draws on sociologist Pierre Bourdieu's theory to construct a global literary field, keeping a balance between the irreducible singularity of literary works and their corresponding positions in a national and translational literary system. The result of two decades' work on modern literature, following a prize-winning book on the transnational author Samuel Beckett (*Beckett the Abstractor*, 1977), Casanova's book looks into the production and circulation of literature in the world from a historical and sociological point of view. Using historian Fernand Braudel's theory of a "world-economy" to bring Bourdieu's notion of a literary field from the national to the global level, Casanova writes a history of the relatively autonomous literary field, a "world republic of letters," that she sees as emerging in the sixteenth century and with Paris as its center. Structured by power relations between the dominant and dominated cultures, the literary field is one in which writers struggle for symbolic capital while fighting the inherent inequities engendered by the center–periphery polarization.

In her essay "Literature as a World," Casanova proposes as conceptual frame a "world literary space" that mediates between historical, political, and economic contexts and the aesthetic autonomy of the text. Arguing for a reconciliation of intrinsic and extrinsic criticism, Casanova defines her notion of the world literary space as a world-structure, different from the level playing field of a flattened "world-system," because it foregrounds the distinction dominant–dominated so as to emphasize the struggles and inequalities that lie at the core of this international space. "My project, then, is to restore the coherence of the global structure within which texts appear ... only to return to the texts themselves."

Pascale Casanova, "Literature as a World" (2005). In *New Left Review* 31 (Jan./Feb. 2005), pp. 71–90.

World Literature in Theory, First Edition. Edited by David Damrosch.
© 2014 John Wiley & Sons, Ltd. Published 2014 by John Wiley & Sons, Ltd.

Customer: God made the world in six days and you, you can't make me a damn pair of trousers in six months!

Tailor: But sir, look at the world and look at your trousers.

quoted by Samuel Beckett

Far, far from you world history unfolds, the world history of your soul.

Franz Kafka

Three questions. Is it possible to re-establish the lost bond between literature, history and the world, while still maintaining a full sense of the irreducible singularity of literary texts? Second, can literature itself be conceived as a world? And if so, might an exploration of its territory help us to answer question number one?

Put differently: is it possible to find the conceptual means with which to oppose the central postulate of internal, text-based literary criticism – the total rupture between text and world? Can we propose any theoretical and practical tools that could combat the governing principle of the autonomy of the text, or the alleged independence of the linguistic sphere? To date, the answers given to this crucial question, from postcolonial theory among others, seem to me to have established only a limited connection between the two supposedly incommensurate domains. Post-colonialism posits a direct link between literature and history, one that is exclusively political. From this, it moves to an *external* criticism that runs the risk of reducing the literary to the political, imposing a series of annexations or short-circuits, and often passing in silence over the actual aesthetic, formal or stylistic characteristics that actually 'make' literature.

I want to propose a hypothesis that would move beyond this division between internal and external criticism. Let us say that a mediating space exists between literature and the world: a parallel territory, relatively autonomous from the political domain, and dedicated as a result to questions, debates, inventions of a specifically literary nature. Here, struggles of all sorts – political, social, national, gender, ethnic – come to be refracted, diluted, deformed or transformed according to a literary logic, and in literary forms. Working from this hypothesis, while trying to envisage all its theoretical and practical consequences, should permit us to set out on a course of criticism that would be both internal and external; in other words, a criticism that could give a unified account of, say, the evolution of poetic forms, or the aesthetics of the novel, and their connection to the political, economic and social world – including telling us how, by a very long (indeed historical) process, the link gets broken in the most autonomous regions of this space.

So: another world, whose divisions and frontiers are relatively independent of political and linguistic borders. And with its own laws, its own history, its specific revolts and revolutions; a market where non-market values are traded, within a non-economic economy; and measured, as we shall see, by an aesthetic scale of time. This World of Letters functions invisibly for the most part, save to those most distant from its great centres or most deprived of its resources, who can see more clearly than others the forms of violence and domination that operate within it.

Let us call this mediating area the 'world literary space'. It is no more than a tool that should be tested by concrete research, an instrument that might provide an account of the logic and history of literature, without falling into the trap of total autonomy. It is also a 'hypothetical model' in Chomsky's sense – a body of statements whose working out (if risky) may itself help to formulate the object of description; that is, an internally coherent set of propositions.[1] Working from a model should permit a certain freedom from the immediate 'given'. It should, on the contrary, allow us to construct every case afresh; and to show with each one that it does not exist in isolation, but is a particular instance of the possible, an element in a group or family, which we could not have seen without having previously formulated an abstract model of all possibilities.

This conceptual tool is not 'world literature' itself – that is, a body of literature expanded to a world scale, whose documentation and, indeed, existence remains problematic – but a *space*: a set of interconnected positions, which must be thought and described in relational terms. At stake are not the modalities of analysing literature on a world scale, but the conceptual means for thinking literature *as* a world.

In his story, 'The Figure in the Carpet' – turning as it does on the aims of interpretation in literature – Henry James deploys the beautiful metaphor of the Persian rug. Viewed casually or too close up, this appears an indecipherable tangle of arbitrary shapes and colours; but from the right angle, the carpet will suddenly present the attentive observer with 'the one right combination' of 'superb intricacy' – an ordered set of motifs which can only be understood in relation to each other, and which only become visible when perceived in their totality, in their reciprocal dependence and mutual interaction.[2] Only when the carpet is seen as a configuration – to use Foucault's term in *Les Mots et les choses* – ordering the shapes and colours can its regularities, variations, repetitions be understood; both its coherence and its internal relationships. Each figure can be grasped only in terms of the position it occupies within the whole, and its interconnections with all the others.

The Persian carpet metaphor perfectly encapsulates the approach offered here: to take a different perspective, shifting the ordinary vantage-point on literature. Not to focus just on the global coherence of the carpet, but rather to show that, starting from a grasp of the overall pattern of the designs, it will be possible to understand each motif, each colour in its most minute detail; that is, each text, each individual author, on the basis of their relative position within this immense structure. My project, then, is to restore the coherence of the global structure within which texts appear, and which can only be seen by taking the route seemingly farthest from them: through the vast, invisible territory which I have called the 'World Republic of Letters'. But only in order to return to the texts themselves, and to provide a new tool for reading them.

Birth of a World

This literary space did not, of course, spring into being in its present configuration. It emerged as the product of a historical process, from which it grew progressively more autonomous. Without going into detail, we can say that it appeared in Europe in the 16th century, France and England forming its oldest regions. It was consolidated and enlarged into central and eastern Europe during the 18th and especially the 19th centuries, propelled by Herderian national theory. It expanded throughout the 20th century, notably through the still-ongoing decolonization process: manifestos proclaiming the right to literary existence or independence continue to appear, often linked to movements for national self-determination. Although the space of literature has been constituted more or less everywhere in the world, its unification across the whole planet is far from complete.

The mechanisms through which this literary universe functions are the exact opposite of what is ordinarily understood by 'literary globalization' – better defined as a short-term boost to publishers' profits in the most market-oriented and powerful centres through the marketing of products intended for rapid, 'de-nationalized' circulation.[3] The success of this type of book among educated Western layers – representing no more than a shift from train-station to airport literature – has fostered belief in an ongoing literary pacification process: a progressive normalization and standardization of themes, forms, languages and story-types across the globe. In reality, structural inequalities within the literary world give rise to specific series of struggles, rivalries and contests over literature itself. Indeed, it is through these collisions that the ongoing unification of literary space becomes visible.

Stockholm and Greenwich

One objective indicator of the existence of this world literary space is the (almost) unanimous belief in the universality of the Nobel Prize for literature. The significance attributed to this award, the peculiar diplomacy involved, the national expectations engendered, the colossal renown it bestows; even (above all?) the annual criticism of the Swedish jury for its alleged lack of objectivity, its supposed political prejudices, its aesthetic errors – all conspire to make this annual canonization a global engagement for the protagonists of literary space. The Nobel Prize is today one of the few truly international literary consecrations, a unique laboratory for the designation and definition of what is universal in literature.[4] The echoes it creates each year, the expectations aroused, the beliefs stirred all reaffirm the existence of a literary world stretching across virtually the entire planet, with its own mode of celebration, both autonomous – not subject, or at least not directly, to political, linguistic, national, nationalist or commercial criteria – and global. In this sense, the Nobel Prize is a prime, objective indicator of the existence of a world literary space.[5]

Another indicator – less readily observable – is the appearance of a specific measurement of time, common to all the players. Each new entrant must recognize at the outset a reference point, a norm against which he or she will be measured; all positions are located relative to a centre in which the literary present is determined. I propose to call this the Greenwich Meridian of literature. Just as the imaginary line, arbitrarily chosen in order to determine the lines of longitude, contributes to the real organization of the world and makes it possible to measure distances and assess positions across the surface of the globe, so the literary meridian allows us to gauge the distance from the centre of the protagonists within literary space. It is the place where the measurement of literary time – that is, the assessment of aesthetic modernity – is crystallized, contested, elaborated. What is considered modern here, at a given moment, will be declared to be the 'present': texts that will 'make their mark', capable of modifying the current aesthetic norms. These works will serve, for a time at least, as the units of measurement within a specific chronology, models of comparison for subsequent productions.

To be decreed 'modern' is one of the most difficult forms of recognition for writers outside the centre, and the object of violent and bitter competition. Octavio Paz brilliantly set out the terms of this strange struggle in his Nobel Prize acceptance speech, the title of which is, precisely, *In Search of the Present*. He describes his entire personal and poetic trajectory as a frantic – and successful, as his receipt of the highest award testifies – search for a literary present, from which he understood early on that, as a Mexican, he was structurally very distant.[6] Texts granted modern status create the chronology of literary history, according to a logic that can be quite different from those of other social worlds. For example, once Joyce's *Ulysses* had been consecrated as a 'modern' work by Valéry Larbaud's 1929 French translation, winning the reviews and critical attention that had so far eluded it in English, it became – and remains, in certain regions of literary space – one of the measures of novelistic modernity.

Temporalities

Modernity is, of course, an unstable entity: a locus of permanent struggle, a decree destined for more or less rapid obsolescence, and one of the principles of change at the heart of the world literary space. All those who aspire to modernity, or who struggle for monopoly control over its attribution, are engaged in the constant classification and de-classification of works – with texts apt to become former moderns or new classics. The recurrent use of temporal metaphors in criticism, airily declaring works to be 'passé' or 'outmoded', archaic or innovative, anachronistic or imbued with 'the spirit of the times', is one of the clearest signs of these mechanisms' functioning. This explains, at least in part, the permanence of the term 'modernity' in literary movements and proclamations at least since 1850 – from the different European and Latin American modernisms, through Italian and Russian futurisms, up to the various postmodernisms. The innumerable claims to 'newness' – 'Nouveau Roman', 'Nouvelle Vague' and so on – adhere to the same principle.

Owing to the inherent precariousness of the principle of 'modernity', a work declared modern is doomed to become obsolete unless elevated to the category of 'classic'. Through this process, some works can escape the vagaries of opinion and disputes over their relative value. In literary terms, a classic stands above temporal competition (and spatial inequality). On the other hand, practices that are remote from the literary present, itself established by the whole system of consecrations at the centre, will be declared long out of date. For example, the naturalist novel is still being produced in the zones furthest from the Greenwich Meridian (whether peripheral literary spaces or the most commercial regions of the centre), even though it has not been considered 'modern' by the autonomous authorities for a very long time. The Brazilian critic Antonio Candido observed:

> what demands attention in Latin America is the way aesthetically anachronistic works were considered valid … This is what occurred with naturalism in the novel, which arrived a little late and has prolonged itself until now with no essential break in continuity … So, when naturalism was already only a survival of an outdated genre in Europe, among us it could still be an ingredient of legitimate literary formulas, such as the social novel of the 1930s and 40s.[7]

This type of aesthetic-temporal struggle is often waged through intermediaries who themselves have an interest in the 'discovery' of authors from abroad. The Norwegian Ibsen was consecrated as one of the greatest European dramatists more or less simultaneously in Paris and London, around 1890. His work, labelled 'realist', overturned all theatrical practice, writing, decor, language and dialogue, leading to a genuine revolution in European theatre. The international consecration of a playwright from a country that had gained independence only a short time before, and whose language was seldom spoken (and therefore seldom translated) in France and England, was secured through the actions of a few mediators – Bernard Shaw in London, André Antoine and Lugné-Poe in Paris – who themselves planned to 'modernize' theatre in their respective countries, going beyond the stale, established norms of vaudeville and bourgeois drama which held sway in London and Paris, and making their own names as dramatists or producers.[8] In the Dublin of 1900, Joyce in his turn made use of the prodigious aesthetic and thematic novelty of Ibsen's work in his struggle against Irish theatre, which threatened, in his view, to become 'much too Irish'.

Much the same applies to Faulkner. Having been lauded from the 1930s on as one of the most innovative novelists of the age,[9] Faulkner himself became a measure of novelistic innovation after receiving the Nobel Prize in 1950. Following his international consecration, Faulkner's work played the role of a 'temporal accelerator' for a wide range of novelists of different periods, in countries structurally comparable, in economic and cultural terms, to the American South. All of them openly announced their use (at least in a technical sense) of this Faulknerian accelerator; among them were Juan Benet in 1950s Spain, Gabriel García Márquez in Colombia and Mario Vargas Llosa in Peru in the 1950s and 1960s, Kateb Yacine in 1960s Algeria, António Lobo-Antunes in 1970s Portugal, Edouard Glissant in the French Antilles of the 1980s, and so on.

Seeing through Borders

But why start from the hypothesis of a world literary space and not a more restricted one, which would have been easier to demarcate – a regional or linguistic field, for instance? Why choose to begin by constructing the largest possible domain, the one entailing most risks? Because to illuminate the workings of this space, and in particular the forms of domination exerted within it, implies the rejection of established national categories and divisions; indeed, demands a trans- or inter-national mode of thought. Once we adopt this world perspective, we can immediately see that national boundaries, or linguistic ones, simply screen out the real effects of literary domination and inequality. The reason for this is simple: literatures the whole world over were formed on the national model created and promoted by Germany at the end of the 18th century. The national movement of literatures, which accompanied the formation of Europe's political spaces from the beginning of the 19th century, led to an essentialization of literary categories and the belief that the frontiers of literary space necessarily coincided with national borders. Nations were considered to be separate, self-enclosed units, each irreducible to any other; from within their autarchic specificity, these entities produced literary objects whose 'historical necessity' is inscribed within a national horizon. Stefan Collini has demonstrated the tautology underlying the definition of 'national literature' for the British – or rather, English – case: 'only those authors who display the putative characteristics are recognized as authentically English, a category whose definition relies upon the examples provided in the literature written by just those authors.'[10]

The national division of literatures leads to a form of astigmatism. An analysis of Irish literary space between 1890 and 1930 that ignored events unfolding both in London (the political, colonial and literary power, in opposition to which the Irish space is constructed) and in Paris (alternative recourse and politically neutral literary power), or passed in silence over the trajectories, exiles, and various forms of recognition offered in the different capitals, would be condemned to a partial and distorted view of the actual stakes and power relations facing Irish protagonists. Similarly, a study of the formation of the German literary space from the end of the 18th century that overlooked its intensely competitive relationship with France would run the risk of completely misunderstanding its structuring engagements.

This is not to suggest that inter-national literary power relations are the only explanatory factors in literary texts, or the sole interpretative instruments we can apply to them; still less that literary complexity should be reduced to this dimension.

Many other variables – national (that is, internal to the national literary field), psychological, psychoanalytic, formal or formalist – have a role to play.[11] The point is rather to demonstrate, in both structural and historical terms, how many variables, conflicts or forms of soft violence have remained undetected and unexplained due to the invisibility of this world structure. Critical writing on Kafka, for example, is often limited either to the biographical study of his psychology or to descriptions of Prague in the 1900s. In this case, the biographical and national 'screen' prevents us from seeing the author's place within other, larger worlds: within the space of the Jewish nationalist movements then developing across central and eastern Europe; in debates between Bundists and Yiddishists; as one of the dominated in the German linguistic and cultural space, and so on. The national filter acts as a kind of 'natural' frontier which prevents the analyst from considering the violence of transnational political and literary power relations as they impact upon the writer.

World Space or World-System

The hypothesis of a world space, functioning through a structure of domination that is, to some extent, independent of political, economic, linguistic and social forms, clearly owes a great deal to Pierre Bourdieu's concept of the 'field' and, more precisely, of the 'literary field'.[12] But the latter has so far been envisaged within a national framework, limited by the borders, historical traditions and capital accumulation processes of a specific nation-state. I found in Fernand Braudel's work, and his 'world-economy' in particular, the idea and the possibility of extending the analysis of these mechanisms onto the international plane.[13]

I would stress, though, the distinction between the 'world structure' that I am proposing and the 'world-system', most notably developed by Immanuel Wallerstein, which seems to me less appropriate to spaces of cultural production.[14] A 'system' implies directly interactive relations between every element, every position. A structure, on the other hand, is characterized by objective relations, which can operate outside of any direct interaction. Moreover, in Wallerstein's terms, the forces and movements that struggle against the 'system' are considered 'anti-systemic'. In other words, they are external to the system and struggle against it from a position 'outside', which is sometimes hard to situate but can potentially be located on the 'periphery'. In an international structure of domination, the opposite is the case: the definitions of 'outside' and 'inside' – that is, the boundaries of the space – are themselves the focus of struggles. It is these struggles that constitute the space, that unify it and drive its expansion. Within this structure, means and methods are permanently disputed: who can be declared a writer, who can make legitimate aesthetic judgements (ones that will endow a given work with a specific value), the very definition of literature.

In other words, world literary space is not a sphere that is set above all the others, reserved exclusively for international writers, editors, critics – for literary actors manoeuvring in a supposedly de-nationalized world. It is not the sole preserve of great novelists, hugely successful authors, editorial produce devised for global sales.

It is formed by all the inhabitants of the Republic of Letters, each of them differentially situated within their own national literary space. At the same time, each writer's position must necessarily be a double one, twice defined: each writer is situated once according to the position he or she occupies in a national space, and then once again according to the place that this occupies within the world space. This dual position, inextricably national and international, explains why – contrary to what economistic views of globalization would have us believe – international struggles take place and have their effects principally within national spaces; battles over the definition of literature, over technical or formal transformations and innovations, on the whole have national literary space as their arena.

The one great dichotomy is between national and international writers. This is the fracture which explains literary forms, types of aesthetic innovation, the adoption of genres. National and international writers fight with different weapons, for divergent aesthetic, commercial and editorial rewards – thus contributing, in different ways, to the accumulation of national literary resources required to enter the world space and compete inside it. Contrary to the conventional view, the national and international are not separate spheres; they are two opposed stances, struggling within the same domain.[15]

This is why literary space cannot simply be imagined as a world geography that might be grasped merely through a description of its regions, its cultural and linguistic climates, centres of attraction and modes of circulation, as Braudel or Wallerstein have done for the economic world.[16] Literary space should rather be conceived in terms of Cassirer's 'symbolic form', within which writers, readers, researchers, teachers, critics, publishers, translators and the rest read, write, think, debate, interpret; a structure which provides their – our – intellectual categories, and recreates its hierarchies and constraints in every mind, thus reinforcing the material aspects of its existence.[17] Differentially so, according to one's position within it (national, linguistic, professional) at any given moment. Literary space in all its forms – texts, juries, editors, critics, writers, theorists, scholars – exists twice over: once in things and once in thought; that is, in the set of beliefs produced by these material relations and internalized by the players in literature's Great Game.

This is another thing that makes the structure so hard to visualize: it is impossible to place it at a distance, as a discrete and objectifiable phenomenon. More: any description or analysis of its workings has to go *against* the vast mass of conventional thought about literature, against the given scholarly or aesthetic facts, and to reconceive every notion, every category – influence, tradition, heritage, modernity, classics, value – in terms of the specific, internal workings of the world republic of letters.

Accumulating Power

The primary characteristics of this world literary space are hierarchy and inequality. The skewed distribution of goods and values has been one of its constituting principles, since resources have historically accumulated within national frontiers.

Goethe was the first to intuit the direct link between the appearance of a *Weltliteratur* and the emergence of a new economy founded on the specific struggles of inter-national literary relations: a 'market where all nations offer their wares' and 'a general intellectual trade'.[18] In fact, the world of literature provides a paradoxical sort of marketplace, constituted around a non-economic economy, and functioning according to its own set of values: for production and reproduction here are based on a belief in the 'objective' value of literary creations – works denominated as 'priceless'. The value produced by national or universal classics, great innovators, *poètes maudits*, rare texts, becomes concentrated in the capital cities in the form of national literary goods. The oldest regions, those longest established in the literary field, are the 'richest' in this sense – are credited with most power. Prestige is the quintessential form power takes in the literary universe: the intangible authority unquestioningly accorded to the oldest, noblest, most legitimate (the terms being almost synonymous) literatures, the most consecrated classics and most celebrated authors.[19]

The unequal distribution of literary resources is fundamental to the structure of the entire world literary space, organized as it is around two opposing poles. At the pole of greatest autonomy – that is, freest from political, national or economic constraints – stand the oldest spaces,[20] those most endowed with literary heritage and resources.[21] These are generally European spaces, the first to enter into transnational literary competition, with large accumulated resources. At the pole of greatest heteronomy, where political, national and commercial criteria hold strongest sway, stand the newcomers, the spaces most lacking in literary resources; and the zones within the oldest regions that are most subordinate to commercial criteria. Each national space, meanwhile, is itself polarized by the same structure.

The power of the richest zones is perpetuated because it has real and measurable effects, notably the 'transfer of prestige' through reviews or prefaces by prestigious writers of hitherto unrecognized books, or of works from outside the centre: Victor Hugo's enthusiastic reviews of Walter Scott, at a time when the first French translations of his novels were appearing; Bernard Shaw's reviews of the first productions of Ibsen's plays in London; Gide's 1947 preface to Taha Hussein's *Livre des jours*; or the complex mechanism of recognition through translation, as in the consecration of Borges when translated by Roger Caillois, Ibsen by William Archer, and so on.

Degrees of Autonomy

The second constitutive feature of the literary world is its relative autonomy.[22] Issues posed in the political domain cannot be superimposed upon, or confounded with, those of the literary space, whether national or international. Much contemporary literary theory seems bent on creating this short-circuit, constantly reducing the literary to the political. A salient example would be Deleuze and Guattari's *Kafka*, which claims to deduce from a single diary entry (25 December 1911), not only a particular political stance – thus affirming that Kafka is indeed 'a political author' – but a political vision that informs his entire oeuvre. Taking up a mistranslated phrase in the French version of the *Diary*, they construct the category of 'minor literature' and attribute to Kafka, via a flagrant historical anachronism, preoccupations which could not have been his before the First World War.[23]

Autonomy implies that the events which take place in literary space are autonomous too: the watershed dates, manifestos, heroes, monuments, commemorations, capital cities, all combine to produce a specific history, which cannot be confused with that of the political world – even if it partially depends upon it, in a form that would require careful attention. Braudel, in his economic history of the world between the 15th and 18th centuries, notes the relative independence of artistic space with regard to the economic and hence the political. Venice was the economic capital of the 16th century, but Florence and its Tuscan dialect were intellectually in the ascendant. In the 17th century, Amsterdam became the great centre of European trade, but Rome and Madrid triumphed in the arts and literature. In the 18th century, London was the centre of the economic world but it was Paris that imposed its cultural hegemony:

> In the late 19th and early 20th century, France, though lagging behind the rest of Europe economically, was the undisputed centre of Western painting and literature; the times when Italy and Germany dominated the world of music were not times when Italy or Germany dominated Europe economically; and even today, the formidable economic lead by the United States has not made it the literary and artistic leader of the world.[24]

The case of the Latin American literatures would be further proof of the relative autonomy of the literary sphere, with no direct link, no cause-and-effect relation between political-economic strength and literary power or legitimacy at an international level. The global recognition accorded to these bodies of work, in the form of four Nobel Prizes, the worldwide esteem for their great names, the established legitimacy of their leading aesthetic model, despite the political and economic weakness of the countries concerned, show that the two orders cannot be confounded. To understand the conditions for the emergence of Latin America's literary 'boom', for example, we need to postulate the relative independence of literary phenomena.[25]

But if the literary world is *relatively* independent of the political and economic universe, it is by the same token relatively dependent on it. The entire history of world literary space – both in its totality, and within each of the national literary spaces that compose it – is one of an initial dependence on national-political relations, followed by a progressive emancipation from them through a process of autonomization. The original dependence is still there to some degree, related to the seniority of the space under consideration; above all at the level of language. Their almost systematic nationalization across the world makes languages an ambiguous instrument, inextricably literary and political.

Forms of Domination

In literary space the modes of domination are thus encased within each other. Three principal forms exert themselves to differential degrees, depending on the position of the given space: linguistic, literary and political domination – this last increasingly taking on an economic cast. The three overlap, interpenetrate and obscure one another to such an extent that often only the most obvious form – political-economic domination – can be seen. Numerous literary spaces are linguistically dependent (Canada, Australia, New Zealand, Belgium, Switzerland, Quebec) without being politically subordinate; others, notably those emerging from decolonization, may have achieved linguistic independence but remain politically unfree. But subordination can also be measured in purely literary terms, independent of any political oppression or subjugation. It is impossible to account for certain types of exile, or changes in written language, temporary or permanent – those of August Strindberg, Joseph Conrad, Samuel Beckett, E.M. Cioran, for example – without hypothesizing the existence of strictly literary forms of domination, forces outside any power-political framework.[26]

The consequences of literary domination for the production, publication and recognition of texts require their own analysis. The inevitable primacy that literary studies accord to psychology, for instance – notoriously based on the incomparable solitude of the writer – often hinders an account of the unnoticed structural constraints that impinge on a writer's production of works, down to their choice of form, genre, language. Take Gertrude Stein: although feminist studies rightly insist on her biographical and psychological particularity, especially her lesbianism, they leave unmentioned her location in world literary space, as if this were somehow self-evident. Or rather, anything relating to her position as an American in Paris is mentioned only in a biographical or anecdotal context. Yet we know that the US was subordinate in literary terms during the 1910s and 1920s, and that American writers came to Paris seeking literary resources and aesthetic models. Here we have an example of specifically literary domination, taking place in the absence of any other form of dependence. A simple analysis of Stein's status as an expatriate poet in Paris – 'immigrant' status being a clear sign of dependence – and the position of the American literary space within the World of Letters would help us understand why Stein was so preoccupied, as was Ezra Pound at the same juncture, with the 'enrichment' of a national American literature. At the same time, her interest in the literary representation of Americans – her gigantic *The Making of Americans* its most striking manifestation – takes on its full significance. The fact that she was a woman and a lesbian in Paris in the 1910s is of course crucial to understanding her subversive impulse and the nature of her whole aesthetic project. But the historically structured relation of literary domination, clearly of primary importance, remains hidden from the critical tradition. As if, as a general rule, there were always some particularity – important no doubt, but still secondary – that concealed the overall pattern of literary power relations.

This form of literary ascendancy – so unusual, so hard to describe, so paradoxical – can in some situations represent a liberation, compared to the aesthetic, or aesthetico-political, imprisonment of archaic spaces that are closed to innovation. Its power is exercised over every text, every writer in the world, whatever their position and however clear their awareness of the mechanisms of literary domination; but all the more, over those who originate from a literary space that lacks autonomy or is located in one of the subordinate regions of the World of Letters.

However, the effects of consecration by the central authorities can be so powerful as to give certain writers from the margins who have achieved full recognition the illusion that the structure of domination has simply disappeared; seeing themselves as living proof of the establishment of a new 'world literary order'. Universalizing from their particular case, they claim that we are witnessing a total and definitive reversal of the balance of power between centre and peripheries. Carlos Fuentes, for instance, writes in *The Geography of the Novel*:

> The old Eurocentrism has been overcome by a polycentrism which ... should lead
> us to an 'activation of differences' as the common condition of a central humanity ...
> Goethe's world literature has finally found its correct meaning: it is the literature
> of difference, the narration of diversity converging in one world ... A single world,
> with numerous voices. The new constellations that together form the geography of
> the novel are varied and mutating.[27]

Multiculturalist enthusiasms have led others to assert that the relation between centre and periphery has now been radically reversed, and that the world of the periphery will henceforth occupy the central position. In reality, the effects of this pacific and hybridized fable are to depoliticize literary relations, to perpetuate the legend of the great literary enchantment and to disarm writers from the periphery who are seeking recognition strategies that would be both subversive and effective.

Modernismo as Re-expropriation

Literary inequality and its relations of dominance provoke their own forms of struggle, rivalry and competition. But the subjugated here have also developed specific strategies which can only be understood in a literary framework, although they may have political consequences. Forms, innovations, movements, revolutions in narrative order may be diverted, captured, appropriated or annexed, in attempts to overturn existing literary power relations.

It is in these terms that I would analyse the advent of *modernismo* in the Spanish-speaking countries at the end of the 19th century. How to explain the fact that this movement, which turned the entire tradition of Hispanic poetry on its head, could have been dictated by a poet from Nicaragua, on the far reaches of the Spanish colonial empire? Rubén Darío, captivated from boyhood by the literary legend of Paris, stayed in the city in the late 1880s and, logically enough, was enthused by the

French symbolist poetry that was just making its mark.[28] He then carried out an astonishing operation, which can only be called an expropriation of literary capital: he imported, into Spanish poetry itself, the very procedures, themes, vocabulary and forms lofted by the French symbolists. This expropriation was asserted quite explicitly, and the deliberate Frenchification of Spanish poetry, down to the phonemes and syntactic forms, designated 'mental Gallicism'. The diversion of this capital towards inextricably literary and political ends[29] was not, then, carried out in the passive mode of 'reception', and still less of 'influence', as traditional literary analysis would have it. On the contrary, this capture was the active form and instrument of a complex struggle. To combat both the political-linguistic dominance of Spain over its colonial empire and the sclerosis that was paralysing Spanish-language poetry, Darío openly asserted the literary domination exercised by Paris at that time.[30] Paris, both as cultural citadel and as potentially more neutral political territory for the subjects of other imperial or national powers, was used by numerous 19th- and 20th-century writers as a weapon in their literary struggles.

The problem at stake in the theorization of literary inequality, then, is not whether peripheral writers 'borrow' from the centre, or whether or not literary traffic flows from centre to periphery; it is the restitution, to the subordinated of the literary world, of the forms, specificities and hardships of their struggles. Only thus can they be given credit for the invention – often concealed – of their creative freedom. Faced with the need to find solutions to dependence, and in the knowledge that the literary universe obeys Berkeley's famous *esse est percipi* – to be is to be perceived – they gradually perfect a set of strategies linked to their positions, their written language, their location in literary space, to the distance or proximity they want to establish with the prestige-bestowing centre. Elsewhere, I have tried to show that the majority of compromise solutions achieved within this structure are based on an 'art of distance', a way of situating oneself, aesthetically, neither too near nor too far; and that the most subordinated of writers manoeuvre with extraordinary sophistication to give themselves the best chance of being perceived, of existing in literary terms. An analysis of works originating in these zones as so many complex placement strategies reveals how many of the great literary revolutions have taken place on the margins and in subordinated regions, as witness Joyce, Kafka, Ibsen, Beckett, Darío and many more.

For this reason, to speak of the centre's literary forms and genres simply as a colonial inheritance imposed on writers within subordinated regions is to overlook the fact that literature itself, as a common value of the entire space, is also an instrument which, if re-appropriated, can enable writers – and especially those with the fewest resources – to attain a type of freedom, recognition and existence within it. More concretely and directly, these reflections on the immense range of what is possible in literature, even within this overwhelming and inescapable structure of domination, also aim to serve as a symbolic weapon in the struggles of those most deprived of literary resources, confronting obstacles which writers at the centre cannot even imagine. The goal here is to demonstrate that what they experience as an insoluble, individual state of dependence, with no precedents or points of comparison, is in reality a position created by a structure that is at once historical and collective.[31] As well as questioning the methods and tools of comparative literary studies, the structural comparativism of which I sketch the outlines here also seeks to be an instrument in the long and merciless war of literature.

Notes

1. Noam Chomsky, *Current Issues in Linguistic Theory*, The Hague 1964, p. 105 ff.
2. Henry James, *The Figure in the Carpet and Other Stories*, Harmondsworth 1986, p. 381.
3. See André Schiffrin, *The Business of Books: How the International Conglomerates Took over Publishing and Changed the Way We Read*, London and New York 2000.
4. See Kjell Espmark, *Le Prix Nobel. Histoire intérieure d'une consécration littéraire*, Paris 1986.
5. The recent award of the prize to the Austrian Elfriede Jelinek – unclassifiable author of violent and experimental prose works and plays, with a radical, and radically pessimist, political and feminist critical stance – is another example of the Swedish jury's total independence in making its choices and conducting its 'literary policy'.
6. 'The modern was outside, we had to import it', he writes, for example. Paz, *La búsqueda del presente. Conferencia Nobel*, San Diego 1990.
7. Antonio Candido, 'Literature and Underdevelopment', in *On Literature and Society*, trans. Howard Becker, Princeton 1995, pp. 128–129.
8. The same 'self-interested use' of the foreign explains the case of the French Romantics cited by Christopher Prendergast – the former 'made use of' Shakespeare and the English theatrical tradition to establish themselves in the French space. See 'Negotiating World Literature', NLR 8, March–April 2001, pp. 110–111.
9. Sartre's famous article on *The Sound and the Fury*, 'La temporalité chez Faulkner', appeared in the *Nouvelle revue française* in June–July 1939; reprinted in *Situations I*, Paris 1947, pp. 65–75.
10. Stefan Collini, *Public Moralists: Political Thought and Intellectual Life in Britain, 1850–1930*, Oxford 1991, p. 357.
11. *Pace* Christopher Prendergast, I do not argue that the ideas of 'nation' or 'national' must necessarily be linked to that of 'literature'. Indeed, it was rather to distinguish them that my *République mondiale des lettres* (1999) proposed the notion of 'national literary spaces', i.e., sub-spaces which are themselves located within the world literary universe. These sub-spaces vie with one another, through the struggles of writers, not for national (or nationalist) reasons, but instead for strictly literary stakes. That said, the degree of literary independence relative to national conflicts and ideologies has a strong correlation to the age of the sub-space. Here the example of Wordsworth – whose œuvre cannot of course be interpreted purely in terms of inter-national rivalry – is a perfect illustration of the fact that it is the oldest and best endowed national spaces which manage gradually to constitute an autonomous literature within their national enclosures, (relatively) independent of strictly literary stakes; that is, a depoliticized and (at least partially) denationalized space. See Prendergast, 'Negotiating World Literature', pp. 109–112.
12. On this point see Pierre Bourdieu, *Les Règles de l'art. Genèse et structure du champ littéraire*, Paris 1992.

13   Fernand Braudel, *Civilisation matérielle, économie et capitalisme – xve–xviiie siècles*, 3 vols, Paris 1979, vol. 3, especially ch. 1, pp. 12–33.

14   Franco Moretti takes up the world-system concept in his 'Conjectures on World Literature', nlr 1, January–February 2000, and in 'More Conjectures', nlr 20, March–April 2003. It allows him first of all to affirm the unity and foundational inequality of the literary system he seeks to describe, a crucial, boundary-defining affirmation to which I wholly subscribe. On the other hand, it seems to me that his use of the Braudelian opposition between 'centre' and 'periphery' tends to neutralize the (literary) violence involved, and so to obscure its inequality. Instead of this spatial dichotomy, I prefer an opposition between dominant and dominated, so as to reintroduce the fact of a power relation. Here I should make clear that this does not imply a mere division into two opposing categories but, on the contrary, a continuum of different situations in which the degree of dependence varies greatly. We could, for example, introduce the category put forward by Bourdieu of 'dominated among the dominants' to describe the situation of the (literarily) subordinate within Europe. The world-systems use of the term 'semi-periphery' to describe this type of intermediary position also seems to me to neutralize and euphemize the dominant–dominated relation, without providing a precise measure of the degree of dependence.

15   In offering a comparative table of the 'institutions of regional, national and world literature in India', Francesca Orsini suggests that there are different and mutually independent 'levels' or 'spheres' within a single national literary space. I would argue that we are dealing with positions that exist only in and through the relations of power in which they hold each other, and not with a rigid, immutable 'system'. See 'India in the Mirror of World Fiction', nlr 13, January–February 2002, p. 83.

16   See notably Wallerstein, *The Modern World-System*, 3 vols, New York 1980–1988.

17   Ernst Cassirer, *La Philosophie des formes symboliques*, vol. 1, *Le langage*, Paris 1972, especially ch. 1, pp. 13–35.

18   J.W. von Goethe, *Goethes Werke*, Hamburg 1981, vol. 12, pp. 362–363. See also Fritz Strich, *Goethe and World Literature*, New York 1972, p. 10.

19   The *Dictionnaire Larousse* gives two complementary definitions of 'prestige', both of which imply the notion of power or authority: '1. Ascendancy stemming from greatness and which seems to possess a mysterious character. 2. Influence, credit'.

20   More precisely, those that have been longest in the space of literary competition. This explains why certain ancient spaces such as China, Japan and the Arab countries are both long-lived and subordinate: they entered the international literary space very late and in subordinate positions.

21   Notably those that can lay claim to (paradoxical) national 'universal classics'.

22   On the notion of 'relative autonomy', see Pierre Bourdieu, *Les Règles de l'art*, Paris 1992, especially pp. 75–164.

23   Kafka's *klein* – suggesting simply 'little literatures' – was overtranslated by Marthe Robert as 'minor literatures', an expression whose subsequent fortunes are well known. See Gilles Deleuze and Félix Guattari, *Kafka. Pour une littérature mineure*, Paris 1975, p. 75; and my 'Nouvelles considérations sur les littératures dites mineures', *Littérature classique*, no. 31, 1997, pp. 233–247.

24   Braudel, *Civilization and Capitalism, 15th–18th Century: Volume iii, The Perspective of the World*, London 1984, p. 68; *Civilisation matérielle*, vol. 3, p. 9.

25   See the debate on this crucial point which has been taking place in Latin America since the 1960s, and which is well reconstructed by Efraín Kristal in 'Considering Coldly ...',

NLR 15, May–June 2002, pp. 67–71. Here we can clearly see that the role of agents of social and political transformation, notably attributed to writers of the 'boom', was largely illusory.

26   August Strindberg briefly became a 'French writer' between 1887 and 1897, writing *Le Plaidoyer d'un fou* and *Inferno* directly in French for the purposes of international recognition.

27   Fuentes, *Geografía de la novela*, Madrid 1993, p. 218.

28   In his *Autobiography*, Darío writes: 'I dreamed of Paris ever since I was a child, to the extent that when I prayed I asked God not to let me die without seeing Paris. Paris was for me like a paradise where one could breathe the essence of earthly happiness'. *Obras completas*, Madrid 1950–55, vol. 1, p. 102.

29   What Perry Anderson has called 'a declaration of cultural independence': *The Origins of Postmodernity*, London and New York 1998, p. 3.

30   Efraín Kristal's analysis of this point is very illuminating and entirely convincing. But he seems to believe that the idea of appropriation or diversion contradicts that of emancipation. Could we not on the contrary put forward the hypothesis that this initial diversion (necessary if it is true that no symbolic revolution can take place without resources) makes possible a creative renewal? After Rubén Darío had played the role of aesthetic accelerator, *modernismo* of course became an entirely separate Hispanic poetic movement, inventing its own codes and norms without any reference to France.

31   This is why I fully subscribe to Franco Moretti's affirmation, which could serve as a motto for a discipline still in its early stages: 'Without collective work, world literature will always remain a mirage.' See 'More Conjectures', NLR 20, March–April 2003, p. 75.

15

Globalization and Cultural Diversity in the Book Market

The Case of Literary Translations in the US and in France (2010)

Gisèle Sapiro

Gisèle Sapiro is Research Director at Centre National de Recherche Scientifique and Director of Studies at the École des Hautes Études en Sciences Sociales, and director of the European Center for Sociology and Political Science of the Sorbonne (CESSP-Paris). Sapiro's studies cover a wide research area: from the sociology of intellectuals, culture, and literature, to the sociology of translation and of international cultural exchanges, social history of the humanities and social sciences. Having worked under Pierre Bourdieu's supervision for her doctoral degree, Sapiro follows him closely through her renowned volume *The Writers' War* (*La Guerre des écrivains (1940–1953)*, 1999), which discusses the symbolic power of words during the Nazi occupation of France. She wrote widely on the intellectuals' relation to the political and literary field, and on the emergence of the aesthetics of modernity, taking these interests to a global context (*L'Espace intellectuel en Europe. De la formation des États-nations à la mondialisation, XIXe–XXIe siècle*, 2009), viewing French literature in the world system of translation, or looking at the role translation plays today in a book market marked by globalization and cultural diversity. In the same range of interests, Sapiro revisits the dynamics of literary exchanges between Paris and New York in the age of globalization and emphasizes the contradictions inherent in the ongoing process of unifying the editorial field (*Les Contradictions de la globalisation éditoriale*, 2008). In *La Responsabilité de l'écrivain. Littérature, droit et morale en France, XIXe–XXIe siècles* (2011), Sapiro looks into the history of subversive literary discourse in France as against public morality and as the agent of reshaping the ethics of literature.

In the following essay from 2010, Sapiro takes Bourdieu's field theory to an international level by analyzing the translation market in the United States and

Gisèle Sapiro, "Globalization and Cultural Diversity in the Book Market" (2010). In *Poetics* 38 (2010), pp. 419–439. © 2010 Elsevier B.V. All rights reserved.

World Literature in Theory, First Edition. Edited by David Damrosch.
© 2014 John Wiley & Sons, Ltd. Published 2014 by John Wiley & Sons, Ltd.

France, combining quantitative and qualitative data covering the time frame 1980–2005. Sapiro shows how the notion of world literature and the practice of translation played a central role in increasing cultural diversity, developed into a strategy by small-scale presses and their publishers to fight the declining linguistic diversity of works brought out in translation by larger, commercially driven presses in both countries. By adding a qualitative analysis to the quantitative data, Sapiro reveals a more nuanced and complex scene than is often supposed in discussions of a flattened global landscape today.

1. Introduction

The oldest among all cultural industries, the book industry also appears the most reluctant to globalization. The reasons are both symbolic and economic: its medium, the written language, has historical links with national identity, and the transnational circulation of books often requires translation, which is costly in time and money. Nevertheless, as shown below, this market underwent major changes in the past twenty years, and has become more global. Yet instead of being interpreted as an opening of the national markets to other cultures, this process has been considered by some of the actors as a menace to cultural diversity. Translation was one of the strategies they developed in order to counter this menace.

Different models have been used to analyze globalization in the realm of culture (Crane, 2002): the world-system theory (Wallerstein, 2004) based on the core–periphery model, the network flows analysis, the reception approach, and cultural policy strategies. Though all of them have proven adequate to describe different aspects of globalization, these models propose different views of the consequences of globalization: the core–periphery model emphasizes its homogenizing effect (Tomlinson, 1991), while the network flows analysis lays stress on hybridization and "indigenization" (Appadurai, 1996; Hannerz, 1996), and the reception approach reveals patterns of appropriation, negotiation and resistance (Regev, 2007); the analysis in terms of cultural policy strategies sheds light on the competition between cultural industries and other actors involved in the process (Crane, 2002).

In this paper, I examine the meaning and effects of globalization in the book market through the case of translations, using the number of source-languages as an indicator of cultural diversity. Though translation can be considered in itself as a form of hybridization of cultures, as publications from one culture are expressed in the language of another, the flows of translation depend both on the structure of the book market and on the system of power relations between linguistic communities as assessed by the number of primary and secondary speakers (De Swaan, 1993, 2001). A quantitative approach to the flows of translations among languages based on the *Index Translationum* data reveals the asymmetrical structure of the world system of translations (Heilbron, 1999; see also Venuti,

1995, 1998): translation flows move mainly from the core to the periphery. The English language occupies a hyper-central position: about half of the translated books in the world in the 1980s were originally written in English. Translations from French, German and Russian represented 10–12% of this market until 1989, these languages thus being central. A few languages had a semi-peripheral position, accounting for 1–3% of the global market (Italian, Spanish, Polish, Danish, Swedish and Czech). The share of other languages was less than 1%; they may thus be considered peripheral.

The core–periphery model provides a useful framework for understanding the flows of translation from the standpoint of the source language. It can also, at least partly, account for the high variations in the rate of translations into different languages. The more a language is central, the smaller the share of translations in its book production: by 1989–1991, it was around 3% in English, 15–20% in French and German, 25% in Spanish or Italian, two semi-peripheral languages, and 60% in a peripheral language like Swedish (Ganne and Minon, 1992). Yet the model does not explain the variations within each language, according to genres, publishers, and series.

In this paper, I will show that though globalization reinforced the domination of English, a closer analysis of the field of publishing in the US and in France using Bourdieu's approach (Bourdieu, 1993:74–111, 2008; Sapiro, 2008a) reveals a more nuanced picture. Whereas the pole of large-scale production is dominated by the English language, the pole of small-scale production in both countries developed a strategy of resistance by translating literary works from an increasing number of languages, in order to promote cultural diversity.

The first section presents the data and the surveys on which the research is based. The second section analyzes the effects of globalization in the book market from the standpoint of the power relations between languages. The third section compares the structure and classification principles of the book industry in the US and in France using Bourdieu's field theory. Literature being the category of books where diversity is the highest, the fourth section focuses on the market of literary translation in both countries.

2. Data and Survey

Empirical evidence is drawn from both quantitative data and qualitative material (interviews). A major problem when studying the market of translation is the lack of reliable data. I used the UNESCO *Index Translationum* database to map the evolution of translation flows for six central or semi-peripheral languages from 1980 to 2005. But although this database proves useful for this purpose, it is not reliable enough to conduct a more precise analysis of the translation market in different countries. For my survey of the French market of translation (Sapiro, 2008d), I therefore turned to other sources: (i) the French professional database

Electre, which was reprocessed to identify new literary books translated from 11 languages from 1985 to 2002 and compare their evolution by genre and publisher; (ii) lists of publishers, or of series of books in translation for the larger firms, from which the ratio of the number of languages per number of books and authors was calculated; (iii) questionnaire data gathered by the French Syndicat national de l'édition on contracts signed by French publishers for buying or selling rights, most of them for the purpose of translation. The questionnaire data can be exploited systematically only from 1997 onward, when the categories (languages, countries, genres) were stabilized. Despite the fact that not all publishers returned the questionnaires, this data source gives an overall picture of the linguistic and national diversity in the French publishing business. Finally, I conducted interviews with French publishers.

Quantitative data are much more difficult to gather for the American book market. The web site *Three Percent* provides a database of new literary translations in 2008 and 2009, which includes the source language, the country and the publishing house.[1] I built a database of literary translations from French published in the US from 1990 to 2003 based on the *Index Translationum* (Sapiro, 2010). However, my account of American publishing in this paper is mainly based on 30 semi-structured, in-depth interviews[2] with American publishers, editors, literary agents, translators, and state representatives. The publishers and editors, on whom I will focus in this paper, were asked to describe their publishing house, their translation policy, the reasons for translating, the way they discover the books they translate, their work with translators, marketing, and publicity.

3. Effects of Globalization in the Book Market

The structure of the book market is characterized by a high concentration on the one hand and a great dispersal on the other. This can be observed at three different levels that, without entirely overlapping, are superimposed: production (conglomerates vs. small firms), spatial relations (core vs. periphery), and circulation (large-scale vs. small-scale). Like very competitive open markets, the book market is concentrated around large conglomerates – oligopolies – while there is a growing number of small independent firms (Reynaud, 1982).

The recent transformations of the book industry are commonly analyzed as a result of rationalization (of the organization and of the costs, mainly through the laying off of staff) and concentration, in relation to the acceleration of the merging/acquisitions of firms (Mollier, 2008, 2009; Piault, 1998; Rouet, 2007; Schiffrin, 2000). Despite the concern of globalization theory with the spatial aspects of social relations, and despite the recent emphasis on the geographic aspects of domination in global capitalism (Harvey, 2001, 2006), little attention has been paid to the configuration of spatial relations structuring the world space of publishing (Sapiro, 2009a). This is all the more strange considering that the book industry is first and foremost a matter of territories, which determine circulation patterns:

linguistic areas, geographic territories of the distribution networks, national borders circumscribing judicial spaces and public policies, and imaginary territories
associating identities with places. Defining the borders is at stake in the competition
and the struggles occurring among these spaces and within them.

The emergence of a transnational market of symbolic goods is not new but goes
back to the development of the book industry in the 17th century. The printing
industry was concentrated from the outset around some cities, like Leipzig,
London or Paris. They became cultural capitals with the help of the political
power that reinforced their monopoly to the detriment of the periphery through
protectionist laws on copyright. In return, the printing industry played a crucial role
in the building of national identities (Anderson, 1983). Paralleling this, the capitalist
impulse to conquer new markets, in association with imperialist cultural policies,
gave birth to transnational book markets in the Spanish, English, German and
French linguistic areas, which were dominated by these same cultural centers.
Like the provinces, the colonized territories as well as the areas under the cultural
hegemony of these centers were relegated to the periphery of the book market.
Consequently, in this market, territories are defined by linguistic areas and the
nation-states together (Sapiro, 2009b).

While this history accounts for the core–periphery structure of the global book
market, the hegemony of the cultural centers, mainly the French and the British
ones, was challenged by the affirmation of national identities. The United States
combatted British hegemony in the anglophone area by developing an autonomous national literature (Casper and Groves, 2007), which emerged in the late
19th century, and a book industry, which succeeded in reversing the power relation in the 1960s. Between 1955 and 1978, book production in the US increased
more than six-fold (from 12,589 to 85,126 titles), more than twice as much as in
France and Germany (from 10,364 to 31,673 in France) (Milo, 1984). The domination of French firms in the francophone area (Chartier and Martin, 1991),
which was challenged by Belgian publishers since the beginning of the 19th
century without success (Durand and Winkin, 1999), is being fought today by
publishers from Québec, thanks to a national policy supporting the local cultural
industry (Vincent, 2007).

As a result of the building of national identities, translation became from the
mid-19th century onward the main mode of transnational circulation of books.
It favored the codification of national languages, the importation of literary models
(Even-Zohar, 1990), and the development of publishing in many countries. Nation-
states became active agents of an "international" book market (Sapiro, 2009a).

After World War II, a global market for movies, records and, more slowly, books,
emerged as exchange was being liberalized within the framework of international
negotiations, notably the General Agreement on Tariffs and Trade (GATT), which
reflected the dominant position the US had acquired. This process accelerated with
the neo-liberal turn in the 1970s, when the idea of "globalization" replaced that of
"development," in order to open the borders to the free circulation of goods and
capital (Wallerstein, 2004).

The Uruguay round of the GATT negotiations, beginning in 1986, aimed at extending the free exchange agreements into the service trade, and hence into immaterial or incorporeal goods, including cultural products (Jennar and Kalafatides, 2007). A dissent arose, led by French representatives, who argued that cultural products were not random commodities and should be protected from purely mercantile mechanisms. In 1993, the European Parliament adopted the principle of "cultural exception." But this notion was considered too protectionist and elitist, since it included only works that had gained legitimacy as high culture in the Western world. UNESCO played a major role in proposing the notion of "cultural diversity," which refers to the anthropological notion of culture and includes linguistic diversity (Gournay, 2002; Mattelart, 2007; Regourd, 2004). It was recognized in 2000 at the G8 Okinawa Summit. In 2001, UNESCO adopted a convention on the protection of "cultural diversity". Being polysemous enough to fit in a wide set of social problems, ranging from cultural production to political matters linked to cultural and social identity, diversity became a key word and what I call an "axiological operator" in the public space in Europe. Although the public debate on "cultural exception" was mainly concerned with audiovisual products, it applied more broadly to culture and to the effects of globalization.

In the book industry, globalization fostered the unification of a global market. The multiplication, since the 1980s, of specific organizations like the international bookfairs, from Peking to Guadalajara through New Delhi and Ouagadougou, is altogether the symptom and one of the mechanisms of this unification. Some agents (publishers, translators, and literary agents) became specialized in intercultural mediation. The literary agents play an increasingly important role in this market: by imposing professional rules and a commercial logic, they contribute by rationalizing and harmonizing its functioning. The fall of the communist regimes and of the dictatorships in Spain, Portugal and Latin America opened the borders and entailed a reconfiguration of the power relations structuring this market, with Russia moving from center to semi-periphery, and Spain strengthening its position. While multinational conglomerates appeared, the role of nation-states, which were formerly central actors organizing that "international" book market, began to decline (this is a more general aspect of globalization; Held *et al.*, 1999), though as we will see, they reaffirmed their role through the defence of the notion of cultural diversity. But denationalization does not mean deterritorializion. On the contrary, the competition on territories of book copyright is harsher than ever (Sapiro, 2009a): English, American, French and Spanish publishers tend to demand exclusive rights for the whole language-speaking area – all the more since the development of sales through the Internet, which solves the problem of local distribution – or they tend to struggle over the list of territories appended to the copyright contracts.

The dynamics of globalization stimulated local cultural industries. As a result, cultural exchange increased. The number of books in translation in the world grew from 50 000 published in 1980 to more than 75 000 in 2000 (+50%), according to the *Index Translationum* database. In the 1990s, the average number of books in translation published annually was 24% higher than in the

Table 15.1 Evolution of the average number of books in translation published per year in the 1980s and 1990s, by original language.

Language	1980–1989	%	1990–1999	%
English	24 251	44.7	39 808	59.1
French	5853	10.8	6609	10.0
German	4678	8.6	6234	9.3
Russian	6213	11.5	1565	2.5
Italian	1595	3.0	1963	2.9
Spanish	893	1.7	1737	2.6
Other	10 655	19.7	9048	14.0
Total	54 138	100	66 964	100

Index Translationum.

1980s. But did this growth imply a diversification as assessed by the number of connections between languages?

In fact, far from favoring diversity, globalization has reinforced the domination of English (Table 15.1): the share of books translated from English reached close to 60% in the 1990s (vs. 45% in the 1980s), and the average amount per year was 64% more than in the 1980s, and it is 2.6% higher than the growth rate of all books in translation (24%). This growth should be related to the drastic decline of the percentage of books translated from Russian after 1989, from 11.5% to 2.5%, leaving only two central languages apart from English: French and German, the positions of which have been more or less steady (see Table 15.1). Among the semi-peripheral languages, Spanish strengthened its position, from 1.7% to 2.6%, while Italian has kept its share around 3%. The share of all the other formerly semi-peripheral languages has fallen under 1% (except for Swedish). Furthermore, contrary to what could be expected in the globalization era, the overall share of the peripheral languages decreased from close to 20 to 14%, and the average number of books translated every year from other languages was even smaller in the 1990s than in the 1980s. Thus, quantitatively speaking, diversity has diminished.

The presence of some Asian countries, mainly China and Korea, has clearly grown, while Japan has strengthened its position largely because of the success of the Japanese comics called mangas.[3] Some areas remain excluded from the exchanges, like many African countries, where the publishing industry is not very developed and the book trade is dominated by large companies from the former colonial states (France and the UK).

Though a correlation can be observed between this unequal structure and the volume of the book production in each country (Pym and Chrupala, 2005), it is not a mechanical reflection of the book trade. Markets are in themselves social constructions, which are not independent from cultural and political factors (Bourdieu, 2005). Some languages owe their position mainly to state policies, and a change in political power relations or the disappearance of such policies can alter this position, as the Russian example illustrates (see Table 15.1).

Table 15.2   Evolution of the share of the translations into French, German, Spanish, English, Japanese and Portuguese within the global market of translations.

Language	1980	1990	2000	2004
French	9.9%	11.2%	13.2%	15.5%
German	17.1%	17.4%	14.0%	6.6%
Spanish	12.8%	17.0%	11.1%	9.3%
English	8.6%	7.0%	4.8%	4.4%
Japanese	4.8%	3.0%	7.2%	8.1%
Portuguese	3.1%	2.8%	4.2%	4.4%
Other	43.7%	41.6%	45.5%	51.7%
Total	50 525	53 740	75 783	82 653

Index Translationum.

Market size can neither explain variations in the share of translations into different languages nor variations between different categories of books. The number of translations grew in all languages but in English, which is indicative of the reinforcement of the American publishing in the global book market. From 1980 to 2000, the number of translations into French doubled, a growth rate two times higher than the world average. This evolution does not merely reflect the growth of the book market. The share of translations in the French book production has increased from 10% in the 1960s to 14% in 1970 and from 15% in 1985 to 18% in 1991. The reverse can be observed in the American book market, where it has fallen from 8.6% in 1960, to 4.95% in 1975, and to less than 2.8% nowadays (Cusset, 2003:617).

Table 15.2 presents the evolution of the global distribution of translations according to the target language. Six languages account for about half of the translations in the world: French, German, Spanish, English, Japanese and Portuguese. In 2004, French comes first, with 15.5% of all translations done in the world (13% of which are published in France, the rest in the other francophone countries), outranking German, which fell from around 17% in the 1980s to 6.6% in 2004.[4] The percentage of translations into English also dropped from 8.6% to 4.4%, whereas Japanese rose in the same proportion (from 4.8% to 8.1%). The share of Spanish is declining after a leap to 17% in 1990, while that of Portuguese has slightly grown.

Variations between and within different categories of books may be indicative of the relative autonomy of cultural fields (Bourdieu, 1993): some languages are endowed with a high literary capital on the international scene (Casanova, 2005) or with a high capital in a specific domain like philosophy (Sapiro and Popa, 2008).

To understand these variations, one has to analyze the structure of the book market, which results from the articulation of economic, political and cultural factors. These different logics are incarnated by various categories of agents (e.g. authors, translators, shareholders, marketing managers, sales representatives, state representatives), some being "double agents" (e.g. publishers and literary agents) conveying both commercial and cultural logics.

4. Large-Scale vs. Small-Scale Circulation

The market of symbolic goods in general and the book market in particular are structured around the opposition between small-scale and large-scale production/circulation (Bourdieu, 1993:74–111, 2008). While intellectual or aesthetic criteria prevail at the pole of small-scale production, the pole of large-scale production is ruled by the law of the market.

This structure can be observed both in the US and in France. Interviews with publishers representative of the small-scale production confirm this opposition. C., a young American publisher of upmarket fiction and politically committed nonfiction, explains:

> We love success. But we don't have shareholders we have to please ... Our fundamental mission is to do good books and raise the level of conversation always. We like success because it helps us survive and we'd like to survive. But our primary goal is neither to survive nor to sell lots of books. We hope to survive and we'd like to make money and we'd like to sell a lot of books. But it is not... We are not just saying: How can we sell a lot of books? We are saying: How can we continue to keep our identity alive and do the things that are worthy to be doing and keep optimistic. (Interview with C., Oct. 3rd, 2008)

Even a French editor who worked at that time in an upmarket imprint belonging to a large conglomerate could say:

> [...] Sometimes we do irresponsible things. I would plead guilty. Sometimes we do totally crazy things [...], because then, you say to yourself if you don't do that, then you are not a publisher. Maybe we will sell 350 [copies], but this we must do. (Interview with N., June 7th, 2002; my translation)

The products of the book market can be polarized along this opposition between small-scale and large-scale production. On one side are best-sellers and other commercial genres such as romance, tourist guides and practical books – all shortsellers that sell tens to hundreds of thousands of copies. On the other are scientific works and upmarket literary works including novels, short stories, poetry or drama, which seldom sell more than ten thousand copies in the first year after publication but can stay alive in the backlist and become longsellers, thanks to the canonization process which turns them into classic works.

Typically, the economy of symbolic goods needs time to accumulate symbolic capital by achieving recognition in the field of cultural production (critical attention, literary awards, academic attention), this symbolic capital being converted in the long run into economic capital (English, 2005). Evoking the successes of the founder of a prestigious American publishing house, an editor explains:

> He believed in *slow* bestsellers, like [X's drama] sold more than a million copies. It was just never like a flash in the pan. [...] He grew up with [a famous poet's] idea

that some truly new kind of writing could take 20 years to catch on. That's a very comfortable editorial margin *[Laughs]*.

[...] I think that when you look at his successes, they were based on being patient, and one thing super-commercial publishing doesn't allow for is patience, they can't ... you know, it's just not their business model. (Interview with A., March 2nd, 2009)

The editor of a foreign literature series in a large French independent publishing house endowed with high prestige, describes this process:

We want to take the time to build an "œuvre," and step by step find the public for this "œuvre" in France. And I have, for these authors who don't sell very well, I have time ahead. I can convince our boss and say: I really believe in that, maybe we'll never have a very large public but we will have a public, and book after book, his/her reputation, renown, has to be built in France. (Interview with L., May 14th, 2002; my translation)

Independent publishers of upmarket books, even those created in the past thirty years, declare that around 50% of their activity is secured by the backlist.

This small-scale economy often relies on financial support from the state or from private bodies. Some national book markets are divided into distinct segments, as in the United States, where the economic organization of nonprofit publishers – mainly university presses, but also independent presses such as The New Press – differs from that of the trade publishers, since the former usually get financial support from philanthropic foundations (Thompson, 2005). Other markets, like the French one, are more unified, but a division can still be observed, notably in the support of the state to the small-scale upmarket production (Surel, 1997). Translations into French, as we will see below, have benefited from this support.

Another condition for maintaining a pole of small-scale circulation is the existence of independent bookstores, since the economic constraints associated with large-scale circulation are increasingly imposed through the concentration of distribution around bookstore chains (Bourdieu, 2008). This is an additional distinctive feature of the French book market as opposed to that of the United States. The survival of a dense network of independent bookstores is due to the implementation in the 1970s of a book policy that included a law on the fixed book price passed in 1981 (Rouet, 2007; Surel, 1997). More recently, in September 2008, these bookstores were awarded a special label from the French government. In the US, independent publishers usually complain about the growing concentration of bookstores around big chains, like Q.:

The problem [...] is that there are almost no more independent bookstores in America now. 80% of the sales are done by the big chains. The big chains, they don't give a damn about the literature or the genre they have... When the independents represented 50% or 60%, they were always ready to take two or three copies, some of them would keep them three months after receiving them, while the chains, if you haven't sold in six weeks, they are back in your stock, which is part of the problem (Interview with Q., Oct. 15th, 2007; my translation).

Moreover, the US chains "don't give a damn about the backlist," as Q. puts it, because managing the backlist requires skills and time which is at odds with the rationalization of profit. This is also the case in publishing conglomerates, as explained by another American publisher who quit an upmarket imprint belonging to a large company when the commercial constraints became unbearable: books in the backlist were required to sell twice as many copies a year than they needed in order to be profitable (Interview with Z., May 27th, 2008).

In the debates around the concentration process in publishing, the large conglomerates were accused by agents located at the pole of small-scale production of stiffening commercial constraints and standardizing cultural production. The notion of standardization, borrowed from Horkheimer and Adorno (1972), and which is also relevant to other sectors of industrial production, was implicitly opposed to innovation, originality, quality, and craftwork. It functioned as a negative axiological operator, allowing the superimposition of a set of oppositions between nonprofit vs. trade publishers, independent vs. non-independent publishers, upmarket vs. commercial literature, high vs. low culture (see, for example, Alberto *et al.*, 2008; Schiffrin, 2000; Vigne, 2008).

Though it is undeniable that conglomerates increase the commercial constraints on the whole book industry, the reality is probably a little more complex regarding standardization, since there are independent publishers selling commercial books, whereas the classification principles within large companies reproduce the hierarchy between "upmarket" and "commercial" books: some imprints are specialized in "very literary fiction," others in mass market products, the format ("hardcover," "paperback," "rack size") being an indicator of the distribution channel (Interview with S., editor of the literary imprint in a large publishing company, October 4th, 2007; on distribution channels in the US, see Coser *et al.*, 1982:333–361).

Yet this shows that the division between high and low culture is still in force in the US as in France, despite both the merging of imprints producing upmarket and mass products, and the increasing role of big chains in the distribution. "Upmarket" and "commercial" are categories literary agents use to classify the books they sell:

> […] when agents sell [rights], they distinguish *fiction* and *nonfiction*. Then, in fiction, you've got *literary fiction, commercial fiction*, and then you have *upmarket commercial, very commercial*, you have *women's upmarket, women's commercial, women's upmarket literate* … (Interview with Be., French editor of a series of foreign literature; March 14th, 2006; my translation).

These categories are not used explicitly in France, where literary agents have not come to play such an important role in the publishing industry, but some equivalents can be found, like the 19th century notions of "belles-lettres" and of "littérature de gare" ("railway station literature"). A good level of observation for exploring the classification principles in the French book production is to compare series. While publishers' catalogues in the US are classified chronologically, in France the booklists are organized around series. Series materialize the main classification principles, like the distinction between "literature" and "non literature", an equivalent of the American "fiction"/"nonfiction" distinction (although they do not completely overlap, since "literature" in France can include literary nonfiction).

Like the imprints in a conglomerate, series can be hierarchized as more or less commercial, more or less upmarket: for instance, at the old prestigious independent publisher Gallimard, the "série blanche" is devoted to upmarket literature in French, while the "série noire" specializes in mystery (though it mainly includes upmarket mystery novels, as compared to more popular mystery series published by other firms, the "black" is still more commercial and less prestigious than the "white" series).

As illustrated by this last example, the compartmentalization in series can more or less overlap with another major classification principle of the literary production, which is genre. Genres like mystery or romance are often published in specific series that differentiate them from the more "universal" upmarket literature series, or in different formats ("pocket" or "rack size").

The field of publishing is thus hierarchized in the US like in France around the opposition between upmarket and commercial, which overlaps with the opposition between small-scale and large-scale production. We will now examine where literary translations are located in this structure.

5. Literary Translation as a Factor of Cultural Diversity

Using field analysis to locate translations reveals a high variation between the pole of large-scale circulation and the pole of small-scale circulation. The English language production is dominant in the commercial genres, both in the US and in France (and everywhere else), while the literary upmarket sector shows a high linguistic diversity. Translating from many languages was a strategy developed by agents at the small-scale production pole to fight the growing hegemony of English. They promoted a different conception of globalization, based on cultural diversity.

Globalization has reinforced the commercial constraints on the world book market, together with the domination of the English language. The increase in the number of translations (see Section 3) is largely due to the pole of large-scale production. Though the *Index Translationum* does not provide data on the number of copies printed or sold, suffice it to consider the single case of Harlequin books: from the 1980s to the 1990s, the number of titles of this publisher translated in all languages has increased by +135% (from 7468 to 17561), which is five-fold or six-fold the average growth rate of translations in the world (24% as mentioned above) and twice the growth rate of translations from English (64%).

Among all categories of books, literature has the highest degree of cultural diversity as assessed by the number of translations and the number of languages translated. Books in translation represent 35 to 40% of the new fiction books published each year in France, twice as much as the overall share of translations in the book production. Between 1997 and 2006, French publishers acquired the translation rights for at least 5113 adult literary works (an average of 568 per year) from 61 languages and more than 80 countries (source: Syndicat national de l'édition). In 1999, according to a survey of the National Endowment for the Arts, 297 new literary translations were published in the US, which was scarcely more than 2% of the new publications of adult fiction and poetry that year (Allen, 2007:25). In 2008, at least 361 fiction and poetry books were translated from 47 languages and 64 countries (see Table 15.3). Though these data are not exactly comparable to the French figures (they include first translations of classical books free from rights), they show the high linguistic diversity in the literary translation market despite the low number of translations.

But linguistic diversity strongly decreases when we move from the upmarket to the commercial pole in the US, as well as France. The English production is dominant at the pole of large-scale circulation, and national diversity is very low: almost all English translations come from the US or England (or Canada for Harlequin books). This holds for the majority of best-sellers, romances, thrillers,

Table 15.3   Number of books in translation published in the US in 2008, according to the original language.

Language	No. of titles
French	58
Spanish	50
German	33
Arabic	27
Japanese	23
Russian	20
Italian	14
Portuguese	14
Chinese	12
Hebrew	12
Swedish	11
Hungarian	8
Norwegian	6
Polish	6
Czech	5
Greek	4
Icelandic	4
Korean	4
Persian	4
Slovenian	4
Danish	3
Dutch	3
Serbian	3
Turkish	3

(Continued)

Table 15.3 (*Continued*)

Language	No. of titles
Various	3
Albanian	2
Bosnian	2
Catalan	2
Romanian	2
Tamil	2
Urdu	2
Afrikaans	1
Belarusian	1
Bengali	1
Bulgarian	1
Burmese	1
Croatian	1
Estonian	1
Finnish	1
Galician	1
Hindi	1
Ukrainian	1
Vietnamese	1
Welsh	1
Yiddish	1
Zulu	1
Total	361

Three Percent database.

and for 90% of the translated mystery novels published in France. In these genres, translations from English are even more numerous than the French products. Three quarters of the 243 books published in Laffont's "Best-sellers" series from 1984 to 2002 (mainly mystery, thrillers and a little science fiction) were originally written in English and about one quarter in French. The average yearly number of new books published in this series doubled from 9 to 18 from 1995 onwards, mainly due to the rise of translations from English.

Between 1985 and 2002, the number of new fiction books translated from English almost tripled, from 433 to 1134. Though this growth occurred in all genres, it was most significant in commercial genres like romance, thrillers, mystery, and in youth literature, where translations from English are dominant (Sapiro, 2008a, b, c, d).

Contrary to the American publishing market where translations are not distinguished from original works in English, and contrary to the pole of large-scale production, French literary upmarket publishing usually separates translations from original works in French into different series. This division implicitly superimposes two criteria, language and nation – literature in translation being traditionally called "foreign literature", while French literature encompasses works from the whole francophone world, a reminder of French hegemony in this area (Sapiro, 2010). In contrast, in the US, the notion of "foreign literature" includes literature of other anglophone countries and not only books in translation, the distinction between nation and language being here, as can be assumed, the result of the struggle of American publishing for its autonomization from English domination during the 19th century.

The French series of foreign literature are representative of the pole of small-scale production. They seldom have best-sellers and typically sell between 800 and 5000 copies, apart from Nobel or other prize winners. It is in the "foreign literature" series of the traditional literary publishers that both linguistic and national diversity reaches its highest point in French publishing. This cultural diversity has been reinforced by globalization. Since the 1980s, the most prestigious foreign literature series, like Gallimard's "Du monde entier" and Le Seuil's "Cadre vert", translated books from 20 to 30 different languages and up to 40 countries (see Table 15.4). Le Seuil was at that time independent, like Gallimard and Albin Michel. Even an upmarket imprint in a large conglomerate like Fayard has a high degree of linguistic diversity, but this is less true of the imprint Grasset, and there is at least one case of an imprint's prestigious foreign literature series being suppressed after it was bought by a conglomerate (Interview with B., March 14th, 2006).

This diversification was fostered by the creation, since the end of the 1970s, of many small independent firms specializing in literary translation. For these newcomers in the publishing field, translating was a way to accumulate symbolic capital (Serry, 2002). The most successful was Actes Sud, which nowadays accounts for 450 publications a year. Its list includes translated literary upmarket works from more than 36 languages.

Though translations from English are still the most numerous in literary upmarket publishing, they are underrepresented compared to the share of English books among all books translated into French: one third of the books in Gallimard and Seuil's foreign literature series are translated from English, as are 25% of the translated books at Actes Sud, while, according to the *Index Translationum*, two thirds of all books translated into French were originally written in English during the same period.[5] Furthermore, national diversity is much higher at the pole of small-scale production even among translations from English; we find not only American or English authors, but also Irish, Indian, African, and Philippine authors.

The ratio of the number of books per number of languages is much lower in these foreign literature series, where it ranges from 9 to 30, than in commercial series like Laffont's "best-sellers", where it reaches 60.8. This is also true of the ratio of number of authors per number of languages: 5 to 13, as opposed to 29 (Table 15.5).

With regards to linguistic and geographic origins of translations, the opposition between homogenization and diversity thus coincides with the opposition between commercial and upmarket. In the competition induced by globalization within the world market of translation, some agents of the small-scale production promoted cultural diversity as a strategy for fighting the growth of commercial

Table 15.4 Number of books in translation published in the series/domains of foreign literature of the big French literary publishers, by original language (1984–2002, except for Le Seuil: 1984–1999[a]).

Original Language	Actes Sud	Gallimard (Du monde entier)	Seuil (Cadre vert)	Fayard (Littérature étrangère)	Albin Michel (Les grandes traductions)	Grasset	Christian Bourgois
Afghan					1		
Albanian	5	2		56	1		1
Arabic	39	6	4	2	1		1
Armenian	1		1		2		
Bengali	1	1					
Bulgarian	6						
Catalan	5	2	2				
Chinese	17	6	1	1	4		5
Korean	24						
Danish	10	9	4	1	1		2
English/American	223	188	79	157	64	108	290
Estonian		1					
Farsi	3			2			
Finnish	8	1					
Frioulan	1						
Frison	1						
Galician		1		1			
Georgian					1		
German	122	80	24	72	26	25	52
Greek	22	10	5	3			1
Hebrew	20	12	4	11	1	1	
Hindi	1	1					
Hungarian	13	7	1		1		
Icelandic	5	1			1		

Italian	55	48	34	52	16	20	39
Japanese	15	25	10	6	5		
Lithuanian	1				1		
Macedonian	1			3			
Malaysian	1						
Dutch	30	14	9		2		
Norwegian	18	2					
Polish	17	7	2	16	6	1	6
Portuguese	16	28	9		13		26
Romanian	6	4		1	6		
Russian	57	44	8	40	27	1	6
Serbian/Croatian	6	6		8			
Spanish	91	71	55	12	11	32	80
Swedish	55	11		1	1	4	5
Czech	2	13	2		4		1
Tibetan				3			
Turkish	3	15	2				
Yiddish	1						

Sapiro (2008b:193–194).

[a]The data for Le Seuil were provided by Hervé Serry, whom I would like to thank here.

Table 15.5 Comparison of series/domains of French publishers: number of books and number of languages translated (1984–2002, except for Le Seuil: 1984–1999).

Publisher (series/ domains)	Number of books	Number of authors	Number of languages[a]	Ratio books/ languages	Ratio authors/ languages
Actes Sud	896	469	36	24.9	13.0
Gallimard (Du monde entier)	618	320	31	19.9	10.3
Seuil (Cadre vert)	256	126	19	13.5	6.6
Fayard (Littérature étrangère)	466	129	20	23.3	6.5
Albin Michel (Grandes traductions)	203	121	22	9.2	5.5
Christian Bourgois	519	196	17	30.5	11.5
Grasset	192	86	8	24.0	10.8
Laffont (best-sellers)	243	116	4	60.8	29.0

[a]The language is here the unit, without distinction of the country. English language counts as one, the same for Spanish and Portuguese. The number of original countries is mentioned in the text when possible.

products, mostly translated from English. They found an ally in the French government: the Centre national du livre (CNL), funded by the French Ministry of Culture, implemented by the end of the 1980s, a policy of financial support for translation of French upmarket books (both fiction and nonfiction) into other languages. Many countries adopted such a policy in order to support the translation of their literature in other languages. The specificity of the French policy is that it also helps translations of contemporary literature and human and social sciences into French. This policy aims at encouraging cultural exchanges with small countries and peripheral languages. From 2003 through 2006, the CNL subsidized the translation of books from more than 30 languages. The CNL also organizes meetings around foreign literatures. This counter-strategy of the French state in the face of the growing hegemony of English contrasts with the strategy of small countries like the Netherlands and Israel, which are eager to follow the dominant trend (75% of translations into Dutch and 90% into Hebrew are from English) (Heilbron, 2008; Sapiro, 2008c).

Paradoxically, while favoring cultural diversity, this commitment of governments in supporting translation strengthened the identification between language and nation, at the very moment when cultural production was on the way to being denationalized with, on the one hand, the emergence of multinational conglomerates, and on the other, the success of the notion of "world literature", which referred to authors coming from the periphery, from ethnic minorities and from migration, who had been marginalized by the national conception of literature (this notion appeared around 1992 when Derek Walcott was awarded the Nobel Prize, Michael Ondaatje the Booker Prize, and the Caribbean writer Patrick Chamoiseau the prix Goncourt).

A similar trend in favor of translation arose more recently in the US. Translating was conceived by some actors in the literary upmarket production as a means to combat the growing hegemony of English in the world and the closure of American culture as revealed by the dramatic fall of the share of translations in the American book production.

Among their reasons for "their increasing reluctance to bring out books by non-American writers" several publishers interviewed by the *New York Times* journalist Stephen Kinzer evoked as a decisive factor "the concentration of ownership in the book industry, which is dominated by a few conglomerates. That has produced an intensifying fixation on profit. As publishers focus on blockbusters, they steadily lose interest in little-known authors from other countries" (Kinzer, 2003). Other reasons mentioned were the lack of staff editors reading foreign languages, the high cost of translation, the local references, and the different writing. My own interviews confirmed these findings. Most translations must be subsidized now, as the head of a literary upmarket imprint in a large conglomerate explains:

> [In the past] a book didn't have to sell *so many* copies to become doable. But now it's impossible, you know, now every book is sort of scrutinized to see whether it can succeed, and it's like tying a large stone around the neck of a book to make it be an unsubsidized translation (Interview with R., Feb. 3rd, 2009).

Moreover, it appeared that when they do publish translations, publishers tend not to present them as such (it is not specified on the cover), out of fear that retailers will "skip" them, as Q. explains:

> Because the big chains, when we arrive with these fiction in translation, they now have what is called a "skip", which means that for instance there is a [chain] which has 1200 bookstores they take zero, not one available copy, among books in translation [...]. (Interview with Q., Oct. 15th, 2007; my translation)

Although traditional prestigious publishing houses which have become imprints in large conglomerates, like Farrar, Strauss & Giroux, Knopf, Harcourt, and Pantheon continue to play a significant role in importing literature from foreign languages, most translations (around 80% in 2008) are published either by nonprofit presses which mention it as part of their mission – such as Overlook, White Pine, Dalkey Archives, The New Press, and also academic presses that publish literary translations, especially Nebraska University Press – or by small independent trade publishers: alongside the older New Directions, founded in 1936, and presses founded in the 1960s–1970s like David Godine, Sun & Moon, or the smaller but influential Burning Deck, a number of small firms appeared in the late 1980s, like Host Publication, Seven Stories, Arcade. Since the end of the 1990s, a new generation of publishers launched small presses, most of them not-for-profit, devoted to what they call "international literature" (a term they prefer to "books in translation"), like Archipelago, Open Letter, which both translate from a wide range of languages, some of them being specialized in areas, like Aflame, which publishes fiction from the Warm World (ex-"Third World"). The terms they use to describe their activity is "mission," "vision," "labor of love," "pleasure," "magical," all terms opposed to the rationalization of profit governing the commercial logic of the large conglomerates. One of them explains:

> Sure, we're, we're a not-for-profit press, set-up, devoted to international literature, um, both fiction and non-fiction, and poetry, um, but we're set up as a not-for-profit just because it, it's, difficult, book sales are low and we wouldn't be able to do the sort of books that we want to do, not just international literature but it's groundbreaking, innovative international literature that's, you know, we're not opposed to things that might be a little bit commercial, but it's really literary, you know, literary books that have a, have a strong voice, a strong spirit. (Interview with I., Feb 17th, 2009).

They could rely, for this purpose, on the support of the nation-states, which implemented, as already mentioned, translation policies. The context was a growing awareness of the need for this international literature in the US, regarding the very low share of translations (the website *Three Percent* was named after this), which they present as "a problem", as "pretty embarrassing". One of these publishers remembers:

> I think since that time, that was like 2002, 2003, like over that period since then, I think there's been like a real growth in the awareness, in like the awareness of litera-ture in translation in the sense that, um, we know now there's a lot of articles about how few books are translated, but then there's also a lot of articles about there are great books that are translated that are flying under the radar and there's kind of a desire among readers now for these books, for something that's like cutting through the noise of crap that's published in America, that there's more genuine and interesting voices that are available. (Interview with B., Feb. 20th, 2009).

This viewpoint was shared by independent literary upmarket publishers from the older generation:

> Um, it just seemed to me increasingly important, that, um, in a country that is so, in some ways, removed, from any other kind of international, I mean, especially under the Bush years, but it's been true in our whole culture, we've been so, unable to assimi-late and learn about other cultures, that it seemed crucial that some few of us keep publishing international literature [...] (Interview with Co., Feb. 11, 2009).

It was also one of the motivations for launching the PEN World Voices festival (in 2005) and the online literary magazine *Words without Borders*, which aims at pro-moting a "globalization" of cultural exchange by bringing foreign voices from other languages to the US:

> Our ultimate aim is to introduce exciting international writing to the general public [...] presenting international literature not as a static, elite phenomenon, but a portal through which to explore the world. In the richness of cultural information we present, we hope to help foster a "globalization" of cultural engagement and exchange, one that allows many voices in many languages to prosper.[6]

The notion of "authentic voices" from the world is opposed to the standardized products that large conglomerates sell under the label of globalization, as D. argues:

> Now you have more interest on the part of the big publishing houses in the world because they just want to have everything. It is a kind of aspect of globalization. It is not that they want to present to the American people, American readers, authentic voices to explain what is really going on in these countries by people who really know, it is not that at all. It is kind of the opposite. It is just they will go wherever they have to go to get a sexy story or the same story with new exotic locations. It is really worse than I can even describe. (Interview with C., Oct. 3rd, 2008)

Yet this defense of cultural diversity through translation can be shared by publishers of upmarket literature within large conglomerates, as exemplified by this excerpt of the interview with S., who is in charge with the American literary imprint in a large company:

> I think networking and word of mouth is very important for discovering books to translate from foreign languages. It is very important to do that in this country and into the English language in general because I do believe there is a kind of imperialism of the English language throughout the world and publishing translations is my way of combatting that. (Interview with S., Oct. 5th, 2007)

As demonstrated in this section, language diversity appears thus to be located in the upmarket literary publishing, as opposed to commercial publishing, both in France and the US. The main difference between American and French publishing is that, in France, where the high linguistic diversity is secured by Actes Sud and by the prestigious "foreign literature" series of the larger literary upmarket publishers, small presses tend to specialize in a few languages and or areas, like Piquier for South-Eastern Asia. In the US, where the concentration process is more advanced, the role of maintaining diversity was taken over by the smaller presses, as the traditional literary publishers were being incorporated in larger conglomerates and expected to produce better sales results.

6. Conclusion

In this paper, translation was used as an indicator of cultural diversity in the book market. This empirical case study provides some answers to the question whether globalization induces more heterogeneity or more homogeneity. Though the increase in the number of translations in the world is an indicator of a higher number of connections, the cultural flows are asymmetrical. Moreover, globalization implied a reduction of the number of interconnections between languages, thus less heterogeneity. But when we pay closer attention to the structure of the book market, it appears that this process is not homogeneous. Using Bourdieu's frame analysis of the field of publishing, I demonstrated that while English is dominant at the pole of large-scale production, diversity according to the source language is very high at the pole of small-scale production, thanks to the historical link between literature, language and nation. In spite of the differences between the American and the French fields of publishing, namely the higher commercial constraints that bear upon publishers in the US, this opposition continues to prevail. Far from fostering diversity, globalization strengthened the hegemony of English and the economic constraints on the world market of translation. This is why globalization was identified with standardization by agents of the small-scale production, who defended the autonomy of intellectual criteria against the law of market. The strategy they adopted in order to counter this trend was precisely the defense of cultural diversity through translation, with the support of the nation-states, the role of which was menaced in this evolution. This explains how the nation-states paradoxically reaffirmed their role in the global market of translation at the very moment – at the beginning of the 1990s – when this market was becoming denationalized.

Although the case of translations seems at first glance to support the reading of globalization as a narrative justifying cultural imperialism (Bourdieu and Wacquant, 1999:42; Mattelart, 1983), it also displays the competition it triggered and the counter-strategies developed by the agents, including nation-states, in what appears to be a global field of struggle between economic, political and cultural forces. Both geographic and imagined territories are more than ever at stake in these struggles. Yet the limits of quantitative analysis must be stressed. The number of languages is not the unique measure of cultural diversity. Translating means interpreting (Toury, 1995), and reception implies not only importation but also appropriation and social uses. In this sense, the case of translation could plead in favor of the hybridization thesis because interpretation and appropriation are not mechanical reproduction. But this is in no way a new phenomenon. If we consider, as already argued, that national cultures were built through translations, the heuristic value of the idea of hybridization to explain globalization diminishes dramatically. Rather than a general statement, empirical studies of the variety of translation practices and of reception processes would provide a better picture of how the transnational circulation of books contributes or not to cultural diversity. Conversely, globalization poses the question of "translatability," a question which transcends that of translation and invites us to study cultural producers' strategies (in rhetorics and in practice) in order to place themselves on the global scene (Apter, 2001), the very notion of "world literature" providing an example of such a strategy.

Notes

1   http://www.rochester.edu/College/translation/threepercent/index.php?s=database.
2   The interviews were conducted in October 2007 and January to April 2009.

3   The average number of books translated every year from Japanese was twice as high in the 1990s than in the 1980s: around 400 vs. 200, and their share in the world market of translation has risen from 0.6% at the beginning of the 1990s to 0.9% in 2002.

4   German book production has grown much faster than the number of translations in German. My hypothesis, which needs to be verified, is that it results from the concentration of publishing around conglomerates and the rationalization process (Schalke and Gerlach, 1999), whereby translations are considered as not profitable enough.

5   Please note that our data on series count only new publications, whereas the *Index* data include reprints. But according to the SNE data, 62% of the books for which the rights were acquired by French publishers between 1997 and 2006 were written in English, 30% were published in the US, and 22% in the UK.

6   http://www.wordswithoutborders.org/?lab=AboutUs.

References

Alberto, R., Combes, F., Hazan, E., Faucilhon, J., 2008. *Le livre: que faire?* La Fabrique, Paris.

Allen, E., 2007. Translation, globalization and English. In: Allen, E. (Ed.), *To Be Translated or Not to Be*. PEN/IRL Report on the International Situation of Literary Translation. Institute Ramon Lull, Barcelona, pp. 17–33.

Anderson, B., 1983. *Imagined Communities: Reflections on the Origin and Spread of Nationalism*. Verso, London.

Appadurai, A., 1996. *Modernity at Large: Cultural Dimensions of Globalization*. University of Minnesota Press, Minneapolis, MN.

Apter, E., 2001. On translation in a global market. *Public Culture* 13(1), 1–12.

Bourdieu, P., 1993. In: Johnson, R. (Introd. and Ed.), *The Field of Cultural Production: Essays on Art and Literature*. Polity Press, Cambridge, UK.

Bourdieu, P., 2005. *The Social Structures of Economy*. Polity Press, Cambridge, UK (English transl.).

Bourdieu, P., 2008. A conservative revolution in publishing. *Translation Studies* 1 (2), 123–153 (English transl.).

Bourdieu, P., Wacquant, L., 1999. On the cunning of imperialist reason. *Theory, Culture and Society* 16 (1), 41–58.

Casanova, P., 2005. *The World Republic of Letters*. Harvard University Press, Cambridge, MA (English transl.).

Casper, S.E., Groves, J.D. (Eds.), 2007. *The Industrial Book (1840–1880)*. University of North Carolina Press, Chapel Hill, NC.

Chartier, R., Martin, H.-J., 1991. *Histoire de l'édition française*. Fayard/Cercle de la librairie, Paris.

Coser, L.A., Kadushin, C., Powell, W.W., 1982. *Books: The Culture & Commerce of Publishing*. Basic Books, New York.

Crane, D., 2002. Culture and globalization: theoretical models and emerging trends. In: Crane, D., Kawashima, N., Kawasaki, K. (Eds.), *Global Culture: Media, Arts, Policy, and Globalization*. Routledge, New York, pp. 1–28.

Cusset, F., 2003. Made in USA: la fabrique éditoriale. *Critique* 59 (675–676), 606–617.

De Swaan, A., 1993. The emergent world language system. *International Political Science Review* 14 (3).

De Swaan, A., 2001. *Words of the World: The Global Language System*. Polity Press, Cambridge.

Durand, P., Winkin, Y., 1999. Des éditeurs sans édition. Genèse et structure de l'espace éditorial en Belgique francophone. *Actes de la recherche en sciences sociales* 130, 48–65.

English, J., 2005. *The Economy of Prestige: Prizes. Awards and the Circulation of Cultural Value*. Harvard University Press, Cambridge, MA.

Even-Zohar, I., 1990. The position of translated literature within the literary polysystem. *Poetics Today* 11 (1), 45–52.

Ganne, V., Minon, M., 1992. Géographies de la traduction. In: Barret-Ducrocq, F. (Ed.), *Traduire l'Europe*. Payot, Paris, pp. 55–96.

Gournay, B., 2002. *Exception culturelle et mondialisation*. Presses de Sciences Po, Paris.

Hannerz, U., 1996. *Transnational Connections: Culture, People, Places*. Routledge, London.

Harvey, D., 2001. *Spaces of Capital: Towards a Critical Geography*. Routledge, New York.

Harvey, D., 2006. *Spaces of Global Capitalism: Towards a Theory of Uneven Geographical Development*. Verso, London.

Heilbron, J., 1999. Towards a sociology of translation: book translations as a cultural world system. *European Journal of Social Theory* 2 (4), 429–444.

Heilbron, J., 2008. L'évolution des échanges culturels entre la France et les Pays-Bas face à l'hégémonie de l'anglais. In: Sapiro, G. (Ed.), *Translatio. Le Marché de la traduction en France à l'heure de la mondialisation*. CNRS Editions, Paris, pp. 311–332.

Held, D., Mc Grew, A., Goldblatt, D., Perraton, J., 1999. *Global Transformations. Politics, Economics and Culture*. Polity Press, London.

Horkheimer, M., Adorno, T., 1972. *Dialectic of Enlightenment*. Herder and Herder, New York.

Jennar, R.M., Kalafatides, L., 2007. *L'AGCS. Quand les Etats abdiquent face aux multinationales*. Raisons d'agir, Paris.

Kinzer, S., 2003. America Yawns at Foreign Fiction. *The New York Times*, July 26, on line: http://ww.nytimes.com/2003/07/26/books/26book.html?pagewanted=1.

Mattelart, A., 1983. *Transnationals and the Third World: The Struggle for Culture*. Bergin and Garvey, South Hadley, MA.

Mattelart, A., 2007. *Diversité culturelle et mondialisation*. La Découverte "Repères", Paris.

Milo, D., 1984. La bourse mondiale de la traduction: un baromètre culturel. *Annales* 1, 92–115.

Mollier, J.-Y., 2008. *Édition, presse et pouvoir en France au XXe siècle*. Fayard, Paris.

Mollier, J.-Y., 2009. Les stratégies des groupes de communication à l'orée du XXIe siècle. In: Sapiro, G. (Ed.), *Les Contradictions de la globalisation éditoriale*. Nouveau Monde, Paris, pp. 27–44.

Piault, F., 1998. De la "rationalisation" à l'hyperconcentration. In: Fouché, P. (Ed.), *L'Édition française depuis 1945*. Éditions du Cercle de la Librairie, Paris, pp. 628–639.

Pym, A., Chrupala, G., 2005. The quantitative analysis of translation flows in the age of an international language. In: Branchadell, A., Lovell, M.W. (Eds.), *Less Translated Languages*. John Benjamins, Amsterdam, pp. 27–38.

Regev, M., 2007. Cultural uniqueness and aesthetic cosmopolitanism. *European Journal of Social Theory* 10, 123–138.

Regourd, S. (Ed.), 2004. *De l'exception à la diversité culturelle*. La Documentation française, Paris.

Reynaud, B., 1982. La dynamique d'un oligopole avec frange: le cas de la branche d'édition de livres en France. *Revue d'économie industrielle* 22, 61–71.

Rouet, F., 2007. *Le Livre. Mutations d'une industrie culturelle*. La Documentation française, Paris.

Sapiro, G., 2008a. Translation and the field of publishing: a commentary on Pierre Bourdieu's "A conservative revolution in publishing" from a translation perspective. *Translation Studies* 1 (2), 154–167.

Sapiro, G., 2008b. Les collections de littérature étrangère. In: Sapiro, G. (Ed.), *Translatio. Le Marché de la traduction en France à l'heure de la mondialisation*. CNRS Editions, Paris, pp. 175–210.

Sapiro, G., 2008c. De la construction identitaire à la dénationalisation: les échanges intellectuels en la France et Israël. In: Sapiro, G. (Ed.), *Translatio. Le Marché de la traduction en France à l'heure de la mondialisation*. CNRS Editions, Paris, pp. 371–394.

Sapiro, G. (Ed.), 2008d. *Translatio. Le Marché de la traduction en France à l'heure de la mondialisation*. CNRS Editions, Paris.

Sapiro, G., 2009a. Mondialisation et diversité culturelle: les enjeux de la circulation transnationale des livres. In: Sapiro, G. (Ed.), *Les Contradictions de la globalisation éditoriale*. Nouveau Monde, Paris, pp. 275–302.

Sapiro, G. (Ed.), 2009b. *Les Contradictions de la globalisation éditoriale*. Nouveau Monde, Paris.

Sapiro, G., Popa, I., 2008. Traduire les sciences humaines et sociales: logiques éditoriales et enjeux scientifiques. In: Sapiro, G. (Ed.), *Translatio. Le Marché de la traduction en France à l'heure de la mondialisation*. CNRS Editions, Paris, pp. 107–143.

Sapiro, G., 2010. French literature in the world system of translation. In: McDonald, C., Suleiman, S. (Eds.), *French Literary History: A Global Approach*. Columbia University Press, New York, pp. 298–319.

Schalke, C., Gerlach, M., 1999. Le paysage éditorial allemand. *Actes de la recherche en sciences sociales* 130, 29–47.

Schiffrin, A., 2000. *The Business of Books*. Verso, New York.

Serry, H., 2002. Constituer un catalogue littéraire. *Actes de la recherche en sciences sociales* 144, 70–79.

Surel, Y., 1997. *L'État et le livre: les politiques publiques du livre en France: 1957–1993*. L'Harmattan, Paris.

Thompson, J.B., 2005. *Books in the Digital Age: The Transformation of Academic and Higher Education Publishing in Britain and the United States*. Polity Press, Cambridge, UK.

Tomlinson, J., 1991. *Cultural Imperialism: A Critical Introduction*. The Johns Hopkins University Press, Baltimore, MD.

Toury, G., 1995. *Descriptive Translation Studies and Beyond*. John Benjamins, Amsterdam.

Venuti, L., 1995. *The Translator's Invisibility: A History of Translation*. Routledge, London.

Venuti, L., 1998. *The Scandals of Translation: Towards an Ethics of Difference*. Routledge, London.

Vigne, E., 2008. *Le Livre et l'éditeur*. Klincksieck, Paris.

Vincent, J., 2007. Book policy in Quebec. In: Gerson, C., Michon, J. (Eds.), *History of the Book in Canada, vol. III: 1918–1980*. University of Toronto Press, Toronto, pp. 45–51.

Wallerstein, I., 2004. *World-Systems Analysis: An Introduction*. Duke University Press, Durham, NC.

16

From Cultural Turn to Translational Turn

A Transnational Journey (2011)

Susan Bassnett

One of the most influential contemporary translational theorists, Susan Bassnett is herself a translator and a poet, as well as Professor of Comparative Literature at the University of Warwick. With a multilingual education and a transnational academic career, Bassnett began teaching in Italy and continued in the United States before coming to Warwick. She is the author of more than 20 books; her *Translation Studies* (1980) continues to have a major impact on expanding the field of translation studies to encompass a broad engagement with culture. Bassnett's approach has shifted from arguing in the 1990s for a leading role for translation studies to reinforce a comparative literature still struggling to make peace with postcolonial studies (*Comparative Literature*, 1993), to rethinking translation in the context of a global market. In *Reflections on Comparative Literature in the Twenty-First Century* (2006), she argued that world literature gives the translator a pre-eminent role as agent engaged in the circulation and re-production of literature.

Bassnett's changing views on translation studies mirror the discipline's history in the past three decades, from the periphery of comparative literature to a mode of reading world literature, as "translation is effectively rewriting." Bassnett argues that world literature theory can strengthen and broaden what used to be an insular discipline of translation studies. In the 2011 essay given here, Bassnett looks back at the history of the field as it has evolved from a marginal position through the cultural turn in the 1990s to its repositioning at the heart of world literature in a global era, in which translation can be seen "as negotiation, as intercultural mediation, as a transcultural process."

Susan Bassnett, "From Cultural Turn to Translational Turn: A Transnational Journey" (2011). From Cecilia Alvstad *et al.*, eds., *Literature, Geography, Translation* (Newcastle upon Tyne: Cambridge Scholars Publishing, 2011), pp. 67–80.

Not so long ago literature, geography, and translation would have been seen as three distinct and separate fields of research, remote from one another. That they should today, in the twenty-first century, be seen as interconnectable, testifies to the radical shifts of perception that have taken place over the last decades of the twentieth century and the first decade of the new millennium. This interconnectedness has come about in part because of great changes within the subjects themselves: the study of literature is today contextualised in ways unimaginable before the postcolonial era; the study of geography has changed so completely that human and physical geographers now consider themselves as belonging to different disciplines, the former in the social sciences, the other in the physical sciences; and the study of translation has risen in status to the point where some claim that they work in a distinctive discipline called translation studies. All three fields, however, are concerned today with the movements of peoples, and with processes of import and export that are not only commercial but also aesthetic and intellectual. Any study of translation necessarily involves a geographical dimension, and the movement of literatures through translation requires an awareness of changing contexts of textual production.

In the immediate aftermath of World War II, research in the arts and humanities appeared to have changed very little since the earlier part of the century. Philology retained its importance, literary criticism followed formalist or New Critical methods, the canon was still intact, and disciplinary boundaries remained much as they had been in the 1930s. Degree programmes tended to be offered still in single subjects, and the concept of interdisciplinarity was viewed largely as radical and esoteric. Yet by the mid-1960s, that picture had changed in the English-speaking world and disciplinary certainties were being called increasingly into question. Sociological subject fields were emerging, new methodologies were developing, and entirely new areas were coming into being and asserting their right to autonomy, including subjects such as film studies, theatre studies, cultural studies, socio-linguistics and, closely following, women and gender studies. The European student protests of 1968 were primarily about the urgent need to rethink the old educational structures and certainties in a changing world, but there was also a powerful intellectual demand for innovation and reform. It was in this historical moment of transition and contestation that translation studies as a distinctive field of research also began to emerge.

It is important to remember when and how the subject started, and in what context, as we consider nearly forty years later its progress and development. For today, translation studies is at a watershed: those who term themselves translation studies specialists are still very few in number, yet interest in translation as a cultural phenomenon has never been greater. In her 2007 book Bella Brodzki makes claims for the importance of translation in today's world, arguing that translation "underwrites all cultural transactions, from the most benign to the most venal" (2007, 2). She points out that just as it is impossible today to ignore the impact of gender when studying "authorship, agency, subjectivity, performativity, multi-culturalism, postcolonialism, translationalism, diasporic literacy and technological literacy" (2007, 2), so it is impossible to ignore the integral role of translation in all discursive fields. This is a statement that would have been inconceivable when translation studies first began to appear on the academic stage in the 1970s. Brodzki is effectively saying that translation is at the heart both of all forms of communication and of all endeavours to analyse those forms. The idea of translation as central to international transactions on so many levels is light years removed from earlier ideas that defined translation as a secondary, second-class activity, as a derivative rather than a creative literary act, as a technical procedure of limited social importance.

At a conference in Leuven in 1976, which brought together a miscellaneous group of scholars, including myself, who later came to be labelled as the "poly-systems theorists" and still later as "the manipulation school", André Lefevere was given the task of writing a short manifesto of translation studies, based on a radical rethinking of the more traditional relationship between theory and practice. Instead of applying theory to the study of translation, translation studies would seek to investigate translation itself and then apply that knowledge to literary and linguistic theory: "The goal of the discipline is to produce a comprehensive theory which can be used as a guideline for the production of translations" (Lefevere 1978, 234). The key to this new disciplinary utopia was integration of theory and practice, with translations viewed both as text products and as text producers. And a first step in its establishment would be a radical revision of literary history, so as to determine the development of norms and conventions and most import-antly, to challenge received wisdom about the historical role of translation. The next phase of development in translation studies saw a focus on historical research, a kind of mapping that considered the role played by translation in different literary histories. This map-making exercise shed a lot of light on canonical assumptions about originality and literary transfer, and called seriously into question some of the claims for the autonomy of national literatures. Reading literary history through the lens of translation has enabled us to see more clearly that the development of any literary system involves complex processes of import and export.

Looking back, it is clear that what was taking place as translation studies started to emerge was also happening in other fields. Translation studies shared with other new fields a contestatory function, as young scholars challenged the academic estab-lishment, calling into question the literary canon, promoting interdisciplinarity and pursuing an almost evangelising mission to rediscover lost histories. The question of history was pre-eminent, perhaps because a new generation was looking with dis-quiet at the histories bequeathed to them by their parents and grandparents. In Britain and Commonwealth countries this was particularly important in the light of the demise of the old British Empire, while in the United States the Civil Rights movement had forced a rethinking of the history of slavery in the forging of the nation. Across Europe, complex histories of occupation, collusion, resistance, and collaboration were highlighted by the accelerated post-war reconstruction processes and by the prospect of a new European market. In the universities, new subject fields were reassessing history in terms of class, race, nationality, religion, and gender.

In an important essay from 1978, which deserves to be much more widely read, the Israeli systems theorist Itamar Even-Zohar pointed out that translation has played a different role in different cultures and at differing historical moments, being seen as a high status activity at certain times and as a marginal activity at others. In that essay, he advanced the view that there are distinct social circumstances that affect the production of translations. A literature in the early stages of its development, for example, is likely to translate far more than a literature that perceives itself as solidly established and self-sufficient, as also is a literature that is undergoing a period of extreme change or one that perceives itself as marginal, or in Even-Zohar's terms, "weak". The importance of Even-Zohar's essay is that he set out a skeletal framework for a cultural approach to translation, stressing the importance of the historical context and advancing thinking about the ways in which texts travel across borders and are received in new cultural contexts. His approach was framed within his theory of the polysystem, which conceived of all literary production ("high" and "low", canonical and popular, innovative and conservative) as an aggregate of diverse sub-systems in a given culture. Within such a model, translation could be shown to have played a highly significant role at particular moments in time. It may seem a grandiose claim, but Even-Zohar's polysystems theory offered a radical way of rethinking earlier Formalist theories and hence opened up possibilities for exploring new pathways through literary history.

The polysystems approach appealed particularly to literary scholars seeking to reposition translation in the epistemological hierarchy, where it occupied a low-status position. In an essay published in 1986, for example, Maria Tymoczko made an important claim for the significance of polysystems theory in reassessing major textual shifts in the Middle Ages. Focussing on the twelfth-century transition from epic to romance, Tymoczko argues that this period saw massive changes in genre and character typologies, equally massive formal and stylistic changes, and a major ideological shift from a warrior ethos to the celebration of courtly romantic love. However, a full understanding of how and why this happened can only come about by an investigation into the role played by translation:

> The history of translation in twelfth-century French literature and its connection with the development of the genre of romance is a case study supporting a poly-systems approach to literary dynamics [...]. A theoretical perspective has been needed to show [...] the patterned workings of a system of translation within a dynamic literary system. A polysystem framework for translation theory in this case can serve to rewrite the literary history of twelfth-century France. (Tymoczko 1986, 21–22)

The enthusiasm for the polysystems approach that dominated translation studies in the English speaking world during the 1980s can be explained by essays such as Tymoczko's. Even-Zohar's theory offered a way of rethinking traditional literary history through a lens that put translation into sharp focus, and it also emphasised the ideological dimensions of translation. Theo Hermans' collection of conference papers published in 1985, provocatively entitled *The Manipulation of Literature*, led to some suggestions that a new "manipulation school" of translation studies had come in to being, where the emphasis was on tracing the fortunes of a text in the target culture and on the complex processes of text production that characterise the transfer of a piece of writing from one culture to another. André Lefevere's *Translation, Rewriting and the Manipulation of Literary Fame*, published in 1992, can be seen as the high point of this line of historical research. Lefevere discusses patronage, editing, anthologising, and what he terms "rewriting" and states bluntly:

> Literary histories, as they have been written until recently, have had little or no time for translations, since for the literary historian translation had to do with "language" only, not with literature – another outgrowth of the "monolingualization" of literary history by Romantic historiographers intent on creating "national" literatures preferably as uncontaminated as possible by foreign influence. (1992, 39)

By the time Lefevere published his book, it was clear that the dominant approach to translation in the English-speaking world was determined by ideological issues. Bassnett and Lefevere had brought out a collection of essays in 1990 in which they argued that translation studies was undergoing a cultural turn, a point emphasised by Edwin Gentzler in his survey of the field, *Contemporary Translation Theories*, published in its second edition in 2001 (it had first appeared in 1993). Gentzler declared that one of the two most important theoretical shifts in translation in the latter part of the twentieth century was the shift from source-oriented to target-text-oriented theories. Interestingly, Genztler's second most significant shift was the inclusion of cultural factors as well as linguistic elements in the teaching of translation, a reference to the German functionalist approach that has been so successful internationally and which also, though in a rather different manner, focussed on the target culture.

More recently, expanding research in what is termed world literature also serves to highlight the significance of translation in literary transactions. It appears self-evident that the transmission of texts across cultural boundaries should also have a linguistic dimension, yet studies of literary transmission tended for a long time to play down or disregard the role of translation. This is understandable once we pause to reflect on the link between the construction of national literary histories in the nineteenth century, an age characterised by passionate struggles to establish clearly defined and coherent national identities across Europe. We can see the Czech or Finnish cases as analogous to the imperial British mission in this respect: the drive to create a national literature directly linked to a sense of new national identity, which had at its heart the importance of literature produced in the national language, is not so far removed from the drive to reaffirm the greatness of a colonising power around the world. Lord Macaulay's (in)famous Indian minute, wherein he stated that all the libraries of India and Arabia were not worth one shelf of a good European library, can be read alongside statements by Czech revivalists such as Josef Jungmann, who claimed boldly that "in the language is our nationality" (Macura 1990).

One of the problems of emphasising the national basis for literary production is that translations tend to be seen as immigrants, not quite worthy of the status accorded to texts produced within a given literary tradition. This is a partial explanation for the downgrading of translation in literary histories, despite the huge role it has played. What is significant today about the growth of world literature is that it offers a reappraisal of the significance of translation and proposes a shift of focus onto interconnectedness, on global literary and cultural flows on the one hand, and on questions of agency on the other. But at the same time, despite the spread of programmes calling themselves translation studies and despite the interest in translation globally, the most innovative thinking about translation is not coming from within the field itself, nor does translation studies appear to be having much impact outside its own boundaries. Indeed, it could be argued that developments in world literature have been moving parallel to work in translation studies, and that where we must turn today for the most innovative thinking about translation is to scholars who see themselves as comparatists, as postcolonialists, as world literature people. Research in translation studies continues unabated, but much of it is still utilising antiquated methodologies.

There has been a great deal of debate since translation studies first emerged as a field of study back in the 1970s as to whether it constitutes a distinctive discipline in its own right. Over the years, I have contributed to the debate, at one stage suggesting, with André Lefevere, that translation studies should be redefined as an overarching discipline into which comparative literature should be accommodated. Today, I find such debates tedious and outmoded; both translation studies and comparative literature are not disciplines – both are methods of approaching the study of texts. In all areas of literary transfer, there is interconnectedness, and it is this that we should be investigating. Sherry Simon, for example, has recently published a book entitled *Translating Montreal* and is working on a further book that will take this idea of "translating cities" still further. Significantly, her book is subtitled "Episodes in the life of a divided city", and here storytelling, the theme of reconciliation, and a spatial dimension are all encompassed. Simon explores what she calls "the sensation of living among competing codes" (2006, 218), focussing not on conflict but on constructive encounters. "Languages," she tells us in her conclusion. "take on density when they touch", and from that increased density comes an excitement that "keeps attention from settling" (2006, 219).

In a talk given at the University of Warwick in 2009, Harish Trivedi attacked what he perceives as the undermining of translation understood as a literary act involving more than one language. He takes issue with Salman Rushdie, Homi Bhabha, and any number of scholars who use translation metaphorically. Bhabha, says Trivedi, does not at all mean literary translation involving two texts from two different languages and cultures [...] what he means by translation instead is the process and condition of human migrancy [...] the condition of Western multiculturalism brought about by Third World migrancy. (2009)

Trivedi's critique reflects his anxiety about the hegemony of global English, and he has been expressing that anxiety for some time. But in his Warwick speech he introduced a new line of attack: what had translation studies specialists been doing for the last 15–20 years, he asked, how had they seemingly failed to notice this rapid growth of a whole alternative narrative with all kinds of ideological implications centred apparently around something termed translation? It is a good question to ask, and a timely one.

My response to that question is that translation studies, which began as contestatory, has been so intent on establishing itself as a distinct field, or discipline as some would have it, that it has turned inwards. The proliferation of programmes in translation studies disguises the fact that often this is a catch-all term used by university administrators in a restructuring of modern languages. Translation is sexy, so the amalgamation of several language units can be rebranded as an Institute or Centre for Translation Studies. In some cases, translator training programmes have been similarly rebranded. The term translation studies, which had no credibility prior to the 1980s, is now marketable, regardless of what that term covers. Moreover, concern about the inward-looking nature of the field is also reflected in some of the publications that have been appearing. I sometimes feel that if I have to read one more doctoral thesis or article that offers a bit of regurgitated translation theory, usually citing all the old guard (including Bassnett, Toury, Lefevere, Baker, Pym, Venuti, Vermeer, Nord, and Gentzler) and followed by a totally untheorised case study, I will toss the text out of the nearest window. How can any field retain its contestatory role if it is seeking to become an establishment itself, with its own canonical list of names and a restricted methodology?

Let us assume, as Doris Bachmann-Medick posits, that there is currently something she defines as a "translational turn" going on in literary studies. Translation is chic, it is the term of the moment, the idea of translation is becoming integrated into research in the humanities more generally. We may, like Harish Trivedi, disapprove of this trend, lamenting that monolinguals are also seeing themselves as translators, or we may rejoice that translation as metaphor is becoming more widely employed, but the question remains as to where this translational turn places translation studies in its next stage of travel. The cultural turn of the early 1990s focussed attention on the broader, translinguistic aspects of translation, including translation as negotiation, as intercultural mediation, as a transcultural process, but the translational turn is not happening within translation studies, it is taking place outside the field.

Lest this become too pessimistic, let us now consider two major exciting new areas of exploration that are starting to open up, both of which revolve around new ways of thinking about the age-old dichotomy of original versus translation/copy/

imitation, and both of which involve a return to the central positioning of texts that can involve scholars from outside and inside translation studies. For if we stray from the actual processes of translation, we risk losing touch with what translation actually means, and it is worth reminding ourselves, as Umberto Eco has done, that nothing really new has been said about translation since Cicero and St. Jerome distinguished between word for word and sense for sense, between taking the text to the reader or taking the reader to the text.

In 2009 Esperança Bielsa and I published *Translation in Global News*, which is based on a three-year research project into the politics and economics of translation in the transmission of global news. Through our investigation into news translation, into how information moves not only across linguistic and cultural boundaries but also along electronic pathways, we found ourselves compelled to recognise the impossibility of thinking about translation as a relationship between source and target, because the source was plural, undefinable, multifaceted. We started out looking at news agencies; we ended up questioning the definition of translation itself. Today, news and media translation is an important area of enquiry, as researchers explore the complexities of internet translation, for example, and find themselves faced with the difficulty of deciding whether what they are considering is translation at all. In short, the traditional frameworks within which we have thought of translation start to break down when the methods of production deny us any clear sense of what a source text might be. And all the arguments about acculturation as possibly less desirable than foreignisation go out of the window when we consider that news translation is totally target-focussed, hence accultura-tion is the only option conceivable. Research into translation and global flows in this age of accelerating electronic communication is still in its infancy, but is full of promise, and here perhaps methodologies from translation, literature, and geography can assist one another.

My particular interest at present, though, is to explore the boundaries of translation from a writer's perspective. I am increasingly engaged in the production of texts, not only in their analysis. I find myself going back time and again to Borges, when he says with such superb irony

> I do not write, I rewrite. My memory produces my sentences. I have read so much and I have heard so much. I admit it: I repeat myself. I confirm it: I plagiarise. We are all the heirs of millions of scribes who have already written down all that is essential a long time before us. We are all copyists... (Borges in Kristal 2002, 135)

Borges' irony is reassuring. It also invites us to rethink the categorising of translation as something less than other forms of writing, for what he is effec-tively suggesting is that all writing is a form of translation. We could equally say that all translating is a creative act, for translation involves a double act of interpretation and reshaping. If we are indeed all copyists and plagiarists, then what is important is for the plagiarism to be well done and to constitute, in its own way, an original version.

In her preface to a fascinating recent translation of the Anglo-Saxon poem *The Wanderer*, the English poet Jane Holland justifies her decision to change the sex of the protagonist from male to female. She explains that she wanted this translation to provide a centrepiece for her latest collection of poetry, and that as a woman writing in the twenty-first century, a thousand years away from the world of the original poem, she found that "the traditional male-male relationship of the lord and his faithful retainer (took) on a strongly homoerotic charge when read with a modern sensibility and […] as a female poet" (2008, 6). Holland here highlights something that is often overlooked when we talk about translations: the stage of creating a translation that involves close reading. That act of reading then conditions our response to the work, and the reading is then re-encoded in the translation itself.

Jane Holland explains that for her, the process of reading shaped her translation, but that she had not foreseen this – it happened naturally and she did not resist. Her translation also changes the metrical rules of the Anglo-Saxon and moves away from traditional rhetorical devices such as alliteration, besides the most obvious gender change. But for other writers, the decision to translate may be a conscious means of altering one's own writing style, a means of expanding the range of inner possibilities through a relationship with another writer.

One of the strangest things about writing is that although you do it in order to reach out to readers, you are always surprised by readers' reactions. In 2008 Paschalis Nikolau and Maria-Venetia Krytsi edited a collection of essays on the translator as agent, *Translating Selves. Experience and Identity between Languages and Literatures*. In Nikolau's essay on literary translation and life-writing, I was surprised (and very flattered) to find him discussing my collection of poems and translations, *Exchanging Lives*, in a way that had never occurred to me when I was writing it, but which made a great deal of sense. At one stage he says:

> Bassnett's work in particular shows awakenings of narrative, illustrates that even in the apparently inhospitable environs of translation, there are stories and memories – so often incited by other writing(s) – that emerge from within us, weave their way into the ontology of translation, and are told through its various "betrayals". Settings of translation, and the twilight hours between translation and original are what an auto-biographical imperative will often turn to, specifically demand and further help to effect; especially when the experience to be communicated may be too painful or inti-mate for either autobiography or even "proper" creative writing. (2008, 66)

His analysis touches a nerve: he suggests that translating can be a form of autobiographical writing, a means of writing the self at one stage removed, as it were, a means of writing creatively about pain or trauma assisted by the cloak of the words of a writer from another time and another place. This would certainly make sense as to why it is that so many writers choose also to translate, often at times of crisis; Ted Hughes, for example, the founder of the journal *Modern Poetry in Translation* back in the 1960s, sought to understand the Holocaust and the horrors of World War II through translating such writers as Janos Pilinsky. Hughes had no Hungarian, so worked with a native speaker, Janos Csokits, who produced word-for-word drafts that Hughes took and worked on. Csokits admired Hughes' capacity to get to the heart of the poem even in his crudely produced first literal drafts:

> It is almost as if he could X-ray the literals and see the original poem in ghostly detail like a radiologist viewing the bones, muscles, veins and nerves of a live human body…The effect is not that of a technical device; it has more to do with extra-sensory perception. (Csokits in Bassnett 2009, 87)

The general perception of Ted Hughes is that he was an archetypal English poet of the twentieth century, the Poet Laureate who wrote magnificently about the savagery of the natural world and who can be placed in a long tradition of English nature writers going back through Thomas Hardy, William Wordsworth, and Shakespeare (*King Lear*) to the great early medieval poets. But throughout his life Hughes translated, from ancient and modern languages, from the one language he knew (French) and from other languages he did not know. In the last years of his life, as illness took hold, he translated more than ever, just as Queen Elizabeth I, with death approaching, translated Boethius and other Latin writers, day after day, scribbling her English version in a shaky hand testifying to her fears that time was running out for her. What is it, we may ask, that gives translating such power and makes it such a compulsive activity for people who apparently have no need to do it? This is an important question, but not one that was asked until recently, as we have come to rethink the status and importance of translation and translators.

The Irish poet, Michael Longley, describes himself as having been "Homer-haunted for fifty years". Longley is one of a growing number of writers who is using translation in creative new ways, in a process of recontextualisation. So for example his poem "Ceasefire", written after the IRA declared a ceasefire in Northern Ireland in August 1994, both is and is not a translation from Homer. The final couplet of Longley's sonnet is spoken by King Priam, who has just dined with Achilles, the man who killed his son Hector: "I get down on my knees and do what must be done / And kiss Achilles' hand, the killer of my son" (1995, 39). Commenting on this poem, Longley notes how it had a massive impact when it came out, being cited by politicians and priests alike, and says simply: "[I]t was Homer who spoke to us across the millennia. I was only his mouthpiece" (Longley in Harrison 2009, 105).

Josephine Balmer is another poet who returns to ancient Greek and Latin poetry as a source of inspiration. What characterises Balmer's work is the way in which she blurs the boundaries between traditional notions of "translation" and other forms of writing. She states simply that translating classical writers inevitably involves creative (re)writing. Not only do we often know very little or nothing at all about the original writer, but we have only a tenuous sense of the context in which they wrote in the first instance. Moreover, in many cases the texts exist either as fragments, with great gaps in them, or have been edited over the millennia in all kinds of ways, so that there is no definitive source text from which to begin translating, but rather a range of variations of a putative source. What is a translator to do in the absence of a clear source text and the lack of contextual information, except to use his or her own creative powers to forge a version for and of their own time, in other words, to recontextualise.

Balmer's latest collection builds confidently on this interface between writing and translating. Entitled *The Word for Sorrow*, it is in one respect a version of parts of Ovid's *Tristia* and *Epistulae ex Ponto*, works written during his exile to the Black Sea. In her preface, she recounts how one afternoon, by chance, she stopped to wonder about the former owner of her Latin dictionary, whose name is inked on the flyleaf. Playing around with internet search engines, she discovered that the original owner had fought at Gallipoli in 1915, crossing the Dardanelles that Ovid had written about in his poems. A connection was made: "*The Word for Sorrow* took shape, a series of poems exploring the story of an old second-hand dictionary and its owner alongside versions of the texts it was helping to translate" (Balmer 2008). The collection thus weaves together two stories of exile and pain, the Roman poet lamenting his banishment and the young soldier finding himself in one of the bloodiest theatres of war of the early twentieth century. Balmer brings together two narratives, two histories, separated by time, space, and language.

By what definition can her work be called translation? This kind of writing invites us to go beyond that term, which has come to acquire such a restricted meaning, so as to reconceptualise translation as movement between and across, not simply as a transaction between a source and a target text. Just as media translation calls into question the relationship between source and target, so too does recontexualising literary translation. The interest in translation globally, the use made of the term metaphorically, is surely not due to the emergence in the 1970s of a small field of study that called itself translation studies, but rather to the greater sense of fluidity that marks the world we inhabit and the texts being produced at this time. The idea of transposition is etymologically present in the word "translation", which implies movement across time and space and, as Brodzki has pointed out, translation underwrites all our cultural transactions in this multifaceted, globalised world of ours. The systematic study of translation has been an important field of research for several decades; what needs to happen now is for translation studies scholars to engage with colleagues in other disciplines, so that thinking about cultural translation, research into translation processes, and creative translation practice can provide nourishment for one another.

Works Cited

Apter, Emily. 2006. *The Translation Zone: A New Comparative Literature*. Princeton: Princeton University Press.
Bachmann-Medick, Doris. 2009. "The translational turn". *Translation Studies* 2 (2): 2–16.
Balmer, Josephine. 2009. *The Word for Sorrow*. Cambridge: Salt Publishing.
Bassnett, Susan. 2002a. *Translation Studies*. 3rd edn. London and New York: Routledge.

Bassnett, Susan. 2002b. *Exchanging Lives. Poems and Translations*. Leeds: Peepal Tree.

Bassnett, Susan. 2009. *Ted Hughes*. Tavistock: The Northcote Press.

Bhabha, Homi. 1994. *The Location of Culture*. London and New York: Routledge.

Bielsa, Esperança, and Susan Bassnett. 2009. *Global News Translation*. London and New York: Routledge.

Brodzki, Bella. 2007. *Can These Bones Live? Translation, Survival and Cultural Memory*. Stanford: Stanford University Press.

Eco, Umberto. 2001. *Experiences in Translation*. Trans. Alastair McEwen. Toronto: University of Toronto Press.

Even-Zohar, Itamar. 2000. "The position of translated literature within the literary polysystem." In Lawrence Venuti (ed.), *The Translation Studies Reader*, 192–197. London and New York: Routledge.

Gentzler, Edwin. 2001. *Contemporary Translation Theories*. 2nd edn. Clevedon and Philadelphia: Multilingual Matters.

Hermans, Theo. 1985. *The Manipulation of Literature*. London: Croom Helm.

Holland, Jane. 2008. *The Lament of the Wanderer*. Coventry: Heaventree Press.

Kristal, Efrain. 2002. *Invisible Work. Borges and Translation*. Nashville: Vanderbilt University Press.

Lefevere, André. 1978. "Translation studies: The goal of the discipline." In James Holmes, Jose Lambert, and Raymond van den Broeck (eds.), *Literature and Translation. New Perspectives in Literary Studies with a Basic Bibliography of Books on Translation Studies*, 234–35. Leven: ACCO.

Lefevere, André. 1992. *Translation, Rewriting and the Manipulation of Literary Fame*. London and New York: Routledge.

Longley, Michael. 1995. *Ghost Orchid*. London: Jonathan Cape.

Longley, Michael. 2009. "Lapsed classicist." In S. J. Harrison (ed.), *Living Classics. Greece and Rome in Contemporary Poetry in English*, 97–113. Oxford: Oxford University Press.

Macura, Vladimir. 1990. "Culture as translation." In Susan Bassnett and André Lefevere (eds.), *Translation, History and Culture*, 64–70. London: Pinter.

Nikolaou, Paschalis, and Maria Venetia Kyritsi (eds.). 2008. *Translating Selves. Experience and Identity between Languages and Literatures*. London: Continuum.

Simon, Sherry. 2006. *Translating Montreal. Episodes in the Life of a Divided City*. Montreal and Kingston: McGill-Queen's University Press.

Trivedi, Harish. 2009. "Translating culture versus cultural translation." Working paper delivered at the University of Warwick, June 2009.

Tymoczko, Maria. 1986. "Translation as a force for literary revolution in the twelfth-century shift from epic to romance." *New Comparison* 1 (Summer): 7–27.

Part Three

Debating World Literature

Stepping Forward and Back
Issues and Possibilities for "World" Poetry (2004)

Stephen Owen

Stephen Owen is the James Bryant Conant University Professor at Harvard University and a world-renowned name in the study of classical Chinese literature. He has written extensively on Chinese poetry and poetics (*Traditional Chinese Poetry and Poetics*, 1985; *The Making of Early Chinese Classical Poetry*, 2006; *The Late Tang*, 2006) and has co-edited the volumes *Ways With Words: Writing about Reading Texts from Early China* and the *Cambridge History of Chinese Literature* (2010). He has long been interested in comparative literature and comparative poetics, the subject of his book *Mi-lou: Poetry and the Labyrinth of Desire* (1989), and he served as editor of Chinese literature for *The Norton Anthology of World Literature* (2003).

In a controversial 1990 article, "What Is World Poetry?," Owen questioned the value of poetry written for an international audience but cut off from its own linguistic and literary traditions. In "Stepping Forward and Back: Issues and Possibilities for 'World' Poetry" (2004), Owen revises and expands on his earlier argument, discussing the challenges of reading as well as writing lyric poetry in a global market. While still embedded within the national literary establishment, "world poetry" raises the problem of canonization or international recognition, which in turn is embedded within the problem of translation, all the more visible in the case of poetry. "There can indeed be a 'world poetry,'" he concludes, "so long as we understand that this is not the whole world of poetry."

A dozen years ago I reviewed a translation of Bei Dao's poetry for *The New Republic*. The review was submitted without a title; but the editor, in his wisdom, saw fit to give it the fatal heading "World Poetry." The review stirred a fair amount of reaction,

Stephen Owen, "Stepping Forward and Back: Issues and Possibilities for 'World' Poetry" (2004). In *Modern Philology* 100:4 (2004), pp. 532–548. © 2003 by The University of Chicago. All rights reserved.

World Literature in Theory, First Edition. Edited by David Damrosch.

not a little of which was wrathful, from the community of contemporary Chinese poets and those who study them.[1] The argument of the review was a simple one, one that in fact touched on Bei Dao's poetry only as a case of a larger issue of contemporary poetry in languages other than English and those languages we recognize as "international." Of all literary forms, lyric poetry has been most closely tied to the particularities of national languages; at the same time, insofar as a lyric poet is seen as part of an international community of poets and readers, there is a pressure for linguistic fungibility. As national recognition seeks the supplement of international recognition, a literary text not only has to be translated, it has to be able to claim that its essential values are still present in translation. Like movie dialogue with subtitles, novels often shrug off the potential problems here. This presents a special problem for lyric poetry, however, a problem commonly solved by the assumption that, no matter how good the translation, there is an original that is always still better – sometimes located on a facing page, but more often to be found only in major research libraries. Such an implicit claim for all translated poetry has its obviously troubling aspects: the reader or critic who might feel confident facing a translated novel modestly defers both judgment and pleasure when facing translated poetry; the poem comes to us as existing elsewhere. The only escape from this peculiar doubling of poetry's other and greater meaning would seem to be a new identity for lyric poetry, one that is not dependent on any particular national language. This is a troubling possibility for lyric poetry, but a not uninteresting one.

The theme of this centenary issue of *Modern Philology* ("Toward World Literature") seems an appropriate occasion to revisit some of these issues in light of a dozen years of continuing change. The central question is one of how poetic value is and can be constituted across language boundaries. Perhaps because of lyric poetry's ties to national languages and to a history of poetry in a particular national language, it encounters problems when situated in the context of world poetry. I would like to follow the old argument a bit further, then to consider how things have changed in the past dozen years, and finally to take what may seem an odd detour, in the poetry I know best, Chinese.

I readily concede that contemporary poetry still operates primarily in the context of national literatures and national languages. If international recognition is a force, it is a force only on the edges of a national literature, pressing in different degrees and different ways. It is, to my knowledge, not a force at all on poetry in English. Cultural power is not evenly distributed, and the poet writing in English (or French) can work in blithe self-confidence regarding the universal adequacy of his or her linguistic community. "International recognition" means recognition by certain centers of cultural power and recognition in English or one of the other international languages. For a young Korean poet to be translated into Tagalog and acclaimed in Manila is, no doubt, a matter of satisfaction; but it has less cachet than to be translated into English or French and invited to New York or Paris. It is unfair, but it is a fact. The cultural globe, like the financial globe, has capitals, but the capitals of the cultural globe are far less evenly distributed over the demographic globe.

Within particular national literatures, the structures of recognition and literary valuation remain much as they have been throughout modern times and earlier. Circles of recognized poets and critics discover new poets – and sometimes neglected older ones. University students and young intellectuals have their favorites, and such poets sometimes enter the more formalized structures of recognition in national literatures (perhaps because university students and young intellectuals join national literary establishments). Sometimes there are national institutions that recognize a poet of lasting achievement – poet laureates, permanent or transient – which is often a gift of honor received only ambivalently. Established poets enter anthologies and literary histories, sometimes to stay and sometimes as mere visitors. Collectors of used books in the various national languages can accumulate a rich array of anthologies of recent poetry from across many decades and observe the remarkable changes in the fates of poets. Competition for prominence and survival – what commonly gets called "canonization" – is an issue, and an issue that few feel comfortable addressing as a sociological question in contemporary poetry (though it is a commonplace question in the academic representation of the past).

Actors real and fictional may have claimed credit for having performed before the crowned heads of Europe, but international recognition is a relatively new constituent in the politics and economics of poetic judgment. Such recognition does not always mean translation, but it often does. International recognition and translation can bring substantial financial rewards for novelists; for poets they bring only prestige. The full structure of international recognition is complex, but in the cultural imagination of many writers it has been embodied first and foremost in the Nobel Prize for literature. Young poets in many countries are encouraged to aspire to this, and works that receive the prize are not only quickly translated, but even studied to understand where world literature is at the present moment and what sorts of things are valued. The prize has become a cultural force in ways never imagined in its founding, which may be the common fate of all prominent and long-established institutions.

As the world grew increasingly integrated in the second half of the twentieth century, the Nobel Prize entered the imagination of cultural communities outside the core circle of literatures in the main European languages (including Russian). Within this enlarged horizon of contenders, one factor became prominent. Although I am not privy to their discussions, I strongly suspect this has also been a factor in the deliberations of the prize committee itself. This is a presumed right of representation: "It is time for a writer from country X to get the Nobel Prize." I have heard and read this many times, with only the "X," the variable nationality, changed. This was certainly long a sentiment in China. Literary communities in various countries feel that one of their best authors ought to be chosen, representing them among the Nobel laureates from other countries. Unlike the Olympics, the other great example of structured international competition, neither winning nor failing to win the Nobel Prize for literature is a self-evident judgment.

The problem with representation in this context is the question of who gets to choose the representative. We will return to this question in greater length later;

here we may simply observe that this choice of an imagined "best in the world" may reveal itself as a judgment of the best by a small group of people in a faraway country. If a writer from some other country wins the Nobel Prize, then a national literary community can read the works of the winner and hope for their own success in the following year. If, however, the winner of the Nobel Prize implicitly represents a particular national literature and yet the person chosen is not someone well known or admired by the literary establishment or readership in that country, then the members of that community suddenly realize that they have no say in world literature.

In this way an imagined right to be represented can easily turn into a demand for self-representation. Not only does no structure for this exist in the global cultural community, but it is hard to see how such a structure could be created. It is, however, one of those nice cases where irreconcilable values meet. We can easily understand why a large community of writers and intellectuals within a particular national culture might resent their literature being celebrated in a choice made by a group of even very thoughtful and conscientious Swedes – if that choice ignores all the writers they consider important. At the same time, the mind pauses in quiet horror at the thought of a "United Nations" of poets, each elected by writers' associations in the constituent countries, taking annual turns as a Global Poet Laureate. We have here a conflict of legitimate values for which there is no possible reconciliation.

Literature, in both the original language and in translation, has been moving across cultural and national borders ever since literature existed. Nevertheless, many national literatures still have distinct histories and distinct values. It is therefore worth considering what an international structure of value would have to look like. Since literature is a matter of taste, in the several senses of the phrase, I will take food as my metaphor – though I am not sure whether it is merely a metaphor or the instantiation of a structure of value that operates on many levels. I need a location where international food comes together. If I find such a location in the food court of a mall, I hope it will not seem too demeaning to the claims of literature in general and of poetry in particular.

Food courts have certain rules that function within the grammar of mall planning. Before the construction of any particular mall is completed, the planners design a structured representation of food types, a large proportion of which are recognized international types. In the planning stage various individuals or chains may compete to represent the type (the decision on who is allowed to represent a type being left in the invisible hands of the mall planners); but once the structure is realized, the competition for consumer attention is displaced from the relative quality within any particular type to the competition among types. The consumer may choose to patronize an "Italian" fast food stall (pizza, spaghetti, and lasagna), a Chinese stall, an Indian stall, a Japanese stall, a Mexican stall, a New York deli, a hamburger stall, or a stall that serves "healthy food." I believe most of my readers will be familiar with the range and variations. The size of the mall determines the extent of choices, and one can outline a rather clear hierarchy of the types that will be added as the size expands. Not all national cuisines are represented – only those with constituencies.

In observing such a cultural structure, it is always worth noting possibilities so habitually excluded that they eventually become all but invisible. What you do not generally find is competition between restaurants of the same type. Choice is displaced from a hierarchical judgment of quality to a lateral preference for a certain type – a matter of taste, in one of the possible senses of the phrase. It is easy to see in this an allegory of American culture, but it has become an international form as well.

Each of the limited number of national cuisines here represented is, in its native context, actually constituted of a wide range of often very divergent regional styles. While one may find upscale restaurants featuring regional cuisines of other countries in large cities, as a general cultural phenomenon regional variation is replaced by a national style – indeed, a national style of cuisine that exists only in relation to a specified set of other national cuisines. Like that of the nation-state itself, the coherence of a national cuisine exists with perfect clarity only outside its own borders. This national style of cuisine is further mediated by the local taste of the place in which the mall or restaurant is located. There is no "Chinese food" in China; there are only regional and local cuisines and specialized types of food that transcend region. Chinese food does indeed exist outside of China, but it is not quite the same in Boston, Prague, or Madrid.

Within any national cuisine (as a collective of local cuisines), there are many things commonly eaten in other countries, if not universally. If you break an egg and whirl it in a hot pan, the same thing happens in whichever country the egg is broken, no matter how long that country's cultural history. National cuisines also contain dishes and foods that no one in another country would willingly eat, except for a broad-minded intellectual determined to expand his or her gustatory horizons. These extremes – the too common and the too exotic – have no place in the stalls of the food court. Chinese food stalls in food courts, like most Chinese restaurants catering to an American clientele, serve neither steamed bread buns (*mantou*, which are, indeed, just bread) nor shredded pig's belly nor seasoned jellyfish. To function as a commensurate map of different food types, including the international, the cuisine of the food court has to exist on a comfortable margin of difference – with plastic knives and forks provided.

The choice of a commercial and popular cultural form as the analogy for a high cultural enterprise may seem to verge on the satirical, but it remains a persuasively minimalist model for an empirically possible structure of valuation within historically diverse cultural sets. University students, like the Nobel Prize Committee, hear only of those literatures for which there are talented translators and academic brokers. The literature in question can be neither too common nor too exotic; it has to be on some comfortable margin of difference for the target audience. What seems satirical in the shadow of the food court analogy becomes simple pragmatism when trying to talk about non-Western literary traditions to scholars of European literature, not to mention students. When you deal with texts from China or Japan or the Indian subcontinent or the Islamic world, you are dealing with cultures with histories that are as deep as everything you know or don't know about Europe; and they know much about European cultural history as well. To do any one of these literary cultures well takes a lifetime.

Our culinary map of the food court is not all that far from planning a syllabus for a course on world literature – or even from planning a syllabus for a course on a single literature that presents formidable cultural difficulties. The model is not identical: we modify it out of the larger hopes of our university system. We may challenge the taste and expectations of our student consumers more strenuously than a Chinese or Indian fast food stall in a food court challenges the hungry shopper. We will try to include texts that are valued in the cultures that produced them, despite the difficulties – though we may flavor them a bit differently. These are important differences. But underneath lie intractable problems of constituting global culture or world literature; it is always constituted in a local "somewhere," creating a structure of commensurability that maps and essentializes easily attainable margins of difference. This is not a local problem of the United States or Europe; the Chinese also tend to generalize about the West in ways that forget history and regional difference, as an imagined entity that exists only on a Chinese cultural map.

* * *

Critics and scholars working within the context of a single national literature have the luxury of innocence: they can read a set of poems and judge poet X to be the best. If poet X can sustain a history of such judgments, he or she may enter the canon. At this point the poet moves beyond effective judgment in any radical sense (witness the attempts to jettison Milton in the first half of the twentieth century). Rather, the canonical poet becomes a constituent in the evolving values by which other works are judged. The truly canonical poet cannot be extracted without destabilizing the whole system. Shakespeare is not self-evidently a great poet – he certainly was not such to French neoclassical critics – rather, his works historically came to instantiate certain values, values by which other works were judged over a continuing history. When those works entered a canon, they became a set that defined a certain range of literary values, with the consequence that those values appeared self-evident.

This is the old model of value formation in national literatures – and, indeed, Shakespeare played an important role in initially imagining national literature. Our food court model suggests an important change in the structure of value – a change, we have argued, that is one of the fundamental rules of the food court. Rather than asking whether poet X in category A is better than poet Y in category B, we presume that poets X and Y are best in their own categories (which can be a problematic assumption, allowing that poets X and Y have been brought to our attention because they fit into a system in which they are understandable and comparable). We are not allowed to say that category A is better than category B: we may prefer Chinese beef and broccoli to chicken koorma, but we may not say that it is superior. When neoconservatives proclaim the superiority of Western civilization (not asking how and when that category came to be constituted), the liberal academy is scandalized: one simply prefers to read Wordsworth; it is not that one believes Wordsworth "superior" to Du Fu. While it is silly on the level of the food court, such a concession to the possibility of different values – however naively and habitually made – is a profound step in understanding the historicity of values that have come to seem as if natural.

This brings us back to the Nobel Prize. Even with the pressure to represent different national literatures, the judgments of the Nobel Prize Committee are claims of value and not of preference. If the Nobel Prize Committee chooses a Romanian writer over a Chinese writer, such a choice cannot possibly mean that Romanian literature is better than Chinese literature. How do we explain it? This writer is better than that writer. But in the context of comparing writers from different cultures, isn't that an old-fashioned failure to understand context and cultural difference?

We need to underscore the fact that within any national culture there is no hesitation or embarrassment in declaring this writer better than that writer. And there are national structures of cultural power that are perfect analogues to structures of international cultural power. A young poet in provincial Guangxi is on a different footing than the favorite young poet of Beijing University. The rules seem to change only on the level of comparing national cultures, of however recently the nation-state has been constituted. On this level, comparative evaluative judgments become problematic. And the Nobel Prize Committee braves those problems every time it makes a decision. They are trying to play the old game of literary judgment in a new world.

* * *

The price of common global structures of value is that much of the world must play the game by rules (including those of literature) that are not of their making and in whose making they have no say. This is a serious price, but in many areas it is a price well worth paying for the advantages gained. In most global venues of judgment, spokespersons for the "rest of the world" at least participate: in Olympic committees, world courts, the United Nations, and so on. In literature, however, and particularly in poetry, the issue of national language returns as the remnant of indigestible difference.

It is not fair that a Russian air traffic controller has to speak English and an Indonesian pilot must understand it. We do, however, understand that air traffic controllers and pilots must have a mutually comprehensible language, and we are exceedingly grateful if they can understand one another. To find a common ground to reflect on world poetry is something else again. If we decide – as pragmatically we must – to work through translation, we have opened a Pandora's box of problems that call the very enterprise into question. Suppose we take the leap and accept that we must work through translation. Who then is competent to comment and judge? Should this be restricted only to native speakers of the language of translation? If we have a translation from Japanese, why should an Arab speaker of English be less qualified than a native speaker of English? And what is being read in these translated poems – the English or the poetic ideas and images?

When it comes to the prizes that have come to symbolize global values in literature, the question comes back to who is doing the choosing. The choice of

Gao Xingjian for the Nobel Prize in literature sparked a strong response in China and on Chinese Web sites. Politics played some role. Gao Xingjian is intensely opposed to the Communist government and is much admired by a segment of the exile community and in Taiwan. Certainly the Chinese government's disapproval of the choice was political. The generally negative response by intellectuals in China, however, went much deeper.[2] Gao Xingjian prides himself on being an international writer, which for all intents and purposes means a European writer who uses the Chinese language. His plays were known in Beijing for a time, but his subsequent work was almost unknown. Political reasons were an important factor in this ignorance of his work; but the poetry of Bei Dao, who was also considered for the Nobel Prize, was also politically sensitive yet well known in China. There were also quite a few other writers widely known and admired in China who were passed over for consideration time and again. The conclusion, obvious yet invisible earlier, was foregrounded with perfect clarity in the choice of Gao Xingjian for the Nobel Prize: this was a European choice and not a Chinese one – or, in a term often repeated, a "Swedish prize." There seems a new awareness in China that there can be no world literature or world poetry except as constituted locally, from some center that mediates and judges according to its own values – in Europe or the United States.

We have problems here that admit no solution – except by throwing away the questions and the historical institutionalization of literature that generates them. Once we let go of a certain kind of story of poetry that we are used to telling, we find some interesting things.

* * *

What has changed since 1990 is, of course, the remarkable expansion of the Web – with its textual fluidity, its monstrous capacity to archive (a technological "Funes the Memorious"), its proliferation of centers located in e-space rather than quotidian geography, its democratic lack of judgment, and its interest groups. Poetry has taken on a new and strange life here. All one needs to do is to go on-line and do a search for "Turkish poetry" or "Hindi poetry," and so on. The implementation of Unicode as a standard has solved the considerable problems of non-Roman scripts on the Web. Exile and émigré communities have often played a significant role in literature; they are active here too but with a new twist: works from the exile/émigré community mix with works from the home country instantly and usually invisibly. Often one cannot tell where a Web site actually originates (Yahoo! China does have an interesting function that allows one to select only those Web sites from China itself, a function that bespeaks the inability to distinguish them otherwise).

On the Web we see clearly the resurgence of national language communities detached from nation-states. Although more authoritarian states seek to control the political dimensions of this, as in the recent Chinese crackdown on unlicensed Internet cafes, it seems to be an endeavor that is hopeless in the long run. Politics and pornography are the obvious favorite targets, but poetry is one too. Clear hierarchies of authority in literary judgment have been replaced by interest groups of invisible membership and scattered through terminals everywhere. In place of the cultural establishments of nation-states, charged with defining literary history and canon (these have their Web sites as well), we have an immaterial medievalism of shifting texts and authors, working in an e-space that is peculiarly local. In this space, diaspora dissolves, and Romanized Yiddish poetry continues in an e-shtetl.

Few of the critics and academicians with curatorial oversight over national literatures would be so heartless as to deny grandmothers the right to compose poems in their favorite language and post them for their far-flung friends. Those same critics and academicians, however, might be troubled by the thought that this could be poetry's future (even though it bears some similarities to medieval poetry before the latter was integrated into national canons). When I look at a nicely constructed Turkish Web site with the poetry of an individual or an anthology of recent poems, I have no idea how those poets are considered (if at all) by the Turkish national literary establishment.

Sometimes here we see the hope of international readership. Introductions in English are provided, and sometimes there are translations. This is, to some degree, a function of English keywords in the search. If one types in keywords in the national language, what one thought before was a flood turns out to be only a modest pond. Insofar as lyric poetry, with its ties to particular languages, resists globalization, it is, in its relative brevity, the ideal form for the Internet and is thriving there.

At this point it might occur to us that in looking for world poetry, we have been looking for the wrong thing. We want poetry to be important in a way that helps define and represent a national culture, a poetry that can contribute to a story of canonical writers, the very best of which may emerge on some global horizon with the best of other national literatures. These can provide resources for courses in contemporary poetry in the academy. We want a literary Olympics, the apotheosis of the food court. We may want to change a judgment here or there, but we do not want ten thousand names and hundreds of thousands of poems in every language with a community that is plugged into the Net. The very idea of world literature depends on the continued power of national literary establishments sorting and recommending, giving us representatives. The moment we abrogate that structure (the structure of the Olympics and other transnational institutions), the moment we recognize the talented exile poet who comes to see us personally, is the very moment we have to start reading the Web and local publications.

Those who deal with contemporary poetry know that it is, unfortunately, as much a social venture as an aesthetic one. If we admire the venturesome contemporary Chinese poet who appears in Germany and do not know of the no less poetically bold contemporary poets in Beijing, we become brokers in an exceedingly troubling game of reputation that is centered in the West.

If, in the United States, we are particularly interested in world literature or world poetry, that is very much a function of one aspect of our own national culture, both local and imperial. The national literary establishments that can provide us material for world poetry are very much alive and well in most of the world. They have their centers and their provinces, their hierarchies and ventures on canonicity; they have complex structures of national prizes, recognition, and status that still serve to articulate prominence. We may see the talents to which they are blind – but those talents appear through our local history of values.

The system of national recognition is the way poetry works as we have known it, and it has served us well in finding memorable poets in a morass of versifying. It is not a bad system, so long as we understand its historicity and historical contingency. I will honor my role as broker for one particular national literature in this system by suggesting that China has recently been producing poets truly worthy of international note, such as Bei Dao and, more recently, Yu Jian, a poet whose rejection of world poetry and the national literary establishment has, ironically, contributed to his prominence.

* * *

Negation, of course, includes what it negates: to reject world poetry, even with the greatest sincerity, is to remain within its vast purview. Is there another level, however, where poetry flourishes beneath conceivable international notice? By noticing the unmentionable, I run the risk of another round of wrath from colleagues. Yet the "world of poetry," in the sense of the poetry actually being written and enjoyed worldwide, deserves some small note as well as "world poetry."

Although I will discuss primarily the Chinese case, the phenomenon I will describe appears throughout the old civilizations of Asia, though in different ways in different countries. A little background in cultural history is necessary here. In the late nineteenth and twentieth centuries, European culture, including European poetry, collided with the great civilizations of Asia, each of which had an indigenous poetry with a long history and established traditions. The process of influence and change was remarkably similar in a wide variety of quite different literary cultures. First, there was an attempt to extend the old, indigenous poetics to account for modern realities. This was followed by a "new poetry," often in free verse, that rejected the metrics, imagery, poetic language, and social ethos of the older poetry. The new poetry was often created by Western-educated intellectuals or by intellectuals in major urban centers where Western influence was strongest. In some countries the indigenous elite poetry disappeared altogether – as in Korea, whose elite poetry was composed in Chinese, and in Turkey. In both these countries the language reform was radical. By now the new poetry has taken root everywhere; it has matured and developed its own histories, from China and Japan to the Arab world. When we think of world poetry, we are always thinking of the new poetry in these countries.

We may then ask: What happened to the older poetry, which often inspired immense affection and whose practice carried great cultural prestige? The answer to this question differs by country, as does the relation between the new poetry and the continuing practice and popularity of classical verse. The Urdu *ghazal*, for example, apparently continues to flourish as a serious form, with satisfying compromises between tradition and modernity. In Japan modern haiku and modern *waka* flourish as an autonomous sphere of traditional poetry, with huge contests and recognized modern masters. Although the new poets often hold such verse in a certain contempt, it has remained a recognized part of Japanese poetry in the twentieth century and continues into this new century. It has even entered English anthologies of modern Japanese literature. It exhibits the tensions that the oxymoron "modern classical poetry" shows everywhere: a debate between traditional poetics on the one hand and new themes and language on the other, and a certain joy in the interplay between the two.

Nowhere is the tension between the new poetry and modern classical poetry greater than in China. The "new poets" and their spokespersons at once have contempt for contemporary classical poetry and feel the threat that a widespread affection for the older classical poetry presents. The new poetry is institutionalized in government supported writers' associations, in the university, and in textbooks (not to mention translation into other languages and representation in the foreign academy); but Mao Zedong wrote classical song lyrics that are widely known by heart. *Shikan* (*Poetry*), the official poetry journal of the National Writers' Association, has a column for classical poems, but it is essentially a journal of the new poetry. The new poetry has its passionate admirers and its brilliant poets. At the same time, those who love the new poetry are well aware that many people do not like it and will privately admit that many people are still writing classical poetry, perhaps more than the new poetry. Thus, despite its nearly complete institutional dominance, the new poetry often feels embattled in a struggle for domestic acceptance even more than for international recognition.

To those who have read modern Chinese poetry outside China, the continued flourishing and popularity of classical poetry is a well-kept secret. It lives primarily in provincial capitals, which in turn represent most of China. This is not the poetry of the young intellectuals of Beijing and Shanghai. A few home pages of the more technologically advanced practitioners of modern classical poetry and yearbooks (*nian-jian*) will reveal the names of a large number of journals devoted to contemporary classical poetry, some with long and regular runs going back to the end of the Cultural Revolution; even a very large Chinese library like Harvard's has only a handful of these, most of which are unread and safely off to the depository as soon as they arrive.

The new poets might criticize modern classical poetry for being out of touch with modern realities. But Chinese classical poetry has long been engaged with the particulars of everyday life – one might even say all too engaged. In opening at random *Dangdai shici* (*Contemporary Classical Poetry and Song Lyric*) 4 (1984), one of the longest running of these journals, I encounter a song lyric modeled on a twelfth-century predecessor with the following subtitle: "On October 5, 1980, I received a long-distance call from my son asking for a tape recorder under the pretext of studying foreign languages; I wrote this to admonish him." A few pages earlier I note another lyric, modeled on a different twelfth-century lyricist, indignantly subtitled:

"On hearing that the Japanese Ministry of Education has revised its school text-books" (on the issue of removing references to the Japanese war in China). There are long and learned poems responding to various television series. Then there is an unforgettable long poem on a neighbor building a new home replete with Sanyo appliances; at the house-warming party, the neighbor is carried away by the police (for crimes that led to his wealth), the guests disperse like "startled swans," and the poem concludes with an allusion to the pop singer Teresa Teng:

> The tape recorder knows not the pain of him who leaves;
>   it still is singing: "When will be the day that you come back again?"[3]

Framing the line from the Teresa Teng song, every modestly educated Chinese reader will here recognize an allusion to a famous poem of the ninth century. We should ask: What is going on here?

While contemporary classical poetry remains in large measure occasional, the more recent pages of journals such as *Jiangxi shici* (*Jiangxi Classical Poetry and Song Lyric*) tend to avoid these more outrageous occasions of the early 1980s. The journal does, however, provide an outlet for moments of spontaneous patriotism, as well as for commemorating sites visited on one's vacation. There is something embarrassing about this poetry to the higher levels of the Chinese elite.

In this phenomenon of continuing and even resurgent Chinese classical poetry, we can again find collisions of values that cannot be reconciled. We can see at once the reasons why supporters of the new poetry generally hold modern classical poetry in contempt. Although there is much poetry that is quite wonderful by the standards of classical poetry, it often carries the unmistakable whiff of poetry one wrote on one's vacation. This poetry suggests elderly gentlemen practicing a craft that will soon expire along with their persons (and elderly gentlemen are indeed well represented). Contrary to expectations, the craft is not expiring, and the writers are often young and female.

We also see that many people are having a good time with this poetry and using it to deal with life's little ups and downs – in an old craft that rubs in moving or humorous ways against modern realities. It is a poetry that apparently has a significant readership. These journals are not vanity publications. The first issue of *Contemporary Classical Poetry and Song Lyric* (despite its general title, a local Guangzhou journal) had a print run of 36000 copies and sold out in less than two months; the second issue was down to 33600 – enough to make any publisher of a journal of contemporary poetry envious.[4] Most journals of new poetry come nowhere near such numbers, even the major state-sponsored ones.

For someone like myself who loves both the older classical poetry and that world poetry of which the Chinese new poetry is a part, the conflict of irreconcilable values is particularly sharp. Modern Chinese classical poetry basically is of the same kind as the old canonical poetry of the Tang and Song in China. Looking back from the vantage point of modern classical poetry, we can see Tang poets giving pious advice to their sons, expressing their reaction to current political events, and writing poems on the sites visited on their vacations. Since those vacations were taken twelve hundred years ago, they have acquired a certain patina, not to mention a considerable body of commentary. What charms us about that poetry in the past – its imaginative engagement with the particulars of life in a shared poetic ethos – is what troubles us about the same poetry continuing in the present. These poems are not going to make it into my syllabus of world poetry; for one thing, they would require too many footnotes. These poems will never be presented to the Nobel Prize Committee, who would not know quite what to make of them. Many poets who write classical poetry live abroad, but I can't imagine any one of them presenting himself as an exile poet. Like most of their predecessors in the Tang and Song, people who write classical poetry do other things for a living – even if writing poetry is what they most care about. The "poet" as a profession seems restricted to those who write new poetry. Writers of modern Chinese classical poetry can get no grants; universities will not support them so that they can continue writing poetry. In the world of poetry, they are invisible, except to a community of classical poetry lovers in China. It is a poetry with much hack writing but also a poetry with much that is valuable – "valuable" only in a separate sphere of a classical something we must still call poetry.

Contemporary poetry is sometimes supposed to be difficult. If modern classical Chinese poetry is too difficult for a non-Chinese reader to appreciate, it is a worthwhile reminder that the difficulty of contemporary poetry, like its liberty, is in fact strictly governed by many unspoken rules. These rules, like many other international rules, were created in the West. They have now become naturalized in many countries; they have been extended and are no longer a foreign import. There can indeed be a "world poetry," so long as we understand that this is not the whole world of poetry. Other kinds of poetry stubbornly continue outside the scope of world poetry. This is poetry for internal consumption.

* * *

Journals of modern classical poetry usually contain a section of prose essays, both on the problems of contemporary classical poetry and on particular writers. In a fairly recent issue of *Jiangxi Classical Poetry and Song Lyric* we find the reprint of a preface by Shu Wu, an important figure in the Chinese literary establishment and not someone one would expect to be prefacing a 1998 anthology of contemporary classical poetry.[5] Judging from the preface, Shu Wu was himself a bit surprised to find himself in this role. After reciting the impressive classical literary lineage of his family (reminding us of the prestige that this confers, even on an establishment writer in the vernacular), Shu Wu expressed his surprise that these poets were writing "well," referring to the mastery of craft that readers look for in classical poetry. He seemed no less surprised to find that the anthology included young people, as well as aging gentlemen educated in another era. Shu Wu is a professional writer and intellectual; he discovered that the authors of these classical poems included "an air-force pilot, an electrician, and a woman worker at the Capital Airport." Although Americans may willingly give the benefit of the doubt to poetry by insurance executives, poetry by an electrician is more charming as a possibility than an actuality. In the Chinese context, the composition of poetry by people other than intellectuals has a weight and resonance, both in the premodern context and in the Communist modern context. What is at stake here is the kind of poetry being composed by electricians: classical poetry.

Shu Wu knows quite well that composing classical poetry has no official status. No twenty-four-year-old can be recognized as an "important young poet" if he writes classical poetry. The literary establishment reserves fame for those who write the new poetry. He concludes – with an admiration that also has historical resonance – that these people can be writing only for the love of the art, because it gives them pleasure.

The preface is a nice moment in which a member of the Chinese literary establishment, which basically supports the new poetry as a form, confronts the continued existence of classical poetry, indeed its continued flourishing. The flavor of his discomfort has its delights. He attacks the classical poetry that occurs commonly in magazines on occasional topics – perhaps he saw the father's poem of rebuke to his son who had called long-distance to ask for a tape recorder. If Shu Wu is going to be compelled to acknowledge that modern classical poetry exists, he is going to demand "pure poetry" and "serious poetry." He offers a long list of the "best writers" of modern classical poetry and concludes – with a shocking radicalism in this context – that perhaps the best classical poetry should be included as a part of the history of modern poetry.

Modern classical poetry has, of course, never been part of the "history of modern Chinese poetry." Its death was legislated long ago. What is of particular interest is that Shu Wu can name an impressively long list of the "best writers" of modern classical poetry, from the early Republic on through the present. We realize that he has obviously read them all before and is quite familiar with their work. Through this acknowledgment, Shu Wu comes out of the closet, suggesting that all of these poets he probably admires may be worthy of consideration as "serious," as part of Chinese poetry.

* * *

This discussion is not meant to be a brief on behalf of modern Chinese classical poetry – or for modern *waka*, haiku, and *ghazals*. The areas of our interest are, rather, the nature of national literary establishments and how poetry, in various ways, has found a life outside of national literary establishments. Insofar as they are national in the modern sense, these literary establishments exist in an international context. Through them (or explicitly against them, as in the exile poets or the "poetry of the common man," *minjian shi*, represented by Yu Jian) there is indeed a rich literature that is world literature. It can win prizes and be recognized by the academy. These poems can appear in a university course syllabus or in an anthology of world poetry in many countries. This is a poetry with its canons, hierarchies, and a narrative of change that we call literary history.

There are, however, other poetries, invisibly flourishing. These poetries sometimes have a far more enthusiastic readership than the poetry in the academy. They are on the Web. In the Chinese case this means primarily the new poetry, though classical poetry is there as well with increasing frequency. Young poets put up their work and get responses. They have readers and fans. Texts get reproduced with uncertain accuracy.

There is also a world of older poetry, happily continuing outside the notice of those who take a global overview of contemporary poetry. Writers of new poetry on the Web generally do not read the new classical poetry, and writers of the new classical poetry tend not to be interested in the new poetry. There is no unity, except in the domain of the literary establishment and the academy. Poetry is going off on its own in many directions. Both the new poetry on the Web and the older poetry (sometimes on the Web, but primarily in special journals) belong exclusively to national language communities. We will see, someday, how this all plays out and where poetry, in our new century, is. Perhaps it is in all these places.

Notes

1 Stephen Owen, "World Poetry," a review of Bei Dao's *The August Sleepwalker*, trans. Bonnie McDougall, *New Republic* (November 19, 1990), pp. 28–32. The best-known early Chinese reply was Michelle Yeh, "Chayi de youlü – yige huixiang," *Jintian* (*Today*) (1991.1), pp. 94–96. See also Rey Chow, *Writing Diaspora: Tactics of Intervention in Contemporary Cultural Studies* (Bloomington: Indiana University Press, 1993), pp. 1–4; Gregory B. Lee, *Troubadours, Trumpeters, Troubled Makers: Lyricism, Nationalism, and Hybridity in China and Its Others* (London: Hurst, 1996), pp. 93–101; Huang Yunte, *Transpacific Displacement: Ethnography, Translation, and Intertextual Travel in Twentieth-Century American Literature* (Berkeley: University of California Press, 2002), pp. 161–182.
2 Since the government strongly discourages comment on Gao Xingjian, there is little in the public media; most of the response appeared soon after the decision in Web forums. It is also a topic of private conversation.
3 *Dangdai shici* 4 (1984): 7.
4 *Jiangnan shici* was running at about 20 000 an issue. *Jiangnan shici* (1989.2), p. 1.
5 *Jiangxi shici* 49 (1998.2): 173–187.

18

To World, to Globalize
World Literature's Crossroads (2004)

Djelal Kadir

A leading figure in comparative and world literary studies, Djelal Kadir is the Edwin Erle Sparks Professor of Comparative Literature at the Pennsylvania State University. Born in Cyprus, Kadir was educated in England and then at Yale University and the University of New Mexico, then taught at Purdue University and the University of Oklahoma, where he was editor of the journal *World Literature Today* in the 1990s. Kadir has written extensively on hemispheric American studies in post-colonial perspective, in books including *Columbus and the Ends of the Earth: Europe's Prophetic Rhetoric as Conquering Ideology* (1992) and *The Other Writing: Postcolonial Essays in Latin America's Writing Culture* (1993), and he has extended these interests as founder of the International American Studies Association. His subsequent work has focused on intersections of language, identity, and power in world literature and culture, notably in his 2011 book *Memos from the Besieged City: Lifelines for Cultural Sustainability*. Among other collaborations in the fields of Latin American and world literature, he is the co-editor of *Other Modernisms in an Age of Globalization* (2002), *Literary Cultures of Latin America: A Comparative History* (3 vols., 2004), and the *Longman Anthology of World Literature* (6 vols., 2004; 2009).

Kadir's wide-ranging essay "To World, to Globalize: World Literature's Crossroads" calls into question the role and responsibility of practitioners of world literature, pointing out the representational nature of "world" in the phrase "world litera-ture." To look at literature globally and in worldly perspective implies giving it "a particular historical density," by rebinding it in a self-legitimizing narrative, which Kadir traces back far before Goethe, to Herodotus. Drawing on examples from *The Epic of Gilgamesh* to Wallace Stevens, Kadir argues for attention to the theoretical

Djelal Kadir, "To World, to Globalize: World Literature's Crossroads" (2004). In *Comparative Literature Studies* 41:1 (2004), pp. 1–9.

World Literature in Theory, First Edition. Edited by David Damrosch.

awareness already inscribed within literature, and for the need for greater critical self-awareness on the part of the theorist in turn.

The onus is on us, the practitioners of comparative literature, to examine the degree to which recurrent patterns of historical coincidence, between what we do and what is happening in the world, might entail a necessary complicity on our part. While we cannot deny that we are in the world, we can and do differ on how we are of it. A continuous self-examination and critical alertness to our place in the world is our only glimpse into our relationship to the world. Such reflection is also what defines what we do and the nature of the consequences of our doing it.

Comparative literature is neither a subject, nor an object, nor is it a problem. Comparative literature is a practice. It is what its practitioners do. These practitioners are subjects, they objectify their material, and their practices may well be problematic. But first and foremost comparative literature is defined not by a corpus, a subject matter, an object, or an immutable set of problems. Rather, comparative literature takes on its significance by what is done in its name and by how those practices become ascertained, instituted, and managed.

The verb "to manage" spans a wide register. It reaches from husbanding and cultivation to command and control to maintaining a level of precarious sustainability, especially when uttered in the future tense and in the first person plural, i.e., "we'll manage." There are fields defined by practice and fields defined by the corpus or object on/in which that field's practitioners operate. An example of the first would be the dancer and of the second the physician; dance is defined by the acts of performance, medicine by the body or physic on which the physician works. One could say that literature is a corpus on and in which the comparatist performs, but literature's corpus is itself an outcome constituted by acts of management and negotiated processes of cultivation. As such, literature is a product of practices with identifiable practitioners and definable consequences. Management in fields defined by practice gravitates toward the more precarious end of the manageability spectrum. Perhaps this is the inevitable result of the toll exacted by the need to constantly scrutinize and justify the practices themselves, as well as actually practicing them. Such dual action is more imperative at historical junctures when the practitioner of comparative literature senses the convergence of certain historical processes with his or her own practices.

We are now, at the beginning of the twenty-first century, at such a juncture. Hence the need for us to examine what our role might be between what is happening in the world and our intensified focus on world literature. The re-emergent conjunction between the globalization of the world from decidedly local and uncontestable sites of power and self-interest in ways that fit the pattern of imperial hegemony, on the one hand, and the upsurge of a discourse of/on world literature and globalization among practitioners of comparative literature, on the other hand, is a coincidence that bears examination.

In pursuing this examination, it might be apposite to the discussion of world literature and globalization to take the word "world" as verb, and to read globalization not as boundless sweep but as bounding circumscription. *To world* and *to globalize*, then, would have to be parsed in light of their subject agencies and their object predicates. World and globalization, thus, would be imputable actions, rather than anonymous phenomena. The virtue of imputability resides in the prospect of being able to trace responsibility and consequence, not as mechanical cause and effect necessarily, but as motivation and outcome in an object relation of subject agency as it affects a phenomenon and makes it a/the world.

Literature, as already noted, is itself the outcome of cultural practice, and to world literature is to give it a particular historical density. Globalization is a process that binds a sphere by the circumference it describes. In the case of literature, the compelling question becomes, who carries out its worlding and why? And in the instance of globalization the inevitable issue is the locus where the fixed foot of the compass that describes the globalizing circumscription is placed. Where the foot of the compass rests is inexorably the center. And, since all actions are motivated, the worlding of literature is not random, though the outcomes of the action, as with the potential of all actions, could well be unintended and accidental. A discussion of world literature and globalization, then, may well yield greater explicatory possibilities if viewed through these practical considerations.

Conventionally, we are wont to date the notion of "world literature" to Goethe. We are also given to see the world of Goethe's "world literature" as circumscribed by the geographical fulcrum of Europe. In reality, neither the historical ascription nor the geographical parameters are altogether accurate. The world, and certainly the notional world of narrative, were already subject to a certain critical revisioning and territorial displacement as early as the fifth century BC, when Herodotus' perception of a shifting *oikoumene*, or world as home, led him to compose the inquiring narratives that would form the founding acts of Western historiography and of the narrative genre of history.

Herodotus referred to his narratives in the plural, *historie*. And that plurality could well serve as index to the multiplication of the Greek world in its relations to the words around it. Herodotus experienced that shift first hand as alert observer in a public sphere whose subtle accommodation of Greek and Anatolian syncretisms suddenly became culturally and ethnically refracted as his native city of Halicarnassus passed into imperial Persian governance. The world of the Greeks, the *oikoumene*, would undergo a transcultural metamorphosis in ontological, political, and epistemic ways. The *oikoumene* would no longer be the "home as the world." It would thenceforth mean the challenging process and vicissitudes of "feeling at home in the world." For Herodotus himself, we know, the shift would prove an insurmountable shiftlessness that precluded his ever feeling at home anywhere again, a peripeteia that would lead eventually to his exilic death in Thurii in southern Italy's "Magna Graecia," the westernmost periphery of what had been the Greek "home as the world."

As in Herodotus' world and, a millennium later, as with Montesquieu's ironically translocal and self-consciously transcultural *Lettres Persanes* of 1721, Goethe's 1827 pronouncement of the now seminal *Weltliteratur* in the journal *Über Kunst und*

Altertum also has its Persian catalyst embedded within Goethe's own work. This is the medieval Persian poet Hafiz, whose reading by Goethe some ten years earlier inspired the German poet to begin learning Persian at age sixty-five and led to his *Westöstlicher Divan* of 1819.

Bridging Goethe to Herodotus forms a link to a third dimension, a dimension that historically corresponds to our contemporary world and the nagging questions of critical correlation between worldliness and globality. Just as with Goethe in our comparative literature seminars, Herodotus has had a resurgence in our "new world order" and its historiographic and cultural studies curriculum, despite what some see as our historical moment's blithe presentism. Throughout history, Herodotus has been read and remarked most intensely at historical moments of intensified imperial hegemony, as in the Hellenistic era of Alexander the Great and his eastward conquests, and during the so-called Age of Discoveries that accompanied the westward transatlantic movement of Europe and its Renaissance. There is a continuity between such imperial ventures and what elicits the inquiries of Herodotus in the fifth century BC, namely, the sharpened conflict between Greek colonial expansion and the westward reach of Persian imperialism. At mid-point between the time of Herodotus' *historie* in the middle of the fifth century and the appearance of the Mede, as Xenophon referred to the Persians, on the Greek horizon in 546 BC, lies the Battle of Marathon in the year 490. As a result of that victory against overwhelming odds, Greek culture felt justified to differentiate itself from the non-Greek in self-privileging ways that forged what has proved to be a template for a primal scene of identity politics and cultural essentialism. Hence, the opening question of Herodotus' narrative, which the nine books that ensue seek to answer in a relational way: Why do Greeks and non-Greeks go to war?

The larger question, of which Herodotus himself becomes symptomatic, is what happens to the locus of the *oikoumene* when it ceases to be tantamount to *the* world and becomes yet another locus *in* the world? In the concept of world literature, Goethe, not unlike us, would countenance the same question, and, not unlike Goethe, we are still straining to interrogate and chart the multivalent space that encompasses and that is encompassed by what we call the world, a space where the local and the global continue to contend. For it should be noted that Goethe's coinage of *Weltliteratur* in 1827 was in direct response to his own "globalization" of sorts, when he was responding to a review of one of his works in the Paris *Globe*. The 1790 work in question itself has a globalizing subject, as its title, *Torquato Tasso*, avers, Tasso having been the globalizer whose millenarian *Gerusalemme Liberata* and its apocalyptic vision prefigure many future struggles in the region over the ownership of history and the future alike.

I do not mean, with this excursus, to assimilate the situated worldliness of our world literature to the worldliness in the world literature of Goethe necessarily. Nor, for that matter, am I intending a structural or culturalist homologation of the modern worlds and the proto-historiographic world of Herodotus. What I do wish to foreground is the consistency with which the invocation of something referred to as "world" repeatedly correlates ideologically with cultural and political thresholds at traumatic cusps of history. In the case of Herodotus, that convergence comes literally at the threshold of what Westerners would come to know as history. In Goethe's post-Napoleonic case, such invocation coincides with the potential coalescence of disparate cultures and discursive sites into a cosmopolitan agora whose promising ecumenism was shattered by what we will subsequently come to know as national literatures. Those formations throughout Europe shortly after Goethe's coinage proved to be a nationalist coalescence into discrepant chauvinisms. These are the units of culture that would, in fact, precondition and define what we have come to know as comparative literature, inasmuch as comparative literature as a field has traditionally been predicated on the basic units of national literatures and the contrapuntal legacy of national discourses.

And in our case, here, today, our narratives of worlding and expanding discourse on world literature take on their sense of urgency as we are poised between a putatively flattened world of economic globalization and an array of counter-movements of heightened inequality, cultural and religious conflict, and expansionist realpolitik emanating from multiple locales around the globe. What, then, do world and world literature mean in an unprecedented era so redolent with historical precedents?

If history itself be a guide, the response to this question would oblige us to countenance the possibility that we may well inhabit a momentary interregnum between epochs of even greater historical trauma. We would be obliged to consider the possibility that our globalizing world, especially after the 1989 demise of the materiality of the would-be "one world" and "world literature" prognosticated in the 1848 *Manifesto* of Marx and Engels, may be virtual in more than one sense. That our world's spatiality, that is, may well be the locus not of a global hamlet, but the façade of a virtualized Potemkin village managed by the Office of Strategic Information: a global *oikoumene* of sanitized imagistic dematerialization forged by satellite signals and sustained by fiber optic nerves and laser-guided weapons. And, if history be a guide, we would have to face the possibility that today's increasingly shrill assault on anything truly and ethically cosmopolitan could well be something other than an exclusive reaction-formation on the part of the local against the hegemonic ambition of the global. More than likely, we may be facing a nascent reassertion of the factious and the return of the repressed as discrepant ethnonationalism in the name of cultural identity in tandem with the resurgence of imperial hegemony in the ostensible spirit of liberation of the oppressed and spiritually unregenerate, whether located in Iraq, or in Palestine, or in Chechnya, or in Tibet, or in the Democratic Republic of the Congo.

These events may well lead us to conclude that world literature may be nothing more than a product of our engagement in notional or narrative acts of worlding. If we should still be possessed of any quotient of ethical awareness and a certain grammatical intuition, we may well experience a nagging realization to what extent the term "world" is no longer merely a nominal noun or an expansive adjective. That "world" is, in fact, a highly repercussive and consequential verb. We were alerted to this repercussive possibility of worlding at yet another significant moment in the traumatic history of traumas. That occurred in Martin Heidegger's 1935 essay "The Origin of the Work of Art," where Heidegger explored the notion of worlding at the threshold of a would-be "one world" and "a new world order" with the messianic ideology of what would apocalyptically and post-historically call itself The Third Reich. Its un-seasonal, millenarian hubris notwithstanding, that untimely worlding left its baleful ravages. It has left, as well, its enduring legacy, often in the least expected places.

If "world" in world literature, then, is a verb, we who do the worlding arrogate to ourselves not only the verb's subject agency but the world itself. And our actions' object predicate consists not only of the world but also of its literatures and cultures. There is, unmistakably, something inevitably proprietary in the transitive impulse of such productive action, whose reach constructs, defines, and inexorably appropriates its objects. World literature, in this sense, is invariably a product of our optic and grasp. And, though our contemporary insight belatedly proscribes a self-justifying Archimedean point, no critique of the panopticon seems to be able to dissuade us from the conviction that we command an empyrean view and behold a global totality within which "world" as adjective in the phrase "world literature" is now privileged, yet again, as it has been in regular intervals in human history, particularly at moments of imperial stirring. And though we may have come to realize that the act of worlding is not uniquely ours, the recrudescent chatter on the topic of world literature in our critical present, in tandem with imperial moves that circumscribe the world into manageable global boundedness, may not be insignificant and certainly begs for examination.

We had already come to the realization some time ago that the universality of whatever may have been deemed universal by the various cultural accommodations of world literature, particularly by mid-twentieth-century American and East European comparatists, does not reside in the world or in the literature. Rather, we realized that any such universality is merely a function of the universalizing impulse in the cultural optic and subject agency of those doing the worlding. All this realization notwithstanding, Goethe's notion continues to exert its magnetism, even as we invoke it not necessarily for celebration but for its historical reassessment. I suspect, then, that an intensified discourse on world literature re-emerges at this time, as I have intimated already in recalling Herodotus and history's inception, for reasons of historical trauma which find us at a moment analogous to Goethe's era following the fractiousness of Napoleonic Europe and, as history would prove, just prior to the rise of an even deeper moment of contention through ethnonationalisms and imperial adventurism that would ensue in the second half of the nineteenth century as Europe set off on a new imperial era.

The fact that we have recently emerged from a half-century's worldwide Manichaean contest and into a spider's world wide web of global disproportions with political/economic asymmetries may not be altogether irrelevant to our renewed interest in Goethe. As to what might ensue from this historical (re-)turn, there is no lack of ominous portent in the infelicities spawned by mythoi of ethnocentric symbolizations and inflicted through fratricidal acts of nationalist righteousness, in spite of the vaunted threat to national sovereignty that some diagnose in globalization. National formations may indeed be mutating, but in their new transformation into franchises of predatory capital with local/parochial rootedness and global reach, world and world literature will be no less the interested outcome of those in a position to assume the subject agency of the verb "to world."

As a verbal term that denotes simultaneously world and globalization, the French "mondialization" may be most suggestive in this regard. The term's conflating of world and globe redoubles the emphasis on the way asymmetries inflect not just the virtual and the metaphoric. Such a conflation aggravates and deepens, as well, the actual repercussions of acts on their objects. In this sense, the global in globalization is defined by the grasp of the globalizing processes' subject agencies, the vested interests of ubiquitous capital, and the virulent local reaction formations that these processes provoke. Likewise, there has been a very limited world in world literature, and no more literature in the world than what has been allowed by the historically constructed optic and parameters of specific and shifting cultural criteria that precondition our world-generating impulses and the market viability of their cultural products. A claim for anything more than this in either the world or in the literature is a fetish of our worlding desire, or an alibi for a realpolitik that we embody, symptomatically or opportunistically. The question for us as comparatists who are party to the resonant discourse on world literature, then, is what our own role might be in this worlding, a question fundamental to the theorizing of world literature today.

19

For a World-Literature in French (2007)

Michel Le Bris *et al.*

On March 16, 2007, the liberal and internationalist Parisian newspaper *Le Monde* published a manifesto, "Pour une littérature-monde en français," whose 44 co-signers proclaimed the rebirth of French literature as a global and no longer national literature. Organized by the French writer and editor Michel Le Bris (co-founder of "Étonnants Voyageurs," an annual world literary festival) and by novelist Jean Rouaud (winner of the prestigious Prix Goncourt), the manifesto hailed the decentering of French literature in terms of "a Copernican revolution" and proclaimed the death of the colonial narrative of *la francophonie*, centered on Paris as the arbiter of cultural value. "The center," the manifesto declares, "is from now on everywhere, in all four corners of the earth. The end of la francophonie. And the birth of a World Literature in French."

A key tactic of the manifesto was to break down the division between "francophone" literatures (those of the former colonies) and "French" literature proper (that of "the Hexagon," the imperial center). Though few of the manifesto's 44 signatories were French by birth, a third had made their careers in France, including J.M.G. Le Clézio, winner of the Nobel Prize the following year. The manifesto sparked a major controversy, prompting a range of responses that give a very different sense of the political as well as cultural stakes of a mode of world literature widely discussed beyond the Anglo-American sphere, as can be seen from the three essays that follow the manifesto, first by France's then-presidential candidate Nicolas Sarkozy, and then by two scholars of French and francophone literature.

In time, this might be looked on as a historic moment: in the same autumn, the Goncourt, the Grand Prix for the Novel of the French Academy, the Renaudot, the

Michel Le Bris *et al.*, "For a World-Literature in French" (2007). Trans. Delia Ungureanu from "Pour une 'littérature-monde' en français," in *Le Monde*, March 16, 2007.

Femina, and the Goncourt for high school students were awarded to writers born outside France. Just a coincidence among publishers' catalogs, unusually concentrating the talents emerging from the "periphery," or a mere meandering before the stream returns to its riverbed? We believe it's just the opposite: a Copernican revolution. Copernican, because it reveals what the literary field already knew, though without admitting it: the center, that point from which a purely French literature was supposed to emanate, is no longer the center. Until now, the center, though less and less often, had an absorptive capacity that compelled writers coming from the outside to strip off their foreignness before melting in the crucible of the center's language and national history. This fall's awards tell us that from now on the center is everywhere, in all four corners of the earth. The end of francophonie. And the birth of a World Literature in French.

The world is returning, and this is great news. Hasn't it been for too long notably absent from French literature? The world, the subject, meaning, history, the "referent": for decades, they have been bracketed off by our great thinkers, inventors of a literature with no other object but itself, which was, as they said back then, "performing its own critique in the very process of enunciation." The novel was too serious an enterprise to be entrusted to novelists alone, guilty of "using language naively," and so they were asked to recycle themselves in academic linguistic exercises. Since these texts would then connect only with other texts, in an endless game of combinations, there could come a time when the author would find himself – and with him, the very idea of creation itself – hollowed out, leaving the field free for the commentators and exegetes. Instead of staying in touch with the world to absorb its life, its vital energies, the novel had nothing better to do than to watch itself writing itself.

The fact that writers could survive at all in such an intellectual climate should make us optimistic about the novel's capacities to resist any attempt to deny it or enslave it …

We can date historically this new desire to find once more the pathways of the world, this going back to literature's incandescent powers, this felt urgency for a "world literature": they are simultaneous with the violent fall of grand ideologies, more precisely … the return of the subject, meaning, History to the world's stage; that is to say, through the effervescence of the antitotalitarian movements, in the West and in the East as well, that would soon bring down the Berlin Wall.

A return, we must observe, through intersecting paths and circuitous routes, even as such a route had been so strongly resisted! It is as though, once their chains had been broken, everyone had to learn to walk anew; and also to have a taste for the dust of the roads, for the enticement of the outdoors, and for meeting a stranger's eyes. The stories of these amazing travelers, appearing in the mid-1970s, became the sumptuous gateways through which the world returned to fiction. Others, wanting to write about the world in which they lived, turned to noir fiction, as Raymond Chandler or Dashiell Hammett had done before them with the American city, following Jean-Patrick Manchette.[1] Others turned to the pastiche of the popular novel, the detective novel, the adventure novel, a sly or prudent strategy to recover narrative while playing wittily with the "the novel of the forbidden." And others, story-tellers, infiltrated the comics, following Hugo Pratt, Moebius, and a few others. And attention turned again to francophone literatures, especially of the Caribbean, as if far away from the sclerotic French models, a novelistic poetic effervescence whose secret seemed lost could be reborn there, heir to Saint-John Perse and Aimé Césaire. And this despite the blinders of a literary field that pretended to wait only for a few new hot spices, archaic or Creole words – so picturesque, indeed – good for reviving a gruel which had become too tasteless. 1976–1977: the indirect routes for a return to fiction.

But at the same time, a new wind was blowing from across the Channel, carrying news of a new literature in English, uniquely harmonized with a world about to be born. In an England mired in its third generation of Woolfian novels – which meant the air was becoming stagnant – some young troublemakers were turning to the world beyond to take a deep breath of fresh air. Bruce Chatwin left for Patagonia and his story took the shape of a manifesto for a new generation of travel writers ("I'm reading reality using the narrative techniques of the novel, to give back to reality its novelistic dimension").[2] And then, in an impressive hubbub, a series of noisy, multi-colored, hybrid novels began to appear, which conveyed, with a rare force and in new words, the noisiness of those exploding metropolises where cultures from every continent clashed, shuffled, mixed. At the heart of this effervescence were Kazuo Ishiguro, Ben Okri, Hanif Kureishi, Michael Ondaatje – and Salman Rushdie, who explored with acuity the emergence of what he called "translated men": people born in England, no longer living in nostalgia for a forever lost homeland, but who still experienced the state of living in between two worlds, with a foot in each camp, and who were somehow trying to turn this intermingling into the beginning of a new world. For the first time, a generation of emigrant writers, rather than melting away in the host culture, chose to write by starting from this plural identity, in the vague and unstable territory of these frictions. And by doing so, as Carlos Fuentes empha-sized, they were less the product of decolonization than the heralds of the twenty-first century.

How many French-language authors, caught in between two or more cultures, wondered at this strange disparity which relegated them on the margins as "franco-phones," a barely tolerated exotic hybrid, while the children of the former British Empire took fully legitimate possession of English letters? Should we stipulate a con-genital degeneration on the part of the heirs of the French Colonial Empire, as com-pared to those of the British Empire? Or should we rather admit that the problem had to do with the literary field itself, with its strange poetics spinning around itself like a whirling dervish, and with this vision of francophonie, in which France, mother of arts, arms, and laws, continued to spread its light, the universal benefactor intent upon bringing civilization to the people living in darkness? So the Antillean, Haitian, African writers who appeared then had no reason to be jealous of their English language colleagues. With the concept of "creolization" that brought them together, through which they stated their singularity, one would have had to be deaf and blind, looking into the other only to find one's own echo, not to see that this was nothing less than language gaining autonomy.

Let us be clear: the conscious emergence of a world literature in French, open to the world, transnational, signs francophonie's death warrant. No one speaks "francophone" or writes in francophone. Francophonie is the glimmer of a dead star. How can the world care about the language of a virtual country? And yet it's the world that invited herself to the autumn award banquets. From this we understand that the time has come for this revolution.

It could have begun earlier. How could we ignore for decades a Nicolas Bouvier, with his so perfectly entitled *Usage du monde*?[3] Because the world, back then, hadn't been given a residence permit. How couldn't we recognize in Réjean Ducharme one of the most important contemporary authors, whose 1970 *L'Hiver de force*, strengthened by an extraordinary poetic inspiration, overwhelmed everything that was afterwards to be written on the consumption society and all its libertarian stupidities? Because back then we looked down on "La belle Province," Quebec, we expected nothing from it apart from its savory accent, and its words that kept the perfumes of old France. And then we could cherry-pick the African or Antillean writers, equally kept in the margins; how can one be surprised when the concept of creolization itself is reduced to its opposite, mistaken for a United Colors of Benetton slogan? How can one be surprised if people are keen on postulating an exclusive bodily connection between the nation and the language that expresses its unique genius – since, at heart, the concept of francophonie presents itself as the last avatar of colonialism? What these autumn awards confirm is just the opposite: that the colonial pact is broken, that this liberated language has become everyone's concern, and that, if we stand firm, this could also be the end of the era of contempt and self-satisfaction. The end of "francophonie" and the birth of a world literature in French: these are the stakes, to whatever degree writers accept them.

World literature, because it is clear that the French literatures spread all over the world today are multiple and diverse, forming a huge network whose ramifications enlace several continents. But world literature also because all these literatures talk about the world that emerges right before our eyes, and by doing so, they find again, after decades of "the forbidden in fiction," what has always been the object of artists, novelists, creators: the task of giving voice and visibility to the unknown of the world – and to the unknown in ourselves. Finally, if we perceive everywhere this creative effervescence, it's because something in France itself started to move, as the young generation, liberated from the age of doubt, seizes without hesitation the ingredients of fiction to open up new novelistic roads. So it seems a renaissance has arrived, of a dialogue in a vast polyphonic ensemble, without worrying over who knows what struggle for or against the pre-eminence of this or that language or of any such "cultural imperialism." With the center placed amid the other centers, we witness the formation of a constellation in which language, liberated from its exclusive pact with the nation, free from any power except for those of poetry and the imagination, will no longer have any frontiers than those of the spirit.

Signed (in alphabetical order) by: Muriel Barbery, Tahar Ben Jelloun, Alain Borer, Roland Brival, Maryse Condé, Didier Daeninckx, Ananda Devi, Alain Dugrand, Edouard Glissant, Jacques Godbout, Nancy Huston, Koffi Kwahulé, Jean-Marie Laclavetine, Dany Laferrière, Gilles Lapouge, Michel Layaz, Michel Le Bris, J.M.G. Le Clézio, Yvon Le Men, Amin Maalouf, Alain Mabanckou, Anna Moï, Wajdi Mouawad, Nimrod, Wilfried N'Sondé, Esther Orner, Erik Orsenna, Benoît Peeters, Gisèle Pineau, Jean-Claude Pirotte, Grégoire Polet, Jean-Luc V. Raharimanana, Patrick Rambaud, Patrick Raynal, Jean Rouaud, Boualem Sansal, Dai Sitje, Brina Svit, Lyonel Trouillot, Anne Vallaeys, Jean Vautrin, André Velter, Gary Victor, Abdourahman A. Waberi.

Notes

1 A left-leaning crime novelist (1942–1995), credited with revitalizing crime fiction in France.
2 Referring to Chatwin's vivid, quasi-fictional travelogue *In Patagonia* (1977).
3 *The Way of the World*, a novel published in 1985 by Swiss traveler and writer Nicolas Bouvier.

20

For a Living and Popular Francophonie (2007)

Nicolas Sarkozy

A week after *Le Monde* published the manifesto "Pour une littérature-monde en français," Nicolas Sarkozy, then running for election as President of France, published a critique of the manifesto in *Le Monde*'s conservative counterpart, the newspaper *Le Figaro*. Sarkozy had himself entered French public life from a complicated cultural-political background. Son of an émigré Hungarian aristocrat and a French mother of half-Jewish heritage, Sarkozy grew up in comfortable circumstances (his father became wealthy as founder of a leading advertising agency) but often felt looked down upon for his mixed heritage. He embraced French culture with enthusiasm, and made his way in conservative political circles by dint of charisma, eloquence, and financial acumen, rising to become head of France's leading center-right party, the Union pour un Mouvement Populaire (UMP). His response to the manifesto probably represents the first occasion when theories of world literature have figured in a presidential campaign, which Sarkozy won two months later, serving as President of France from May 2007 until May 2012. In his plea "Pour une francophonie vivante et populaire" – a title echoing the name of his party – Sarkozy argues that global francophonie must be supported as a bulwark against monolingual Americanization. Agreeing with the manifesto's authors that "a language carries also a political message, a certain representation of the world," he proposes a very different political program, to reform education through the study of francophone cultures "to keep literary talents" at home.

La Francophonie isn't dead. During my travels abroad these past few months, I have been moved to see that everywhere around the world, the French language

Nicolas Sarkozy, "For a Living and Popular Francophonie" (2007). Trans. Delia Ungureanu from "Pour une francophonie vivante et populaire," in *Le Figaro*, March 22, 2007.

World Literature in Theory, First Edition. Edited by David Damrosch.

enjoys the same prestige as always. More than ever, this enthusiasm bestows a sense of obligation on us. Because the decline of French over against English is not an inevitability.

Now, as we celebrate the centenary of the birth of Léopold Sédar Senghor,[1] our country will be honored to pay the formulator of Négritude and founder of francophonie the homage which it should have paid at the time of his death. With no publicity at all, I was the leading French politician to visit his grave. I would like today to confirm this homage paid to this man who was one of those most devoted to spreading our country's influence. That's why I proposed to have his name inscribed in the crypt of the Panthéon, next to those of Charles Péguy and Toussaint L'Ouverture.[2]

We must return to a francophonie according to the spirit of Senghor. For this, we, the French, must involve ourselves all the more in this francophonie whose spokesmen are sometimes foreign authors, those who defend it so courageously yet so alone, in the absence of those who should have been its real advocates: the French themselves. Least of all our young people, who don't always understand this necessity.

I'd like us to enrich our school curricula with a significant francophone section and to create centers for francophonie in the cities, living homes for art and culture, where our youth can "get in touch" with the originality of francophone cultures. It's equally important to let them discover the richness of the cultures in the South with the help of a civic service matched with a francophone section.

The French youth who have come in through immigration will have their place in this dialogue of cultures, since the French language has also been voiced by writers from the Maghreb and sub-Saharan Africa. It is no coincidence that among the countries I've recently visited, Senegal and Algeria have given our Academy[3] two of the most ardent devotees of French, Assia Djebar and Senghor.

Concerning our system of higher education, it is urgent that we begin to think about creating chairs in francophone literature, which now scarcely exist in France, so that we can keep literary talents such as Maryse Condé, Alain Mabanckou, or Achille Mbembe, who have ended up having to exile themselves to the United States. The very heart and future of Francophonie are less and less French, but paradoxically become more and more Anglo-Saxon. Francophonie saved by America? That takes the biscuit!

A language carries also a political message, a certain vision of the world. Since it is spoken by such different peoples as those of Lebanon, Niger, or Vietnam, French is the story of a community destined to be formed between "us and them." I deplore the fact that, sometimes, this is confiscated by groups who, pretending to defend the French language, seek to promote their own personal interests. As long as *la francophonie* is suspected of a whiff of such motives, people will feel very distrustful about it and will be tempted to throw out the baby (France) with the bath water (francophonie). For in its origins, francophonie wasn't a colonial concept; quite the contrary. Not wanting to be suspected of neocolonialism, General de Gaulle began by interrogating it before Léopold Sédar Senghor would define it as "the daughter and sister of independence," as "a cultural symbiosis between states united by French, which is all the more humane because it is so rich, bringing together the most opposite values."

In France, we must do away with a Jacobean idea of a francophonie that crushes and suppresses: it is pointless to oppose the French language to "the languages of France." How can we claim our cultural distinctiveness over against English and not admit it for our own regional cultures, threatened to disappear? Local languages, including overseas ones such as Creole, must be offered to students in the territories where enough parents desire this.

From the local to the global, francophonie happily crosses all borders, but without always knowing where she's going. We have to view this as a means for the French language to stand up to English without embarrassment. This entails that our administrations address themselves to international bodies in French, and that French, the language of law, be the language of reference for European documents.

The European Union's expansion toward the East should not challenge our privileged partnership with countries in the South. Thus, just a few days ago, France's ratification of the International Convention for Cultural Diversity allows for local languages to be established on an equal basis along with French, especially in Africa: despite its present difficulties, through the linguistic dynamism inherited from its misunderstood precolonial history, the Black Continent can make an important contribution to the production of universal values.

Notes

1   Senghor (1906–2001), major Senegalese poet and cultural theorist, a key figure in the Négritude movement championing African culture. He served as president of Senegal from 1960 to 1980, and was instrumental in the formation of "La Francophonie," an organization of 57 nations with substantial French-speaking populations.
2   Sarkozy envisions Senghor's name in the company of two very different figures: a classic modern French writer, Charles Peguy (1873–1914), and Toussaint L'Ouverture (1743–1803), leader of the Haitian revolution for independence from France.
3   The Académie Française, the elite body of 40 "immortals" charged with safeguarding the French language and its development.

21

Francophonie and Universality
The Ideological Challenges
of Littérature-monde *(2009)*

Jacqueline Dutton

Jacqueline Dutton is senior lecturer in French at the University of Melbourne, Australia. Her research areas extend from modern French literature to utopian theory and literature to travel writing. Her 2003 book, *Le Chercheur d'or et d'ailleurs: L'Utopie de J.M.G. Le Clézio,* opens up a dialogue between francophone and postcolonial studies and recent discussions on a world literature in French by looking into the example of the 2008 Nobel laureate, Le Clézio. In "Francophonie and Universality," Dutton analyzes the ideological challenges of reinventing francophonie through the common project of a world literature in French, in the wake of the volume *Pour une littérature-monde* based on the manifesto printed in *Le Monde*. Dutton contextualizes the 2007 manifesto through previous approaches taken in French and francophone studies, arguing that it is less radical than its signers suggest. She sees their views on francophonie and universality as bound up with concepts that are ideologically compromised within a neocolonial project, and argues for a more nuanced stance, redefining these terms in the global narrative of world literature.

'The World is an Amazing Place'

In 2007, France saw the world come back into literary focus when the manifesto 'Pour une littérature-monde en français' (Le Bris and Rouaud 2007a) blazed across the pages of *Le Monde des livres*. 'Le monde revient' declared the article ['The world is returning'], heralding the return of the wider world, of diversity and plurality, to shake up the exclusive and elitist domain of French literature from the Hexagon.

Jacqueline Dutton, "Francophonie and Universality: The Ideological Challenges of *Littérature-monde*" (2009). In *International Journal of Francophone Studies* 12:2–3 (2009), pp. 425–438. Quotations given by Dutton in French have been translated into English.

World Literature in Theory, First Edition. Edited by David Damrosch.

In 2008, on the other side of the planet, Australian television audiences saw the world slip out of focus when the major multicultural broadcasting authority, SBS, replaced its highly successful slogan 'The World is an Amazing Place', introduced to promote the new SBS Television channel in 1994, with the current branding 'Six Billion Stories and counting ...'

Although these two cultural phenomena may seem entirely unrelated – juxtaposing the radical literary movement against the media-marketing machine – they reveal similar motivations to encourage diversity and analogous attempts to encapsulate in pithy slogans the ideological challenges they are seeking to advance. On one hand, the *littérature-monde* manifesto endeavours to banish the notion of francophonie as an outdated and divisive term that segregates French language literatures written by authors of non-French origins from metropolitan French writers and proposes a more inclusive category to encompass all writing that can speak of/to the world: speaking the world. On the other hand, the rebranding of SBS strives to remove the impersonal reference to the world 'at large' as an externalized reality that the audience views outwardly, to privilege the plethora of personal accounts that add up to represent the cultural diversity of the world.[1]

Both of these examples of French and Australian representations of diversity engage with popular ideological tensions to convey their messages pertaining to francophonie, universality, and multiculturalism. However, the ways in which they invoke the 'world' in their arguments are fundamentally different. While the world comes back to save literatures in French from the hierarchical structures of editing, publishing and distribution that dominate French language markets, the world is not enough for the Australian small screen – access to the individual story is more important than a generalizing interpretation or evaluation of the global environment.

As suggested through this initial comparison of the term 'world', the same desire to express diversity can lead to opposing readings and receptions in different cultural contexts. The apparently inclusive terms of francophonie and universality can be equally ambiguous in certain circumstances, and the *littérature-monde* manifesto highlights their exclusionary functions in the context of French language literatures. The manifesto and volume of essays entitled *Pour une littérature-monde* (Le Bris and Rouaud 2007) therefore present ideological challenges to the institutionalized interpretations of francophonie and universality, in an effort to engage with these nebulous and at times, nefarious expressions. Whether the contributors and signatories of these texts reject, contest or reconsider the roles of francophonie and universality in French language literatures, they all question the ideological underpinnings of these notions in their various attempts to reclassify their own and others' writings as *littérature-monde*.

This article will examine the particular challenges to francophonie and universality raised by the *littérature-monde* authors, comparing their distinctive reactions that are not all aligned with the dramatic stance of the initial manifesto. By exploring how such boundaries and constraints are stretched and modified, it may be possible to determine whether *littérature-monde* can effectively circumvent or overcome obstacles to inclusion for all writers of French language literatures.

Francophonie and Universality

Francophonie and universality have been in the international spotlight for a number of years, under suspicion for hegemony, neo-colonialism, and various other charges. To cite but one recent reference to the growing discontentment with official French policies on the subject demonstrates the force of the counter-argument:

> Francophonie? It's old-fashioned, out of date. The remainder of the colonial empire and of France's grandeur. Nostalgia for a world vision that no longer exists. In fact, a form of neocolonialism which, under the guise of defending the language, wishes to conserve an outdated influence. And anyway, what is it beyond Africa and a few acres of snow in North America? Just a glaze of sorrow. English won everywhere. With the globalization, the battle of languages is a battle of the rearguard. Francophonie is a bit out of fashion today in the 'hour of Europe', the opening up of the financial markets, and the triumph of the Internet. Why prop yourself up with a language? It's both a ridiculous Maginot line and a denial of modernity. When one has to deal with global-ization and learning to live together it's not the moment to wrap yourself up in lan-guages. It's difficult enough as it is, without having to hide yourself in your little linguistic bunker. (Wolton 2006: 15)

The *littérature-monde* manifesto does not therefore break new ground by simply disputing the currency of francophonie and universality in contemporary global literary and cultural contexts. The specific ideological challenges that the *littérature-monde* movement poses are nevertheless innovative and original. Multiple per-spectives and modes of expression emanate from a wide range of contributors to constitute a cohesive unit defending a common cause – equality and diversity in French language literatures. It is via this polyphony of voices from within the movement that *littérature-monde* displays its most powerful provocation, defying a uniform approach to the argument and instead reinventing francophonie and universality with a series of different propositions.

This study will consider the two principal angles adopted by the *littérature-monde* movement to present ideological challenges to francophonie and univer-sality. First, it will track how francophonie can either be rendered obsolete by embracing *littérature-monde*, or rehabilitated as a term that includes metro-politan French writers in the category of 'Francophone' writers, thus overcoming the entrenched distinction between 'French' and 'Francophone'. Second, it will look at how some authors dismiss universality and its imperialist connotations by eliding it with francophonie, while others interpret it as a synonym of *littérature-monde*, recasting universality in different forms to enable a new way of being in the world. Each of these strategies will be replaced in the context of current criticism of francophonie and universality to demonstrate the variety of different viewpoints that are encompassed in the *littérature-monde* essays, as well as the inherent diversity of ideological alternatives that underpin the movement.

The Death of Francophonie

Beginning with *littérature-monde*'s first and most violent attack, the manifesto opens fire on francophonie, pronouncing its death as a *fait accompli*, as evidenced by the fact that it has no practical relevance in contemporary life: 'The emergence of a world literature in French, consciously affirmed, open to the world, transnational, signs francophonie's death certificate. No one speaks 'francophone', or writes in francophone. Francophonie is the glimmer of a dead star' (Le Bris and Rouaud 2007). The total erasure of francophonie from any agenda is alluded to in the introductory paragraphs of Michel Le Bris's eponymous contribution to the volume *Pour une littérature-monde*, where he sums up the reactions of Alain Mabanckou, Anna Moï and Abdourahman A. Waberi as an 'adieu à la francophonie' (Le Bris 2007: 24). But Le Bris's declaration of francophonie's disappearance is nuanced here through reference to a specific strain of francophonie:

> The death certificate of a certain idea of francophonie, perceived as a space over which France cast its light for the benefit, one must infer, of masses still living in darkness. The end of this kind of francophonie and the emergence of a world literature in French. (Le Bris 2007: 24)

However, his inherent disgust for the relic of an imperialist past resurges in later lines: 'I no longer feel like the defender of a former French Empire, final vestige of our grandeur, even if it's disguised in the tattered rags of "francophonie"' (Le Bris 2007: 42), and he even predicts the complete eradication of the adjectival form from literary vocabulary: 'these writers in French whom we still call (but not for long, I think) "francophones"' (Le Bris 2007: 32). Jean Rouaud takes up the partial condemnation of francophonie in his essay entitled 'The Death of a Certain Idea' (Rouaud 2007: 7) and Jacques Godbout asks: 'Does Francophonie rhyme with scorn [mépris]?' (Godbout 2007: 105). Tahar Ben Jelloun decries the obvious neo-colonialism of a 'francophonie' label for writers that persists in spite of the public's ability to appreciate good and bad literature regardless of the colour or origins of the author: 'Since then, we know that francophonie has returned to its original status, that of a political area maintaining a barely overcome (or, better, disguised) colonial memory' (Ben Jelloun 2007: 117). Raharimanana's categorical refusal of the epithet condemns Onésime Reclus for coining the neologism 'francophonie' and therefore for its continuing pejorative connotations:

> Shall I consider myself to be francophone as a Reclus wanted me to be, under his
> heel, inferior, a servant of the French Empire, eternally indigenous, shut up inside the
> frontiers and sub-cultures he assigned me to, while he grants himself the world to
> shine out upon? No, thanks! (Raharimanana 2007: 308)

These are the 'grave-diggers of francophonie' to whom Abdou Diouf, Secretary
General of the International Organisation for Francophonie, refers in his response
to the *littérature-monde* manifesto (Diouf 2007). In many ways, the authors cited
above are expressing in extreme and personal ways the same frustration that
has pushed scholars to demonstrate their own dissatisfaction with the terms used
to describe their research and teaching. In the special issue of *Yale French Studies*
entitled 'French and Francophone: The Challenge of Expanding Horizons', Réda
Bensmaïa crosses-out the very term 'francophonie' in a dramatic gesture to
represent the de-negation of both the critical and creative space that complicates
'French' and 'Francophone' literatures (Bensmaïa and Waters 2003: 17–23). As a site
that offers scholars and writers an opportunity to go beyond the hierarchical
and other constraints of the French/Francophone paradigm, Bensmaïa's crossed-
out francophonie may in some ways be considered a more cerebral precursor to
littérature-monde, given its ambition to efface and replace the outmoded concept of
francophonie. Mireille Rosello also questions the need to align oneself with either
'French' or 'Francophone' studies, categorically refusing two fundamentally flawed
visions of francophonie that correspond to those rejected by the *littérature-monde*
movement:

> One that would imagine a hegemonic status of French linked to a colonial power as
> if by some sort of perverse umbilical cord, and a second definition that would suspect
> non-European Francophone writers of alienation if they choose to write in French.
> (Rosello 2003a: 131–132)

In spite of the surprisingly forceful manner in which francophonie's death is
framed, the *littérature-monde* authors who forecast such a grim finale are simply
building on previous predictions that francophonie cannot last as political or
cultural point of reference, and perhaps not even as a linguistic one. What distinguishes the *littérature-monde* movement's contributions to the debate is their
unbridled passion to divest themselves definitively of this burden and move
on to embrace a new model that is potentially just as fraught with risk as
francophonie.

Rehabilitating Francophonie

While the manifesto expresses an unflinching resolve to bury francophonie forever,
some of the *littérature-monde* authors obviously have doubts about jettisoning francophonie so quickly. They propose ways of eliminating the neo-colonial and hierarchical elements of the concept through stretching the boundaries of its definitions

and common usages. The most pressing imperative for rehabilitating francophonie to transform it into an acceptable term for use in contemporary discourses is to abolish the separation of 'French' from 'Francophone'. In order to address the hierarchical dilemma that places the former before the latter in many instances – ranging from simple word order to media perceptions to editorial practices – 'French' has to be subsumed within the category of 'Francophone'. There is no other way of removing the superiority complex surrounding 'French', but as this is a profoundly ingrained position that is perpetuated from both within French language communities and often more blatantly by Francophiles who are somewhat removed from the Francophone field, the successful effacement of this binary would be a highly improbable undertaking.

However, posing it as a possibility or a potential pathway is a sign that the contributors to the *littérature-monde* essays have not condemned francophonie without considering its road to redemption. Jacques Godbout presents a pessimistic point of view regarding the fatal division between 'French' and 'Francophone' in his essay 'La Question préalable', laying out the conditions for francophonie's rehabilitation, as well as *littérature-monde*'s future prospects:

> How can one believe in a world literature in French when, for more than forty years, the Hexagonals, though they generally celebrate the existence of 'francophonie', never see themselves as part of it. The 'francophones' would be then a separate race that one encounters in Africa, in America, and in the peripheral territories of Belgium or Switzerland. There's no such thing in France, except now and then when we invite them to sing during the Francofolies Festival or at the Francoffonies of the Salon du Livre at the Porte de Versailles [in Paris].
>
> Rather than pretending that the institution of French literature belongs to a real world literature, Philippe Sollers, Philippe Labro or Bernard-Henri Lévy should see themselves as 'writers in French' – that is, as 'francophones'. (Godbout 2007: 105–106)

Godbout's stance is powerfully unequivocal, and his alignment with the most militant of the *littérature-monde* authors is demonstrated by his epigraph featuring Alain Mabanckou's forceful statement from his article 'Francophonie, yes; a ghetto, no!'; 'French literature is a national literature. It is this literature that should join the great francophone whole' (Mabanckou 2006). Mabanckou also reiterates such points from his *Le Monde* article in his *Pour une littérature-monde* essay, citing his previous definition of a Francophone writer, 'definition in which I would include as well, without equivocation, the French writer':

> To be a francophone writer is to be a depository of cultures, of a whirlwind universe. To be a francophone writer is certainly to be an inheritor of French letters, but above all it's to bring one's own personal touch to the grand ensemble, that touch that breaks frontiers, blots out races, reduces the distance between continents only in order to establish a brotherhood through language [...]. The francophone brotherhood is on its way. We'll no longer come from one or another country or continent, but rather from

a particular language. And our creative neighborhood will be nothing other than the universe. (Mabanckou 2007: 56)

Like Godbout, Ben Jelloun names the metropolitan French authors who should be included in the Francophone canon in order to validate francophonie as a truly inclusive representation of those who use the French language:

> Sometimes I wanted to rebel against the so ambiguous and narrow notion of francophonie. The francophone writer is the half-breed who comes from abroad and is asked to stick to his status of belatedness as against the writers of French origin. This notion of origin is just as unpleasant as that of francophonie. This distinction exists, you can find it in the dictionaries, it's used by the media and by politicians. It almost sounds like discrimination. But we'll let it pass as well and we'll ask the official representatives of francophonie to show a bit of imagination and include in French literature everyone who writes in French, knowing well that there are various ways to use this language, starting with Marcel Proust and Louis-Ferdinand Céline and going on through Aimé Césaire and Kateb Yacine, among others. (Ben Jelloun 2007: 117)

As mentioned above, the manifesto does not engage with the specific contributions that metropolitan French writers could or should make to the *littérature-monde* movement. Whether such a distinction regarding the background of the authors should be made or not is highly debatable, but it is nevertheless interesting to observe certain tendencies that may have some relevance to *littérature-monde* authors' arguments with regard to redefining the borders of francophonie. One of the salient strategies of the manifesto was to include a selection of signatories from all over the world, and it was of course crucial to list both 'French' and 'Francophone' partisans of *littérature-monde* to lend the movement credence. Of the 44 signatories, fifteen are from France, although they may profess other significant cultural or regional affinities. Evidently, these fifteen authors identify more readily with the other signatories than with those authors whose 'littérature franco-française' is the target of derision in the manifesto, described as 'an endless game of combinations', 'with no other object but itself', with 'its strange poetics spinning around itself like a whirling dervish'. In fact, many of them demonstrate their desire to distance themselves from the designation of 'French' writer, seeking acceptance instead under the broader umbrella of *littérature-monde*. The 2008 Nobel Laureate in Literature, J.M.G. Le Clézio, is a prominent example of such attitudes, downplaying his French identity to emphasize his Mauritian heritage and citizenship and his attachment to literature as a mode of cultural expression – a tendency that President Nicolas Sarkozy chose to overlook in claiming Le Clézio's Nobel Prize as a coup for France's cultural and political influence in the globalized literary marketplace! The relative representation of 'French' authors in the *Pour une littérature-monde* essays is greatly reduced – only three of the 27 contributors – two of whom are the editors of the collection (Michel Le Bris and Jean Rouaud) and the third, Patrick Raynal, centres his essay on the *policier* genre rather than cultural appartenance or language issues. It would seem therefore that the suggestion to rehabilitate francophonie – by including metropolitan French writers together with authors of various different origins – is favoured more by those authors for whom 'Francophone' has been an adopted or imposed identity than for 'French' writers, who embrace more readily the step towards a new designation as practitioners of *littérature-monde*.

The idea to reform an exclusive interpretation of francophonie through including 'French' and 'Francophone' cultural actors and representatives under the same rubric is not new to followers of the debate either. The *littérature-monde* authors carry on the argument that many critical commentators have observed, including Michel Tétu (1997), David Murphy (2002) and Charles Forsdick (2003). Many of the contributors to Kamal Salhi's edited volume *French in and out of France* (2002) make similar suggestions, but Gabrielle Parker asks the question most directly: 'Is France a member of *la Francophonie*?' (Parker 2002: 33). While the title of Tom Conley's article in *Yale French Studies* responds in no uncertain terms: 'All French Literature is Francophone' (2003: 166–176), Mireille Rosello is more measured in her interpretation of the question:

> If I ask, for example, whether 'French studies' include 'Francophone studies' or whether 'Francophone studies' include 'French studies', a different answer obtains when I am writing an entry for an encyclopedia, or when I am discussing interviewing techniques with a student who has applied for a position [...] Theoretically, Hexagonal literature is a branch of Francophone studies. (Rosello 2003a: 131)

In any event, general practice has not followed the development of the theory, and although there has been much discussion of the topic in critical and creative arenas, it seems more likely that a designation such as *littérature-monde* would encourage self-identification by authors from any origins who write in French. The last hurrah for francophonie proposed by several members of the *littérature-monde* movement therefore seems unlikely, at best.

Universality under Attack

If francophonie is dead, as some of the *littérature-monde* writers claim that it is, then universality is also under serious threat. The manifesto lays the foundations for the case against universality, conflating the ideological underpinnings of francophonie and universality, which are condemned as invalid excuses for defending France's cultural superiority and its 'civilizing mission'. It rejects 'this vision of francophonie, in which France, mother of arts, arms, and laws, continued to spread its light, as universal benefactress intent upon bringing civilization to the peoples living in darkness' (Le Bris and Rouaud 2007). Several of the essays echo these sentiments, such as Jean Rouaud's text that mocks 'these inexhaustible voices who lecture us on French literature, with their pretense to universality' (Rouaud

2007: 11), and sarcastically asks, 'how can one renounce this drunkenness which used to shape glorious destinies, this dead star which turned France into a light-house of civilization?' Michel Le Bris elaborates further on the self-proclaimed universality of French literature: 'the one and only, ultimate reference, eternally admirable, model bestowed upon humanity', a fallacy maintained by interested parties: 'the unbelievable morgue of those pawns who were on top then, imposing their norms, dictating good taste and who to reject, self-proclaimed clerks of the universal' (Le Bris 2007: 25). He goes on to repeat the manifesto's message that links francophonie and universality in an inextricable knot: 'the end of fran-cophonie [...] Yes, if we understand by this a space over which France, mother of arts, repository of the universal, continued to spread its light' (Le Bris 2007: 45). Alongside the fiery rampages of the volume's editors, a more playful and subtle repudiation of universality in conjunction with francophonie prevails. Raharimanana scorns France's myths that uphold the Abbé Grégoire's brand of universality[2] and the neo-colonialist strand of francophonie as the saving graces of 'primitive' peoples:

> I'm told that Abbé Grégoire is my ancestor, I'm told that the geographer Onésime Reclus is my grandfather. The abbé was the first to plead for Black literature and to say that thanks to this we think and we write [...] Thank you, dear abbé! My fathers were in darkness, there was no way their languages could save them or enlighten them. (Raharimanana 2007: 307–308)

Michel Layaz minimizes the value of the universal, by praising 'a world which escapes the coarseness of the "universal report"' (Layaz 2007: 277), and Edouard Glissant warns against the flight from a colonial past towards the very concept that engendered such devastation: 'It was first necessary to deal with the problem of colonialism, a situation inherited from the 19th century [...] one shouldn't retreat in advance into some sort of abstract universal' (Glissant 2007: 77). Lyonel Trouillot criticizes France's use of universalism to promote its language and literature as the standards of civilization and culture, ending with the probing question that features as the epigraph to the present article:

> Language isn't a referent, [...] French literature isn't a referent, and [...] there's no ref-erent more universal than another. We also had to take a hard look at the notion of universal. Who was it who created the universal? (Trouillot 2007: 198)

Trouillot's question emphasizes the hegemonic nature of universality, that has been examined at length by Judith Butler, Ernest Laclau and Slavoj Žižek in *Contingency, Hegemony, Universality* (2000). The complex relationships between these three concepts have been interrogated in more sophisticated arguments than could be considered in the *littérature-monde* essays, but those authors who refute universality's authority concur with Laclau (and Gramsci) saying that the only universality society can achieve is a hegemonic universality – a universality contaminated by particularity (Butler *et al.* 2000: 51). Žižek determines how the 'battlefield' for hegemony is predicated upon the existence of a certain 'empty' form of universality (Butler *et al.* 2000: 110), the recognition of which seems to be the premise for *littérature-monde*'s attack on the traditional values of French universalism, now perceived to be void of relevance in the current debate. Butler, however, offers more optimistic avenues to explore the terrain of 'competing universalities' that arise from breaking up dominant regimes rooted in particularity to allow alternative versions of universality (Butler *et al.* 2000: 179). Not all critics of universality are as hopeful for change. Roger Celestin and Eliane Dalmolin refer to 'Universalism in Crisis' as the key thread in their overview of political, social and cultural transformations in France's history from 1850 to the present. Paul Dirkx is one of the most consistent and methodical detractors of 'franco-universalisme', a *doxa* that insidiously attempts to hide its imperialist underpinnings by denying the socio-historic roots that anchor it in the most exploitative ambitions of the French Republic – colonial annexation, obliteration of origins and total erasure of local and regional particularities. Gabrielle Parker concludes her thorough analysis of the conjoined notions of francophonie and universality on a pessimistic tone with the remark that 'French discourse itself has to be interrogated to deconstruct the opposition between metropolis and "the rest"' (Parker 2003: 100). This massive enterprise is also suggested in Mireille Rosello's assessment of France's gradual renegotiation of its fundamental tenets through introducing 'tactical universalism' and 'Republican multiculturalism' (Rosello 2003b: 144).

Alternative Modes of Universality

Essentially, there is more optimism surrounding the notion of universality than francophonie in both the *littérature-monde* movement and in focused critical debate on the subject. Complete condemnation of universality is rare, though blistering criticism of the French or European models that constitute the current reference point for the term abounds. Alain Mabanckou challenges the relevance of these western versions of universality in a world of diversity and multiculturalism:

> Therefore, no authority whatever should assume the right to dictate what is universal and what is not. The universal is the assessment we reach through our own intelligence, our encounters and the mixing of our cultures. Consequently, the universal forming a totality, we no longer have a universal if this totality is deprived of the elements which, brought together, form a *disparate*, but *coherent* totality! In the end, and we already know this, the universal is 'the local, minus the walls'. Is it necessary to add that the world literature in French should be included in this attempt? (Mabanckou 2007: 63–64)

Proposing new ways of defining universality, taking into account the fluid variability required to allow for the diverse elements and ideals that make up *littérature-monde* is Mabanckou's aim and the philosophy behind this approach to universality appears much more reasonable and acceptable than a hegemonic and outmoded Eurocentric one. Other authors display more confidence in universality as a basic concept, perhaps due to its historical reinventions as opposed to the stasis of francophonie as an institution. Anna Moï valorizes universality as a positive entity to strive for: 'the spectrum of peoples who contribute to constructing this universality' (cited in Le Bris 2007: 47); Gary Victor describes world literature as 'a necessary human quest, for universality', one of the jewels that it has to offer (Victor 2007: 320). For Nancy Huston, the specific and universal qualities of literature are simply points on a spectrum that identifies the miraculous nature of the creative experience: 'Any good novel is a miracle. I'd like to be able to choose [...] between a miracle that conveys specificity and another that conveys universality' (Huston 2007: 152). Nimrod is the one who explicitly elides universality and *littérature-monde* to reinforce his argument in favour of a literature that promotes dialogue with the Other: 'A literature which translates such truthfulness wins, from all points of view, its claim to the universal – a term used even before the invention of littérature-monde' (Nimrod 2007: 233).

The varying fortunes of universality have already been alluded to above, along with the opening of possibilities for its recasting in different moulds. In addition to these prospects, Margaret Majumdar's studies also demonstrate universality's versatile forms as she traces the notion from its roots in French Enlightenment and the universality of human reason to the *mission civilisatrice* and assimilation policies of the nineteenth century, through to a Sartrean perspective of universality as a proletarian project. The advent of institutionalized francophonie in the aftermath of decolonization signified a departure from the socio-historical evolution of the term to create a 'virtual paradigm of the abstract universal defined in idealistic terms' (Majumdar 2005: 22). And the politico-economic dimension produced by the *exception culturelle* that led to the coupling of universalism and exceptionalism is the incarnation that Majumdar deems to be the most adaptable and resilient form yet (Majumdar 2005: 28). Immanuel Wallerstein goes further to determine a programme for action to substitute the partial and distorted view of democracy that he defines as 'European universalism' with a new model of 'universal universalism' that is realizable and egalitarian in its aims and its outcomes. He underscores the urgency of such a project:

> The struggle between European universalism and universal universalism is the central ideological struggle of the contemporary world, and its outcome will be a major factor in determining how the future world-system into which we shall be entering in the next twenty-five to fifty years will be structured. (Wallerstein 2006: xiv–xv)

Interestingly, the favoured option that he proposes is inspired by Léopold Sédar Senghor's 'rendez-vous between giving and receiving': 'a multiplicity of universalisms that would resemble a network of universal universalisms' (Wallerstein 2006: 84).

The ideal of creating a new universality that corresponds to the diverse cultures and experiences to be found in today's globalized communities is precisely what the *littérature-monde* movement seeks to accomplish. Of the ideological challenges that the manifesto and collection of essays poses to francophonie and universality, the call to reinvent universality is the most powerful and potentially achievable. Whereas the goal to rehabilitate francophonie by integrating metropolitan French literatures into the Francophone fold may be accomplished on a small scale, the recasting of a new universal universality is far more attainable on a larger scale.

Conclusion

This exploration of the ideological challenges to francophonie and universality that are posed by the contributors to the *littérature-monde* manifesto and volume of essays has therefore established that the proposal to renegotiate the boundaries and constraints of universality is the most promising one for promoting inclusion rather than exclusion amongst French language literatures. Such an initiative forms a sound grounding for *littérature-monde* to develop further as a concept that encourages equality and diversity. But to return to the initial observations that open this article, does the *littérature-monde* movement embrace the 'world' to the detriment of the individual story, privileging the universal over the particular, in a shift that seems to oppose the trend witnessed in the repositioning of SBS Television in the Australian multicultural marketplace? Could this be a reminder of the tendency towards the universal in traditional French logic and the emphasis on the particular in anglophone multicultural policies? Many commentators would support this culturally biased interpretation of the apparently contradictory inclinations in French and Australian methods for contesting homogeneity and hierarchies, but there may be another level at which this juxtaposition can be read.

In challenging the ideological underpinnings of francophonie and universality, the *littérature-monde* movement essentially espouses both of the slogans that SBS has used over the past 25 years to promote the television network's opening to multicultural and multilingual programming. *Littérature-monde* combines the impetus to look outward and see that 'the world is an amazing place', capable of inspiring and completing the evolution of 'French' and 'Francophone' literatures in an inclusive gesture 'that speaks the world'. By the same token, *littérature-monde* demonstrates its support for a literary movement that allows for expression of the particular. Every author, no matter what colour or origin, has their own tale to tell and all of the 'six billion stories and counting …' that capture the lives of the world's populations are equally valuable in themselves, albeit of variable quality and appeal when transcribed into literary and artistic forms.

In the end, the 'Pour une littérature-monde en français' manifesto is not so different from the Australian TV network's branding, except that it serves to incorporate both of the SBS slogans into its hyphenated form. If, as Michel Le Bris has suggested, the space that exists between 'littérature' and 'monde' can be transformed into a place for perpetually redefining the parameters and the applications of the term, then perhaps it can also accommodate new visions of universality that encourage both global representations and multi-cultural models of French language literatures to flourish.

Notes

1 For more information on the history and initiatives of SBS, see Lang *et al.* (2008), *The SBS Story: The Challenge of Diversity*.
2 See Alyssa Goldstein Sepinwall's (2005) biography of the Abbé Grégoire for a detailed background to this reference.

References

Ben Jelloun, T. (2007), 'La Cave de ma mémoire, le toit de ma maison sont des mots français', in M. Le Bris and J. Rouaud (eds.), *Pour une littérature-monde*, Paris: Gallimard, pp. 113–124.

Bensmaïa, R. and Waters, A. (2003), 'Francophonie', *Yale French Studies*, 103, pp. 17–23.

Butler, J., Laclau, E., and Žižek, S. (2000), *Contingency, Hegemony, Universality. Contemporary Dialogues on the Left*, London: Verso.

Celestin, R. and Dalmoulin, E. (2007), *France from 1851 to the Present: Universalism in Crisis*, New York: Palgrave Macmillan.

Conley, T. (2003), 'From Detail to Periphery: All French Literature is Francophone', *Yale French Studies*, 103, pp. 166–176.

Diouf, A. (2007), 'La francophonie, une réalité oubliée', *Le Monde*, 19 March, http://www.etonnants-voyageurs.com/IMG/pdf_Le_Monde.fr___diouf.pdf. Accessed 9 February 2008.

Dirkx, P. (2006), *Les 'Amis belges'. Presse littéraire et franco-universalisme*, Rennes: Presses Universitaires de Rennes.

Forsdick, C. and Murphy, D. (eds.) (2003), *Francophone Postcolonial Studies*, London: Oxford University Press.

Glissant, E. (2007), 'Solitaire et solidaire', in M. Le Bris and J. Rouaud (eds.), *Pour une littérature-monde*, Paris: Gallimard, pp. 77–86.

Godbout, J. (2007), 'La Question préalable', in M. Le Bris and J. Rouaud (eds.), *Pour une littérature-monde*, Paris: Gallimard, pp. 103–112.

Huston, N. (2007), 'Traduttore non e traditore', in M. Le Bris and J. Rouaud (eds.), *Pour une littérature-monde*, Paris: Gallimard, pp. 151–160.

Lang, I., Hawkins, G., and Dabbousy, L. (2008), *The SBS Story: The Challenge of Diversity*, Sydney: University of New South Wales Press.

Layaz, M. (2007), 'Billet pour la vie', in M. Le Bris and J. Rouaud (eds.), *Pour une littérature-monde*, Paris: Gallimard, pp. 269–278.

Le Bris, M. (2007), 'Pour une littérature-monde en français', in M. Le Bris and J. Rouaud (eds.), *Pour une littérature-monde*, Paris: Gallimard, pp. 23–54.

Le Bris, M. and Rouaud, J. (2007a), 'Pour une littérature-monde en français', *Le Monde des livres*, 16 mars, http://www.etonnants-voyageurs.com/spip.php?article1574. Accessed 29 January 2008.

292 *Jacqueline Dutton*

Le Bris, M. and Rouaud, J. (eds.) (2007b), *Pour une littérature-monde*, Paris: Gallimard.

Mabanckou, A. (2007), 'Le chant de l'oiseau migrateur', in M. Le Bris and J. Rouaud (eds.), *Pour une littérature-monde*, Paris: Gallimard, pp. 55–66.

Mabanckou, A. (2006), 'La francophonie, oui, le ghetto: non!', *Le Monde*, 19 March.

Majumdar, M. (2005), 'Exceptionalism and Universalism: The Uneasy Alliance in the French-Speaking World', in T. Chafer, and E. Godin, (eds.), *The French Exception*, New York and London: Berghahn Books, pp. 16–29.

Moï, A. (2007), 'L'Autre', in M. Le Bris and J. Rouaud (eds.), *Pour une littérature-monde*, Paris: Gallimard, pp. 243–250.

Murphy, D. (2002), 'De-centring French Studies: towards a postcolonial theory of Francophone cultures', *French Cultural Studies*, 13: 2, pp. 165–185.

Nimrod (2007), '"La Nouvelle Chose française". Pour une littérature décolonisée', in M. Le Bris and J. Rouaud (eds.), *Pour une littérature-monde*, Paris: Gallimard, pp. 217–236.

Parker, G. (2003), '"Francophonie" and "universalité": evolution of two notions conjoined', in C. Forsdick and D. Murphy (eds.), *Francophone Postcolonial Studies*, London: Oxford University Press, pp. 91–101.

Parker, G., (2002), 'The Fifth Republic and the Francophone Project', in K. Salhi (ed.), *French in and out of France*, Oxford: Peter Lang, pp. 11–34.

Raharimanana (2007), 'Le Creuset des possibles', in M. Le Bris and J. Rouaud (eds.), *Pour une littérature-monde*, Paris: Gallimard, pp. 305–314.

Rosello, M. (2003a), 'Unhoming Francophone Studies: A House in the Middle of the Current', *Yale French Studies*, 103, pp. 123–132.

Rosello, M. (2003b), 'Tactical Universalism and new multiculturalist claims in postcolonial France', in C. Forsdick and D. Murphy (eds.), *Francophone Postcolonial Studies*, London: Oxford University Press, pp. 135–144.

Rouaud, J. (2007), 'Mort d'une certaine idée', in M. Le Bris and J. Rouaud (eds.), *Pour une littérature-monde*, Paris: Gallimard, pp. 7–22.

Salhi, K. (ed.) (2002), *French in and out of France*, Oxford: Peter Lang.

Sepinwall, A. G. (2005), The Abbé Grégoire and the French Revolution. *The Making of Modern Universalism*, Berkeley, Los Angeles/London: University of California Press.

Tétu, M. (1997), *Qu'est-ce que la Francophonie?*, Paris: Hachette Edicef.

Trouillot, L. (2007), 'Langues, voyages et archipels', in M. Le Bris and J. Rouaud (eds.), *Pour une littérature-monde*, Paris: Gallimard, pp. 197–204.

Victor, G. (2007), 'Littérature-monde ou liberté d'être', in M. Le Bris and J. Rouaud (eds.), *Pour une littérature-monde*, Paris: Gallimard, pp. 315–320.

Waberi, A. A. (2007), 'Ecrivains en position d'entraver', in M. Le Bris and J. Rouaud (eds.), *Pour une littérature-monde*, Paris: Gallimard, pp. 66–76.

Wallerstein, I. (2006), *European Universalism: The Rhetoric of Power*, New York/London: The New Press.

Wolton, D. (2006), *Demain la francophonie*, Paris: Flammarion.

22

Universalisms and Francophonies (2009)

Françoise Lionnet

A past president of the American Comparative Literature Association, Françoise Lionnet is a professor of French and Francophone Studies and director of the African Studies Center at the University of California, Los Angeles. Her books extend from comparative and francophone literatures on the politics of representation (*Autobiographical Voices: Race, Gender, Self-Portraiture*, 1989) to postcolonial studies and African and African-American studies (*Postcolonial Representations: Women, Literature, Identity*, 1995). Lionnet challenges disciplinary boundaries within the context of a global market, arguing both for a comparative feminist criticism and for a comparative study of the margins of anglophone and francophone literatures, giving birth to what Lionnet calls "minor transnationalism" in her co-edited volume of that name (2005). More recently, looking into the intellectual and political overlapping of disciplines and methodologies that too often seem separate, Lionnet and Shu-mei Shih have argued for a "creolization of theory" aware of the legacy of colonialism (*The Creolization of Theory*, 2011).

Lionnet's "Universalisms and Francophonies" responds to the 2007 *Le Monde* manifesto. She examines the negative reactions that the manifesto provoked and proposes instead to speak, in the plural, of "francophonies," which would stress their universality in difference in a decentered and multilingual world. She emphasizes the concept's broader encompassing of a diversity that goes globally beyond French literature and escapes the manifesto's Manichean opposition between "littérature-monde" and "littérature francophone." Lionnet suggests that pluralized "francophonies" would enable a theoretical dialogue with Goethe's *Weltliteratur* and with anglophone world literature, "both of which imply an understanding of the *world of* literature as fundamentally transnational and polyphonic."

Françoise Lionnet, "Universalisms and Francophonies" (2009). In *International Journal of Francophone Studies* 12:2–3 (2009), pp. 203–221. © Intellect Ltd 2009. Passages quoted by Lionnet in French have been translated into English.

> The narrative fiction of globalization
> is produced by people always in motion,
> by deracinated people, by people without a country.
>
> (Joël des Rosiers, 'Entretiens' 1998: 37)

French literature is no longer 'French,' nor is it yet 'global'. The manifesto 'Pour une littérature-monde en français' published in *Le Monde des livres* on 16 March 2007 (Le Bris *et al.*) is but a belated recognition of the creative decentring of the French literary world, and a flawed if confident diagnosis of its currently 'depressed' state.[1] If literature is in a searching mood, and seems at pains to define itself, the French language, by contrast, with its many regional and global inflections, remains a capacious and fertile terrain irrigated by many local idioms and the lively vernacular cultures they translate. French is present on all continents, practiced by 200 million speakers, only a fraction of whom (primarily those living in France) are monolingual. A palimpsest under the pen of the bilingual Francophone writers who wrestle with it, transform it, and keep it polyphonically alive, French bears the traces of its innumerable encounters with other oral and written traditions. When produced by writers whose everyday lives are awash in multilingual environments, Francophone literature is a vehicle that raises to a new global level its readers' awareness of a long-standing philological feature of literary language, namely, its polysemy, and the distinct subjective dynamics of such textured palimpsestic creativity in a 'minor' mode.[2]

The manifesto acknowledges, and aims to promote, the 'returned' presence of the 'world' on the literary scene ('le monde revient'), but oddly enough, it fails to address the nature of language as the hybrid medium that brings this world into being. It focuses on thematic, generic, and categorical issues, but is silent on the quality of the linguistic innovations that have served to anchor literature in specific landscapes and transnational critical geographies. It raises timely cultural issues. But more than half a century after Erich Auerbach first proclaimed that 'our philological home is the earth: it can no longer be the nation' (Auerbach 1969: 17), a statement variously echoed in the works of Edward Said and Edouard Glissant, the manifesto seems surprisingly indifferent to the intricate layering of linguistic codes and rhetorical practices that are the philological hallmark of many Francophone texts.[3]

Or rather, the manifesto ironically evokes the burden of Francophone literature's exotic appeal: 'a few new hot spices, archaic or Creole words – so picturesque, indeed'. But it does so without openly acknowledging that this perceived liability is linked to the colonialist and paternalistic gaze that some critics and readers have fastened on that literature without regard for the complex ways in which a text's *difference* requires a reorientation of *their* gaze. The solution proposed is to do away with the term 'Francophone' as though the cure is to modify the *object*, and not the offending gaze.

But does this not sound like a familiar assimilationist agenda that seeks the integration of the other into the same? The burden is put on the 'other' to change its appearance, to rename itself, in order *not* to be perceived as 'exotic', not to be classified among the 'minor' or less-than-significant practices of contemporary letters. Thus: to fit in. To appear modern and sophisticated. And indeed, to accede to the universal – but as defined by the dominant voices, instead of striving for a productive re-interpretation of the concept from within a broad and all-inclusive frame.[4] These are surely the unintended consequences of the manifesto's rhetorical moves, its unexamined assumptions.

There is an uncomfortably dogmatic quality to the document; a clumsiness to its formulations that alternatively baffles and appals. How is it that the distinguished Francophone writers who have transformed the world of contemporary literature can be so blindsided into endorsing this call for a normalized and normalizing approach to the globalized present of literary discourse? Given the deep respect that the remarkable figures who signed this call can command, it is with no small measure of trepidation that negative views are aired here.

Writers such as Maryse Condé, Ananda Devi, Assia Djebar, Edouard Glissant, Jean-Marie G. Le Clézio, Alain Mabanckou or Abdourahman Waberi (all signatories of the manifesto, except for Djebar) strive for a universalist understanding of poetic value. They are acutely aware of the pitfalls of a politicized or racialized aesthetics that can restrict creativity, and of the limitations of labels such as 'minor', 'minority', 'marginality' or 'littératures de l'exiguïté' (Paré 1992). Some have endeavoured, with mixed success, to repudiate exoticism and the romanticization of alterity. Others refute the charge of political oppositionality with its simplistic anti-colonial rhetoric. Edouard Glissant's *Traité du Tout-Monde* (1997) is an appealing theoretical, ethical, and poetic statement about the dangers of exclusionary categories. But it is not clear why the label 'Francophone', which is already 'global' and all-encompassing given its primary linguistic meaning (about which more later), should be perceived by *these writers* as a restrictive designation of identity or talent.

To be sure, the term 'Francophone' has served to marginalize non-hexagonal writers, to ghettoize them. And by endorsing the manifesto's claims, the writers declared their adhesion to a positive idea of *global French* that would usher in the demise of the institutions of 'francophonie' with their dubious historical origins in imperialist geographies. But if French is a 'global language, with an international vocation' as the linguist Claude Hagège (2009) puts it, echoing the official political stance of both governmental and non-governmental agencies since Onésime Reclus,[5] it is also a vehicle that is re-appropriated and transformed by its many users. If the term 'Francophone' evokes for some the inconvenient colonial baggage of second-class, regional, and identitarian connotations imposed by the conventions and traditions of French letters since the Enlightenment, it is also true that it indexes diversity in a way that 'French' does not.[6] Furthermore, the history of anti-colonial representation is founded on successful modes of *reversal* and re-appropriation of devalued or denigrated categories, the expression 'Black is Beautiful' being the most famous and successful among those. So, why not embrace the term Francophone, which has acquired such powerful purchase around the globe precisely because it has created a space in which *French* colonial legacies have been exposed and successfully opposed, and the language appropriated for the purposes of decolonization?

This essay is an attempt to think through some of these paradoxes and what they reveal about the internalization and subsequent reproduction of old colonial paradigms. It will briefly address the formal question of the manifesto as a performative genre, and focus on the intellectual debates that have emerged as a result of the document's declarations and denunciations in the wake of France's cultural decline and the serious racial and social issues that underlie its Republican ideology of universalism.[7] The goal here, then, is to try to understand what is at stake in the newly intensified search for cultural meaning and definitions, and in the discussions sparked by the manifesto's (and its follow-up volume of essays') Manichean opposition between 'littérature-monde' and 'littérature francophone' (Le Bris and Rouaud 2007).

National Capital, Transnational Prestige

French nationalist literary history put a high premium on the purity of language. But that history came to a dead-end by the mid-twentieth century post-colonial era and the subsequent emergence of Francophone literatures, a development paralleled in the English-speaking world by the explosion of British Commonwealth literatures. One way to begin exploring these issues might be to transpose the question posed by Gauri Viswanathan in an essay she published in 2000 in *ARIEL: A Review of International English Literature*: 'Precisely where is English literature produced?' (Viswanathan 2000: 22). Hence we might also consider: precisely where is *French* literature actually *written*, and how is it now taught, classified, and canonized? Where does it acquire recognition and social purpose? The answer, of course, is: not just in France, not just by French citizens, as the plethora of successful and award-winning Francophone writers demonstrate, and as the pedagogical success of that literature confirms.

As an institution, French literature has been part of a disciplinary formation that furthered the secular and 'nationalist goal of civic education' (Wolff 2001: 248) during the nineteenth and twentieth centuries. But today, it increasingly relies on diverse and peripheral sites of cultural production and on pedagogical protocols that give centrality and visibility to voices and writing practices that have transformed the field into a truly transnational arena, even if Paris remains its symbolic, editorial, and financial hub. That hub continues to enshrine a hierarchical stratification of writers. As Pascale Casanova has argued, Paris remains for many 'the capital of this Republic without frontiers or limits, a universal country devoid of any patriotism […]: the universal Republic of Letters' (Casanova 1999: 49). For her, the belief in this cosmopolitan ideal reinforces the symbolic importance of the capital in the global marketplace of ideas and values: 'Paris is doubly universal: through the belief in its universality and through the real effects which this belief produces' (Casanova 1999: 50).

The manifesto simultaneously acknowledges *and* interrogates the role of Paris as universal model and inevitable principle of mediation. Choosing *Le Monde des livres* as its vehicle, rather than any number of more popular electronic or other media, the manifesto proclaims its highbrow status and seriousness of purpose. By declaring, in Paris, that the centre is now everywhere, it stresses the capital's debt to the periphery, but reinforces by the same token the city's role as a site of cultural prestige that can grant distinction and visibility to writers in accordance to the regulatory principles of literary modernity with their well-established systems of coveted awards.[8] Indeed, the document begins by stating that the autumn 2006 literary prizes were in fact the primary impetus for its publication, the 'Copernican revolution' to which it aims to respond.[9]

Immediate controversies have ensued, in large part because the manifesto affirmed the *fact* of the existing denationalization of literature, and the aesthetic and social consequences of this transformation. These are not mere questions of definition rooted primarily in a *querelle de mots*. They expose a much more serious struggle over historical legacies, and the eruption of a long-standing epistemological problem, one that revolves around contested notions of the 'literary', especially with regard to the textures of linguistic practice and the aesthetic choices they presuppose. Such questions have far reaching consequences about institutional arrangements and the power of these arrangements to refigure the relationship between not just language and culture, but also literature and identity, unity and multiplicity, colonial pasts and racialized presents. Hence the acuity of the reactions among public figures and academics – across the French-speaking world and in some American French departments – to the declarations made in this *manifeste des 44*, signed by 44 writers of varying renown and origins.

Written under the impulse of Michel Le Bris, a critic and writer well known in France as the visionary power behind the Francophone literature festival 'Etonnants Voyageurs' (an expression borrowed, incidentally, from the last poem of Baudelaire's 1857 *Les Fleurs du mal*), the manifesto is the latest instalment in a long history of declarations of literary independence. These have included the 1549 Pleiade's *Défense et Illustration* of the French language, Victor Hugo's 1827 *Preface de Cromwell*, André Breton's First (1924) and Second (1930) *Manifeste du Surréalisme*, Alain Robbe-Grillet's 1963 *Pour un nouveau roman*, and Jean Bernabé, Patrick Chamoiseau, and Raphaël Confiant's 1969 *Eloge de la créolité*. All have crystallized cultural, ideological, and political issues related to identity and language, and all are critical *monuments* to the extent that they have earned a place, a *lieu propre*, in the history of French literature.

But some manifestoes can be the expression of extreme 'position-takings' that are politically expedient and provide quick publicity, precisely because they oversimplify complex issues. By the same token, the radical nature of their statements can lead to unwise generalizations that provoke and deserve satirical treatment. The 2007 vintage leaves itself open to criticism because it exhibits a lack of conceptual clarity that contradicts the best and most thoughtful aspects of the oeuvres of its most distinguished signatories.

That is why one should bear in mind what Tristan Tzara, the Franco-Roumanian iconoclast, had to say about the genre of the manifesto. He gives a tongue-in-cheek definition, in his 1918 *Manifeste Dada*, of what such a document is supposed *to be and do*:

> A manifesto is a communication to the whole world, with no pretense other than the discovery of the means to heal instantaneously the syphilis in the political, astronomic, artistic, parliamentary, agronomic and literary domain. It can be gentle, good-humored, it's always right, it's strong, vigorous and logical.
>
> Speaking of logic, I think I'm very likeable. (Tzara 1973: 55)

Tzara's satirical approach hides an important truth. Literary manifestoes have a perfomative function, they bring new categories into existence, but they should not take *themselves* too seriously since they embody contradictions and bring to the surface cultural inconsistencies inherent in the political nature of the message they forcefully communicate 'au monde entier', with 'vigour' and 'logic'. Manifestoes are an intervention whose success depends on their visibility. They enter a literary field of forces structured by transformative debates and conflicts, and within which disagreements about language and contests over definitions can bring to the players in the field new levels of Bourdieuian 'distinction' (Bourdieu 1979). Concepts such as 'littérature-monde', *weltliteratur* or 'world literature' are not new, but the 2007 manifesto raised awareness and found an immediate (both negative and positive) echo. Hence its success.

As a 'communication to the whole world', *le manifeste pour une littérature-monde* could not have been better titled since it stemmed from a genuine desire to be truly inclusive and to extend French *literary* citizenship to all those who write with talent in that most precious of *patrimoines*, the French language ...! But rather than undoing the centre-periphery dichotomy that structures the colonial difference, and the presumed apartheid between France and the larger Francophone world, the manifesto proclaims instead that it is time to rename the field – as though it were still 'emerging' – and to bury the old formulations:

> 'the emergence of a world literature in French ... signs francophonie's death certificate. *No one speaks "francophone" or writes in francophone.* Francophonie is the glimmer of a dead star. How can the world care about the language of a virtual country?' (emphasis added)

Francophonie lacks distinction; it is not 'real' but 'virtual': hence it is high time to announce its impending demise and call for the normalization or mainstreaming of those literatures from the so-called peripheries. The manifesto, however, signals its own provincialism by the use of such terms as 'émergence' for a literature that has been in existence for a century (or more, depending on how one 'counts'). It broadcasts its own lacunae, namely, its ignorance of a rich literary history, one that is always already assimilated with and into that of the *métropole*, once it becomes part of a certain definition of the 'canon' with *its* criteria for distinction and inclusiveness.

Building on Pierre Bourdieu's notion of distinction, James English has argued that the 'economy of prestige' that structures the field of cultural production is dependent on what he terms the 'feverish proliferation' of awards in today's cultural domains, be it literature, film, music or art (English 2005: 2). As previously mentioned, the manifesto confidently asserts that the 2006 awards caused a 'revolution'. It is true that every autumn in Paris literary awards raise writers' and readers' expectations, and determine the relative standing of new books, their status within the field of contemporary letters. Reversals of fortune can cause mini 'revolutions'. But for a long time now, (beginning at least with the 1921 Goncourt to René Maran's *Batouala*), the most prestigious of these awards (the Goncourt, the Renaudot, the Femina, the Grand Prix de l'Académie, the Prix Max Jacob, among many others) have gone to writers who are not 'Franco-French' figures of cultural identity. Those may have either chosen to live in France or been forced into a relationship with the French language as a result of a variety of historical circumstances. Their geographic and ethnic origins underscored then and now the worldwide francophonies that continue to exist in countries scattered across the former empire, as well as in parts of Eastern Europe, the Middle East, and Western Europe, where the term Francophone remains valued and appreciated because of the diversity it subtends.[10]

Some were dissident intellectuals who may have voluntarily left their countries or escaped in search of greater freedom: figures such as the Roumanian Eugène Ionesco, the Haitian René Depestre or the Cuban Eduardo Manet come to mind. Others may use the French language because their position within a long history of colonial entanglements made possible their mastery of that idiom while restricting their access to other rightful linguistic legacies and historical memories: the Martinican Aimé Césaire, the Mauritian Edouard Maunick or the Algerian Leïla Sebbar would fall into that category. Yet others such as the Algerian Assia Djebar, the Vietnamese Linda Lê or the Djiboutian Abdourahman Waberi might belong to both categories. But, if it has been customary to refer to writers from the former colonies, as well as from Romania, Belgium, Luxembourg or Switzerland as 'Francophone', the term began to pose a problem as a political, institutional, and analytic concept once the field of Francophone studies began to expand (in the United States, the United Kingdom, and in France) as a result of several factors. These included, in the 1980s and early 1990s, the influence of American ethnic studies and anglophone postcolonial studies, initially viewed negatively by the mainstream of French studies as too 'politically correct' or 'communitarian', and thus irrelevant to European concerns. During the following decade, new approaches to transnationalism and creolization have highlighted the horizontal or 'minor' forms of transcultural exchanges which serve to circumvent mediation by a major metropolitan centre. Currently, in the late 2000s, it is the comparative study of the 'margins' that is truly taking off. Comparative Anglophone and Francophone, as well as lusophone, hispanophone or even sinophone literatures together constitute new forms of 'minor transnationalism', as was argued in a book with the same title edited by Françoise Lionnet and Shu-mei Shih, and as a conference on the Caribbean demonstrates.[11]

These are the stimulating academic developments that have accompanied the institutionalization of francophonie in the university curriculum. But since these have also destabilized traditional notions of French studies and comparative European studies, they have led to cultural controversies over the merits of the term Francophone. Such controversies are a symptom of the anxieties that trouble Parisian intellectuals in the face of this ongoing pedagogical revolution. The de-nationalization of literature has been proceeding apace for half a century if not more, but what is different now is that it has become *official* and very public, as a result of the manifesto, which is itself now the subject of articles, conferences, books, and special issues of journals that are thus causing much ink to flow.[12]

By putting forth the concept of 'littérature-monde *en français*', the signatories decry two distinct moments and movements: first, they denounce the self-referential, highly intellectualized, and to their mind, alienated approach of modernist and post-modernist writers; and second, they announce the 'death' of francophonie because it carries the stigma of the 'pittoresque' and the 'exotique' and is a linguistic category that is nothing but 'the language of a virtual country'. The overall intention is positive: the authors wish to advance a progressive and all encompassing approach to literary identity in the age of globalization. The goal is to link changes in the literary field to a vast swath of political changes, from increased cultural creolization everywhere to the fall of the Berlin wall, all of which results, for them, in the collapse of grand ideologies and the concomitant 'autonomisation de la langue'. But the manifesto falls far short of that goal, and it would have been much more far-sighted to propose instead that the term *francophonies* (in the plural) be maintained in order to underscore the geographic and historical multiplicities that it conveys, thus enabling a more interesting dialogue with the Goetheian concept of *weltliteratur* and the English 'world literature', both of which imply an understanding of the *world of* literature as fundamentally transnational and polyphonic. As Elisabeth Mudimbe-Boyi asks in her editor's 'Introduction' to the volume *Empire Lost: France and Its Other Worlds*, 'Does a more global, transcultural, and transnational, or transcontinental francophonie, as practiced in the academic space, allow for escaping from the rigid and reductive binaries of Self and Other, Center and Periphery?' (Mudimbe-Boyi 2009: xvi). Put another way, does francophonies invoke greater diversity and multiplicity than *littérature-monde en français*? And if so, how and why?

Citizens, Foreigners, and Literary Belonging, or the Paradoxes of Francophonie

The basic common sense understanding of the term 'Francophone' is a purely linguistic one: those who use the French language. But by that definition, Eugène Ionesco, Ahmadou Kourouma, and Khal Torabully would all belong together in a category that would simply serve to set them apart from a *nationalist* understanding of French literature, an understanding that readily absorbs Ionesco into the pantheon of French authors, but not Kourouma or Torabully. The appropriation and assimilation of non-hexagonal authors goes back centuries: but no one ever called the Swiss Jean-Jacques Rousseau a 'Francophone' writer; nor does the 2008 Nobel Prize winner, J.M.G. Le Clézio, born in Nice during World War II, and raised first in what was then the Italian-occupied border region of France, then in Nigeria, usually count as 'Francophone'. But in point of actual fact, he is the offspring of a Mauritian family with roots in Brittany that had emigrated to the Ile de France (a.k.a Mauritius) in the eighteenth century. Rousseau, Ionesco, and Le Clézio count among what can, without controversy, be called 'canonical' figures within the French tradition, even if their respective lineages suggest francophonie rather than a strictly hexagonal understanding of literary history.

One of the rare poetic movements of the prose-rich eighteenth century, a movement that helped renew the genre and opened the way for both Romanticism and Symbolism, is an all-but-forgotten group of three Francophone Creole poets. Two from the island of Reunion, Evariste Parny and Antoine de Bertin, and one from Guadeloupe, Nicolas Germain Léonard. They travelled to and worked together in Paris, as soldiers in the king's army, and as libertine poets and members of a literary group called *La Caserne*. Parny and Bertin went on to Boston and New Orleans, Haiti, Brazil, the Cape of Good Hope, and India. Parny had a lasting impact on Chateaubriand, Lamartine, Baudelaire, Ravel who put his *Chansons madécasses* to music, and especially Pushkin who considered him his favourite poet. Baudelaire, who is seldom forthcoming about his sources, confesses, in March 1846 in a letter to his sister-in-law, Félicité, that his ambition is to 'follow in the footsteps of a Petrarch or a Parny' (Baudelaire 1973: 135). But there exist no studies of Baudelaire that investigate the link between his brand of erotic lyricism and Parny's 1778 *Poésies érotiques* about a young Creole woman from the same island Baudelaire visited in 1841. Parny's 1787 *Chansons madécasses* are considered the first examples of French *poèmes en prose*, hence also inaugurate a genre that Baudelaire would perfect in *Le Spleen de Paris* (Vincent-Munnia et al. 2003). The echoes and borrowings are too rich and interesting to continue to ignore. Parny's iconoclastic rhetoric and his abolitionist sympathies eventually caused him to fall into disfavour among later nineteenth century writers and critics although Sainte-Beuve devotes a long study to his many volumes of poetry (Sainte-Beuve 1844). In the United States, the most recent critical works on the literature and culture of the slave trade make no mention of the poet's early denunciations of black servitude and his pointed understanding of slavery's role in shoring up Enlightenment ideologies.[13]

Whereas Rousseau and Le Clézio are classified by readers and critics as French, most likely because their individual identities are racially unmarked and they thus easily fit into a common sense 'national' understanding of Frenchness, the rare French literary anthologies that do include Parny hasten to characterize him as a *Creole* poet, thus marking him as different and 'other' (Tadié et al. 2007: 230–32). By contrast, for Slavicists and Russianists who have come to know and appreciate him via Pushkin's writings,[14] Parny is simply one of the minor *French* poets of the eighteenth century. In general, one can state that all non-white non-hexagonal writers tend to be defined by circumlocutions. André Breton felt obliged to refer to Aimé Césaire as a 'great Black poet' (Breton 1944), and not as 'a great French poet' and *Wikipedia: the free encyclopedia* (2009) describes Maryse Condé as a 'French-language author of historical fiction', not as a French author *tout-court*. Césaire and Condé are citizens from Martinique and Guadeloupe, respectively. But they continue to be classified, in anthologies, reference works, and on bookstore shelves, in the 'ghetto' of non-white authors from outside the hexagon, which can also include numerous Francophone *non-citizens* from Senegal, Vietnam, Algeria, and some four-dozen other multilingual countries.

A bit like the Commonwealth, which is an association of 53 independent states, most of them from the former British colonial empire, the Organization Internationale de la Francophonie is an association of 55 member states, 32 of which use French as an official language, while in fourteen others, French is one language among several; the OIF's motto, echoing with a significant difference that of the French Republic, is 'equality, complementarity, solidarity'. The OIF is a truly global organization that encourages cooperation in the areas of culture, science, economy, justice or peace. That is its official role. To the extent that one of its goals is to offer serious resistance to the imperium of 'global English', it provides a space and a forum where alternative histories, viewpoints, and cultural priorities can be opposed to the neo-liberal encroachments of a predatory globalism.

In many of the Francophone countries, French is present as a result of a long history of colonial expansion dating back to the fifteenth century: Quebec City, for example, celebrated its 400th anniversary in 2008 and its proud identity as the oldest North American city. Because North American French-speaking communities are a linguistic minority in the vast continent of English-speakers, their status, fierce defence of their language, and protection of their Francophone cultural specificities take on a very different valence when compared to the place that the French language occupies in the former colonies of Africa and Asia, where the might and money of the French government continues to exert an influence that often serves to mute if not erase completely local vernacular cultures and languages. That is the interesting and multifaceted role of French on the global scene today, the context and the horizon that should ground any discussion of francophonie.

These contradictions create frustrations in inverse proportion to the increasing interest that the French literary market place has been taking for some time in the ethnic and cultural provenance of books that appeal to a reading public much more invested in questions of race, diversity, equality, and geographic origin. If the traditional universalist approach to literary quality and value focused primarily on matters of form and on the use of standard French as a means of transcending the determinations of one's origins, today literary belonging is undergoing a healthy and contested process of redefinition, one that needs to take into account not just writers', and certainly not just professional critics' perspectives, but also the responses that various 'interpretive communities' can bring to a text, as Stanley Fish argued back in 1976 (Fish 1980). Fish stresses the constructed and culturally specific conventions that communities of readers bring to the act of reading and to their encounter with a given writer's works. Such encounters can lead to forms of reciprocity as writers respond in turn to readers' expectations and to the new interpretive communities that the pedagogical institutionalization of this literature generates.

The question remains, however: if it is not just language and readers, then is it race, nationality, history or geography that determines who you are *as a writer*?

In the United States, since the early 1990s, intersectional feminist criticism has argued that all of these overlapping categories must be taken into account in order to arrive at a properly comprehensive, rather than reductive, understanding of cultural, social or literary identity.[15] But at the height of the vital international feminist movement which gave birth to the dialectical forms of 'French feminist theory' in the 1970s and 1980s, non-hexagonal writers such as Julia Kristeva (from Bulgaria), Luce Irigaray (from Belgium), Hélène Cixous (from Algeria) could affirm that it is literature and the language they choose to write in that constitute their true homeland, the place where they feel most free from social, biological, geographical, and historical constraints. By focusing, as Simone de Beauvoir had done, on the socially constructed nature of femininity, they were able to clear a space for a more engaged critique of social conventions, thus allowing women writers to feel freed from both biological determinations and the patriarchal rules of grammatical expression since Boileau. The pied-noir Marie Cardinal was the first to unpack with devastating precision this question of form and grammar in her autobiographical novel, *Les Mots pour le dire*, a title that was in dialogue with Boileau's 1674 'Art poétique' and that became an instant feminist and psychoanalytic success in 1975.[16]

But, if literature can indeed be such a freeing home for those who have had to resist oppression and abandon dangerous and destructive nation-states, the 'pleasures of exile', to use George Lamming's ironic formulation (Lamming 1991), are not equally distributed, and 'exile in language' yields levels of transnational or creolized creativity that can only become legible in terms of various dissymmetries and their performative functions at the level of both identity and linguistic competences. The binary French/Francophone has now led to such a hierarchized approach that one can well understand why Francophone writers are motivated to reject the contested cultural and political label of francophonie. They argue that it minoritizes and segregates them in a discursive space that denies them access to the Republican ideal of unmarked identity, to a literary glory comparable to that of native-born French luminaries or, as in the case of the 1970s and 80s feminists, to the joys of intransitive writing and purely poetic transcendence.

Resistance to the concept of francophonie takes many forms because it also sets up a dichotomy between foreign-born French speakers who acquire the language *in situ* and French citizens from the *départements d'Outremer* who are classified among non-citizens. Patrick Corcoran's timely 2007 *Cambridge Introduction to Francophone Literature* opens by stressing that the winners of those 'prestigious French literary prizes have included a significant number of "francophone" writers.' But then, he proceeds to identify some by geographic origin: 'the Moroccan Tahar Ben Jelloun, the Martinican Patrick Chamoiseau, the Lebanese Amin Malouf' in contrast to 'a string of writers such as Jonathan Littell […], Dai Sijie, François Cheng […], and Andreï Makine […] *who are at best French by "adoption",* and therefore foreigners rather than simply francophone' (Corcoran 2007: 1, emphasis added). These foreigners' arrival on the scene, their *venue à l'écriture* in French is the result of a choice generally made in adulthood, and a function of their place on a Parisian map of merit that usually predates their renown as *global* French writers. As a result, the label Francophone is arguably as ill-suited to them as it is to the expatriate English-Canadian and 2006 Prix Femina, Nancy Huston, or the exiled Afghani and 2008 Prix Goncourt, Afiq Rahimi.

Or is it?

The question of labels, and the hierarchies they underwrite, has become increasingly uncomfortable for those Paris-based writers who are part of a cosmopolitan scene in which the use of French tends toward a renewed appreciation of the universalism of a 'world Republic of Letters' centred in the European capital, and aspiring to rival global English and the planetary vitality of that language in the works of such postcolonial anglophone writers as Ben Okri, Amitav Ghosh, Arundhati Roy or Salman Rushdie. The situation seems particularly challenging for the critics who pontificate each year on these matters, and who would like to set the rules by which writers and editors play the autumn games of literary value and competitive schmoozing, and who now raise questions not just about the intrinsic literary value of particular novels but also about numerous extrinsic considerations that may remain unstated publicly, because the field of the literary is supposed to remain, at least nominally, 'autonomous'.

The manifesto's strange appeal resides precisely in its ability to merge opposing formulations: the extrinsic and the intrinsic, the national and the global, the referential and the non-referential, that is, on the one hand, the world of the real: 'le grand absent', 'le monde revient'; and on the other, words freed from all constraints: 'language liberated … free from any power except for those of poetry and the imagination'. The document thus blithely resolves all contradictions in a utopian declaration of faith in a world of fiction that 'n'aura plus de frontières que celles de l'esprit'.

The underlying questions that this approach raises tend to fall into various patterns of comparative and historical valuation: how are 'we' (French critics) to name this 'new' global literature and its contributions to 'our' universal canon? Is there a common denominator among these users of the French language? Do they represent the emergence of a new trend, a new style of *appartenance* that combines specifically French as well as global sensibilities? Or is this the contemporary incarnation of a familiar Enlightenment ideology, namely, a twenty-first century universalism in the era of *mondialisation*? If *littérature française* and *littérature francophone* are no longer acceptable categories, then does *littérature-monde* do a better job of describing and conceptualizing the intellectual and creative challenges of the field? Does it translate better the realities of today?

In other words, these are reflections that go to the heart of the French understanding of literary modernity, an understanding that constructs literature as a field of forces with intrinsic and unique rules where writing, reading, and translation (in the many senses of that word) must conform to their own regulatory principles in order to participate fully in the democratic public sphere in which actors compete for recognition and status. As stated earlier, Paris plays a crucial and central role in this ideology of literary modernity. The manifesto tries to distance itself from that ideology, but it keeps falling back into a defensive return to the power of pure poetry and the liberated imagination, both of which are universalized in terms of the system of value that underwrites modernity *en français*.

Performing Francophonies, Translating Universalisms

It is naïve to think that language and power can be so readily de-coupled. The prescriptive efforts to bury the concept of francophonie and to urge writers to grab on to the stakes of world literature *in French*, did not sit well with Abdou Diouf (2007), the Senegalese secretary general of the OIF, who published an immediate response in *Le Monde* stating that the declarations of these 'grave-diggers of francophonie' can only serve to reinforce French condescension toward Francophone writing. He writes: 'The French language doesn't belong only to the French, it belongs to all those who have chosen to learn it, to use it, to fertilize it with the accents of their own cultures, of their own imagination, of their own talents' (Diouf 2007). In a somewhat different vein, Lilian Kesteloot, the grande dame of African literary criticism from the 1960s, writing from Dakar, published a joint response with Amadou Lamine Sall, in which they both argued that liberation from the nation was emphatically not a sufficient answer for writers whose very use of French constitutes a form of alienation from their native cultures and languages, however successful they are at transforming the idioms of the borrowed colonial tongue into a truly 'world' language that carries an array of exogenous cultural connotations and inflections, hybridized with local vernaculars (Sall and Kesteloot 2007).

Setting up 'francophonie' as a field of multiple idioms, a heteroglossic and creative medium, Diouf and Sall/Kesteloot proceed from different ideological positions, the former emphasizing the world-wide 'ownership' of a language that was never tied to a 'national' identity if your perspective on it is a non-hexagonal one; and the latter cautioning against any easy evacuation of national moorings for the creative writer whose imaginative and poetic potential is necessarily mediated by language and geography.

What these eminent Africanists dwell on is the oppositional dyad francophonie/ *littérature-monde* that the manifesto sets up, thus legitimizing a false model of opposing singularities, as though there were only two monolithic entities face to face: the French language on the one hand, and the colonial field of francophonie on the other, the suffix-phone becoming the index of an embarrassing status ('No one speaks "francophone" or writes in francophone') that reinforces the linguistic hegemony and purity of French, despite protests to the contrary. Indeed, the suggestion, reiterated and developed by Michel Le Bris in his own expanded essay 'Pour une littérature-monde en français' in the collection published by Gallimard a few months after the manifesto (Le Bris and Rouaud 2007), is that French is sufficiently universal to become the ideal vehicle of the 'translated men' à la Rushdie. It is especially interesting to note that the initial title of both the manifesto and the expanded essay is 'Pour une littérature-monde en français' whereas the 'en français' has been deleted from the title of the book, thus making it echo the more obviously comparative concepts of *weltliteratur* and 'world literature' (which refer to literatures in *all* languages), and thus making it appear to endorse the cosmo- politan character of literary production in a truly 'global' Republic of Letters. Such an echo however, is thoroughly disingenuous and misleading because Le Bris and Rouaud have in mind 'le monde *en français*'. And what might that mean? That French is so capacious as to be able to render accurately, poetically as well as imaginatively, the cosmopolitanism so admired by the heirs of Enlightenment ideologies and the proponents of a multilingual, planetary field of literary achieve- ments? Perhaps it is, but then it is no longer just 'French'. It becomes the very practice of francophonie in its diverse manifestations that Abdou Diouf (2007) eloquently defends, and that this essay began by pointing out in regard to the palimpsestic nature of the writing practices of bilingual authors who explore new notions of space, of interiority and exteriority, and of belonging and difference in non-binary ways.

The Lebanese writer, lawyer, and literary journalist, Alexandre Najjar, in a piece that he entitles, after a Lebanese proverb, 'Explaining water as water', also bemoans the short sighted and disingenuous nature of the manifesto. He states that it is 'doubly distressing' because it is signed by the same Francophone writers who are now trying to make the term 'tacky', thus sowing doubt in readers' minds about the health of a lively field, 'while at the same time most of them are part of francophone institutions or juries of francophone prizes' (Najjar 2007). Najjar points out that francophonie had just been celebrated the previous year during a very successful Salon du livre in Paris, and he adds:

> [The manifesto] includes, on the other hand, unacceptable errors which need to be corrected: the fact that the major French prizes were awarded this year to writers 'outside France' is by no means a 'Copernican revolution'. This phenomenon is nothing new [...] The notion of world literature in French means nothing, it's nothing but a periphrase for francophonie, which is the totality of those who, in all four corners of the earth, share in the use of French. 'He explained water as water', says a Lebanese proverb. This is just what all this is about. For what is francophonie if not the French language 'open to the world and transnational', the very same definition they want to give to 'world literature in French'? (Najjar 2007)

Finally, the longest and most sustained engagement with the ideas and rhetorical moves of this manifesto comes from Camille de Toledo's *Visiter le Flurkistan ou les illusions de la littérature monde*, a thought-provoking, at times devastating, at others poignant, close reading of the document. He makes many excellent points about its lack of critical and conceptual clarity, but he too fails to address the special status of bilingual writers and the distinct relationship they have with a language that is not their mother tongue. He writes: 'In this respect, the writers from "the inside" and those from "the outside" are in almost complete agreement concerning the rules, the practices, the material' (Toledo 2008: 57). He adds, 'Car tous, nous fûmes, un jour ou l'autre, colonisés par une langue' (Toledo 2008: 58), thus falling into an all too familiar model of universal trauma – the violence of language – without regard for the 'gigantic inequality' (Balibar 2011: 207–225) that material dissymmetries and different histories of loss invariably generate.

Toledo's statements assume an implicit understanding of and agreement with the Lacanian distinction between the Imaginary and the Symbolic whereby the acquisition of language marks the child's entry into the paternal phallic order, 'the name of the father' (Lacan 1968: 41). But many Francophone texts destabilize that universalizing distinction, since a multilingual subject's relation to language is necessarily different from that of a monolingual speaker, and the affective and creative use of a language varies according to *how* it was learned: on one's 'mother's knees'; as a result of a more or less forcible 'wrenching' or 'deracination' (Toledo 2008: 57) through colonization and education in the 'other's' colonial idiom; or by a decision freely made to add it to one's repertoire. These radically different contexts cannot all produce an 'almost complete agreement concerning the rules, the practices, the material', as Toledo puts it (Toledo 2008: 57). Each of the above situations of 'colonization' by language needs to be understood as singular and contextually specific, all the more so in multilingual sites. Saint Augustine already knew this and wrote eloquently in his *Confessions* about having been forced to learn Latin and Greek under the constant threat of 'cruel punishments' that he contrasts with the playful and affectionate apprenticeship of his mother tongue (Saint Augustine 1979: 35).[17]

To argue, therefore, in favour of the term francophonies, in the plural, is to cut through the false universalisms that unexamined theories of trauma such as Toledo's (2008) can lead to. Francophonies has always suggested that 'French' when used in different parts of the world acquires local specificities, which is what Diouf (2007) means when he explains that the language belongs to all those who 'have chosen to learn it, to use it, to fertilize it'. Francophone literatures, like anglophone, sinophone, lusophone or hispanophone literatures, are not metropolitan literatures, they represent many decentered sites of creative energies, contestations, and post- as well as de-colonial activities. The suffix -phone serves to undermine the hegemonic implications of 'French', English', 'Spanish' or 'Chinese' as powerful national traditions *into* which might be incorporated the marginal writers whose talent wins them a seat at the banquet of canonical games or at the *Académie française*, that ever vigilant guardian of the standard language, even if its role is also to accept – and legislate – poetic deviations from the norms.

What seems clearer at this point in the discussion is that the idea of francophonies may need to be deployed and developed in the direction indicated by a recent anthology edited by Dohra Ahmad (2007) and published by Norton. It is entitled

Rotten English, after Ken Saro-Wiwa's expression to refer to non-standard English and to 'what would have once been derogatorily termed "dialect literature", [...] slang, creole, patois, pidgin' as the book cover explains (Ahmad 2007). The anthology includes examples of classics of Southern American writing (Mark Twain and Zora Neale Hurston), Jamaican English (Louise Bennett, Claude McKay), Dominican- or Chicano-American 'Spanglish' (Junot Diaz, Gloria Anzaldúa), Irish writing (Roddy Doyle), Nigerian English (Uzodinma Iweala, Chinua Achebe), and the idioms of a Pakistani-Londoner (Gautam Malkani), as well as a Maori poet (Patricia Grace). Useful cultural contexts are given, thus 'translating' for readers unfamiliar with non-standard uses of English.

Similarly, 'translating' between vernacular *Frenches* and French can be a more successful way of opening up literature to a new universality: one that is inclusive of these transnational differences. According to Zygmunt Bauman (1999), true universality is the actual ability to translate differences into an acknowledgement of diversity. He writes:

> Far from being a peculiar pastime of a narrow set of specialists, 'translation' is woven into the extreme of daily life and practised daily and hourly by us all [...] In this common ability to reach effective communication without recourse to already shared meanings and agreed interpretation the possibility of universalism is vested. Universality is not the enemy of difference; it does not require 'cultural homogeneity', nor does it need 'cultural purity' and particularly the kind of practices which that ideological term refers to. The pursuit of universality does not involve the smothering of cultural polyvalence or the pressure to reach cultural consensus. Universality means no more, yet no less either, than the across-the-species ability to communicate and reach mutual understanding – in the sense, I repeat, of 'knowing how to go on', but also knowing how to go on in the face of others who may go on – have the right to go on – differently. (Bauman 1999: 201–202)

Francophonies names the terrain on which effective communication happens among agents who do not possess in advance common meanings and interpretations. They might share a language, a basic frame of reference, but in each context that language fragments into a multiplicity of possible meanings and idioms, each related to other local vernaculars that irrigate, destabilize, or complicate it. Hence the concept offers a rich potential for an open understanding of universality. It is the forms of that new, inclusive, universality that will need to be further investigated in order for a properly 'global' concept of francophonies to come into being, and to take its own, *relative*, place in the world-literature system. Thus conceived, francophonies, in the plural, is the concept that would enable the kind of 'mutual understanding' called for by Bauman (1999). It would acknowledge that all users of the language have 'the right to go on – differently'. It would imply respect for and recognition of epistemological and ontological diversity. Such respect is, ultimately, the only viable ground of the search for meaning, of which contests over linguistic definitions are but a displaced intimation.

Notes

1 For a sharp rebuke about that state of depression, see John Jefferson Selve's interview with Camille de Toledo (Toledo 2007). All unreferenced citations are from the manifesto 'Pour une littérature-monde en français'.

2 Among many others, see Deleuze and Guattari (1975); Derrida (1996); Donadey (2000); Gauvin (1999); Lionnet (1991); Medded (1985); and Zabus (1991).

3 Glissant, who signed the manifesto, also insists that one writes today in the presence of 'l'imaginaire des langues [...] toutes les langues du monde [...] On ne peut plus écrire son paysage ni décrire sa propre langue de manière monolingue' (Glissant 1996: 112–113).

4 For a recent French articulation of the need for just such a reorientation of the western perspectives on modernity and universality, see Guillebaud (2008) and Lambert, Mongin and Padis (2009). In addition Bauman (1999) and Lionnet (1998) develop similar points from different angles.

5 In a brief interview on the 'Journal de France 2', on 10 April 2009, rebroadcast on TV5 Monde, about his new book, *Dictionnaire amoureux des langues* (Hagège 2009). The imperial political agenda of 'francophonie' dates back to the colonial geographer Onésime Reclus who coined the term in his book *France, Algérie et colonies* (Reclus 1886).

6 Alain Mabanckou, in 'La francophonie, oui ... le ghetto, non!' (Mabanckou 2006), argues for the inclusion of France into the 'grand ensemble' of francophonie. He provides a good critique that is subsequently cancelled out by his adhesion to the collective position adopted in the manifesto.

7 The 2005 *banlieue* riots, and the 2009 general strikes in the *départements d'Outremer* are recent examples of this problem. For a critique of the French Republican ideology of unicity, see Lionnet (2008b).

8 For a full discussion of this phenomenon, see English (2005).

9 Alexandre Najjar contests the validity of that expression, as explained and developed below (Najjar 2007).

10 For example, Laulan and Oillo (2008) and Wolton (2006).

11 Lionnet and Shih (2005). In November 2009, an international conference in Lisbon, Portugal focused on 'Going Caribbean'. The call for papers stated: 'This conference aims to open up new perspectives through the comparative study of Fiction and Art from the broader Francophone, Hispanic, Dutch, and Anglophone Caribbean as well as their respective Diasporas'. The work of Kathleen Gyssels (2006) has been instrumental for Caribbean studies.

12 Conferences have been organized in Algeria in 2008, in Florida in 2009, and volumes are in preparation, including this one.

13 An example of this oversight is Miller (2008: 122 ff.) He briefly mentions the Indian Ocean and Mauritius, but quotes selectively from Diderot's *Encyclopedia* and hence misunderstands the role of what was then known as the 'East Indies' in the dynamics of the 'Atlantic triangle'. For a discussion of 'The Indies', see Lionnet (2008a).

14 Wachtel (2006).

15 A term first used by Kimberlé W. Crenshaw (1991), and later by Valerie Smith (1998) in literary criticism.

16 'Ce qui se conçoit bien s'énonce clairement/Et les mots pour le dire viennent aisément' is Boileau's well-known formulation, learned by rote by many French and Francophone

school children (Boileau-Despréaux 1966: 227–229; Cardinal 1975). For a complete discussion, see Lionnet (1989: 194ff.)

17   For a detailed reading of that episode, see Lionnet (1989: 19–20, 35–66).

References

Ahmad, Dohra (2007), *Rotten English: A Literary Anthology*, New York: W.W. Norton.

Auerbach, Erich ([1952] 1969), 'Philology and *Weltliteratur*', *The Centennial Review*, 13: 1, pp. 1–17.

Augustine, Saint, Bishop of Hippo ([397–398] 1979), *Confessions* (trans. R.S. Pine-Coffin), New York: Penguin.

Balibar, Etienne (2011), 'Toward a Diasporic Citizen? From Internationalism to Cosmopolitics', in Françoise Lionnet and Shu-mei Shih (eds.), *The Creolization of Theory*, Duke University Press.

Baudelaire, Charles (1973), *Correspondance*, vol. 1, jan. 1832–fév. 1860, Claude Pichois and Jean Ziegler (eds.), Paris: Gallimard/Pléiade.

Bauman, Zygmunt (1999), *In Search of Politics*, Cambridge: Polity Press.

Boileau-Despréaux, Nicolas ([1674] 1966), 'Art Poétique', in Françoise Escal (ed.), *Oeuvres complètes*, Paris: Gallimard/Pléiade, pp. 227–229.

Bourdieu, Pierre (1979), *La distinction: critique social du jugement*, Paris: Minuit.

Breton, André (1944), 'Martinique, charmeuse de serpents : Un grand poète noir', *Tropiques*, 11, pp. 119–126.

Cardinal, Marie (1975), *Les mots pour le dire*, Paris: Grasset.

Casanova, Pascale (1999), *La République mondiale des Lettres*, Paris: Seuil.

Corcoran, Patrick (2007), *The Cambridge Introduction to Francophone Literature*, Cambridge: Cambridge University Press.

Crenshaw, Kimberlé W. (1991), 'Demarginalizing the Intersection of Race and Sex: A Black Feminist Critique of Antidiscrimination Doctrine, Feminist Theory, and Antiracist Politics', in Katharine Bartlett and Roseanne Kennedy (eds.), *Feminist Legal Theory*, Boulder, Co.: Westview Press, pp. 57–80.

Deleuze, Gilles and Guattari, Felix (1975), *Kafka: Pour une littérature mineure*, Paris: Minuit.

Derrida, Jacques (1996), *Le monolinguisme de l'autre ou la prothèse d'origine*, Paris: Galilée.

Des Rosiers, Joël (1998), 'Entretiens' with Catherine Le Pelletier', in *Encre noire: La Langue en liberté*, Guadeloupe: Ibis rouge, pp. 32–39.

Diouf, Abdou (2007), 'La francophonie, une réalité oubliée', *Le Monde*, 20 March.

Donadey, Anne (2000), 'The Multilingual Strategies of Postcolonial Literature: Assia Djebar's Algerian Palimpsest', *World Literature Today*, 74: 1, pp. 27–36.

English, James F. (2005), *The Economy of Prestige: Prizes, Awards, and the Circulation of Cultural Value*, Cambridge: Harvard University Press.

Fish, Stanley ([1976] 1980), 'Interpreting the Variorum', *Is There A Text in This Class?*, Cambridge: Harvard University Press, pp. 147–174.

Gauvin, Lise (1999), *Les langues du roman: Du plurilinguisme comme stratégie textuelle*, Montréal: Presses de l'Université de Montréal.

Glissant, Édouard (1996), "L'imaginaire des langues." Interview with Lise Gauvin in *Introduction à une poétique du divers,* Paris: Gallimard, pp. 111–143.

Glissant, Edouard (1997), *Traité du Tout-Monde*, Paris: Gallimard.

Guillebaud, Jean-Claude (2008), *Le commencement d'un monde: vers une modernité métisse*, Paris: Seuil.

Gyssels, Kathleen (2006), *Passes et impasses du comparatisme postcolonial. Parcours transfrontaliers de la diaspora africaine aux Amériques*, Thèse d'Habilitation en Littérature générale et comparée, Paris: Université de la Paris III/Sorbonne-Nouvelle.

Hagège, Claude (2009), *Dictionnaire amoureux des langues*, Paris: Plon/Odile Jacob.

Lacan, Jacques (1968), *Speech and Language in Psychoanalysis* (trans. Anthony Wilden), Baltimore: The Johns Hopkins University Press.

Lambert, Julie, Mongin, Olivier, and Padis, Marc-Olivier (2009), 'Entretien avec Jean-Claude Guillebaud', *Esprit*, 352, February, pp. 51–60.

Lamming, George ([1960]1991), *The Pleasures of Exile*, Ann Arbor: University of Michigan Press.

Laulan, Anne-Marie and Oillo, Didier (eds.) (2008), *Francophonie et mondialisation*, Paris: CNRS.

Le Bris, Michel, *et al.* (2007) 'Manifeste pour une littérature-monde en français', *Le Monde des livres*, 16 March, p. 2.

Le Bris, Michel (2007a), 'Pour une littérature-monde en français', *Pour une littérature-monde*, Sous la direction de Michel Le Bris et Jean Rouaud, Paris: Gallimard, pp. 23–53.

Le Bris, Michel and Rouaud, Jean (2007b), *Pour une littérature monde*, Paris: Gallimard.

Lionnet, Françoise (1989), *Autobiographical Voices: Race, Language, and Self-Portraiture*, Ithaca: Cornell University Press.

Lionnet, Françoise (1991), Anamnèse et utopie', in Charles Bonn (ed.), *Autobiographie et récits de vie dans les littératures africaines. Itinéraires et contacts de cultures*, 13, Paris: L'Harmattan, pp. 117–134.

Lionnet, Françoise (1998), 'Performative Universalism and Cultural Diversity', in Goux, Jean-Joseph and Wood, Philip (eds.), *Terror and Consensus: The Cultural Singularity of French Thought*, Stanford: Stanford University Press, pp. 119–132.

Lionnet, Françoise (2008a), '"The Indies": Baudelaire's Colonial World', *PMLA*, 123: 3, May, pp. 723–736.

Lionnet, Françoise (2008), 'Continents and Archipelagoes: From *E Pluribus Unum* to Creolized Solidarities', *PMLA*, 123: 5, October, pp. 1503–1515.

Lionnet, Françoise and Shih, Shu-mei (2011), *The Creolization of Theory*, Durham: Duke University Press.

Lionnet, Françoise and Shih, Shu-mei (2005), *Minor Transnationalism*, Durham: Duke University Press.

Mabanckou, Alain (2006), 'La francophonie, oui … le ghetto, non!', *Le Monde,* 19 March.

Medded, Abdelwahab (1985), 'Le palimpseste du bilingue', in Abdelkébir Khatibi (ed.), *Du bilinguisme*, Paris: Denoël, pp. 125–140.

Miller, Christopher L. (2008), *The French Atlantic Triangle: Literature and Culture of The Slave Trade*, Durham: Duke University Press.

Mudimbe-Boyi, Elisabeth (2009), 'Introduction', in Elisabeth Mudimbe-Boyi (ed.), *Empire Lost: France and Its Other Worlds*, Lanham: Lexington Books, pp. xi–xxiii.

Najjar, Alexandre (2007), 'Contre le manifeste 'Pour une littérature-monde en français': *Expliquer l'eau par l'eau*', http://www.najjar.org/litteratureMondeEnFrancais.asp. Accessed 25 September 2013.

Paré, François (1992), *Les littératures de l'exiguité*, Hearst, Ontario: Le Nordir.

Reclus, Onésime (1886), *France, Algérie et colonies*, Paris: Hachette.

Sainte-Beuve, Charles Augustin (1844), 'Poètes et romanciers modernes de la France—L. Parny', *Revue des Deux Mondes*, 8, pp. 816–843, http://fr.wikisource.org/wiki/Poètes_et_romanciers_modernes_de_la_France_-_L._Parny. Accessed 10 April 2009.

Sall, Amadou Lamine and Kesteloot, Lilyan (2007), 'Un peu de mémoire, s'il vous plaît', *Le Monde*, 6 April.

Smith, Valerie (1998), *Not Just Race, Not Just Gender: Black Feminist Readings*, New York: Routledge.

Tadié, Jean-Yves (ed.) with M. Delon, F. Mélonio, B. Marchal, J. Noiray, and A. Compagnon, (2007), *La littérature française: dynamique et histoire*, vol. II, Paris: Gallimard/Folio.

Toledo, Camille de (2007), 'Contre une littérature déprimée et/ou nombriliste'. Interview with John Jefferson Selve, http://bibliobs.nouvelobs.com/2007/10/02/contre-une-litterature-deprimee-et-ou-nombriliste. Accessed 10 April 2009.

Toledo, Camille de (2008), *Visiter le Flurkistan ou les illusions de la littérature monde*, Paris: PUF.

Tzara, Tristan ([1918] 1973), 'Dada manifeste sur l'amour faible et l'amour amer', *Lampisteries précédées de sept manifestes dada*, Paris: Pauvert.

Vincent-Munnia, Nathalie, Bernard-Griffiths, Simone, and Pickering, Robert (2003), *Aux origines du poème en prose français: 1750–1850*, Paris: Champion.

Viswanathan, Gauri (2000), An Introduction: Uncommon Genealogies', *ARIEL: A Review of International English Literature*, 31: 1–2, January, pp. 13–31.

Wachtel, Michael (2006), 'Pushkin's Long Poems and the Epic Impulse', in Andrew Kahn (ed.), *The Cambridge Companion to Pushkin*, Cambridge: Cambridge University Press, pp. 75–89.

Wikipedia: the free encyclopedia (2009), entry on 'Maryse Condé', http://en. wikipedia.org/wiki/Maryse_Condé. Accessed 10 April 2009.

Wolff, Mark (2001), 'Individuality and l'Esprit Français: On Gustave Lanson's Pedagogy', *MLQ: Modern Language Quarterly*, 62: 3, pp. 239–257.

Wolton, Dominique (2006), *Demain la francophonie*, Paris: Flammarion.

Zabus, Chantal (1991), *The African Palimpsest: Indigenization of Language in the West African Europhone Novel*, Amsterdam: Rodopi.

23

Orientalism and the Institution
of World Literatures (2010)

Aamir R. Mufti

Aamir R. Mufti is a professor of comparative literature at the University of California, Los Angeles, where he has taught since completing his doctoral thesis under Edward Said's supervision at Columbia University. His work builds on Said's methodology and postcolonial approach as described in his influential *Orientalism*, extending his analysis to a fuller account of the role of religion in a secularizing world. Mufti looks at the secularization thesis from a comparative perspective, analyzing Islam, modernity in India, and the cultural politics of Jewish identity in Western Europe. In 1997, Mufti co-edited the collection *Dangerous Liaisons: Gender, Nation, and Postcolonial Perspectives*, which focuses on the interdisciplinary crossings between gender, nation, identity, and history within postcoloniality. His book *Enlightenment in the Colony: The Jewish Question and the Crisis of Postcolonial Culture* (2007) examines the late nineteenth-century conflict in India between Hindus and Muslims as a non-Western variation of the crisis of Jewishness in Europe, concluding that modernization rises globally with the national awareness which defines itself against an alienated minority.

In the essay given here, Mufti challenges world literature studies as a depoliticized mode of reading: "world literature is fundamentally a concept of exchange … that recodes an opaque and unequal process of appropriation as a transparent one of supposedly free and equal interchange and communication." Mufti analyzes the case of colonial India to sketch "the formidable structure of cultural domination" imposed by the West on much of the world. Mufti argues that in India's case, the Orientalists' cultural agenda produced the narrative of India as a single nation with a distinct voice in world circulation, decades before Goethe's naming of this practice as *Weltliteratur*. Mufti goes on to look into the global relations of force that are at the

Aamir R. Mufti, "Orientalism and the Institution of World Literatures" (2010). In *Critical Inquiry* 36:3 (2010), pp. 458–493. © 2010 by The University of Chicago.

World Literature in Theory, First Edition. Edited by David Damrosch.
© 2014 John Wiley & Sons, Ltd. Published 2014 by John Wiley & Sons, Ltd.

heart of the concept of world literature, initially imagined within a nationalist project, to the detriment of the true diversity of culture in the Indian subcontinent. Mufti concludes by proposing "a concept of world literature (and practices of teaching it) that works to reveal the ways in which 'diversity' itself – national, religious, civiliza- tional, continental – is a colonial and Orientalist problematic."

What Is World Literature?

In the current revival of the concept of world literature, something of considerable importance appears to be largely missing: the question of Orientalism. Despite the reputation of Edward Said's *Orientalism* as a sort of foundational text for concern with cultural relations on a planetary scale, the specifics of that book's conceptual armature or the archive with which it engages do not seem to play a significant role in this renewed discussion and intensification of interest in the effort to comprehend literature as a planet wide reality.

This is the case for instance with Pascale Casanova's *The World Republic of Letters*, which presents an argument about the emergence of international literary space in Europe in the early modern era and its expansion across the continent and beyond over the last four centuries.[1] The overall armature of the book rests on the identification of three key moments in the development of this international literary space and seems to follow fairly closely the chronology established by Benedict Anderson in *Imagined Communities*. The first, its moment of origin, so to speak, is the extended and uneven process of vernacularization in the emerging European states from the fourteenth to the seventeenth centuries. The next turning point and period of massive expansion comes, she argues, again following Anderson's periodization, in the "philological-lexigraphic revolution" starting in the late eighteenth century and the widely dispersed invention of national traditions that ensued.[2] Casanova argues that the new practice of literature to emerge in the late eighteenth and early nineteenth centuries, linked to a new conception of language and its relationship to its community of speakers, emerged within and as a modality of a massive shift and expansion in European world literary space. The third and, for Casanova, ongoing, period in the expansion of this world literary space is linked to the historical "event" of decolonization in the post-World War II era.

My point of entry into this formulation is what I take to be its most consequen- tial misconception: for Casanova, non-Western literary cultures make their first effective appearance in world literary space in the era of decolonization in the middle of the twentieth century. Casanova thus fails to comprehend the real nature of the expansion and rearrangement of this until then largely European space in the course of the philological revolution. It is through the philological knowledge revolution – the "discovery" of the classical languages of the East, the invention of the linguistic family tree whose basic form is still with us today, the translation and absorption into the Western languages of more and more works from Persian,

Arabic, and the Indian languages, among others – that non-Western textual traditions made their first entry *as literature*, sacred and secular, into the international literary space that had emerged in early modern times in Europe as a structure of rivalries between the emerging vernacular traditions, transforming the scope and structure of that space forever. This moment, which she reads almost entirely through Herder, is mistaken by Casanova for a redrawing of the internal cultural map of Europe rather than as a reorganization that is planetary in nature, in the sense that this emerging constellation of philological knowledge, perhaps best known to us now from Said's reading of it in *Orientalism*, posits nothing less than the languages and cultures of the entire world as its object in the final instance. As is well known, in his writings of the 1770s, including the *Treatise on the Origin of Language*, Herder began to mark a break with conceptions of the origin of language that had been dominant in the eighteenth century, which viewed the origin and development of language as such as part of the history of humanity; we need only think here of the well-known works of such contemporaries of Herder's as Rousseau, Condillac, and Mendelssohn. He argued instead that human intelligence always took a historical form and could only be exercised in language, in particular languages in particular places at particular times. The consequences of the rise and acceptance of some of these ideas about the boundedness of thought in language, from the emergence of secular methodologies of interpretation of the scriptures ultimately to romantic notions about the imagination and history, and even, over a century later, in the forms of cultural relativism that are foundational to British and American anthropology – both Franz Boas and Bronislaw Malinowski had received the German Herderian heritage as part of their intellectual formations – are too well known to require rehearsing here.[3] My point here is a more circumscribed one: the nearly exclusive focus on Herder's writings of the early 1770s, which predate the infusion into the European intellectual-literary sphere of the properly Orientalist ideas of linguistic and cultural diversity, allows Casanova to formulate her argument about the transformation of (European) world literary space without reference to the gestalt shift made possible by the assimilation of the Oriental exempla that became increasingly available to European reading publics in large numbers for the first time from the 1770s gradually onward.[4] (I return shortly to the history and modalities of this dissemination.)

Because Casanova misses this initial charting of non-Western traditions of writing on the emerging map of the literary world (as in fact in many of the recent discussions about transnational literary relations), such figures as Kateb Yacine, V.S. Naipaul, and Salman Rushdie and the psychology of *assimilation* into metropolitan languages and cultures typify the non-Western writer (as they all do for Casanova). Such models of cultural change as creolization and *métissage* consequently become the privileged mode of understanding literatures originating outside the metropolis, and the far more complex and elusive tensions and contradictions involved in the emergence of the modern non-Western literatures disappear from view altogether.

In other words, I propose we take seriously what would appear to be a rather obvious historical claim but one that has not been rigorously present in a great deal of contemporary critical discussion, namely, that the deep encounter between English and the other Western languages and the languages of the global periphery as media of literary expression did not take place for the first time in the postcolonial era, let alone in the supposedly transnational transactions of the period of high globalization but, especially, at the dawn of the modern era itself and fundamentally transformed both cultural formations involved in the encounter.

The effects of the reorganization of culture and knowledge in the course of the philological revolution were far-reaching, not just for the European intelligentsia, but for those very colonized and semicolonized societies, and more specifically the textual traditions, that were now brought under the purview of these new knowledge practices. In order to comprehend the structure of literary relations that is now a planet wide reality, we need to grasp the role that philological Orientalism played in producing and establishing a method and a system for classifying and evaluating diverse forms of textuality, now all processed and codified uniformly as literature. As Vinay Dharwadker has argued in a pioneering essay, the forms taken by "British and European representations of literary India ... lie not so much in the 'nature' of the Indian materials as in the intellectual contexts of European literary thought."[5] The (now universal) category of literature, with its particular Latinate etymology and genealogy, marks this process of assimilation of diverse cultures of writing, a process only partially concealed by the use of such vernacular terms as *'adab* (Arabic, Persian, Urdu) and *sāhitya* (Hindi and a number of the Indian vernaculars) to signify the new literariness.

In this essay, I attempt to suggest ways of thinking critically about the profound consequences of these new structures of knowledge for language, literature, and culture, and more broadly for the politics of identity, in the Indian subcontinent in the course of the nineteenth century. Such a project is a response to suggestions in *Orientalism* – as I read it, against a great deal of contemporary Said reception, I might add – that the critique of Orientalism must ultimately take us to the Orientalized spaces themselves. For Orientalism in Said's sense consists of those Western knowledge practices in the modern era whose emergence made possible for the first time the notion of a single world as a space populated by distinct civilizational complexes, each in possession of its own tradition, the unique expression of its own forms of national "genius."[6] A precise, aphoristic formulation of this question comes in one brief sentence in Said's luminous essay on the late works of Jean Genet: "Imperialism is the export of identity."[7] Orientalism is for Said the name for the vast cultural (and, more specifically, philological) machinery in modern Western imperialism for the establishment of identitarian truth-claims around the world. Said's critique of Orientalism is thus directed as much toward "readers in the so-called Third World" as anyone else, and for them "this study proposes itself as a step towards an understanding not so much of Western politics and of the non-Western world in those politics as of the *strength* of Western cultural discourse, a strength too often mistaken as merely decorative or 'superstructural.' My hope is to illustrate the *formidable structure of cultural domination* and, specifically for formerly colonized peoples, *the dangers and temptations of employing this structure upon themselves or upon others.*" Recalling Gramsci's assertion, in the *Prison Notebooks*, of the "imperative" to produce an "inventory" of the "infinity of traces" that the historical process has left upon the critical subject itself, Said concludes that in "many ways my study of Orientalism has been an attempt to inventory the traces upon me, an Oriental subject, of the culture whose domination has been so powerful a factor in the life of all Orientals." Thus, far from ignoring the possibility of historically autonomous action on the part of the colonized, and far from viewing Orientalism as a totalizing and absolute system of representation, as careless readers have sometimes suggested over the years, Said's critique of Orientalism amounts to a *call* to precisely such action, an invitation to historical self-transformation in the very process of the "critical elaboration" of the self.[8]

Said places the rise of modern Orientalism within the general process of secularization of Western culture in the early modern era. His account of this process is of some interest to us here:

> Modern Orientalism derives from secularizing elements in eighteenth-century European culture.... But if these interconnected elements represent a secularizing tendency, this is not to say that the old religious patterns of human history and destiny and "the existential paradigms" were simply removed. Far from it: they were reconstituted, redeployed, redistributed in the secular frameworks just enumerated. For anyone who studied the Orient a secular vocabulary in keeping with these frameworks was required. Yet if Orientalism provided the vocabulary, the conceptual repertoire, the techniques – for this is what, from the end of the eighteenth century on, Orientalism *did* and what Orientalism *was* – it also retained, as an undislodged current in its discourse, *a reconstructed religious impulse*, a naturalized supernaturalism. [*O*, p. 121; emphasis added]

Said's critique of Orientalism is thus in essence a criticism of its "naturalized supernaturalism," of its remapping of humanity in terms of supposedly secular cultural logics whose Manichean modalities with respect to human collectivities, and in particular those societies that are Christianity's traditional antagonists, can only be understood as a "reconstructed religious impulse." In this sense, *Orientalism* may be said to offer an account of the cultural logic of (Western) bourgeois society in its global or outward orientation, in its encounter with and reorganization of human societies on a planetary scale. Against this, as it were, *false* appearance of the secular in history and its attendant antagonisms – a fundamentally localized (that is, Western) emergence that simultaneously carries the force of the universal in history – Said points not so much to a utopian and distant future without those, as it were, theological antagonisms as to the possibility in the historical present of "surviving the consequences" of these structures and logics "humanly" (*O*, p. 45). Said conceives of this antiidentitarian imperative as the classically *secular* critical task, concerned with the here and now, attentive to the dense and ultimately unassimilable fabric of society – which would barely require repeating, were it not for some remarkably fanciful characterizations of his project current today. It is no accident that "Secular Criticism" is the main conceptual essay of the first book that follows *Orientalism*, for it may in some important ways be read as a methodological reflection on the critical project of the latter. As I have noted elsewhere, the figure of Erich Auerbach exiled in Istanbul that provides a sort of running leitmotif in that essay is an exemplary figure for secular criticism in Said's terms precisely because, as a figure of displacement and dispossession, it marks a certain distance and fissure from the transcendentalization of cultural authority, forms of reckoning cultural transmission and descent that are based, as it were, on the "quasi-religious authority of being comfortably at home among one's people."[9] The critique of Orientalism (and of imperialism more broadly) is inseparable for Said from criticism of the religious as such, understood as all those cultural forms, both the traditionally religious and the conventionally secular, whose appeal to authority is placed outside the fabric of social interest and the possibility of historical transformation. Secular criticism is in that sense a radically historical practice, opposed in concrete and detailed ways to metaphysical grounding and authorization of culture, both secular and religious, constantly unearthing its social filiations and affiliations and identifying the "human" costs of failing to subject to such criticism the process of critical thinking itself. This basic aspect of Said's project is lost on those of his current readers who have found their way to the emerging orthodoxy of the "postsecular" in the humanistic disciplines and yet cannot quite let go of the radical cachet of this eviscerating book even as they take more and more conservative positions, producing self-interested and spectacular (even gymnastic) contortions, with the Saidian text marshaled in the interest of projects and purposes far removed from its own explicit and implicit commitments and affiliations.[10] Taking up once again this foundational concern of *Orientalism*, I am concerned here ultimately with the significance of historical Orientalism for the fabrication, in non-Western societies in the course of the nineteenth and twentieth centuries, of forms of cultural authority tied to the claim to authenticity of (religious, cultural, and national) "tradition" – *turāth*, *rivāyat*, or *paramparā* in some of the languages that will concern us here – and thus for the emergence of the kinds of social fissure that have often accompanied such transitions. In this sense both religious and secular traditions in the modern era – the Arab tradition and Islamic orthodoxy, for instance, or Indian civilization and Hinduism – are products of the Orientalist conjuncture and, far from excluding the religious, the secular complexes have themselves been produced by their anchoring in religious elements configured in majoritarian terms.

This, I want to suggest, is the suppressed element in the concept of world literature from its inception, namely, the far-reaching refashioning of the cultures and societies of the world in the new phase of colonial expansion that accompanied and followed from the Industrial Revolution. By the time Goethe coins the term *world literature* in the last years of his life in the late 1820s – his first reported use of it is in the context of his having recently read a "Chinese novel" – it represents a retrospective look, with the global shifts in the structures of "literary" knowledge it is intended to reference having already been a long established reality, including of course in the life of the poet himself, who, as is well known, was deeply affected in 1791 on reading a translation of Kalidasa's *Śakuntalā* – well before his better known encounter with the verse of Hafiz in the second decade of the next century, to which I return below. And by the time the term is resurrected by Marx and Engels more than a decade after the publication of the *Conversations with Eckermann*, which had reported its earliest use by Goethe, it is relatively speaking an old story indeed, appearing within a historical account of the rise and growth of the bourgeoisie as a global social force.[11] It is the effects of these shifts on the colonized societies themselves, which constitute the objects, properly speaking, of the Orientalists' endeavors, that I am concerned with here. Whether we view world literature (with Franco Moretti) as a conceptual organization rather than a body of literary texts or (with David Damrosch) as a special kind of literature, that which circulates beyond its "culture of origin" – and this tension is inherent in and as old as the term itself – we cannot ignore the global relations of force that the concept simultaneously puts in play and hides from view.[12]

And, finally, taking seriously these scenarios of *domination* that emerged in the era of the birth of modern Orientalism will require some fairly dramatic revisioning of the model of national *competition* proposed by Casanova for what she calls the world republic of letters. The ongoing discussion about world literature, in the singular and plural, is both hugely encompassing and strangely timid; it seems unaware of the enormous role played by the institution of literature in the emergence of the hierarchies and identities that structure relations between societies in the modern world. The integration of widely dispersed and heterogeneous sociocultural formations into a global ensemble has taken place, especially at the most decisive periods in this historical process, disproportionately on and through this terrain. The concept and practices of world literature, far from representing the superseding of national forms of identification of language, literature, and culture, thus emerged for the first time precisely alongside the forms of thinking in the contemporary Western world that elsewhere I have referred to as nation-thinking – that is, those emergent modes of thinking in the West that are associated with the nationalization of social and cultural life and point toward the nation-state as the horizon of culture and society.[13] Our larger task is to comprehend the precise nature of this extended literary-philological moment, in which often-overlapping bodies of writing came to acquire, through a process of historicization, distinct personalities as literature along national lines. The institution of literature, which has not received as much scholarly attention in colonial studies as such practices as the census and ethnography, is chiefly significant for the historical role it played in the formation of the new colonial-national intelligentsias, formed in many colonized societies through the destruction of heterogeneous and ancient cultures of reading and writing.[14]

Orientalism and the Institution of Indian Literature

The role of the new Orientalist studies in the emergence of intellectual and literary cultures of a romantic bent in the West in the late eighteenth and early nineteenth century, and in the emergence of literature as such in the romantic and modern sense is not a developed subject of investigation today, but this has not always been the case, and in fact the role can hardly be overestimated. The influence is by no means limited to those famous (and numerous) romantic works – from *Vathek* (1786/1787) to *Kubla Khan* (1797?), *Lalla Rookh* (1817), the *West-Östlicher Divan* (1819/1827), *Confessions of an English Opium Eater* (1821), *Don Juan* (1819–1824), and beyond – that explicitly adopt Oriental themes, locales, or forms as their own but may be equated with the emergence of an entire cultural horizon, which Raymond Schwab famously conceived of as nothing less than a second, "Oriental" Renaissance in the West. The arrival in Europe and into the European languages of works originating in the classical languages of Asia and the Middle East had far-reaching effects on generations of writers in the West. Starting in the mid-1780s, Sanskrit works were added to the Persian and Arabic, soon superseding both in their ability to cause a "mania" among literary publics across Europe. Schwab, whose *La Renaissance orientale* (1950) remains to date the most detailed mapping of the emergence and development of this cultural horizon from the late eighteenth to the late nineteenth century, went so far as to view the rise of romanticism as little more than the extended "literary repercussions" of the Orientalist knowledge revolution.[15] And M.H. Abrams noted a few years after Schwab in his classic study of romantic aesthetics that the first systematic statement of what he called the emerging "expressive theory of poetry," seeking to establish lyric verse as the poetic norm, was penned by William Jones and appended to his first published collection of poetry, *Poems, Consisting Chiefly of Translations from the Asiatic Languages* (1772). This understanding of the origins of romanticism in the Orientalist conjuncture, routinely expressed by many of the writers themselves and restated at key moments in the history of romanticism studies, by such key figures as Schwab and Abrams, is with few exceptions the great forgotten of the discipline in our own times.[16]

Jones, whose enormous influence in the nineteenth century on several generations of writers and intellectuals on several continents is also largely forgotten today, played an almost unique role in both phases of the early development of modern Orientalism, first with his "imitations," in *Poems*, from classical Arabic, Persian, and Turkish poetry – most famous among them a *ghazal* of Hafiz – then with his Persian grammar and the *Histoire de Nader Chah*, his French translation of a contemporary Persian history of the marauding eighteenth-century Iranian ruler, and finally of course as the leading figure of the new Sanskrit studies to emerge from Calcutta after his arrival there in 1784. *Asiatick Researches*, the chief organ of the Calcutta Orientalists (launched by Jones in 1788), was republished and translated repeatedly in Europe, its diverse contents further disseminated through numerous reprintings and summaries in the popular press, and became the vehicle of their soaring celebrity. As Said put it memorably in his essay on Schwab, "the job of displacement was apportioned to the great capitals: Calcutta provided, London distributed, Paris filtered and generalized."[17] A huge range of writers in Europe and America, most famously Goethe, absorbed both these Orientalist waves, if not always in the chronological order of their unfolding. In Germany alone, during the so-called Indo-mania of the 1790s, triggered by Georg Foster's translation of *Śakuntalā* (1791) from Jones's English translation (1789), this icon of the new knowledge found its way into the work of Herder, Goethe, Schlegel, and Novalis, among numerous others, leading Schwab to refer to the entire age as a "*Śakuntalā* era."[18] The fabrication of Kalidasa as the "Indian Shakespeare," which took place first of all in Germany, marks perhaps the first assimilation of Sanskrit textual materials to the new category of literature and was to become instrumental in the nineteenth century in the repatriation, so to speak, of *Śakuntalā* to the emerging colonial-nationalist intelligentsia in India as "their" greatest contribution to world literature.[19] An unelaborated notion, if not always an explicitly formulated concept, of world literature itself became a feature of nationalist culture from the late nineteenth century onward. World literature was seen as the stage for the reconciliation of all that is specifically Indian with universal and human values as such – as suggested for instance by Rabindranath Tagore in "World Literature" ("Biśwasāhitya"), a well-known lecture first delivered in 1907.[20] And when Tagore extolled the greatness of the play, comparing it to *The Tempest*, he did so in part on the authority of Goethe.[21] In fact, since its appearance in the Orientalist canon *Śakuntalā* has been a cornerstone of that powerful and persistent modern narrative concerning the Orientalists' great "gift" to the Indian people of their own past and tradition – a narrative featured not merely in the official historiography of Orientalism into our own times but also in a wide range of nationalist writing in India itself, including, most famously perhaps, Jawaharlal Nehru's *The Discovery of India*: "To Jones and to the many other European scholars India owes a deep debt of gratitude for the rediscovery of her past literature."[22] And the early role played by Germany in this process should help us understand Orientalism itself as a pan-European system of relays that cannot be reduced to an unmediated logic of colonial *raison d'état*, a position that Said's critics have sometimes incorrectly attributed to him.[23]

The precise historical context for the birth of the new Orientalism in Calcutta, however, is more clearly colonial in an immediate sense, namely, in the ascendancy of British rule in India in the second half of the eighteenth century and the conquest of Bengal in particular. With the victory in the Battle of Plassey in 1757, the British found themselves for the first time in possession of a large contiguous territory populated by an expanse of agriculturalists and, having seized the revenues of Bengal in 1765, felt the need for systematic knowledge of Indian society, whose economic dimension was described over forty years ago by Ranajit Guha in his *A Rule of Property for Bengal*, a pioneering study of knowledge forms and their role in the transformation of colonized societies.[24] On his appointment as the first governor-general of India, Warren Hastings, whom Edmund Burke was to help impeach more than two decades later, began to create the first official and institutional context for the new Indological studies to emerge. Hastings is the first great patron and facilitator of this new philology emerging from Calcutta, and Jones, Nathaniel Brassey Halhed, Henry Thomas Colebrook, and Charles Wilkins were all officials of the East India Company under his administration.[25]

These early forays into the world of Sanskrit textuality betray anxieties about what was at least initially a near-blind reliance on the native practitioners and specialists of what appeared to the emerging Orientalists to be an ocean of indigenous learning. The "secretiveness" of the Brahmins is a constant anxiety in Jones's private correspondence, and the story of his gradual entry into the Sanskrit universe is often told as one of his winning over their trust and even love.[26] The relationship between the European scholar-administrator and his pundits, as they came to be called, constitutes the core institution of this early Indology, an institution that survived to some extent the great shift of the 1820s. Already by the first decade of the century, Indian philology had begun to acquire a more firmly textual basis in Europe itself. In the 1780s Jones and Wilkins could have acquired Sanskrit only in India; in 1803 Schlegel did so in Paris. Through the 1770s, the linguistic focus of the new research in Calcutta had remained on Persian, the language through which the British had largely come to know the history of India.[27] It is only gradually in these decades that these early scholars became acquainted with Sanskrit textual traditions, whose very existence had largely been a matter of rumor and sometimes of wild speculation until then.[28]

What this early generation of Orientalists encountered on the subcontinent was not one single culture of writing but rather a loose articulation of different, sometimes overlapping but often mutually exclusive, systems based variously in Persian, Sanskrit, and a large number of the vernaculars, often more than one in a single language, properly speaking.[29] Their writings reveal both a sense of elation as well as apprehensions at this encounter with an unknown of almost sublime proportions. I think we may speak here of a sort of philological sublime, a structure of encounter with a linguistic and cultural complexity of infinitesimal and dynamic differentiations and of seemingly infinite proportions. Sympathetic chroniclers of these intellectual developments, even into the twentieth century, cannot resist the language of incalculability. "He stood," writes Cannon of Jones at the threshold of his study of Sanskrit, "the pioneer and orienter, before a huge, unexplored knowledge." Jones's famous third-anniversary address to the Asiatic Society in Calcutta in 1786, in which he broached for the first time the claim for a genetic "affinity" between Sanskrit and Greek and Latin – the germ of the idea of the Indo-European family of languages – was itself intended as the first of five annual discourses that would elaborate a vast comparative anthropology of, as Cannon puts it, "titanic scope" to encompass the ancient continent:[30]

> The *five* principal nations, who have in different ages divided among themselves, as a kind of inheritance, the vast continent of *Asia*, with the many islands depending on it, are the *Indians*, the *Chinese*, the *Tartars*, the *Arabs*, and the *Persians*: *who* they severally

were, *whence*, and *when* they came, *where* they are now settled, and *what advantage* a more perfect knowledge of them may bring to our *European* world, will be shown, I trust, in *five* distinct essays; the last of which will demonstrate the connection or diversity among them, and solve the great problem, whether they had *any* common origin, and whether that origin was *the same*, which we generally ascribe to them.[31]

The famous prospectus of research that Jones had already penned during his passage to India is similarly expansive, covering such fields as flora and fauna, astronomy, geography, numismatics, and archeology.[32] And in these early records of his Eastern discoveries, at least, it is not simply "India" that is referenced, but India, Asia, and the East more broadly, in a series of synechdocal enlargements. It is only in later decades that the idea of Indo-European affinity came to function explicitly as part of the cultural apparatus of colonial governance, mutating in the course of the nineteenth century into the full-blown theory of the Aryan conquest, in which race, language, and culture became indistinguishably fused.[33]

In her now classic study, *The Rhetoric of English India*, Sara Suleri has spoken of Burke's famous involvement with the impeachment of Hastings as the occasion for an elaboration of what she calls the Indian sublime. Implicit in the workings of the sublime in colonial culture, Suleri writes, is an "overdetermined fearfulness that the colonial imagination must experience in relation to its Indian novelty." To reduce experience to a list or itinerary thus becomes the "driving desire" of Anglo-Indian narrative, such forms of the "catalog" becoming the modality of "colonial self-protection" in the face of the sublime. Suleri calls attention to Burke's insistence on the failure of colonial description, to "the colonizer's pained confrontation with an object to which his cultural and interpretative tools must be inadequate."[34] The various philological "projects" (to borrow a term from Said) of the long nineteenth century that emerged from these early excavations of Jones and his contemporaries, through the linguistic inventions of the College of Fort William, to which I return shortly, and culminating in the monumental cultural cartography of G.A. Grierson's *Linguistic Survey of India* (1898–1928) are linked by their participation in the philological version of this overdetermined sublime and mark a variety of attempts to grapple with the unrepresentability of the sociocultural reality of the subcontinent in the terms of contemporary Western intellectual systems at various points in the history of its subsumption into the imperial domain.

It is in the new Orientalist studies and in their wider reception that the subcontinent is first conceived of in the modern era as a single cultural entity, a unique civilization with its roots in the Sanskritic and more particularly Vedic texts of the Aryans. It is in the new Indology that the contemporary Western frames of thought that I have referred to as nation-thinking are first brought to bear upon culture and society in the subcontinent. I cannot put it more starkly than this: the idea that India is a unique *national* civilization is first postulated on the terrain of literature, that is, in the very invention of the idea of Indian literature in the course of the philological revolution. The dissemination throughout the European intellectual world of the new researches that began to emerge from Calcutta in the 1780s therefore constitutes the *first significant dissemination anywhere* of the Indian national idea.

This invocation of an "Indian" tradition of sublime appearance and proportions consisting of both sacred and secular elements – this invention of the sacred-secular *Indic complex* as such – functioned as a massive, collective act of interpellation, calling up into existence a specifically Indian intelligentsia for the first time and assuring its inculcation in the procedures and methods of nation-thinking. That this particular historical consciousness, this emergent understanding of language, culture, society, and history, did eventually take hold, as it were, within certain elite sectors of society in India itself later in the century is an extremely complex story, being reconstructed in bits and pieces by literally dozens of scholars across several disciplines but still best understood in the formation of a new literary culture among the Bengali Hindu *bhadralok*, the first properly colonial and thus first modern intellectual culture in India and perhaps Asia, which came eventually to refer to itself as the Bengal Renaissance.

The role of Orientalist knowledge in the fabrication of this colonial elite and the first, properly speaking, Indian intelligentsia in the subcontinent is copiously documented but understood largely in terms of the historiographic category of influence. The narrative that lurks close to the surface in most of these accounts, as I have already noted, represents this cultural transaction as a selfless gift, from colonizer to colonized, of the latter's past conceived as History. Two generations of scholars of modern Hinduism – such as Partha Chatterjee, Tapan Raychaudhuri, and more recently Brian K. Pennington, Srinivas Aravamudan, Amit Ray, and Anustup Basu – attempting precisely to break free of this profoundly colonial narrative, have shown in recent years that the most famous products of the translation labors of the Calcutta Orientalists, such as Wilkins's *Bhagvat-Geeta, or Dialogues of Kreeshna and Arjoon* (1785) and Jones's *Sacontalá; or, the Fatal Ring: An Indian Drama* and the *Institutes of Hindu Law, or the Ordinances of Menu* (1794), were acts of invention with far-reaching consequences of a different sort for the colonized society.[35] They acquired a prominence and uniqueness within its conception and practices of the Indian "tradition" that had little or nothing in common with their authority and place in precolonial cultures in the subcontinent, in Bengal or elsewhere. This is true equally of forms of writing now deemed sacred as of those deemed secular. And the process reveals the mutual interdependence between emergent secular-national and Hindu-religious formations. The conception of the *Gita* as a distinct and core scriptural text of the Hindus, for instance – a conception that allowed Gandhi even to juxtapose it to the scriptures of the monotheistic religions in his publicly ostentatious practice of religious ecumenicism – cannot be understood outside this, precisely speaking, *Orientalist* process of its extraction from its textual and social contexts and reconstellation at the core of a newly fashioned Indian national tradition. More broadly speaking, Orientalism placed selected Brahmanical texts and practices at the core of the civilization of the sub-continent as a whole, establishing hierarchies between not merely diverse textual traditions but between these various elite forms of textual authority and a vast range of lived religious forms – hierarchies that continue to help reproduce elements of the colonial social order in postcolonial times. The founders of modern *savarṇa* (literally, "same color") or upper-caste Hinduism – figures such as Bankimchandra Chattopadhyay, Swami Vivekananda, and Keshub Chander Sen – were enthusiastic readers and devotees of the European Orientalists.[36] The awe and even reverence in which these early "moderns" in the subcontinent held such late eighteenth- and nineteenth-century European codifiers of this "Indian" tradition as Jones, Wilkins, Colebrooke, and Max Müller is an index of the Orientalists' *invention* of Indian literature and its insertion into an expanded and transformed world literary space. We might even say that the acquisition of this structure of feeling – a sense of awe and reverence for the labors of the Orientalists – is what it meant to be modern for the first time in different regions and languages of the subcontinent at different times in the course of the nineteenth century.

Thus when it began gradually to emerge in different parts of the country from the middle decades of the nineteenth century, the colonial-nationalist intelligentsia found fully formed a body of writing understood as Indian literature and a body of knowledge and cultural system for configuring language, literature, and culture in national terms. Put differently, this emergent intelligentsia was in a strong sense schooled in Orientalism, which constituted for it the very horizon of modern, Western, humanistic knowledge. The nineteenth century in India can thus be conceived of in cultural and intellectual terms as the period of the long emergence of the category of the *indigenous* and its installation at the core of a new middle-class intellectual culture of increasingly pan-subcontinental scope. Both the secular and the religious types of nationalism in modern times share this ground of the indigenous as facilitator of the authenticity of tradition *(paramparā)*, the shared ground that explains the ease of movement over the modern era from the one to the other political and cultural formation – from the religious to the secular in the early decades of the twentieth century and in the opposite direction in our own times. The notion of world literature itself came to have a significant place in this culture of nationalism, stressed to varying degrees by different writers and thinkers, as that universal space to which India may be said to have made, in the form of its ancient Sanskritic culture, a distinct national contribution, as I have already noted with respect to Tagore.

But my larger interest here, to which I return in more detail below, is that this mode of insertion of the colony into the space of world literature, this distinctly *nationalist* resolution of the question of literature and culture, set the stage for the elaboration of contradictions between national and nonnational social imaginaries in the subcontinent, in particular between the Indic complex and the Indo-Persian ecumene, of which the "Urdu" version of the northern vernacular (as opposed to its "Hindi" version) may be said to carry the most visible linguistic trace in modern times. Let us briefly consider the case of *Payām-e mashriq* (Message of the East, 1924), the great response in Persian to Goethe's *Divan* produced by Muhammad Iqbal, Tagore's approximate contemporary, in which "the East" as a whole is produced above all as a transnational Islamicate sphere. If Goethe's *Divan* of 1819 may be said, in its detailed and close engagement with the (fourteenth century) *dīvān* of Hafiz, to be the instantiating gesture of the emerging European practice of world literature, taking the "national" literary complex of "Persia" to be a synecdoche for the "East" more broadly, Iqbal's collection returns the gesture by placing an *Indo-Persian* (and by implication, Indo-*Muslim*) literary and theosophical complex, in whose elaboration he himself had played a key role for some two decades already, at the center of this "message" in response.[37] In *this* practice of world literature on Indian soil, the tradition (*rivāyat*) of the Indo-Muslim poet leads back to the Persian Hafiz – a fundamentally nonnationalist resolution – and the "indigenous" cultural materials of the Indian-*national* literary complex certainly make an appearance from time to time, but as a framed (rather than framing) element.

Later in this essay, I shall return at length to the question of the divided vernacular of the North, that is, Hindi-Urdu, whose history is a record of a series of effects of the emerging logic of indigenization in the nineteenth century. But let us turn first to an Anglophone context for the early elaboration of the topos of the nation and consider briefly the case of Henry Derozio, the poet and famously charismatic teacher of literature at Hindu College in Calcutta. A young "half-caste" of mixed English, Portuguese, and Indian parentage, Derozio got caught up in the late 1820s in one of the first controversies in colonial India concerning the effects of Western-style education and will perhaps forever remain associated with the image of his students, the sons of upper-caste Hindu families, allegedly consuming liquor and meat openly and ostentatiously in the marketplace. It is conventional to regard Derozio as a leading member of the generation known as Young Bengal and as the first Indian to write poetry in English. Hindu College itself was an early attempt to negotiate between Hindu orthodoxy and the new education. But this new culture of reading and writing became immediately associated with the scandal of iconoclasm and the breaking of caste rules. The new practice of reading literature is in tension here with fealty to a textually authorized religious orthodoxy. A mere four decades later, as Partha Chatterjee has shown in his reading of Bankimchandra Chattopadhyay, this seemingly insurmountable tension would become, for certain classes of people in certain places in colonial India, a distant memory; for Chatterjee, Bankim is both the leading figure of the new Bengali literature that emerged in the second half of the nineteenth century and among the founders of a modern Hindu neoorthodoxy.[38]

The classical references of Derozio's English models are reproduced in his poems of the 1820s, but they become subject here to a fundamental ambiguity. Are the "barbarous hordes" in "Thermopylae" the Persians knocking on Europe's door or Europeans who have come to subjugate Persia's ancient neighbor? Are "Sparta's sons" defending Europe against the Asiatic horde or a model for Asia's sons themselves that shows them how "liberty in death is won"? Is the "patriot sword" in "Freedom to the Slave" a *gift of* the English language or *lifted against* it? But more important for our purposes perhaps is the appearance in Derozio's verse of language that is in keeping with the Orientalist conventions available to contemporary literature, conventions that, for instance, Jones's Indian verse, especially the hymns to the figures of the Hindu pantheon – which appeared in several editions of his collected poems in the quarter century from 1799 on – had helped to popularize.

Derozio repeatedly invokes an Indian Golden Age. This is, for instance, the case with "To India – My Native Land":

> My country! In thy day of glory past
> A beauteous halo circled round thy brow,
> And worshipped as a deity thou wast.
> Where is that glory, where that reverence now?
> …Well, let me dive into the depths of time,
> And bring from out the Ages that have rolled
> A few small fragments of those wrecks sublime,
> Which human eye may never more behold.[39]

Indian *national* sentiment arises out of a *Western* and in fact *English* literary model here, which in itself is the product of an encounter between literature in the new sense and the Orientalists' philological labors. And a constitutive ambiguity is already at work in this very early, properly speaking, nationalist text, revealing the ambiguous and ambivalent reliance of nationalist culture on the structures of colonial knowledge – how could "India" appear to one of its "native" sons as an ocean full of "wrecks sublime"?

The historical trajectory I am interested in here, leading from the birth of the new Orientalism in the late eighteenth century to the fitful and regionally uneven emergence of a colonial-nationalist intelligentsia in the course of the nineteenth, is far from being a linear or unidirectional one and cannot be said to conform to any notion of historical necessity. And it unfolded across a social field marked by contradictions at various levels. Most importantly, this process of acculturation to indigenizing notions and practices was directed ultimately at a small class constituted mostly from the precolonial social elites rather than the subaltern mass of the people, turning the latter into the popular object of their project of national elaboration. And this intelligentsia came eventually to turn this national complex, including the myth of a lost Indian golden age we have just encountered in Derozio's verse, against colonial rule. The imperial overlords, furthermore, remained as a whole highly ambivalent about these cultural developments, split in the late nineteenth century, for instance, between the posture of selfless tutelage and savage disdain of these "chattering" classes, both of which we encounter, for instance, in Rudyard Kipling's writings. But the fact that nationalist intellectuals appropriated the work of the Orientalists selectively and in effect ironically,[40] or with a view to their own perceived interests, does not in any way lessen the significance of a distinctly Orientalist pedagogy in their very emergence as a pan-subcontinental, "Indian" class.

The logic of indigenization, first put to work as I am arguing here in the assembling of the Sanskrit-centered Indic complex, had far-reaching effects across the cultural and social field that came into being under the impact of colonial rule and across a range of contemporary vernacular formations. But Orientalism's linguistic and literary invention of India has in fact to be understood as a complex two-part, nonsynchronous process: the assembling of the Indic complex (Jones and his contemporaries and the wider discourse initiated by their work) and then, following the first significant transition in the history of this early Indology, the invention of the modern vernaculars through an enormous and multipronged project. This second phase of Orientalism's Indian "project" involved in these early years such colonial institutions as the College of Fort William in Calcutta (about which more below), the College of Fort St. George in Madras, and the Baptist mission at Serampore in Bengal – the latter undertaking a massive printing project in a large number of the Indian vernaculars, inventing movable type for the first time for several of the languages and dialects of India. One tectonic impact of this dual process of indigenization in colonial culture – the Sanskritization of tradition, on the one hand, and the invention of the modern vernaculars, on the other – was the rapid decline and disappearance of Indo-Persian civilization, whose forms of cosmopolitanism, once the culture of vast segments of the literate classes in the subcontinent across the lines of religious affiliation, could now only appear under the sign of the nonindigenous, the elite, and thus alien.

By far the most dramatic instance of this process of indigenization on the terrain of language, not surprisingly, is the effort to produce a linguistic and literary *center* for the emerging nation space – the invention of modern *śuddha* ("purified") Hindi as the language of the nation precisely under the sign of the indigenous. And if modern Urdu may be described for our purposes as the version of the northern vernacular that most visibly carries traces of the now-disappeared Indo-Persian culture, then the concept of indigenization helps clarify for us the distinct situation of Urdu since the middle of the nineteenth century as a set of linguistic, literary, and social practices at odds with the emerging practices of the nation. The larger issue here is not simply that the fabrication of an Indian tradition was anchored by a (modern) Hindu religio-political identity but rather that these shifts in the con-tours of knowledge, language, and culture produced *two increasingly distinct social groups and social imaginaries* among the new, urban middle classes across the subcontinent, each marked by a newly standardized religious identity, one of which came to see itself as being in possession, in a strong sense, of that classical Sanskritic and more broadly "Indic" heritage, and the other, because it could not replicate that *strong* claim to possession, came to see itself, and of course was seen by others, as not quite Indian. The emergence of polarized religio-political identities in India in modern times, and of the two distinct and rival forms of the north Indian vernacular associated with them, that is, modern Hindi and Urdu, itself is decisive for the course of the larger processes that precipitated the final partition of India in the middle of the twentieth century along religious lines and is thus in a strong sense a colonial development. This is a historical judgment that must not be confused with the more popular, and distinctly nationalist, habit of assigning the "blame" for the political split to British policies of divide and rule. But the precise unfolding of these processes of partition across the cultural, social, and political fields cannot be understood without reference to the conditions of colonial rule in the subcontinent. The entire dialectic of the indigenous and the alien, Hindu and Muslim, that is so defining of the cultural history of the second half of the nineteenth century is put into motion for the first time in the slow and massive realignment of the gears of knowledge and culture at its beginning.

Orientalism and "the Language of Hindoostan"

At least two levels of interaction are significant here, if we may return for a moment to the terms of analysis introduced by Casanova: first, this linguistic and cultural conflict may be viewed as evidence of a struggle to achieve preeminence in an emerging *national* literary space in the subcontinent in the course of the nineteenth century, a literary space whose (evolving) political milieu is provided by the development of the structures of the colonial state; and, second, the emergence of this national space itself is inseparable from the process of its insertion into the *international* literary space in the period of the latter's massive expansion across the globe. Of course, to a large extent this process in India parallels developments in language and literature in Europe since the middle of the eighteenth century, from the ubiquitous collections of folktales across the continent to the recovery of "bardic" traditions.[41] And a celebrated "forgery" scandal like the Macpherson-Ossian controversy in fact reveals the inventive nature of *all* philological fabrications of national traditions. But the paradox of the Indian situation is this: the process of vernacularization that we know to be inseparable from modernization – and, outside of Europe, we may think of such language revolutions as the May 4th movement in China, *genbun ichi* in Japan, the *nahḍa* in Egypt and Greater Syria – produced in India not one but two claimants to the status of lingua franca. To put it more precisely, it produced two versions of the same language complex, the northern Indian vernacular – and in fact two lexically different versions of the same *kharī bōlī* ("upright speech") morphological subset of the vernacular of Western Uttar Pradesh and eastern Punjab, which the armies and Sufis of the Mughal sphere had helped to establish as the northern Indian lingua franca – in conflict and rivalry with each other over claims to social reach and social distinction in the emerging national literary space. There is no name for this more encompassing and contradictory linguistic formation – whether Hindi, Urdu, or Hindustani – that is not subject to the terms of the conflict itself. To acquire one or the other of these supposedly distinct languages is therefore not simply to learn a language as such. It is to learn ways of participating in a language field constituted as a *polemic*.

Urdu cannot be conceived of as just another Indian language among others, as it were, since part of its historical reality over the last two hundred years has been precisely that it creates difficulties of a particular sort for the very terms in which the Indianness of language and literature have come to be conceived, difficulties that have repeatedly produced an embittered response in those committed to the production of a philology or literary history of a nationalist orientation.[42] In this connection, we may consider briefly the history of Urdu's relationship as a cluster of language practices and a textual corpus in the northern vernacular to the *mārga/dēśī* polarity (literally, "the way"/"of the place, local") operative in nationalist philology and literary history. A feature of Sanskritic culture since its rise to hegemonic status as the cosmopolitan cultural order in the subcontinent early in the first millennium of the Common Era, this polarity acquired a radically new valence and functionality in colonial-nationalist culture. Sheldon Pollock, the leading scholar of the Sanskrit world in our time, has translated this polarity into English as "cosmopolitan/vernacular" and analyzed with brilliant clarity its ability to give an account of the relation between Sanskrit and the rise of the vernaculars toward the end of the first millennium.[43] Since the early nineteenth century, however, this conceptual binary has been subject to the logic of indigenization I have been attempting to describe here and played a central role in Orientalist-nationalist philology. In the foundational work of such figures as Suniti Kumar Chatterji, for instance, it functions entirely within the terms of the Hindi-Urdu polemic, with *both* the "cosmopolitan" and "vernacular" functions and orientations (read "Sanskrit" and the "New Indo-Aryan languages" like Hindi respectively) now carrying the force of the indigenous as against the hybrid and alien forms of Urdu and the Indo-Persian cultural sphere more broadly. Any attempt to conceptualize linguistic–literary relations between different cultural formations in contemporary South Asia in terms of the conceptual structure of *mārga/dēśī*, as in G.N. Devy's *After Amnesia: Tradition and Change in Indian Literary Criticism*, which is a pioneering and brilliant attempt to envision a practice of literary criticism that is capable of thinking against and beyond what he calls the "epistemological stumbling block" of colonial culture, finds its own stumbling block in the forms of anomaly that from the perspective of nationalism seem to coalesce in Urdu.[44]

The single most important institutional setting for an understanding of the inventiveness of Orientalism in its second, "vernacular" phase is the College of Fort William, which embodied this first transition in the history of Calcutta Orientalism from the decade of Jones and deserves a closer look from our discipline than it has gotten. (From Said's account of the developments in Calcutta, it is missing entirely; see *O*, pp. 77–79.) The college was formed in 1800 as the first formal institutional attempt to train the future officers of the East India Company. If Governor-General Hastings is the patron of the first, that is, Sanskritic, phase of Orientalism, Wellesley is that of the second, vernacular one. In the course of a few years at the beginning of the century, a small group of European lexicographers and translators, including John Gilchrist, Edward Warring, and the Baptist missionary William Carey, along with their teams of native assistants, including Mir Amman, Mir Sher Ali Afsos, Lalluji Lal, and Ramram Basu, produced the models for standardized prose in several of the vernacular languages of India.[45] The very organizational structure of the college, which grouped its personnel into European "professors" and "teachers," on the one hand, and native *munshis* ("scribes"), on the other, was thus an articulation of vastly different intellectual cultures, subjectivities, and social temporalities – as European intellectuals with the most "advanced" contemporary forms of Western humanistic education from such institutions as Oxford supervised the work of *munshis* of various sorts, who were trained in the traditional manner of the late Mughal Empire, in the first formal institution of "modern" education in India.[46]

The effects of the college's work for language and literature in north India in particular were far-reaching. Under the explicit instructions of Gilchrist, appointed Professor of Hindostani in 1800, these individuals produced, for use as textbooks in the linguistic education of the young British recruits of the East India Company, a handful of prose works in two distinct forms of the north Indian vernacular, to be called Hindi and Hindostani respectively, which Gilchrist viewed as separate Hindu and Muslim languages, the one with an emphasis on Sanskrit as lexical source and the other on Persian and Arabic.[47] In aligning religion, language, and literature in this manner Gilchrist was simply reproducing the terms of a wider Anglo-Indian discourse since at least the middle of the eighteenth century. In these early decades, the British often used the word *Moor* to refer to Muslims in India and *Moor's* for their purported language. Jones himself, in his 1786 address, distinguished between the "Hindostani" language and the "Bhasha," and the Serampore missionaries, among them Carey, who joined the college as teacher of Sanskrit and Bengali, had already begun to highlight in their publications two distinct variants of the northern vernacular. The Fort William College narratives are thus the first instance anywhere of the standardization of the vernacular in two distinct forms marked by religious difference. And the fact that these works were published with native individuals identified as *authors* of the works is already an indication of the at least minimal inroads toward the installation of a specifically literary space in India – a far cry from the anonymous "pundits" of Jones and his contemporaries when they started out a mere twenty years earlier. The Fort William College project thus represents one attempt to impose order of a particular sort, in line with the methods of nation-thinking, on the "infinitely varied common tongue" of north India, as Alok Rai has put it quite memorably.[48] A critical reception history of the "Hindi" and "Hindostani" narratives produced at the college, which comprehends the modes by which these profoundly colonial texts entered and shaped the emerging vernacular literary cultures in northern India – their entry into school and college curricula, their canonization in the works of the new literary history – still remains to be written, as does a careful comparative philology that seeks to place these early colonial linguistic-literary projects – the Serampore and Fort William College texts above all – alongside the range of contemporary literary practices at various degrees of remove from colonial institutions.

As Shamsur Rahman Faruqi has shown, the term *Hindustani* had no such fixed currency within the indigenous culture itself, with the poets and *tazkira* (biographical anthology) writers of the period using a range of designations – including *rēkhta* ("scattered" or "mixed"), *zabān-e urdū-e muʿallā* ("speech of the exalted camp/court"), *Hindavi* or *Hindui*, and even simply *Hindi* – to designate the language of their compositions, which was seen to be in varying ways distant from or proximate to a number of dialects and registers – Braj-bhasha (or bakha), Avadhi, and Bhojpuri among numerous others. Let us consider briefly the case of Inshallah Khan Insha's *Kahānī Rānī Kētakī aur Kuñvar Uday Bhān kī* (The Tale of Queen Ketaki and Prince Uday Bhan; 1803?), for instance, a text whose probable period of composition makes it a contemporary of the Fort William College narratives but whose social milieu lay at a relative distance from the social orbit and temporalities of the emerging colonial state and that played a not negligible role in the production of the self-conception of Hindi nationalism in the twentieth century as having arisen out of a long indigenous tradition.[49] This Hindi canonization of Insha's tale is at the very least paradoxical, since he is widely regarded as one of the great codifiers of the Urdu tradition, above all in his Persian-language prose work, *Daryā-e laṭāful* (The Ocean of Refinement; 1808), which, in its very effort to establish rules of *bon usage* in the northern vernacular, constitutes perhaps the most fecund source for an understanding of the range and emerging hierarchy of linguistic practice in north India in the early nineteenth century. This latter text of Insha's has been subject to repeated excoriation in Hindi literary history as evidence of the tangential nature of Urdu to the mainstream linguistic development of north India.[50] But in the story Insha appears to have proceeded with the opposite intention: to purge writing in the vernacular, as a sort of feat of linguistic prowess, of all "foreign" vocabulary originating in Arabic, Persian, and Turkic. It is of course this linguistic conceit that makes it available for later appropriation by Hindi nationalism: "it occurred to me one day to tell a story in which besides Hindavi no mixture of another way of speaking [bōl] should be encountered.... Neither any foreign speech [bāhar kī bōlī] nor the rustic [gañvārī] should be present in it." But what is meant by the "rustic" here is itself quite revealing, as we are told that a respectable older acquaintance of the author's had expressed his skepticism about the plausibility of such a linguistic adventure, in which "Hindaviness [Hindavi-pan] would not be removed" – that is, by "foreign" lexical elements – "but the *bākhā* would not come bursting in."[51] In this text written at a certain remove from the workings of the properly colonial logic of indigenization (in Lucknow, outside formal British sovereignty, at the turn of the century), a very different sort of cultural logic seems to be at work. The danger inherent in the quest for "Hindaviness," that is, for a lexically de-Persianized and de-Arabicized practice of the *kharī bōlī* form of the vernacular, "as spoken formerly [pahlē] by the best people [achchhōñ sē achchhē] amongst themselves," is this eruption of the *bākhā*, coded as "rustic" speech. (And Insha's boastful response of course is that he is equal to the challenge of overcoming this peril.) In other words, the register we now identify as Urdu is the guarantor here of the purity and social prestige of *kharī bōlī* as such and is on a continuum with the register that is characterized here by "Hindavi-ness," both forms needing to be vigilant about the popular and "rustic" forms identified collectively here as the *bakha*. The properly colonial logic of indigenization (and alienization) at work in the contemporary Fort William College project is nowhere to be seen in Insha's text, which is shaped instead by the tussle between the refined and the rustic or vulgar. Taking a longer historical view, we might say that the Fort William College project shatters this linguistic continuum by positing, with the certainty inherent in the state-Orientalist truth-claim, the existence of distinct and vastly different, indigenous and alien, traditions of spoken and written language marked by religious difference. The later retroactive Hindi assimilation of Insha's text under the sign of the indigenous and popular, as part of a continuous historical development that also seamlessly includes the Fort William College narratives, thus misconstrues the fractures of this historical moment entirely, papering over the still vast gulf separating the indigenizing logic of the colonial state from the precolonial logics of linguistic and cultural differentiation and stratification operating in vast segments of society in the subcontinent.

Modern Hindi thus emerged in conflict and competition, on the one hand, with Urdu, which, under the sign of the nonindigenous, it wished to eject from the space of the nation, but also, on the other, with a range of *other* forms of the northern vernacular about which it remained instead fundamentally ambivalent, wishing to incorporate them into its own pre-history, but as premodern and thus *superseded* forms of the indigenous vernacular, inadequate to the linguistic and aesthetic demands of the modern world. This is the case above all with Braj, which was, along with Urdu, one of the two dominant literary traditions in the eighteenth and early nineteenth centuries in the northern language zone, but which now could only appear in Hindi nationalist culture under the sign of a premodern and popular "sweetness" of expression (*miṭṭha*) whose temporality is incommensurable with the, properly speaking, historical time of the nation.[52] This inability of early Hindi nationalists to see anything but *khaṛī bōlī* as the appropriate idiom – more precisely, as the only appropriate and authentic morphological base – for the speech of the nation in its modernity is thus in large measure the result, ironically, to say the least, of the already established and officially canonized modernity of *khaṛī bōlī* in its Urdu version, which was from 1837 a language of the colonial state in its function as the language of the law courts in north India. Put differently, because modern Hindi occupied the same morphological ground as Urdu it replicated the morphological hierarchy of *bon usage* codified in the earlier emergence of Urdu in the late Mughal eighteenth century and in its standardization in the nineteenth as a language of the colonial state, reproducing Urdu's classification of Braj as primitive and rustic speech. We might even say, in other words, that at its moment of emergence "Hindi" *is* "Urdu" in the process of being indigenized.

The process of linguistic differentiation and realignment was thus a gradual and laborious one and by no means linear. This fact may be judged in an anecdotal way from a small event from 1847 reported by a historian of the language conflict. A group of Hindu students at Benares College – which a mere four decades later would emerge as one of the centers of the Hindi movement – responded to the linguistic admonishments of their exasperated British educator by noting that because there were numerous forms of the spoken language, they did not understand what he meant by pure Hindi and that in order to know which words to expunge in an effort to purify their language as he was requiring them to do they would have to learn Arabic and Persian. Even if it were apocryphal, this story would be enormously useful for understanding the logic of linguistic indigenization; for the native speaker, the route to the discovery of that which is meant to be properly one's own is a circuitous one, leading through precisely that which is to be rendered foreign and alien. The overall process of the emergence of Urdu and Hindi as rival linguistic and literary registers identified with distinct and mutually conflicted religious identities represents a massive rearrangement of a layered, performatively contingent, and dynamic linguistic reality into a structure of binary oppositions.[53] It is only quite late in the nineteenth century – as the notion of a lexically Sanskritized version of the northern vernacular, built on the same *kharī bōlī* morphological ground as Urdu, gradually gained ground among a segment of the intelligentsia as the only legitimate lingua franca – that the terms *Hindi* and *Urdu* came to acquire their present differentiations and meanings. A *post*-colonial philology of this literary and linguistic complex can never adequately claim to be produced from a position uncontaminated by the language *polemic* that now constitutes it and can only proceed by working through its terms.

   Finally, any attempt to give an account of the contemporary social situation of Urdu and Hindi as literary languages must confront the paradoxical fact that no literary history, properly speaking, can fail to locate their modern origins in the Fort William College narratives, written expressly not for an Indian reading public but rather for the linguistic and cultural training of young British officers of the East India Company. There was a lag of several decades after their initial publication before they became available to "Urdu" and "Hindi" reading publics. Even some three decades later, the ornate language of Rajab Ali Beg Suroor's *Fasāna-e 'ajā'ib* (1831?) was intended precisely as a repudiation of the purportedly conversational and pedestrian Fort William College style. The very foundational acts of historicization that sought to produce for the first time the terms of distinct and independent histories for these two traditions – I am thinking here of such late nineteenth- and early twentieth-century figures as Muhammad Husain Azad (Urdu) and Ramchandra Shukla (Hindi) – thus represent at the same time their anchoring in this colonial and Orientalist logic.[54] In a very real sense, then, prose traditions in the languages we have come to read and write as "our own" – I am speaking here as a person formed in the Hindi-Urdu polemic as a "native" speaker of "Urdu" – were invented for the purpose of colonial governance, and the task of criticism today is at the very least the untangling and rearranging of the various elements presently congealed into seemingly distinct and autonomous objects of divergent literary histories. The critical task of overcoming the colonial logics persistently at work in the formation of literary and linguistic identities today is thus indistinguishable from the task of pushing against the multiple identitarian assumptions, colonial and Orientalist in nature, of Hindi and Urdu's mutual, religiously marked distinctness and autonomy.

   This secular-critical task, furthermore, corresponds not simply to some image of a heterogeneous past but to the contradictory contemporary situation of language and literature itself. For, the laborious historical process of creating two distinct language identities – a historical labor undertaken, as I have tried to show, first by Orientalists and then by Indian nationalists (and Muslim separatists) – still remains ongoing and incomplete. Despite the countless efforts at differentiation and countless applications of identitarian pressure across the linguistic and literary field in this enormous cultural zone in the subcontinent for well over a century, Urdu and Hindi remain intimately proximate and available to each other in a whole range of media and forms – in spoken language forms, in the so-called "Hindi" films of Bollywood cinema, but above all in literary writing itself. A desire for Urdu – coded as refined and cosmopolitan – is inherent to modern Hindi, and a desire for Hindi – coded as popular and vernacular – is inherent to modern Urdu itself. That this encounter takes place through a haze of misconceptions – after all, in Pakistan, at least, the institutionalization of Urdu as the national language has been achieved by sundering nearly all its former associations with the mannered *ashrāf* elite, and modern standard Hindi can hardly be equated with any genuinely popular form of the spoken language – does not diminish the fact that it takes place daily. In this sense, Hindi-Urdu remain articulated as the elements of a single formation in contradiction, and the more the contradiction is heightened – by a myriad of nation-alizing processes operative at numerous social locations – the more the singularity (in contradiction) is affirmed and renewed, even though at yet one further level of remove from the phenomenal levels of social experience.

In sum, then, Orientalism may be understood as a set of processes for the reorganization of language, literature, and culture on a planetary scale, which effected the assimilation of heterogeneous and dispersed bodies of writing onto the plane of equivalence and evaluability that is literature, fundamentally transforming in the process their internal distribution and coherence, their modes of authoriza-tion, and their relationship to the larger social order and social imaginaries in their places of origin. In its historically received forms, therefore, world literature is fundamentally a concept of exchange (and, as Marx and Engels understood, a concept of bourgeois society) – that is, a concept that recodes an opaque and unequal process of appropriation as a transparent one of supposedly free and equal interchange and communication. And the Latinate term *literature*, and the set of its cognates in the Western languages, together with a number of calques (or loan translations) in the languages of the global South, now provide the dominant, universalizing, *but by no means absolute* vocabulary for the comprehension of verbal-textual expression worldwide. As my analysis of the Orientalizing process in India, and in the specific case of Hindi-Urdu, has attempted to show, this is an ongoing and open-ended process, a determinate logic of the late capitalist world, so that the critique of Orientalism too is best understood as open-ended and ongoing rather than engaged in and accomplished once and for all.

Global English and the Vernaculars

While the Hindi-Urdu conflict I have been examining here represents at many levels a fairly particular, if not exactly unique, historical trajectory, the broader historical situation of the Indian vernaculars outlined above, and their relation to English as literary language and cultural system, reflects a larger and now planet wide reality. (Some of this applies to lesser and varying degrees to a number of the other Western languages, above all French, but I am bracketing off that question here entirely in order to focus on English.) Having consigned the languages of the global South, including formerly extensive and dispersed cultures of writing, to narrowly conceived ethnonational spheres, English now assumes the mantle of exclusive medium of cosmopolitan exchange.[55] The many signs of this dramatic shift – and I have charted some others in detail in the foregoing pages – can be found in patterns of circulation and access to literary works beyond their immediate societies of origin. To take one concrete example, a hundred years ago at least some intelligentsias in the vast stretch of societies from the eastern Balkans, through Anatolia and Persia proper, including swathes of Central Asia and Afghanistan, and stretching across the northern belt of the subcontinent, may have encountered their textual creations in the original and directly – that is, in Persian, Arabic, or Ottoman Turkish. Today, readers in India, Pakistan, Iran, or Turkey will typically encounter each other's literatures only in translation in English (or in further translation from English), thus only if the works have received that metropolitan recognition. (The overwhelming majority of translations of world literature into the Indian languages, for instance, are actually translations from the English.) Naguib Mahfouz's Nobel Prize and the spate of translations that followed certainly did help introduce modern Arabic literature to many Western readers for the first time, but this is also true of readers in many societies formerly part of the Perso-Arabic sphere as well, in which modern literariness has been instituted precisely through the sundering of the erstwhile link to Persian and/or Arabic – most dramatically perhaps in modern standard Hindi and the Turkish that emerged from the Kemalist language "reforms" in the early decades of the republic. (Both of these languages have been instituted in large measure through a nationalistic de-Persianization of an existing linguistic formation.) Iqbal, who is generally regarded as the founder of the Pakistan idea, wrote much of his poetic output in Persian in the first half of the twentieth century, a far cry from the situation today, where writers in Pakistan, to say nothing of the larger reading public, may well have encountered *Reading Lolita in Tehran* in the original or in Urdu translation but are almost entirely unaware of contemporary Iranian literature in Persian. But these are largely surface phenomena that indicate the deeper tectonic shifts in language, literature, and culture I have been concerned with here and that are the long legacy of the colonial empires and their logics of Orientalization. As I have argued at some length, this entire question of the expansion of the Western European languages or, more accurately, of the question of their assimilation of non-Western cultures of writing – a process I have identified here as Orientalism – is largely ignored in contemporary accounts (such as Casanova's) of the emergence and expansion of world literary space and in such frameworks for the consideration of literary and linguistic diversity as Anglophone literatures or global English.

With respect to English and the Indian vernaculars, a now-notorious statement published some years ago by Salman Rushdie might inadvertently offer us some further clarity about the contemporary situation. In the introduction to an anthology of postindependence Indian fiction, Rushdie offered his readers his considered opinion that the only contemporary Indian literature of significant worth was being written in English: "prose writing … by Indian writers *working in English*, is proving to be a stronger and more important body of work than most of what has been

produced in the 16 'official languages' of India, the so-called 'vernacular languages' …
and, indeed, this new, still burgeoning, 'Indo-Anglian' literature represents perhaps
the most valuable contribution India has yet made to the world of books."[56] At least
a dozen of these vernaculars happen of course to be major literary cultures, some of
them with traditions of writing up to a millennium old, of none of which Rushdie
could be entirely unaware. Rushdie's remarks came clothed in a mood of sincerity
frustrated; the editor of a projected anthology, having searched exhaustively, was
forced to admit in the end that there was nothing in these literary languages that
was worth including in the volume. The one exception to this general rule, Rushdie
informed his readers, was the Urdu short story Ṭōbā Ṭēk Siṅgh," by Saadat Hasan
Manto, a translation of which was consequently included in the collection – not
exactly an original selection, nor the result of particularly strenuous deliberation,
given the story's mass popularity in the subcontinent and the fact that it had
been produced as a short film and shown on Channel Four in Britain a decade
earlier for the fortieth anniversary of the Partition.

Rushdie's is not, if we are to be precise, an Orientalist statement, but rather an
Anglicist one, to use the terms of the great imperial debate in the early nineteenth
century about colonial governance and education.[57] If there are echoes of Macaulay
here, this is far from being accidental. Macaulay's famous judgment of 1835 about
the relative merits of Occidental over Oriental literatures had expressed the
distinctly *colonial* logic inherent in Europe's encounter with its Asiatic possessions.
Critical as it was of the Orientalists' case for continuing the natives' education in
Asiatic languages and traditions of writing, it had nevertheless relied on and
reproduced precisely the terms of the Orientalist reinvention of the world literary
system and the placing of the "literatures of the East" within it: "I am quite ready,"
Macaulay writes in his well known "Minute on Indian Education," "to take the
Oriental learning at the valuation of the Orientalists themselves." Macaulay's formulation stated precisely the relative hierarchy and discrepancy of power in the colonial
era between, on the one hand, the European languages and above all English and, on
the other, the major languages of Asia and the Middle East so that "the whole native
literature of India and Arabia" could be judged in terms of and therefore *assimilated*
into "a single shelf of a good European library."[58] In Rushdie's comments, Macaulay's
judgment is updated for the twenty-first century – in a precise sense, giving expression to the now *global* logic through which the Indo-English novel has come to be
represented to the outside world in recent years as the authentic and *authenticating*
literature of India. Rushdie, whose *Midnight's Children* first introduced world audiences to the global ambitions of the Anglophone Indian bourgeoisie at the threshold
of the neoliberal restructuring of the Indian economy, establishes the proper relationship in the world literary system between English and the Indian vernaculars as
medium of Indian literary expression. The Indo-English novel has become in recent
decades a global form and tradition with a vast accumulation of cultural capital,
with British and American editors descending routinely on the major Indian cities
in a frenzied search for the next big first novel, the next *God of Small Things*, a process that is now a routine part of the lives of aspiring young Anglophone writers,

affecting in all kinds of concrete ways the writing that gets produced. Remarks such as Rushdie's represent the naturalization of the asymmetrical situations, the vastly different symbolic resources, of English and the vernaculars of the subcontinent – including Hindi and Urdu, the putative national languages, respectively, of India and Pakistan – not just globally but within South Asia itself.[59] English here shapes the identity of the Anglophone intelligentsia as, properly speaking, the *national* (rather than a regional) one precisely through the circulation of its cultural products in *world* literary space (Rushdie's "world of books").

Significantly, the remarks are an attempt at disavowing the heterogeneity of the Anglophone novel's own linguistic environment in places such as India (and, we might add, Africa) – English (or for that matter French) in Asia and Africa never exists out of hearing range of a number of its linguistic others – a heterogeneity that often gets packaged within the form itself as one of its supposedly exotic pleasures, most famously in Rushdie's own works, whose characteristically "Indianized" English stages the presence of modes of speech that the author and the novels themselves repeatedly characterize as the street Hindustani of Bombay.[60] This mode of appearance of the vernaculars within the discourse of the Anglophone novel marks an attempt to manage linguistic (and social) heterogeneity through ethnicized assimilation. But it gets packaged as linguistic diversity in the interests of a global cultural system in which the Anglophone elite now wishes to participate on equal terms and is an asymmetrical process unimaginable in reverse; that is, it is impossible to imagine a similarly instrumental assimilation of English into the discourses of vernacular fiction. Anglicism (Macaulay et alia) and Orientalism (Jones et alia), which are viewed historically as antagonists in the great imperial debate, in fact represent two moments in the unfolding of the same colonial logic. This logic has been reinscribed in our own postcolonial times, at one level, in the argument (of unequals) about the respective rights, representativeness, and value of English and the vernaculars, an argument that now gets staged globally, not just within the nation-states of the subcontinent.[61] On the one hand, Anglophone literary expression, the end product of an epochal historical process of assimilation, is packaged in the world literary system – including in departments of English in the West – as an instance of pure diversity; on the other, Indian languages, especially in the nationalized forms of Urdu and Hindi, stake their claim to authentic national expression against the alien presence of English. In fact neither end of this polarity can do the work it is marshaled to do within the globalizing cultural logics of the late-capitalist world. Neither framework allows an understanding of the Indian vernaculars themselves as "conscripts of modernity," conscripted into the cultural system of English and the other culturally dominant European languages.[62] While exilic and dislocated subjectivity is much touted by Rushdie as the great problematic of the Anglophone novel, it is in fact no less pertinent (and poignant), perhaps more so, for our understanding of the vernacular literary traditions themselves.

How then do we revisit the concept of world literature today, given these disjunctures and relations of force, at various levels of world literary space, between the global metropolitan languages and the languages of the global South? We have to move beyond appeals to diversity here because, if we are to take seriously the historical constellation of Orientalism – which made possible, as I have argued, the appearance of the latter group of languages and textual traditions for the first time within the structures and terms of the former – what would be needed is a concept of world literature (and practices of teaching it) that works to reveal the ways in which "diversity" itself – national, religious, civilizational, continental – is a colonial and Orientalist problematic, though one that emerges precisely on the plane of equivalence that is literature. What we have to teach when we teach world literature is precisely the history of these relations of force and powers of assimilation. The universalism that is inherent in the task of rethinking the concept of world literature and its usefulness (or not) in our own times – and I believe that question remains still an open one – thus has to be confronted with linguistic heterogeneity and the concept itself uncoupled from the effects of standardization and homogenization both within and across languages and cultures that come masked as diversity. That such a critical project cannot take the form exclusively of the "distant reading" Moretti proposes should be clear, but neither can it take the form of close reading for its own sake. What is needed is *better* close reading, attentive to the worldliness of language and text at various levels of social reality, from the highly localized to the planetary as such. In this sense Said's project at least from *Orientalism* onward implies not a rejection but rather a radicalization of philology – that is, it calls for a radically historical understanding of language and the forms of its institution in literature, culture, and society. Philology in this sense is thus an indispensable element of the practice of secular criticism as Said conceives of it. An elaboration of this philology after Orientalism, if I may call it that, is one of the core and most urgent tasks of the critical humanities in our time.

Notes

1 See Pascale Casanova, *The World Republic of Letters*, trans. M.B. DeBovoise (Cambridge, 2004).

2 *Ibid.* p. 48; for the phrase in the original, see Benedict Anderson, *Imagined Communities: Reflections on the Origin and Spread of Nationalism* (London, 1983), p. 80.

3 See, for instance, Isaiah Berlin, *The Roots of Romanticism*, ed. Henry Hardy (Princeton, NJ, 2001). Michael F. Brown has recently revisited the uniquely anthropological notion of cultural relativism in "Cultural Relativism 2.0," *Current Anthropology* 49 (June 2008): 363–383.

4 Concerning Herder's later engagement (in the 1790s) with the Indological studies and translations, especially the *Bhagavad Gita*, see Saverio Marchignoli, "Canonizing an Indian Text? A.W. Schlegel, W. von Humboldt, Hegel, and the Bhagavadgita," in *Sanskrit and "Orientalism": Indology and Comparative Linguistics in Germany, 1750–1958*, ed. Douglas T. McGetchin, Peter K.J. Park, and D.R. SarDesai (Delhi, 2004), pp. 248–251.

5 Vinay Dharwadker, "Orientalism and the Study of Indian Literatures," in *Orientalism and the Postcolonial Predicament: Perspectives on South Asia*, ed. Carol A. Breckenridge and Peter van der Veer (Philadelphia, 1993), p. 160.

6   For an early, in fact pioneering, study along these lines, which seeks to identify the northern European, phil-Hellenic reinvention of Greece as a colonial event, and which is influential for me here, see Stathis Gourgouris, *Dream Nation: Enlightenment, Coloniza-tion, and the Institution of Modern Greece* (Stanford, Calif., 1996).

7   See Edward W. Said, "On Jean Genet's Late Works," *Grand Street* 36, no. 9 (1990): 38. On Genet and this remarkable essay of Said's, see Gourgouris, *Does Literature Think? Litera-ture as Theory for an Antimythical Era* (Stanford, Calif., 2003), pp. 249–291.

8   Said, *Orientalism* (New York, 1978), pp. 24, 25; emphasis added; hereafter abbreviated *O*.

9   Said, "Secular Criticism," *The World, the Text, and the Critic* (London, 1983), p. 16. See Aamir R. Mufti, "Auerbach in Istanbul: Edward Said, Secular Criticism, and the Question of Minority Culture," *Critical Inquiry* 25 (Autumn 1998): 95–125. On secular criticism and "detranscendentalization," see Gourgouris, "Transformation, Not Transcendence," *Boundary* 2 31 (Summer 2004): 55–79.

10 See, for instance, Gil Anidjar, "Secularism," *Critical Inquiry* 33 (Autumn 2006): 52–77. Modesty is not among the many weaknesses of this somewhat careless essay. Anidjar sets himself the task of instructing Said in the real significance of his critique in *Orientalism*, regretting that Said failed to realize that, following the logic of his own argument in that book, he should have been a postsecularist. It is really too bad (I have sometimes thought since reading it) that this instruction was not undertaken while Said was alive.

11 See Stefan Hoesel-Uhlig, "Changing Fields: The Directions of Goethe's *Weltliteratur*," in *Debating World Literature*, ed. Christopher Prendergast (London, 2004), pp. 26–53. Goethe's earliest known use of the term occurs on 31 January 1827; see *Conversations of Goethe with Johann Peter Eckermann*, trans. John Oxenford, ed. J.K. Moorhead (New York, 1998), pp. 164–166. On Goethe's reading in Orientalism and travel literature, see Walter Veit, "Goethe's Fantasies about the Orient," *Eighteenth-Century Life* 26 (Fall 2002): 164–180, and Fritz Strich, *Goethe and World Literature* (1945; London, 1949), chap. 9. On Goethe's reading of Hafiz and the writing of the *Divan*, see Jeffrey Einboden, "The Genesis of *Weltliteratur*: Goethe's *West-Östlicher Divan* and Kerygmatic Pluralism," *Lit-erature and Theology* 19 (Sept. 2005): 238–250.

12 See David Damrosch, *What Is World Literature?* (Princeton, NJ, 2003), p. 4, and Franco Moretti, "Conjectures on World Literature," *New Left Review* 1 (Jan.–Feb. 2000): 54–68.

13 See Mufti, *Enlightenment in the Colony: The Jewish Question and the Crisis of Postcolonial Culture* (Princeton, NJ, 2007).

14 See the pioneering historical studies of Bernard S. Cohn, *"An Anthropologist among the Historians" and Other Essays* (New York, 1987) and *Colonialism and Its Forms of Knowledge: The British in India* (Princeton, NJ, 1996), and Nicholas B. Dirks, *Castes of Mind: Colonialism and the Making of Modern India* (Princeton, NJ, 2001). On the teaching of literature in colonial India, see Gauri Viswanathan, *Masks of Conquest: Literary Study and British Rule in India* (New York, 1989).

15 See Raymond Schwab, *La Renaissance orientale* (Paris, 1950), trans. Gene Patterson-Black and Victor Reinking under the title *The Oriental Renaissance: Europe's Rediscovery of India and the East, 1680–1880* (New York, 1984), and Said, "Raymond Schwab and the Romance of Ideas," in *The World, the Text, and the Critic*, p. 252.

16 See M.H. Abrams, *The Mirror and the Lamp: Romantic Theory and the Critical Tradition* (1953; New York, 1971), pp. 87–88. I am grateful to Jennie Jackson for pointing out this passage to me. See also Fatma Moussa-Mahmoud, *Sir William Jones and the Romantics* (Cairo, 1962).

17 Said, "Raymond Schwab and the Romance of Ideas," p. 250. See Schwab, *The Oriental Renaissance*, pp. 52–57.

18 See Schwab, *The Oriental Renaissance*, pp. 57–64; Garland H. Cannon, Jr., "Sir William Jones and the *Sakuntala*," *Journal of the American Oriental Society* 73 (Oct.–Dec., 1953): 198–202; and Dorothy Matilda Figueira, *Translating the Orient: The Reception of Śākuntala in Nineteenth-Century Europe* (Albany, NY, 1991).

19 See David Kopf, *British Orientalism and the Bengal Renaissance: The Dynamics of Indian Modernization, 1773–1835* (Berkeley, 1969). The earliest articulation of this notion that I can identify is in a letter of Jones's, written during the process of mastering the Sanskrit text in 1787. See William Jones, *The Letters of Sir William Jones*, ed. Cannon, 2 vols. (Oxford, 1970), 2: 682, and Cannon, *The Life and Mind of Oriental Jones: Sir William Jones, the Father of Modern Linguistics* (Cambridge, 1990), pp. 274–275.

20 See Rabindranath Tagore, "World Literature," in *Selected Writings on Literature and Language*, ed. Sukanta Chaudhuri (Oxford, 2001), pp. 138–150. On Tagore and Orientalism, see Amit Ray, *Negotiating the Modern: Orientalism and Indianness in the Anglophone World* (New York, 2007).

21 See Tagore, "*Shakuntala*," in *Selected Writings on Literature and Language*, p. 237.

22 Jawaharlal Nehru, *The Discovery of India* (New York, 1946), p. 317. See also Cannon, *The Life and Mind of Oriental Jones*, pp. xv–xvii; Kopf, *British Orientalism and the Bengal Renaissance*, p. 275; Thomas R. Trautmann, *Aryans and British India* (New Delhi, 2004); and Nirad Chaudhuri, *Scholar Extraordinary: The Life of Professor the Rt. Hon. Friedrich Max Müller, P.C.* (London, 1974).

23 See Trautmann, *Aryans and British India*, pp. 21–22. For Said's anticipation and refutation of such arguments, precisely with reference to Germany's nonimperial relationship to India, see *O*, pp. 18 –19. For a useful collection of historical studies of German Indology, see *Sanskrit and "Orientalism."* Suzanne Marchand's much-awaited study of German Orientalism will doubtless alter our understanding of it in significant ways.

24 See Ranajit Guha, *A Rule of Property for Bengal: An Essay on the Idea of Permanent Settlement* (1963; Durham, NC, 1996). It is a remarkable but hardly noted fact that this book, written at least fifteen years before the publication of Said's *Orientalism*, anticipates elements of its argument in rather uncanny ways. So far as I know, Said was not familiar with the existence of Guha's study when he wrote his own book in the 1970s, which had largely disappeared even from Indian debates after its initial publication by Mouton in 1963, though of course in *Culture and Imperialism* it provides one of the main instances of the latest phase of the global anticolonial "culture of resistance," the phase Said refers to as "the voyage in" (Said, *Culture and Imperialism* [New York, 1993], p. 216).

25 It is one of the smaller ironies of this historical moment that one of the sources Burke relied upon for the ideas about Indian legal reform that made their way into Fox's ill-fated India Bill in 1783, which proved to be only the first salvo in the attack on the practices of the East India Company that was to culminate in the trial of Hastings, was none other than Jones, who may well have been the author of the early drafts of some of the sections of the bill that are attributed to Burke. See Cannon, "Sir William Jones and Edmund Burke," *Modern Philology* 54 (Feb. 1957): 165–186. On the Hastings trial and Burke's role in it, see Dirks, *The Scandal of Empire: India and the Creation of Imperial Britain* (Cambridge, Mass., 2006). Amit Ray provides a fine narrative of these scholarly, administrative developments in Calcutta under the tutelage of Hastings; see Ray, *Negotiating the Modern*, pp. 29–53.

26 See, for instance, Cannon, *The Life and Mind of Oriental Jones*, pp. 229–230, and Nehru, *The Discovery of India*, p. 317.

27 Some of the translations from this period whose ultimate source is a Sanskrit text or set of texts, such as Halhed's well-known compilation *The Laws of the Gentoos*, were translated from Persian versions of the Sanskrit originals, themselves often at more than one remove. Halhed's Persian original is itself thought to have been a written translation of an oral account given by a Brahmin in Bengali. See Cannon, *The Life and Mind of Oriental Jones*, p. 231, and Trautmann, *Aryans and British India*, p. 28.

28 On Jones hearing rumors, before his discovery of Śakuntalā, of the existence of a form of writing called *nāṭaka*, see Cannon, *The Life and Mind of Oriental Jones*, pp. 273–274.

29 On knowledge systems in precolonial India, see "Forms of Knowledge in Early-Modern South Asia," a special issue of *Comparative Studies of South Asia, Africa, and the Middle East* 24, no. 2 (2004), ed. Sheldon Pollock.

30 Cannon, *The Life and Mind of Oriental Jones*, pp. 137, 142.

31 Jones, "On the Hindus," *Discourses and Essays*, ed. Moni Bagchee (New Delhi, 1984), p. 5.

32 See Cannon, *The Life and Mind of Oriental Jones*, pp. 197–198.

33 See Thomas R. Metcalf, *Ideologies of the Raj* (Cambridge, 1997). For a collection of studies of the Aryan thesis into our own times, where it has become entangled in the politics of right-wing Hindu nationalism, see *The Aryan Debate*, ed. Trautmann (Delhi, 2005). Unfortunately, and in marked contrast with such historians of ancient India as Romila Thapar, Trautmann remains apologetic and equivocal in face of the Hindutva politicization of historical and archeological evidence and claims.

34 Sara Suleri, *The Rhetoric of English India* (Chicago, 1992), pp. 33, 30, 31.

35 See Partha Chatterjee, *Nationalist Thought and the Colonial World: A Derivative Discourse?* (Minneapolis, 1986); Tapan Raychaudhuri, *Europe Reconsidered: Perceptions of the West in Nineteenth-Century Bengal* (Delhi, 1988); Brian K. Pennington, *Was Hinduism Invented? Britons, Indians, and Colonial Construction of Religion* (New York, 2005); Srinivas Aravamudan, *Guru English: South Asian Religion in a Cosmopolitan Language* (Princeton, NJ, 2006); Ray, *Negotiating the Modern*, chap. 2; and Anustup Basu, "Hindutva and Informatic Modernization," *boundary* 2 35 (Fall 2008): 239–250.

36 See, among numerous other works, Chatterjee, *Nationalist Thought and the Colonial World*; Sudipta Kaviraj, *The Unhappy Consciousness: Bankimchandra Chattopadhyay and the Formation of Nationalist Discourse in India* (Delhi, 1995); Chaudhuri, *The Autobiography of an Unknown Indian* (London, 1951) and *Scholar Extraordinary*; Raychaudhuri, *Europe Reconsidered*; and Kopf, *British Orientalism and the Bengal Renaissance*.

37 On Goethe and Hafiz, see Einboden, "The Genesis of *Weltliteratur*."

38 See Chatterjee, *Nationalist Thought and the Colonial World*, chap. 3.

39 Henry Louis Vivien Derozio, "To India – My Native Land," in *Early Indian Poetry in English: An Anthology: 1829–1947*, ed. Eunice de Souza (New Delhi, 2005), p. 6. On early editions of Jones's verse, see V. de Sola Pinto, "Sir William Jones and English Literature," *Bulletin of the School of Oriental and African Studies, University of London* 11, no. 4 (1946): 686–694.

40 See Rosinka Chaudhuri, *Gentlemen Poets in Colonial Bengal: Emergent Nationalism and the Orientalist Project* (Calcutta, 2002).

41 See, for instance, Katie Trumpener, *Bardic Nationalism: The Romantic Novel and the British Empire* (Princeton, NJ, 1997).

42 For a characteristic argument about Urdu as a conscious rejection of the indigenous, see Amrit Rai, *A House Divided: The Origins and Development of Hindi-Urdu* (Delhi, 1984).

43 See Sheldon Pollock, "The Cosmopolitan Vernacular," *Journal of Asian Studies* 57 (Feb. 1998): 6–37.

44 G.N. Devy, *After Amnesia: Tradition and Change in Indian Literary Criticism* (Hyderabad, 1995), p. 59. See Suniti Kumar Chatterji, *Indo-Aryan and Hindi* (1942; Calcutta, 1960), chap. 3.

45 See Kopf, *British Orientalism and the Bengal Renaissance*, and Sisir Kumar Das, *Sahibs and Munshis: An Account of the College of Fort William* (New Delhi, 1978).

46 See Das, *Sahibs and Munshis*; Kopf, *British Orientalism and the Bengal Renaissance*; and Muzaffar Alam and Sanjay Subrahmanyam, "The Making of a Munshi," *Comparative Studies of South Asia, Africa, and the Middle East* 24, no. 2 (2004): 61–72.

47 See Sadiqur-Rahman Kidwai, *Gilchrist and the "Language of Hindoostan"* (New Delhi, 1972). Gilchrist was a member of the Asiatic Society; he arrived in Calcutta in 1783, a year before Jones's arrival and founding of the society, and he is listed as a member of the society in the first volume of *Asiatick Researches* (1788).

48 Alok Rai, *Hindi Nationalism* (New Delhi, 2001), p. 24.

49 See, for instance, Vijayendra Snatak, *Hinī adab kī tārīkh*, trans. Khursheed Alam (New Delhi, 1999), p. 214.

50 See Rai, *A House Divided*. On Amrit Rai's polemical use of Insha, see David Lelyveld, "*Zuban-e Urdu-e Muʿalla* and the Idol of Linguistic Origins," *Annual of Urdu Studies* 8 (1993): 71–81.

51 Inshallah Khan Insha, *Kahānī Rānī Kētakī aur Kuñvar Uday Bhān kī*, ed. Maulvi Abdul Haq (Aligarh, 1975), pp. 11–12.

52 I owe this latter point to Rashmi Bhatnagar's superb presentation at MLA 2008 and to our subsequent conversations.

53 This story is told by Christopher R. King, *One Language, Two Scripts: The Hindi Movement in Nineteenth-Century North India* (New York, 1994), pp. 90–91; see also Alok Rai, *Hindi Nationalism*, pp. 65–66. On performativity in the precolonial northern vernacular, see Sumit Guha, "Transitions and Translations: Regional Power and Vernacular Identity in the Dakhan, 1500–1800," *Comparative Studies of South Asia, Africa, and the Middle East* 24, no. 2 (2004): 23–31.

54 On Azad, see Shamsur Rahman Faruqi, "Constructing a Literary History, a Canon, and a Theory of Poetry: *Ab-e Ḥayāt* (1880) by Muhammad Husain Āzād (1830–1910)," *Social Scientist* 23 (Oct–Dec. 1995): 70–97. For Shukla, see Milind Wakankar, "The Moment of Criticism in Indian Nationalist Thought: Ramchandra Shukla and the Poetics of a Hindi Responsibility," *South Atlantic Quarterly* 101 (Fall 2002): 987–1014.

55 The term is Gayatri Spivak's. See Gayatri Chakravorty Spivak, *Death of a Discipline* (New York, 2003).

56 Salman Rushdie, introduction to *Mirrorwork: Fifty Years of Indian Writing, 1947–1997*, ed. Rushdie and Elizabeth West (New York, 1997), p. viii.

57 On the historical debate, see Kopf, *British Orientalism and the Bengal Renaissance*, and Eric Stokes, *The English Utilitarians and India* (Oxford, 1959).

58 Thomas Babington Macaulay, "Minute on Indian Education" (1835), in *From the East India Company to the Suez Canal*, vol. 1 of *Archives of Empire*, ed. Mia Carter and Barbara Harlow (Durham, NC, 2003), p. 230: "I have no knowledge of either Sanscrit or Arabic. – But I have done what I could to form a correct estimate of their value. I have read translations of the most celebrated Arabic and Sanscrit works. I have conversed both here and at home with men distinguished by their proficiency in the Eastern tongues. I am quite ready to take the Oriental learning at the valuation of the Orientalists

themselves. I have never found one among them who could deny that a single shelf of a good European library was worth the whole native literature of India and Arabia."

59 For a superb analysis of some of these asymmetries, see Francesca Orsini, "India in the Mirror of World Fiction," in *Debating World Literature*, pp. 319–333.

60 An important exception in recent fiction is Amitav Ghosh's *Calcutta Chromosome*, which confronts precisely this ghostly presence of the vernacular in Angophone practices. See Bishnupriya Ghosh, *When Borne Across: Literary Cosmopolitics in the Contemporary Indian Novel* (New Brunswick, NJ, 2004).

61 Indeed, Amit Chaudhuri responded to Rushdie's proclamations with an anthology of his own, expanding its range to include precisely the vernacular literatures Rushdie had so summarily left out. See *Picador Book of Modern Indian Literature*, ed. Amit Chaudhuri (London, 2001).

62 I borrow the phrase from David Scott from a somewhat different context. See David Scott, *Conscripts of Modernity: The Tragedy of Colonial Enlightenment* (Durham, NC, 2004).

24

Against World Literature (2013)

Emily Apter

Emily Apter is Professor of French and Comparative Literature at New York University, having previously taught at UCLA and several other American universities after receiving her PhD from Princeton. Apter works on nineteenth- and twentieth-century French and comparative literature, feminism, and relations of literature, politics, and psychoanalysis, as in her book *Feminizing the Fetish: Psychoanalysis and Narrative Obsession in Turn-of-the-Century France* (1990). Subsequently, she explored the multi-national nation (*Continental Drift: From National Characters to Virtual Subjects*, 1999), and has increasingly engaged with the world-systems theory propounded by Immanuel Wallerstein and applied to literary studies by Franco Moretti. In *The Translation Zone: A New Comparative Literature* (2006), Apter analyzes the theory of literary world systems and the translatability of genres, arguing that translation is a critical form of intellectual labor in a world increasingly marked by "oneworldedness." Her work has focused increasingly on the difficulties of the labor of translation in light of the thorniness of language and the alterity of works even in "the original." The following essay is adapted from the introduction to *Against World Literature: On the Politics of Untranslatability* (2013), a book inspired in part by her work on a paradoxical translation project, an English version of French theorist Barbara Cassin's *Vocabulaire européen des philosophies: Dictionnaire des intraduisibles*.

World Literature, as a disciplinary rallying point of literary criticism and the academic humanities, became increasingly prominent from the mid-1990s on. Between 1991 and 1997, under the editorial stewardship of Djelal Kadir, the journal *World Literature Today* cast World Literature as a hosting ground to literary

Emily Apter, "Against World Literature" (2013). Introduction to Emily Apter, *Against World Literature: On the Politics of Untranslatability* (New York: Verso).

World Literature in Theory, First Edition. Edited by David Damrosch.
© 2014 John Wiley & Sons, Ltd. Published 2014 by John Wiley & Sons, Ltd.

postcolonialism. Pascale Casanova's watershed book *La République mondiale des lettres* sparked renewed interest in World Literature in France after it appeared in 1999 despite an opening salvo that sounded anxieties over whether it was even legitimate to speak of World Literature. In its second life in English as *The World Republic of Letters* (published in 2004 in the series "Convergences: Inventories of the Present" edited by Edward Said), the book became a flashpoint in literary and cultural studies, especially with respect to arguments over reiterated Eurocentrism and the status of so-called peripheral nations. *Debating World Literature*, a collection of essays edited by Christopher Prendergast in 2004, assessed the impact of Casanova's book as well as Franco Moretti's influential essay "Conjectures on World Literature" (2000) as it set out to rescue the "literature" half of the World Literature configuration from the de-aestheticizing jaws of globalization. A conference held at Istanbul Bilgi University in December 2008 titled "World Literature in Between," which kicked off with a conversation between David Damrosch and the Nobel-prize winning Turkish author Orhan Pamuk, served as prelude to the launch of the Institute of World Literature, spearheaded by David Damrosch at Harvard University. The Institute held its inaugural session at Peking University, Beijing in 2011 and on the same occasion marked The First Congress of the World Literature Association with a special focus on "The Rise of World Literatures." As anthologies, volumes of critical essays and specialized studies with a world literary focus propagate – some emphasizing networks and systems oriented around Marx's hypothetical of a literary International, others emphasizing a Goethean lineage adjusted to an era of global finance capital – the disciplinary construct that is here designated with upper case has secured its foothold in both the university institution and mainstream publishing. It stands in contrast to lower-case "world literature," which may be considered a descriptive catchall for the sum of all forms of literary expression in all the world's languages.

In titling this essay *Against World Literature: On the Politics of Untranslatability*, an interrogation shadows the provocation of the fore-title: if one is *against* the revival of World Literature in some of its new institutional guises, then what is one *for*? Certainly, I endorse World Literature's deprovincialization of the canon and the way in which, at its best, it draws on translation to deliver surprising cognitive landscapes hailing from inaccessible linguistic folds (what R.A. Judy, citing the eleventh-century Islamic philosopher Ibn Sina, refers to as the "arousal" and "wonder" [*takhyil*] sparked by poetic syllogisms).[1] However, I do harbor serious reservations about tendencies in World Literature toward reflexive endorsement of cultural equivalence and substitutability, or toward the celebration of nationally and ethnically branded "differences" that have been niche-marketed as commer-cialized "identities." As Simon During states convincingly: "The interest in world literature obviously follows the recent rapid extension of cross-border flows of tourists and cultural goods around the world, including literary fiction." During gleans "a complex dynamic between literature's increased participation in the gen-teel leisure industry and the relative decline of literary writing's importance both in the education system and in the market."[2]

I have been left uneasy in the face of the entrepreneurial, bulimic drive to anthologize and curricularize the world's cultural resources, as evinced in projects sponsored by some proponents of World Literature. Studies of broad ambition like the richly synthetic volume *The Routledge Companion to World Literature* (2012), whose programmatic reach (as its back cover proclaims) covers "the disciplinary relationship of World Literature to areas such as philology, translation, globalization and diaspora studies," fall prey inevitably to the tendency to zoom over the speed bumps of untranslatability in the rush to cover ground.[3] In a counter-move, I invoke untranslatability as a deflationary gesture toward the expansionism and gargantuan scale of world-literary endeavors.

A primary argument here is that many recent efforts to revive World Literature rely on a translatability assumption. As a result, incommensurability and what has been called the Untranslatable are insufficiently built into the literary heuristic. Drawing on philosophies of translation developed by Jacques Derrida, Gayatri Chakravorty Spivak, Samuel Weber, Barbara Johnson, Abdelfattah Kilito and Edouard Glissant, as well as on the way in which the Untranslatable is given substance in the context of Barbara Cassin's *Vocabulaire européen des philosophies: Dictionnaire des Intraduisibles* (whose English translation I supervised with co-editors Jacques Lezra and Michael Wood), my aim is to activate untranslatability as a theoretical fulcrum of comparative literature with bearing on approaches to world literatures, literary world systems and literary history, the politics of periodization, the translation of philosophy and theory, the relation between sovereign and linguistic borders at the checkpoint, the bounds of non-secular proscription and cultural sanction, free versus privatized authorial property, the poetics of translational difference, as well as ethical, cosmological and theological dimensions of worldliness. These problematics unfold with reference to a central thesis about the interest of an approach to literary comparatism that recognizes the importance of non-translation, mistranslation, incomparability and untranslatability.

Translation studies' particular appeal derived from its ability to respond to a planetary remit without sacrificing engagement with the world's languages. The number of publications, books, book series, articles in journals about, and journals devoted to the practices and theory of translation spiked from 2000–2012, attesting to the combination of excitement and disaggregation characteristic of the emerging discipline.[4] Translation studies gained traction in the humanities because it was interdisciplinary without diluting a disciplinary formation in comparative literature. It drew on the tradition of *translatio studii* in Renaissance humanism (so important to comparative literature's foundation as a discipline), reworking it for a contemporary global education. Among the substantive issues that transferred most obviously from early periods to the present, I would mention knowledge transmission; philosophies of "world," "humanity" and "human rights"; the idea of a "classic"; aesthetic judgment and its critique; vernacularization and linguistic ethnocentrism in tension with cosmopolitan culture. Such topics go to the heart of what is of direct concern to graduate students preparing to teach subjects in the humanities at a difficult juncture in the economy of education. As teachers in training, graduate students have an obvious stake not only in acquiring pedagogies (competence in the translation *practicum* and the related subfield of translation theory), they also need to identify problems and topics that clearly communicate why the humanities matter in contemporary society. Translation remains one of those areas that relates to a larger public without sacrificing intellectual nuance. It is also the kind of paradigm – the translational humanities – whose global relevance has just begun to be understood in relation to public policy, legal theories of authorship and intellectual property, and international security, and whose implications as a language technology for media theory ask to be more fully explored. Finally, as a practice that lends itself to collaborative pedagogy, translation opens up questions of how to teach literature in the humanities now, especially when there is a need to ford the divisions between World Literature and theory that have led to unproductive rifts.[5]

As momentum increased in translation studies, *Weltliteratur* – with its Euro-Romantic, neo-Hegelian, Marxist and humanist pedigree, from Goethe to Lukács, Auerbach to Said – also gained renewed attention. Franco Moretti's "Conjectures on World Literature" induced a non-apologetic swerve away from close reading toward distant reading. Another essay, "Evolution, World-Systems, *Weltliteratur*" (2006), after noting the dearth of viable concepts and hypotheses in the study of World Literature, proposed using evolutionary theory and world-system analysis in the name of a unitary perspective that reveals (as it does with the system of capitalism) the "one and unequal" playing field of national and local literatures. *Death of a Discipline* (2003) by Gayatri Chakravorty Spivak introduced the concept of "planetarity" for a critical, non-"globalized" area studies. Bruce Robbins and Pheng Cheah, drawing on the work of Etienne Balibar, married political theories of citizenship to the politics of cosmopolitanism in forging their notion of "cosmopolitics" (1998). David Damrosch's *What Is World Literature?* (2003) used a text's translational circulation as a metric of World Literature's worldliness. Katie Trumpener modeled the ascendant geopolitical ascription of World Literature in her contribution to a 2006 volume *Comparative Literature in an Age of Globalization* (edited by Haun Saussy) that grew out of the 2004 American Comparative Literature Association Report on the State of the Discipline. "Modernism in the World" was the title theme of a 2006 essay by Simon Gikandi critiquing postcolonial emulations of high modernist literature. In an essay on translations of Kazuo Ishiguro (2007) Rebecca Walkowitz introduced the notion of "unimaginable largeness" to characterize "the New World Literature." The World Novel acquired currency as a unit of analysis in Joseph Slaughter's *Human Rights, Inc.* (2007), a book that calibrated the rise of the Bildungsroman with the emergence of international charters. Wai Chee Dimock's *Shades of the Planet: American Literature as World Literature* (2007) imposed the prospect of a planetarized America, as did *A New Literary History of America* (2009), edited by Werner Sollors and Greil Marcus. Postcolonial criticism – galvanized by Edward Said, Ato Quayson, Homi Bhabha, Achille Mbembe, Mary Louise Pratt, Gayatri Chakravorty Spivak, Walter Mignolo, Robert Young, Gauri Viswanathan and countless others – assumed the world literary purview as a given, integral to oppositional theoretical paradigms.

In France, the resurgence of engagement with World Literature had a lot to do with the impact of Pascale Casanova's *World Republic of Letters* (1999). The book projected a new model of World Literature by assailing the old universalist form. The author showed how France's success in defining the World Literature canon in the nineteenth and early-twentieth centuries guaranteed its national prestige and its dominance as a geographic axis of cultural capital. Casanova also underscored the role of translation in assigning national authors and literary works a place in the world literary system of publication, distribution and critical review (despite failing to account for the "re-arrangement of world literary space in philological work on classical languages of the East prior to Herder's writings on language in the 1770s," as Aamir Mufti has argued).[6] Though no utopian program of a retrofitted World Literature was explicitly promulgated, the book pointed implicitly in the direction of a galaxy of micro-mondes in translation, in which the role of hegemonic societies in the management and mediation of literature was curtailed. More recent work in France, all of which bears Bourdieu's imprint, focused on the migration of ideas and the displacement and re-formation of intellectual networks (Laurent Jeanpierre, Yves Chevrel), the sociology of translation (Gisèle Sapiro, Blaise Wilfert) and the genealogy of *Weltliteratur* as a Goethean "situated universalism" with prophetic resonance for contemporary translation studies (François Xavier Landrin's "La sémantique historique de la *Weltliteratur*: genèse conceptuelle et usages savants.") In 2012 Jérôme David's *Spectres de Goethe. Les métamorphoses de la "littérature mondiale"* [Specters of Goethe. The Metamorphoses of "World Literature"] – a tour de force of critical ventriloquism in the manner of Goethe's conversations with Johann Peter Eckermann – attested to *Weltliteratur*'s renewed piquancy as a literary paradigm.

Both translation studies and World Literature extended the promise of worldly criticism, politicized cosmopolitanism, comparability aesthetics galvanized by a deprovincialized Europe, an academically redistributed area studies and a redrawn map of language geopolitics. Partnered, they could deliver still more: translation theory as *Weltliteratur* would challenge flaccid globalisms that paid lip service to alterity while doing little more than to buttress neoliberal "big tent" syllabi taught in English. Unfortunately, though, translation studies and World Literature, even in their renewed and best-intentioned guises, inevitably fell short of such objectives. Their institutional forms could not escape being too pluralistic, too ecumenical, insufficiently hard-line in the face of appropriation by universities seeking to justify the downsizing of national literature departments or the cutting of "foreign" language instruction. A course in translation – carrying a distinguished imprimatur as a professional training that could even produce measurable "outcomes" – was often deployed as a patch for "humanities lite" and for literary education that was politically *appauvri* in its amenability to soft diplomacy and its default to models of oneworldedness freighted with the psychopolitical burden of delusional democracy. Here, the psychopolitics of planetary dysphoria were itself definable as the depression of the globe or the thymotic frustration of the world.

Both fields, moreover, were unable to rework literary history through planetary cartographies and temporalities despite their recourse to world-systems theory. Shaped by classical genre theory, Renaissance humanism, Hegelian historical consciousness, Goethean *Weltliteratur*, Diltheyan *Geistesgeschichte* and the Marxist ideal of an "International of letters," literary history has been beset by what

Christopher Prendergast, following Arjun Appadurai, calls the "Euro-chronology problem." This is a problem arising from the fact that critical traditions and disciplines founded in the Western academy contain inbuilt typologies – "epic," "classicism," "Renaissance," "realism," "the avant-garde," "the postmodern" – adduced from Western literary examples.

In addition to giving short shrift to temporality and periodization, translation studies and World Literature ignored problems more internal to their theoretical premises. With translation assumed to be a good thing *en soi* – under the assumption that it is a critical praxis enabling communication across languages, cultures, time periods and disciplines – the right to the Untranslatable was blindsided. In a parallel way, at its very core World Literature seemed oblivious to the Untranslatable – as shown by its unqueried inclusion of the word "world." World was famously interrogated by Heidegger alongside "finitude" and "individuation" in his *Fundamental Concepts of Metaphysics*. It was defined as that which humans (as opposed to animals or stones) richly "have." In having world – that is to say, in having the capacity for world made possible by language and subjective accessibility – beings become human. The concept of world, Heidegger affirms, "means the accessibility of beings as such rather than beings in themselves." Aside from the dichotomies of animal/human or living/non-living – they are juggernauts of critical theory at the current pass – the philosophization of world remains a fundamental problem demanding the rephilosophization of literary history through the history of translation. "The history of philosophy," as Abdelfattah Kilito reminds us with reference to the historic importance of Averroës's translation and exegesis of Aristotle, "is at its core the history of translation."[7] The expression "history of translation" from my perspective implies a decided emphasis on when and where translation happens, and, especially, on how and why it fails.

Translation failure – one of Walter Benjamin's obsessions and a concept whose richness has been plumbed by translation studies far less than his famously enigmatic notion of *reine Sprache* (pure or transparent language) – invites elaboration alongside other iterations of the non-translatable: "lost in translation," the mistranslated, unreliable translation and the *contresens*, an impassive condition that would seem to nest in language; sometimes discernible as a pull away from language norming. We see this last effect in Kilito's characterization of cases in which the target language refuses to cooperate with the translator, especially where devilishly difficult phrases in Arabic like *amma ba'ad* (roughly, "so now," "as to what follows," "that said") and *layta chi'ari* ("if only my knowledge," "if only I knew") are concerned.[8] Glossolalia, or speaking in tongues – or language that bars access to translation – represents yet another form of translation failure. What we have in this instance, as Daniel Heller-Roazen points out, is speech that preserves only the envelope of semantic intention. "Glossolalia," he recalls, "is a technical expression referring to a variety of speech act whose name derives from the Greek term for speaking in tongues … Giorgio Agamben has commented that such speech consists not so much in the "pure uttering of inarticulate sounds" as in a "'speaking in *gloss*'; that is, in words whose meaning one does not know." To hear such sounds is to know they mean something without knowing exactly what such a "something" might be; in other words, it is to discern an intention to signify that cannot be identified with any particular signification."[9] For Heller-Roazen, glossolalia posits a non-signifying model of communicability against the grain of language's inherent profit motive. The conventional economic ends of communication – transactions, deals, exchanges, investment returns – are put out of action and, in their stead, we find a pure language that plays off disinterested communicative gestures.

In Heller-Roazen's ascription, glossolalia is not wide of the mark of Wittgenstein's nonsense, with its attendant lexicon of *das Unsagbare* (the Unsayable), *das Unverständlich* (the Un-understandable) and *das Unaussprechliche* (the Inexpressible) introduced in the *Tractatus Logico-Philosophicus*. Each of these terms demarcates where logic fails; where propositions that lack sense (*sinnlos*) and direction (*sens*) must be identified; where inexpressible things put pressure on speech; or where the nonsense of mysticism and metaphysics prevails. The idea that nonsense is the result of the "failure to understand the logic of our language" implies that language can make sense of a proposition like "Green is green," as long as humans grasp the logic of the sentence (as long, that is, as "Green" is understood as the proper name of an individual who has turned green due to sickness, a skin condition or the inebriation of the beholder).[10] For Wittgenstein, translation is the mechanism by which language logic is tested. And, in translation studies, the limits of sayability and expressibility are increasingly a focus, conjugating logic and philology, with the latter understood in Werner Hamacher's ascription as an "inclination (or disinclination) to that which is said and not said."[11] Wittgenstein's understanding of nonsense (*unsinn, bedeutungslos*) – qualifed as gibberish or as pseudo-propositions about the world – holds further potential for analyzing poetic opacity: he defines it as the outer edge of intelligibility in language; the limitrophe of a discrete tongue; or inflections of madness, schizo-language and autism. From here, it is but a short step to translation theory filtered through Saul Kripke's Wittgensteinian "private language argument" (*Wittgenstein on Rules and Private Language*) or Nelson Goodman's "new riddle of induction" (*Fact, Fiction, and Forecast*), which argues that, with time factored, a given object could meaningfully be *grue* or *bleen*.

Where the Untranslatable in language philosophy directs one to the logic of grammar, the limits of reference, the outer reach of thinkability or the difference between meaningful and meaningless propositions, in semiology it connotes grand abstractions – Logos, God, Truth, Marx's General Equivalent – nouns, in short, at their greatest distance from material referents. These transcendental signifieds emphasize how questions of untranslatability are rooted in theology, hermeticism, hermeneutics and epigraphy, which associate them with such notions as *alêtheia* (hidden being, truth), "glossolalia" (speaking in tongues), gnomic or apodictic utterances, the differend, the nonpareil, the sublime, the exception and the sovereign. Foregrounded here are questions concerning the theological grounding of "language as such" posed by early Benjamin, as he countered Kantian pure reason through recourse to Hamann's theory of creation that suggests it to be the physical imprint of the divine word.[12] Of parallel importance is the last seminar given by Derrida in 2002 organized around the theme of "The Beast and the Sovereign."

Derrida designated Christ the master translator of the Logos, and, from thence, of "man as a *zoon*, as a living animal possessed of *logos* who gives rise to an entire tradition of rational man" as the "calculating animal." He attributes the logo-centrism of monotheistic religions to "forced translations" that form the basis of "sovereign hegemony." Located, then, at the core of political theology, translation carries with it this weight of coercion, this residual history of forcing, tangible in legislation against blasphemy or historic prohibitions on the vernacularization of sacred texts.[13] So we have the Latin Bible proscribed in English in the early Middle Ages; the German Bible, translated by Luther, initially condemned as a travesty; and Arabic-only strictures applied to the Quran. The theological ban on the portage of holy words from one language to another extends, in secular contexts, to a *force de frappe*. This is evinced in the injunction issued (albeit somewhat ironically) by Kilito: "Thou Shalt not Translate Me!" Kilito's fables of translational impropriety add density to recent efforts by Naomi Seidman (in *Faithful Renderings*), Daniel Heller-Roazen (in a prospective project on "secret language" and idiolects that are off limits to tourists and travelers) and Saba Mahmood (in *Politics of Piety*) to rethink secular criticism in terms of theologies of translation. Kilito is no anti-secularist, but he refuses to delegitimate the force of translational interdiction in sacred language by dismissing it as dogma or traditionalism or subordinating it to culturalist accounts of divine authority.

Mahmood, by contrast, adopts a culturalist approach, arguing that piety is always already a politics, situationally localized and personally negotiated. Glossing Talal Asad, she notes: "Asad shifts from an understanding of scripture as a corpus of authoritatively inscribed opinions that stand for religious truth, to one which divine texts are one of the central elements in a discursive field of relations of power *through which* truth is established."[14] Judith Butler, for her part, circumvents the impasse between religious absolutism and cultural relativism by transforming the critique of judgment into the problem of adjudicating translatability. For Butler, cultural translation as a practice "would be a condition of such judgment, and that what is being judged is not only whether the question of whether a given action is injurious but also whether, if it is, legal remedies are the best way to approach the issue, and what other ways of acknowledging and repairing injury are available."[15]

Cultural translation, in these terms, shifts the politics of offense, blasphemy, moral injury, dogma, religious truth and the culture of belief from the obdurately dichotomized framework dividing piety and secularism (mired in ongoing wars of religion as well as the intractable Western/non-Western culture wars) to one of law and language. Butler has recourse to translation to explicate how scriptural and legal truths become grounded in universals, legally sanctioned or situationally overdetermined. There is a pragmatics of translatability built into this approach but therein lies its limitations; for in proposing just "to translate" the translational interdiction as part of a larger grammar of linguistic judgment calls, the boundaries of untranslatability are perforce traduced and sacral untranslatability as such is no longer taken seriously. The difficulty remains concerning how to take sacral untranslatability at its word without secularist condescension. I make no pretense of resolving the issue, only to ensuring that it be recognized as a major heuristic challenge for the interpretive humanities.

Theological untranslatability – a property of non-controversion vested in "theological onomasiology" (God-naming), and associated historically with the way polytheistic, intercultural translations of the gods' proper names gave way to Judeo-Christian strictures that held any translation of God's name to be apostasy – often functions as an adhesive of bonded community and the hegemony of monotheistic religions. But François Noudelmann has given it different connotations in the guise of "disruptive kinship," where elective as opposed to genetically ordained affinities are the rule. Disruptive kinship implies an *air de famille* minus the *lien de parenté*: it refers to blood ties that have been broken, thwarted orders of nature, queer families, subcultures, soul mates, monsters, the progeny of Virgin birth, spirits born of metempsychosis, or, in the case of language, Untranslatables that stand outside of language families. Derrida initiated thinking along these lines in "Des Tours de Babel," with reference to the breakdown of kinship models in nineteenth-century historical linguistics:

> The allusion to the maturation of a seed could resemble a vitalist or geneticist metaphor; it would come, then, in support of the genealogical and parental code which seems to dominate this text. In fact it seems necessary here to invert this order and recognize what I have elsewhere proposed to call the "metaphoric catastrophe": far from knowing first what "life" or "family" mean whenever we use these familiar values to talk about language and translation; it is rather starting from the notion of a language and its "sur-vival" in translation that we could have access to the notion or what life and family mean. This reversal is operated expressly by Benjamin.[16]

Sundered filiation leads to orphaned, dispossessed literary properties, which is the unifying idea in the book's last section, "Who Owns My Translation?" Building on Derrida's articulation of linguistic dispropriation in *Monolingualism of the Other; or, The Prosthesis of Origin* ("I speak only one language and it is not my own"), I conjecture that one reason why literary studies falls short as anti-capitalist critique is because it insufficiently questions what it means to "have" a literature or to lay claim to aesthetic property. Literary communities are gated: according to Western law and international statute, authors *have* texts, publishers *have* a universal right to translate (as long as they pay), and nations *own* literary patrimony as cultural inheritance. Translation, seen as authorized plagiarism, emerges as a form of creative property that belongs fully to no one. As a model of deowned literature, it stands against the swell of corporate privatization in the arts, with its awards given to individual genius and bias against collective authorship. A translational author – shorn of a singular signature – is the natural complement, in my view, to World Literature understood as an experiment in national sublation that signs itself as collective, terrestrial property.

If the conditions of property-value and economic privatization underwriting contemporary literary world-systems are crucial to analyzing literature's material assets, they also inflect the economy of comparison. The Hellenist Marcel Detienne, whose *Comparer l'incomparable* (2000) engages with the heuristics of the Untranslatable in the comparative human sciences, takes us in this direction when he examines the comparatist's *art de monnayer* – the ability to traffic in differential civilities, in "incomparable" sacred and patrimonial objects. Incomparables and Untranslatables are thus set about in a world in which mobile social placing and terrestrial property-lines both affirm and trump national heritage claims. Disputes over art restitution or access to archeological sites, seen in this light, provide insight into the material stakes of "having" something culturally unique, nationally branding, or personally self-defining, and I have experimented with looking at these topics in relation to literary property.

Working "against World Literature" has led to an array of loosely affiliated topoi – oneworldedness, literary world-systems, terrestrial humanism, checkpoints, theologies of translation, the translational interdiction, pedagogy, authorial deownership, possessive collectivism. These topoi – hardly exhaustive – provide so many ways of looking at how untranslatability plays out in literary studies. Hardly programmatic, they nonetheless imply a politics of literature critical of global literary management within corporate education, testing the hypothesis that translation and untranslatability are constitutive of world forms of literature. Consider, for instance, how Tolstoy gained admission to the precinct of the "world novel" by opening *War and Peace* in French. This gambit may look paradoxical – to attain greatness as a Russian novelist, write in French! – but it confirms that one function of foreign languages is to certify the novel's non-provincialism; its bona fides as *Weltliteratur*. As Richard Pevear, co-translator with Larissa Volokhonsky, of the 2007 Knopf English translation of the novel notes:

> The book opens in French – not with a few words of French (as in those English versions that do not eliminate the French altogether), but with a whole paragraph of French, with only a few phrases of Russian at the end. This mixing of French and Russian goes on for another five chapters or more, and occurs frequently throughout the rest of the book. There are also some long letters entirely in French, as well as official dispatches, and quotations from the French historian Adolphe Thiers. There are passages in German as well. For all of them Tolstoy supplied his own translations in footnotes, as we do. But that made the question still more problematic, because Tolstoy's translations are occasionally inaccurate, perhaps deliberately so. The amount of French in the text is smaller than some early critics asserted – not a third, but only about two percent. But there is a great deal of gallicized Russian, either implying that the speaker is speaking in French, or showing that upper-class ladies like Julie Karagin are unable to write correctly in their own language.[17]

Tolstoy arguably trademarked the world novel as a chronicle of political instability and crisis by leaning heavily on untranslatability, whether in the guise of non-translated passages in French and German, Russian-inflected French, or unreliable translations of textual segments earmarked for translation in the notes. Pevear implies that the Untranslatable performs a metafunction in the novel, tormenting its would-be translator with the impossibility of the task at hand; demonstrating, with a certain realism, how language-savvy aristocratic society lives in a world in which blunted comprehension and linguistic subterfuge are the norm; and contributing to an effect that Pevear suggests occurs throughout, namely a compositional heterogeneity that "disrupts the fictional continuum."

The "invasion" of French onto the territory of the Russian language in *War and Peace* reiterates the plot structure, which devolves around the Napoleonic incursion and its consequent shake-up of the old social order. It may not be too great a stretch to say that Tolstoy's heteroglossic micro-society, with its subterranean revolutionary urges multilingually channeled, foreshadows *The Communist Manifesto* circulating the world over in multiple translations. This idea of a translational International leads us to a free translation of World Literature as "screwed-up literature" based on a passage of *The Communist Manifesto*. Marx and Engels wrote: "In place of the old local and national seclusion and self-sufficiency, we have intercourse in every direction, universal interdependence of nations. And as in material, so also in intellectual production. The intellectual creations of individual nations become common property … and from the numerous national and local literatures, there arises a world literature." Jonathan Arac notes:

> So much of the business of this passage is condensed in the single word translated "intercourse": German *Verkehr*. A standard dictionary lists the meanings for this word in sequence as: traffic, transportation, communication, commerce, intercourse in its sexual as well as other senses, and communion. It is all but communism (in German, *Kommunismus*), for which Marx and Engels required recourse to a Latin, rather than a Germanic, derivation, perhaps to signal the movement's internationalism. The related verb, *verkehren*, means to turn over, with the usual off-key sense carried by the prefix *ver-*, so to put it colloquially, to screw up. *Die verkehrter Welt* is the world turned upside down, which in the metahistory of Marx and Engels is just what the bourgeoisie does by means of its *Verkehr*.[18]

Verkehrte Weltliteratur, or screwed-up literature, has precisely the right impertinent coding. For in standing the world on its head, it encourages the literatures of the world to mess with World Literature, turning it into a process of translating untranslatably. It beckons one to run the experiment of imagining what a literary studies contoured around untranslatability might be.

It may seem counter-intuitive to argue for untranslatability in the era of a translational turn. Certainly there are critics who consider such a move to be unconvincing, if not downright folly. In his *Is That a Fish in Your Ear? Translation and the Meaning of Everything* (2011), the critic and accomplished translator David Bellos insists that nothing is *un*translatable. "The circulation of novels," he writes, "among all the vehicular languages of the world and their incontestable conversations with one another demonstrate without a shadow of a doubt that style does survive translation … In sum, the widespread notion that style is untranslatable is just a variant of the folkish nostrum that a translation is no substitute for the original."[19] Bellos treats the idea that certain contents are ineffable or ungraspable with similar skepticism, arguing with clever reverse logic, that "the ineffable is [not] a problem for translation, but translation is one big problem for the ineffable" (152). Here, he is positioning himself contra Jerrold Katz's Wittgensteinian *axiom of ineffability* (which states that "What cannot be expressed in any human language … lies outside the boundaries of translation and … outside the field of language too"). For Bellos, "One of the truths that translation teaches us – is that everything is effable" (153). In this sense, the view that everything is effable implies a faith in the limitless capabilities of rationalism to appropriate (aligned with what Heidegger would insist is the capacity to turn the earth into a world). Such a categorical statement about the conditions of optimal cognizability does not in itself necessarily offer a disproof of linguistic ineffability or untranslatability. It would seem that Bellos' opposition to untranslatability is guided by his role as a professional translator having to overcome difficult hurdles. Thus a joke visiting card signed "Adolf Hitler – Fourreur," encountered in a shop by a character from Perec's novel *Life: A User's Manual*, is translated by Bellos as "Adolf Hitler – German Lieder." The match here works off the French term for "furrier," homo-nymically close to a French pronunciation of Führer (leader), and the German word for "songs" (*Lieder*), whose English pronunciation sounds out the English "leader." Bellos comments: "It may well be not the only or the best possible translation of Perec's joke visiting card, but it matches well enough in the dimensions that matter … It doesn't preserve all dimensions of the original – what ever does? – but matches enough of them, in my honest but not very humble opinion, to count as a satisfactory translation of a self-referring, meta-linguistic, and interlingual joke" (279). While this maximal translation may be justified under the special constraints imposed by humor, in dismissing the untranslated as a "dimension that doesn't matter," Bellos leaves hanging the question of what matters. Perhaps it would be more accurate to understand the Untranslatable, not as pure difference in opposition to the always translatable (rightly suspect as just another non-coeval form of the romantic Absolute, or fetish of the Other, or myth of hermeneutic inaccessibility) but as a linguistic form of creative failure with homeopathic uses.

Alain Badiou's opposition to philosophical untranslatability proves harder to contend with, coming as it does from a philosopher recently turned translator whose ideas have been much with me. Badiou's "hypertranslation" of Plato's *Republic* (*La République de Platon*, 2012) is a true adventure in philosophy. He theatricalizes the mise-en-scène of Platonic discourse (in a cross between Brecht and Beckett). He introduces French slang and he takes liberties with Plato's content to the point of inventing a new female character. Throughout, there is an attempt to stage an encounter with "the real" through recourse to colloquial diction; a diction contributing to the translation's political intention. Badiou valorizes equality (rather than liberty or freedom of expression, associated with "the politics of appearance and opinion") alongside the text's potential for a contemporary politics of justice.[20] According to him, "I turned to the *Republic*, the masterwork of the Master, to allow its power to scintillate the present."[21] As Susan Spitzer, the translator of the text into American English, intimates, Badiou's

Republic may be seen as an exercise in "communist" translation whose "fidelity" to the Greek original should be gauged in political terms:

> "Hypertranslation" is the word Alain Badiou has used, in *The Communist Hypothesis* and elsewhere, to describe his treatment of Plato's *Republic*. Not a "simple" translation into French of the Greek original, then, and still less a scholarly critique of it, Badiou's text transforms the *Republic* into something startlingly new by expanding, reducing, updating and dramatizing it, leavening it with humor and revitalizing its language with his own philosophical lexicon. Yet, for all the plasticity of the hypertranslation, its freewheeling appropriation of the source text, it still remains an adaptation based firmly on his painstaking translation of Plato's language into modern French.[22]

Badiou's approach to translating involves "absolute comprehending": "I start by trying to comprehend the text, absolutely, in its own language" (xii).

He broke this process down by doing line readings of the original Greek, consulting three (standard but very dated) French translations, and making notes on specific passages, some dating back to the earliest years of his philosophical education. A series of procedures that avoid excessive recourse to scholarly tools allowed him to channel Plato directly. The result, he avows, is not a "translation" in the strict sense of that term but a faithful philosophical transcription; a translation that militantly refuses "capitulation" to editorial normalization in the name of staying constant to the text's "eternity." Badiou modernizes images (the cave becomes a moviehouse) and adds anachronistic references (to the Paris Commune, World War I, Freud, AIDS, Jean-François Lyotard, etc.). This "faithful" infidelity, jarring though it may be, supports the creation of "Badiou-Plato": a sublation or philosophical event referring to a politics of Truths and an ontology of the Subject. It is this construct that authorizes Badiou's strong translation of Plato's "Idea of the Good" (*Idée du Bien*) as "Truth" (*Vérité*); "soul" (*âme*) as "Subject" (*Sujet*); "God" (*Dieu*) as "Big Other" or "Other" (*grand Autre, Autre*); and "Republic" (*République*) – a notoriously difficult Untranslatable going back to the Greek *Politeia*, commonly construed as "constitution" – as "State" (*Etat*) or "politics" (*politique*).[23] In his introduction to the English translation, Kenneth Reinhard associates this pattern of over-translation with a unique form of sublimation that he poses as

> a sublime – *hypselos* – place of new topological proximities, unmappeable according to the conventional metrics of history and geography. The hyper-space opened up by Badiou's translation is a realm of ideas, but it is no heavenly empyrean; Badiou's *Republic* is neither a philosophical purification nor a literary modernization of Plato in the sense of being an attempt to reduce historical distance for the sake of making an ancient text more familiar, a part of our world. On the contrary, Badiou's "hyper" translation *sublimates* Plato's text, in Lacan's sense of sublimation as "the elevation of an object to the status of a Thing," which is precisely to *de*-familiarize it, to bring out its strangeness – at least from the perspective of current opinion about Plato and Platonism. (xii)

Badiou's translational practice marshals Plato's opposition to sophistics in the service of his own. He groups lines 336b–357 from book 1, for example, into a chapter captioned "Reduce the Sophist to Silence" to emphasize Socrates's relentless smack-down of the Sophist Thrasymachus (a vain pugilist and champion of "Might makes right"). Bruno Bosteels links this aspect of Badiou's Platonism to his general refusal of the linguistic turn in philosophy:

> For Badiou, subordinating the doctrine of being to the logic of the signifier or to a linguistic anthropology amounts to reducing philosophy to sophistics – ontology then becomes what Barbara Cassin, following Novalis, calls 'logology'. Aside from his polemics against the great modern sophists that would include everyone from the second Wittgenstein to the late Lyotard, the fact remains that there is a rather glaring absence of any theory of language in Badiou's philosophy of the event ....

> Badiou also never indulges in play on etymologies and alleged un-translatables, nor does he in any way privilege the aura of the original, mostly Greek or German texts of philosophy, as has become customary in much post-Heideggerian thinking. For Badiou, the French language would be utterly foreign to such auratic philosophical uses ...

> Cassin's overarching aim in recognizing the protagonism of sophistics is to give the history of philosophy a different beginning by reverting the decision of sense away from the principle of univocity and back to linguistic equivocation.[24]

Barbara Cassin herself wishes to avoid reductive dichotomies: "Anti-Platonism seems like such an outdated notion! But anti-sophistics, too, seems so outdated!" Acknowledging that Badiou is committed to a form of Platonism that refuses to "recognize the constitutive character of the linguistic variation," Cassin suggests that he nonetheless retains the structural function of the sophist idea of Truth as an empty set within his own definition of Truth as a void in the situation, as "withdrawal" from the authority of language.[25]

Badiou may recognize that sophistics makes philosophy stronger, but his anti-sophistic elevation of univocity over equivocation, of idea over language, of transparency over opacity, of transmission over hermeneutics, results in the subordination of translation to philosophy. This explains why he could rely without apology on an old mimeographed copy of Etienne Balibar's "teaching" translation of Wittgenstein's *Tractatus Logico-Philosophicus* when writing his book on *Wittgenstein's Antiphilosophy* rather than on published scholarly editions in French and English. The translation's quality is not at issue, it is the communication of the Idea that counts. The "Communist Idea," as evental form, is contingent on furthering access to philosophy to the non-initiate. In this respect, Badiou's democratic and demotic translation targets a point of pride held dear by the academic guild: expertise in reading works of philosophy in the original. According to Badiou: "Specialists from all disciplines love to seek shelter behind the old destroyed Babel. Who has not heard the objection that, not knowing the language – from Greek to formal logic via German or Hebrew – they could not hope to understand anything whatever of what was said therein? Only to be followed by organizing an interdisciplinary conference on translation, without in any way moving the lines."[26]

If there is a philosophy of untranslatability in Badiou, it has little to do with language. It derives from an *incommensurability* at the heart of mathematical Platonism. To cite Kenneth Reinhard's introduction to Badiou's *Republic* yet once more, at issue is "a subjective construction that begins with the thesis that there is something incommensurable about all existing measures, something similar to the irrational relation between a diagonal and the sides of a square. But, unlike the exponents of mystical Platonism, Badiou insists that it is incumbent on us to *determine* this non-relation, to construct a new measure for the immeasurable."[27] Arguably, between Badiou's example as a translator of Plato and his philosophical commitment to a Platonic mathematical ontology that activates the incommensurable, one can posit a philosophical Untranslatable. It may be identified with a sublime gesture of hyper-translation – convertible into a matheme – that denominates a subjective "inexistent." It might also be thought of (after Graham Harman) as an action of "vicarious causation" that makes the Idea appear when contiguous but non-communicating objects, qualia and ontic states are brought into relation.[28] Badiou's philosophical translation, indifferent to language and sworn to mathematical ontology (in which the Subject lines up structurally with Parmenides's suprasensible form of the One), sits at the antipode of Cassin's "philosophizing in languages," where the politics of linguistic difference is availed to unhorse language nationalisms.[29] As I have already intimated, Cassin's dictionary of Untranslatables constitutes a venture in sophistical philosophizing with and in translation as its heuristic of choice.

Cassin's practice of untranslatability in the *Vocabulaire* has deepened more recently into a theory of equivocal symptoms in language; historically stigmatized as the mark of radical evil in translation. In "Homonymy and Amphiboly or Radical Evil in Translation," she has argued that homonymy destabilizes language in its very structure. Noting that we are used to viewing homonymy as an accident of language, or one of those tricks that language plays on the translator, similar to "false friends" (*faux amis*: words or expressions that sound the same across languages but that have very different significations), Cassin recognizes that it nonetheless expresses something about language's very essence. For Aristotle, she notes, it served as a paradigm of the transcendental illusion; an evil that could be temporarily neutralized but that would continuously return. She suggests that for Aristotle the evil of homonymy is compounded by amphiboly: a form of ambivalent syntax that normalizes the expression of logical fallacies and grammatical anomalies. An oft-cited example in English hails from Groucho Marx in *Animal Crackers*: "One morning I shot an elephant in my pajamas. How he got into my pajamas I will never know." Here, semantic ambiguity and humorous effect are produced by the phrase "in my pajamas," which modifies both the subject of the sentence, "I," and the elephant.

For Cassin, Parmenides' famous enunciations on the condition of "to be" or "being" – *ontôs on, to ti ên einai* – reveal this troubling aspect of the amphiboly. The fact that the Greek word *esti* produces a grammatical sentence without a verb yields a host of amphibolies that to modern readers look like so many ontological brain teasers. Parmenides's famous *Poem* is rife with them: "The what it was to be"; "the 'is' is what it is to be"; "the One, that it is and that it is not possible for it not to be … the other that it is not and that it is necessary for it not to be"; "What is is; for it is to be / but nothing it is not." These formulations may not qualify as amphibolous in the strict syntactic sense but they produce the same effect of intelligibility within nonsense that one finds, say, in the phrase "Helicopter powered by human flies" or in Molière's "Et de même qu'à vous je ne lui suis pas chère," which I would be tempted to render very freely in English as: "I am cheap because I'm not his dear." What we experience here is the shock of a logical enconomy that permits a "twofer" (two for the price of one); itself a kind of *double-bind* or state of exception in syntax and semantics. Amphiboly, as Cassin intimates, makes an error of meaning acceptable even as it arouses conscious suspicion of something off-kilter or terribly wrong within language. It is not by chance that from Aristotle to Kant, amphiboly has been treated with suspicion. In *The Amphiboly of Concepts of Reflection*, Kant would cast amphiboly as an obstruction to the apprehension of things in themselves, a grand deception of phenomena. In Lalande's gloss on Kant, "the imputation of conceptual predicates to sensible phenomena results in ignorance of the conditions proper to the sensible."[30] Though stigmatized by the philosophers, Cassin wants to recuperate homonymy and amphiboly as strong forms of equivocity for a fully performative sophistics whose ultimate goal – following a path leading from Gorgias to Lacan and J.L. Austin – is a "consequential relativism."

Following this path, we face the difficult prospect of trying to conjugate Cassin *with* Badiou; which is to say, linguistic relativism with subjective truth; logology with matheme; the unconscious with logics of worlds; deterritorialized languages with the genius of language in one tongue. For literary studies more broadly, this endeavor involves an effort to relate linguistic pluralism (inherent in translation as a liberal art) to a practice of *Weltliteratur* that takes full measure of linguistic constraints and truth conditions in the investigation of singular modes of existing in the world's languages.

Notes

1   R.A. Judy, "Discrepant Diaspora, Inchoate Reflections on a Neo-Humanist Style." Precirculated essay draft, contemporary literary theory seminar, Department of English and Comparative Literature, Columbia University. Session took place February 18, 2011.
2   Simon During, *Exit Capitalism: Literary Culture, Theory and Post-Secular Modernity* (London: Routledge, 2009), 57–58.
3   Theo D'haen, David Damrosch, and Djelal Kadir, eds., *The Routledge Companion to World Literature* (London and New York: Routledge, 2012).
4   Works like *The Routledge Companion to Translation Studies* (Jeremy Munday, 2009); *Key Terms in Translation Studies* (Palumbo, 2009); *Introducing Translation Studies: Theories and Applications* (Munday, 2008); *The Routledge Encyclopedia of Translation Studies* (Baker, 2008); *Translation and Creativity: Perspectives on Creative Writing and Translation Studies* (Loffredo and Perteghella, 2008); *A Companion To Translation Studies* (Kuhiwczak

and Littau, 2007); *The Translation Zone: A New Comparative Literature* (Apter, 2005); *Nation, Language, and the Ethics of Translation* (Bermann and Wood, 2005); *The Translation Studies Reader* (Venuti, 2004); and *Translation Studies* (Bassnett, 2002) built on earlier collections, including *Postcolonial Translation: Theory and Practice* (Bassnett and Trivedi, 1999); *Gender in Translation* (Simon, 1996); and *Descriptive Translation Studies and Beyond* (Toury, 1995).

5 Revathi Krishnaswamy is one of many to note that the field of "world literary theory" or "non-Western literary theory before European colonialism" is paltry. Even work on classical non-Western languages coming out of comparative poetics tends to have little influence on the critical projects associated with theory. [See Krishnaswamy's essay included in this volume – Ed.]

6 See Aamir Mufti, "Orientalism and the Institution of World Literatures," in this volume. [Ed.]

7 Martin Heidegger, *The Fundamental Concepts of Metaphysics: World, Finitude, Solitude*, trans. William McNeill and Nicholas Walker, Bloomington: Indiana University Press, 1995, 280 (original German text: *Grundbegriffe der Metaphysic: Welt-endlichkeit – einsamkeit*); Abdelfattah Kilito, introduction to *De la traduction*, by Abdessalam Benabdelali, trans. (from Arabic) Kamal Toumi (Morocco: Editions Toukbal, 2006), 9.

8 *Ibid*. My thanks to Omar Berrada for his help with the approximative translations of *amma ba'ad* and *layta chi'ari*.

9 Giorgio Agamben, *The End of the Poem: Studies in Poetics*, trans. Daniel Heller-Roazen, Stanford, CA: Stanford University Press, 1999, 66; "To hear such sounds …": Daniel Heller-Roazen, "Glossolalia"; entry commissioned for the English edition of the *Vocabulaire européan des philosophies: dictionnaire des intraduisibles* (ed. Barbara Cassin, Paris: Seuil, 2006). English edition: Emily Apter, Jacques Lezra, and Michael Wood, eds., *Dictionary of Untranslatables: A Philosophical Lexicon* (Princeton, NJ: Princeton University Press, forthcoming).

10 Ludwig Wittgenstein, *Tractatus logico-philosophicus*, trans. D.F. Pears and B.F. McGuinness (London: Routledge, 1997), 19 and 16, respectively.

11 Werner Hamacher, "From 95 Theses on Philology,'" *PMLA* 125: 4, October 2010, 997. "Thesis 57" states: "What belongs to philology – besides the inclination to that which is said – is the courage for what is not said."

12 Peter Osborne and Matthew Charles develop this point in their summary of Benjamin's anti-Kantianianism. They note: "In the essay 'On Language as Such and the Language of Man' (c. 1916), Benjamin offers a theological conception of language which draws on Hamann's discussion of Creation as the physical imprint of the divine Word of God," to claim that there "is no event or thing in either animate or inanimate nature that does not in some way partake of language" (Walter Benjamin, *Selected Writings* vol. 1, 1913–1926. Eds. Marcus Bullock and Michael W. Jennings (Cambridge, MA: Harvard University Press), 62–63. Peter Osborne and Matthew Charles, "Walter Benjamin," in *The Stanford Encyclopedia of Philosophy*, Spring 2011 edition, ed. Edward N. Zalta.

13 Jacques Derrida, *The Beast and the Sovereign*, trans. Geoffrey Bennington (Chicago: University of Chicago Press, 2009), 450; *ibid.*, 455; "Located … at the core of political theology": see Ernesto Laclau, "On the Names of God," in *Political Theologies: Public Religions in a Post-Secular World*, ed. Hent de Vries and Lawrence Eugene Sullivan (New York: Fordham University Press, 2006), 137–147.

14 Saba Mahmood, *Politics of Piety* (Princeton, NJ: Princeton University Press, 2005), 116.

15 Judith Butler, "The Sensibility of Critique: Response to Asad and Mahmood," in *Is Critique Secular? Blasphemy, Injury, and Free Speech*, ed. Talal Asad *et al.* (Berkeley: The Townsend Center for the Humanities, University of California Berkley, 2009), 103.

16 Theological untranslatability: see Jan Assmann, "Translating Gods: Religion as a Factor of Cultural (Un)Translatability," in *The Translatability of Cultures: Figurations of the Space Between*, ed. Sanford Budick and Wolfgang Iser (Stanford, CA: Stanford University Press, 1996), 26 and 31–33; see François Noudelmann, *Pour en finir avec la généalogie* (Paris: Léo Scheer, 2004), and François Noudelmann, *Les Airs de famille, une philosophie des affinités* (Paris: Gallimard, 2012); Jacques Derrida, "Des Tours de Babel," trans. Joseph F. Graham in *Difference in Translation*, ed. Joseph F. Graham (Ithaca, NY: Cornell University Press, 1985), 178. Jacques Derrida, *Le Monolinguisme de l'autre ou la prothèse d'origine* (Paris: Galilée, 1996), 15. Translation (my own) of "*Oui, je n'ai qu'une langue, or ce n'est pas la mienne.*" In *Monolingualism of the Other; or, The Prosthesis of Origin* (Stanford: Stanford University Press, 1996), 2, the translator Patrick Mensah renders this phrase as: "*Yes, I have only one language, yet it is not mine.*"

17 Richard Pevear, translator's introduction to Leo Tolstoy, *War and Peace*, trans. Richard Pevear and Larissa Volokhonsky (New York: Alfred A. Knopf, 2007), x–xi.

18 Karl Marx and Frederick Engels, *The Communist Manifesto*, ed. Eric Hobsbawm, trans. Samuel Moore (London: Verso, 1998), 39; Jonathan Arac, "Global and Babel: Language and Planet," in *Shades of the Planet: American Literature as World Literature*, ed. Wai Chee Dimock and Lawrence Buell (Princeton, NJ: Princeton University Press, 2007), 21.

19 David Bellos, *Is That a Fish in Your Ear? Translation and the Meaning of Everything* (New York: Penguin Books USA, 2011), 290.

20 Alain Badiou, *The Adventure of French Philosophy*, trans. Bruno Bosteels (New York and London: Verso, 2012), 311.

21 "Je me suis donc tourné vers *La République*, oeuvre centrale du Maître, précisément consacrée au problème de la justice, pour en faire briller la puissance contemporaine." Alain Badiou, *La République de Platon* (Paris: Fayard, 2012), 10.

22 Susan Spitzer, "Translator's Preface," in Alain Badiou, *Plato's Republic: A Dialogue in Sixteen Chapters, with a Prologue and an Epilogue*, trans. Susan Spitzer (Cambridge, UK: Polity Press, 2012), xxiv.

23 Badiou, *Plato's Republic*, 13–14.

24 Bruno Bosteels, Translator's introduction, Badiou, *The Adventure of Philosophy*, xlvii–xlviii.

25 Barbara Cassin, "Who's Afraid of the Sophists? Against Ethical Correctness," trans. Charles. T. Wolfe, *Hypathia* 15: 4, Fall 2000, 116. She refers to Alain Badiou, *Conditions* (Paris: Seuil, 1992), 72–76.

26 Badiou, *The Adventure of Philosophy*, 344.

27 Reinhard, "Introduction," Badiou, *Plato's Republic*, x.

28 See Graham Harman, "On Vicarious Causation," in *Collapse* 2, May 2007, 190.

29 As a pendant to Cassin's return to sophistics, see Pascal Quignard's *Rhétorique spéculative* (Paris: Gallimard, 1995), which seeks to rehabilitate the Sophist position against neoplatonic tendencies of mathematization.

30 "What is is; for it is to be / but nothing it is not" (French translation: *L'étant en tant qu'étant, l'étant étantiquement, le ce que c'était que d'être*; German translation: *Das Sosein, das, was es war, sein*, ou *das Wesenwar*). Molière: Mélic, II, 3. "The Amphiboly of Concepts of Reflection" (*Amphibolie der Reflexionsbegriffe*). André Lalande, *Vocabulaire critique et technique de la philosophie* (Paris: Presses Universitaires de France, 1996), 50.

25

Comparative Literature/
World Literature
A Discussion (2011)

Gayatri Chakravorty Spivak and David Damrosch

One of the most important debates at the heart of comparative studies today concerns the philological, methodological, and ideological status of the opening up of the discipline by the study of world literature. Gayatri Chakravorty Spivak and David Damrosch discussed the challenges that comparative literature faces in the age of globalization, and the sometimes uneasy relationship between comparative and world literary studies, in a plenary session at the annual meeting of the American Comparative Literature Association held in Vancouver in April 2011. The following text is the transcription of this session, at which the speakers debated the goals, politics, and ethics of this reshaping of the discipline from different perspectives.

Gayatri Chakravorty Spivak is University Professor and a founding member of the Institute for Comparative Literature and Society at Columbia University. One of the leading figures in postcolonial theory and criticism, Spivak advocates a socially grounded view of comparative and world literature, integrating literary and area studies. Having first become prominent as the translator of Jacques Derrida's *Of Grammatology*, Spivak has continued to develop a distinctive approach to literary and cultural studies, drawing on deconstructionist, feminist, and Marxist theories. Her books look into the cultural politics and the underlying ideological projects that inform literary institutions and disciplines in the age of globalization (*In Other Worlds: Essays in Cultural Politics*, 1987; *Thinking Academic Freedom in Gendered Post-Coloniality*, 1993; *Outside in the Teaching Machine*, 1993; *A Critique of Postcolonial Reason: Towards a History of the Vanishing Present*, 1999; *Death of a Discipline*, 2003; *Other Asias*, 2005). David Damrosch, the editor of the present volume, is Ernest Bernbaum Professor of Literature in the Department of Comparative Literature at Harvard University, and is a past president of the American

Gayatri Chakravorty Spivak and David Damrosch, "Comparative Literature/World Literature: A Discussion" (2011). In *Comparative Literature Studies* 48:4 (2011), pp. 455–485. Copyright © 2011 The Pennsylvania State University, University Park, PA.

Comparative Literature Association; he is also the founding director of the Institute for World Literature. His books include *What Is World Literature?* (2003), *The Buried Book: The Loss and Rediscovery of the Great Epic of Gilgamesh* (2007), and to *How to Read World Literature* (2009). He is the founding general editor of the six-volume *Longman Anthology of World Literature* (2004, 2009) and of *The Longman Anthology of British Literature* (4th ed., 2009), as well as editor of *Teaching World Literature* (2009), and co-editor of *The Princeton Sourcebook in Comparative Literature* (2009).

[*David Damrosch*]: I'm happy to be here with my old friend and longtime colleague Gayatri Spivak, with whom I've shared productive disagreements that continue to this day, so I'll try to think about that a little bit with you today. Certainly, we have seen an extraordinary sea change – but you may think I'm speaking of the Aquatic Activity Caucus, our water-borne action group. We do try to do something each year, and we went kayaking yesterday, but beyond the ACLA/AAC, there has been a real sea change in the discipline since we of the older generation were in school, when comparative literature really meant the study of a very few, mostly Western European major literatures. As the Swiss comparatist Werner Friederich said in 1960, "World literature is a presumptuous and arrogant term. Sometimes, in flippant moments, I think we should call our programs NATO literatures. Yet even that would be extravagant, for we do not usually deal with more than one quarter of the NATO-nations."[1] Or as Sukehiro Hirakawa has written of studying at Tokyo University in Japan's first comparative literature program, reading Wellek and Curtius and Auerbach in the 1960s: he describes being tremendously impressed with these great scholars, but it seemed to him and his colleagues in Japan that comparative literature "was a sort of Greater West European Co-Prosperity Sphere."[2] Interesting analogy…

Of course, what comparative literature really meant, first and foremost, was to have a really good *accent* in French and German. This was the price of admission, and then you might do theory or you might not, you might study one or another period, but the accent was really what became a marker of excellence and a sort of security. I remember, in graduate school, coming out from a seminar taught by Paul de Man; one of my fellow students was clearly rather insecure, as I was, about whether we were really following de Man's incredibly rich and intricate exposition. She comforted herself by declaring: "But, you know, his French really isn't very good." Well, what she meant was that he was Belgian – a native speaker of French but not with a Parisian accent. This stuck in my mind, as neither could I follow his theories properly, nor was my French accent very good either, and so I couldn't take that level of comfort. But it's been a great thing that the world has opened up to a much broader set of nations, both larger and smaller, both in Europe and outside, so that the *Longman Anthology* now includes Gayatri's sparkling translation of Mahasweta Devi's *Breast-Giver*, plus translations from Nahuatl, Sumerian, Middle High German, Polish, and Vietnamese, the kinds of thing that were rarely in comparatists' view before, and I think we can have much to celebrate here.

I myself think that there are really only three problems with the newly expanded world of comparative studies today. I know I share an interest in these problems with Gayatri; perhaps we have a different perspective on them. The three inter-twined problems are that the study of world literature can very readily become culturally deracinated, philologically bankrupt, and ideologically complicit with the worst tendencies of global capitalism. Other than that, we're in good shape.

There has been no one more attentive to these problems than Gayatri Spivak, as we can see in the preface to her influential *Death of a Discipline* of 2003. There she says that "between the presentation of the Wellek Library Lectures of May 2000 and the final revision of the book in May 2002, the discipline of comparative liter-ature in the United States underwent a sea change" – so the sea change metaphor is already there, and the Aquatic Activities Caucus will have to get Gayatri into a kayak next year in Providence. She continues: "Publishing conglomerates have recognized a market for anthologies of world literature in translation. Academics with large advances are busy putting these together." (Who *are* these academics with large advances for their anthologies? I wish I knew!) She goes on to say that

> the market is international. Students in Taiwan and Nigeria will learn about the literatures of the world through English translations organized by the United States. Thus institutionalized, global educational market, only teachers, presumably the graduate discipline of comparative literature will train these teachers. The book you are about to read is therefore out of joint with the times in a more serious way than were the Wellek Library Lectures of May 2000. I have changed nothing of the urgency of my call for new comparative literature. I hope this book will be read as the last gasp of a dying discipline.[3]

Gayatri's preface has already formulated all three of my concerns: the philological one of translation, the methodological one of American specialists presuming to put together world anthologies, and the ideological one of the publishing conglomerates trying to Americanize the world.

The moral force of this statement is not compromised by the fact that this critique is not in fact correct. These world literature anthologies, to my knowledge, have never been published for the global market, not from any wish to avoid spreading American visions of the world but simply for market reasons: permission costs are too high. You have two ways to get anthology permissions: you can get North American rights or global permissions. To get global rights costs twice as much as the North American rights, and none of the major survey anthologies has opted for the higher expense of global permissions, because there's not yet enough of a market outside North America. So that what we are really purveying through these anthologies is a vision of the world for a North American audience. The critique of these anthologies does apply quite well in relation to the Canadian market, where students are being given versions of world literature that have a good number of selections from the United States but little or nothing from Canada. Outside North America, though, if some students in Nigeria or Taiwan get hold of these anthologies it is through websites that Longman and Bedford and Norton don't control and don't figure into their marketing or their publishing plans. So capitalism itself has an interesting way of protecting the wider world from the invasion of American world literature anthologies.

Even so, there is a real issue here, in that Gayatri's critique taps into a long-running debate that began in the 1950s as world literature courses began to gain visibility in the United States. There was an important conference held at the University of Wisconsin, Madison, in 1959 on the teaching of world literature. You can see it as a conference volume published the following year, *The Teaching of World Literature*, edited by Haskell Block. And what is revealed if you look at the volume is a deep divide between comparative literature and world literature. It was fully in place there, and it's a divide along lines of class and of geography.

What you had in the late 1950s and early 1960s was the elite East Coast schools with strong language departments, where comparative literature departments expected that students would come in to their graduate programs knowing French and German and Latin – the same three languages that were commonly taught in prep schools. If you wanted to work in another language, the surrounding language departments would provide that training, and if the university didn't offer, say, Bengali or Nahuatl, then you simply wouldn't work on those literatures, as these programs had a real distaste for translation. And then you had the populist public universities, mostly in the Midwest, the South, and the Rocky Mountain states, in which world literature was growing like Topsy. With some embarrassment, the speakers at the Wisconsin conference talk about how their enrollments had been growing in the 1950s from forty to four hundred in just a few years in one case at Iowa, with the encouragement of the dean of the Business School, who started requiring his *business* students to take a world literature course. One can see already smoke coming out of Gayatri's ears as I say this, and I understand the reason and share that concern.

But it's very interesting that in all this whole debate, the world literature people are mostly from midwestern and southern schools. One of the opening speakers at the Wisconsin conference regretted that they didn't have more people "from farther away," but I think he was really regretting that no one had come from any of the elite East Coast schools – and no one from either coast, as a matter of fact: no speakers from Stanford, Berkeley, or UCLA. The proponents of world literature were well aware that their thriving new survey courses were coming under attack as linguistically and culturally amateurish. When Werner Friederich noted that most programs were teaching only "NATO literatures," he wasn't saying that the sense of comparative literature should be expanded. Just the opposite: he went on to advocate abandoning the term "world literature" outright, because comparatists only really wanted to talk about one quarter of the NATO literatures.

Friederich then clarified the nature of his opposition. In his essay in the conference volume, called "On the Integrity of Our Planning," he noted that

> I am bitterly opposed to sweeping survey courses such as The Novel in World Literature, three hours per week, in one semester. . . . It is because of courses like these that the bricks have kept on flying from the left and from the right, from the solid

language departments snorting that this is the flimsiest kind of sheer amateurism, and from the solid comparatists complaining that it is because of such courses that Comparative Literature, ever since the 1920s, has gotten a black eye and an ill repute from which it has yet not completely recovered.[4]

He went on to say that the concept of integrity "must be applied most strictly in our planning, and – if an all-too-enthusiastic World Literature teacher is not capable of such self-discipline and renunciation – that the course committee on his own campus must restrain him most emphatically and insist on the inviolability of fairly stiff academic standards." Translation per se was not Friederich's problem but the very concept of the survey: "At North Carolina," he concludes, "we have about eight or ten translation courses: the Greek drama, French classicism, Goethe – but we do not have a single Survey of World Literature; our people would not stand for it."

Now it was shortly after this conference that the ACLA commissioned the first "report on standards" for which Friederich was calling, chaired by Harvard's Harry Levin. So you have the elite schools in the Northeast – Harvard, Yale, Princeton, Columbia, Cornell, Amherst and so on, Werner Friederich's UNC being very much an outpost of that elite pattern – allying themselves against large public universities in the heartland, schools like Iowa, Wisconsin, Colorado, from which the attendance was largely drawn for Haskell Block's world literature conference. When ACLA set up the first Committee on Standards, they put Haskell Block on the committee to pull him back in line, to get him back with the program, as indeed he did.

In the very first paragraph of his ACLA report, issued in 1965, Harry Levin declared that

> a preliminary question arises as whether it is necessary, desirable or practical for Comparative Literature to be represented in every institution, whether it does not make special demands in the way of linguistic preparation and intellectual perspective which ought to reserve it for the more highly qualified students. And whether it does not presuppose an existing strength in language departments and literature and libraries, to which not very many colleges and indeed not every university can be fairly expected to measure up.[5]

Even more restrictive was the second "Report on Standards," chaired by Yale's Thomas Greene in 1975 – the year I entered the graduate program in his department at Yale. Greene's report noted the rapid growth of programs around the country in recent years and even nodded toward a novel vision of world literature. "It is a vision," Greene said, "which will soon begin to make our comfortable European perspectives parochial." Soon, perhaps, but not yet. Greene continued:

> There is cause, we believe, for serious concern, in transforming our discipline, that we not debase those values on which it is founded. The slippage of standards, once allowed to accelerate, would be difficult to arrest and in at least some colleges and universities, Comparative Literature seems to be purveyed in the style of a smorgasbord at bargain rates. At the undergraduate level, the most disturbing recent trend in the universities is the association of comparative literature with literatures in translation.[6]

Greene's critique hit home. No self-respecting program in his day could wish to be seen as the educational equivalent of the food court in "the Mall of America."

We can best understand this geographical and class divide if we take a postcolonial approach, for which we're so indebted to Gayatri and to Edward Said and others. A decade before the publication of Said's *Orientalism*, in fact, the colonial dynamics of American higher education were already noted in Christopher Jencks and David Riesman's *The Academic Revolution* (1968). There they talk about the rise of higher education during the boom years of the postwar era, looking particularly at Catholic colleges, historically black American colleges, and public colleges generally. And they make a really interesting analogy: they say that American graduate programs treat comprehensive colleges and undergraduate institutions in much the way that colonial powers used to treat their colonies. They get raw material – undergraduates – produced by the colonies, they bring them to the metropolitan center for reprocessing, and they send them back out again to the colonies, value-added, to teach the undergraduates. So in 1968 Jencks and Riesman were very perceptive in seeing the comprehensive state schools and the colleges as existing in a colonial relation to the imperial graduate programs. I think that Gayatri's critique of world literature in the beginning of *Death of a Discipline* actually maps rather well onto the limitations of traditional comparative literature in the United States and Canada *before* the rise of the contemporary study of world literature, and the problem today may be that the opening up of the global canon may not in itself have solved the deeper structural problems long besetting comparative study overall.

How do we advance beyond this neocolonial situation, if we accept the seriousness of the critique that when it's done badly, the teaching of world literature is, in fact, methodologically naïve, culturally deracinated, philologically compromised, and ideologically suspect? I would like to set out three proposals to start the conversation: one on the philological level, one on the methodological level, one on the ideological level.

On the philological level, I think we need, in fact, more languages and more language study. As a consequence, we need a more of a *sliding scale* of language study. The old model for comparatists was to acquire "near native fluency" in a couple of languages beyond English – usually French and then German or perhaps Italian, Spanish, or Russian, or very occasionally another "minor" European language such as Norwegian or a "major" language elsewhere such as Chinese. In this way, you were going to be as good as those otherwise narrow-minded people in the national literature departments: we'll show that we can do what they can do, and then we do it better when we add in the cultural capital of high-value literary theory.

It is certainly great to have near-native fluency in one or two languages beyond your native tongue, but there are a lot more languages out there. And from my point of view, the way to deal with this is in fact to study more languages. Particularly for those who have not grown up multilingual as the Swiss-born Werner Friederich did, this will usually mean learning languages on a sliding scale of fluency. The fundamental thing is to no longer have to be prisoner of translations, so that you can check a translation against the original. That's the first level, and it's often very useful, even before you have the time to get the near-native linguistic fluency or the greater cultural fluency gained by living abroad. So I would like to propose that we encourage much more language study in our programs, and at a more varied level, not so much trying to imitate the national literature departments' faculty in their specialized knowledge at every point. I think ideally every student will have such a near-native grasp of one language but then a range of competence in several others.

Methodologically, it seems to me that we need much more collaborative scholarship, as well as collaborative teaching, particularly insofar as world literature is no longer simply or possibly even primarily pursued at the level of the introductory survey course. As interested as I am in the challenges of the sophomore-level survey course, I think the discussion fixates too much on that beginning level. The study of world literature is percolating at many levels today, as we can see in hundreds of papers being delivered here in Vancouver. Increasingly in our scholarship, as in upper-level undergraduate work and advanced graduate study, world literature frames many discussions of comparative literature, including classic comparisons of two or three works read in their original languages.

The new scholarly importance of a broad outlook on the world's literatures means that we have to get serious about moving beyond the limited ability that any of us can have in more than a few languages. We are going to have to do much more collaborative work, which we still lag far behind most of the social sciences in doing. A new emphasis on collaboration will have consequences for teaching as well as for research, and it should entail a refashioning of the authority relation between professor and student. This begins to get us into the ideological issues. Rereading the debates of the 1960s and 1970s over comparative literature against world literature, one striking commonality emerges on both sides of the controversy. Universal in all those documents – the Wisconsin world literature volume as much as the Levin and Greene reports – is the assumption that the only person in the classroom who really knows another language is the professor. The teacher is always represented as having to bring the original into class, and the real debate concerns whether such knowledge on the professor's part is necessary or only desirable. There seems to have been no thought that some other person in the class would possess a language that the teacher doesn't know. This can hardly have been the case even in the 1960s, and it is still less true today on more and more campuses, both in North America and in many parts of the world. Many of us find that our students collectively know many more languages than we do, and often they have substantial cultural knowledge that we do not have. Rather than struggle to work up a little "background" on unfamiliar literary cultures, we can collaborate with our students.

In my own undergraduate world literature survey course, instead of requiring two papers each semester as I always used to do, I now require one paper and one wiki. For each week, two or three students collaborate to produce a wiki for the week's reading. Very typically, one of the students will be someone who has some special linguistic knowledge or cultural background, either by heritage or because they've started taking courses in the area, and it's quite remarkable to find how many languages can be accessed by students. The other students in the wiki group may have no linguistic knowledge but merely an active interest in the material, and they often prove to be extremely adept at finding good information to present on the wiki.

This is not at all a feature only of Ivy League schools; I hear similar reports at the University of Nevada at Las Vegas, where the *Longman Anthology* is used, and at Auburn University in Mississippi, places that a generation ago had not nearly so much of a cultural range among their students. So it allows us to explore a different kind of methodology, which involves also the possibility of using new technologies such as wikis to encourage the collaborative work that gives students a new purchase on our authors. And there's nothing like such collaborative work for giving the students a sense of access and power. In a great moment in my class last year, a student recited from memory a verse by Hafez, in Persian. This was a sophomore from the Dominican Republic, with no heritage background at all; he was just taking second-year Persian and he had memorized this poem; his recitation earned him a standing ovation from the class. We have a whole other world right in front of us in our classrooms today.

Finally, on the ideological level, I think we really need a great deal of pluralism. We will always have ideological divisions and debates in our field. I myself am a liberal humanist and proud of it, and there are many comparatists to my left and also to my right in the sense of more traditional in what they study, but I think that where all of us are very much on common ground is on needing to push back against the market at every possible opportunity. All of the best world literature anthologies, for example, are in fact deeply concerned to try to push the market from within, to really push against the limitations of American myopia and to help faculty move beyond the linguistic and cultural comfort zones of the sixties and seventies.

Comparatists based in the United States have a particular challenge in combating what Gayatri has criticized as "multi-culti" American exceptionalism, the unexamined belief that a nation of immigrants can celebrate some Disneyfied diversity without doing the hard work of learning anything substantial about other cultures. This is certainly an American problem, but I would say that there are very few countries where there's not a covert exceptionalism, a cryptonationalism or even open jingoism, deeply engrained within comparative studies. It takes a different form in different countries, both ideologically and institutionally, but whatever our location, our job is to use world literature to shake comparative literature out of its dogmatic slumber, to critique its nationalist self-involvement, and to really push back against the market at every opportunity. So a good anthology, or a good course, or a good research project challenges the reigning doxa, pushing against the euphorias of national self-satisfaction.

The other thing to emphasize is that world literature, taught well, will inspire more language learning, more genuine understanding of the world, more difficult engagement. And actually courses in world literature can help promote language learning even better at the schools that Levin and Greene were writing off, the schools they thought shouldn't even have comparative literature programs because they didn't have enough serious scholars doing enough languages. Our host for this conference, Simon Fraser University, seems to me an absolutely striking example of how world literature can work when it's done well. When the faculty here were deciding how to build literary studies at the new satellite campus in Surrey, they considered setting up a standard comparative literature program, but they decided instead to establish a world literature program, with the inspiration of Paulo Horta and his dean and their colleagues; in the older model, you couldn't really have done a comp lit program at Surrey because you don't have enough languages offered on campus and probably also not sufficient interest among the school's largely working-class population in the kinds of high European theory that had become so central in the discipline during the seventies and eighties. So they developed their world literature program in view of their student body, at once very local and also very international, with dozens of countries of origin. After just a few years the program is thriving, with enrollments triple of what they had expected and a hundred majors today.

Their courses rely heavily on translation, yet the program is also activist about providing students with language possibilities well beyond what the small Surrey campus can offer. The two students who picked me up at the airport were complaining that there are not many languages offered at the Surrey campus, but the program is helping one to go to Italy and helped the other to go to Japan to do their work. The success of the program is also putting pressure on the administration to have more language offerings on campus, but meanwhile it's not a bad learning experience to live with a host family in Japan, which is what one of these two students had done, or to go to Italy and eat really well, as the other is about to do. What's not to like about that?

To sum up, I think the critiques of world literature that we see today are actually also critiques of comparative literature when either is done badly. The challenge for us is to forge our divergent approaches into an active relation, in which we reframe comparative study in a global context, using it to spread the study of languages and cultures and to push back at every possible stage against the vagaries of the global capital market.

[*Gayatri Chakravorty Spivak*]: David and I go back a long way, and he has persuaded me to the extent that I now think the approach that I would like to represent would persistently "supplement" (I cannot bring myself to use the word "collaborate") the efforts of the enlightened world literature-ists. However, I would like to start on a note of protest against the polarization between the high theory that comparative literature was supposed to have required in its heyday, and the inbuilt populism of world literature, which is implicit in much of David's presentation. The supplementation of the world literature effort is all the more necessary, because the idea that world literature is more populist is itself vanguardist, an idea belonging to our moment. In Beijing, at David's invitation, I spoke of "supplementing the vanguard." Believe me, I taught at Iowa for twelve years, leaving as director of comparative literature, and we were not unable to run the program – established by René Wellek, with Rosalie Colie, Ralph Freedman, and Geoffrey Hartman on its founding faculty. Haskell Block was my friend. While I was teaching there, I got an offer from Brown, which I refused, I got an offer from the University of Massachusetts at Amherst, which I refused, because, in fact, Iowa was not so different from the East Coast, with its "nose up in the air." But I was not into that sort of regionalist prejudice, not even then. (I might add here that the University of Las Vegas holds Wole Soyinka and financed the extraordinary International Center for Writing and Translation headed by Ngũgĩ wa Thiong'o, whose stunning Conference on Global Conversations: A Festival of Marginalized Languages in October 2007 came from a position that questions the idea of world literature as such, that the University of Alabama at Tuscaloosa was frequently visited by Derrida because Richard Rand taught there.) To think that there is something "charmed" about the Ivy League even as we patronize (in every sense) the populism of the "other" schools is not a good idea. I should know. I am a graduate of the University of Calcutta who, to quote my dear ironic friend Edward W. Said, "inched her way up to the Northeast," landing on Columbia's doorstep six months short of fifty. I almost didn't make it; a colleague (who will forever remain nameless) split the ad hoc. The students raised a hue and cry. Hardly an elite entry – quite like my position on world literature.

Certainly it is a great idea to acknowledge the linguistic and cultural diversity of a US classroom. It is also a good exercise to create wikis and applaud the ability of a Dominican student to memorize Hafez in Persian. As someone with her feet in both worlds, however, I propose a test. Would the linguistic capacity and cultural knowledge of the student from elsewhere qualify for tertiary education in the country of the student's origin? If not, the student is not an appropriate informant for the class. This absolutely does not mean that we refuse to acknowledge diversity. But if we do so, we must earn the right to be able to judge what the student brings to the class.[7]

I have been counseling against the double standard that ignoring this question led to for many decades, before globalization called for the epistemological change that is now part of my argument. I think it might not be impertinent to quote myself from 1992 here:

> What actually happens in a typical liberal multicultural classroom "at its best"? On a given day we are reading a text from one national origin. The group in the classroom from that particular national origin in the general polity can identify with the richness of the texture of the "culture" in question. (I am not even bringing up the question of the definition of culture.) People from other national origins in the classroom (other, that is, than Anglo) relate sympathetically but superficially, in an aura of same difference. The Anglo relates benevolently to everything, "knowing about other cultures" in a relativist glow.[8]

We must, of course, and also, keep track of how first generations flow into later ones, become American in uneven ways, unless we want world literature studies – however much it travels hither and yon – always to be geared toward new immigrants, not a good argument for serious disciplinary change.

I should also add that I am not considering the issue from the point of view of increasing enrollment. That consideration is indeed crucial, especially when we speak at professional organizations. But I have to believe that there is room for epistemological arguments even when they do not seem practical in the short run.

Let such arguments play a supplementary role? "It is the strange essence of the supplement not to have essentiality," Derrida wrote. "It may always not have taken place. Moreover, literally, it has never taken place: it is never present, here and now.... Less than nothing and yet, to judge by its effects, much more than nothing."[9] Our work, supplementing, is para-sitical on world literature ideas. I have always insisted that we earn the right to supplement by the most painstaking intimacy. John Drabinski's comment on the passage, not disclosing that care, does, however, show the other side of the double bind of supplementation ably. This too is importantly true: "A conception of an addition to that which *pretends* to be self-sufficient, which then unravels self-sufficiency with a constitutive contingency." Supplementation is not necessary, it is contingent. Without us, you'll be more popular. With us, an abode of bliss.

The point of view that I represent, then – not a very popular point of view at the moment – should see itself as supplementing the stakes of world literature rather than anything else. I'm of course sorry I hadn't checked the facts about world distribution and the Longman's anthology.[10]

Our concern is not how to situate the peaks of the literary production of the world on a level playing field but to ask what makes literary cases singular. The singular is the always universalizable, never the universal. The site of reading is to make the singular visible in its ability.

Kant thought the world and self were "as if" 's. Derrida thought this was the reason why Kant could not solve the problem of world government today. Yet it is also true that this thinking of world and self as "as if" 's can take on board Marx's insistence that the material determines the mental. To step into a world literature by ourselves today – because everything is opening up – and to say that it's the message of capitalist globalization is not to be tendentious but to point out that this moment is conjuncturally similar to the time of Goethe and Kant. A sudden access to a world, and they start talking about *Weltliteratur* and *cosmopolitheia*, in the same way, but with a great difference as well, that we talk about world literature and cosmopolitanism.

But if Kant the philosopher knew the world was "as if," Kant the political writer wrote as if he did not. That is, to act out part of the architectonic of the programming of practical reason, but I can't go there now. Let us just say that *we* forget the "as if" in a less systemic way and posit a worldliness in search of the same, to see in what ways the past, the present, and the future of the literary impulse in the world can share. It is, alas, that false promise of a level playing field that we in our sanctioned ignorance (seeing only capital's social productivity, not its persistent subalternization), act out, the ideological damage controllers of the economic sphere of globalization: the material determines the mental, ideology shifts. In that forgetfulness of the "as if," the politics of identity can overcome the ethics of alterity. Thinking of any international student as an authority on globality because of his/her identity is like thinking all Americans abroad are experts on Melville.

I don't think we can hold back the stakes of a world literature. But we, who are interested in the singularity of the literary production, can always try to remain short of that final coding. Into a "universal," the "world" as adjective. I agree with David, my classical Greek is awful and I often hit my head against it, and my students know this, yet I can use it to ask questions. Even my French and German are not good – I fell upon them because I couldn't get financial aid in English in 1961, before Lyndon Johnson lifted the quota on alien registration, because I was not a native speaker. I had had six months of French at the Alliance Française in Calcutta at the Centre Culturel and three months of German with the German widow of a Bengali freedom fighter. I had borrowed money to get to Cornell and had no work permit, so certainly I didn't have the money to go back either. De Man had just become head of comp lit and had soft money slots for financial aid, thought that I was smart enough that I could perhaps manage. He could take a chance because, in those days, if I goofed, he could put it down to cultural difference, right? So he, in fact, took the risk because at Cornell I could not go into language courses if I was working for a PhD in comp lit. This is why this is all the French and German I know. I've never made a secret of it, and therefore I agree with David that one should really try to proceed with what one has rather than try to be as good as one can be in a single language. I have recently said that one should, on the other hand, assume that all languages can be a first language, that they can get the ethical moving, because a first language is learnt before reasonableness and primes the metapsychological. This is not to be confused with locating experts in the global classroom.

We might, then, as a globally dispersed and diversified collectivity, supplement that seemingly practical will to hold the world in a grid. I don't mean survey courses; I mean the presuppositions of world literature. Supplementing, remember, is to figure out the exact shape of a place that is empty in what is to be supplemented, zooming out, but not in competition with zooming in. We might ask Jean Genet's question about the essence of art: "What remains of a Rembrandt, torn into four equal pieces and flushed down the toilet?" The four equal pieces can be read in the politics of identity, voting blocks, Melissa Williams's view of multiculturalism, systemic grids, competing cultures. And in the ethics of alterity, we can imagine the other – here, a hero named Rembrandt, or in the case of Joe Diebes, the Canadian-US composer, Bach – as singular, universalizable, but never universal.

This is a brand of provincializing Europe – from dispenser of signs to mere trace – that most of us cannot think of, because we the "other"s are caught within the politics of identity and can only offer as a substitute something coming from our own neck of the woods. This is what one expects from the so-called global classroom. We are going to be all critical of universalization, but not of ourselves, we're not Eurocentric. But on the other hand, this global classroom lets us all be self-interested and provide for little identitarian enclaves. I've made this kind of critique of the human rights folks, so much so that Didier Coste actually suggested in print that rather than listen to Gayatri Spivak one should substitute the classical multiculturalism of Europe à la Étiemble.

Let us speak for Rembrandt and Bach as universalizable but never universal. That rethinking is hard. And, in the end, I'll try to regionalize another case if I have enough time: the great Indian model, and that's Tagore. These are placeholders here for singular cases where the politics of practicing suspension of cultural identity as an examined or self-conscious cultural difference takes over. Even for the European, preparing for the ethical reflex calls for wasteful spending rather different from tax deductible write-offs of purchased virtue. We will come to the peculiar idea of wasteful spending in a bit.

People here and there have commented favorably on my remark that in globality we are in an island of signs, in an ocean of traces – this compares to what you also were saying, David. A sign system promises meaning. We can follow that promise only in a few languages – and I agree with you that we should expand that – with the promise of meaning. A trace does not promise anything. It is something that seems to suggest that there was something before. In globality, we're in an island of signs, in an ocean of traces, and I could give you many examples, but the boring part of it is – and this is not in globality, but long before – when you don't understand a language, to simply say "Oh, the handwriting looks beautiful, it sounds wonderful" – that is legitimizing by reversal the reason why barbarians were called barbarians.

In my judgment, Joe Diebes, as the clip I'll show will show, tends to protect the trace from the promise of the sign, a kind of reversed grammatology, tracing the score by hand in real musical time, acting out iteration.[11]

The score is virtually phonocentric, a visual graphic reserving the sound of music, inviting its turning into sound, in real time, articulated as usual by the play of the blanks and the spacing. I saw this machine tracing, iterating, while the supposed original, another site of contingency, was remotely played by another kind of machine, empirically recognizable as such.

In other words, the artist was tracing printed musical scores, tracings which were almost like a sign system, like writing, meaning the contours of the music and the time of performance, so that finally an object remained which did not resemble the mere sanity of the score. This is the kind of earned intimacy that goes away when we're trying to approach remote things and to give them a certain standing and signification. This is an example, a miming, of how the ethical as such suspends the subject in the other's text, here, a musical score tracing.

If signifying is to turn into sign, tracing is to take us to the remains as trace. Was there music here? Joe's description is as follows:

> Each page of Bach's six suites for solo cello is traced on vellum in real-time. I perform these drawings in step with the Mstislav Rostropovich 1991 recording and videotape the process. The video documents the impossible attempt to write out the score in real musical time. As in my previous music installations I am interested in merging the time of writing/composing into the continuous present of performance.

The second page that the link above will open for you shows the final remains, a mute answer to the question of the essence of art – what remains? – disclosed by iteration, not systematization as such.[12] Bach is not here modified or universalized as a world artist or a world-class artist. The machine of the hand must know the machine of the score well enough to be able to trace it and fail. Post-theoretical ethical practice and globality: the hand is a mechanical part object. The trace generates remains that cannot move up to systemic coding, calling for supplementation as task.

Marx thought of the trace as insufficient, incomplete because the representation theories never conclude. For him, the general equivalent, money, shedding its thingliness, became something like a numeric system. Yet he took us heuristically back into understanding traces. The fetish character of the commodity and the coat talking the language of commodities are the two best known. For only that will transform the quality of the detail of our lives, make the spirit uneasy, training for change without waiting for vanguardism to transgress the collective spirit. In spite of all the wikis and twitters that can create a systemic intimacy, in this space of learning you play to lose.

This is for me an important conversation, and so I quote myself again, something I wrote recently for a book catalog:

> The bottom line of teaching literature as such is to teach how to read, in the most robust sense. The bottom line of teaching philosophy as such is to teach how to think, again, in the most robust sense. It is to teach an activism of the imagination and intellect. It is to teach how to play oneself as an instrument – distanced yet connected – reading, thinking. It is only a few (an unexpected joy for the teacher) who slide into being taught to play to lose, the only way you can be a teacher in the humanities. What is loss here? Do you want to lose when you play to lose? Did Socrates? Does the parent or the teacher in *Putrāt shishyāt parājayam*? But *qui gagne perd* – a lesson I learnt (I think) from deconstruction. A *mise-en-abyme*, a hall of mirrors, gain to loss to gain to loss – but what remains?[13]

In order so to play, to turn the humanism of the humanities around in these hard times, you must be completely inside the intimacy of humanism itself, and you can't get around that one by polarizing East Coast language learning and Middle West moral imagination.

Gramsci will epistemologize Marx, calling for an incandescent political passion in the collectivity of workers with class consciousness. Nietzsche complicates matters by commenting on the actual move from trace to sign as the disclosure of arbitrary systemic determination: "The entire history of a custom can, in this way, be a continuous sign chain of ever new interpretations and revisions, whose causes don't even have time to be related to one another, but, on the contrary, in some cases succeed and alternate with one another in a purely chance fashion."[14] In other words, trace masquerading as sign. Kant systematized the trace as the necessity for the transcendental deduction.[15]

Encyclopedic world literature impulses fall within this systemic tradition, this good systemic tradition, the best of what I have called "the restraining of the future anterior." Unfortunately, it also works – in the discussion, perhaps one of you will ask me a question – it also works to finesse certain kinds of historical tracings, in the interests of systematicity, most significantly the retracing of the map of West Asia, in the early years of the last century, creating a certain kind of world, an episode in the vicissitudes of Byzantium, whose latest examples are the events in Mazar-i-Sharif. When Terry

Jones says we are not responsible for their actions, we comparatists cannot dismiss him as an obscure fanatic, forgetting not only the "as if"'s, but also that history is larger than personal good will. So however much we say that a kind of unranked collectivity of languages and literatures has come because of the increase of immigration, however much we posit Mesopotamia as the origin of literature, we cannot undo this. No amount of Chinese culturalism will undo the Chinese appropriation of Euroteleology in Africa.

As we measure the casualties of the UN compound in Mazar-i-Sharif in April 2011, we must not forget that Eleanor Roosevelt eased out W.E.B. Du Bois when he had dared to suggest that the United Nations repeats the old colonial power lines. You cannot know the whole world. You make certain kinds of choices, taking the imperialist anti-imperialist position, adroitly analyzed by Raymond Williams as the Bloomsbury Fraction.

Those of us who represent the supplementary antisystemic position must not be thought of as "naysayers." We are what Rabindranath Tagore called "the wasteful spenders," the *bajey khorcheys*. In a piece that struggles with transcendentalism, chiastic balance like Schiller transforming the Kantian critique and reproductive heteronormitivity, there are two transgressive moments in Tagore that made that very piece unclear then to the Indian common reader in 1906.

The unexplained but declared translation of the English phrase "comparative literature," which he cites, in English, in his essay, is *"bishsho shahitto*, world literature," he says, without any explanation at all: "You have asked me" in Bengali he writes, "to talk about comparative literature, but I will call it 'world literature.'"

[Looking at David] It's worth looking at. And at what the range is between the general atmosphere of the liberal humanist essay and the transgressive moments – (a) the repeated metaphor of *bajey khoroch*, or "wasteful spending," and (b) the intimations of singularity, to which I cannot pay attention here.

Tagore was at every step self-distanced from the Shinpei Goto style, embattled Pan-Asianism of the early years of the last century. His attitude was cosmopolitan and critical toward mere nationalism – and I think David is right in saying that world literature can go against mere nationalism – and it combined with his love of what he perceived to be the possibility of a humane India. He thus had a serious engagement with India's nationalist message to the world. Yet, in the mistranslated name of world literature, he theorizes the imaginative creative bond that travels across national boundaries as *bajey khoroch*, wasteful spending, a powerful metaphor for what in the imagination goes above, beyond, beneath, and short of mere rational choice toward alterity. The uncertain intimacy open to ethical alterity is "wasteful."

The world is in bad shape with the loss of emphasis on the humanities. This message of Tagore – that what goes across is not immediately profitable or evaluable does not give us greater numbers, etc., that it is "value-added" in an incommensurable sense with no guarantees – this lesson is hard to learn, in the face of the will to institutional power, through knowledge management. Tagore's examples range from the opposition of Egyptian dervishes, as he calls them – it's the Mahdists – to the British in the 1880s – he calls it "literary" because of this wasteful spending of their lives, comparable to the Ghost Dance of the Sioux against the US cavalry at Wounded Knee. He defines that worldliness beyond, beneath, above, and short of not only merely rational choice but also the verbal text. This can take on board the Kantian impulse to place the possibility of judgment in the aesthetic. In globalization, where all impulses of judgment, including "ethical waivers" claimed by government officials are managerial, this is an impulse worth subverting and sabotaging for a worldliness in the literary rather than restraining the future anterior – something (else) will have happened – by diagnosing and systematizing items to see how they qualify for our rubric.

Why should we endlessly quote Goethe? A magisterial writer but historically undoubtedly informed by that imperialist anti-imperialism which I already cited as the Bloomsbury Fraction. Marx is another story. If we remain focused on the North American context saying, hey, this is not about the world market, this is about North America, we forget to ask that kind of question because we can present ourselves as the tousled hair, erratic kind of "great" teacher, unable to imagine that we are folded and held within the terrible greed of rampant capitalism. It reminds me of all the romantic pieces in national media about the authenticity of the rural American way of life, the farm philosophy of the United States, our wonderful grandparents and how they lived very differently from the way in which this unrestricted greed is making us live, without once mentioning the subsidies. Those pious pieces never ever talk about, let's say, how Brazil, India, and China together in the Cancun Group tried to fight against the subsidies, never talk about the fact that American agribusiness is a site of global conflict.

It's the same way if we say, "Hey, we're just talking about how well we're doing in North America." We have to think about this as we endlessly go on quoting the eighteenth and nineteenth century and talk about opening up the global classroom and study non-European antiquity.

I imagine rather a globally diversified collectivity of scholars, teachers supplementing and training to supplement, the epistemological performance of a world literature, how it constructs its object of knowledge, how it teaches the students to construct their object of knowledge. In other words, what David has very correctly supplied to us is how we should, indeed, undo the limits of old-style comparative literature and the pride of the national literatures, though it's very hard to try to fight against comp lit and the national literatures when, in a budgetary way, they're really not having a good time at all.

That kind of construction of the object of knowing, in the literature classroom, it seems to me, has to be supplemented in some way, and not just by reading the same old, same old with good language skills but by trying to read the same old, same old texts by undoing them, taking them away from the universal and give them the kind of singularity that Diebes is trying to give, and Genet, with the Rembrandt and the Beethoven and the Bach. If it's really for North America, let's hit the mainstream. This is not the Culture Wars. Augmenting the canon arithmetically is not the only task on the agenda. It's a time to singularize rather than provincialize the European context of comp lit, simply offering a substitute, a picture of North America within its boundaries and its global classrooms, giving us something called world literature that constructs its object in this way.

[*Damrosch*]: I guess I should say a few more words in response, and there would be a lot of things to discuss. It is certainly the case that Gayatri's work is so extraordinarily varied that one can't represent her accurately simply by quoting a passage from her work. I think that's part of her Goethian aspect, reminding me of what Eckermann says about Goethe: "He's a diamond that presents a different facet each way you look." That's certainly true of Gayatri.

I agree that Tagore is extremely interesting. I just finished this week collaborating with my friends Theo D'haen and Djelal Kadir in editing *The Routledge Companion to World Literature*, in which we have essays on Goethe and on Tagore in our opening section on foundational statements. And again, I never heard of Tagore's essay when I was in graduate school. It simply wasn't there in the curriculum.

I really liked Gayatri's emphasis on singularity, and I think this is intriguing for "comp lit" versus "world lit," because when world lit is done badly the world is flat, it's Thomas Friedman on a bad day, and even Thomas Friedman on a good day can lead to a flattening or a leveling out, a kind of a mush of the global. We certainly don't want that. What's interesting to me is that when it's done well, world literature actually reframes the singular in new ways. A rather high proportion of the papers at this conference, for example, involve a single writer. That was not our teachers' comp lit. Comp lit used to be like my mother's dinner plates: something red, something white, and something green, sort of like eating the Italian flag for dinner every night. So you needed something French, and something German, and something English or possibly Italian or Russian. Nor was the textual range so great even within the favored few literatures. At the time I was writing my dissertation at Yale, half of all dissertations in progress in the department involved Henry James, or Balzac, or both. It was like that Monty Python restaurant where you can get a frog on a peach or a peach on a frog; that was sort of what it was.

But what's interesting is that the comp lit of that era had a particular problem with singularity, because you'd have to put two or three things together to be a comparatist. A couple of years ago I did a book on the *Epic of Gilgamesh*, and it's a book on one text as a work of world literature, thinking about the chain of significations that circulates from Babylon up into Assyria and that from there gets recovered in the Victorian era. My book has two modern heroes: the first important Iraqi archaeologist, Hormuzd Rassam, who discovered the library of Ashurbanipal with its decisive trove of tablets, and the epic's decipher, George Smith, a fascinating working-class British guy who never went to high school, much less college. By studying *Gilgamesh*'s circulation out into the world, I was able to look closely into issues of race, class, imperial politics, and the singularity of a unique literary work and its exceptional history.

We can also use such studies to try to intervene in our culture, whether academically or beyond. The Gilgamesh book came from the distress that I felt following the events of 9/11, when there was a lot of very loose talk about a "clash of civilizations," this Samuel Huntington type of thing. And I asked myself what I could work on to show that if you really go back, there's only one common civilization underlying both Western and Middle Eastern cultures. "Okay," I decided: "the general public needs a book on the *Epic of Gilgamesh.*" This wasn't the old kind of comp lit, but I told it as an adventure story, hung on the biographies of Rassam and Smith, about how the epic developed and circulated. What I was finding was the multiple singularity of that text, it was not one thing. The epic was a different thing in the court of Ashurbanipal than it had been in Babylon, and it became something different when it was dug up, and it becomes something else again when it circulates back into the Middle East today. I can't say that I had any great success in intervening in Donald Rumsfeld's discourse, but it was prob ably the only book centered on the Neo-Assyrian Empire that has been reviewed in *Entertainment Weekly*, and I hope that some readers saw the cultural-political lessons within the adventure story; I don't know, but one has to push.

And just to add a note on the question of language. I'm very interested by Gayatri's remarks on the limited French and German available to her as a student in India. The language I could not study in my high school in New York City was Spanish. This is kind of unbelievable, if you think about it now. Spanish was being spoken on the street outside the school, New York has one of the largest Spanish-speaking populations of any city in the world, it was in my own neighborhood, all around me. But because I attended a parochial school that wanted to send kids to the Ivy League, I could study French, German, and Latin, and only those languages. Sure enough, these were the three languages on which I had to pass language exams when I entered my graduate program in comp lit.

I did study Spanish in graduate school, as it happens, and this was because of what you might think of as the worst kind of superficial "Let's plug in a little bit of multicultural stuff" in a freshman-year art history survey course. Typical of the early seventies, the course dealt only with Western art, from the Greeks through Leonardo and on up to abstract expressionism. My particular seminar leader, though, happened to be a Mesoamericanist, Arthur Miller, a recently hired assistant professor. He was impatient with the Eurocentrism of the course, and he put in a week on Mesoamerican art, which I just thought was incredibly interesting to see. I decided to write my ten-page term paper on the uncanny statue of the goddess Coatlicue at the Museo Nacional de Antropología in Mexico City. I discovered a book on *Aztec Thought and Culture* by Miguel León-Portilla, which quoted a lot of poetry to illustrate Aztec ideas. I thought this was the most amazing poetry, even in an English translation of León-Portilla's Spanish translations of the Nahuatl originals. This was a new world I'd never seen. I was deeply moved, and I thought, "If I get a chance, I'd love to study this language."

Four years later, in graduate school, I discovered that a Nahuatl course was being offered in the anthropology department. When I asked Bart Giamatti, my director of graduate studies, whether I could take this course for credit, he threatened to throw me out the window, which was then on the seventh floor of Bingham Hall. This produced a little moment of vertigo, but to his credit, he did let me take it for credit. The enrollment doubled when I signed up. And it was because of studying that language that I realized I had to learn Spanish, because I couldn't work on the Nahuatl otherwise, since so many of the editions and the scholarly studies are in Spanish. So I studied Spanish, as a result of which I can now use the Spanish text of Cervantes when I'm teaching my world literature class. So we have a return of the once déclassé language that was below my private school's radar screen, via Nahuatl, thanks to a brief exposure to translated poetry in a survey class.

Such experiences can occur at any time. My middle child, Eva, changed schools after eighth grade in order to go to a high school where she could study Japanese, all because in third grade she'd had a class trip to a Japanese tea ceremony. And she studied Japanese for four years in high school and lived with families in Japan for two summers. You don't know what's going to spark someone's potentially lifelong interest. The main thing about that is to not stop at the level of the superficial first acquaintance. Our students will find what hits them, and then you can encourage them to go as far as possible with it. That I think is a real moral imperative for us as teachers and scholars, to press that singularity in a globally and politically aware context.

[*Spivak*]: Edward Said, in his revision of *Orientalism*, quietly wrote that national liberation movements showed that subalterns were speaking, suggesting that upper-class bourgeois leaders, such as Nehru and Gandhi, were, in fact, subalterns. I only saw this by chance, because of course I had the first edition of *Orientalism*, which my dear friend and ally had given me when it came out. Because I couldn't find it in the wreck that is my office, I bought a second copy. And I saw that he had written this in the added "afterword." He never told me because he knew I would not agree and he certainly didn't give me a footnote – this idea of subalternity simply being non-European and colonized is a bad idea, which you also see in Michael Hardt and Antonio Negri's phrase "subaltern nation," since by Gramsci's classic definition, still useful in working at the relief map of a playing field that isn't level at all, the subaltern classes are those who are de facto not constituted into a (nation-)state.

The fact that a young North American student had not heard of Tagore, David – and I'm not saying anything personally – has nothing to do with the fact of this Nobel laureate poet being known exceedingly broadly. Let me share the unread bit with you because I think it's necessary for us to regionalize these national figures who are put together with – who did you say? Tagore and who?

[*Damrosch*]: Goethe.

[*Spivak*]: Goethe, there we go. So Tagore is a Goethe type of figure, I said, didn't I, transcendentalism, reproductive heteronormativity, the chiastic balance like Schiller undoing Kant's critique, etc., and then there are these transgressive moments which the Indian reading public did not understand. I mean Tagore himself cites this, so he has to explain. Therefore, please let's not think of him as a subaltern figure because he happens to have written in another language. As Amartya Sen has recently written, in the West Tagore is thought of as a kind of Kahlil Gibran in drag.

In a paper presented in Baroda, in February, Professor E.B. Ramakrishnan suggested that we regionalize the multilingual Indian literatures, that we not try endlessly to find one example and translate it into English and put it side by side with something else. He asked us rather to "regionalize" these – his word – multilingual Indian literatures by way of context and language in order paradoxically to restore their Indianness that is at best a theoretical geopolitical fiction like "Europe," pleading perhaps for comparative literature, all world literature, to include something called "Indian" as a historical sign system to be traced post-theoretically rather than sketched in here through global English alone. In Baroda, I tried to follow Professor Ramakrishnan's directive with reference to the massive figure of Tagore. I poached from what I had done in my hometown three months before Baroda.

Speaking of Tagore in Calcutta as a bit of a mischievous feminist iconoclast, I segued into my subject by way of Jayasree Roy Chowdhury, now Jayasree Nath, a school friend from a small girls' school in Calcutta, who had continued on to Brabourne, a small women's college where we had both been students for the first two years (1955–1957) of undergraduate studies. In college, she and I would sit down at a harmonium and sing Tagore songs or "Rabindra Sangeet" on every possible occasion.[16] I should mention that these songs form a stock of occasional songs for groups and institutions in West Bengal and Bangladesh, and each one of them would be readily recognized by the entire reach of the middle class. So "Bhora thak" we sang at farewells, "Jibono jakhono" ("When Life") at deaths, "Nutan juger bhorey" ("At the Dawning of a New Era") on Independence Day, "Morubijoyer" ("Desert Conquering") on 25 *boishakh* (Tagore's birthday in the Indian calendar).

And I think at the end of the day, I'd said last December, asked to celebrate Tagore on his 150th anniversary, in Calcutta, "in spite of all of the grandeur of the poet's trajectory" – and they would have been very surprised that at his 150th anniversary, with extensive celebrations in Japan, and of course in all of the states in India, that he was being discovered for world literature in North America – "in spite of all the grandeur of the poet's trajectory, it is this intimacy," I said, and I was being subversive in my hometown, "in our girlish souls, established now into examined lives, which 'mean' Tagore for us. Always a better articulation of our own feelings." Not just us. I remember my mother saying her college generation grew up on *Shesher kobita*, a slim love story of the deliberate end to an affair, where Tagore takes himself on in the name of a poet of a younger, rebellious generation. "This," I said, "is my Tagore, giving soul-shape to middle-class women," often mistaken for women as such. This is not the Tagore you will read when you compare him to Goethe, although Goethe's own contributions in this field are abundantly recognized.

To show how much of this is generally internalized in cultural production today, I was going to show some clips from a film by Moinak Biswas called *Sthaniya sambaad*, "local news." But you get my point. When you regionalize him – and if I had shown the clip, you would have seen the Bengali stuff coming on – it's not because you need to know Bengali in order to understand Tagore but because in order to regionalize him, singularize him rather than keep him as one of those figures we declaim so that world literature can be selectively worldly. You really have to think about singularity in a collectivity and put geopolitics over against this. Not only the secession of the global elite, not only the globetrotting preservationists, whom we haven't talked about at all in terms of a "world" supporting the unexamined culturalism of the metropolitan migrant elite, but also the call-center workers about whom Shehzad Nadeem has written: "Workers must be able to pass as American or British."

I should mention here that "singularity" doesn't necessarily imply single texts. It simply implies that what is singular in any text is the universalizable. We must be in search of this -ability. (I am thinking of Samuel Weber's excellent recent book with that title, but not then transgress into making the singular universal, place it on a grid. Weber deals with this task beautifully.)[17]

This is the other side. We used to say about the European Enlightenment, cutting a postcolonial riff on Adorno and Horkheimer, that the other side of the dialectics of the Enlightenment is the dark part of the colonies. Benjamin talking about civilization and its other side: barbarism. In the same way, the other side of that worldliness, in North America embracing the world via Goethe, there in the call centers, Nadeem has written, "workers must be able to pass as American or British and maintain their composure in the face of sometimes racist abuse by irate customers. It is simply part of the job." Thus the animating paradox of their condition, Nadeem writes, is that "they are reaping the benefits of the corporate search for cut-rate labor but" – the other side – "also bearing the burden." "They are" he writes, "upwardly mobile cyber-coolies."[18] Now when you think of that figure passing as American, outsourcing, think of insourcing and the opposite of what would be the antonym of "cyber-coolies" in the videotic classroom. Think about the two things together. This is one of the exercises that I would ask you to perform as you train your imagination to supplement the impulse to world lit.

David and I will probably – to quote him – duke it out again. The task is too import-ant for both of us. And we'll probably say different things next time. In Turkey – we were very reverent and polite toward each other. Today we have said that we are going to supplement. I agree with him, he agrees with me, there was a little abuse right in the beginning of his talk, but it's nothing, we like each other. This is not the end of the conversation. You come again, to see how we step toward each other. Thank you.

Questions

Question One: Thanks very much to you both. It was a fascinating conversation. I have a question for David regarding a comment that you've made at the end of your introductory talk, which was that the imperative is to push back against the market. And I wanted to push you a bit on that one. Is what you're talking about pushing back against the market, or is it in a sense enhancing the market? Is there a way to talk about the differences between those two, particularly if you talk about, for example, sending students on exchange programs, or deans expanding the availability of foreign language classes? How does one actually talk about the differences in a world literature context between pushing against the market and enhancing it? Thank you.

[*Damrosch*]: It's a really tricky question and one that certainly any anthologist thinks about very hard. Just to talk about my experience, my best education in the market came in my years as an assistant professor, when an old college roommate and I invented a board game called "True Love." The object was to get from "First Date" all the way to "Meaningful Relationship" while accumulating more points than your partner. It wasn't a very playable game, but it was a nice concept, and we got in to see various people at large game companies. The situation there is like the textbook industry, only much more so. The equivalent at these companies of an acquisitions editor is the vice president for marketing, so that's very clear. And the most interesting case was when we talked with the vice-president at Milton Bradley. We had the good fortune to get in to see him on a Friday afternoon when he was tired and he just felt like musing. He told us that he often felt he knew exactly what his customers wanted, but he couldn't sell to his customers, he had to sell to the distributors. "If only I could kill my distributors," he said with a sad smile, "then I could really sell to my customers!" So here he was, a marketer who would only take a game if it would sell three quarters of a million units a year – extremely successful at what he was doing – and yet he was a prisoner in a sense of his own distribution mechanism.

And I thought of this conversation when I started to do the anthology work, because it's a similar thing. As scholars, we sell to our consumers – the graduate students or colleagues who will read us. But as textbook editors, we sell to our distributors, the faculty who teach the course. They aren't the people who actually buy the book, which they get for free as a desk copy; they assign the book to the people who buy it, the student consumers. So pushing the market means pushing the distribution mechanism. And it means that we anthologists can't simply include what we believe from our experience will be the best works to excite undergraduates, the works that they will love and that will teach them about the world. Instead, it's a question of what we can get the faculty to teach, to assign – people who have often been trained differently, under the older NATO-literatures model, and they're often out of their comfort zone when they're going beyond what's common. So major literature anthologies these days are about one-third non-Western and two-thirds Western. The proportion is completely distorted by the market. But again, we push away from 100 percent Western or 95 percent Western, which is what the proportion was not so long ago, and if we're now at 66 percent Western, we're getting somewhere.

I think that pushing the market can also be said to enhance the market, as it certainly does. The textbook publishers are now having to put out new editions at an insane rate of revision because of the used book market, which is a whole separate issue and problem, and it enhances the new edition to have some new texts in it. You can't find a new work by Dante that people want to use, but if you can tell them "You need this Vietnamese text, which is really cool," it enhances the market for the next edition of the anthology, even as it entices the faculty to try new things. To me, this is a kind of both/and situation, since it makes the publisher willing to include the works I'm eager to have there. When I speak of world literature as works in circulation, this could be just giving in to the market, but in fact I'm always pushing because I'm putting things into the anthologies that haven't been circulated before. So I think this should enhance the market against its own mindless principles toward a more mindful opening out.

Question Two: Hi, my question is to David. First of all, I'm not sure I understood your distinction between comparative and world literature. It seems to me you were saying what used to be comparative literature is now world literature, and if I'm wrong, please do correct me. But my second question has to do with your response to Gayatri's question about ethics in studying world literature. I'm not sure whether you really grappled with that question, and what I want to put to you was maybe one way to make you answer that question, which many of us have. Who wants to study world literature, you know, these sort of fictional thousands of students who want to study world literature, who are they, why do they want to at this moment study world literature and what kinds of literatures do they want to study? And that might in some way bring in the whole notion of politics and ethics which Gayatri was emphasizing.

[*Damrosch*]: An extremely important question, as we were both saying, and thank you for giving me the chance to clarify this. Every now and then, in the field of comparative literature you get someone making an imperialist claim for their particular thing and saying that the discipline has to become this, for example that comp lit has to be replaced by translation studies. And translation studies has come in and it's very important, but this would not be the whole of comp lit. I wouldn't want to be seeming to say "comp lit is now world literature." I think rather that we have a dynamic interplay in which world literature can help reframe comparative study. Comparative study is still a fundamental part of what we do. My department is still called Comparative Literature; I think the term has a history we should honor, and I often do compare actually, and comparison across literatures will remain a very viable mechanism in our discipline.

I also think you have a kind of figure/ground reversal between world literature and national literature, because, in one sense, world literature is prior to the creation of most national literatures, but in another sense, world literature exists only *within* a national space for any given reader. So in this sense world literature is actually a function of national systems and needs to be thought about that way. National literature, comparative literature, world literature exist in a dynamic interplay, and no one of these can eat the others up.

On the ethical question, I have to admit: I am a structuralist in recovery. I'm ethically challenged as result of my formalist training in the seventies, though this is somewhat paradoxically overlaid or underlaid with the fact that I'm also a preacher's kid. As a result, I'm very evangelical, though an evangelist without an ethics is sort of like Benjamin's Marxism, you might say, a paradoxical Marxism of someone who doesn't believe in progress. But I think it's a kind of ethical stand at some deep level to press for a more capacious study of the world's literatures, but this does very much involve asking who is studying and why. We also need to think really seriously about the opening up of the power relations between teacher and students, and part of the ethical question is to take seriously the modes in which people come to studying comparative and world literature and the kinds of dialogue that can emerge.

Question Three: [My question is] to both of the learned speakers here. Self-realization means to introspect and to be able to understand the meaningful relationship with God and humanity. But self-realization is also to build oneself in worldly circumstances. Now how would you define that self-realization in the world literature context, especially when you want to go into the text, subtextual meaning and intertextual meaning?

[*Spivak*]: Self-realization … now let me ask you if you would like to think of that English phrase in as many different languages as you can think of. I mean, you and I are obliged to speak here in English. I'm not making a silly remark here.

At the end of his book called *Rogues*, Derrida offers a task and he says: try to translate in all the languages of the world, beyond Latinity, what you think in your language is the difference between "reasonable" and "rational," which is an impossible request.[19] But the importance of the request is that these words come combined with a package that tells you something within the language, the nature of that language.

I don't know how I would agree with you that literature helps you to realize yourself. On the other hand, I could agree with you by saying what I was trying to say: that the ethical reflex is to go toward the other, and literature doesn't teach you that, but literature allows you to train for that in the way in which if you get the capacity to be able to trace a text, that is already a kind of training in the sort of thing that you need to have in this world of ours in order not to be like Nicholas Kristof, all the innumerable NGOs, etc. You said in introducing me, Haun, that I was doing some incredible work improving the lives of people, which I would be very shocked to think that that's what I was doing. That particular impulse is something that we ought to question a little bit.

So if you think about self-realization in that way, I suppose I would go along with you. But for me, the problem is that it's an English phrase. You look like you are perhaps from South Asia. If you go to that thing which the Hindutwa people quote often: "*Na vā arē jāyāyai kāmāya jāyā priyā bhavati/ātmanastu kāmāya jāyā priyā bhavati*" and so on (that your wife does not become beloved because you desire your wife but because you desire your *ātman* – or the other way, the *ātman* in-forming you as a desiring-machine, as it were – that's why your wife becomes beloved, and so on with many important nouns – husband, knowledge, etc.). If you translate that *ātman* as *Self*, capital "S," you're into that "self-realization in English" bag.

On the other hand, if you try to trace it and you see that it's cognate with *atmos* and it probably means something like that sort of *signifiance* conveyor belt, not meaning*ful*, which allows the possibility of meaning, so that Benjamin can speak at the end of "The Task of the Translator" of the *reine Sprache* without meaning which makes translation possible, then you get a completely different program from self-realization. So I would remain caught within that assumption because I would think of the many different ways in which self-realization can come to us given the world's wealth of languages. Think of Africa and the wealth of its languages, for example.

I was just looking at that sentence where Tagore talks about world literature and comparative literature – no, not of translation – "The responsibility that you've given me for a discussion in English you have given it a name: 'comparative literature.' I will call it '*Bishsho Shahitto*' in Bengali."[20] *Vishwa sahitya* (in the Sanskritized form) is not world literature, of course, because *sahitya*, as you know, is precisely collectivity, whereas literature is something like letters. So where are you going to find an answer to questions of this sort?

That's why I was saying let's not ignore the stakes of world literature, as self-realization seems to be a nice good goal, if you expand the self so that all of the world's different languages can be included. If you realize that the "self" is made up in language – that too is self-realization. But let's supplement it with those kinds of worries that I've just shared with you in this long answer of mine. The literary is wasteful spending. That's why I so catch on to that. It won't lead you to a systemic coding, that's why I showed you those pictures. So if you're not satisfied with my answer, it's not a problem, we can talk more.

Question Four: My name is Natasha. Actually, I'm an undergraduate student with the world literature program at the Simon Fraser University and one thing that I realized particularly with the undergraduate panel that occurred at the ACLA for the first time this year was that most academic institutions do teach quite a variety of different theories, narratives, prose, poetry. What I wonder is, could there possibly be a level playing field across academic institutions in North America? What are your opinions on that?

[*Damrosch*]: The great thing about the multiplicity of North America's system is that it's so much more varied than most countries' systems are. And, in particular, the comparative literature programs are best when they are localized to the interests and possibilities of the institution, and no one program does or should do just what the others do, so that variety is so much better than a leveling out. At the same time, I do think we have a much more even playing field these days, insofar as there isn't so much the hegemony of a few programs that there used to be. I think that's a welcome opening out, let's say, rather than leveling out, of programs and of events like this very ACLA meeting here. Not only do our eighteen hundred speakers reflect the extraordinary variety of the institutions in North America, but we probably we have people from forty different countries here. This is an extraordinary kind of opening out. This is the very opposite of a leveling, but it is an opening of the playing field to a much wider variety of players than we used to see, which is one of the most extraordinary things that's happening today.

[*Spivak*]: She was talking about funding and what is being taught. Now, when you talk about funding, of course you know that in this country, in Canada, and in the US, the situations are not exactly similar, but in the United States, since you have private institutions, public institutions, community colleges, and then university systems with many colleges, some of which are flagship colleges, the other are not so, etc., it would be very difficult to talk about funding. The budget of Harvard for example is bigger than some small third world countries …

[*Damrosch*]: Before the crisis …

[*Spivak*]: Yes, yes, even with the crisis. You know, I'm not fighting. Princeton is much smaller than Columbia, but it has a budget which is somehow bigger. So it's even within the biggies … I think that the answer to your question is a "no," and I'm glad you asked the question, but we should discuss why the question is impossible. You know, it's the same as why "it's opening up," etc., ignores these details. And we should talk about it. That's why I think in fact of Marx's third thesis, there is a difference between teachers and students. It's not a power difference, it's more like I'm my students' servant, because I have a little bit more experience. They can teach me things, but I can teach them a little something too. For example, on the question of funding here.

   And the other thing would be to teach the same things everywhere. I think you asked the question in a good spirit, and I am glad you asked it. But again, if you sit down to think about it, it might be better if they didn't all teach the same thing. So that you can go to Arizona to learn more about Native American stuff and you can go to Middlebury to do a little more with languages, so a little diversity might be better than uniformity. This is a good question and we can talk more about it now that I know what you meant by it. Thank you.

Notes

1 Werner P. Friedrich, "On the Integrity of Our Planning," in *The Teaching of World Literature*, ed. Haskell Block (Chapel Hill: University of North Carolina Press, 1960), 14–15.

2 Sukehiro Hirakawa, "Japanese Culture: Accommodation to Modern Times," *Yearbook of Comparative and General Literature* 28 (1979): 47.

3 Gayatri C. Spivak, *Death of a Discipline* (New York: Columbia University Press, 2003), xii.

4 Friedrich, "On the Integrity of Our Planning," 15.

5 Harry Levin *et al.*, "Report on Professional Standards," http://www.umass.edu/complit/aclanet/Levin.html (accessed 7 Oct. 2011).

6 Thomas Greene *et al.*, "Report on Professional Standards," http://www.umass.edu/complit/aclanet/Greene.html (accessed 7 Oct. 2011).

7 Colloquium style classes can help here, but if I remember right, my main point in April in Vancouver had been epistemological. These issues do not for me address the problem.

8 Gayatri Chakravorty Spivak, "Teaching for the Times," *Journal of the Midwestern Modern Language Association* 25.1 (1992): 183.

9 Jacques Derrida, *Of Grammatology*, corr. ed., trans. Gayatri Chakravorty Spivak (Baltimore, MD: Johns Hopkins University Press, 1997), 314.

10 We are inhabiting the register of truth rather than the register of exactitude (as Lacan would put it), I had said in Vancouver, trying to cover up a lapse in fact checking. So, my apologies to David.

11 Here Gayatri Spivak plays the clip, showing a hand overwriting the score, on a page of the printed musical score of Bach's six suites for solo cello, while Mstislav Rostropovich's 1991 recording plays concurrently (http://www.joediebes.com/works/one2one.html [accessed 29 Sept. 2011]).

12 Referring to http://www.joediebes.com/works/one2one.html.

13 "Playing to Lose," in "Loss," written for the Seagull Press's annual catalog (Kolkata, India).

14 Friedrich Nietzsche, *On the Genealogy of Morals and Ecce Homo*, trans. Walter Kaufmann (New York: Vintage, 1989), 77.

15 The Marx-Kant-Gramsci bit comes from my forthcoming book *An Aesthetic Education in the Era of Globalization*. The bit on the multicultural classroom is also from there.

16 There were plenty of Bengali speakers in the ballroom in Vancouver. I mentioned the initial phrase of many songs, beginning with "Bhora thak" or "Let it Be Full."

17 Samuel Weber, *Benjamin's –abilities* (Cambridge, MA: Harvard University Press, 2008).

18 Shehzad Nadeem, *Dead Ringers: How Outsourcing Is Changing the Way Indians Understand Themselves* (Princeton, NJ: Princeton University Press, 2011), 2.

19 Jacques Derrida, *Rogues: Two Essays on Reason* (Stanford, CA: Stanford University Press, 2005), 159.

20 Rabindranath Tagore, "World Literature," trans. Swapan Chakravorty, in Rabindranath Tagore, *Selected Writings on Literature and Language*, ed. Sisir Kumar Das and Sukanta Chaudhuri (New Delhi: Oxford University Press, 2001), 141. (Translation modified.)

Part Four

World Literature in the World

26

The Argentine Writer and Tradition (1943)

Jorge Luis Borges

A world-renowned writer, essayist, poet, and translator, Jorge Francisco Isidoro Luis Borges Acevedo (1899–1986) is best known for his short fictions which challenge the limits of genre, playing on dreams, possible worlds, literary theories, and an encyclopedic range of intertexts, most notably in the stories collected in *Ficciones* (1944) and *El Aleph* (1949). A master of parody, pseudo-scholarship, and enigmatic detective stories, Borges influenced the South American magic realism of the 1960s and much work in literary theory since then. Born in Buenos Aires to parents of mixed Spanish, Portuguese, and English descent, Borges gained fluency in several languages, reinforced when his family moved to Europe in 1914. He returned to Argentina in 1921, bringing home the latest avant-garde trends in European litera-ture, which shaped poems and essays that he published in surrealist journals. Over the years, he translated many works from English, French, and German, including writing by Poe, Kafka, Hesse, Woolf, Gide, and Faulkner. Both anti-fascist and anti-communist, he opposed the populist authoritarianism of Argentina's president Juan Perón during the decade 1946–1955, losing his position at a municipal library as a result. Following the fall of Perón, Borges was appointed Professor of Literature at the University of Buenos Aires and director of the National Library – a somewhat ironic honor, as he had begun losing his sight in the late 1930s and was entirely blind by then.

Always an exceptionally cosmopolitan writer, Borges enjoyed worldwide fame beginning in the 1960s, influencing writers such as Gabriel García Márquez in Colombia, Italo Calvino in Italy, and Abe Kobo in Japan. In the essay given here, Borges envisions the European cultural tradition as a whole seen from abroad. He rejects "local color" as an imported value in favor of a universalism in which one's

Jorge Luis Borges, "The Argentine Writer and Tradition," trans. Esther Allen. From Jorge Luis Borges, *Selected Non-Fictions*, ed. Eliot Weinberger (New York: Penguin, 2000), pp. 420–427.

World Literature in Theory, First Edition. Edited by David Damrosch.

national character will be most deeply revealed. Anticipating Pascale Casanova's emphasis in *The World Republic of Letters* on peripheral writers' ability to challenge and change the canon of world literature, Borges asserts that "we can handle all European themes, handle them without superstition, with an irreverence which can have, and already does have, fortunate consequences." His world-encompassing understanding of what tradition should be – "we should feel that our patrimony is the universe" – foregrounds today's global span of literature.

I would like to express and justify certain skeptical propositions concerning the problem of the Argentine writer and tradition. My skepticism is not related to the difficulty or impossibility of resolving the problem, but to its very existence. I think we are faced with a rhetorical theme, suitable for pathetic elaboration, rather than a true cerebral difficulty; it is, to my mind, an appearance, a simulacrum, a pseudo-problem.

Before examining it, I would like to consider its standard expressions and solutions. I will start with a solution that has become almost instinctive and presents itself without benefit of any rationale: the one which affirms that the Argentine literary tradition already exists in *gauchesco* poetry. Consequently, the lexicon, techniques, and subject matter of *gauchesco* poetry should enlighten the contemporary writer, and are a point of departure and perhaps an archetype. This is the most common solution, and for that reason I intend to examine it at some length.

It was proposed by Lugones in *El payador*; there we read that we Argentines possess a classic poem, *Martín Fierro*, and that this poem should be for us what the Homeric poems were for the Greeks. It seems difficult to contradict this opinion without detriment to *Martín Fierro*. I believe that *Martín Fierro* is the most lasting work we Argentines have written; I also believe, with equal intensity, that we cannot take *Martín Fierro* to be, as has sometimes been said, our Bible, our canonical book.

Ricardo Rojas, who has also recommended the canonization of *Martín Fierro*, has written a page, in his *Historia de la literatura argentina*, that appears to be almost a platitude, but is quite shrewd.

Rojas studies the poetry of the *gauchescos* – the poetry of Hidalgo, Ascasubi, Estanislao del Campo, and José Hernández – and finds its origins in the poetry of the rural improvisational singers known as *payadores*, that is, the spontaneous poetry of the gauchos themselves. He points out that the meter of this popular poetry is octosyllabic, the same meter used by the authors of *gauchesco* poetry, and he concludes by considering the poetry of the *gauchescos* to be a continuation or magnification of the poetry of the *payadores*.

I suspect that this claim is based on a serious mistake; we might also call it a clever mistake, for it is clear that Rojas, in order to give popular roots to the poetry of the *gauchescos*, which begins with Hidalgo and culminates with Hernández, presents it as a continuation or derivation of the poetry of the gauchos; therefore

Bartolomé Hidalgo is not the Homer of this poetry, as Mitre said, but only a link in the sequence.

Ricardo Rojas makes a *payador* of Hidalgo; nevertheless, according to the same *Historia de la literatura argentina*, this supposed *payador* began by composing lines of eleven syllables, a meter that is by its very nature barred to *payadores*, who do not perceive its harmony, just as Spanish readers did not perceive the harmony of the hendecasyllabic line when Garcilaso imported it from Italy.

There is, to my mind, a fundamental difference between the poetry of the gauchos and *gauchesco* poetry. One need only compare any collection of popular poetry with *Martín Fierro*, *Paulino Lucero*, or the *Fausto*, to become aware of this difference, which exists equally in the lexicon and in the intent of the poets. The popular poets of the countryside and the outskirts of the city versify general themes: the pain of love and absence, the sorrow of love, and they do so in a lexicon that is equally general; the *gauchesco* poets, on the contrary, cultivate a deliberately popular language that the popular poets do not even attempt. I do not mean that the idiom of the popular poets is a correct Spanish, I mean that whatever may be incorrect in it results from ignorance. In the *gauchesco* poets, on the contrary, there is a quest for native words, a profusion of local color. The proof is this: a Colombian, a Mexican, or a Spaniard can immediately understand the poems of the *payadores* – the gauchos – but needs a glossary in order to reach even an approximate understanding of Estanislao del Campo or Ascasubi.

All of this can be abbreviated as follows: *gauchesco* poetry, which has produced – I hasten to repeat – admirable works, is as artificial as any other literary genre. The first *gauchesco* compositions, the ballads of Bartolomé Hidalgo, attempt to present themselves in accordance with the gaucho, as if spoken by gauchos, so that the reader will read them with a gaucho intonation. Nothing could be further from popular poetry. When they versify, the people – and I have observed this not only among the *payadores* of the countryside, but also in the neighborhoods of Buenos Aires – do so in the conviction that they are engaging in something important; therefore they instinctively reject popular words and seek out high-sounding words and turns of phrase. In all likelihood, *gauchesco* poetry has influenced the *payadores* by now, so that they, too, abound in Argentinisms, but initially this was not the case, and we have evidence of that (evidence no one has noted) in *Martín Fierro*.

Martín Fierro is written in a *gauchesco*-accented Spanish, and for a long while the poem does not allow us to forget that the person singing it is a gaucho; it abounds in comparisons taken from life in the grasslands; and yet there is a famous passage in which the author forgets this concern with local color and writes in a general Spanish, speaking not of vernacular subjects but of great, abstract subjects: time, space, the sea, the night. I am referring to the *payada*, the improvised musical face-off between Martín Fierro and El Moreno that occupies the end of the second part. It is as if Hernández himself had wished to demonstrate the difference between his *gauchesco* poetry and the genuine poetry of the gauchos. When the two gauchos,

Fierro and El Moreno, start singing, they forget all *gauchesco* affectation and address philosophical issues. I have been able to corroborate this by listening to *payadores* in the surroundings of Buenos Aires; they reject the idea of versifying in street slang, in *orillero* and *lunfardo*, and try to express themselves correctly. Of course they fail, but their aim is to make of poetry something high, something distinguished, we might say with a smile.

The idea that Argentine poetry must abound in Argentine differential traits and in Argentine local color seems to me to be a mistake. If we ask which book is more Argentine, *Martín Fierro* or the sonnets in *La urna* by Enrique Banchs, there is no reason to say that the former is more Argentine. It will be said that in Banchs' *La urna* there are neither Argentine landscapes nor Argentine topography nor Argentine botany nor Argentine zoology; nevertheless, there are other specifically Argentine conditions in *La urna*.

I can recall a couple of lines of *La urna* that seem to have been written expressly to prevent anyone from saying that this is an Argentine book; the lines are:

> *El sol en los tejados*
> *y en las ventanas brilla. Ruiseñores*
> *quieren decir que están enamorados.*

> *[The sun glints on the tiled roofs/and on the windows.*
> *Nightingales/mean to say they are in love.]*

A denunciation of "the sun glints on the tiled roofs and on the windows" seems inevitable here. Enrique Banchs wrote these lines in a house on the edge of Buenos Aires, and on the edges of Buenos Aires there are no tiled roofs, there are flat, terrace roofs; "nightingales mean to say they are in love"; the nightingale is not so much a real bird as a bird of literature, of the Greek and Germanic tradition. Nevertheless, I would maintain that in the use of these conventional images, in these incongruous tiled roofs and nightingales, although neither the architecture nor the ornithology is Argentine, there is the Argentine reserve, the Argentine reticence; the fact that Banchs, in speaking of a great sorrow that overwhelmed him, of a woman who left him and left the world empty for him, makes use of conventional, foreign imagery such as tiled roofs and nightingales, is significant: significant of a reserve, wariness, and reticence that are Argentine, significant of the difficulty we have in confiding, in being intimate.

Furthermore, I do not know if it needs to be said that the idea that a literature must define itself by the differential traits of the country that produces it is a relatively new one, and the idea that writers must seek out subjects local to their countries is also new and arbitrary. Without going back any further, I think Racine would not have begun to understand anyone who would deny him his right to the title of French poet for having sought out Greek and Latin subjects. I think Shakespeare would have been astonished if anyone had tried to limit him to English subjects, and if anyone had told him that, as an Englishman, he had no right to write *Hamlet*, with its Scandinavian subject matter, or *Macbeth*, on a

Scottish theme. The Argentine cult of local color is a recent European cult that nationalists should reject as a foreign import.

A few days ago, I discovered a curious confirmation of the way in which what is truly native can and often does dispense with local color; I found this confirmation in Gibbon's *Decline and Fall of the Roman Empire*. Gibbon observes that in the Arab book *par excellence*, the Koran, there are no camels; I believe that if there were ever any doubt as to the authenticity of the Koran, this lack of camels would suffice to prove that it is Arab. It was written by Mohammed, and Mohammed, as an Arab, had no reason to know that camels were particularly Arab; they were, for him, a part of reality, and he had no reason to single them out, while the first thing a forger, a tourist, or an Arab nationalist would do is bring on the camels, whole caravans of camels on every page; but Mohammed, as an Arab, was unconcerned; he knew he could be Arab without camels. I believe that we Argentines can be like Mohammed; we can believe in the possibility of being Argentine without abounding in local color.

Permit me to confide something, just a small thing. For many years, in books now fortunately forgotten, I tried to compose the flavor, the essence, of the outskirts of Buenos Aires; naturally I abounded in local words such as *cuchilleros, milonga, tapia*, and others, and in such manner I wrote those forgettable and forgotten books; then, about a year ago, I wrote a story called "Death and the Compass," which is a kind of nightmare, a nightmare in which elements of Buenos Aires appear, deformed by the horror of the nightmare; and in that story, when I think of the Paseo Colón, I call it Rue de Toulon; when I think of the *quintas* of Adrogué, I call them Triste-le-Roy; after the story was published, my friends told me that at last they had found the flavor of the outskirts of Buenos Aires in my writing. Precisely because I had not abandoned myself to the dream, I was able to achieve, after so many years, what I once sought in vain.

Now I wish to speak of a justly illustrious work that the nationalists often invoke. I refer to *Don Segundo Sombra* by Güiraldes. The nationalists tell us that *Don Segundo Sombra* is the characteristic national book; but if we compare *Don Segundo Sombra* to the works of the *gauchesco* tradition, the first things we note are differences. *Don Segundo Sombra* abounds in a type of metaphor that has nothing to do with the speech of the countryside and everything to do with the metaphors of the Montmartre salons of that period. As for the plot, the story, it is easy to discern the influence of Kipling's *Kim*, which is set in India and was, in its turn, written under the influence of Mark Twain's *Huckleberry Finn*, the epic of the Mississippi. In making this observation, I do not wish to devalue *Don Segundo Sombra*; on the contrary, I wish to emphasize that in order for us to have this book it was necessary for Güiraldes to recall the poetic technique of the French salons of his time, and the work of Kipling, which he had read many years before; which is to say that Kipling and Mark Twain and the metaphors of the French poets were necessary to this Argentine book, to this book which is, I repeat, no less Argentine for having accepted those influences.

I wish to note another contradiction: the nationalists pretend to venerate the capacities of the Argentine mind but wish to limit the poetic exercise of that mind to a few humble local themes, as if we Argentines could only speak of neighborhoods and ranches and not of the universe.

Let us pass on to another solution. It is said that there is a tradition of which we Argentine writers must avail ourselves, and that tradition is the literature of Spain. This second piece of advice is, of course, a bit less narrow than the first, but it also tends to restrict us; many objections can be made to it, but two will suffice. The first is this: Argentine history can unequivocally be defined as a desire to move away from Spain, as a willed distancing from Spain. The second objection is that, among us, the pleasure of Spanish literature, a pleasure I personally share in, is usually an acquired taste; I have often loaned French and English works to people without any particular literary erudition, and those books were enjoyed immediately, without effort. However, when I have suggested that my friends read Spanish books, I have found that these books were difficult for them to enjoy in the absence of special training; I therefore believe that the fact that certain illustrious Argentine writers write like Spaniards is not so much a testimony to some inherited capacity as it is evidence of Argentine versatility.

I now arrive at a third opinion on Argentine writers and tradition, one that I read not long ago and that greatly astonished me. This is the opinion that we Argentines are cut off from the past; that there has been some sort of rupture between ourselves and Europe. According to this singular point of view, we Argentines are as if in the first days of creation; our search for European subject matters and techniques is an illusion, an error; we must understand that we are essentially alone, and cannot play at being European.

This opinion strikes me as unfounded. I understand why many people accept it: such a declaration of our solitude, our perdition, and our primitive character has, like existentialism, the charms of poignancy. Many people may accept this opinion because, having done so, they will feel themselves to be alone, disconsolate, and in some way, interesting. Nevertheless, I have observed that in our country, precisely because it is a new country, there is a strong feeling for time. Everything that has happened in Europe, the dramatic events there in recent years, has resonated deeply here. The fact that a given individual was on the side of Franco or the Republic during the Spanish Civil War, or was on the side of the Nazis or the Allies, was in many cases the cause of very serious disputes and estrangements. This would not happen if we were detached from Europe. As for Argentine history, I think we all feel it deeply; and it is only natural that we should, because that history is very close to us, in chronology and in the blood; the names, the battles of the civil wars, the war of independence, all of it is, in time and in family traditions, quite near.

What is Argentine tradition? I believe that this question poses no problem and can easily be answered. I believe that our tradition is the whole of Western culture, and I also believe that we have a right to this tradition, a greater right than that which the inhabitants of one Western nation or another may have. Here I remember an essay by Thorstein Veblen, the North American sociologist, on the intellectual preeminence of Jews in Western culture. He wonders if this preeminence authorizes us to posit an innate Jewish superiority and answers that it does not; he says that

Jews are prominent in Western culture because they act within that culture and at the same time do not feel bound to it by any special devotion; therefore, he says, it will always be easier for a Jew than for a non-Jew to make innovations in Western culture. We can say the same of the Irish in English culture. Where the Irish are concerned, we have no reason to suppose that the profusion of Irish names in British literature and philosophy is due to any social preeminence, because many of these illustrious Irishmen (Shaw, Berkeley, Swift) were the descendants of Englishmen, men with no Celtic blood; nevertheless, the fact of feeling themselves to be Irish, to be different, was enough to enable them to make innovations in English culture. I believe that Argentines, and South Americans in general, are in an analogous situation; we can take on all the European subjects, take them on without superstition and with an irreverence that can have, and already has had, fortunate consequences.

This does not mean that all Argentine experiments are equally felicitous; I believe that this problem of the Argentine and tradition is simply a contemporary and fleeting version of the eternal problem of determinism. If I am going to touch this table with one of my hands, and I ask myself; "Will I touch it with the left hand or the right?" and I touch it with the right hand, the determinists will say that I could not have done otherwise and that the whole prior history of the universe forced me to touch the table with my right hand, and that touching it with my left hand would have been a miracle. Yet if I had touched it with my left hand, they would have told me the same thing: that I was forced to touch it with that hand. The same occurs with literary subjects and techniques. Everything we Argentine writers do felicitously will belong to Argentine tradition, in the same way that the use of Italian subjects belongs to the tradition of England through the work of Chaucer and Shakespeare.

I believe, moreover, that all the foregoing discussions of the aims of literary creation are based on the error of supposing that intentions and plans matter much. Take, for example, the case of Kipling: Kipling dedicated his life to writing in accordance with a given set of political ideals, he wanted to make his work a tool for propaganda, and nevertheless, at the end of his life he had to confess that the true essence of a writer's work is usually unknown by that writer; and he remembered the case of Swift, who while writing *Gulliver's Travels* wanted to raise an indictment against mankind and instead left behind a children's book. Plato said that poets are the amanuenses of a god who moves them against their will, against their intentions, as the magnet moves a series of iron rings.

Therefore I repeat that we must not be afraid; we must believe that the universe is our birthright and try out every subject; we cannot confine ourselves to what is Argentine in order to be Argentine because either it is our inevitable destiny to be Argentine, in which case we will be Argentine whatever we do, or being Argentine is a mere affectation, a mask.

I believe that if we lose ourselves in the voluntary dream called artistic creation, we will be Argentine and we will be, as well, good or adequate writers.

27

Cultures and Contexts (2001)

Tania Franco Carvalhal

An important figure in the shaping of Latin American comparative studies, Tania Franco Carvalhal (1943–2006) was Professor of Comparative Literature at the Federal University of Rio Grande do Sul in Brazil. Carvalhal held a PhD in literary theory and comparative literature from the University of São Paulo and also taught at the Sorbonne and at Indiana University. A founding member and former President of the Brazilian Comparative Literature Association, at the time of her death Carvalhal was President of the International Comparative Literature Association. In her scholarly work, Carvalhal argued for a global opening of the discipline, looking into the relation between comparative literature and Goethe's *Weltliteratur*, as well as concepts in translation theory and reception theory, with a special interest in Latin American and especially Brazilian literature. Her books challenge the traditional comparative literature practice in Latin America of looking reverently at European literatures as a source and model for the Latin American ones. Carvalhal moved from a historical view of the discipline in *La Literatura Comparada* (1996) to analyzing contemporary changes in the discipline's theories and methodologies in a global age in such works as *Entre dois mundos: comparatismo e globalização* (1998) and *Culturas, contextos, discursos – limiares críticos no comparatismo* (1999). The essay included here, translated for this volume, is an account of the two-way transatlantic traffic of modernism and the uses of modernist ideas in Brazil. Carvalhal examines the relation of French modernism to Brazilian literatures in both directions, stressing the interchanges between cultures, contexts, and identities and arguing that a plural identity can encompass both the local and the universal.

Tania Franco Carvalhal, "Cultures and Contexts" (2001). Trans. Delia Ungureanu from Eduardo Coutinho, *Fronteiras imaginadas: Cultura Nacional / Teoria Internacional* (Rio de Janeiro: Aeroplano), pp. 147–154.

"Paris, cultural capital of Latin America." With its implicit irony, this phrase is effective because it synthesizes what we already know and what the history of Latin American cultures already confirmed: that is the strong and decisive French presence in shaping the intellectual physiognomy of the nations of the New World. It is a known fact that, for intellectuals, to leave South America for Paris was an ideal (when it was not attainable) in the first decades of the 20th century, in forms of migration or voluntary exile which reappeared in the 1970s as compulsory exile imposed by the military coups in Brazil, Argentina, Uruguay, and Chile.

In his study "Paris, Literary Capital of Latin America" (1999),[1] Pierre Rivas pointed out that this city stood out as the center of the consolidation of Latin American thought, since for Latin America, France was a factor of unification, even though also an alienating one. This meant that while it alienated the Latin American writers from their cultural origins, it also provided them with a similar formation that brought them together, uniting their views on the world and thought. Rivas looks into what the Paris "détour" meant for the Latin American writer: the myth of Latin identity, a space of exile, neutral territory, but also the space in which one rediscovers his own country with the lucidity which emerges from being at a distance. Therefore, the "détour" becomes a "retour," a strategy to go back to the colonial heritage, to cut the umbilical cord that connected the writer to the European womb, being at the same time a space for international recognition and legitimation.[2]

At this point, Pascale Casanova's reflections from her recent *République Mondiale des Lettres* (1999) could be useful: not only those on the consecration of literary texts through translation into a prestigious language,[3] but especially those initial considerations where she states that "only literary texts manifest themselves through a singularity emerging from the totality of the structure that has allowed for its manifestation." In other words, an author comes to have a market value through the performance of a cultural mediator such as Valéry Larbaud, who was the first to think of an "intellectual international," in other words, through the emergence of an international literary criticism, which breaks away from the national customs which had created "the illusion of singularity, specificity and insularity" (Casanova, p. 16).

This context of interchanges between contexts, cultures, and identities is no doubt aptly referred to by Jules Supervielle in his poem "Champs-Elysées"[4] dated April 1946, included in the volume *Oublieuse mémoire* (1948), which reads as follows:

> *Savez-vous que chaque jour cent poètes d'Amérique*
> *Remontent sans être vus l'avenue de Champs-Elysées,*
> *Et cent autres la descendent,*
> *Pendant le défilé, les marronniers cèdent la place à*
> *Des palmiers hauts sur pieds.*

> *[Did you know that each day a hundred poets from America*
> *Ascend the Champs-Elysées without being seen*
> *And another hundred walk down,*
> *During the procession, the chestnut trees give way to*
> *Palm trees standing tall.]*

And then:

> *Mais quel est donc ce bruit sourd sur les côtes d'Amérique?*
> *Ce sont les poètes de France qui débarquent là-bas leurs doubles.*
> *Ohé Pablo et Alfonso, Jorge Luis, Carlos, Roberto,*
> *Ohé Mario et Manuel et Augusto Frederico,*
> *Ohé Sara et Gabriela, ohé Silvina et Juana, ohé Orfila et Cecilia*
> *Voici les amis de France!*
> *Interpellons-nous à voix forte à cause de ces espaces*
> *Qui voudraient se mettre entre nous,*
> *Même dans sa chambre, un poète est entouré de ses fôrets,*
> *Ouvertes, les portes, les fenêtres, pour laisser passer la nature.*
>
> *[But what is this muffled noise on the American coasts?*
> *It's the poets of France disembarking their doubles down there.*
> *Hey, Pablo and Alfonso, Jorge Luis, Carlos, Roberto,*
> *Hey, Mario and Manuel and Augusto Frederico,*
> *Hey, Sara and Gabriela, hey, Silvina and Juana, hey, Orfila and Cecilia*
> *Here are the friends of France!*
> *Let's call them loudly because these spaces try to come between us,*
> *Even in his room, a poet is surrounded by his forests,*
> *The doors, the windows, opened to let nature in.]*

Next to this large contingent of Latin Americans in France (many of them referred to in the poem) we must cite as a counterpart the French in Latin America, including familiar names such as those of Valéry Larbaud, Blaise Cendrars, Claude Lévi-Strauss, Henri Michaux, Bernanos, Roger Caillois, Drieu La Rochelle, Le Clézio, Régis Debray, Darius Milhaud, Paul Claudel, Roger Bastide …

The great interest taken by these intellectuals in Latin America was no doubt a response to the knowledge and spreading of Latin American realities in Europe, beginning in the 1930s, when they were already linked to the initial exoticism, but gaining a strong utopian meaning as "the land of the future." From Blaise Cendrars in 1933, the 21st century was said to be "the century of Latin America."

This to and fro between Europeans and Latin Americans allowed, in some cases, someone to sporadically venture out only to get back not to his usual solitude, but to be more knitted together with others. And since then, we encounter next to the diplomatic performances of Neruda, A. Reyes, O. Paz, Carlos Fuentes, the academic presence of Latin American intellectuals in European and North American universities. Despite the still reduced space granted to the teaching of Brazilian literature in this context (see the article of Walnice Nogueira Galvão, "Brazilian Studies," in his most recent book, *Desconversa*, 1998),[5] Latin American Studies has kept a certain importance, preserving some essential spaces as one can see in the volume edited by Susanne Klengel on *Contexts, Histories and Transfers in European Latin American Studies: The Cases of Germany, Spain and France*, 1997,[6] which provides material for a comparative history of these studies, with information on the cultural mediation routes and the different dynamics and reception modes of literary texts.

The Self / The Alien

The republication in 1997 of Roger Bastide's book *Poetas do Brasil*,[7] published initially in the 1940s by Guaira Press in Parana, invites us to reflect on a constant theme in Brazilian criticism: the relations between France and Brazil, and consequently, the relations between the self and the alien. As Susanne Klengel points out in "Comparative Histories, Crossed Histories," "the studies on the imagological nature of the proper and the alien proved how much the forms of production owe to their historical and cultural context, and to their correspondent traditions of discourse" (Klengel, p. 5).

Object of theses and dissertations and a central focus of research projects, these relations which get back to the images each culture produces when faced by another have been thoroughly analyzed, and yet so much more remains to be explored in this field of study. In the case of France, this is due to the importance I have already pointed out which this literature and culture had for Latin American countries at the moment of their formation and at other moments that followed; it is our task now to find a theoretical basis and exemplification of critical practices across the ocean to incorporate French suggestions.

These changes and interchanges, focused on the singularity of the self when confronted by the alien diversity, appear in Mario Carelli's 1993 volume *Cultures croisées: histoire des échanges culturels entre la France et le Brésil de la découverte aux temps modernes*.[8] In the preface to the volume, Gilbert Durand stresses the question of the "reflected images" of cultures and cites the advice once given by Bastide: "Va au Brésil, c'est l'Empire de l'Imaginaire …!" ("Go to Brazil, it's the Empire of the Imaginary …!")

Two Meanings of the Cultural Exchanges

"Attentive to the Other almost to the point of conversion," as Durand describes him, "precursor of mutual anthropology," to use Mario Carelli's words, Roger Bastide advocated cultural relations being aware of the need to leave prejudices behind and to adopt new concepts and forms of perception to be able to understand (and know) the Other. Therefore, in his analysis of Brazilian poets' work, the French critic sought to emphasize the singularity of each poet and his struggles to differentiate and liberate himself from European influences. For instance, he identifies in Sergio Milliet's trajectory an initial and distinct phase, when the poet wrote in French; this was the basis on which his poetical itinerary would unfold and which led to the poet's rediscovery (which he names his "apprenticeship") of Brazil. In Guilherme da Almeida he finds a conquest of rhythm which, he writes, "emerges from a tropical land, from the races brought together in a solar embrace and who writhe on the Tree of the Cross," the catchphrase of Portuguese missionaries, "the stump around which dance the Indians, the trunk on which the flesh of Black slaves moans" (Bastide, p. 86).

As one can see, in this encounter of three races, the poet found Brazil. In the same way, he identifies Bandeira as "the poet of the Recife," while Drummond is the poet of Minas Gerais and of its old churches, and Mário de Andrade, the poet of São Paulo. A poet of the city, Mario's lyrical poetry, according to Bastide, "was not a Romantic lament, moving rather towards theater" (77–78). He sees this lyrical poetry as a dialogue and a dance, and "this is what makes it very Brazilian, because it has the precision of Brazilian dance" (78).

But beyond stressing the Brazilian particularities of each of the poets he studies, Bastide deals also with the counterpart of these influxes – the Brazilians' presence in French letters, identifying a curious analogy in the strategies of appropriating the other on both sides of the Atlantic. It's worth transcribing below what he writes in his study, which would become a book, *Incorporating Brazil in Contemporary French Poetry*:

> It seems that contemporary France's poetical discovery of Brazil emerged from two essentially different sources: the appearance of the South (and through this, the route to the Tropics) in literature and a methodology of a global possession of the world (which went from the "Prose of the Trans-Siberian" to "The Sixth Day of Creation" in America).

And Bastide continues:

> What Denis barely perceived when he wanted to prove the influence of a tropical climate on Brazilian literature, a Durtain, a Cendrars, even a Claudel would accomplish. These hawkers of poetry were trading in Praça Onze in Rio, in Bolsa de Café in São Paulo the modern tendencies in French literature as tropical fruits, mixing their juice and honey, their sugary taste and terebenthene with the local poetry. (156–157)

We should take into account that Bastide referred only to the French authors who were in Brazil, who were in contact both with the country and with the intellectuals of the time and who literally incorporated what was transformed (or what they had heard or read) in their own literary production. In this case, the example of Blaise Cendrars is striking.

And it is charming that there are other aspects to emphasize. First of all, Bastide associated two substantial elements in his discovery of Brazil: on the one hand, the rediscovery of the South – a European south, a sunny Mediterranean – as a counterpart of the North (hazy and full of fog), described previously; on the other hand, an escape from immediate reality (a troubled post-war world) into another world which was embodied by America. Hence, southern poetry met the Tropics and tried to acclimatize the European poets in the same way in which it wished to find another "Pasárgada" (as Manuel Bandeira did), becoming in this context a factor which favored at the same time the opening towards a new reality.

It is clear that Bastide identifies the strategies adopted by the French poets in Brazil: the incorporation of themes and scenes with their own modern technical devices. Therefore, we witness a sort of "exchange," one diametrically opposed to the one used by the Brazilian writers who explored their own self (their themes and local scenes) through the incorporation of the alien (the European technique). Just as striking is the fact that both were acting from the perspective of Machado Assis' "theory of the sauce," cited by Afrânio Coutinho, where we read that the artist "can go and search for a new spice abroad, but that he must blend it in a sauce of his own making."[9]

The interest of Bastide's book lies in the form in which he treats his themes rather than with the themes themselves. That is the critical course of his readings, whose sociological inclinations go back to two concepts which are today fundamental for the study of intercultural and interliterary relations: the concept of culture and that of context. In his preface to the book, Antonio Candido observes that Bastide wasn't too preoccupied to distinguish "the good from the bad," as he wanted to be more a sociologist than a critic, emphasizing, at the same time, that for him, "the text is a sum of meanings and signs which, when valid, justify a certain interest" (Bastide, p. 13). This statement, associated with what Candido writes that Bastido said: "don't make value judgments, but reality judgments," points out the two reasons why "culture" and "context" lie at the core of his critical approach. On the one hand, they should be thought of as social mechanisms which underlie cultural and literary manifestations; on the other hand, they allow for the reading of these manifestations as symptoms of more profound movements, which are rooted in experienced reality.

Today, the concept of cultural "appropriation" (or "incorporation") is different from the one employed by Bastide to emphasize above all the inexistence of a "pure, endogenous cultural nucleus" (see Bernardo Subercaseaux's "La apropriación cultural en el pensamiento latinoamericano" ["Cultural Appropriation in Latin American Thought"]).[10] The Chilean critic states that there is no longer a dichotomy between central and peripheral countries, and hence there is no longer the possibility to build interpretations on the landmark of a dichotomy which opposes the national to the foreign. As he said when referring to the post-modern,

> It is the postmodern line of thought that expresses a new world situation, one in which cultural borders no longer coincide with political borders and in which this dichotomy can no longer therefore be conceived in Manichean terms.[11]

Such a statement emphasizes that intercultural and interliterary relations must take into account the new configurations arising from the fact that interchanges which were made previously only in one direction – and it was not rare that the traffic was blocked – now are no longer going in a single direction. Aware that only a theoretical contribution conceived in their own culture can offer the Latin American critic the possibility to move beyond his condition of consumer of foreign theoretical schemes, writers from the continent have addressed the relations of mutual appropriation. The inclusion of Latin American writers in European theoretical studies (let us recall here Umberto Eco, Hans Robert Jauss, Gerald Graff, Gérard Genette, Douwe Fokkema) shows that it is no longer possible to study the fiction of the last three decades without taking these writers into account.

On the other hand, the reality of an opened, ecumenical Latin American culture, in a continuous reshaping, existed already in Bastide's thought. When he said that getting to know Brazil "triggers an unpredictable enrichment," he may have been alluding to the fact that under its cultural blend, as Gilbert Durand points out,

Le Brésil est porteur, sans complexes, de ce message d'anthropologie culturelle, indiquant à chaque culture qu'elle ne peut trouver son identité et conforter ses espérances qu'en se replongeant dans la saga imaginaire, foisonnante, plurielle qui l'a fondée.

[Brazil is the bearer, without any complexes, of this message of cultural anthropology: that no culture can find its identity and realize its hopes if it doesn't plunge back in the imaginary rich plural saga which founded it.][12]

I have cited in French an idea that we still have to circulate: the richness of the varieties which form a plural identity, and for this very reason its analysis has become an object of interest for comparative studies.

Notes

1 Pierre Rivas, "Paris como capital litéraria de America Latina" ["Paris as Literary Capital of Latin America"], in Flavio Aguiar and Ligia Chiapinni Moraes Leite, *Literature e história na América Latina* [Literature and History in Latin America] (São Paolo: EDUSP, 1993).

2 Pascale Casanova, *La République Mondiale des Lettres* (Paris: Seuil, 1999).

3 On translation as process of "literarization" see Casanova, *La République Mondiale*, 188ff.

4 Jules Superveille, *Oeuvres poétiques complètes* (Paris: Gallimard, 1996), 52–21.

5 Walnice Nogueira Galvão, *Desconversa* (Rio de Janeiro: Ed. UFRJ, 1998).

6 Susanne Klengel, ed., *Contextos, histórias y transferencias en los estudios latinoamericanistas europeos: los casos de Alemania, España y Francia* [Contexts, Histories and Transfers in European Latin-American Studies – the Cases of Germany, Spain and France] (Madrid: Iberoamericana, 1997).

7 Roger Bastide, *Poetas do Brasil* [Brazilian Poets] (São Paolo: EDUSP/Duas Cidades, 1997).

8 Mario Carelli, *Cultures croisées: Histoire des échanges culturels entre la France et le Brésil de la découverte aux temps modernes* [Crossing Cultures: The History of Cultural Exchanges between France and Brazil from the Discovery to Modern Times] (Paris: Nathan, 1993).

9 Afrânio Coutinho, "Machado de Assis na Literatura Brasileira" ["Machado de Assis in Brazilian Literature"]. In *Obras completas* (Rio de Janeiro: Aguilar, 1965), vol. 3, xix.

10 Bernardo Subercaseaux, "La apropriación cultural en el pensamiento latinoamericano" ["Cultural Appropriation in Latin American Thought"], *Mundo* 1:3 (Summer 1987).

11 Bernardo Subercaseaux, "Nueva sensibilidad y horizonte 'Post' en Chile," *Nuevo Texto Critico* 6 (1990), 143–144.

12 Gilbert Durand, Preface to Carelli, *Cultures croisées*, 11.

28

An Idea of Literature
South Africa, India, the West (2001)

Michael Chapman

Michael Chapman is Professor Emeritus of English Literature at the University of KwaZulu-Natal in Durban, South Africa, and editor of the journal *Current Writing*. He has written widely on Southern African literatures from a postcolonial perspective, exploring the intercultural changes between the world's metropolitan centers and what Chapman calls the "edge" literatures of South Africa and India (*South African English Poetry: A Modern Perspective*, 1984; *Southern African Literatures*, 1996; *Art Talk, Politics Talk*, 2006; *Postcolonialism: South/African Perspectives*, 2008). In "An Idea of Literature," Chapman analyzes the case of South African and Indian literatures in relation to the West, proposing "a method of comparison that is based on mutual recognitions of worth and value" between the metropolitan center and the "edges," inspired by Wolfgang Iser's idea of "recursive looping." Arguing that intercultural dialogue functions with greater difficulty at the edge than in Europe or the United States, Chapman seeks to develop a wider understanding of what can be regarded as world literature: "we need to develop a critical language sympathetic to the style of a great deal of literature from Africa, India and South America: a style that could be designed as 'oral.' "

The new century suggested new possibilities for comparative study. The end of the Cold War, the symbolic end of racism in the demise of apartheid, the potential of information-age communication, taken together, could have been conducive to comparison as a mode of constructing, enlarging and enriching the cultural life. Instead of flexible interchanges, however, millennial reactions often remind us of Charles Bernheimer's observation that comparison is too often productive of anxiety.

Michael Chapman, "An Idea of Literature: South Africa, India, the West" (2001). In *English Studies in Africa* 44:1 (2001), pp. 47–58. Reproduced with permission of the copyright owner.

World Literature in Theory, First Edition. Edited by David Damrosch.

Certainly it was the competitive model that prevailed in the heated exchange that followed Salman Rushdie's remarks in a special fiction issue of *The New Yorker* (1997). The issue 'India Focus' marked the fiftieth anniversary of Indian independence and provoked the comment by Rushdie that Indian literature in English represents perhaps the most valuable contribution India has yet made to the world of books.

In his response in the *IndiaStar Review of Books* C.J.S. Wallia pointed angrily to the condescending title of Rushdie's article ('Damme – This Is the Oriental Scene for You') and concluded that not only does Rushdie disdain India's thirteen highly developed languages, but that *Midnight's Children* is not the utterly original work as so often cited in the West. We are reminded of the early assessments of the Indian critics Feroza Jussawalla and Uma Parameswaran, both of whom drew attention to Rushdie's imitation of G.V. Desani, a writer who showed how English could be bent and kneaded until it spoke in an authentic Indian voice. Wallia is pleased, at least, that in the article under attack Rushdie, albeit grudgingly, concedes that he learned a trick or two from Desani (5).

Such reactions of 'them' and 'us' have unfortunately come to characterise comparative study of the centre and the edge, or the metropole and the periphery, or the rich North and the poor South, to use the terms of postcolonialism, whether the South be India, South America, Africa, or even – I suspect – the former Eastern Europe. We are reminded of comparison continuing to produce anxiety. Instead of transcending the divide of the colonial, or colonised experience, argument continually re-inscribes the dichotomy. Instead of centres and edges finding open conversation between different understandings, different vocabularies, and different cultural paradigms, antagonists remain locked in reactive response. The voice of the metropole, often the self-exile of diasporic inclination, empties experience at the edge of its politics and history in the textual inflections of Western academic and literary pronouncement. Or, so the critic at the edge might charge. Thus Aijaz Ahmad – like Wallia – sees postcolonial studies as essentially a fashion of the centre while Arif Dirlik typecasts the postcolonial figures – the Rushdies, Spivaks and Homi Bhabhas – as a set of elite transnational intellectuals who from the comfort of the metropolis enunciate further discourses that marginalise the problems and struggles of those who remain the victims of Euroamerican power. As far as critics like Ahmad and Dirlik are concerned, the impact of *Midnight's Children* has not to do so much with its contribution to Indian literature in English; rather it is that behind terms such as hybridism and creolisation – terms associated with the colonised native of the South – Rushdie employed a less radical, a more familiar method: that of modernist or postmodernist style, a style usually associated with the self-referring art worlds, even the art religions of the West.

As Wallia reminds Rushdie, the 'style' of *Midnight's Children* does not accord with the styles of very many major Indian writers including Ghosh, Desai, Seth and Narayan. In these writers the life experience of people is rooted in the realism of tradition, or folk wisdom, before it is rudely wrenched into yet another adaptation of the self-exile: that of magical realism. To which Arnab Chakladar adds that the Indian literature favoured by the first-world academy is that which most closely approximates Western postmodernism's image of itself: an observation that could be

applied no doubt to writing from South America, or even Africa. (My slight qualifica-
tion concerning Africa is deliberate. Decolonisation in ex-settler colonies drew sharp
attention to literature as a vehicle of nationalist political struggles.) Rushdie's coinage
'the Empire writes back to the centre'[1] has become not so much a manifesto of emancipation in the poor South as a formula for further imitation of the master's voice.

How the South moves beyond reacting to the latest fashion, or -ism, or -post of
the metropole is of course not a simple matter when regimes of truth, influence and
dissemination occupy the metropolitan space. Even Ahmad and Dirlik operate on
the terrain of the postcolonial theory that they attack. Their objections are
philosophical, methodological, and familiar to the Marxist European tradition.
Again, we encounter not so much relocation as retaliation. The Euroamerican power
raids the alien territory and the native fights back usually having to utilise the very
weapons, theories and texts of the dominating presence. Yet in Ahmad's case, simple
retaliation is not the whole story. In his chapter, ' "Indian Literature" ...', he avoids
Wallia's tendency to confuse the voice of analytical understanding with the voice
of the creative writer. Instead of his arguing emotively for the value of all of India's
thirteen languages, or that an Indian language rather than English be the vehicle
of the Indian mind or sensibility, Ahmad argues for a multilingual conception
of Indian literature: a multilingual conception in which relationships between
the various languages, cultures and traditions are analysed. It is an approach
that points to a way beyond the Empire's always having to write back. For it
reminds us at the outset that shaping forces at the edge, whether political or
cultural, are not simply imitative of, but are often quite distinct from, forces at
the metropolitan centre.

I am seeking here a method of comparison that is based on mutual recognitions
of worth and value. Such a project of relocation need not avoid the consequence of
colonialism: that the centre and the edge, in reaction, have illuminated and contaminated each other's histories for over 400 years. The project takes seriously, however,
what Iser refers to as the 'recursive looping' between cultures (296). To take an
example from South Africa, the Xhosa were the earliest Africans to have had to
sustain contact with European settlers. On the eastern frontier of the Cape Colony
British missionaries by 1799 had already influenced the Xhosa praise poet Ntsikana
to experience a dramatic conversion in which his Christianity involved a direct
relation to a god rather than to his ancestors. Composing hymns, Ntsikana introduced Christian content at the same time as his style remained close to traditional
oral praise poetry: God not the Chief was praised in the catalogue of names that
recognised the Creator and Preserver. An archaic language carried the authority of
the past into the new situation: that of the story of the frontier in its subsequent wars,
betrayals and migrations; in short, in its modernisations and modernities. The point
is that Xhosa literature would not have taken the form it did had it not encountered
a British settler presence on its ancient land. Neither would South African literature
in English have followed the forms it did had it not at the beginning encountered a
clash of races and cultures. It was the hard content of the frontier, for example, that
enabled Thomas Pringle, a Scottish poetaster of late Augustan strain, to find the new

human subjects and themes – slavery, war, exile, miscegenation – that would lend
purpose and resonance to his voice.

The recursive looping of cultures can be complicated: in spreading the Scriptures
missionaries were inevitably part of a vast literacy project which extended the
Bible to vernacular springs of creativity. The result among the Xhosa was not only
good African Englishman, but the first consciousness of African nationalism. If the
'translation' of one culture into another can be regarded as an act of dispossession, it
can also be regarded as an act of empowerment, and it is difficult today to
separate Xhosa literature from the wider delineation, South African literature. One
might retain the distinction by focusing on language. But as soon as one invokes a
multilingual concept one identifies several features of early Xhosa literary activity
that characterise the general literary life. There is the composite figure of the author-
politician-journalist, a feature still of a society of thin literary culture. The newspaper and journal, as on the eastern Cape frontier, continue to occasion the outlet
for a great deal of expression. Forms of political discussion, biography, and obituary
as moral exemplum continue to assist in the restructuring of African identities in
rapidly modernising times. The Xhosa intellectual tradition produced the leadership
of both the ANC and Black Consciousness, movements that would assimilate a range
of ideas and ideals including Christianity, Fanon's anti-colonialism, US Black Power,
and African ubuntu or sharing in community. The comparative model I am sketching
is marked, creatively, by both Westernism and Africanism. A common characteristic
ultimately is not division, but the potential of a revindicated humanism.

My example is drawn from South Africa; similar examples, however, could be identified at other edges. Whereas multiclass literacy usually in a single, national language
grants assurance to the centre, the periphery is characterised by small, literate communities which grasp at Western-style communication amid resilient but economically
marginalised oral-majority speech. There is often a mismatch between the nation-state
as a European bourgeois-colonial formation that is predicated on linguistic, religious
and ethnic homogeneity and the heterogeneity of the Indian, or African, or Brazilian
situation. A further characteristic is a history of uneven development resulting in
the pre-modern, the modern, and the postmodern existing almost simultaneously
in a condition of differentiated modernity. This too has consequence for the range and
form of the expression according to which customary voices – separatist church songs,
for example – are likely to be alive and strong alongside cultures of the book.

Mainstream literary-cultural study, however, privileges not only the book, but more
specifically the novel. Accordingly, Bill Buford, editor of the special issue of *The New
Yorker* to which I referred earlier on, finds it unproblematic that Indian literature be
characterised almost entirely by its novels in English. South American literature for its
part tends to be identified, in metropolitan reading circles, again almost entirely in
translations of magical realist novels by writers who mostly live outside of their home
countries. South African literature, too, relies heavily for its literary reputation abroad
on its novelists. There are the 'airport' African adventures of Wilbur Smith and the
serious novels of Nadine Gordimer, J.M. Coetzee and André Brink. Yet the novel is
probably the most precarious form in societies of uneven development. Or, at least,

the rise of the novel as in the eighteenth-century bourgeois drawing-room tradition. Life at the edges of the world is insufficiently stable, insufficiently educated to invest long durations of time in the extended fictional work. What is more likely to be heard are forms of instant poetry: praising is probably Africa's original form, a form eminently adaptable to modern conditions in its passage from Shaka's court to the political rally: Mighty One [Shaka] who thunders across the ground!, or Wise One [Mandela] who leads us to Freedom!. The fictional form most likely to be read is the short story, and while one can identify in Gordimer's superb short stories the modern European inheritance, there are other ways to understand storytelling.

To consider again the recursive looping between cultures, a particularly powerful storytelling tradition is to be found among the Zulu, several of whose stories were recorded and translated into English in the 1860s by the Rev. Henry Callaway. Having travelled from England to Natal in 1858 to work under Bishop Colenso, Callaway studied the language isiZulu, set up a printing press, and between 1866 and 1868 published his still authoritative compilation of Zulu narratives, *Nursery Tales, Traditions, and Histories of the Zulus*. Some of Callaway's respondents would still have had living memories of the spectacular events that had characterised the reigns of Shaka and Dingana, including Shaka's military campaigns and his violent dispersal of his rivals across the interior.

A particularly compelling story was performed for Callaway by Lydia umkaSetemba, who was regarded by her Zulu contemporaries as an impressive teller of tales. Assuming the role assigned in traditional Zulu culture to the woman, usually to the grandmother as the storyteller, educator and entertainer of young and old alike, Lydia umkaSetemba tells of Umxakaza-wakogingqwayo (the name of the central character) who passes from girlhood to womanhood, rites of passage being a common thematic and structural feature of the folk tale. She journeys from the land of her father, where her foolish, youthful vanity had encouraged him to destroy cattle stolen from neighbours, to the terrible regions of the cannibals, where she is then adopted and grows fat and grotesque. In the story the cannibal King is an inverse image of her father who, in killing the cattle, had driven his community to starvation. In the region of cannibals, therefore, the moral ugliness of the child is given concrete form, and on her return to the familiar land she encounters the trials of wizards and physical deformities – she grows a huge head packed with her vanities – before the love of a prince's sister initiates Umxakaza-wakogingqwayo into her true adult beauty. After the tribulations of a journey – from the community to the veld and, as a wiser, more considerate person, back to the community – the story ends as one has grown accustomed to expect in folk tale, with her marriage to the prince.

Callaway's recording indicates concise, memorable opening and closing formulas in a three-part repetition of episodes. While character and situation develop around a single thematic 'core' cliché (in the form of a proverb, a song, or a chant for memorisation), the lesson expands into a narrative the movement of which parallels the moral journey of the heroine. The broad theme, of course, is equilibrium in behaviour and cohesion in society, but the audience learns not through the dry abstraction of moral verities but through emotional involvement in an imitative action that gives opportunity for considerable invention: in matters of character portrayal, in combinations of images and episodes, in symbols suggesting a credible psychology of creative and destructive energies vying for predominance, and in disguises and trans- formations as correlatives of different states of mind. With the basic plots of folk tales familiar to the community – it was the act of telling that introduced the unexpected twists and insights – stories tended to be stored in memory, encouraging the listeners to raid the storehouse of tradition in filling in gaps, arguing about apparent discrepancies between one rendition of the story and another, and entering as participants into what in effect were 'texts' as the generators of the experience. The tale finds its consequence in the conditions of its reception: the interchange may be regarded almost as 'post-structural'.

The aesthetic of the folk tale – we understand – does not follow the conventions of naive realism. Instead, the stories have the potential to create rather than merely record the experience to be explored. We learn where contemporary magical realism might have learned its own trick or two: in the imagination in community which, amid life's hardships, conjures up a plenitude of possibility in the emotion-saturated, surprising language of dream and desire. When we look broadly at fiction at the edge, the folk tale can be seen to be a formative text, the adaptability of which has been exploited in modernity. Bessie Head from Botswana, for example, reinvents tradition in settings that yield present-day versions of ancient tales concerning the authority of the generations, the roles of women and men, and the tensions of conservation and change. The journeys in folk tales from the known to the unknown remind us not only of how convenient early missionaries found Bunyan's *The Pilgrim's Progress* as a bridging text in Christian education, but how the mythic, the fabulous, and the oral tendency of recur- rence in the episode have remained important considerations in response to a range of fiction at the edge, in which the romance mode has had to serve the social intent.

In South Africa there are the 'Jim comes to Joburg' stories which in journeys from the simple to the complicated life include Alan Paton's *Cry, the Beloved Country*. Angola and Mozambique boast the talents of among others José Luandino Vieira, Luis Bernado Honwana, and Mia Couto. Schooled in the literary influences of Brazilian neo-realism and modernism, in which the strange incident may suddenly disrupt the prose of life, Vieira, a former MPLA activist and political prisoner, is equally familiar with the rich resources of local kiMbundu oral storytelling. Utilising the opening and closing formulas of the folk tale, personifying the setting so that the natural elements seem to reinforce the mood of the human drama, and affecting the intimate, colloquial delivery of the 'community storyteller', Vieira twists the most mundane situation – an argument over the ownership of an egg, for example – into spirals of pathos and comedy that encourage our sympathy for ordinary people in their coping with pompous officialdom or, generally, a hard life. In creolised language and form the stories are paradigmatic of Vieira's desire to break down divisions between Europeans and Africans as well as between the 'classes' of Angolan society.

I have been cautious in emphasising so-called oral features. Nevertheless, so long as we avoid the habit of categorising the written text as automatically more profound and analytical than its 'emotional' oral counterpart, there are useful distinctions to be made between the oral and the written in seeking outside the metropole for an appropriate style of fiction. We need to be vigilant at the outset of a still wide-spread tendency in literary study to dismiss as 'not fully achieved' those stories and novels that do not comply with the formal realist criteria of the written, analytical narrative of climax and closure, in which 'rounded', psychologically inward characters think through, rather than act out, their destinies. We might recognise, instead, that an oral 'residue' can manifest itself to effect in strong storylines, episodic plots, recurrent, copious repetitions, aggregative, additive thought, and closeness to the 'life world' that preserves several traditional values. The story might find as appropriate a hyperbolic, participatory style that is empathic, subjective, and situational rather than objective or abstract. It might find appropriate also characters who are somewhat flattened into types, and dialogue that hovers between originality and the formula. The argument is that in countries where written culture is uneven and where communities in rural areas or city townships retain considerable face-to-face contact, the oral style has real and continuing validity. The style should feature, certainly, in the formulation of an aesthetic that hopes to understand literature as having the stamp of experience at the edge in forms of stories, novels, poems, plays, and testimonies. Such an argument for the oral as serious expression, of course, contains an element of political intervention, particularly as the written is still too easily attached to the 'civilised' West and the oral to various forms of barbarism, or at least peasantry. Yet we need to develop a critical language sympathetic to the style of a great deal of literature from Africa, India, and South America: a style that could be designated 'oral'.

The focus on the influence of folk tale is a reminder that the multilingual, differentiated model at the edge cannot simply start with the literate tradition. The equivalent in the West would be a need to recover in the literary culture the seriousness of the fairy tale, or nursery rhyme. Such recovery however assumes urgency perhaps only when one's humanity remains subject to theories about the dark and savage mind. It is understandable, therefore, that the folk tale in Africa, India and other countries on the periphery has received astute attention from 'mainstream' literary and cultural criticism. One of the objectives has been to retain connection between myth and history. The cannibal figures in Zulu folk tale, for example, are seen not as evidence of innate savagery but as literary-psychological projections of the social environment in the years of trouble in the 1820s when, as a result of Shaka's military conquests, famine threatened large areas of Zulu territory. Although trickster-figures feature in most traditions in Africa, the Zulu trickster has lost some of the laughter associated with a deity of misrule and in keeping with the harsher temper of the stories is often completely callous and selfish as, standing half inside, half outside society, he cruelly exposes the weaknesses of human nature.

Nothing I have described here, of course, is so peculiarly 'local' as to lose universal recognition, and it might be valuable for Western tradition to remove, say, Cinderella from romanticism or, more latterly, Disneyfication to return the story to its deeper human significance: Cinderella leaves home to live with her stepmother because her own mother having on her deathbed forbade her father to love anyone less beautiful than his dying wife has at the same time left the man with recourse only to committing incest with his beautiful daughter. The plague witnessed an increase in stepmothers;

gender roles were fixed, punishments were cruel – barbaric! – and the evil stepmother is forced at the end to dance on red-hot metal shoes until she drops dead. To misquote Rushdie, Damme – This Is the European Scene for You! Neither the centre nor the edge has sole claim to civilisation; neither is the exclusive heir of the savage mind.

   The comparative model towards which I am struggling has consequences for the teaching of literature and culture. In this respect it is interesting to compare the approaches of William Walsh and Aijaz Ahmad to the 'idea' of Indian literature. In his study *Indian Literature in English* Walsh focuses on English-language literature by both Indians and non-Indians while in the background, somewhere, the *Indian* India beckons like the Marabar Caves. Before he returns like Forster's Fielding to the supposedly rational universe of English influence, Walsh in his introduction observes an 'age-old settlement of religious belief, thought-pattern, emotional system and symbolic pattern [that] produces an unusually coherent, individualised and confident personality, at least as it is manifested in art and literature' (16).

   Ahmad would however probably describe this as the argument of the centre. Literary culture is drained of its usability. In the case of India, the temptation is to regard traditions of Orientalist High Textuality as immune to human experience, or Indian spirituality as incompatible with Western rationality. This has prompted Amartya Sen to defend both Eastern and Western reason and Ahmad to remind us of the danger of divorcing a textual object like the *Bhagavad-Gita* from the very humanity that it has lent to the teachings of the Veda. What is required at the edge, in contrast, is less 'English Studies' in the tradition of canonicity; greater development of English Studies as a 'subdiscipline within a much broader, more integrated Historical and Cultural studies' (82). Walsh's study is the product of 'English Studies', in which texts are regarded as having minimal context. Literary culture at the edge, however, demands a thick description of context. For societies at the edge enjoy little autonomy, or self-possession. Accordingly, Ahmad's idea of Indian literature – relocated at the edge – derives its unity not from 'some transhistoric metaphysic nor from the territoriality of the existing nation-state, nor by simply assembling discrete histories of the different linguistic traditions' but, as he continues, by tracing

> the dialectic of unity and difference through systematic periodisation of multiple linguistic overlaps and [grounding] that dialectic in the history of material productions, ideological struggles, competing conceptions of class and community and gender, elite offensives and popular resistances, overlaps of cultural vocabularies and performative genres, and histories of orality and writing and print. (265)

Such a formulation may shift us decisively from text to context. But, as I have remarked, Ahmad's multilingual model is not free of its own reaction to the metropole. It is a reaction to the non-politics of textuality by a strong Marxist intervention. The abstraction of the language – stiff, often jargon-ridden – almost robs Marx of his own human dimension. The consequence is that writers who irritate Ahmad get short shrift and are reduced to parody. One such writer is Rushdie. Whereas the centre adjudges Rushdie to have given appropriate form in allegory, epic and folk tale to the Indian experience, the edge – Ahmad suggests – might in turn adjudge Rushdie's India hardly to have cohered beyond an accumulation of smells and caricatures. Politics is too often reduced to buffoonery; women are either whores or virgins; communities exist in social degradation; and the East remains a figment of the postcolonial imagination. It is an imagination that remains 'colonised' by its own sense of superiority. Despite his laudation in Western literary capitals, Rushdie enjoys little certainty of belonging. Rather the author's appearance as the ever-sophisticated migrant reveals a tragic paradox: the postmodern style in its restless discontinuity ends up celebrating the human inability to experience life as more than a virtual reality. At least, that would seem to be Ahmad's summary of Rushdie.

There is at one level no real advance here beyond the reaction of the Empire having had to write back. But, as I have argued, Ahmad makes the valid general point that the multilingual model of the edge is not simply an imitation of the preoccupations of the centre. There is a tension at the heart of his riposte. On the periphery English has to act as the unifying intellectual language while – bound to print culture – it is least suitable for crossing into the field of oral-majority speech where culture is not confined to the history of the book, but in popular manifestation is performative and ritualistic. It links the rural to the urban and the traditional to the modern. In the case of South Africa, indeed any African country, or India, we might derive a certain unity in superimposing the 'idea' of South Africa, or Nigeria, or India on an aggregate of discrete language-literature traditions. The danger is the simplification of the complex layerings of the society in favour of a dream of nationhood. The point is that the potential for common reference, unity of structure, indeed intercultural conversation, remains more difficult at the edge than in Europe or Europe's offshoots in North America.

At the same time, the danger of the heterogeneous, very unequal society not to seek unity, or at least a set of common values within diversity, is the divisiveness of ethnicity, apartheid, or Balkanisation. It is also to ignore the fact that the North and the South can benefit mutually from each other's distinct insights. The antidote to the metropolitan theorist, or the travelling self-exile, is not the indigene who 'knows' the local and global as absolute, essential oppositions. Poets at the edge do not only recite praise poems; many utilise forms of the sonnet. The story of frontier in South Africa, to which I have referred, imported the big ideas of the eighteenth-century Enlightenment. The novel continues to be written at the edges of the world. American pop culture pervades the South. South Africa is not simply an amalgamation of Africa and the West: the country has the largest Indian (or, South African Indian) population outside of India. During his twenty-year stay, Gandhi formulated and practised his philosophy of soul power in the hurly-burly of South African ethnic politics, a philosophy that influenced ANC passive resistance in the Defiance Campaign of the 1950s. Today Bollywood film stars are celebrities on South African screens.

My references to South Africa, India and the West, I hope, raise several questions that could encourage conversation beyond the stereotypical response, or reaction. Does Africa have only an ethno-exotic culture? My answer is implied in my discussion of universal plots and motifs within Zulu storytelling. Suffice it to say that human recognitions occur in unexpected places. Is the mystique of India unaffected by the detritus of the contemporary scene? Seth would answer, definitely not. Is the South undifferentiated, backward, and unmodern? Its differentiated modernity suggests a complicated interchange of influences and experiences according to which we are reminded of the intrusiveness of the South. Patchy modernisation, the interface of orality and literacy, the elusiveness of intercultural communication are, after all, phenomena experienced not only in Africa or India, but in London's Brixton, in migrant communities in the United States and Germany, and in many parts of the former Soviet bloc.

In attempting to move beyond a competitive model of comparison, we discover something more significant than imitation: that in many respects the South has gained the confidence of its own particularity. The power of critical contextualisation or re-contextualisation, as in Ahmad's analysis, is certainly indebted to Western discourse. The strength of his local commitment, nonetheless, encourages crucial adaptations. A key question in literary culture is how art objects achieve what they are meant to achieve in their cultural contexts, or when relocated in different cultural contexts. An equally important question involves negotiations between metropole and margin about the complete acceptance or the complete rejection of modern theories, both intellectual and aesthetic. To return to the opening argument, how do we avoid having to pit Rushdie's postcolonial pronouncements against the voices of many major Indian writers? As I suggest in my discussion of Xhosa literature, we may seek points of contact, in Rushdie's case, between the community inhabitant and the metropolitan voyager.

If Rushdie seems ever restless, the 'local' writer R.K. Narayan might have been more securely located: *The Vendor of Sweets* easily entertains both renunciations of the world and the need to keep the shop open. We should not, however, be tempted to find self-possession when in Narayan's view the *dharma* is precarious in the contemporary world. Jagan, the protagonist of *The Vendor of Sweets*, might feel reassured by the warmth of surrounding community. But Narayan the author identifies an unmitigated loneliness as the only truth of life. Both the individual and the community reveal aspects of a modern sensibility that in different degrees we all share, whether in Narayan's Malgudi or Rushdie's cosmopole. The power of English may enable us to cross many barriers while we attend to the problem of maintaining regional value in information-age economies. This foregrounds translation both as an art form and a practical means of making a range of languages, cultures, and beliefs available to a mode of explication.

In 1941 the great Bengali writer and Nobel prizewinner Rabindranath Tagore observed that his 'direct contact with the larger world was linked up with the contemporary history of the English people.... It was mainly through their mighty literature that we formed our ideas' (Nehru 321). Looking back Harish Trivedi, Professor of English at the University of Delhi, places such comments in a new context of understanding: the way writers in India reacted indicated the 'historically necessary but now also historically exhausted stimulus' of English literary studies (176–177). This is perhaps a rhetorical overstatement. Trivedi's point is however that equality of interchange demands more than the study of 'Indo-Anglian literature' as a 'half caste' curiosity alongside the Anglo-American canon. It requires instead a fully fledged comparative programme involving the study of the several literatures together 'in relation to each other, and in interpenetration with each other' including 'English Literature', 'English Literature from Elsewhere', as well as 'Literature in a modern Indian Language', according to a range of approaches, including 'Indigenous and Post-Colonial, favouring both Local and International Literatures' (210–216).

The Empire – in Trivedi's response – does not write back. Instead, it reaches across without erasing the differences upon which postcolonial debate is currently posited. Comparative study may be made to embody again a human agenda: a re-humanising of those who have been dehumanised wherever we locate the edge, wherever we locate the centre.

Note

1   Rushdie's 'postcolonial' identification – 'the Empire writes back to the centre' – serves as the epigraph of Ashcroft, Griffiths and Tiffin's study (1989).

Works Cited

Ahmad, Aijaz. '"Indian Literature": Notes towards the Definition of a Category'. *In Theory: Classes, Nations, Literatures*. London: Verso, 1992. 243–285.

Ashcroft, Bill, Gareth Griffiths and Helen Tiffin. *The Empire Writes Back: Theory and Practice in Post-Colonial Literatures*. London: Methuen, 1989.

Bernheimer, Charles. 'Introduction: the Anxieties of Comparison'. *Comparative Literature in the Age of Multiculturalism*. Ed. C. Bernheimer. Baltimore: Johns Hopkins University Press, 1995. 1–17.

Buford, Bill. 'Declaratione of Independence: Why are There Suddenly So Many Indian Novelists'?' *The New Yorker* 73.17 (1997): 6–7.

Callaway, Henry. *Nursery Tales, Traditions, and Histories of the Zulus*. Springvale: John A. Blair; London: Trübner and Co., 1868. Rpt Westport, Connecticut: Negro Universities Press, a Division of Greenwood Press, 1970.

Chakladar, Arnab. 'The Postcolonial Bazaar: Marketing/Teaching Indian Literature'. *Ariel: A Review of International English Literature*, 31:1 & 2 (January-April 2000): 183–201.

Dirlik, Arif. 'Postcolonial Aura: Third World Literature in the Age of Global Capitalism'. *Critical Inquiry*, 20:2 (1994): 328–357.

Head, Bessie. *A Collector of Treasures*. London: Heinemann, 1977.

Iser, Wolfgang. 'Coda to the Discussion'. *The Translatability of Cultures: Figurations of the Space Between*. Ed. S. Budeck and W. Iser. Stanford: Stanford University Press, 1996. 294–302.

Narayan, R.K. *The Vendor of Sweets*. Mysore: Heinemann, 1967.

Nehru, Jawaharlal. *The Discovery of India*. Bombay: Oxford University Press, 1969.

Rushdie, Salman. *Midnight's Children*. New York: Knopf, 1981.

Rushdie, Salman. 'Damme – This Is the Oriental Scene for You'. *The New Yorker: Fiction Issue*. 73:17 (1997): 50–58.

Sen, Amartya. 'East and West: The Reach of Reason'. *New York Review of Books* (20 July 2000) 33–38.

Trivedi, Hamish. *Colonial Transactions: English Literature and India*. Manchester: Manchester University Press, 1995.

Viera, José Luandino. *Luuanda*. London: Heinemann, 1964.

Wallia, C.J.S. *IndiaStar Review of Books*. http://www.indiastar.com/wallia6.htm, 1997.

Walsh, William. *Indian Literature in English*. London: Longman, 1990.

29

The Deterritorialization
of American Literature (2007)

Paul Giles

Paul Giles is Challis Chair of English at the University of Sydney and one of the leading names in American Studies today, analyzing American literature and culture through the theory and practice of transnationalism. As director of the Rothermere American Institute, University of Oxford (2003–2008) and President of the International American Studies Association (2005–2007), Giles has promoted the study of international relations which shape American history, culture, and politics. His book *The Global Remapping of American Literature* (2010) builds upon the concept of different spatial configurations of American literature, from the nationalist project of the nineteenth century to its opening out in the age of globalization as a renegotiation of its boundaries. In *Transnationalism in Practice: Essays on American Studies, Literature and Religion* (2010), Giles analyzes the transnational turn in American Literary Studies, its change of methodology and practice, in a global market and economy.

Drawing on Gilles Deleuze's and Félix Guattari's notion of deterritorialization, the essay included here remaps American literature through the concept of geographical space and its representations. Giles looks into the nationalistic project beginning in 1865 and going through 1980, when the transnational turn reshapes its configuration in a global era, and asks for a rethinking of the idea of American national identity. Intriguingly, Giles argues that "the current transnational phase actually has more in common with the so-called early national period between 1780 and 1860, when national boundaries and habits were much less formed and settled."

Paul Giles, "The Deterritorialization of American Literature" (2007). In Wai Chee Dimock and Lawrence Buell, eds., *Shades of the Planet* (Princeton: Princeton University Press), pp. 39–61.

World Literature in Theory, First Edition. Edited by David Damrosch.

The theme of this essay is the relationship between American literature and physical space. My concern will be not only with fictional works that are organized, explicitly or implicitly, around particular conceptions of place, but also with how these texts are informed by other kinds of geographical projection, of the kinds found in cartography and other forms of mapping. My thesis will be that the relationship between American literature and geography, so far from being something that can be taken as natural, involves contested terrain, terrain which has been subject over the centuries to many different kinds of mutation and controversy. I will argue these instabilities have too frequently been overlooked in the ways the subject of American literature has been codified and institutionalized, especially over the past hundred years. David Harvey wrote in 1989 about the desirability of reconstructing a matrix of "historical-geographical materialism" within which cultural conditions can be analyzed, and to reconsider American literature in the context of geographical materialism is to think through the variegated forms of its imaginary relations to the real dimensions of space.[1] More specifically, I will contend that the association of America, and by extension the subject of American literature, with the current geographical boundaries of the United States is a formulation that should be seen as confined to a relatively limited and specific time in history, roughly the period between the end of the American Civil War in 1865 and the presidency of Jimmy Carter, which ended in 1980. In the early years of the republic, I shall suggest, the more amorphous territorial framework of the United States engendered parallel uncertainties about the status and authority of American discourse, whereas since 1980 the effects of globalization have impelled us to reexamine the premises of US national identity in a quite different light.

There are two significant theoretical considerations to address before proceeding with this argument. The first is the problem of periodization. It is important to acknowledge how any boundary that historians draw, in time or in space, must inevitably be arbitrary in some way, but it is also important not to lose sight of the valuable cultural work that a retrospective process of chronological remapping can perform. As Fredric Jameson observed in his classic essay "Periodizing the 60s," the value of this kind of historicization lies in the way it can bring to light structural analogies between apparently disparate events within particular eras. This has the beneficial effect of moving narratives of the past away from both anecdotal self-indulgence and sentimental forms of nostalgia through a contrary insistence that, in Jameson's words, "History is necessity," that the past "had to happen the way it did, and that its opportunities and failures were inextricably intertwined, marked by the objective constraints and openings of a determinate historical situation."[2] In this regard, Arjun Appadurai has similarly described the identification of "isomorphic" correspondences between disparate points on a grid as a way of bringing into illuminating juxtaposition events that might otherwise have been considered entirely unrelated, thereby bringing to light correspondences that would otherwise have remained hidden.[3]

The second theoretical caveat emerges from Paul Ricoeur's observation, in *Time and Narrative*, of how cultural historians have no choice other than to read time backward, as what Ricoeur calls "retrodiction" rather than prediction. This method inevitably involves projecting from effect to cause, rather than the other way around. This means not only that all history is narrative, but also that we reconfigure such narratives in the light of what Ricoeur calls a "redistribution of horizons," changing our view of the past in accordance with revised expectations about the present and the future.[4] This in turn lends all historical remapping a reflexive dimension, since scholars necessarily find themselves imitating the formula that Edgar Allan Poe ascribed to the writing of detective stories, starting at the conclusion and then retracing forward what had already been traced backward. This kind of structural double bind has manifested itself recently in the manifold attempts to change the genealogy of American literary history, to revise beginnings rather than ends: Cyrus Patell, to take just one recent example, discovers the precursors to multicultural twenty-first-century America in the Dutch ethnic legacy of cosmopolitan New York, rather than in the time-honored Puritan origins of New England.[5] The teleology we impose upon the past, in other words, is embedded necessarily in concerns of the present.

This recognition of the inevitably perspectival slant of institutional narratives, however, can also serve beneficially to demystify the old institutional narratives associated with American Studies. At the beginning of the twenty-first century, it becomes increasingly apparent that twentieth-century narratives of American cultural history, framed as they were by assumptions about the country's national destiny, became accustomed to looking out for phenomena that seemed to anticipate the national power of the United States, a power that had only been consolidated in hegemonic terms relatively recently. The very category of the "early republic" is itself an anachronistic term, of course, implying there was a later republic into which these anterior events naturally led. This is why, for example, the Puritan poet Edward Taylor was often celebrated in the last century as a harbinger of the tortuous romantic spirit of Emily Dickinson, in the same way that Anne Bradstreet was hailed as an honorary ancestor by post-1945 writers such as John Berryman, who prized her confessional aspects, and Adrienne Rich, who emphasized her sturdy spirit of feminist independence.[6] All of these misprisions involve a creative and interesting use of the past, but in a historical sense they are manifestly misleading, since they tend to gloss over Taylor's Calvinist silences and Bradstreet's courtly, Renaissance conservatism in the interests of aligning them with a national narrative that is projected backward so as to validate American national culture of a later time.

There is, however, little to suggest such a sense of national triumphalism appeared a fait accompli to Americans themselves in the first half of the nineteenth century, when their structures of governance and tentative moves toward political cohesion were based on what many at the time considered to be the dubious theoretical hypothesis of federal union. In the first sixty years of US history, in the aftermath of the colonial period, the country's sense of national identity was as uncertain, as provisional, as its cartography. Matthew Lotter's map of Philadelphia in 1777 symptomatically illustrates the gaping discrepancy between a tiny rational grid at the heart of the city center and the sprawling, amorphous terrain in the unmapped, unregulated countryside of surrounding Pennsylvania.[7] The western part of the present-day

United States was even more inchoate: to look at a historical map of Latin America in 1830 is to see the territories of Mexico extending up through present-day California, Arizona, and New Mexico, with the shape of the nation itself appearing very different from the "sea to shining sea" model with which we are familiar today.[8] The point here, quite simply, is that when Ralph Waldo Emerson writes in 1844 about America being a "poem in our eyes," it is precisely that, a hypothetical or imaginative conception, or at least one that has not yet achieved any firm sense of territorial grounding or enclosure.[9] Walt Whitman's national poetry in the 1850s similarly has a tentative, optative dimension, something that is frequently overlooked because of the blustering and hortatory tone of his verse. All of the political investments in notions of Manifest Destiny in the 1840s and 1850s, the drive to expand westward and to claim the land in the name of the Stars and Stripes, speak to a desire to, as it were, fill in the blank spaces on the map, to subjugate the continent in a cartographic as well as a military sense. Indeed, the frequent US wars at this time – with the British in 1812 culminating in the Battle of New Orleans, with the Mexicans in the 1840s over Texas and the Southwest territories, and with Native Americans over the question of Indian removal – all of these speak to an impulse to redescribe the map of the nation. This is one reason maps themselves were so popular in American education in the early nineteenth century, as Martin Brückner has shown, and why geography came to be considered a basic, compulsory subject in American schools; the textbook *Geography Made Easy*, produced by the "father of American geography" Jedediah Morse in 1784, had gone through twenty-two editions by 1820, and geographical writing at this time was, in Bruce Harvey's words, a "patriotic genre."[10] The reciting of place names became as familiar in American educational contexts at this time as the learning by rote of spelling or multiplication tables in other countries, and it testified to the pioneering attempt imaginatively to appropriate what was, of course, a dauntingly large and unsettled continent.

To talk of early-nineteenth-century American culture in relation to deterritorialization, then, is to suggest that its way of identifying itself as something different did not necessarily involve simply a mimetic reflection of locality. The writings of Ralph Waldo Emerson have traditionally been thought of as a source for the national identity of American literature because of his principled emphasis on what he calls in "Nature" (1836) an "original relation to the universe."[11] But there is, in fact, very little description of the natural world in this or any other part of Emerson's writing, and the way he marks his originality is not through mimesis but through intertextuality, through taking icons and ideas from classical European culture and spinning them round in a new way. The exuberantly weightless quality of Emerson's prose thus derives from the way he remaps nineteenth-century American culture in relation to the classical monuments of the past. Just as Handel's biblical oratorios of a hundred years earlier rehouse epic mythologies of the past within a radically disjunct neoclassical environment, a form of "sacred parody" that flaunts ebulliently the gap between past and present, so Emerson presents himself in a deliberately belated fashion as the intellectual heir of Plato and Montaigne, someone whose project involves the vertiginous transformation of one culture into another.[12] It is perhaps unfortunate that Emerson was designated by the twentieth-century critical tradition of American Romanticism most closely associated with Harold Bloom as the institutional progenitor of American literature – the ultimate source of Transcendentalism, Pragmatism, William James, Wallace Stevens, and so on – without an equivalent emphasis on what Emerson describes in his essay "Experience" (1844) as the inherently intertextual quality of perception: "Life is a train of moods like a string of beads," he writes, "and, as we pass through them, they prove to be many-colored lenses which paint the world their own hue, and each shows only what lies in its focus." "Experience," with its emphasis on what Emerson calls the attainment of a soul's "due sphericity," exemplifies ways in which, for a person living in the United States in the 1840s, her home appeared to be positioned in a paradoxical situation somewhere between the empirical and the abstract, between place and placelessness.[13] It is one of the burdens of Emerson's writing that location itself is always relative and arbitrary, that Goethe is his neighbor as much as the man in the next street, that, as he remarks in his 1844 essay "The Poet," banks and tariffs are "dull to dull people" but in fact rest on "the same foundations of wonder as the town of Troy, and the temple of Delphi."[14] To read Emerson in intertextual terms, in other words, is to deterritorialize him, to extract him from the limiting circumference of antebellum New England and to think about ways in which he attempts deliberately to reconceptualize Enlightenment universalism within an alternative New World environment.

In the 1850s, geography itself increasingly became part of the rhetoric of Manifest Destiny in the United States. The American Geographic Society was established in 1851, three years before Arnold Guyot, the most influential American geographer of his era, took up the chair at Princeton he was to occupy for the next thirty years. Emerson himself owned the 1851 edition of Guyot's *The Earth and Man*, in which the author's project was to develop a theory of hemispheric evolution as providential and thus as entirely consonant with the exceptionalist qualities of US national identity. The "vital principle" of geography, asserted Guyot, was the "mutual exchange of relations" between "inorganic nature" and "organized beings," so that the physical world should not be seen merely as an inert or inanimate object, but as a phenomenon "organised for the development of man." According to "the decrees of Providence," he claimed, "nature and history, the earth and man, stand in the closest relations to each other, and form only one grand harmony." Guyot's conception of hemispheric symmetry was of a piece with his narrative of westward historical progression, the notion that the center of civilization, which had originated in Asia, was now passing from Europe to North America. Guyot further verified the cultural superiority of North to South America by presenting this hemispheric antithesis as analogous to that which appertained in Europe: "The contrast between the North, mitigated in the temperate regions of the mother country, is reproduced in the New World, more strongly marked, and on a grander scale, between North America, with its temperate climate, its Protestant and progressive people, and South America, with its tropical climate, its Catholic and stationary population."[15] It is not difficult to see why this version of geographical providence would have appealed especially to Emerson in the 1850s, after the war with Mexico, the annexation of Texas, the evacuation of the British from the Pacific Northwest, and the American incorporation of the Oregon Territory. In a journal entry of 1853, Emerson notes how "Columbus was the first to discover the equatorial current in the ocean," and he cites with approbation a passage from *The Earth and Man*, where Guyot declares it "beyond a doubt ... that the waters of the ocean, move with the heavens; that is, in the direction of the apparent course of the sun and stars, from east to west."[16]

What crucially changed the cultural and political landscape of the United States was, of course, the Civil War, which after its conclusion in 1865 consolidated the geography of the nation by ensuring it would henceforth be integrated into one political territory. It is not surprising that scholars, particularly in the United States, have kept returning compulsively to the Civil War as a turning point of national destiny because, despite all of the internecine regional and racial conflicts it highlighted, the outcome of the war also facilitated the emergence of the United States as the world's leading economic power in the second half of the nineteenth century. It was then that the country began to take the continental shape that we know today: California was admitted to the union in 1850, Oregon in 1859, Kansas in 1861, Nevada 1864, Nebraska 1867, Colorado 1876, the Dakotas, Montana and, Washington in 1889, Idaho in 1890, and so on. The joining together of the North and the South, in other words, ran in parallel with the joining together of the East and the West; America was metamorphosed from a series of local economies into an imposing continental edifice. Given the simultaneous growth in communications and technology at this time, the expansion westward of the railways, the development of the telegraph, and so on, it becomes easy to see how the United States could understand itself as a coherent political and economic entity by the year 1900 in a way that simply had not been possible when Emerson wrote "Nature" in 1836.[17]

This vision of the United States as a culturally and politically unified entity had, of course, been anticipated during the Civil War by Abraham Lincoln. In his Gettysburg address, Lincoln invoked a self-replicating, circular representative structure of "government of the people, by the people, for the people," as though the model of the country were predicated upon a mythic form of egalitarian democracy, something that was certainly very far from the minds of the Founding Fathers eighty years earlier. Not coincidentally, it was around Lincoln's time that the *United States* began to take on the form of a singular noun, rather than the plural noun that had been conventionally used in the first half of the nineteenth century, with this shift from plural to singular exemplifying again the consolidation of the nation into a state of indivisible unity. It was also around the turn of the twentieth century that the notion of the land as bearing inherent national values came to be invested with a sacred aura. Florida and New Orleans, for instance, were bartered and traded quite happily in the early nineteenth century, but after the Civil War the idea of the United States as a national space was mystified in such a way that no politician would dare henceforth to think of paying off the national debt by, say, simply selling off the Florida Keys or southern California to the highest bidder.[18]America's purchase of Alaska from Russia for $7.2 million in 1867 was, in this sense, the last commercial transaction of its kind.

Much of the critical language in this era of burgeoning US nationalism tended to involve a justification of American difference, of the particular qualities of American scenes and locations, such as we see in the novels of Theodore Dreiser, William Dean Howells, and others. This was also the era of the mythology surrounding Ellis Island, through which immigrants were to be socially assimilated and homogenized into American citizens. The high-water mark of immigration to the United States was 1.3 million in 1907, the year before Israel Zangwill produced his play *The Melting Pot*, which reproduced the mythology of America as a land of immigrants even in critiquing its efficacy. This kind of double vision, constructing and deconstructing an image of America as promised land simultaneously, was characteristic of the way American Modernism tended to be wrapped into a rhetoric of nativist utopia, a rhetoric that served as the foundational basis and underlying grid for all of the texts' subsequent vacillations and ironies.[19] Although Randolph Bourne's essay "Trans-National America," published in 1916, starts off in its first sentence by proclaiming "the failure of the melting pot" in the face of "diverse nationalistic feelings" among the American immigrant population during the First World War, the penultimate paragraph of Bourne's essay looks forward prophetically to a new version of the United States predicated upon a greater tolerance of ethnic diversity, what Bourne calls "a future America, on which all can unite, which pulls us irresistibly toward it, as we understand each other more warmly."[20]

American literature of the late nineteenth and early twentieth centuries thus tends not only to be saturated in locality but also to understand that locality as a guarantee of its own authenticity and its patriotic allegiance, something articulated most explicitly by the polemical essays of Howells in defense of the methods of realism. This is the realm of what Philip Fisher has called "hard facts," where the relationship between the local and the national becomes self-allegorizing, in the sense that the value of particular places, Willa Cather's Nebraska or Robert Frost's New England or William Carlos Williams's New Jersey, is validated not by their specific local characteristics or phenomenological qualities but from their synecdochic embodiment of a national impulse, their sense of being, as Williams put it, "in the American grain."[21] Tom Lutz's work on literary cosmopolitanism has emphasized the extent to which regional writing in late-nineteenth- and early-twentieth-century America was mediated by an external perspective that sought to integrate region and nation as the geographical corollaries of each other, as patriotic manifestations of what Howells called "our decentralized literature." John Dewey's 1920 essay "Americanism and Localism" paradoxically declared "locality" to be "the only universal" aspect of American national identity, while Carrie Tirado Bramen, in *The Uses of Variety*, has described how an emphasis on diversity, both ethnic and regional, became an "inviolable sign of national exceptionalism" for twentieth-century American culture.[22] Tracing this discourse of material and spatial abundance back to William James's writings on pluralism in 1909, Bramen shows how, so far from opposing identitarian politics, James became the precursor of latter-day theorists such as Cornel West who, even now, imagine a commitment to diversity to be emblematic of the way in which an open US culture differentiates itself from the more repressive, restrictive systems of other countries.

This move to integrate and reconcile local variation within a larger national matrix was perpetuated in the early twentieth century through the rationalized industrial methods perfected by Henry Ford and others, which were based around a factory system where the national model was reproduced in every state of the union. The defining issue in John Dos Passos's novel *USA*, published in 1938, is how by this time national similarities have become more important than regional differences, how an industrial model of mass production and consumption has permeated every corner of the United States. (The title of the first volume of this trilogy, *The 42nd Parallel*, is taken pointedly from the geographical line of latitude that extends east to west across the US.) All of this generated tremendous political cohesion and economic wealth for the country in the middle part of the twentieth century, enabling it to intervene decisively in the Second World War and to establish itself iconically, particularly in Europe, as an emblematic land of the free, a Cold War alternative to both the brutality of Fascism and the poverty of Communism. It was of course in the aftermath of the Second World War that the American Studies Association was founded in the United States, in 1951. Most of the American studies programs in Europe also originated around this time, trading off the idea of America as an exemplary and exceptional nation, a beacon both of material regeneration, through its laissez-faire economic system, and also of cultural modernity. Such modernity was thought to emerge through a stylistic emphasis on colloquial informality, typified in the 1950s by jazz and other forms of popular culture, as well as in the incisive vernacular of Saul Bellow and the beat writers, all of which seemed to imply a welcome escape from the ossified class structures and social hierarchies of Europe. In a cover story of 1941, Henry Luce, editor-in-chief of *Time* magazine, famously described the twentieth century as the American century. As Neil Smith has observed, such a prophecy on Luce's part necessarily involved an assumption of "geographical amnesia," a putative triumph over the coordinates of physical space, the replacement of an imperial design based on territorial possession by one driven instead by a liberal internationalism, through which American economic and cultural ideas would penetrate overseas markets.[23]

What I want to suggest, though, is that the United States has now moved in significant ways beyond this national phase and that since about 1980 the country has entered what we might call a transnational era, one more centered around the position of the United States within global networks of exchange. In attempting to give some form of historical specificity to transnationalism, I'm drawing on the idea of deterritorialization first broached in 1972 by the French theorists Gilles Deleuze and Félix Guattari, in their psychoanalytical work *Anti-Oedipus*, to describe the flows of desire that traverse the boundaries of distinct, separate territories:

> The decoding of flows and the deterritorialization of the socius thus constitutes the most characteristic and the most important tendency of capitalism. It continually draws near to its limit, which is a genuinely schizophrenic limit.... [C]apitalism,

through its process of production, produces an awesome schizophrenic accumulation of energy or charge, against which it brings all its vast powers of repression to bear. ... Far from seeing in the State the principle of a territorialization that would inscribe people according to their residence, we should see in the principle of residence the effect of a movement of deterritorialization that divides the earth as an object and subjects men to the new imperial inscription, to the new full body, to the new socius. ... The State can no longer be content to overcode territorial elements that are already coded, it must invent specific codes for flows that are increasingly deterritorialized.[24]

The term "deterritorialization" has subsequently been used in a broader cultural and political context by critics such as Caren Kaplan, who has related it to the experience of women and ethnic minorities in "becoming minor," or living on the edge, and by Appadurai, who has discussed it more specifically in relation to the processes of globalization:

the world in which we now live – in which modernity is decisively at large – [involves] a theory of rupture that takes media and migration as its two major, and interconnected, diacritics and explores their joint effect on the work of the imagination as a constitutive feature of modem subjectivity. ... [M]y approach to the break caused by the joint force of electronic mediation and mass migration is explicitly transnational – even postnational. ... [I]t moves away dramatically from the architecture of classical modernization theory, which one might call fundamentally realist insofar as it assumes the salience, both methodological and ethical, of the nation-state. ... Until recently ... imagination and fantasy were antidotes to the finitude of social experience. In the past two decades, as the deterritorialization of persons, images, and ideas has taken on a new force, this weight has imperceptibly shifted.[25]

Speaking in 2004, a senior diplomatic figure in the US Embassy in London expressed the view that the crucial political shift within his own professional lifetime was not the transition in 2000 from Bill Clinton to George W. Bush, but the country's move in 1980 from Jimmy Carter to Ronald Reagan. All such dividing lines in history are of course arbitrary and approximate, as noted earlier, but this one might be more plausible than most, because it was in the 1970s and 1980s that the economic infrastructure of the United States began to change decisively. Richard Nixon anticipated this shift toward a global economy in August 1971 when he announced that the United States would no longer redeem currency for gold, thereby effectively abandoning the gold standard and ushering in an era of fluctuating exchange rates. David Harvey dates the decline of "the Fordist regime" from 1973, the same year that money became "de-materialized," as a fully floating system of currency conversion was adopted so that money no longer had "a formal or tangible link to precious metals."[26] With the loss of the mechanism that effectively regulated the growth rate of the country's money supply, the United States, like other nation-states, found itself increasingly drawn into the marketplace of global exchange, something given greater momentum by the free-market philosophies of President Reagan in the 1980s, and in the 1990s by the dramatic growth in information technology that made it increasingly possible to transfer capital around the globe at a moment's notice. These developments were replicated slightly later in other parts of the world: in Britain, for instance, Margaret Thatcher became prime minister of Britain in 1979, bringing to an abrupt end the postwar years of liberal social consensus in that country, but the key symbolic event in Europe was the fall of the Berlin Wall in 1989, which not only effectively ended the Cold War but also fatally undermined the social and economic cohesion of what had been postwar Europe's most successful corporate state, West Germany. Michael Denning sees the fall of the Berlin Wall as heralding the crucial break between what he calls the age of three worlds, demarcated according to the discrete geopolitical zones that dominated area studies in the Cold War era between 1945 and 1989, and the subsequent era of globalization. Denning makes the point that it was pressure from the International Monetary Fund and the transfer of finance capital across national borders that crucially destabilized at this time the autonomy of self-enclosed political regimes of all kinds, Manley's social democratic Jamaica as well as De Klerk's South Africa.[27]

It is important to emphasize how these forces of deterritorialization have also operated powerfully to disturb and dislocate the national identity of the United States itself, in particular the relationship between its domestic space and the rest of the world. In *Empire*, produced not coincidentally at the height of the neoliberal boom in 1999, Michael Hardt and Antonio Negri describe international capitalism as "a *decentered* and *deterritorializing* apparatus of rule that progressively incorporates the entire global realm within its open, expanding frontiers," and they suggest this was a "new imperial form of sovereignty," one not to be identified with any particular "nation-state." But such a version of imperialism would appear to be oddly reminiscent of a disembodied transcendentalism, wherein finance capital, rather than Emerson's transparent eyeball, has become the force field whose center is everywhere and its circumference nowhere: in the words of Hardt and Negri, "Empire presents a superficial world, the virtual center of which can be accessed immediately from any point across the surface."[28] By rendering spatial geography redundant, Hardt and Negri implicitly mimic the rhetoric of empire in the way they render territorial formations obsolete; according to Neil Smith, their "recognition of empire remains clouded by the lost geography ideologies that should be its target."[29] Within the world of geographical materialism, however, the actual experience of deterritorialization manifests itself as much more jagged and fractious, bound up with tensions and inconsistencies that cannot be subsumed merely within global systems or regimes of capital accumulation.

One fictional representation of this fraught state can be found in the novel *Primary Colors* by Joe Klein, published as an anonymous account of Bill Clinton's election campaign in 1992. The presidential candidate, called there "Jack Stanton," addresses a group of workers in Portsmouth, New Hampshire, and tells them he's not going to delude them into thinking he can protect their jobs for life in a new situation where transnational corporations can swiftly pull investment in and out of the country in a way that would never have occurred to Henry Ford sixty years earlier:

> "So let me tell you this: No politician can bring these shipyard jobs back. Or make your union strong again. No politician can make it be the way it used to be. Because we're living in a new world now, a world without borders – economically, that is. Guy can push a button in New York and move a billion dollars to Tokyo before you blink an eye. We've got a world market now. And that's good for some. In the end, you've gotta believe it's good for America. … I'll fight and worry and sweat and bleed to get the money to make education a lifetime thing in this country, to give you the support you need to move on up. But you've got to do the heavy lifting your own selves. I can't do it for you, and I know it's not gonna be easy."[30]

Stanton, or Clinton, deliberately positions himself here in relation to the flexible conditions of the global marketplace, the realm of outsourcing and transnationalization, where American corporate interests can be served just as easily, often more easily, by relocating service or production industries to Mexico or Asia, where wages are lower and costs are cheaper, rather than through domestic investment. What this has meant is that the stable patterns of middle-class prosperity and security that characterized the earlier Henry Ford era have all but evaporated; corporate profits have of course increased rapidly, but their growth is not related directly to or shared by large sections of the working population, as it tended to be in the mid-twentieth century, when corporations such as Ford usually took a benevolent, patriarchal interest in the welfare of their employees.

The relationship between American culture and globalization is a vast topic that touches upon telecommunications, media, and the expansion of transnational corporations; the main point to be made here is simply that it happened. For example, the hamburger chain McDonald's only opened its first two foreign outlets, in Canada and Puerto Rico, in 1967, but by 1999 overseas sales for McDonald's had actually overtaken domestic sales, and today a majority of their outlets, approximately seventeen thousand out of thirty thousand, are located outside the territorial boundaries of the United States.[31] Indeed, the relationship between geographical location and cultural identity has changed so radically in the wake of recent changes in communications technologies that Linda Basch has argued the traditional distinction between migrants and immigrants no longer holds good. She points, for example, to the Grenadian constituency in New York who remain socially, politically, and often economically part of their ancestral domain; in fact, of Grenada's population of ninety thousand only thirty thousand of them actually live there, and this has led to a new construct of what Basch calls a "deterritorialized" nation-state within which people can remain active electronically in their old countries. Such two-way relationships have increasingly been legally formalized: since the late 1980s, for example, the Philippine state has continued to collect income tax on all Filipino citizens residing abroad on a special overseas visa issued by the government. This has meant also that the US Congress has found itself increasingly under direct pressure from Filipino voters in the United States to get involved directly in Filipino domestic politics, with the consequence that the traditional distinctions between domestic and foreign have come to appear increasingly unclear. Nor should this Filipino example be seen as especially anomalous; in *The Transnational Villagers* (2001), Peggy Levitt offers a case study of how migrants from Miraflores, a town in the Dominican Republic, to Jamaica Plain, a neighborhood of Boston, participate in the social, political, and economic lives of their homelands and their host society simultaneously.[32] The transnational village, in Levitt's sense, functions not through spatial proximity but through cheap telecommunications and airfares, and to conceive of a nation-state that stretches beyond its traditional geographical boundaries is also to imagine, by a reverse projection, an American state whose territory is no longer automatically synonymous with the interests of US citizens.

None of this is intended to present neoliberalism or globalization as a simple fait accompli, nor to suggest that local or national politics have no part to play in the organization and redistribution of resources. What it is to argue, in relation to the study of American literature and culture, is that since about 1980 the rules of engagement have changed so significantly that old area studies nostrums about exceptionalist forms of national politics and culture, pieties about American diversity or whatever, have become almost irrelevant. In terms of ways in which this move toward a transnational infrastructure has manifested itself in American literature, some of the most illuminating instances occur in the works of writers such as Douglas Coupland and William Gibson – one brought up in Vancouver, Canada, but who writes about the Pacific Northwest as a transnational region; the other born in South Carolina, but resident in Vancouver since 1972 – whose representations of American digital culture are organized obliquely around parallel computer universes. There is an extended treatment of the theme of deterritorialization in Gibson's novel *Pattern Recognition* (2003), whose heroine works for a public relations company called Blue Ant, described in the book as "more post-geographic than multinational." As she shuttles across national boundaries, Gibson's heroine thinks back to her father, who for twenty-five years had been "an evaluator and improver of security for American embassies worldwide" and whose watchword had always been "secure the perimeter." However, the old Cold Warrior is lost in Manhattan on the morning of 9/11, with his wife saying "that when the second plane hit, Win's chagrin, his personal and professional mortification at this having happened, at the perimeter having been breached so easily ... would have been such that he might simply have ceased, in protest, to exist."[33]

Gibson's novel highlights the way in which 9/11 has become for the United States the most visible and haunting symbol of the new permeability of its borders, its vulnerability to outside elements. In this sense, it is no surprise how the enormous stress on "homeland security" in the administration of George W. Bush should operate as a reaction against this widespread sense of dislocation and trauma. To turn a home into a "homeland" is, by definition, to move from a zone in which domestic comforts and protection could be taken for granted to one in which they had to be anxiously and self-consciously guarded; in that sense, the very phrase "homeland security" is almost a contradiction in terms, since it evokes the very insecurity it is itself designed to assuage. As Jean Baudrillard has said, terrorism might be seen as an almost inevitable counterpart to the development of liberal market economies, since its enabling structures are almost identical, based as they are around the exploitation of computer and aeronautic technologies, rapid capital transfers, the wide dissemination of scientific and other kinds of information, and the all-encompassing power of a global media: above all, terrorism trades off a culture of spectacle.[34] Whereas for most Americans the Second World War and the subsequent Cold War took place in alien locations, the distant world of European battlefields or the shadowy realm of spies coming in from the cold, the most uncomfortable thing about 9/11 was the way it demonstrated how borders separating the domestic from the foreign can no longer be so easily policed or, indeed, even identified. Such permeability became conflated in the minds of many Americans both with a threat to Christian fundamentalist values and with the loss of job security for large numbers of people in what Edward Soja has called a "postfordist" economic landscape, one driven by internationally mobile capital and technology, rather than by labor and more traditional forms of production.[35] The powerful impact of 9/11 might thus best be understood not in terms of how it appeared as an entirely unexpected event, a bolt from the blue, but, on the contrary, how it resonated as a symbolic culmination of the various kinds of deterritorializing forces that had been gathering pace since the Reagan years.

Considered in the light of these transnational pressures, the back-formation of nationalist reaction in twenty-first-century US politics becomes less surprising. To regard the loss of a liberal, democratic idea of America as some kind of betrayal of inherent national values is simply to conflate the mythic version of exceptionalism that sustained American Studies in the mid-twentieth century with a just and accurate representation of the country as a whole. Moreover, to refer twenty-first-century politics back simply to the framework of an internecine conflict within the United States between conservatives and liberals – "a cold civil war," as Hortense Spillers called it in 2004 – is to misunderstand how this situation has been brought about in large part by the way foreign bodies are interfacing uncomfortably with US national interests.[36] To imagine the current situation in the US simply as another civil war is to redefine it in domestic, nineteenth-century terms as a Manichaean conflict between emancipation and slavery, enlightenment and oppression; it ignores the more significant ways in which both the red and the blue states have become mutually self-defining in the way they square up against each other dialectically, comprising a protective circle within which each recognizes the other as the enemy. In this sense, the idea of a new civil war becomes a curiously comforting notion, one that assumes your antagonist is an old, familiar foe rather than one that is new and harder to recognize. There is also a danger within the liberal academy of superciliously dismissing the conservative agenda as simply intellectually backward, though the obstreperous rejection of deracination and cosmopolitanism as elitist conceits in the aggressively demotic poetry of Robert Pinsky suggests how anxieties about cultural, economic, and religious displacement are by no means confined merely to tub-thumping evangelicals.[37]

The larger framework here relates to the diminution rather than the agglomeration of US power. Political theorist Immanuel Wallerstein has concluded that the relative decline of American hegemonic power over the next fifty years is inevitable, not because of any particular policies pursued or not pursued by US presidents, but because of more structural reasons, in particular the increasing modulation of domestic economies within a transnational axis of geopolitical space. The amorphous processes associated with globalization will affect the United States politically as well as economically: as Niall Ferguson has pointed out, any nation is less powerful politically if it has a thousand nuclear weapons when every other nation has one than if it has one and other nations none at all. One of the policies being pursued by George W. Bush's administration, a policy surely doomed to long-term failure, is to freeze nuclear "proliferation," as they call it, at a stage most favorable to the United States.[38] This is a familiar enough ploy within the annals of imperial history, going back to the ancient Romans, who attempted strenuously to prevent potential enemies from getting their hands on all kinds of dangerous weapons. But given the way that the Internet has speeded up global exchanges of information, so that scientific knowledge is no longer locked within Cold War vaults but dispersed among many different centers, such an ambition of exceptionalist superiority and isolationism, geared toward preserving American world domination, would appear to have no chance at all of long-term success. Nor is it at all likely that, for all of its politically calculated rhetoric about the "axis of evil," the US government itself is unaware of how this balance of power is slowly shifting. Indeed, one of President Bush's own advisory bodies, the National Intelligence Council, produced in December 2004 a report entitled *Mapping the Global Future*, which describes globalization as "an overarching 'mega-trend,' a force so ubiquitous that it will substantially shape all the other major trends in the world of 2020," so that "how we mentally map the world in 2020 will change radically." The report goes on to predict openly that although the United States will continue to be "the most important single country across all the dimensions of power," by 2020 it will also see "its relative power position eroded."[39]

In this light, one of the most interesting aspects of contemporary American literature is how it represents ways in which these pressures of deterritorialization are being internalized and understood affectively. John Updike, for instance, made his name in the 1960s and 1970s by chronicling the fortunes of Harry Angstrom in the Rabbit series of novels, and especially for the way he drew analogies between the fate of his main character and the contemporary condition of the United States. Thus, *Rabbit, Run* (1960) comments on the impulse toward romantic freedom among the beat writers of the late 1950s, *Rabbit Redux* (1971) sardonically observes the Apollo moon landings and the swinging sixties, and so on. Part of the structural difficulty with this Rabbit sequence, though, as many critics have observed, is that the parallels between the life of a white Pennsylvania automobile worker and the fate of the country as a whole seem ultimately to become forced and exclusionary.[40] Updike's Rabbit novels are attuned specifically to the nationalist ethos of a post-World War II era when white middle-class America was assumed to represent the fate of the country at large, and when the national radio and television networks, which function as a kind of chorus in Updike's novels, imagined themselves to be speaking on behalf of a unified people. However, in *Seek My Face* (2002) there is a specific meditation on what Updike's narrator calls "the fading Protestant hegemony" and on the erasure of the national security that formerly went along with a clearly defined sense of American identity. Ensconced at the age of seventy-nine in her house in Vermont, the painter Hope Chafetz thinks of how "owning this house restored her to certain simplicities of childhood, when houses and yards demarcated territories of safety and drew upon deep wells, mysterious cisterns brimming with communal reserves." She also watches the evening news on television and sees in place of the regular NBC newscaster, Tom Brokaw, what she calls "a perfectly stunning young woman, light topaz eyes as far apart as a kitten's," whose "name wasn't even Greek, it was more like Turkish, a quick twist of syllables like an English word spelled backwards. The old American stock is being overgrown," she thinks: "High time, of course: no reason to grieve."[41] The elegiac tone in this novel is related not only to Hope's personal sense of aging but also to her recognition of how the old American order itself is passing, how the traditional iconography of national identity now appears to be as insecure as the superannuated charms of Christian theology, whose demise, in typical Updike fashion, is also lovingly chronicled in this book.

Another kind of map is provided by Leslie Marmon Silko as a preface to her 1991 novel *Almanac of the Dead*, a narrative that ambitiously rewrites the history of America from the standpoint of Native American communities. Centered on Tucson, Arizona, this "five hundred year map" extends from the Laguna Pueblo Reservation in the north to Mexico City in the south, and it represents the current US–Mexico border as incidental to the flow of human and cultural traffic across this land over the centuries. The novel itself, like the cartographic image that precedes it, encompasses a perspective of deliberate inversion that involves redrawing the map of the United States in space as well as time. Silko's novel deliberately eschews the chronologies of US history to establish for the Arizona region an entirely different kind of cultural vantage point, seeing the American Southwest in the context of Aztec civilizations and the Apache wars, thereby rendering the familiar national narrative of the United States contingent and reversible. This in turn works as a corollary to the chronology of "the people's history" in the last section of this book, which foregrounds slave history and deliberately overlooks the celebrated landmarks of established US history.[42] Silko herself has described the US government as an illegitimate enterprise founded on land stolen from Native American peoples, though *Almanac of the Dead* represents American culture more in terms of a complex legacy of mixed ancestries, a hybrid concoction of Spanish and other indigenous cultures interlinked with the apparatus of the global village. Elsewhere, Silko has written of the shift in emphasis after 1980 by agencies of the US government from the "Iron Curtain" to "Border Patrol," as the Immigration and Naturalization Service sought to prevent free travel not only across but also within US borders, especially in the American Southwest, and to construct the kind of defensive mechanisms against a perceived threat of mass migration and "illegal aliens" that anticipated the current fetish of "homeland security."[43] Indeed, Native American culture offers an interesting microcosm and symbol of the current fate of US culture, since the concept of deterritorialization was forcibly applied to Native American people in the early nineteenth century, when Andrew Jackson, president of the United States between 1829 and 1837, urged the nation to accept the loss of Indian tribes as inevitable. In

The Pioneers (1823), James Fenimore Cooper represents the breakup of the ice on Lake Otsego as an organic analogue to the historical dispossession of Native American peoples, a process that the author thereby tries to naturalize.[44] Indeed, one might say that the loss of territorial security that was visited upon Native Americans in the nineteenth century has now become, in different ways and under different circumstances, something that is afflicting US culture as a whole.

My general hypothesis, then, is that the nationalist phase of American literature and culture extended from 1865 until about 1980, and that the current transnational phase actually has more in common with the so-called early national period, between 1780 and 1860, when national boundaries and habits were much less formed and settled. The geography scholar Robert David Sack has linked the idea of territory above all to themes of power, protection, and political control, control that is sometimes projected onto the territorial formation itself, as in the familiar notion of something being "the law of the land." He has also written of how the notion of territory has frequently been endowed with an idea of mythical content, as in the way the ancient division of the Chinese Empire into four quarters was fondly imagined to be a mirror of cosmic order.[45] Such forms of sublimation involve what Deleuze and Guattari called a process of "reterritorialization," where the appropriation of territory is designed to occlude its own material flux, an approach that manifests itself, often in circuitous ways, even in contemporary readings of American literature.[46] For instance, in *Landscape and Ideology in American Renaissance Literature* (2003), Robert E. Abrams invokes the idea of what he calls "*negative* geography" in order to explain the resistance of Thoreau and others to rationalistic cartographies, cartographies that Abrams understands as alien impositions from the European world on a pristine American scene. In this reading, the escape from abstract geographical mapping into what Abrams calls "a sense of indefinite existential promise" becomes an implicit guarantee of an American literary nationalism that justifies itself by its escape from "the hallucinatory authority of centralized, panoptic vision" and defines itself instead by its relationship to the unmapped sublime.[47] Abrams thus critically recapitulates the classic Transcendentalist move whereby the erasure of specific locations in history and geography becomes the sign of the writer's separatist self-reliance and American authenticity. To place culture and geography in this kind of mutually exclusive relationship is, of course, to overlook ways in which their narratives are inextricably intertwined. In this sense, Abrams's version of "negative geography" operates much like a traditional form of dehistoricization, a transliteration of material conditions into a version of mythic idealism within which time and space are frozen out. Geographical materialism, by contrast, would seek to restore these spatial dynamics to American literature.

In an era of global warming and various forms of transnational circulation, when issues of the environment cannot be reduced simply to local or national specificities, such a dissolution of space into "negative geography" must surely appear merely parochial. One of the conceptual problems with the study of US literature and culture has always been its tendency toward a relatively narrow theoretical matrix, its distinct preference for familiar nationalistic terms of reference enjoying a supposedly "natural" affinity with the native soil, a self-perpetuating loop through which American writers were critically validated for being identifiably American. By contrast, the conceptual displacement of US territorial autonomy has opened up intriguing new possibilities for the international study of America's place within the world today, and there are two European theorists of transnationalism whose work might usefully, if provocatively, be read against the grain of the American polis. The first is the German philosopher Jürgen Habermas, whose book of essays *The Postnational Constellation* (2001) is one of the best investigations so far of the challenges posed by the contemporary world to social democratic models of community based around the secure foundations of a welfare state. Habermas goes on in this book to consider ways in which forms of representative democracy might be reconfigured within a new era of digital technology and genetic engineering, switching the arguments away from a religious fundamentalist focus by offering interesting observations on whether human cloning might be considered a new version of political slavery. He also raises important questions of how individual choice might be preserved within a postliberal environment, where, pace Thomas Jefferson, freedom can no longer be seen as a natural or inherent right linked organically to any particular national soil.[48] Habermas's rigorously secular philosophy forms a valuable transnational counterpoint to current American debates about multiculturalism and diversity, debates that too frequently assume an implicitly nationalistic and metaphysical dimension, shadowed as they are by the old patriotic ghost of *e pluribus unum*.

Another European theorist of transnationalism who might be said to open up crevices in the monolithic US domain is French political thinker Etienne Balibar. Balibar's *We, the People of Europe? Reflections on Transnational Citizenship* (2004) discusses ways in which nations have traditionally attempted to guard their borders so as to preserve the integrity of their public sphere and have consequently defined themselves primarily through various mechanisms of exclusion, although he also points out how, in the twenty-first century, these borders are no longer "entirely situated at the outer limit of territories" but are – through international media, finance, and so on – dispersed everywhere within them, so that "border areas … are not marginal to the constitution of a public sphere but rather are at the center."[49] The central concern of Balibar's book is the changing political system in Europe and its slow evolution into something more like a federal union, but, by Ricoeur's logic of "retrodiction" that I invoked earlier, it's entirely possible these altered conditions in Europe will force us to reexamine the literature and culture of the nineteenth- and twentieth-century United States in a new light. Prophecy is always a risky business, but it would appear likely that over the next fifty years Europe will gradually evolve into a more integrated political state within which English will emerge as the dominant language, even though, as David Crystal suggests, this use of English as a lingua franca will exist alongside a range of other European languages historically embedded in particular national cultures.[50] What this will produce is a model of political union where multinationalism and multilingualism are the norm, and this may well induce scholars in the twenty-first century to take another look at American literary history of earlier eras, when the official rhetoric of melting-pot assimilation and monolingualism tended simply to gloss over aspects of US culture that did not conform to these hegemonic ideals. Rather than seeing Europe as positioned in the kind of conceptual opposition to America that characterized the exceptionalist impulse of American Studies in the twentieth century, this transnational matrix will force scholars to think of Europe and the United States in terms of more complex relations of analogical convergence and divergence. Just as scholars today look back with a touch of condescension on the 1950s generation that equated American literature exclusively with books written by white males, so scholars in 2050 may look back in equal bemusement upon the generation of scholars around the turn of the millennium that understood American literature to be synonymous with literature written in English.

Deterritorialization as the term was used by Deleuze and Guattari had a quite specific psychoanalytical meaning, but the term can be extrapolated to make some suggestive observations about ways in which subjects of all kinds, both individual and national, find themselves compelled to relate to what Appadurai calls the "theory of rupture that takes media and migration as its two major, and interconnected, diacritics."[51] This is why I would see some of the recent work on American empire, which has become prominent recently within the world of American studies, as problematical. The concept of "United States imperialism" seems often to extrapolate a view of American influence abroad from the realist epistemologies associated with the nationalist era at home, thereby simply extending the familiar domain of US nationalism around the globe. Its locus classicus is the Theodore Roosevelt paradigm of the strenuous frontier life, which certainly helped to galvanize American territorial excursions during the Spanish-American wars of the 1890s; but it is far from clear that the expansionist dimensions of US imperialism at the turn of the twentieth century can be translated smoothly into the ubiquitous border conditions of a hundred years later.[52] David Harvey has written of the dialectic between a territorial and a capitalist logic of power within the "new imperialism," and of how "[i]n practice the two logics frequently tug against each other, sometimes to the point of outright antagonism."[53] This is the internal contradiction of twenty-first-century empire that the idea of deterritorialization effectively mediates. Rather than merely conflating America and empire and understanding US power to be a "colossus," in Niall Ferguson's imperious phrase, there is an important sense in which we should read the United States itself as one of the objects of globalization, rather than as merely its malign agent, so that all of the insecurities associated with transnationalism are lived out experientially within the nation's own borders as well.

By restoring a matrix of historical and geographical materialism to the United States at the beginning of the twenty-first century, we come to understand how the idea of American culture has always been bound up inextricably with particular configurations of space, configurations that have changed their shape many times over the past two hundred years. From a critical point of view, deterritorialization, like transnationalism, is a doubled-up, recursive term that seeks to bracket off or contradict the trope associated with a prior metanarrative: territory, nation, or homeland. It speaks to a paradoxical situation where affective loyalties, local affiliations, and subliminal legacies are ironically traversed by larger vectors of political and economic disenfranchisement, vectors that threaten to push the nation further and further away from the representative center of its own imagined community. To speak of American literary culture under the rubric of deterritorialization is thus not simply to encumber it with the monolithic categories of globalization or imperialism but, rather, to think of it as a socially constructed, historically variable, and experientially edgy phenomenon, whose valence lies in the tantalizing dialectic between an illusion of presence and the continual prospect of displacement.

Notes

1 David Harvey, *The Condition of Postmodernity: An Enquiry into the Origins of Cultural Change* (Oxford: Blackwell, 1989), 359.

2 Fredric Jameson, "Periodizing the 60s," in *The 60s without Apology*, ed. Sohnya Sayres, Anders Stephanson, Stanley Aronowitz, and Fredric Jameson (Minneapolis: University of Minnesota Press – Social Text, 1984), 178.

3 Arjun Appadurai, *Modernity at Large: Cultural Dimensions of Globalization* (Minneapolis: University of Minnesota Press, 1996), 182.

4 Paul Ricoeur, *Time and Narrative*, vol. 1, trans. Kathleen McLaughlin and David Pellauer (Chicago: University of Chicago Press, 1984), 135; and *Time and Narrative*, vol. 3, trans. Kathleen Blamey and David Pellauer (Chicago: University of Chicago Press, 1988), 173.

5 Edgar Allan Poe, "The Philosophy of Composition" (1846), in *Essays and Reviews* (New York: Library of America, 1984), 13; Cyrus Patell, "A New Capital for American Literary History," paper presented at the Modern Language Association Annual Convention, Philadelphia, December 30, 2004.

6 For critiques of this teleology in relation to "early American literature," see R.C. De Prospo, "Marginalizing Early American Literature," *New Literary History* 23 (1992): 233–265; and William C. Spengemann, *A New World of Words: Redefining Early American Literature* (New Haven: Yale University Press, 1994).

7 William Boelhower, "Inventing America: A Model of Cartographic Semiosis," *Word and Image* 4, no. 2 (April – June 1988): 495.

8 On the instability of US nationalism in the West in the early nineteenth century, see David Waldstreicher, *In the Midst of Perpetual Fêtes: The Making of American Nationalism, 1776–1820* (Williamsburg, Va. and Chapel Hill: Omohundro Institute of Early American History and Culture and University of North Carolina Press, 1997).

9 Ralph Waldo Emerson, "The Poet," in *Essays: Second Series*, vol. 3 of *Collected Works*, ed. Alfred R. Ferguson and Jean Ferguson Carr (Cambridge: Harvard University Press, 1983), 22.

10 Martin Brückner, "Lessons in Geography: Maps, Spellers, and Other Grammars of Nationalism in the Early Republic," *American Quarterly* 51 (1999): 311–343; Bruce A. Harvey, *American Geographics: US National Narratives and the Representation of the Non-European World, 1830–1865* (Stanford, Calif.: Stanford University Press, 2001), 28.

11 Ralph Waldo Emerson, "Nature," in *Nature, Addresses, and Lectures*, vol. 1 of *Collected Works*, ed. Robert E. Spiller and Alfred R. Ferguson (Cambridge: Harvard University Press, 1971), 7.

12 Ronald Paulson, *Hogarth's Harlot: Sacred Parody in Enlightenment England* (Baltimore: Johns Hopkins University Press, 2003), 214–222.

13 Ralph Waldo Emerson, "Experience," in *Essays: Second Series*, 30, 46.

14 Emerson, "The Poet," 21–22.

15 Arnold Guyot, *The Earth and Man: Lectures on Comparative Physical Geography, in Its Relation to the History of Mankind*, trans. C.C. Felton (London, 1850), 17, 19, 294–295, 28–29, 284.

16 Ralph Waldo Emerson, *The Journals and Miscellaneous Notebooks, vol.* 13, 1852–1855, ed. Ralph H. Orth and Alfred R. Ferguson (Cambridge: Harvard University Press, 1977), 5, 169.

17 On the cultural and economic development of the United States in the late nineteenth century, see Alan Trachtenberg, *The Incorporation of America: Culture and Society in the Gilded Age* (New York: Hill and Wang, 1982).

18 Benedict Anderson, "National Citizenship, Private Property, and Domestic Migration: Witches' Brew?" paper presented at University of Oxford, October 13, 2004.

19 On the complementary aspects of racial identity and textual irony in American modernist narratives such as *The Great Gatsby*, see Walter Benn Michaels, *Our America: Nativism, Modernism, and Pluralism* (Durham, NC: Duke University Press, 1995), 41–42.

20 Randolph Bourne, "Trans-National America," in *War and the Intellectuals: Collected Essays, 1915–1919*, ed. Carl Resek (New York: Harper and Row, 1964), 107, 123.

21 Philip Fisher, *Hard Facts: Setting and Form in the American Novel* (New York: Oxford University Press, 1985); William Carlos Williams, *In the American Grain* (New York: Boni, 1925).

22 Tom Lutz, *Cosmopolitan Vistas: American Regionalism and Literary Value* (Ithaca: Cornell University Press, 2004), 38; John Dewey, "Americanism and Localism," in *The Middle Works, 1899–1924*, vol. 12, 1920, ed. Jo Ann Boydston (Carbondale: Southern Illinois University Press, 1982), 15; Carrie Tirado Bramen, *The Uses of Variety: Modern Americanism and the Quest for National Distinctiveness* (Cambridge: Harvard University Press, 2000), 1.

23 Neil Smith, *American Empire: Roosevelt's Geographer and the Prelude to Globalization* (Berkeley and Los Angeles: University of California Press, 2003), 17, 460.

24 Gilles Deleuze and Félix Guattari, *Anti-Oedipus: Capitalism and Schizophrenia*, trans. Robert Hurley, Mark Seem, and Helen R. Lane (1972; reprint, London: Athlone Press, 1984), 34, 195, 218.

25 Caren Kaplan, "Deterritorializations: The Rewriting of Home and Exile in Western Feminist Discourse," in *The Nature and Context of Minority Discourse*, ed. Abdul R. JanMohamed and David Lloyd (New York: Oxford University Press, 1990), 357–368; Appadurai, *Modernity at Large*, 3, 9, 53.

26 Niall Ferguson, *Colossus: The Rise and Fall of the American Empire* (London: Allen Lane, 2004), 102; Harvey, *Condition of Postmodernity*, 140, 297.

27 Michael Denning, *Culture in the Age of Three Worlds* (London: Verso, 2004), 24–26, 46.

28 Michael Hardt and Antonio Negri, *Empire* (Cambridge: Harvard University Press, 2000), xii, xiii–xiv, 58.

29 Smith, *American Empire*, 458.

30 Anonymous [Joe Klein], *Primary Colors* (London: Chatto and Windus, 1996), 161–162.

31 Ferguson, *Colossus*, 18.

32 Linda Basch, Nina Glick Schiller, and Cristina Szanton Blanc, *Nations Unbound: Transnational Projects, Postcolonial Predicaments, and Deterritorialized Nation-States* (Amsterdam: Gordon and Breach, 1994), 226–227, 258–269; Peggy Levitt, *The Transnational Villagers* (Berkeley and Los Angeles: University of California Press, 2001).

33 William Gibson, *Pattern Recognition* (London: Viking Penguin, 2003), 6, 44, 351.

34 Jean Baudrillard, "L'Esprit du Terrorisme," trans. Michel Valentin, *South Atlantic Quarterly* 101 (2002): 409.

35 Edward W. Soja, *Postmodern Geographies: The Reassertion of Space in Critical Social Theory* (London: Verso, 1989), 3.

36 Hortense Jeanette Spillers, "African Americanist Criticism and the State in the Age of Terror," paper presented at the Modern Language Association Annual Convention, Philadelphia, December 28, 2004.

37 Bruce Robbins, "The Village of the Liberal Managerial Class," in Vinay Dharwadker, ed., *Cosmopolitan Geographies: New Locations in Literature and Culture* (New York: Routledge, 2001), 15. In particular, Pinsky has taken exception to Martha Nussbaum's essay "Patriotism and Cosmopolitanism," which argues for recognition of the rights of noncitizens. See Joshua Cohen, ed., *For Love of Country: Debating the Limits of Patriotism* (Boston: Beacon Press, 1996), 87–88.

38 Immanuel Wallerstein, *The Decline of American Power* (New York: New Press, 2003), 207–208, 287; Ferguson, *Colossus*, 299.

39 *Mapping the Global Future: Report of the National Intelligence Council's 2020 Project* (Washington, DC: Government Printing Office, 2004), 10–11.

40 See, for example, Jay Prosser, "Under the Skin of John Updike: *Self-Consciousness* and the Racial Unconscious," *PMLA* 116 (2001): 579–580.

41 John Updike, *Seek My Face* (London: Hamish Hamilton, 2002), 70–71, 81, 11.

42 Leslie Marmon Silko, *Almanac of the Dead* (1991; report, New York: Penguin, 1992), 14–15, 742–746.

43 Leslie Marmon Silko, "The Border Patrol State" (1994), in *Yellow Woman and a Beauty of the Spirit: Essays on Native American Life Today* (New York: Simon and Schuster, 1996), 115–123.

44 David C. Lipscomb, "'Water Leaves No Trail': Mapping Away the Vanishing American in Cooper's Leatherstocking Tales," in Helena Michie and Ronald R. Thomas, ed., *Nineteenth-Century Geographies: The Transformation of Space from the Victorian Age to the American Century* (New Brunswick, NJ: Rutgers University Press, 2003), 55–71.

45 Robert David Sack, *Human Territoriality: Its Theory and History* (Cambridge: Cambridge University Press, 1986), 1, 33, 77.

46 Deleuze and Guattari, *Anti-Oedipus*, 258.

47 Robert E. Abrams, *Landscape and Ideology in American Renaissance Literature: Topographies of Skepticism* (Cambridge: Cambridge University Press, 2004), 2, 12, 78.

48 Jürgen Habermas, *The Postnational Constellation: Political Essays*, trans. Max Pensky (1998; reprint, Cambridge: MIT Press, 2001), 58–112, 163–172.

49 Etienne Balibar, *We, the People of Europe? Reflections on Transnational Citizenship* (Princeton: Princeton University Press, 2004), 1–2.

50 David Crystal, *English as a Global Language*, 2nd ed. (Cambridge: Cambridge University Press, 2003), 5–7.

51 Appadurai, *Modernity at Large*, 3.

52 See, in particular, Amy Kaplan and Donald E. Pease, ed., *Cultures of United States Imperialism* (Durham, NC: Duke University Press, 1993); and Amy Kaplan, *The Anarchy of Empire in the Making of US Culture* (Cambridge: Harvard University Press, 2002). For a discussion of the different stages of US imperialism, contrasting "the acquisitive, classically colonial wars of 1898" with the "peculiarly anti-geographical ideology of post-nineteenth-century Americanism," see Smith, *American Empire*, 5, xiii.

53 David Harvey, *The New Imperialism* (Oxford: Oxford University Press, 2003), 29.

30

Islamic Literary Networks
in South and Southeast Asia (2010)

Ronit Ricci

Ronit Ricci is lecturer in Asian Studies at the Australian National University and holds a PhD in comparative literature from the University of Michigan. Her research areas extend from alphabet histories in Indonesia, India, and Sri Lanka, to translation studies and comparative and world literature. Ricci's works focus on literary and religious transformations in India and the Indonesian–Malay Archipelago from a global perspective, looking into translation as a means to configure a Muslim world market both transculturally and translinguistically. She has co-edited the collection *Translation in Asia: Theories, Practices, Histories* (2011) and is the author of *Islam Translated: Literature, Conversion, and the Arabic Cosmopolis of South and Southeast Asia* (2011), from which the present essay is adapted. Here Ricci analyzes the forms of literary transmission and translation as Islam spread through South and Southeast Asia, configuring a premodern global cultural community from North Africa to India to the Philippines. Ricci explores the Javanese, Malay, and Tamil adaptations of an Arabic conversion narrative, *The Book of One Thousand Questions*, from the sixteenth century onward, exploring modes of transmission and production that developed the "Arab cosmopolis" of the Muslim world.

Introduction

From its birthplace in Arabia, in the seventh century, Islam spread over vast geographical and cultural distances, emerging as a cosmopolitan religion. Through broad networks of travel, trade and learning, combined with a shared faith and

Ronit Ricci, "Islamic Literary Networks in South and Southeast Asia" (2010). In *Journal of Islamic Studies* 21:1 (2010), pp. 1–28.

World Literature in Theory, First Edition. Edited by David Damrosch.

legal system, people from multiple world regions joined in a universal community. This community had a beating heart in the form of the sacred city, for 'daily and annually across time and space, the history of Islam flows from Mecca and back to Mecca. It flows through myriad networks. They connect individuals and institutions, at once affirming and transforming them.'[1]

Although the central status of Makka cannot be disputed, in this article I discuss a different yet pivotal part of the Muslim world and the history of its networks, which too have served to connect and transform. South and Southeast Asia have been, and remain, crucially important in terms of linguistic and cultural diversity as well as intellectual and literary output. They are also home to the majority of the world's Muslims. A better understanding of the nature of contacts, exchange and transmission between and within these regions offers insight on the broad contours of Islamic history as well as its very local manifestations.

In my discussion I focus primarily on the Tamil-speaking region of Southeast India and the Indonesian-Malay Archipelago with a stress on Sumatra and Java. However, the Islamic cosmopolitan sphere I examine was clearly larger, spanning parts of Sulawesi and Madura, parts of the Philippines and the Subcontinent, communities in Sri Lanka and southern Thailand, much of present-day Malaysia and beyond.[2]

Different kinds of networks, often intertwined, traversed these regions, forging connections between and among individuals and communities. To the oft-mentioned networks of travel, trade, and Sufi brotherhoods, often presented in the scholarship as the paths by which Islam spread and flourished in these regions, I propose adding the literary networks: these connected Muslims across boundaries of space and culture, and helped introduce and sustain a complex web of prior texts and new interpretations, crucial to the establishment of both local and global Islamic identities.

The literary networks I consider were comprised of many shared works, including stories, poems, genealogies, histories, and treatises on a broad range of topics; they also included the readers, listeners, authors, translators and scribes who created the texts, translated and transmitted them, and engaged with them in various ways, thus facilitating the networks, enhancing their reach and significance. Beyond particular texts and individuals, thinking about literary networks also means exploring the multi-layered histories of contacts, selection, interpretation and serendipity that shaped the networks as we have come to know them today.

The literary works I address were told and re-told in local languages which were profoundly influenced and shaped by the influx of Arabic, defined broadly as the bearer of new stories, ideas, beliefs, scripts, and linguistic and literary forms. Such inscribed texts, as well as oral sources, poetics and genres, were to a large extent shared by Muslims across these linguistically and culturally diverse regions. They contributed to the rise of a common repository of images, memories and meaning that in turn fostered a consciousness of belonging to a trans-local community.

The two way connections many literary works had – both to a larger Islamic world and to very local communities – made them dynamic sites of interaction, contestation, and negotiations of boundaries. Competing agendas (as, for example, between creative and standardizing impulses), often played out between their pages.

Islamization was an on-going process in South and Southeast Asia, as it was in many regions. Literary texts of various kinds played an important role in enhancing and shaping this process by introducing those who converted to Islam to their newly acquired faith, history, practices and genealogies as well as by reaffirming the truths of Islam for those who were already members of the universal *umma*. As Muslim societies expanded, additional texts were translated and composed, further enhancing Islamization.

Literature produced within local Muslim communities, and the literary networks that extended across and beyond the local – especially when studied comparatively – provide new insights into the history of Islam in these regions, the balance between local and global elements privileged by particular Muslim authors and societies, and the roles played by literary transmission and translation in their histories.

In the following pages I first briefly discuss Islamization processes in South and Southeast Asia with an emphasis on these regions as interconnected nodal points of material and cultural exchange. I then elaborate on a literary example, the textual tradition of the *Book of One Thousand Questions*, a well known Islamic book, and its translations and adaptations into three major languages of these regions – Javanese, Malay and Tamil – between the sixteenth and twentieth centuries. The *Book of One Thousand Questions* (hereafter the *One Thousand Questions*) provides a lens through which to examine questions of Islamization, networking, and literary and linguistic transformation. It offers a model for the kind of literature, and literary networks, we might study in an attempt to address these broad themes. The *One Thousand Questions* will be explored as an element of what I term, following Pollock's theorization of the Sanskrit cosmopolis, the 'Arabic cosmopolis' of South and Southeast Asia, a trans-local Islamic sphere in which language and literature played major roles.

Islamization in the Indonesian Archipelago and Southeast India and Contacts between These Regions

The spread of Islam in the Indonesian-Malay region was a complex process that has been much debated by scholars, both local and foreign. These have suggested various theories regarding Islam's arrival and acceptance by indigenous populations, based for the most part on archeological findings, travellers' accounts, and local chronicles.

Historical evidence taken together points to a slow and gradual process of Islam's spread: by the end of the thirteenth century it was established in North Sumatra; in the fourteenth century in Northeast Malaya, Brunei, parts of East Java and the Southern Philippines; in the fifteenth century in Malacca and other areas of the Malay Peninsula; and in the sixteenth century the coastal areas of central and East Java were mostly Islamic while its western region and much of the interior was not.[3]

Turning to the Tamil land, archeological evidence suggests an Islamic presence – rooted in Arab trade – in the Coromandel region of Southeast India since the eighth century AD.[4] Nearby Sri Lanka, with its old-rooted Muslim-Tamil population, has also long been associated with the important pilgrimage site of Adam's Peak, the place where, according to early Arab traditions, Adam was believed to have fallen from paradise to earth.[5] Further evidence of the spread of Islam and Muslim life in the region comes from traveller accounts, including those of Marco Polo and Ibn Baṭṭūta.[6]

The influence of Sufis has been viewed as central to the spread of Islam in the Archipelago and South India. With their focus on personal devotion, healing and the charismatic power of teachers and saints, Sufis provided a bridge between the beliefs of non-Muslims and Muslim worship, as they did in many other regions of South and Southeast Asia. Tomb shrines, often associated with Sufi masters, have given rise to devotional cults, which served as a critical force in the expansion of Islam.

Contacts of many kinds provided the material 'backbone' for the emergence of the Islamic literary networks. The coasts of Southeast India and Indonesia were part of the Indian Ocean's commercial networks where goods and shared texts and values crossed the seas carried by Muslim merchants, pilgrims, soldiers and scholars, and where coastal towns, which functioned as important trade centres and ports, developed into major centres of Islamic learning and culture.

For example, in the sixteenth and seventeenth centuries the Sultanate of Banten on Java's northern coast had extensive trade contacts with the Chulias, Muslim traders from the Coromandel coast, many of whom settled in the town.[7] Iron, steel, diamonds and fabrics were exported to Aceh via Masulipatnam from the Persianized kingdom of Golconda in the seventeenth century, in exchange for benzoin, camphor and pepper.[8] Shipping records from Malacca and Nagapattinam in the eighteenth century show the continuing strength of trade from Coromandel to Southeast Asia even in the face of growing European competition, pointing to a 'remarkable persistence of old forms of trade'.[9]

Besides trade, the Muslims of South India and the Archipelago shared a variety of relationships: at least as early as the seventeenth century they had a shared set of pilgrimage sites, some of which are still popular today. Well known in South India is the lineage of the seventeenth century Sufi mystic sheikh Sadaqatullah of Kayalpattinam, whose tomb continues to attract devotees from Malaysia and Indonesia; members of the two communities intermarried, with the Maraikkāyyar, claiming descent from Arab seafarers, preferring intermarriage with the Muslims of the Archipelago over marriage with the lower strata of Tamil Muslim society.[10]

The *madhhab* followed by Javanese and South Indian Muslims living along the coast was one and the same (Shafiʿi); contacts in the sphere of Islamic education appear to have been strong, with similar institutions emerging in Tamil Nadu, Sumatra and Java;[11] Indonesian pilgrims on their way to Arabia used to stop in the Maldives,[12] and in the eighteenth century a Coromandel mosque existed in Batavia. Under colonial auspices contacts – whether through trade or the deployment, employment or exile of subjects – continued.[13]

Of special interest to my discussion are the contacts between Southeast India and the Archipelago as portrayed and understood in literature. Various localities in the Archipelago are mentioned in early Sanskrit and Tamil texts.[14] The lands of Indonesia figure in a significant number of South Indian Sufi legends and chronicles as the place a guru must go to perform feats of forest asceticism, portrayed as a 'sort of exotic wild terrain to test his power to the utmost extent'.[15] India is often mentioned in Javanese and Malay literature as the land 'above the winds' (M. *atas angin*) contrasted with the lands 'below the winds' (M. *bawah angin*), connoting the Archipelago. Bayly notes the similarities between the Javanese tales of the *wali sanga* (the nine 'saints' credited with bringing Islam to Java) and of Tamil teachers fulfilling the same mission.[16]

Following the evidence for sustained contacts between Muslims in Tamil Nadu and the Archipelago and the mutuality of a flow of people, ideas and practices that is found in examples such as those mentioned above, I turn now to a more detailed discussion of the roles played by literary texts that, to a large degree, were shared by Muslims from linguistically and culturally diverse communities in the region. Such works enhanced a sense of common ground and familiarity with a particular vocabulary, idiom and belief system; they also, concurrently, inspired local creativity and provided a means to address local concerns and agendas. For scholars in the present such literature provides a site for examining the ways particular societies articulated how and why Islam was initially accepted, why professing Islam remains important, and how these processes were remembered and understood.

Reading the literature means, in part, being attentive to how language is employed within it and considering what particular modes of usage may suggest. The spread of Islam in the regions discussed here, however distant from the Middle East culturally and geographically, cannot be fully grasped without seriously considering the role of Arabic and the profound changes that its incorporation – at many levels – into local vernaculars has brought about. 'Arabic' must be considered not in a narrow linguistic sense but broadly, including ideas about its sanctity, its resulting un-translatability, and the range of ideas and stories it carried along as its legacy.

A discussion of literary production in Muslim communities, of translation, transmission, literary networks and the emergence of an Islamic cosmopolitan sphere in these regions – shaped to a large degree by language and literature – must include a close look at the impact of Arabic.

I now introduce the lens through which I will examine these issues, the afore-mentioned *Book of One Thousand Questions*. The discussion draws on its myriad versions in Javanese, Tamil and Malay, three languages that to date have not been the focus of a comparative study.[17]

The *Book of One Thousand Questions*: An Introduction

The narrative frame of *One Thousand Questions*'[18] is rather straightforward: a Jewish leader in seventh century Arabia by the name of Abdullah bin Salām[19] meets with the Prophet and informs the Prophet that he wishes to ask him some questions and, should he be convinced by the replies, he and his people will embrace Islam. The questions – spanning multiple topics, from the afterlife to mysticism – are then posed and answered, and the Jews, on realizing that this Prophet is indeed the 'seal of the prophets', convert. Most likely reflecting the intellectual and doctrinal struggle between Jews and Muslims in the early days of Islam's development, the *One Thousand Questions* – with conversion issues at its heart – later circulated far and wide.

The way the story was told and re-told in different languages and cultural contexts provides some insight into the histories and shifting agendas of Muslim communities that emerged far from the birthplace of this story and of their religion. The questions, and the replies, present us with the issues deemed central at particular moments, by particular authors, in particular places, pointing above all – through the conversion narrative – to why one should choose to become and remain a Muslim.

The *One Thousand Questions'* variations – across languages and periods – are numerous and complex. Often the same question, presented by Ibnu Salam to the Prophet in different versions, received different replies – very much context-bound – in different languages. For example, his question about who is destined for hell in the afterlife provided different authors with the opportunity to present depictions of sinners and their punishments in hell. Such depictions, in turn, helped define the boundaries of permitted and forbidden behaviours in living, worldly Muslim societies. In the Tamil region, where Muslims were a small minority, the *One Thousand Questions* emphasized the dire consequences of following non-Muslim local customs like 'praising as God idols of copper and stone'[20] or weeping, falling to the ground and beating one's chest over the body of a deceased relative, as well as listening to music of any kind.

On Java, on the other hand, where versions of the *One Thousand Questions* were inscribed for the most part in the eighteenth and nineteenth centuries when the majority of Javanese professed Islam, authors were less concerned with setting the boundaries between Islam and other traditions. Hell does not figure prominently in these *One Thousand Questions* versions and the list of sinners is quite formulaic, including, among others, Jews, Christians, polytheists, fire-worshippers, and hypocrites. The focus of Javanese authors seems to have lain elsewhere, more in the realm of intra-Muslim, rather than inter-religious debates, showing a tendency to subordinate many themes to an elaborate examination of mystical teachings.

The *One Thousand Questions*: A Brief Translation History

The tenth-century Arabic work first recounting the dialogue between the Prophet and the Jew Ibn al-Salām did not emerge out of the blue.[21] Several centuries of prior texts, circulating in the form of *ḥadīth* (traditions) and Qur'ānic commentaries, lay at its foundations.

The tradition of encounters between the Prophet and the Jews goes back to Qur'ānic passages in which the Prophet is posed with hypothetical questions, and with recommended replies, should the questions be asked. Muslim commentators have interpreted the questions as being posed by challenging Jews, and mention of a Jewish convert to Islam has been taken to refer to Ibn al-Salām, the protagonist of our story.[22] The Qurʾānic citations were later elaborated by some of the earliest writers of Islamic history including Ibn Hishām, Muslim, and al-Tabarī. And so, although the Arabic text of the *One Thousand Questions* dates from the tenth century, tradition locates the germ of the story in the very early and formative period of Islam, and in the context of its most sacred scripture.

The story as told in Arabic changed over time so that a corpus, rather than a single text, must be taken into consideration in any discussion. I mention here some of the significant topics appearing in the Arabic and reappearing – centuries later – in Malay, Javanese and Tamil versions.

The dialogue is framed by the Jews coming to Madina to discuss their questions with the Prophet, who converses with Abdullah until the latter is convinced and converts by uttering the Muslim profession of faith. Qurʾānic quotations are used to support the Prophet's replies. The topics raised include, among many others, prior prophets, God's unity, letter mysticism, and Jerusalem as the navel of the earth.

Interestingly, the first translation of the Arabic text was not into another Muslim language but into Latin, as part of Peter the Venerable's twelfth-century translation project, created to encourage acquaintance with and study of Muslim religious doctrine and literature in Christian Europe, engaged at the time in the Crusades' Holy War. The project, known today as the 'Toledo Collection' included five texts, among them the Qurʾān and the *Book of One Thousand Questions*, translated as *Doctrina Mahumet* by Herman of Dalmatia in 1143.[23]

The Latin version of the text was then translated in the sixteenth and seventeenth centuries into several European languages, including Portuguese, Dutch, Italian, German and French.[24]

Significantly, in several cases, the *Doctrina Mahumet* was published bound in a single volume with the Qurʾān, as had been done originally in Peter the Venerable's project. The Dutch and German editions were printed in the same manner. This suggests that the text was viewed and used in Christian Europe as a supplement to, or commentary on, the Qurʾān, according it great authority. And indeed Bobzin views the text as most influential in shaping European conceptions of Islam.[25]

Also significant, in a similar vein, is the fact that sections of the Latin *One Thousand Questions* were added as a supplement to a 1598 Dutch travel account of the Moluccas (the 'Spice Islands'). Depicted in the travelogue are a local funeral, circumcision and other rituals. The editors used sections of the Latin translation to attempt a better understanding of the culture described.[26] This reliance by the Dutch on the Latin version to explain Islam in Indonesia points once more to this text being viewed as authoritative and comprehensive. This example also shows the non-linear, roundabout ways in which the story travelled and was used and understood. Over a century before Valentijn reported a familiarity with the Malay *One Thousand Questions* on Ambon, its Latin version was incorporated into a Dutch book in that same region.

Throughout the sixteenth to eighteenth centuries the text travelled east and was further translated into additional languages, to be retold across great geographic and cultural distances. Retaining its basic narrative structure and the question and answer format, it differed in many details and emphases in its local tellings, in accordance with specific concerns and agendas. Its title, length, number of questions and some thematic elements were altered as it circulated across regions. The *One Thousand Questions* was translated into Persian, Turkish, Urdu and Tamil.[27] In the Indonesian Archipelago, besides the versions in Javanese and Malay, the text appeared also in Sundanese and Bugis.

In 1847 an Arabic version of the *One Thousand Questions* was translated into English by a Christian missionary working in North Africa, who chose to frame it for his readers with the inaccurate, if provocative, title 'The Errors of Mohammedanism Exposed'.[28]

I now come to the translations of the *One Thousand Questions* that form the focus of my discussion. The single Tamil version, *Āyira Macalā*, was composed by Vaṇṇapparimaḷppulavar, known also by his Muslim name Ceyku Mutali Icukākku. It is considered the earliest complete Muslim text that is extant in Tamil today and has been held in high esteem for several centuries.

The Tamil author of the text based himself on a version by a scholar well versed in Arabic and Persian, in what was likely a collaborative process of translation known also from other Tamil works.[29] Although not stated explicitly the remarkable similarity between the Tamil and Malay versions – based on Persian sources – and the identical title, suggest the Tamil *One Thousand Questions* was based on a Persian source as well, likely one produced in South India itself.[30] It was first read in public in the traditional introductory ceremony of *araṅkērram* in the Madurai court in 1572. The Tamil *One Thousand Questions* is a very poetic work. It reflects the perspective of a minority community that had endured hardship during the period of Portuguese presence in South India (1501–1575). The *One Thousand Questions* is still in print and was last published in 1984 in Madras.

In Javanese the *One Thousand Questions* survives in at least two dozen manuscripts and a print edition from 1913.[31] The earliest extant version dates from the late seventeenth or early eighteenth century, while most manuscripts available today were copied in the nineteenth century. As is typical of Javanese works, it is not uncommon that a date and place of inscription, source language or author remain unmentioned, making it difficult to follow the text's history with certainty. Although many of the questions appearing in other languages appear also in Javanese, its emphasis is on mystical teachings.

Malay poses no less of a complex picture. When Valentijn visited the Moluccas in the early eighteenth century he found there a copy of the Malay text.[32] Pijper lists fifteen manuscripts of the work, kept in the libraries of Leiden, Jakarta and London, with written and published versions appearing from Cairo to Singapore.[33] Several versions claim explicitly to be based on a Persian source, and almost all attribute their origin to the Prophet's uncle ʿAbbās. The story was composed in different genres, including *shāʿir*, *kitāb* and *ḥikāyat*.[34]

Possible shared sites of production for Malay and Javanese versions – like Palembang or Banten – hint at potentially fruitful interactions between authors/translators working in the two languages. A shared claim to a Persian ancestry of Malay and Tamil versions likely accounts for some striking similarities between them.

I have noted how the *One Thousand Questions* travelled far and wide. Let me reiterate the rationale for selecting it as a site for thinking about the role of literature and literary networks in Islamization processes, and in the way Islam was understood and represented in different periods and places.

The *Book of One Thousand Questions* played a role in the inclusion of its audiences within a geographically and culturally diverse Muslim world by introducing and disseminating stories, dialogues, questions, historical and mythic characters, Arabic/Islamic terminology and vocabulary, Qurʾānic quotes, and a gallery of shared images. It was especially well-suited to this role by way of the astonishing scope of materials and issues it raised and addressed; the many intertextual links of these materials to other scriptures, texts, translations and oral traditions; its appeal both to converts and long-time Muslims; the authority of the Prophet lying at its centre; and its dissemination across many cultures and languages.

The *One Thousand Questions*: Forging a New Past for the Present

I now turn to an example of such inclusive roles played by the *One Thousand Questions* across a landscape of expanding literary networks. In particular, I note how intertextuality and the evoking of prior text were widely used by its authors. By 'prior text' I refer, following Alton Becker, to the weaving of older bits of language, stories, figures and events into a text in ways that conjured those earlier materials and associations in the listener.[35] The broad question I address here has to do with how societies in transition, undergoing a profound change such as Islamization, gradually amassed for themselves the textual sources allowing an engagement with, and commitment to, a history only recently adopted; and how translators and authors assembled for their audiences pieces of this long history, initially foreign, in which these audiences would eventually come to be included and which they could begin calling their own.

We may look to a series of questions that I will refer to here as the 'number questions' as an example. Ibnu Salam asks the Prophet what is one, not two ... what is two, not three ... going from one to thirty; he then continues in the same vein, proceeding by tens and asking what is thirty, not forty ... what is forty, not fifty ... all the way to one hundred.[36]

These number questions, in various forms, appear in early Arabic *One Thousand Questions* versions, in the twelfth-century Latin translation, and in other languages, including Tamil and Malay. The questions in the latter two languages are almost identical. When they do differ it is mostly in detail, style or emphasis, not theme.

The replies to the 'number questions' in Tamil and Malay – thirty-seven in all – offer a brief mapping of several domains that in turn gain their own references from additional textual sources. The themes addressed include, among others, God's unity, cosmology, cosmogony, histories of the prophets, and a Muslim understanding of time. The latter two topics occupy the prominent positions within this condensed presentation of Islam.

There are seventeen questions – almost half of the total number – that address the lives and deeds of the prophets: for example, the number nine stands for the number of times God revealed himself to Moses; eleven are Joseph's brothers; Moses was born on the twenty-second of the month of Ramaḍān, while on its twenty-seventh day Jonah was swallowed by the fish. The brief presentation of these prophets offers the kernel of their life story – Jonah and the fish, Idrīs ascending to the sky – as known and elaborated in the much longer, detailed and popular renditions of the prophets' biographies.

Addressing Muslim notions of time occurs through, for example, the replies on the number five (number of daily prayers), six (days of creation), seven (days of the week), twelve (months of the year), and, most notably, the various days of the month of Ramaḍān on which auspicious events occurred: the fifteenth (the Prophet received the Qurʾān), the twentieth (David received Pslams), the twenty-first (Solomon received his ring), the twenty-second (Moses' birth), the twenty-third (Jesus received the Gospel), the twenty-fifth (Moses crossed the Red Sea, escaping Pharaoh's army), the twenty-sixth (the Torah was revealed to Moses), and the thirtieth (God spoke to Moses).

Found here is an incorporation of various dimensions of time, from the divisions of a single day to the days of the week and the annual cycle of months, to a larger sacred history condensed into the holy month of Ramaḍān, during which so many events significant to Muslim history are said to have occurred. The first theme – that of the prophets' lives – is linked to notions of time through the days of Ramaḍān, with Moses providing the most pronounced connection due to his frequent mention. Audiences attentive to this list of questions and answers received an abbreviated introduction to their prophets, the structures of time that guide Muslim lives and to the way the two are intertwined in the ritual and moral observances of the fasting month.

Other matters are addressed only briefly in this question series, yet together the 'number questions' and their replies strengthen the impression that for the reader/ listener an entire picture emerged, its details ranging from the four holy scriptures to the punishment of one hundred blows inflicted on those who commit *zinā*.[37]

In their intertextual drawing on Qurʾānic verses, the canonical tradition and Islamic law, the 'number questions' present a web of meanings and associations in which history and memory play a major role. The connection made between the days of Ramaḍān and so many central events and figures collapses the boundaries between past and present and draws the listener closer to a past of mythical proportions with which he can now more strongly identify. The 'number questions' are a 'mini-guide' of sorts or, even more pertinently, we may see in them a 'mini-*Book of One Thousand Questions*' in which the important facets covered in the text as a whole are put forth in abbreviated form, appropriate for both new converts and practising Muslims.

The *One Thousand Questions* includes many additional instances of linking together past and present, familiar and foreign. It presents not only the on-going dialogue between the Prophet and Ibnu Salam but an entire set of figurative dialogues among prior texts and contemporary events, overlapping and interacting, connecting and diverging in subtle and explicit ways. The letter from the Prophet inviting Ibnu Salam to a debate in the *One Thousand Questions'* opening scene resonates with a powerful and consistent thread within the Muslim imagination: accounts of letters from the Prophet – addressed to kings, potential converts and subsequent generations of Muslims – appeared in the canonical *ḥadīth* collections, law books and local literary works, with one such letter, known in nineteenth century Java as *serat wasiat* ('last testament of the Prophet') circulating widely.[38]

Written in simple Arabic, then translated into Malay, it originated in Islam's centres in Arabia and contained a message from the Prophet, transmitted via Abdullah, the guardian of his tomb. The message was revealed in a dream and depicted a dialogue between the Prophet and God in which the former requested divine intervention on behalf of all Muslims, listed moral and sinful behaviours and warned of the approach of the Final Judgment. The letter circulated widely in West Java in 1884 and a similar one appeared in 1891. This latter document was copied by hand and also printed for wider dissemination in Singapore and Penang.[39]

The two examples discussed, the 'number questions' and the Prophet's letter, highlight how the story told in the *One Thousand Questions* was connected in multiple ways to other textual (and, most likely oral) sources, providing its audiences with important links to a larger cultural landscape and to a sense of the depth and richness of their shared history. In both examples the bonds of time and space were loosened so that this shared history – with the Prophet as its axis – became more accessible to contemporary Muslims in distant lands. For scholars, examining the details of this web of meanings offers clues to linguistic and literary dissemination histories and genealogies and geographies of transmission.

The *One Thousand Questions* not only reached outward, towards broader, translocal Muslim frames of reference, but was, in some ways, also inwardly directed, moving towards the local, the culturally specific. An elaborate account of fetal development throughout the nine months of pregnancy and a comparison between human gestation and divine creation included in Javanese *One Thousand Questions* versions ring familiar from popular texts like the *Niti Mani*; we also find echoes of the *Serat Kridhaksara*, a treatise on the origin and meaning of the Javanese alphabet in sections that map Arabic, rather than Javanese, letters onto the human body.[40]

The engagement of these themes in the Javanese *One Thousand Questions* is an instance of how this trans-regional story also put down strong local roots. It provides an example of how prior, non-Islamic Javanese text (on cosmogony, the alphabet) was reshaped and incorporated into a widely known Islamic work, and of how this work – the *One Thousand Questions* – was interconnected with other specifically Javanese texts through common references, allusions and themes.

I have discussed examples of the notions of prior text and intertextuality and how they participated in shaping a multi-layered, interconnected Islamic literary world, presenting audiences with repeated mention of certain ideas, characters and themes that both tied them to their local community and to a wider, trans-local one possessing a common history. I now examine more closely the contours of the latter, larger Islamic sphere, which emerged in South India and the Archipelago, itself part of a geographically even greater Islamic cosmopolitan civilization.

Literary Networks and the Arabic Cosmopolis

To the common discussions of Muslim networks of trade, scholarship, politics and travel I have proposed adding the literary networks, through which Muslims of different places and cultures were – however symbolically – connected. My stress in thinking about these links is centred on the ways in which literature and language participated in creating, forging and sustaining such networks, which extended across both time and space.

When discussing 'language', or 'the linguistic', I am thinking here of the many ways in which Islam, most notably via the Arabic language, has had an impact on Javanese, Tamil and Malay. This impact must be examined in a context in which, for Muslims worldwide, Arabic possesses a unique status among languages. It is considered the perfect tongue, in which God's divine decrees were communicated to His Prophet. Consequently, at least ideally, the Qurʾān is considered untranslatable and Arabic works more generally are held in high esteem.[41]

Muslims in South and Southeast Asia proved no exception in their reverence for the Arabic language, setting up institutions where it could be studied, adopting its script for their own languages, borrowing its religious terminology and everyday vocabulary, praying in it and embracing its literary and historical narratives and forms. As a result, when we consider an Islamic cosmopolitanism in these regions, Arabic features as one of its major elements. Translation, too, emerges as one of its foundational practices.

Sheldon Pollock's work on the 'Sanskrit cosmopolis' provides an inspiring and useful framework for thinking about the diverse regions discussed here, the long time period over which Islamization unfolded in them, and the powerful roles of language and literature in shaping Muslim communities and consciousness.

Pollock introduced the concept of the 'Sanskrit cosmopolis' of 300–1300 AD, claiming a unique political and cultural status for that language, which developed almost simultaneously across large parts of India and Southeast Asia. He then charted the history of the transition from the use of the cosmopolitan Sanskrit in literary works to the emergence of vernacular literary cultures and compared the process to the one that unfolded in Europe, where Latin was replaced by vernacular production.[42] The major goals of his study were to examine the rise and spread of Sanskrit inscriptions, the formation of vernacular literary cultures and the ways the vernacular not only reconfigured the cosmopolitan language but also how the two produced each other in the course of their interaction.[43] I adopt his cosmopolis model, however loosely, to think about the ways in which another cosmopolitan language – Arabic – rose to prominence in some of the same regions at a later period.

Thinking about Arabic in these regions means assessing a continuum or an on-going process. It means looking not only at the scope of materials produced but also at the range of ways in which Arabic's role was played out in particular languages, texts and scripts: from works composed solely in Arabic and the use of the language in private and public spheres, through interlinear translations, to the ways in which Arabic was integrated into the vernacular. The latter category is at the centre of my present analysis. My focus on Arabicized – rather than strictly Arabic – language and literary cultures includes the wide range of instances in which Arabic influence on local languages is evident, with Arabic combining with, rather than replacing, those languages.

This phenomenon is, I believe, strongly linked to the phenomenon discussed by Pollock for an earlier period: throughout South India and Java during the Sanskrit cosmopolis era local languages were absorbing much Sanskrit vocabulary, literary conventions, genres and themes. Works were written, very consciously, in hybrid forms of language. Compositions in *Maṇippiravāḷam*, a metaphorical and linguistic stringing together of Sanskrit 'pearls' (S. *maṇi*) and Tamil 'coral' (T. *piravāḷam*) on a single necklace, highlighted the beauty and expressiveness of both while maintaining a line of distinction.[44] In Java the Kawi language combined an old form of Javanese with Sanskrit, producing literary works considered to this day among the most intricate and captivating of Javanese literature.

Thus the tendency to adopt an initially foreign vocabulary, along with themes, styles, ideas and stories, was not at all new in this region. A long history – not only of linguistic borrowing but of such combined literary production – was already in place when Arabic was introduced by traders, theologians, travellers and translated works. I'd like to suggest that the processes which produced Kawi, for example, prepared the ground in an important way for the elaborate and deep adaptation of Muslim textual models into Javanese. Linguistic change and borrowing are of course not in any way unique to this case but the extent to which they took place – first with Sanskrit, later with Arabic, providing historical continuity – is far-ranging and impressive in its scope. In both cases the combinations emerging from the use of a cosmopolitan language along with a local one opened up new and intriguing possibilities.

An additional way to think of the Arabicized languages is to consider language primarily as a 'mode of discourse that draws on a particular cultural and religious tradition' as Zaman does in his discussion of the language of the ulema, the traditional religious Muslim scholars. Beginning with Ibn Baṭṭūṭa but focusing his study on scholars of the early twentieth century and their 'language', he notes the 'existence and efficacy of a shared and longstanding language of discourse and learning, of shared ideas about what constituted valuable knowledge and how such knowledge was articulated, preserved and transmitted'. The adoption and use of so much Arabic – in both strictly linguistic and broader ways – by Muslim speakers of Tamil, Malay and Javanese, can be understood similarly as a shared meta-mode of discourse.[45]

A major difference between the Sanskrit cosmopolis and the Arabic one had to do with the fact that 'Sanskrit was not diffused by a single, scripture-based religion',[46] a condition which was clearly central to the spread of Arabic. Despite this substantial difference both were similar in that no organized political power, no colonial enterprise, no military conquest, nor large migration were involved in their diffusion. There also seems to have been an affinity between the understanding of both languages as forms of powerful, potent speech capable of altering and affecting human reality.

Pollock coined the term 'cosmopolitan vernaculars' to label emergent regional literary languages like Kannada or Marathi that conformed to a superposed model established in the cosmopolitan Sanskrit tradition in everything from lexicon and versification to figures, genres and themes.[47] As is well known, vernacular writing and literary texts were already in existence in Javanese and Tamil long before the arrival of Islam (a result, in part, of the Sanskrit cosmopolis epoch) and Malay too has recently been shown to have possessed local systems of writing which preceded the use of *jawi*.[48] For Javanese and Tamil especially (for which much more evidence of the early literary traditions survives) no claim can be made that a vernacular literary tradition first arose in the shadow of Arabic, as Pollock claims for Kannada as influenced by Sanskrit. However, there is no doubt that Arabic deeply affected and reshaped linguistic and literary practices, making these languages – as used by Muslim authors and audiences – into vernaculars linked to a different cosmopolitan order than that to which they had previously belonged.

Arabic, then, inaugurated both a new cosmopolitan age and a new vernacular one. In terms of the comparison I draw here its diffusion and impact resemble most closely the developments Pollock describes for the early vernacular age. At that time Sanskrit provided the ultimate code for local literary cultures that, through emula-tion, competition and imaginative selection, were developing in their own, independent directions. The later interactions between Arabic and vernaculars like Tamil or Malay provide an example of 'a strong tendency with wider application, perhaps even a law: it is only in response to a superposed and prestigious form of preexistent literature that a new vernacular literature develops'.[49] Such develop-ments, in turn, are closely related to Pollock's aim of examining not only how the vernacular reconfigures the cosmopolitan or vice versa but how the two produce each other in the course of their interaction.[50]

Rather than think, as has been the common practice, solely of the ways in which, for example, Javanese has been Arabicized by the contact with speakers and writers of Arabic and Islamic sources, we may also think of how Arabic itself, in such a setting, was 'vernacularized'. The spelling, pronunciation and often also the meaning of Arabic words changed markedly when adopted into Javanese, with Arabic literary genres and themes also taking on a local twist. For audiences who were unfamiliar with the vocabulary as well as grammatical and syntactical elements of 'real' Arabic, this form of the language *was* Arabic. Such audiences across South and Southeast Asia were by no means negligible in size and importance and they – along with their forms of vernacularized Arabic – formed an integral component of the cosmopolis.

In addition, many Muslims from these regions participated in networks of shaykhs, Sufi gurus, theologians, reformers and disciples from across the Muslim world who converged on Makka for the ḥajj pilgrimage and often for longer periods of stay and study. We know that the neighbourhood of Southeast Asians in the sacred city, known as *kampong Jawah*, was the largest of any visiting groups in the mid-nineteenth century and that no language besides Arabic was as widely understood there at the time as Malay.[51] From this we may deduce that not only in distant lands but also in Islam's historical heartland, Arabic was being influenced by the various vernaculars as it was in turn changing them.

* * *

Arabic then, with its many manifestations within the literary worlds of Muslims in the region, played a major role in creating and maintaining literary networks within a sphere of shared idioms, ideas and stories. The 'literary' is here considered in a broad sense that encompasses written, oral and aural materials which connected Muslims across the Arabic cosmopolis. The rise and spread of Arabic's influence cannot be significantly gleaned – as is the case for Sanskrit – from royal inscriptions. But examples of its dissemination abound.

The vocabulary of Islamic texts is infused with Arabic; also everyday speech – especially in Javanese and Malay – is laden with it. This includes the language of both the sacred and the ordinary, like daily greetings, the names of the days of the week and personal names. Arabic's influence on grammatical structures – often via inter-linear translation – is evident, as well as its impact on poetics and literary genres.

All three languages discussed here adopted modified forms of the Arabic script, used for translated as well as original writings. An important feature of the cosmopolis, this orthographic transformation allowed Muslims in diverse locales to experience their own languages in the shared, religiously charged form of Arabic.[52]

Beyond the realm of manuscripts and books Arabic script was to be found in the Archipelago above all on tombstones. In the Tamil region Arabic epitaphs in Kayalpatnam, dating from the fifteenth century, record names and Hijri death dates. Some include sections of religious text, genealogies, and occupations like *qāḍī* (judge), *amīr* (military title), *sādr* (local governor) and *tājir* (learned merchant), employing the Arabic titles of the kind routinely adopted by rulers, members of the nobility and literary figures in both Southern India and the Archipelago.[53]

The literary networks that crisscrossed the Arabic cosmopolis of South and Southeast Asia were determined and defined not solely by the use of a certain 'amount' of Arabic but by the type of works disseminated and the extent of that dissemination. Islamic theological, grammatical and moral works were told in local languages, as were the deeds and adventures of early Muslim warriors and kings. A popular example of the latter can be found in the many volumes depicting the life of Amīr Ḥamza, one of the Prophet's uncles, in Javanese and Malay. Tales of the Prophet's Companions and earlier prophets were widespread. The stories narrating the life of the Prophet himself were of course pivotal to such literary networks. Central episodes from his biography – his birth, ascent to the heavens, splitting of the moon, and his death – became cornerstones in an early history that came to be shared by all who followed his path, no matter their mother tongue.

Not only were literary works translated and adapted into regional languages but there is evidence of single textual sources being written in more than one of the region's languages. Complex combinations were created: for example, some Tamil poets composed multi-lingual verses comprised of Arabic, Persian and Urdu, in addition to Tamil. A book on Islamic medicine, inscribed in 1807 and currently in the Indonesian National Library collection, was written in four languages as well: Javanese, Persian, Tamil and Arabic.[54] Such multiple language volumes were an additional contribution to bridging linguistic gaps between Muslims from different communities, which enhanced the creation of shared repositories of knowledge.

Educational institutions played an important role in fostering a sense of shared identity within the cosmopolis. In religious educational centres Arabic and its branches of learning – grammar, syntax, Islamic jurisprudence, Qur'ānic exegesis, ḥadīth – were routinely taught to new generations of pupils. Madrasas in South India and *pesantren* on Java and Sumatra provided a similar structure for learning – from the very basics of Arabic to highly specialized knowledge – and for bonding with Islamic scholars and other members of the community. From their ranks often emerged the religious officials, leaders and teachers who would in turn train and inform their own disciples.

Religious teachers often travelled in a quest to disseminate their knowledge and religious convictions to others, expanding the geographical and cultural limits of the cosmopolis. It is known from the *Sejarah Melayu* ('Malay Annals') that Tamil Muslim teachers were influential in the Malay regions in the fifteenth century. The *Annals* also claim – as does the *Hikayat Raja-Raja Pasai* ('Book of the Pasai Kings') – that the apostles of Islam reached Malay shores from the Coromandel coast.[55] Shuʿayb discusses at length the deeds of Umar Wali, a Tamil 'saint' who spent years in the forests of Sumatra, propagating Islam;[56] Bayly mentions a Tamil *pīr* from Vetalai who, while meditating in a Sumatran jungle, encountered and overcame a fierce elephant. In gratitude the sultan granted him his daughter in marriage and nominated him as successor to the Achehnese sultanate;[57] Javanese nobles and their retinues, exiled to Sri Lanka from the eighteenth century onwards, brought with them – if not in written, certainly in oral form – stories and traditions which were eventually shared with other Muslims on the island.[58] Although the historical accuracy of some of these developments cannot always be determined with certainty, such traditions attest to a sustained memory of participation in promoting Arabicized networks of language, literature and learning that connected Muslims across the region.

In discussing such connecting ties mention must be made of the wide-ranging spiritual and intellectual networks of the Sufis. Individual masters, and to an even greater extent the various schools of mysticism which coalesced into Sufi orders, 'knitted together widely scattered communities with shared literatures and spiritual genealogies'.[59] Similar stories relating the tolerance of Sufi masters towards non-Islamic forms of worship and their powers of healing, their supernatural perceptions and generosity towards the poor, circulate in different regions and strengthen the impression that these figures played a central role in introducing local populations to aspects of Islam that are broadly shared among them, including a reverence towards 'saints' and an emphasis on hagiographic literature.

Although the Muslim communities discussed here no doubt had a strong sense of attachment to their particular locales, there were also ways in which a sense of place or space transcended the local towards the wider region and beyond. A shared notion of sacred space (differing from that found in Western Asia or North India) is evident in the architectural resemblances among the fifteenth century Great Mosque of Demak, the eighteenth century Selo mosque in Yogyakarta, the mosques of South India including those of Kayalpatnam and the Malabar coast (fourteenth century onwards), as well as the eighteenth century Kampong Laut mosque in Kelantan, Malaysia.[60]

In a way parallel to that which I noted for Islamic literature, through which a distant and foreign history gradually became familiar by way of translation and the introduction of bits of prior text, within the sacred space of the mosques an attempt was sometimes made to introduce and recreate a faraway geography of great importance and sanctity for the local, often recently-converted, faithful. For example, the three-lobed *mihrāb*s of the mosques in Madura and Kayalpatnam, of a type uncommon in India, are modelled on the *mihrāb* in Jerusalem's Dome of the Rock.[61] A related yet more remarkable instance is found in Kudus, on Java's Northern coast. The sole place in Java to adopt an Arabic name, it bears that of Islam's third most sacred city, Jerusalem (A. *al-Quds*).

The town's mosque, erected in the sixteenth century by Sunan Kudus, is known to this day as *Mesjid al-Aqsa*, the name of Jerusalem's ancient mosque built on the Temple Mount, where the Prophet is believed to have passed on his Night Journey to the heavens. The mosque's foundational charter, inscribed in Arabic and said to have been brought from Jerusalem by Sunan Kudus himself, may be interpreted as drawing a parallel between this leader in an Islamizing Java and the biblical unifier of Jerusalem, King David.[62]

In Java localization through site names was apparently uncommon, but in this case a distant, sacred city and its holy mosque were erected anew in Java, mapping a centre of Islamic piety and sanctity upon it. Sunan Kudus' journey to Jerusalem represented a venture into a larger Islamic world. It resulted in the enrichment and authentication of the Arabic cosmopolis he belonged to, linking it explicitly to the historical heartland while declaring its own centrality.

The Kudus inscription points us to a political role accorded to Arabic within the cosmopolis as it was chosen, without the more typical translation act, to legitimize the ruler of a new Islamic centre likely modelled on Jerusalem, ruled and rebuilt at the time by another leader of an expanding Islamic power, Suleiman the Magnificent.

Another case in point is the account of the famed Sunan Kalijaga orienting Java's first mosque (1479, Demak) and the mosque in Makka towards one another, figuring in many Javanese chronicles. It too attests to important notions of space, directionality of power within the Muslim world, and the claims made by members of the cosmopolis regarding their place and role within and beyond it as sanctified histories and geographies were adopted as their own.[63]

Taken together, textual accounts, inscriptions and epitaphs attest to the many ways in which Arabic and Arabicized language participated in the creation of new understandings of space, community and authority.

And so, despite the many differences that continued to exist among Muslim communities of various origins within the cosmopolis, they also shared a great deal. Central to trans-local ties were a reverence towards, and certain familiarity with, Arabic language and terminology, Arabic's textual world, and religious figures representing Islam, all of which fostered a common bond. The sheer volume and scope of Arabic and Arabicized materials in the region is testimony to their centrality.

All these instances unfolded within the larger framework not only of the Arabic cosmopolis of South and Southeast Asia where Muslims read and listened to versions of the *One Thousand Questions* in their own languages but also in the context of a global Muslim culture which emphasized the power of language to a great extent: God's creative powers were condensed in and expressed through the single imperative *kun* and His words were recorded for all future generations in the Qurʾān. It is these fundamental beliefs in the power of words that in large part gave rise to, and sustained, the ideals and practices in the linguistic and literary spheres that developed among Tamil, Javanese and Malay Muslims.

Shifting Cosmopolitanisms

These regions of South and Southeast Asia – as a corner of a larger Muslim world and as an area with its own networks and characteristics – were not in any way static. On the contrary, they were constantly shifting, both internally and in relation to other regions of this global sphere. A textual corpus like the *Book of One Thousand Questions* allows us to examine how agendas were set differently for different Muslim communities while, concurrently, a certain process of standardization was taking place, shaping shared perceptions and allegiances.

Not only was the Muslim-Arabic cosmopolis of South and Southeast Asia discussed here shifting according to the specifics of time and place but it was also never a singular entity in the region: overlapping, intertwining, waxing and waning cosmopolitan worlds developed and were not mutually exclusive. Some, like the Sanskrit cosmopolis analysed by Pollock, had language as a central component. Persian is another case in point. As the result of a constant interaction between the 'literary matrices of India, on the one hand, and of Iran, Afghanistan and Central Asia on the other', Persian gradually emerged as the vehicle of rule, poetry and administration in north India, recognized as the language of politics and cultural accomplishment in nearly the whole of the Subcontinent.[64] This linguistic and cultural influence was deeply felt in the Tamil region and beyond, with important textual sources – including the *One Thousand Questions* – translated from Persian into Tamil and Malay. Other cosmopoleis, like the Arabic one, or the Buddhist one studied by Monius, were centred around religion, with language playing a greater or lesser role, depending on the circumstances. A vivid example of how the Islamic cosmopolitan sphere of South and Southeast Asia with its literary networks connected and overlapped with the Arab world is found in the history of the Hadrami diaspora. Its networks based on trade, writing and kinship have long traversed the broad regions here discussed.[65]

Concluding Thoughts

Reading a story like the *Book of One Thousand Questions* – in a way a literary network in its own right – points us to various kinds of interactions. There are those – as in the cases of Javanese and Malay – between the different versions and copies of the story that make up the extended corpus in each language. These offer lessons about changes over time in a local community and different interpretations by speakers of the same language who reside in different places or belong to particular schools of thought.

There are the connections across languages which are highlighted through common use of words and phrases, common themes raised and addressed in the dialogue between Ibnu Salam and the Prophet, and a shared narrative frame and structure. In the *One Thousand Questions* versions such similarities are especially evident in the comparison between Malay and Tamil tellings, which likely hark back to a common Persian source or even contact between Tamil and Malay traders or travellers visiting each other's lands.[66]

In addition to links within and beyond language and place are temporal links that define the story's regional histories. Almost three and a half centuries separate the composition of the Tamil *One Thousand Questions* (1572) and the most recent copies, from the early twentieth century, preserved in Malay and Javanese. These years span fundamental changes in the region among which the domination of colonial European powers over local political and economic systems is no doubt pivotal.

These different types of links that establish a literary network – whether of a single story, a corpus or an array of related texts – create a kind of meta-intertextuality that extends distances both great and small. The distance is not necessarily geographical, since many worlds can exist in one place at one time, as when Muslim and non-Muslim Tamils shared sacred pilgrimage sites and derived inspiration from texts using similar literary conventions but calling upon different divine powers for mercy.[67] The distance can also be physically or temporally vast, as when Ibnu Salam's tale of conversion was recounted in different languages and during different centuries in India and Java. All such connections – in their multiple dimensions – were elements in an on-going process that gave rise to a shared cosmopolis of ideas, beliefs, idioms and stories.

Notes

1   'Introduction' in miriam cooke and Bruce B. Lawrence (eds.), *Muslim Networks from Hajj to Hip Hop* (Chapel Hill: University of North Carolina Press, 2005), 1.
2   I have opted to base my arguments, first and foremost, on the primary sources linguistically available to me. Citing secondary sources on additional Islamic cultures in South and Southeast Asia would expand the range of sites discussed but, in my view, result in more diffuse and less solid claims. It is my hope that further research in additional regional languages will complement and nuance the picture I present here.

3   M.C. Ricklefs, *A History of Modern Indonesia since c. 1300* (Stanford: Stanford University Press, 1993), 4–13.

4   Susan Elizabeth Schomburg, ' "Reviving Religion" ': The Qadiri Sufi Order, Popular Devotion to Sufi Saint Muhyiuddin 'Abdul Qadir Al-Gilani, and Processes of "Islamization" in Tamil', PhD diss. (Harvard, 2003), 19–20.

5   'Ādam', art. *EI²*: i. 176–178, at 177b.

6   Takya Shu'ayb 'Alim, *Arabic, Arwi and Persian in Sarandib and Tamil Nadu* (Madras: Imamul 'Arus Trust, 1993), 21.

7   Claude Guillot, 'Banten and the Bay of Bengal During the Sixteenth and Seventeenth Centuries' in Om Prakash and Denys Lombard (eds.), *Commerce and Culture in the Bay of Bengal, 1500–1800* (New Delhi: Manohar, Indian Council of Historical Research, 1999), 163–181.

8   Denys Lombard, 'The Indian World as Seen from Acheh in the Seventeenth Century' in *ibid.*, 186.

9   Sinnappah Arasaratnam, 'The Chulia Muslim Merchants in Southeast Asia, 1650–1800' in Sanjay Subrahmanyam (ed.), *Merchant Networks in the Early Modern World* (Aldershot: Variorum, 1996), 139.

10 Susan Bayly, 'Islam and State Power in Pre-Colonial South India' in P. J. Marshall, Robert Van Niel *et al.* (eds.), *India and Indonesia During the Ancien Regime* (Leiden: Brill, Comparative History of India and Indonesia, III, 1989), 145.

11 For example, Umar Wali, an eighteenth-century Tamil scholar of Arabic and Islamic law went to Sumatra in 1763 and spent fourteen years there. According to Tamil sources he established a number of madrasas there, locally called *pasenthiran*.

12 Shu'ayb 'Alim, *Arabic, Arwi and Persian*, 26.

13 Raffles noted that native soldiers often served first in India, then Java, and mentioned the quarters of Javanese soldiers in Calcutta. Thomas Stamford Raffles, *The History of Java by the Late Sir Thomas Stafford Raffles*, F.R.S. (London: John Murray, 1830, 2 vols.), i. 224–225.

14 Southeast Asia is mentioned in the second-century Tamil epic *Cilappatikāram*. Even more pertinent here is the suggestion that Maṇimēkalai, heroine of the Tamil epic by that title, was 'an indigenous Southeast Asian deity'. Monius states that 'although the details of the transmission of the story of Maṇimēkalai, *whether from South to Southeast Asia or vice versa*, will probably never be known, the presence of the goddess … in a variety of languages and literary forms is certainly suggestive of a discrete cultural/literary region extending from South India through mainland and maritime Southeast Asia …' Anne E. Monius, *Imagining a Place for Buddhism: Literary Culture and Religious Community in Tamil-Speaking South India* (Oxford: Oxford University Press, 2001), 112 (my emphasis). On references to Southeast Asia in early Sanskrit literature see H. B. Sarkar, 'A Geographical Introduction to Southeast Asia: The Indian Perspective', *Bijdragen tot de Taal-, Land- en Volkenkunden*, 137/2–3 (1981): 293–323.

15 Bayly, 'Islam and State Power in Pre-Colonial South India', 143–164.

16 *Ibid.*, 153–4; Susan Bayly, *Saints, Goddesses and Kings: Muslims and Christians in South Indian Society 1700–1900* (Cambridge: Cambridge University Press, 1989), 74, 117.

17 In an 1883 lecture Snouck Hurgronje proposed that Indonesian Islam's origins lay in South India, an idea he developed further in his 1894 work on Achehnese culture. Seventy-five years later, G.W.J. Drewes lamented that further investigation of the matter had not been attempted: 'New Light on the Coming of Islam to Indonesia?', *Bijdragen tot de Taal-, Land- en Volkenkunden*, 124/4 (1968): 433–459.

18 The major versions consulted are, in Tamil: Cayitu 'Hassan' Muhammad (ed.), *Āyira Macalā: Islāmiyat Tamiḻ Ilakkiya Ulakiṉ Mutaṟ Kappiyam* (Madras: M. Itris Maraikkayar, 1984); in Malay: Edwar Djamaris (ed.), *Hikayat Seribu Masalah* (Jakarta: Pusat Pembinaan dan Pengembangan Bahasa Departemen Pendidikan dan Kebudayaan, 1994); in Javanese (both anonymous): *Serat Samud* (Pura Pakualaman Library Yogyakarta, 1884), MS. St. 80, *Serat Suluk Samud Ibnu Salam*, Museum Sono Budoyo Library (Yogyakarta, 1898; transcribed 1932), MS. P173a. Additional versions are mentioned below.

19 In Malay he is known as Abdullah bin Salām; in Tamil as Aptullā Ipuṉu Calām; and in Javanese as Ibnu Salam or Samud. For the sake of convenience I use Abdullah or Ibnu Salam when discussing the non-Arabic texts.

20 Muhammad (ed.), *Āyira Macalā*, verse 555.

21 Arabic texts recounting this story possess various titles. For the purpose of this article I have consulted *Kitāb Masāʾil Sayyidi ʿAbdillāh ibn al-Salām li-l-Nabī* (Cairo: al-Yūsufiyya, *ca.* 1920). On Arabic versions see Guillaume Frederic Pijper, *Het Boek Der Duizend Vragen* (Leiden: Brill, 1924), 35–54.

22 For mention of this convert, see Qurʾān 46. 10.

23 This was the first complete translation of the Qurʾān into any language. James Kritzeck, *Peter the Venerable and Islam* (Princeton: Princeton University Press, 1964).

24 On the Portuguese and Dutch see Pijper, *Het Boek Der Duizend Vragen*, 8–9; on the Italian, German and French see Hartmut Bobzin, *Der Koran im Zeitalter Der Reformation* (Stuttgart: Steiner, 1995), 334–335.

25 *Ibid.* I thank Gottfried Hagen for his assistance in translating relevant passages from German.

26 Karel A. Steenbrink, *Dutch Colonialism and Indonesian Islam. Contacts and Conflicts 1596–1950*, trans. C. Jansen and H. Steenbrink (Amsterdam: Rodopi, 1993), 31–33.

27 The Persian texts possessed various titles, among them *Hazār Masālah* (One Thousand Questions). The Turkish was known as *Kerk Sual* (Forty Questions) and the Urdu as *Hazār Masālah*. On the Tamil version see below.

28 N. Davis, *The Errors of Mohammedanism Exposed or, a Dialogue between the Arabian Prophet and a Jew* (Malta: G. Muir, 1847).

29 See Muhammad, *Āyira Macalā*: verse 29 in the Invocation. For several examples of such 'collaborative translation' see Schomburg, '"Reviving Religion"', 650–664.

30 On Persian versions, including those produced in South India, see Pijper, *Het Boek Der Duizend Vragen*, 55–62.

31 For an annotated list of these sources see Ronit Ricci, 'Translating Conversion in South and Southeast Asia: The Islamic *Book of One Thousand Questions* in Javanese, Tamil and Malay' (PhD diss., University of Michigan, 2006), 405–411.

32 Anthony Reid, 'Islamization and Christianization in Southeast Asia: The Critical Phase, 1550–1650', in Anthony Reid (ed.), *Southeast Asia in the Early Modern Era* (Ithaca: Cornell University Press, 1993), 170.

33 Pijper, *Het Boek Der Duizend Vragen*, 72–78.

34 The text is attributed to a Persian source in, for example, Djamaris, *Hikayat Seribu Masalah*, 18.

35 A.L. Becker, *Beyond Translation: Essays Towards a Modern Philology* (Ann Arbor: University of Michigan Press, 1995), 285–288.

36 This is highly reminiscent of the Hebrew Song *Echad Mi Yodea* ('Who Knows What is One'), appearing towards the end of the Passover Haggadah. This is only one among

several major haggadic elements incorporated into the *Book of One Thousand Questions*. We may mention here that the Haggadah – the text read on the eve of Passover recounting the Israelites' exodus from Egypt – is framed by a set of questions that the child – who is young and inexperienced and can be likened to the disciple Ibnu Salam – asks his parent (likely the father) who is an elder, teacher, authority figure, like the Prophet; the transformative journey from slavery to freedom can be likened to the one from Judaism to Islam; and there are additional thematic and structural similarities.

37 Meaning, fornication or adultery.

38 Sartono Kartodirdjo, *The Peasants' Revolt of Banten in 1888*, ('S-Gravenhage: Martinus Nijhoff, 1966); Verhandelingen van Het Koninklijk Instituut voor Taal-, Land-en Volkenkunde, 50, 167.

39 Karel A. Steenbrink, *Beberapa Aspek Tentang Islam Di Indonesia Abad Ke-19* (Jakarta: Bulan Bintang, 1984), 254–267.

40 Anonymous, undated *Serat Kridhaksara*, Museum Sono Budoyo Library (Yogyakarta), MS. P93. The *Niti Mani* was composed in 1886; Arya Sugonda, *Niti Mani* (Surakarta: Albert Rusche and Co., 1919).

41 On the question of the Qurʾān's translatability see A.L. Tibawi, 'Is the Qurʾān Translatable?', *The Muslim World* 52 (1962): 4–16.

42 Much had been written, although theoretically more implicitly, about the existence of a trans-local Sanskrit sphere before Pollock's important work on this notion: Gonda in his 1952 encyclopedic study *Sanskrit in Indonesia* traced the linguistic influence of Sanskrit in the Archipelago; Sarkar in *Indian Influences on the Literatures of Java and Bali* (1934) discussed the spread of Sanskritic literary notions far beyond India; Wales (1961) in *The Making of Greater India* viewed large parts of South and Southeast Asia as coming historically under Indian – in this case Sanskritic – cultural influence.

43 Sheldon Pollock, 'The Cosmopolitan Vernacular', *The Journal of Asian Studies* 57/1 (1998), 6–8.

44 On *Maṇippiravāḷam* see K. Venkatachari, *Maṇipravāḷa Literature of the Śrivaiṣṇava Ācāryas* (Bombay: Ananthacarya Research Institute, 1978). Speculating on this hybrid of Tamil and Sanskrit Monius (*Imagining a Place for Buddhism*, 131) suggests that the status of Tamil as a 'merely regional or local language is raised in the process'.

45 Muhammad Qasim Zaman, 'The Scope and Limits of Islamic Cosmopolitanism and the Discursive Language of the 'Ulama'', in cooke and Lawrence (eds.), *Muslim Networks*, 103.

46 Pollock, 'The Cosmopolitan Vernacular', 12.

47 Sheldon Pollock, *The Language of the Gods in the World of Men: Sanskrit, Culture, and Power in Premodern India* (Berkeley: University of California Press, 2006), 322.

48 Uli Kozok, *The Tanjung Tanah Code of Law: The Oldest Extant Malay Manuscript*. (Cambridge: St Catharine's College and the University Press, 2004), 10–12.

49 Pollock, *The Language of the Gods*, 328.

50 Pollock, 'The Cosmopolitan Vernacular', 6–8.

51 On *Kampong Jawah* see Snouck C. Hurgronje, *Mekka in the Latter Part of the Nineteenth Century* (transl. J.H Monahan; Leiden: Brill, repr. 1931), 215–292. On the prevalence of Malay in Makka see Martin Van Bruinessen, *Kitab Kuning, Pesantren Dan Tarekat: Tradisi-Tradisi Islam Di Indonesia* (Bandung: Mizan, 1995), 41.

52 On the profound influence of Arabic on Malay see P.S. Van Ronkel, *Mengenai Pengaruh Tatakalimat Arab Terhadap Tatakalimat Melayu* (trans. A. Ikram, vol. 57; Jakarta: Bhratara, 1977).

53 Mehrdad Shokoohy, *Muslim Architecture of South India. The Sultanate of Maʿbar and the Traditions of Maritime Settlers on the Malabar and Coromandel Coasts (Tamil Nadu, Kerala and Goa)* (London: Routledge, 2003), 275–290.

54 Shuʿayb ʿAlim, *Arabic, Arwi and Persian*, 105–106.

55 Stuart Robson, 'Java at the Crossroads', *Bijdragen tot de Taal-, Land- en Volkenkunden*, 137 (1981), 262.

56 Shuʿayb ʿAlim, *Arabic, Arwi and Persian*, 502.

57 Bayly, 'Islam and State Power in Pre-Colonial South India', 155.

58 B.A. Hussainmiya, *Orang Rejimen: The Malays of the Ceylon Rifle Regiment* (Bangi: Universiti Kebangsaan Malaysia, 1990), 38–42.

59 Richard M. Eaton, *The Rise of Islam and the Bengal Frontier 1204–1760* (New Delhi: Oxford University Press, 1993), 28.

60 Shokoohy, *Muslim Architecture of South India*, 249.

61 *Ibid.*, 55, 91.

62 On the Kudus mosque and inscription see Claude Guillot and Ludrik Kalus, 'Kota Yerusalem Di Jawa Dan Mesjidnya Al-Aqsa. Piagam Pembangunan Mesjid Kudus Bertahun 956 h/1549 m', *Inskripsi Islam Tertua Di Indonesia* (Jakarta: Kepustakaan Populer Gramedia /EFEO, 2008), 101–132.

63 A depiction of the Demak episode appears in the anonymous, nineteenth-century *Serat Walisana*, Pura Pakualaman Library (Yogyakarta), MS. Pi. 32. 129.

64 Muzaffar Alam, *Languages of Political Islam: India 1200–1800* (London: C. Hurst, 2003), 121.

65 On the Hadrami networks see Engseng Ho, *The Graves of Tarim: Genealogy and Mobility across the Indian Ocean* (Berkeley: University of California Press, 2006).

66 On linguistic contact between Malay and Tamil, see P.S. Van Ronkel, 'Tamilwoorden in Maleisch Gewaad', *Tjidschrift van het Bataviaasch Genootschap* 46/6 (1903): 532–557.

67 An example of the former is the tomb shrine of the prominent Muslim 'saint' Shāh al-Ḥamīd (d. 1570 in Nagur, Tamil Nadu), the most frequently visited` in the region and attracting Muslims and non-Muslims alike. Many genres of writing in Tamil are shared across religious communities. On Tamil-Muslim works written in these genres see M.M. Uwise, *Muslim Contribution to Tamil Literature* (Kilakarai: Fifth International Islamic Tamil Literary Conference, 1990): 151–164.

31

Rethinking the World in World Literature

East Asia and Literary Contact Nebulae (2009)

Karen Laura Thornber

Professor of Comparative Literature at Harvard University, Karen Thornber specializes in the literatures and cultures of East Asia in a global context, and her work increasingly extends into South Asia, Africa, and the Middle East as well. Her first book, *Empire of Texts in Motion: Chinese, Korean, and Taiwanese Transculturations of Japanese Literature* (2009), won prizes both from the Association for Asian Studies and from the International Comparative Literature Association. Using hundreds of sources, Thornber analyzes the complex web of circulation and production between Japanese, Chinese, Korean, and Taiwanese literary networks under the Japanese empire (1895–1945). She followed this book with an equally wide-ranging study in the field of ecocriticism, *Ecoambiguity: Environmental Crises and East Asian Literatures* (2012). There, Thornber looks into the contradictory literary responses to environmental crises in East Asian canonical and peripheral poetry and fiction.

In the following essay, Thornber argues for a less Eurocentric focus in comparative and world literary studies. She proposes to examine the inter- and intra-regional relations in East Asian literatures through the interactions following the "(semi)-colonization" and decolonization of Chinese, Japanese, Korean, and Taiwanese literary worlds during the first half of the twentieth century. These interactions create "fluid spaces of transculturation," at once affirming and undermining Japanese cultural authority. Thornber proposes the concept of "literary contact nebulae" to refer to these ambiguous cultural contacts, as East Asian writers negotiate a regional literary legitimacy vis-à-vis the cultural metropolis of Japan and also seek to build a broader literary community.

One of the great ironies of comparative literature is that even as it moved from focusing nearly exclusively on European literatures to including literatures from other world regions the field in many ways solidified its Eurocentrism. Securely

World Literature in Theory, First Edition. Edited by David Damrosch.
© 2014 John Wiley & Sons, Ltd. Published 2014 by John Wiley & Sons, Ltd.

ensconced at the discipline's core, Western literatures now are read not only by themselves but also in conjunction with texts from regions regularly treated as "peripheral": Latin America, Africa, the Middle East, and East, South, and Southeast Asia.[1] Only rarely do scholars of comparative literature, particularly those working on literatures produced since the dawn of European imperialism, discuss intra-regional or even inter-regional relationships among non-Western texts. Not surprisingly, non-Western creative works written in Western languages have gained more notice than creative works in non-Western languages even when the latter far outnumber the former. And Western literatures often remain the standard against which other corpuses are evaluated.

As its name suggests, world literature, despite having long been defined as an established canon of European masterpieces, has come to embrace non-Western literatures more readily than has comparative literature. David Damrosch, for instance, has identified as world literature "all literary works that circulate beyond their culture of origin either in translation or in their original language ... a work only has an *effective* life as world literature whenever, and wherever, it is actively present within a literary system beyond that of its original culture" (4). This definition includes not only texts that circulate among Western nations or between Western and other cultures, but also those inaccessible to Western readers unfamiliar with non-Western languages. In theory, lack of attention from Western translators and readers does not preclude a creative work – presumably even a Hindi-language text that has circulated widely in Malayalam- and Tamil-language translations but not in Western-language translations – from being considered to enjoy an "effective life as world literature."[2] But in practice here too, cultural contacts within and among non-Western regions, especially contacts of the last few centuries, receive much less attention than those where the West figures prominently, most frequently as a source (e.g., Chinese trans-culturating European literatures), but also as a destination (e.g., Europeans adapting Chinese aesthetics). Current debates on world literature – including the recent workshop "Approaches to World Literature: Questions of Critical Methods beyond Eurocentrism" hosted in June 2011 by the School of Oriental and African Studies (SOAS) at the University of London – rightly critique the frequent marginalizing of literatures in Asian, Middle Eastern, and African languages as "local" or "peripheral."[3]

It is clear that despite its recent advances and burgeoning popularity, the field of world literature must continue to adopt more pluralistic understandings of literatures, cultures, and nations. Indeed, one of the greatest challenges facing scholars today is integrating and reconceptualizing conceptions of "local" and "global," where the former currently is presumed to be the bulk of non-Western cultural production and the latter mainly Western creative output or non-Western texts that have found receptive Western audiences. Although not a panacea, analyzing intra- and inter-regional interactions among non-Western literatures is one way to help world literature shed its lingering Eurocentrism and move closer to region-neutrality, where cultural contacts among Western spaces or between

Western and non-Western sites are no longer privileged above those that involve the West only secondarily, if at all.

Twentieth- and twenty-first century East Asian literary contacts are an excellent case in point. The more we examine modern Chinese, Japanese, Korean, and Taiwanese peoples and cultures, the more the diversity and complexity of their deep interconnections become apparent, and the clearer it is that dividing East Asia's creative output along national and linguistic lines can hinder our understanding of the region's vibrant artistic production.[4] Likewise, conventional comparative and world literature studies of twentieth-century East–West cultural negotiation and late twentieth- and early twenty-first century intra-East Asian popular culture flows do not do justice to the full range of (post)(semi)colonial East Asian transculturation.[5] To be sure, with several notable exceptions, in both colonial and post-1945 East Asia contact with Western texts exceeded intra-East Asian literary negotiation. Yet some of the most sustained and vibrant twentieth- and early twenty-first century East Asian artistic relationships developed not within individual East Asian societies or between East Asian and Western literatures, but among the Chinese, Japanese, Korean, and Taiwanese literary worlds.[6] Scholars have written extensively in recent years on the tremendous success of the Japanese writer Murakami Haruki (村上春樹) in China, Korea, and Taiwan. But this Murakami boom is best seen as a celebrated instance of a longstanding cultural dynamic, not as an entirely new phenomenon.[7] Interactions among the Chinese, Japanese, Korean, and Taiwanese literary worlds flourished under the Japanese empire (1895–1945), slowed briefly in the aftermath of Japan's defeat and the de(semi)colonization of China, Korea, and Taiwan, and then resumed as key conduits of artistic exchange.[8]

In East Asia, as in most areas of the world, cultures and cultural products have constantly been in motion, grappling with and interpenetrating one another within and across artistic, ethnic, geographic, linguistic, political, ideological, and temporal frontiers. In so doing, they have created fluid spaces of transculturation, where transculturation is understood as the "many different processes of [their] assimilation, adaptation, rejection, parody, resistance, loss, and ultimately transformation" (Spitta, 24).[9] Simultaneously affirming and undermining cultural capital and authority, transculturating almost always entails negotiating power. It thus can be particularly vibrant in empires and postimperial spaces. In the nineteenth- and twentieth-century Western and Japanese empires and their aftermaths, (post)colonial, (post)semicolonial, and other subjugated peoples and their (former) imperial counterparts engaged with and transformed one another's cultures and cultural products. Often defying binaries and borders, they produced fascinating amalgams of resistance, collaboration, and acquiescence.[10]

Mary Louise Pratt identifies transculturation as a phenomenon of the "contact zone," a term she coined to describe "social spaces where disparate cultures meet, clash, and grapple with each other, often in highly asymmetrical relations of domination and subordination" (7). More specifically, the contact zone as Pratt understands it is "the space of imperial encounters, the space in which peoples geographically and historically separated come into contact with each other and establish ongoing relations, usually involving conditions of coercion, radical inequality, and intractable conflict" (8).

Artistic encounters in modern East Asia have diverged in two principal ways from the zones discussed by Pratt and others.[11] Not unique to the Japanese empire and its aftermath, these differences reveal underexamined facets of transculturation in sites of (formerly) unequal power relationships, particularly empires and postimperial spaces. First, far from occurring solely among peoples geographically, historically, and culturally distant (i.e., China, Japan, Korea, and Taiwan vis-à-vis the United States and Europe), colonial artistic encounters instead were dominated by exchanges among regional neighbors with longstanding relationships. Internal chaos and American and European oppression in China, paired with Japan's emergence as a colonial power at the end of the nineteenth century, radically transformed rather than introduced contacts among East Asian peoples and cultures. Second, intra-East Asian artistic contacts rarely replicated the steep asymmetries promoted by imperial discourse or presupposed by (post)(semi)colonial peoples. Considering their frequent ambiguity and constantly changing internal dynamics, as well as their hazy edges, the spaces of these contacts are better termed "nebulae" (nebulas) than "zones," which suggest distinct areas with clear borders.

The term *artistic contact nebulae* thus designates the spaces where dancers, dramatists, musicians, painters, sculptors, writers, and other artists from cultures in (formerly) unequal power relationships interact with one another and transculturate one another's creative output. One of the most vibrant subsets of artistic contact nebulae are *literary contact nebulae*, active sites both physical and creative of readerly contact, writerly contact, and textual contact, intertwined modes of transculturation that depend to some degree on linguistic contact and often involve travel. In this context, "readerly contact" refers to reading creative texts (texts with aesthetic ambitions, imaginative writing) from cultures/nations in (formerly) asymmetrical power relationships with one's own; "writerly contact" to interactions among creative writers from (formerly) conflicting societies; "textual contact" to transculturating creative texts in this environment (appropriating genres, styles, and themes, as well as transculturating individual literary works via the related and at times concomitant strategies of interpreting, adapting, translating, and intertextualizing); and "linguistic contact" to engaging with the language of the (former) colonizer or colonized.

While colonial period intra-East Asian literary contacts focused largely on reconceptualizing suffering, relationships, and agency (Thornber 2009), their post-1945 counterparts have been concerned primarily with establishing literary legitimacy and literary communities. Colonialism is one of the most abject forms of surrender of one people to another; it is also one of the most ruthless types of cultural abuse of one people by another. The fragmented political, economic, and cultural domination attending semicolonialism also entails exploitation and demands submission. In most cases (semi)colonial oppression does not end with decolonization, since direct rule is often replaced by more veiled forms of control. Literary contacts that develop in empires and their aftermaths constantly renegotiate legitimacy in light of both artistic and geopolitical developments; writers work to solidify a place for themselves and their cultures on the regional and world literary stage.

Creative artists across East Asia also have devoted significant attention to advocating and establishing communities of writers, readers, texts, and ultimately peoples. They have done so in their conversations with one another, as well as in their discussions, translations, and intertextualizations of one another's work. East Asian literary communities, and those since 1945 in particular, have thrived not by suppressing colonial and wartime tragedies but by making atonement for these tragedies a central focus. Outside of East Asia, protracted decolonization and the colonizer's status as one of the victorious allies in World War Two, not to mention the former colony's relative lack of acknowledged cultural legacy, virtually ensured that the cultural, economic, and political orientations of most newly independent postcolonies remained focused on the former Euro-America metropole; typically the former metropole also retained some measure of power over its former colonies. East Asian nations, on the other hand, rapidly developed divergent political, economic, and even cultural reference points defined by the cold war (the United States and Western Europe for Japan, South Korea, and Taiwan; the Soviet Union for North Korea and China). In time this reorientation enabled memories of (semi) colonialism, however constructed, to become powerful; enmity toward Japan for its failure to atone properly for colonial and wartime atrocities eventually flourished.[12] Intra-East Asian cultural and literary exchange not only survived but thrived in this environment; writers and texts jostled for status, addressed atrocity and negotiated atonement, and built communities with one another in the face of turbulent economic, political, and social conditions.

Negotiating Legitimacy[13]

Hierarchies, challenges to hierarchies, and rebuttals to challenges characterize most post(semi)colonial literary contact spaces worldwide. Vying for acceptance and struggling to establish cultural legitimacy reflect desire to be taken seriously as well as anxiety and insecurity about positions in post(semi)colonial spheres. Cultural relations generally are not as asymmetrical as during the (semi)colonial period. But post(semi)colonial writers, particularly those educated in the former metropole and writing in its language, are frequently driven to assert personal and cultural legitimacy. For their part, writers from former metropoles often undercut their post(semi) colonial counterparts, contesting their literary legitimacy, and at times even questioning their right to narrate their own experiences.

Writerly interactions in postwar East Asian literary contact spaces have usually been less hierarchical and more reciprocal than elsewhere, with authors generally respecting one another as individuals. Intra-East Asian literary criticism and translations also are rarely as concerned with asserting or denying legitimacy as are those of other postcolonial sites. On the other hand, intra-East Asian intertextual relationships have often entailed complex internecine status negotiations, particularly when canonical works and writers are involved.

Creative texts such as the *Taiwan Man'yōshū* (Taiwan Collection of Ten Thousand Leaves; 台湾万葉集, 1981–1993) explicitly invite comparisons with Japanese creative works in order both to rectify perceived slights in these works against (post) colonial literary production and to establish local literary legitimacy. The Taiwanese writer Zhu Tianxin's (朱天心) novella *Gudu* (Ancient Capital; 古都, 1996) dynamically engages with Japanese predecessors in a slightly different manner; it highlights differences between postcolonial and postimperial sites and thus the limited relevance of lauded Japanese predecessors to postcolonial cultures. Japanese texts are no less anxious about acclaimed forebears from the region; some creative works, including Dazai Osamu's (太宰治) novella *Sekibetsu* (Regretful Parting; 惜別, 1945) and Nakata Shōei's (中田昭栄) novel *Ai to kanashimi to tabidachi no uta: Ro Jin* [Lu Xun], *Ōgai, Sofia, Akashi, Tōten, to Nichiro sensō* (Song of Love and Sorrow and Going Forth: Lu Xun, Ōgai, Sophia, Akashi, Tōten, and the Russo-Japanese War; 愛と哀しみと旅立ちの歌: 魯迅,鷗外,ソフィア,明石,滔天と日露戦争, 2001) distort predecessors in ways that at once establish Japanese legitimacy in speaking for the formerly colonized and subvert the authority of the latter's narratives. As these texts suggest, negotiating regional literary legitimacy remained a concern of postwar East Asian writers from the 1940s to the turn of the twenty-first century.

Compiled by the Taiwanese physician Kohō Banri (孤蓬万里;Wu Jiantang, 呉建堂), the *Taiwan Man'yōshū* includes approximately 1400 Japanese-language tanka (短歌) by Taiwanese writers.[14] Composing Japanese-language poetry and prose was a popular activity in colonial Taiwan and continued after decolonization, notwithstanding official prohibitions against writing in Japanese. But for the most part this creative output was ignored by Japanese writers and editors, including the compilers of the 20-volume *Shōwa Man'yōshū* (Shōwa Collection of Ten Thousand Leaves; 昭和万葉集, 1979–1980), an anthology of Japanese-language tanka written between 1925 and 1975. Despite the large number of (semi)colonial tanka poets, of the approximately 1500 writers represented in the *Shōwa Man'yōshū* all but a handful are Japanese. Asserting Taiwanese cultural legitimacy as both students and creators of classical Japanese poetry, the title-intertextuality of the *Taiwan Man'yōshū* explicitly positions this anthology alongside the *Shōwa Man'yōshū* and the eighth-century *Man'yōshū* (Collection of Ten Thousand Leaves; 万葉集), the oldest extant collection of Japanese poetry. Specifying place (Taiwan) as opposed to period (Shōwa), the anthology argues for recognizing Taiwan as a legitimate cultural center. This was particularly important in light of Japan's normalization of relations with China; as Japan moved toward recognizing the mainland government (1972) Taiwanese writers expressed dismay at the implied demotion of Taiwan's political and cultural capital.

The *Taiwan Man'yōshū* openly appropriates elements from the *Man'yōshū* in order to actively confront the *Shōwa Man'yōshū*. In the preface, Kohō claims that the poets featured in his anthology "borrow the tanka form of the *Man'yōshū* to lay bare their life's breath" (11). Kohō here indicates indebtedness to early Japan literary production while also asserting the autonomy of contemporary Taiwanese creative expression.

Like their twentieth-century Japanese counterparts, he argues, Taiwanese tanka poets have both assiduously studied the Japanese classics and resisted becoming enslaved by them.[15] The *Taiwan Man'yōshū* declares that Taiwanese writers thus deserve a place in anthologies such as the *Shōwa Man'yōshū*. This late twentieth-century struggle for legitimacy vis-à-vis Japan was a replay of colonial-period relationships, one that as before positioned Taiwanese as continually attempting to catch up with their East Asian neighbors.

Kohō's collection labors to gain postcolonial literary recognition by taking on Japanese textual production and rectifying its perceived slights against Taiwanese counterparts. In contrast, Zhu Tianxin's *Ancient Capital* does so by establishing difference, challenging Japanese predecessors and highlighting their limited relevance to Taiwan. As its title-intertextuality suggests, the novella *Ancient Capital* dynamically intertextualizes the Japanese writer Kawabata Yasunari's (川端康成) novel *Koto* (Ancient Capital; 古都, 1962), one of three creative works cited by the Nobel Committee that awarded Kawabata the Nobel Prize in Literature in 1968. Zhu Tianxin's novella also includes quotational and onomastic allusions to its Japanese namesake; the narrator explicitly interweaves discourse from a number of predecessors but calls greatest attention to her intertextualization of Kawabata's novel. Inviting comparisons between postwar Japan and Taiwan, Zhu Tianxin's active reconfiguring of Kawabata's text creates space for Taiwanese cultural production.

Kawabata's novel tells the story of a young woman (Chieko) separated from her twin sister (Naoko) at birth and briefly reunited with her years later. This text interweaves Chieko's struggles to come to terms with her background with lyric descriptions of Kyoto and its many temples, shrines, and festivals. The Taiwanese novella reconfigures the confrontations with bloodlines depicted in its Japanese predecessor as encounters with both cultural identities and physical and literary spaces. Ni (you), the narrator and a second-generation Chinese mainlander, is a 1990s *flâneuse* of both Taipei and Kyoto and a reader of texts from around the world, including Japanese literature and maps. Disoriented in contemporary Taipei, she portrays Kyoto as a more desirable yet still problematic place.

At the same time that it venerates Japan's cultural capital (both the city of Kyoto and cultural capital in the Bourdieuian sense), Zhu Tianxin's *Ancient Capital* establishes Taiwanese textual capital (legitimacy). It does so in part by strategically incorporating into its fabric nine passages from Kawabata's novel. Many of these passages, scattered across the midsection of Zhu Tianxin's text and set off with dashes, concern Chieko's fractured identity. Chieko's displacement is contrasted with Ni's displacement, which transcends the personal: the woman between families in Kawabata's novel becomes the woman between cultures in Zhu Tianxin's intertextualization. Ultimately, the Taiwanese *Ancient Capital* exposes the inability of its Japanese predecessor to express Taiwan's complex and more painful experiences.

Taipei is described repeatedly in Zhu Tianxin's novella as a labyrinthine jungle. The past, both personal and cultural, is increasingly difficult to locate, and maps and memories serve primarily to confuse; paradoxically, Taipei's only real anchors are its colonial edifices, which are rapidly being devoured by new construction. The contemporary clutter of buildings, consumer goods, and cultural products from around the world makes Chinese-Taiwanese feel even more out of sorts; for second generation main-landers such as Ni the "old capital" is actually in China, and its simulacrum in Kyoto increases the appeal of the Japanese city. But although Ni finds some solace in Kyoto, even there her incessant layering of memories makes it nearly impossible to feel at home; the Kyoto she experiences is very different from the one described in Kawabata's novel not because it is part of the former metropole but instead largely because of her family circumstances and China's own civil war.

In the Taiwanese novella anxiety over family becomes anxiety over cities and cultural identities, and the traumas of not belonging are magnified; Ni invokes her Japanese literary predecessor and particularly its focus on Chieko's angst and her friends' questions about her background to underscore the inapplicability of Kawabata's text to Taiwanese experience. The incompleteness (from the Taiwanese perspective) of the Japanese novel is highlighted by the narrator's quoting, three-quarters of the way through her own work, Kawabata's final lines: "– Chieko held onto the Bengara lattice door, watching her sister Naeko walk away. Naeko did not look back. A few delicate snowflakes fell on Chieko's forelocks and quickly disappeared. The town was, as expected, still fast asleep. (End of the full text) – *Ancient Capital*. The plane left at ten in the morning" (210). The Japanese creative work is silenced, its body ejected and supplanted but traces left behind in part to remind readers of its incongruity, while the Taiwanese text forges ahead, with Ni on an airplane back to Taiwan. By citing Kawabata's final lines well before its own conclusion, the Taiwanese novella points to the inadequacies of the Japanese narrative in guiding Taiwanese cultural projects.

The shuffled citations from Kawabata's novel signify the Taiwanese text's simul-taneous subordination of a venerated Japanese cultural product and assertion of Taiwanese creative legitimacy. They also counter East Asian, including Chinese and Taiwanese, enthrallment with Kawabata. Not only was Kawabata the first East Asian writer awarded the Nobel Prize in Literature, he also has retained star status in China and Taiwan. His *Ancient Capital* has enjoyed particular acclaim. By the time Zhu Tianxin published her novella in 1996, Kawabata's text had been translated into Chinese at least six times, more than into any single Western language; the novel remains a popular object of transculturation in China and Taiwan in the twenty-first century. The narrator of *Ancient Capital* thus boldly performs vivisection on a literary work that is flourishing, indeed multiplying, outside its country of origin. She declares her novel to be more applicable to contemporary Taiwan than the Japanese work (Kawabata's novel) parading in Chinese clothes (translation).[16]

Both the *Taiwan Man'yōshū* and Zhu Tianxin's *Ancient Capital* establish Taiwanese creative legitimacy while reaffirming Japanese cultural capital. But their intertextual-izations also declare Japanese literary predecessors insufficient – whether purposely (*Shōwa Man'yōshū*) or inadvertently (Kawabata's *Ancient Capital*) – without denying Japanese literary legitimacy.[17] In contrast, Dazai's *Regretful Parting* and Nakata's *Song of Love* intertextualize the Chinese literary giant Lu Xun's (魯迅) famed essay "Tengye xiansheng" (Mr. Fujino, 藤野先生, 1926) in ways that seriously deflate Chinese literary authority. One of the best-known Chinese accounts of life as an exchange student in early twentieth-century Japan, "Mr. Fujino" describes Lu Xun's experiences as a young man studying medicine in Sendai during the Russo-Japanese War. He depicts the staff at the medical college, his anatomy teacher Mr. Fujino (Fujino Genkurō; 藤野源九郎), and some of his classmates as extremely helpful and compassionate. But not everyone in Japan is so kind. Some of Lu Xun's classmates taunt him mercilessly and accuse him of cheating on the final exam. In addition, they not only criticize China and the Chinese but also enthusiastically view slides of Japanese executing Chinese spies.

Unlike Zhu Tianxin's *Ancient Capital*, which highlights differences between Taiwanese and Japanese experiences, both *Regretful Parting* and *Song of Love* use interfigurality as well as onomastic and quotational allusions to distort Lu Xun's depictions of his own experiences. In so doing, they imply that even one of the founders of modern Chinese literature cannot accurately narrate his own story. That this tale concerns the young Chinese intellectual's relationships with Japanese has even more troubling implications: Japanese recastings of "Mr. Fujino" depict Lu Xun as more indebted to Japanese than did Lu Xun himself. In constructing distorted scenarios of Chinese–Japanese solidarity, postwar Japanese writers paradoxically minimize Chinese agency.

Regretful Parting was commissioned by the Japanese Naikaku Jōhōkyoku (Cabinet Information Bureau; 内閣情報局) and Nihon Bungaku Hōkokukai (Japan Literary Patriotic Association; 日本文学報告会); in 1944 these groups asked Dazai to create a work embodying "Independence and Amity." The novella itself depicts these phenomena, but it does so by undermining Lu Xun's story from its beginning. Dazai's narrator features a reporter whose dissatisfaction with "Mr. Fujino" leads him to the elderly Japanese doctor whose memoir forms the bulk of Dazai's novella. The narrator pays homage to Lu Xun near the conclusion of *Regretful Parting* by inserting a lengthy passage from "Mr. Fujino" on the inspiration the Chinese writer still receives from the photograph of Fujino that his Japanese mentor gave him at their parting. In so doing he suggests that the doctor's story cannot fully replace Lu Xun's own text, even though the former is many times longer. More complex is his reference, also at the conclusion, to Lu Xun's request, when asked, that his essay be included in a Japanese anthology of his works in translation, as indeed it was, many times over. Here Dazai paints a pleasant portrait of respectful Japanese translators seeking and following the desires of the beloved Chinese writer. Yet quoting Lu Xun as claiming, "it's fine for you to pick my stories freely, at your own discretion" (127) proves troubling, particularly on the heels of his admission that only the portrait of his Japanese teacher gives him the strength to write his most controversial texts. Adept rearrangement of Lu Xun's own words reconfigures him as relying on Japanese for both the inspiration and the distribution of his work. Intertextualizing "Mr. Fujino" and expanding greatly on, even distorting some of its key scenes, *Regretful Parting* also manages to depict Lu Xun as far more dependent on Japanese wisdom than he actually was, all the while portraying him as the embodiment of Sino-Japanese peace and understanding.

Similarly, in the preface to *Song of Love*, Nakata notes that he long had been intrigued by Lu Xun's move from medicine to literature but that the more he learned about Lu Xun's experiences, the more he also wanted to write about the difficulties facing Lu Xun and his contemporaries (i). The result is a voluminous text that discusses revolutionaries from several nations. But *Song of Love* greatly dramatizes the friendships between Lu Xun and Japanese, friendships sketched ever so briefly or sometimes not at all in "Mr. Fujino." For instance, in Nakata's text Lu Xun and his Japanese friends forlornly face his imminent departure: "Sugimura's eyes, Suzuki's eyes, Yamazaki's eyes, Aoki's eyes, and Lu Xun's eyes all were filled with tears" (494). The young men then go to a photo studio to have a commemorative picture taken. In contrast, the narrator of "Mr. Fujino" discusses his departure only with Fujino. Reappropriating and distorting one of the most dominant voices of early twentieth-century China, *Regretful Parting* and *Song of Love* question the legitimacy of Chinese narration even while emphasizing Sino-Japanese amity. They reveal both fascination and unease with Lu Xun's writing long after his death.[18] They also point to the desire to construct East Asian communities.

Building Community

By intertextualizing "Mr. Fujino" as they do, *Regretful Parting* and *Song of Love* destabilize the very solidarity that they imagine. But the fundamental premise of these narratives – that individuals *should* be bonding and in fact *can* bond no matter how deep the cultural and political divides – characterizes much postwar intra-East Asian literary contact. From the early years of decolonization this longing for literary and ultimately human community has typified personal interactions among writers, discussions of literatures from other parts of the region (often included as the paratexts of translations), as well as intra-East Asian translations and intertextualizations. Focal points have shifted with the times. Literary contacts of the early postwar decades paid considerable attention to forging alliances that by defying colonial experiences and cold war coalitions would help shape a future different from that imagined by world political leaders. More recent readerly, writerly, and textual contacts have demonstrated solidarity regarding the need for Japanese to atone for colonial and wartime atrocities.

Intra-East Asian cultural liaisons recovered far more rapidly than official relations. The excitement with which Japanese greeted the Chinese writer Guo Moruo (郭沫若) on his December 1955 visit to Japan and the warm welcome Chinese afforded prominent Japanese literary figures during that decade illustrate the enduring connections between the Chinese and Japanese creative worlds.[19] Such postwar visits frequently were accompanied by reevaluations of cultural production in order to highlight intra-East Asian literary cooperation. For instance, while in Japan in the mid-1930s, the Chinese literary giant Ba Jin (巴金) had scathingly attacked Japanese culture and claimed Japanese literature not worth a second glance ("Ji duan"). But when he visited Japan in April 1980, he revealed that he in fact considered among his teachers a number of leading early twentieth-century Japanese writers ("Wenxue shenghuo"; Kinoshita). It is likely that, just as Ba Jin's earlier comments stemmed from anger at Japan's imperialist program, these latter remarks came more from his desire to be an affable visitor and, secondarily, his frustration with contemporary Chinese literary production, than from overwhelming admiration of Japanese writers. But even so, these statements serve as reminders of the deep complexity and ambiguity of intra-East Asian creative interactions. In their personal relationships and literary transculturations postwar East Asian writers and texts have displayed solidarity not only in condemning Japanese violence and denials of violence but also in celebrating one another's stances on everything from revolutionary fervor to steadfastness to literary agility in articulating zeitgeist and injustice.

Translators, including those in post-1945 East Asia who reconfigured creative work from other parts of the region, have always been drawn to writing they believe will resonate in some way with local readers, by virtue of its familiarity, its foreignness, or most often a combination of the two. But hope of understanding and emulation also has guided much postwar intra-East Asian translation, understanding, and emulation less of particular stylistic trends – a common occurrence in the early twentieth century – than of sentiments, behaviors, and individuals. This was particularly true of translations of Chinese and Korean literatures in the early postwar decades. Most obviously, desire to increase understanding and facilitate emulation colored literary communities constructed in accordance with cold war alliances. Chinese and North Korean translation of each other's output was particularly notable in this regard. For instance, Kim Ilsŏng (金日成), leader of North Korea for nearly five decades, explicitly advocated the study and translation of modern Chinese literature, revealing the impact of texts by writers such as Guo Moruo, Jiang Guangci (蔣光慈), and Lu Xun on his own thought: "When we were in junior high, reading Marx and Lenin, we also read many revolutionary texts, including [Lu Xun's] 'A Q zhengzhuan' [The True Story of Ah Q; 阿Q正傳, 1921] … Through these texts, we recognized even more clearly the corruption and decay of contemporary society, and this solidified our determination to throw ourselves into the revolutionary struggle" (Yang, 526). Likewise, during the 1950s the Chinese translated substantial quantities of colonial period Korean revolutionary literature, as well as texts from the newly created North Korea. In their prefaces and introductions Chinese translators and commentators called attention to the courage of the Korean people.

Vectors of translation defied cold war alliances just as readily as they supported them. For instance, the translation of modern Chinese literature in postwar Japan was initially motivated by admiration of the steadfastness and courage of the semicolonial Chinese literary world, which translators frequently contrasted with the malleability of the Japanese creative orbit, first under Japan's military leaders during wartime and then under American occupation (1945–1952). Scholars and translators of Chinese literature including Lu Xun's famed translator Takeuchi Yoshimi (竹内好) criticized the Japanese literary establishment for advocating militarism and failing to combat American oppression. Even as Japanese writers grew disenchanted with the revolutionary literature produced in 1950s and 1960s China, Lu Xun and other Chinese were held up as models of active resistance against native and foreign oppression (Maruyama, 232–239).

Intra-East Asian intertextualizations of the early postwar decades also sought to establish communities in defiance of colonial experiences and cold war coalitions, forging networks of resilience and revolution. In contrast, interactions of more recent decades have focused on generating networks united in censuring Japanese colonial and wartime atrocities. It was only in the 1960s, with Japan's tacit involvement in the Vietnam War, that Japanese intellectuals began to express concern with Japan's failure to atone for early twentieth-century crimes committed against China, Korea, and Taiwan; in the 1980s this anxiety became intense. Chinese demands for Japanese atonement were also delayed until the 1980s, when the Chinese Communist Party, to blunt criticisms of its market-oriented reforms and growing trade deficit with Japan, adopted anti-Japanese patriotism as its successor ideology to socialism. Until that time, the Chinese government had suppressed narratives on wartime atrocities, shamed by their exposures of Chinese capitulation; cold war imperatives and tight controls over mass media together distracted attention from Japan (He).[20]

Although delayed, discourse on atonement has been more prominent in East Asia than in other postcolonial sites largely because of Japan's defeat in World War Two and opposing cold war alliances in the region.[21] In the last few decades official and popular spheres have condemned Japan's alleged failure to apologize appropriately for colonial and wartime crimes (Dudden; Lind). These historical tensions also have made their mark on contacts among East Asian writers and texts, but with the exception of the immediate postwar period, far from hampering literary exchange, they have been an integral part of it and even stimulated it. Chinese, Korean, and Taiwanese writers and texts continue to express anger over Japan's colonial and wartime atrocities. Yet they generally perceive Japanese writers and texts as their allies in exposing Japanese violence and compelling Japanese authorities to express more heartfelt remorse. Particularly revealing in this regard are recent Chinese-language translations of the Japanese writer Ishikawa Tatsuzō's (石川達三) novella *Ikiteiru heitai* (Living Soldiers; 生きている兵隊, 1938) and the portrayal of Japanese–Chinese artistic friendships in the Chinese novelist Mo Yan's (莫言) novel *Wa* (*Frog*; 蛙, 2009).

Based on Ishikawa's eyewitness observations and interviews with soldiers who participated in the Nanjing Massacre of 1937, Ishikawa's *Living Soldiers* depicts a platoon of patriotic soldiers who slaughter Chinese on the battlefield, ruthlessly murder innocent civilians, rape Chinese women, and loot Chinese homes and shops. Banned in Japan immediately before its distribution, Ishikawa's novella was little more than a title to wartime readers there. But thanks to extensive intra-East Asian readerly and writerly contacts, it circulated in China in multiple Chinese translations during the war (Thornber, 189–192, 201–207).[22] After prohibitions against literary discussion of Nanjing were lifted in China in the 1980s, Zhong Qing'an (鍾庆安) and Ou Xilin (欧希林) published a translation of *Living Soldiers* in Beijing in 1987 (Huozhe de shibing; 活着的士兵); this was followed by a translation by Liu Musha (劉慕沙), the mother of Zhu Tianxin, published in Taipei in 1995 (Huozhe de bingshi; 活着的兵士). These translations adhere more closely to Ishikawa's version of the novella than do their wartime counterparts, depicting an even more gruesome battlescape.

Ishikawa's novella has been criticized in East Asia for whitewashing Japanese military activities in China. Yet its Chinese-language translators have emphasized its important dual role of confirming injustices perpetrated against China and facilitating Sino-Japanese reconciliation. As Zhong Qing'an and Ou Xilin comment in their preface:

> Although the book's descriptions of troops killing people, setting fires, and looting bear little resemblance to what the Japanese actually did in China, considering that era's Japanese fascist white terror, they are extremely praiseworthy. This text offers powerful testimony to Japan's invasion of China and the savage acts performed there, particularly the Nanjing Massacre ... After finishing the work, can one not respect Ishikawa? Don't you think that Ishikawa is not only an outstanding author but also a brave anti-fascist warrior? ... Having this kind of Japanese friend gladdens our hearts. ... If this translation benefits Sino-Japanese friendship, then we will be overwhelmed with joy and consolation. (4–5)

Liu Musha likewise notes in her preface that, "in an era when the Japanese government is repeatedly attempting to alter the historical facts of the Japanese invasion of China and slaughter of Chinese civilians, it appears that this kind of novel, which comes from a great Japanese writer and exposes the Japanese invasion of China and savage acts against Chinese, perhaps provides additional historical testimony" (8). Although relatively tame compared with many narratives of atrocity, Ishikawa's text is posited as an antidote to Japanese denials of wartime maneuvers in China. Chinese-language translators genuinely believed that making this novella accessible to Chinese readers would contribute to Japanese atonement and Sino-Japanese rapprochement. Their prefaces, integral parts of their translations, work to transform Ishikawa's text from an exposé of Japanese wartime maneuvers in China into an explicit argument for Japanese apology.

Dismay over Japanese atrocities in East Asia likewise has colored personal interactions among writers, including the Nobel Prize-winning Japanese novelist Ōe Kenzaburō (大江健三郎) and the celebrated Chinese author Mo Yan, who have been friends and admirers of each other's literary production since the 1990s. In 2002 Ōe went with his Chinese counterpart on a well-publicized visit to Mo Yan's hometown in Northeast Gaomi Township, Shandong Province for an NHK documentary; Ōe also had the opportunity during this sojourn to speak with Mo Yan's aunt, whose story captivated him.

Mo Yan alludes to this visit in *Frog* (December 2009), a novel that exposes the arduous life of his aunt, a rural doctor torn between the mandates of China's one-child policy and the realities of parental longing, repeated pregnancies, and forced abortions. Like many of Mo Yan's narratives, *Frog* was translated first into other Asian languages: into Vietnamese in 2010 as *Éch*, less than a year after appearing in Chinese, and then into Japanese in May 2011 as *Amei* (蛙鳴). The French translation, scheduled for release in August 2011, will be the novel's first configuration into a Western language. So admiring of Mo Yan is his Japanese publisher that the novel's jacket declares him in several places, "The Asian writer closest to winning a Nobel Prize," echoing Ōe's comment in 2000, featured prominently on the English translation of the Chinese writer's *Shifu yue lai yue you mo* (Shifu, You'll Do Anything for a Laugh; 师傅越来越幽默), that, "If I were to choose a Nobel laureate, it would be Mo Yan."

In "Tingqu washeng yipian" (Listening to the Frog's Voice; 聽取蛙聲一片), the preface to the Taiwanese edition of *Frog*, Mo Yan makes clear his anguish over China's one-child policy. Likewise, in the afterword to the Japanese version, which also declares on its cover that this is a *kinsho* (禁書; banned book), Mo Yan's Japanese translator Yoshida Tomio (吉田富夫) celebrates the Chinese writer for grappling so directly with what long has been a taboo topic in Chinese literature. In these paratexts Mo Yan and Yoshida also speak of Ōe's visit to China and the important role he played in the generation of *Frog*, something that, according to Yoshida, is guaranteed to captivate Japanese readers.[23] But what is particularly interesting about Mo Yan's novel from an intra-East Asian perspective is that each of its five parts opens with a letter from the narrator Ke Dou (Tadpole) to his friend the Japanese writer Sugiya Yoshito. The first letter reveals that Sugiya visited Ke Dou and his aunt in China in 2002; Ke Dou indicates that Sugiya's interest in his aunt and longing to know more about her has inspired him to write at length about her life. *Frog* is semi-autobiographical, but more important than the precise identities of the writers featured in the novel is the text's depiction of an intra-East Asian literary friendship with such a disturbing legacy, something not addressed in the paratexts of either the Chinese or Japanese versions of the novel. Subsequent discourse reveals that Sugiya's father was the army commander who captured Ke Dou's aunt and her family, including her grandfather, a celebrated doctor in the Chinese army. Loath to allow this legacy to impede their relationship, Sugiya apologizes to Ke Dou for the crimes committed by his father's generation; Ke Dou not only applauds Sugiya for so doing, claiming him a model for Japanese and Chinese alike, but also asserts that both Sugiya and his father are victims of the war. In another letter Ke Dou reveals that his aunt is particularly eager to speak again with Sugiya and urges him to return to China: "My aunt talks about you every time she sees me; she's sincere about wanting you to return. ... She also says that there are many things in her heart that she'd like to share, yet that there's no one to whom she can open up. But if you come, she'll speak with you and hold nothing back" (219). Elsewhere Ke Dou affirms that Sugiya also will receive a warm welcome from Chinese writers when he next visits the mainland.

Featuring a Japanese writer who is the son of an army commander who harmed his family, a critic of Japanese wartime treatment of Chinese, his beloved friend, a potential family confidante, the first reader of his manuscript, and in fact the spark that led to its creation, Ke Dou demonstrates the possibilities of Sino-Japanese friendships, literary and otherwise. He places a large burden on Japanese and Chinese writers; they are to apologize and accept apologies for the past and then to establish the types of communities, both personal and professional, that in sufficient numbers will make the past virtually unrepeatable. That Ke Dou does so in a novel focusing primarily on the traumas of China's one-child policy points to the urgency of addressing past wrongs: if longstanding injuries remain unhealed, insufficient attention will be devoted to more recent anguish, and suffering will become even more severe. Like intertextualizations, this textualization of a foreign writer – in sharp contrast with the Japanese textualizations of Lu Xun – points to the inspirations literary artists can offer one another across cultural divides without sacrificing creative status or integrity.

In his 1994 Nobel lecture Ōe spoke of solidarity with writers from other parts of East Asia, commenting, "I align myself with writers like Kim Chiha [金芝河; 김지하] of Korea, and Zheng Yi [鄭義] and Mo Yan, both of China. For me the brotherhood of world literature consists in such relationships in concrete terms." Even more significantly, in a 1995 conversation with Kim Chiha, Ōe commented: "I don't think that it was a Japanese person who received the Nobel Prize or that it was given to Japan .... I received it not as a Japanese writer but as an Asian writer" (Ōe and Kim, 287). Although many East Asian intellectuals would be more hesitant than Ōe to forsake national identity so completely, Ōe's eagerness to create East Asian communities, literary and otherwise, has been shared by numerous writers and texts for much of the postwar period. Particularly eloquent on this topic has been Mo Yan himself, during comments he made at the opening ceremony of the Frankfurt Book Fair in 2009:

> The purpose of our coming to this book fair is to practice Goethe's theoretical idea of world literature. In the era of initiating communication and conversation, the communication and conversation among writers are absolutely necessary. Sitting together, having a face-to-face conversation is communication; reading each other's works is also communication, even more important communication … Let me repeat the words I have spoken many times: a writer has a nationality, but literature has no boundary … Let us allow literature to play its key role in fostering communication among countries, nations, and individuals. And let us, in this era of conversation and communication, play the roles we have and play them well. ("A Writer")

Mo Yan exaggerates somewhat – not all writers have clearly defined nationalities, and not all literature is without boundary. But his larger point is apt. And as his own novel *Frog* suggests, literary communities are not homogeneous utopias. They instead are dynamic, diverse, at times nebulous sites where peoples struggle for and can achieve legitimacy and respect. Modern East Asian literary contact nebulae have regularly defied the many divisions artificially constructed by (post)colonial ideologues, divisions nevertheless very real in affecting lives and careers.

The past two decades have witnessed increased scholarship on pre-1945 intra-East Asian literary contacts, but academic discourse continues for the most part to marginalize post(semi)colonial intra-East Asian literary spaces. Many of these nebulae have been effectively obscured from view by geopolitical divides. Remaining strong until the late 1980s were perceptions of China and Japan as irrevocably separated by major ideological and economic fault lines; of Japan and Korea as being relatively isolated from each other, in no sense bound by neocolonial dependence let alone yearning; and of Taiwan as little more than a gateway to China, without much artistic culture of its own worth examining. But since then cold war tensions have relaxed, and restrictions on popular culture imports and on regional and global travel have diminished. In addition, East Asian governments have actively promoted international interest in their cultures. They also have worked to enhance the cosmopolitanism of their own peoples through establishing language programs and student exchanges within and outside the region. All of these developments invite us to think more comprehensively about the diverse and often fraught transculturating taking place in East Asia and beyond from colonization to the present day. Ultimately, we must become more region-neutral and reconceptualize the world as a space of countless complex and captivating literary networks of all configurations, some of which enforce but many of which defy cultural, national, linguistic, as well as academic boundaries.

Notes

1 The term "Western literatures," itself problematic in its suggestion of homogeneity and parity among other factors, here refers simply to what commonly are understood to be the literatures of Europe and the United States, and to a lesser extent Canada. Literature from the United States is a relative latecomer to the field of comparative literature, and Canadian literature continues to be marginalized in some circles.

2 As is made clear by the case of India with its exceptional variety of peoples and official languages, intra-national circulation can readily be inter-cultural.

3 Such marginalizing takes place worldwide. Sukrita Paul Kumar and Malashri Lal lament that bookstores in Asia are often better stocked in translations of Western literatures than in translations of texts from other parts of the region, and that Asian literatures are often more visible in Western bookstores and libraries than in their Asian counterparts (xx, xxii).

4 Unless otherwise indicated, in this chapter the term Korea refers to South Korea and Korean to South Korean when referring to post-1948 phenomena.

5 They also do not do justice to the multiple interactions among modern East Asian literatures and literary worlds on the one hand, and, on the other, those of Latin America, South and Southeast Asia, the Middle East, and Africa, contacts that I analyze in my two current book projects: *Texts in Turmoil* and *Reimagining Regions and Worlds*.

6 East Asian fascination with the Indian Nobel Prize winner Rabindranath Tagore has also been significant.

7 Ultimately, what most separates the Murakami boom is the critical notice it has received; scholarly attention to the multimillion-dollar late-twentieth and early twenty-first century intra-East Asian popular cultural booms has spilled over to the Murakami craze. Other literary booms, such as the Kawabata Yasunari (川端康成) rage in 1960s Korea (with 15 translations of *Yukiguni* (雪国, 1935–1947) published in that decade alone) and the Ōe Kenzaburō (大江健三郎) surge in 1990s Korea (with seven translations of "Shii-ku" (飼育, 1957) and six translations of *Kojinteki na taiken* (個人的な体験, 1964) in that decade alone), ironically followed on the heels of Nobel Prizes but did not take place in the context of major intra-East Asian popular culture flows. For more on postwar Korean translation of Japanese literature see Kim; Yi; Yun 1998, 2008. Kawabata and Ōe also have been translated extensively into Chinese. Kuroko and Kan, 59–63, 69–87; Wang 411–412, 418–420.

8   See my *Empire of Texts in Motion* for extensive discussion of colonial-period intra-East Asian cultural dynamics.

9   Cf. Dingwaney, 8; Ortiz, xi; Peres, 10; Pratt 7; Rama.

10 Nineteenth- and twentieth-century empires were the largest, the most organized, and the most regulated regimes in human history. By the early twentieth century, they together controlled a substantial majority of the earth's surface.

11 See, for instance, Curley; Dobie; Fitz; Green; Lape, 1–18; Pickles and Rutherdale; Reichl, 1–8, 40–45.

12 Since the 1980s enmity toward Japan has been used as a political tool in China, Korea, and to a lesser extent Taiwan to divert attention from unstable economic conditions.

13 The following sections are drawn largely from my article "Legitimacy and Community."

14 Kohō began assembling tanka by Taiwanese poets in the late 1970s, publishing the first volume of the *Taiwan Man'yōshū* in Taiwan in 1981, and the second and third volumes in Taiwan in 1988 and 1993; the Japanese publisher Shūeisha (集英社) reissued the *Taiwan Man'yōshū* in Japan as two volumes in 1994.

15 Kohō himself had studied the *Man'yōshū* with the noted Japanese *Man'yō* scholar Inukai Takashi (犬養孝) in the early 1940s. Inukai also wrote a preface for the *Taiwan Man'yōshū* in which he establishes ties with the original *Man'yōshū*, but in general his discourse paints the Taiwanese as passively inheriting Japanese literary glory.

16 Zhu Tianxin's work has been welcomed by Japanese readers – *Ancient Capital* was translated into Japanese in 2000 – but it does not enjoy the prestige that Kawabata's enjoys in China and Taiwan. See Huang Yingzhe and Zhang for more on the Japanese reception of the Taiwanese *Ancient Capital*, as well as late twentieth-century Japanese interest in Taiwanese literature.

17 Unlike the *Shōwa Man'yōshū*, Kawabata's novel is not an obviously willful omission of other cultural production.

18 Lu Xun's relationship with Fujino has attracted considerable attention among Japanese; there have been a number of monographs on the subject as well as retellings of the Lu Xun–Fujino story.

19 During his three-week stay in Japan, Guo Moruo met with old Japanese friends and made new ones in cities and towns across the country. His welcome and farewell parties, the latter of which brought together about 1000 Japanese, were hosted by multiple Japanese organizations (Liu Deyou; Lü, 412–418). For Japanese impressions of 1950s China see Nakano Shigeharu's (中野重治) essays "Beijing, Shanghai no hon'ya" (Bookstores in Beijing and Shanghai; 北京,上海の本屋) and "Chūgoku no tabi" (China Travels; 中国の旅). During the colonial period Nakano had befriended a number of Chinese and Korean writers (Thornber 52, 183–184). See also Shimamura.

20 The most obvious example of this phenomenon was the censoring of the Chinese writer Ah Long's (阿龍) novel *Nanjing* (南京,1939), the first and for 50 years one of the very few Chinese fictional works dealing with the Nanjing Massacre of 1937. Although the destruction of Nanjing is now a cause célèbre and has a small but important presence in contemporary Chinese literature, for various reasons related to the stability of their own regimes, both the Nationalist Party and the Chinese Communist Party silenced creative writings about it until the 1980s: Ah Long's *Nanjing* was not published until 1987, and then only after it had been considerably abridged and renamed *Nanjing xueji* (南京血跡). The latter text was translated into Japanese in 1994 and has a foreword by Ah Long's son.

21 Victorious nations are less likely to be held accountable for their crimes, as are nations with which there is a more dependent cultural, economic, or political relationship.

22 In contrast, the novel was not translated into a Western language until 1954, with Teru Hasegawa's Esperanto version, published in Tokyo. Its only other Western-language translation is Zeljko Cipris's 2003 English version.

23 The Chinese edition of *Frog*, published in Shanghai the same month as the Taiwanese edition (December 2009), includes neither a preface nor an afterword; a brief write-up on Mo Yan on the cover's inner flap lists some of his other works, the many languages into which they have been translated, and the numerous international prizes they have won. This brief snippet only hints at the power of the work, indicating that *Frog* was many years in the making, and claiming it a masterpiece that "touches the sorest spot of the Chinese people's soul" and "mercilessly analyzes contemporary intellectuals' petty souls." The write-up also does not mention Ōe, speaking only of the letters the narrator Ke Dou sends to "the righteous Japanese author Sugiya."

Works Cited

Ah Long. *Nanjing xueji*. Beijing: Renmin Wenxue Chubanshe, 1987.

Ba Jin. "Ji duan bu gongjing de hua," in *Ba Jin quanji* 12. Beijing: Renmin Wenxue Chubanshe, 1986. 511–515.

Ba Jin. "Wenxue shenghuo wushi nian," in *Ba Jin xuanji* 1. Chengdu: Sichuan Renmin Chubanshe, 1982. 1–12.

Curley, David L. "Maharaja Krisnacandra, Hinduism, and Kingship in the Contact Zone of Bengal," in Richard B. Barnett, ed., *Rethinking Early Modern India*. New Delhi: Manohar Publishers and Distributors, 2002. 85–117.

Damrosch, David. *What Is World Literature?* Princeton: Princeton University Press, 2003.

Dazai Osamu. *Sekibetsu, Dazai Osamu zenshū* 7. Tokyo: Chikuma Shobō, 1990. 3–130.

Dingwaney, Anuradha. "Introduction: Translating 'Third World' Cultures," in Anuradha Dingwaney and Carol Maier, eds., *Between Languages and Cultures: Translation and Cross-Cultural Texts*. Pittsburgh: University of Pittsburgh Press, 1995. 3–15.

Dobie, Madeleine. "Translation in the Contact Zone: Antoine Galland's *Mille et une nuits: contes arabes*," in Saree Makdisi and Felicity Nussbaum, eds., *The Arabian Nights in Historical Context: Between East and West*. New York: Oxford University Press, 2008. 25–49.

Dudden, Alexis. *Troubled Apologies among Japan, Korea, and the United States*. New York: Columbia University Press, 2008.

Fitz, Karsten. *Negotiating History and Culture: Transculturation in Contemporary Native American Fiction*. New York: Peter Lang, 2001.

Green, Renée, ed. *Negotiations in the Contact Zone*. Lisbon: Assírio & Alvin, 2003.

He, Yinan. "History, Chinese Nationalism and the Emerging Sino-Japanese Conflict," *Journal of Contemporary China* 16:50 (2007): 1–24.

Huang Yingzhe, ed. *Taiwan wenxue yanjiu zai Riben*. Taipei: Qianwei Chubanshe, 1994.

Inukai Takashi. "Jobun," in Kohō Banri, ed., *Taiwan Man'yōshū*. Tokyo: Shūeisha, 1994. 15–17.

Ishikawa Tatsuzō. *Huozhe de bingshi*. Taipei: Maitian Chuban Youxian Gongsi, 1995. Trans. Liu Musha.

Ishikawa Tatsuzō. *Huozhe de shibing.* Beijing: Kunlun Chubanshe, 1987. Trans. Zhong Qing'an and Ou Xilin.

Ishikawa Tatsuzō. *Ikiteiru heitai, Chūō kōron* 53:3 (March 1938): 1–105.

Kawabata Yasunari. *Koto,* in *Kawabata Yasunari zenshū* 18. Tokyo: Shinchōsha, 1980. 229–435.

Kim Hŭng-gyu. *Hanguk munhak pŏn-yŏksŏji mokrok.* Seoul: Koryŏdae Minjok Munhwa Yŏn-guwŏn, 1998.

"Kinoshita Junji to no kaiwa," in Ōbayashi Shigeru and Kitabayashi Masae, eds., *Ha Kin* [Ba Jin] *shasaku shōgai.* Sendai: Bungei Tōhoku Shinsha, 1999. 326–341.

Kohō Banri. "Maegaki," in Kohō Banri, ed., *Taiwan Man'yōshū.* Tokyo: Shūeisha, 1994. 8–11, 30.

Kohō Banri, ed. *Taiwan Man'yōshū.* Tokyo: Shūeisha, 1994.

Kumar, Sukrita and Malashri Lal. "Introduction," in Sukrita Kumar and Malashri Lal, eds., *Speaking for Myself: An Anthology of Asian Women's Writing.* New Delhi: Penguin, 2009. xix–xxviii.

Kuroko Kazuo and Kan Dunwen. *Nihon kin-gendai bungaku no Chūgokugoyaku sōran.* Tokyo: Bensei Shuppan, 2006.

Lape, Noreen Groover. *West of the Border: The Multicultural Literature of the Western American Frontiers.* Athens: Ohio University Press, 2000.

Lind, Jennifer. *Sorry States: Apologies in International Politics.* Ithaca: Cornell University Press, 2008.

Liu Deyou. Kaku Matsujaku [Guo Moruo] *Nihon no tabi: zuikōki.* Tokyo: Saimaru Shuppankai, 1992. Trans. Maruyama Makoto.

Lu Xun. "Tengye xiansheng," *Lu Xun ji.* Guangzhou: Huacheng Chubanshe, 2000. 497–503.

Lü Yuanming. *Riben wenxue lunshi: jianji Zhong-Ri bijiao wenxue.* Changchun: Dongbei Shifan Daxue Chubanshe, 1992.

Maruyama, Noboru. "Lu Xun in Japan," in Leo Ou-fan Lee, ed., *Lu Xun and His Legacy.* Berkeley: University of California Press, 1985. 216–242.

Mo Yan. "A Writer Has a Nationality, but Literature Has No Boundary," *Chinese Literature Today* 1:1 (Summer 2010).

Mo Yan. *Amei.* Tokyo: Chūō Kōronsha, 2011. Trans. Yoshida Tomio.

Mo Yan. *Ếch.* Hà Nội: Văn học, 2010. Trans. Nguyên Trần.

Mo Yan. *Shifu, You'll Do Anything for a Laugh.* New York: Arcade Publishers, 2001. Trans. Howard Goldblatt.

Mo Yan. "Tingqu washeng yipian," in *Wa.* Taipei: Maitian Chuban, 2009. 3–6.

Mo Yan. *Wa.* Shanghai: Shanghai Wenyi Chubanshe, 2009.

Mo Yan. *Wa.* Taipei: Maitian Chuban, 2009.

Nakano Shigeharu. "Beijing, Shanghai no hon'ya," in *Nakano Shigeharu zenshū* 23. Tokyo: Chikuma Shobō, 1978. 522–525.

Nakano Shigeharu. "Chūgoku no tabi," in *Nakano Shigeharu zenshū* 23. Tokyo: Chikuma Shobō, 1978. 345–528.

Nakata Shōei. *Ai to kanashimi to tabidachi no uta: Ro Jin* [Lu Xun], *Ōgai, Sofia, Akashi, Tōten, to Nichiro sensō.* Tokyo: Ikuhōsha, 2001.

Ōe Kenzaburō. "Nobel Lecture," http://nobelprize.org/nobel_prizes/literature/laureates/1994/oe-lecture.html.

Ōe Kenzaburō and Kim Chiha. "An Autonomous Subject's Long Waiting, Coexistence." *positions* 5:1 (Spring 1997): 285–314.

Ortiz, Fernando. *Contrapunteo cubana del tabaco y el azúcar.* Caracas: Biblioteca Ayachucho, 1987.

Peres, Phyllis. *Transculturation and Resistance in Lusophone African Narrative*. Gainesville: University Press of Florida, 1997.

Pickles, Katie and Myra Rutherdale, eds. *Contact Zones: Aboriginal and Settler Women in Canada's Colonial Past*. Vancouver: University of British Columbia Press, 2005.

Pratt, Mary Louise. *Imperial Eyes: Travel Writing and Transculturation*, 2nd ed. New York: Routledge, 2008.

Rama, Ángel. *Transculturación narrativa en América Latina*. Mexico: Siglo Veintiuno Editores, 1982.

Reichl, Susanne. *Cultures in the Contact Zone: Ethnic Semiosis in Black British Literature*. Trier: Wissenschaftlicher Verlag Trier, 2002.

Shimamura Kagayaki. "Nakano Shigeharu no 'Chūgoku no tabi,'" *Ajia yūgaku* 13 (February 2002): 19–29.

Shōwa Man'yōshū. Tokyo: Kōdansha, 1979–1980.

Thornber, Karen Laura. *Empire of Texts in Motion: Chinese, Korean, and Taiwanese Transculturations of Japanese Literature*. Cambridge: Harvard-Yenching Institute Monograph Series, Harvard Asia Center Publications Program, 2009.

Thornber, Karen Laura. "Legitimacy and Community: Traveling Writers and Texts in Post-1945 East Asia," *Paradoxa* 22 (2010): 7–39.

Thornber, Karen Laura. "Reimagining Regions and Worlds: Literature, East Asia, and the Indian Ocean Rim" (unpublished book manuscript).

Thornber, Karen Laura. "Texts in Turmoil: Global Health and World Literature" (unpublished book manuscript).

Wang Xiangyuan. *Ershi shiji Zhongguo de Riben fanyi wexue shi*. Beijing: Beijing Shifan Daxue Chubanshe, 2001.

Yang Zhaoquan. *Zhongchao guanxishi lunwenji*. Beijing: Shijie Zhishe Chubanshe, 1988.

Yi Myŏnghŭi. "Ilmunhak pŏn-yŏksŏ ŭi pyŏnchŏn kwajŏng e kwanhan yŏn-gu: 1895–1995 nyŏn ŭi 100 nyŏn-gan ŭi Ilmunhak pŏn-yŏksŏ e kwanhayŏ," *Kyŏnghŭi Taehakkyo Taehakwŏn Il-ŏ Ilmunhakkwa* 7 (July 1997): 70–87.

Yoshida Tomio. "Yakusha atogaki," in Mo Yan, *Amei*. Tokyo: Chūō Kōronsha, 2011. 470–476.

Yun Sang-in et al. *Ilbon munhak pŏn-yŏk 60 nyŏn hyŏnhwang kwa punsŏk: 1945–2005*. Seoul: Somyŏng Ch'ulp'an, 2008.

Yun Sang-in et al. "Ilbon munhak ŭi Hanguk-ŏ pŏn-yŏk hyŏnhwang e kwanhan chosa (1945 1997)." *Hanyang Ilbonhak* 6 (February 1998): 167–272.

Zhang Jilin. "Ribenren kan Zhu Tianxin de *Gudu*," in Li Fengmao and Liu Yuanru, eds., *Kongjian diyu yu wenhua: Zhongguo wenhua kongjian de shuxie yu chanshi* 1.Taipei: Zhongyang Yanjiuyuan Zhongguo Wenzhe Yanjiusuo, 2002. 481–514.

Zhong Qing'an and Ou Xilin. "Yizhe de hua," in *Huozhe de shibing*. Beijing: Kunlun Chubanshe, 1987. 1–5.

Zhu Tianxin. *Gudu*, in *Gudu*. Taipei: Rye Field Publications, 1997. 151–233.

32

Global Cinema, World Cinema (2010)

Denilson Lopes

Denilson Lopes is Professor at the School of Communications at Federal University of Rio de Janeiro. Lopes' main research areas are Latin American and global cinema, the aesthetics of communication, gender studies, cultural studies, and comparative and world literature. The relation between world cinema and worldliness as landscape is the subject of his book *At the Heart of the World: Transcultural Landscapes of Contemporary Cinema* (*No Coração do Mundo: Paisagens Transculturais*, 2012). In *Delicateness: Aesthetics, Experience and Landscapes* (*A Delicadeza: Estética, Experiência e Paisagens*, 2007), Lopes interrogates the possibility of aesthetics in a postmodern landscape, comparing films, novels, and music in different cultures. He is co-editor of *Image and Sexual Diversity* (2004) and editor of *The Cinema of the 90's* (2005), and has been president of the Brazilian Association of Homoculture Studies (ABEH) and of the Brazilian Society of Cinema and Audiovisual Studies (SOCINE).

In "Global Cinema, World Cinema," Lopes argues in favor of advancing the concept of "world cinema" in contemporary cinema studies. Rather than representing a mere process of Hollywoodization or cultural leveling, Lopes sees the "world" in world cinema as "an aesthetic challenge." In a global age, memory and affect are not only themes but structural elements which offer different possibilities for organizing social space and the construction of characters. Lopes analyzes the intersections of world literature, world music, and world cinema through "the search for transcultural landscapes in contemporary cinema, in dialogue with equivalent expressions in literature and music."

In the nineteenth century, at the same time that the concept of a national literature was developing, there also arose a parallel idea: that of a world literature

Denilson Lopes, "Global Cinema, World Cinema" (2010). In *E-compós* 13:2 (2010), pp. 1–14.

(*Weltliteratur*), a term coined by Goethe. More recently, especially since the 1970s, the recorded music industry came to utilize the term *world music*. Not as well known, more recent and with less of an impact in critical debates, at least up to now, is the expression *world cinema*. In the present paper, I will not only seek to delineate the concept of what would be, in today's world, "global art" or "world art," but also to suggest a path, continuous with the search for transcultural landscapes in contemporary cinema, in dialogue with equivalent expressions in literature and music. I will not attempt an exhaustive inventory of the terms "world literature" and "world music", nor of the details of the debates surrounding them; I will merely address elements that are useful in reflecting over contemporary cinema.

One thing worth retaining from Goethe's idea of a world literature is his search for alternatives to what was then an emerging discourse privileging the specificities of national cultures. However, unlike the idea put forth by Goethe, after the diverse criticisms of "universal" totalizing categories made by post-structuralists and also by intellectuals in the area of Cultural Studies, it is uncomfortable, to say the least, to fall back upon a vague humanist discourse that is sustained only by the idea that readers from different cultures may develop a sense of kinship to a culture other than their own, as the result of, or strengthened by, having read works by authors from other cultures.

Since people travel, it is only natural that ideas and works also travel, that they are translated, interpreted and read in the most far-flung places. And in this sense, although Goethe had an essentially Eurocentric frame of reference, he was not a purist in any sense in defending the idea that in translation, the original work takes on new meanings. He even considered comments on *Faust*, made by foreign critics who had read it in translation, to be more interesting than critiques made from within the German-speaking world. What we can take away from Goethe's notion of a world literature is that global art – which certainly includes global cinema – does not refer to a specific school or movement, nor even to a certain body of literature, "a sum of all national literatures," (Guillén, 1993, p. 38, my translation), nor "an object, it is a *problem*, and a problem that asks for a new critical method" (Moretti, 2004, p. 149), another way of seeing.

Also relevant to the present analysis are discussions of world music, for they are marked by a peculiarity also present in the concept of world cinema. If the label *world music*, which arose within the North American recorded music industry, signified the recognition that there was a market for music in languages other than English, whose styles were not linked to North American pop culture, the term also risked creating a kind of ghetto into which a multiplicity of different musical styles were lumped together, according to a generic, vaguely-defined sense of exotic alterity.

In this vein, the expression *world cinema*, utilized in cinema studies in the Anglophone world, would seem to create, with no better conceptual consistency, a grab-bag category that includes any cinematic works that are not European or North American and/or that are in languages other than English, in the same way that the term *world literature* has been applied in literary studies (Damrosch, 2003, p. 282).

World cinema would thus be "analagous to *world music* and *world literature* in that they are categories created in the Western world to refer to cultural products and practices that are mainly non-Western." (Dennison; Lim, 2006, p. 1).

In beginning to address the subject of global cinema,[1] we come to a point not contemplated thus far: the production and distribution circuits of cultural products and works of art. As in discussions of *world music*, especially the collab-orations between Anglophone pop stars with musicians from all over the world (such as the well-known and hotly debated cases of Paul Simon, Peter Gabriel, David Byrne and Sting, to mention only a few), it would be mistaken to consider any film produced with an international cast and crew to be global cinema, since as far back as the 1920s, Hollywood employed professionals from various coun-tries, whose professional styles were modified to fit the demands of the American film industry.

To think of a global art form as "mode of circulation and of reading, a mode that is as applicable to individual works as to bodies of material, available for reading established classics and new discoveries alike" (Damrosch, 2003, p. 5) – certainly is a step forward, but we need to go a bit further in order to utilize the concept of global art, within the historical singularity that emerges in the context of late capitalism, considering not only "literary works that circulate beyond their culture of origin, either in translation or in their original language" (idem, p. 4), created by authors whose books may be translated into other languages within a few years after their original publication, thus reaching audiences that may be much larger than their readership in their home cultures (idem, p. 18).

Even though it is important to recognize that the conditions of distribution – and, I would contend, of production as well – can result in films having crew mem-bers drawn from various countries and in their reaching millions of spectators from around the world, at the same time, this creates a new tension for artists who hope to reach international audiences and who, to that end, are willing to take the risk of self-exoticization (Dennison; Lim, 2006, p. 3).

In reflecting over what constitutes a truly global cinema, I distanced myself from films characterized by mere exoticism or by strictly cultural phenomena, which operate via processes similar to tourism, reducing art to an easy way of getting access to other realities and places, to a product that is consumed before, during or in lieu of travels, offering the possibility of simulating travel without leaving the comfort of home, like the universal fairs so popular at the end of the nineteenth century before the introduction of theme parks exhibiting cultural icons and images. Instead, I sought works that were aesthetically singular, in which the experience of globaliza-tion was configured as part of everyday experience, memory, affect being translated and interpreted, not only as themes but as questions indivisible from the work's creation within a multidirectional network, as suggested by Negri and Hardt, in the context of Empire, in which they deconstruct categories such as First World/Third World and by extension the theory of three cinemas and dichotomies such as *mainstream*/independent. Global cinema would thus have more of a rhizome structure, if we consider it from a Deleuzian perspective. This characteristic is fundamental in the notion of empire as a network, in contrast to the axial structures that are part of the configuration of national cinemas, with their own specific pasts, presents and futures. Regarding rhizome structure, global cinema would be closer to an "atlas," a "map" (Andrew, 2006), or perhaps even being a constellation with multiple possibilities of configuration, constituting itself via "a method, a way of cutting across film history according to waves of relevant films and movements, thus creating flexible geographies" (Nagib, 2006, p. 35).

In reflecting over global cinema, we should bear in mind the political and anti-homogenizing dimensions of discussions of Third Cinema, not necessarily because of their revolutionary content couched in the rhetorical style of the 1960s, but to help to avoid the expression "global cinema" becoming just one more of the entertainment industry's categories of consumption, a neoliberal tool that diminishes specificities by disqualifying any kind of national construct, most notably for countries with less robust economies. The rhetoric of Third Cinema, however, is insufficient for constructing global cinema as a mechanism for opening up to the practices and objects of other cultures. As we will see further on, this concern is expressed in a more sophisticated way in the theoretical and critical debates over some films emphasizing the setting and characters. From the start, we can think of two possible alternatives for global cinema. Naturally, no film could be set in the entire world, but it is possible for one to take place in a number of different places, and for it to be made by a crew that has passed through a number of different countries and continents, with the finished work recreating this experience of movement even if filmed in the studio. Moreover, even if the film is shot in a single location, it can emphasize how this place is marked by references from other cultures, whether because of migrations or images that arrive via mass media. Within these possibilities, I would like to discuss not merely miscegenations, hybridisms and interculturalities, but also how the world is shown, not merely as a synonym for distance, the Other, alterity, but as an inclusive, non-dichotomous construction. In the end, whatever global or world cinema may be, we would like to discuss how the world can be represented to the viewer, who can speak about it and how it is configured as an aesthetic challenge.

A possible starting point is the three categories that Martin Roberts identifies in the global imaginary of Euro-North-American cinema. First, he identifies *global exploitation films* – *Mondo Cane* (1963), for example – which are marked by a Carnivalesque exoticizing, colonialist perspective, to the extent that they present a world that becomes chaotic in the absence of Europe's civilizing presence (Roberts, 1998, pp. 66–67, our translation, summarizing information drawn from the text rather than by direct citation). Next, the author speaks of the *coffee-table globalism* (idem, p. 66) of films such as *Koyaanisqatsi* (1982) and *Powaqqatsi* (1988), both by Godfrey Reggio, or Ron Fricke's *Baraka* (1992). It is on this kind of imaginary that Martin Roberts dwells in his article. These two films have no dialogue or voice-overs, and their soundtracks are omnipresent and primarily instrumental. They juxtapose images from different countries and their peoples, focusing on spectacular, monumental natural and urban landscapes, with an emphasis on religious rituals, crowded streets, working people, without singling out any central characters except for the occasional quick close-up, depicting a kind of global quotidian.

Finally, Roberts points to the existence of a third imaginary, which he refers to as the "conspicuous cosmopolitanism of the international avant-garde" (idem, p. 66), including films such as *Until the End of the World* (Wim Wenders, 1991), *Night on Earth* (Jim Jarmusch, 1991), and *Sans Soleil* (Chris Marker, 1982). Roberts also mentions Werner Herzog, Ottinger, Aki and Mika Kaurismäki, who engage in a "form of detached, sardonic observation of an increasingly transnational world order and cultural change associated with" directors and characters alike self-consciously constituting themselves as "nomads" and "postmodern descendants of Baudelaire's flâneurs, rootless cosmopolitans threading their way around the globe in search of the even new and different," for whom "tourism, tourist sites, tourists themselves are typically subjects of disdain or satire, even though filmmakers and protagonists are no less tourists than anyone else. What is perhaps most memorable about films of this type is their cult of cosmopolitanism, with its accompanying disdain for the parochialism of the national" (Roberts, 1998, p. 67). It is this last type of imaginary, which Roberts does not [develop] in his paper, that I would like to explore here, also mentioning films released after the publication of his paper, such as *Flirt* (Hal Hartley, 1995), and *The Intruder* (Claire Denis, 2004), as well as others produced by cineastes from outside of Western Europe and the United States, including *Here We Are, Waiting for You* (Marcelo Masagão, 1998), *The World* (Jia Zhang-Ke, 2004), and *Babel* (Alejandro González Iñarritu, 2006) – which may perhaps broaden or modify the framework presented by Roberts.

However, before examining films that seek to portray the world, it may be important to pause to consider the return of cosmopolitanism, a term that Roberts uses to refer to such films. Discussions of cosmopolitanism are recurring, in the history of ideas, in the social and political sciences, economics and law, as well as in studies of cultural and intellectual elites, or even of those who were usually excluded from the benefits of globalization – that is to say, unskilled workers and the poor. It is beyond the scope of this paper to fully summarize this debate; I will only mention some questions that may be helpful in better understanding the films that will be discussed in this paper.

Over the past twenty years, parallel to the emergence of discourse on globalization and multiculturalism, cosmopolitanism has reappeared via a variety of conferences, publications and perspectives. Although cosmopolitanism has a long history, one that is older than that of nationalist discourses, its contemporary form has little to do with what appeared in eighteenth-century French philosophy, which designated, above all, "an intellectual ethic, a universal humanism that transcends regional particularism" (Cheah, 1998a, p. 22). Cosmopolitanism today is less a rigorous concept than an open project (Bhabha *et al.*, 2002, p. 1), an "attitude" (Malcomson, 1998, p. 233) whose challenges are not theoretical but practical (idem, 238). At the very least, perhaps, cosmopolitanism is less interesting as an abstract discussion than as a "strategic bargain with universalism" in which there is "a purposeful concern for all humanity without ignoring 'difference'" (idem, 234). Thus, "the term is not as philosophically ambitious as the word *universalism*, though it does the same work. [...] Nor is it as politically ambitious as the word *internationalism*" but it can help to avoid confusion with "an attempt to revive the naïve Third Worldism of the 1960s." So "the term cosmopolitanism better describes the sensibility of our moment" (Robbins, 1998b, p. 260).

Clearly, there are various problems, among them, determining who is in the position of being "empowered to decide who is provincial" (Malcomson, 1998, p. 238). To establish rigid dichotomies between cosmopolitanism and provincialism, or between localism and nationalism, may not be profitable, given the complex relationships between the global and the local that have led, among other things, to the creation of the term 'glocal'. While we may not think of a cosmopolite as someone who belongs nowhere, and even though it may be difficult to imagine "a paranoid fantasy of ubiquity and omniscience," that is, of belonging everywhere, of being everyplace (Robbins, 1998b, p. 260), it is also not worthwhile to recreate the cosmopolite in the so-often criticized way (especially by the left), as someone characterized by "a privileged and irresponsible detachment" (Robbins, 1998a, p. 4). This occurs because, more and more, the importance of global resistance and world citizenship are considered important issues, and there is increasing recognition of the need to move beyond the privilege currently accorded [by theorists] to diaspora as a social construction and also to the politics of hybridism and interculturalities (Cheah, 1998b).

Incorporated into this is the need to understand cosmopolitanism as one of the "cultural forms of the contemporary world, without logically or chronologically presupposing the authority of the Occidental experience or of the models derived from that experience" (Appadurai, 1991, 192, our translation), assuming various forms of cosmopolitanism such as the post-colonial (Parry, 1991, p. 41), the vernacular (Bhabha, 1996, pp. 191/207), the periphery (Prysthon, 2002), the poor classes (Santiago, 2004, pp. 45/63) or even the patriotric (Appiah, 1998, p. 91). Despite the diversity of terms and views pertaining to cosmopolitanism, we could say that one thing they have in common is that they "presuppose a positive attitude in relation to difference, a desire to construct broad alliances and peaceful, egalitarian global communities, with citizens who are capable of communicating across social and cultural frontiers, creating a universal solidarity" (Ribeiro, 2003, p. 17, our translation). This aspect is even more apparent if we understand post-colonialism as a cosmopolitics of intellectuals from former British colonies whose independence came after World War II, with the desire to provincialize Europe; the task of a post-colonialism that includes Latin America, then, would be to provincialize the United States (idem, p. 30).

Another thing that should be noted is that the term cosmopolitan has come to refer not only to cultural and economic elites – because of their historical privileges, in terms of access to travel – but to those who are privy to a wide range of information, involving the possibilities brought by the mass communications media. There is also the cosmopolitan aspect of today's massive intercontinental migratory movement of workers, whose precursors, as James Clifford (1997, pp. 33–34) reminds us, were not only gentlemen travelers but also the servants who accompanied them.

Thus, cosmopolitanism is a kind of reaction, as much to the excesses of local, regional and national provincialism as it is to the experience of migration, of being uprooted, of forever being an outsider, of never belonging anywhere. In fact, cosmopolitanism is another kind of belonging, the result of the formation of multiple ties, through which the world effectively becomes one's home.

In order to understand this possibility more clearly and in greater detail, we will now move on to examining how the world is conceived of from within cinema. Some films tell stories that take place simultaneously in different parts of the globe – such as in the recent *Babel*, in which a rifle that passes from the possession of one person to another forms the basis for a narrative that moves from the United States to Mexico, Morocco and Japan, or in *Night on Earth*, which weaves together different incidents all taking place in taxis on the same night in five different cities. In a certain way, these films are the heirs of a genre of cinematic works dating back at least to the 1920s that seek to present urban daily life via juxtaposed, parallel stories. In the present paper, however, I will focus on two films that utilize different narrative techniques: a global *road movie* and a film that represents international travel in a single location. Our first stop will be Wim Wenders' *Until the End of the World* (1991).

Since the beginning of his career, Wim Wenders has had an obsession for characters in movement – in search of a home, a person, or simply drifting. *Until the End of the World* is his most ambitious film in terms of the scale of the production and also its cost. Filmed in twelve different countries, it features a cast of characters who wander through Europe, Asia, and the United States, finally arriving in the interior of Australia. It is not a matter of a journey though a city, a country or a continent, but over the entire world. More than a set, the world is a space no longer marked by a malaise brought on by German Nazism, nor by an ambiguous relationship with North American culture. This new sentiment, this changed position is defined by Wenders himself as "cosmopolitan" (Wenders, 2001, p. 292).

In the first part of the film, stolen money and credit cards acquired during a robbery enable several characters to begin a voyage in which huge cities seem to be neighbors, different neighborhoods of a single borderless global megalopolis. The journey seems to be as instantaneous as mass-media connections. The robbery brings in elements of detective movies, and there is even a detective, played by Rüdiger Vogler, but the idea is less to create suspense than to develop connections between the various places through which the plot moves. The cities, mostly European, are shown under the sign of excess: excessive movement, information and images.

Little by little, we perceive that this is what the film is about: it examines the relationship between the gaze and the image, a recurring question in Wenders' work. Sam Farber (William Hurt) is a scientist who travels the world in order to record images of his family, which is spread out across the world, so that his blind mother, Edith (Jeanne Moreau), can see them, using a machine created by his father, Henry

Farber (Max von Sydow). But the device, a kind of film camera, tires the eyes and eventually ruins the vision of the person doing the recording. The film resumes an ethical position taken by Wenders: that the excess of images, the excessive desire to see, leads to physical or metaphorical blindness. It is significant that Sam Farber takes up residence in a small village in Japan, where medicinal herbs are applied to his eyes. As though the cure for the excess of images, of the world, could be found in pauses, in withdrawal, in isolated places, or even in writing.

The reappearance of the local comes in an ambiguous way in the film. If the small Japanese town is a place of cure for Sam Farber, the journey's end comes in the arid interior of Australia, where Henry Farber's laboratory is conducting research to develop the machine that will make it possible for the blind to see. The father, a famous scientist, fled from the United States with his family so that the device would not fall into the hands of the military and large corporations. For him, the location is merely a place that permits him a degree of isolation while also making it possible for him to carry on with his work. He does not reflect over the toll that this takes on his family, nor the impact on the local aboriginal community. As a scientist, he embodies a form of knowledge that is unable to see others, one that is blind to other ways of knowing.

Here, the end of the world is more than the spectre of disaster; it is the progressive elimination of places that are distant from everything, with the advance of mass communications media and the technologies associated with them. The end of the world also appears in another way, midway through the film, when a satellite whose malfunctioning has been suggested since the beginning finally falls to earth, causing a global blackout and equipment failure. Cars come to a halt, computers and telephones go dead. Is it the end of the world when people only have knowledge of what is in their physical and geographical proximity? Or is it the end of the technological world, as it came into existence in the second half of the nineteenth century?

The communications networks are re-established, but Henry Farber's research takes another direction. He no longer seeks to make the blind see, but begins working on a way to make dreams visible by transforming them into digital images that reveal to onlookers what was once private and hidden within the individual. With this, his aboriginal assistants abandon the laboratory, in opposition to this transformation of the inner world, while the remaining characters become more and more obsessed with seeing their own dreams, withdrawing into their own worlds, blind to the world outside.

Later, in one of the most redemptive endings in Wenders' work, Sam Farber's girlfriend, Claire (Solveig Dommartin), appears enveloped in what seems to be an aura of light. Now an environmental activist, she travels around the earth caring for the planet, in clear contrast to her situation in the beginning of the film, when she was lost, unable to recognize where she was when she woke up, as though in a succession of nightmares and missed rendezvous. It is her birthday, and she receives congratulatory messages from a number of the film's characters, via screens that are present in the spaceship in which she navigates around the Earth. It is not a happy ending for the couple, but a celebration of the possibilities offered by technology, in terms of maintaining affective ties. It's a gamble.

> I love to look at positive utopias; even if they are sometimes terribly naïve and sometimes just a bit woozy; I still find it more fruitful than dystopias. I have no interest in gloomy views of the future. The end of the world is such common currency nowadays, you can't do anything with it. All that "no future" talk bores me to tears (Wenders, 2001, p. 295).

It is worth pointing out that this gamble involves cosmopolitanism, clearly defined as an existential and ethical attitude that is distinct from irresponsible distancing that is the privilege and prerogative of cultural elites.

Perhaps the most lingering question raised by the film is whether it is possible to speak of a global quotidian, apart from Wenders' utopian perspective, an everyday life unmarked by grandiloquent tones and *tour de force* (and by the production), which leads the characters of *Until the End of the World* to criss-cross the globe, at the same time that a satellite, whose gaze is turned toward the earth as it moves at high speed through space, begins to fall down into the concrete and material world. In Wenders' previous film *Wings of Desire* (1987), the angels believed in the material world as a poetic possibility, abdicating their place in eternity in favor of it; in *Until the End of the World*, on the other hand, the characters seem to be suspended by and within communicative webs, finding their space for encounters, their way of belonging, perhaps their community. In *Until the End of the World*, Wenders seems to gamble on the potential of a cosmopolitanism that is redefined by technology but not subject to its excesses.

In reflecting over this descent to earth, and turning to a vision of cosmopolitanism less luminous than the one presented by Wenders, one that speaks from another place, perhaps we should accept Ernst Bloch's challenge and shift our attention to Jia Zhang-Ke's *The World* (2004): "Things on the margin are beginning to play an increasingly important role. We should pay attention to the little things, look into them more closely. The curious and the strange often tells us the most. Certain things can only be expressed in such stories, and not in a lofty, epic style" (*apud* Grob, 1997, p. 191).

The world, in Jia Zhang-Ke's film, is the name of a theme park in Beijing that boasts famous monuments in miniature: the Eiffel Tower, the Egyptian Pyramids, Lower Manhattan, "still with the twin towers of the World Trade Center," as one guide proudly puts it, as well as Big Ben, the Leaning Tower of Pisa, the Taj Mahal, the Vatican and the Parthenon. Again, the images representing the world come mostly from the Occidental tradition, catapulted by the tourism industry to places of desire. The park is accessible by a kind of train that "passes through the most disparate countries" in fifteen minutes. The characters themselves speak in terms of "going to India," or "going to Japan," as they move from one monument to another. All this is reflected in the park's advertising slogans: "See the world without having to leave Beijing" or "Give us a day and we'll show you the world."

But what kind of world are we shown? Unlike Wenders, who gives us a road movie that sweeps across countries and continents, Jia Zhang-Ke constructs his film without even focusing on the visitors to the theme park; rather, he concentrates on the park's workers, especially its security guards and a group of young women who work in a kind of musical revue that celebrates the different cultures of the world. They are unskilled workers who come from small towns, for whom the biggest voyage of their lives seems to have been the trip from their hometowns to Beijing. In fact, state restrictions make it difficult for them to leave the country, as in the case of one character who finally obtains a visa, years after her husband left the country illegally. It seems to be easier for foreigners to come to Beijing: some of the park's employees are Russian women who were brought into the country under ambiguous circumstances that suggest trafficking in women.

The target of the film is not a simplistic social critique of the world but merely a side of it that is not shown by the ascetic, monumental and pasteurized character of the monuments trasformed into scenario and image. Without being a festive apotheosis of the world of the simulacrum set in a Las Vegas replete with neon in the midst of Fourth of July celebrations, as in Coppola's *One From The Heart* (1982), the park also brings the possibility of a better life for its workers. It is a space of social encounters, a very particular transcultural landscape in which media images of the world take on three dimensions, becoming places for walking, working, and living. In contrast to the adventurous tone of Wim Wenders' film, *The World* emphasizes the everyday, ordinary life in which money is counted and saved, and petty squabbles arise within families and between lovers. There is nothing epic or grandiose in the film, neither in its events nor in its characters. The tone is somewhat melancholy, but there is still a gamble at the end, when the couple who protagonize the film, a dancer named Tao (Tao Zhao) and a security guard called Taisheng (Taisheng Chen), apparently are killed in their sleep by a gas leak. A bitter metaphysical gamble in the face of an impoverished everyday environment? Certainly, this is no longer the Bressonian tone of the director's earlier films, in which he was fascinated by youth who, relegated to the margins of China's economic development, faced difficulties in entering the workforce, as in *Xiao Wu* (*Pickpocket*), made in 1998, and *Unknown Pleasures* (2002). *The World* may be Jia Zhang-Ke's most ambitious film. For the first time, he had support from a state producer, which facilitated distribution within China, and he also obtained resources from France and from a Japanese company, Takeshi Kitano. But the film also marks stylistic and technical changes in Jia Zhange-Ke's approach. Cuts diminish the length of the takes, and the scene alternates between a few stark interior living spaces and outside shots of Beijing and the park. Yu Lik-wai's beautiful cinematography contrasts with the grandiosity of the locations, the construction sites and wide expanses of highway which are deserted at night, endangering the characters' lives, a relationship that Jia Zhang-Ke continues to explore in *Still Life* (2006). The presence of a soundtrack – the first in Jia Zhange-Ke's work – composed by Giong Lim, utilizes electronic effects, accentuating the film's aesthetic distance from a certain spareness and frugality in the director's previous work, which was marked by long, rough takes and which utilized only

diegetic sound, techniques exploited fully in *Platform* (2000), a historical anti-epic
that follows a group of young people in a theater group as they travel from one
small Chinese town to another. In *The World*, we also find elements of animation,
especially when the characters are talking on cell phones, which accentuates the
rapidity of communications media associated with transportation, and shows the
fleeting contact by characters who float, fly, and get lost among the world of sets in
which they live, as Tao (Tao Zhao), who spends her days cooped up in an airplane
that simulates flight, succinctly puts it, when she says that she is afraid of turning
into a "ghost." The use of this term is not by chance. The film's characters search to
find their own space in society, but end up becoming lost in the anonymous masses
of unskilled workers. Feeling pressured by their families to send money and at the
same time seeking to construct new lives at the margins of the underworld, they
supplement their meager salaries by resorting to robbery and prostitution. Even
affective relationships, marked by uncertainty and ephemerality, fall under this
ghostly shadow, as in the friendship that develops between Tao and Anna (Allá
Shcherbakova), although the latter is Russian and the two women do not speak
each other's language. The fragility of human relations is also seen in the encounter
between Tao and her ex-boyfriend (Jin Dong Liang). When he visits her on his way
to Ulan Bator in Mongolia, only a vague memory of the experiences they once
shared seems to remain. There is also the stylist Qun (Yi-qun Wang) with whom
Taisheng becomes involved, but their relationship is interrupted when Qun receives
a visa to visit her husband, whom she has not seen since he left to become an illegal
immigrant in Paris a decade ago. At a certain point in the film Tao, who lives in the
midst of people who come and go, says that she has never met anyone who has been
on an airplane, and when she picks up a passport to have a look at it she is unable to
understand how to read it. She has a sense of instability that developed without
even travelling, in a physical sense. Images and people come and go, but she remains
in the same place.

The end of the film, perhaps, brings another kind of meaning. When Tao and her
lover Taisheng are found apparently dead, victims of a gas leak, the screen goes
dark and we hear two voices speaking, the last of the film. He asks, "Are we dead?"
and she replies "This is only the beginning." With no intent of facile allegory, this
exchange seems to intensify what the film has presented, but it is unclear what will
be next or what the consequences are.

In Brazilian cinema, too, we are only beginning to speak of the world, as in Marcelo
Masagão's 1998 film, *Here We Are, Waiting for You [Nós que aqui estamos por vós
esperamos]*, a delicate collage of twentieth century history, a journey via images that
synthesize, in a few moments and a few words written onto the screen, great stories
of ordinary people and ordinary stories of great people, guided by a melancholy
soundtrack by Wim Mertens. The film ends in a cemetery, in some part of Brazil, over
whose entrance is written the beautiful title of the film, the director's reply to part of
a poem by Mayakovski – "They say that someplace, apparently in Brazil, there is a
man who is happy," which are quoted, at the same time that we see Buster Keaton
onscreen, serious and serene, being taken away by a train. But to where?

It is not a matter of representing the world, but of finding ways of living in it. We are truly only beginning. Neither periphery nor center. The world. *Here we are, waiting for you.*

Note

1 Because of the problems surrounding the term world cinema, in this paper I will use global cinema as an alternative.

Bibliography

Andrew, Dudley. An atlas of world cinema. In: Dennison, Stephanie; Lim, Song Hwee (eds.). *Remapping World Cinema*. London: Wallflower, 2006.

Appadurai, Arjun. Global ethnoscapes: notes and queries for a transnational anthropology. In: Fox, Richard (ed.). *Recapturing Anthropology*. Santa Fe: School of American Research Press, 1991.

Appiah, Kwame Anthony. Cosmopolitan Patriots In: Robbins, Bruce; Cheah, Pheng (eds.). *Cosmopolitics*. Minneapolis: University of Minnesota Press, 1998.

Appiah, Kwame Anthony. *Cosmopolitanism: ethics in a world of strangers*. New York: W. W. Norton, 2006.

Bhabha, Homi. Unsatisfied notes on vernacular cosmopolitanism. In: Pfeiffer, Peter; Moreno, Laura (eds.). *Text and Narration*. Columbia: Camden, 1996.

Bhabha, Homi. *et al.* Cosmopolitanisms. In: Bhabha, Homi *et al.* (eds.). *Cosmopolitanism*. Durham: Duke University Press, 2002.

Cheah, Pheng. The Cosmopolitical: today. In: Robbins, Bruce; Cheah, Pheng (eds.). *Cosmopolitics*. Minneapolis: University of Minnesota Press, 1998a.

Cheah, Pheng. Rethinking cosmopolitical freedom in transnationalism. In: Robbins, Bruce; Cheah, Pheng (eds.). *Cosmopolitics*. Minneapolis: University of Minnesota Press, 1998b.

Clifford, James. *Routes*. Cambridge: Harvard University Press, 1997.

Damrosch, David. *What is World Literature?* Princeton: Princeton University Press, 2003.

Dennison, Stephanie; Lim, Song Hwee. Situating world cinema as a theoretical problem. In: Dennison, Stephanie; Lim, Song Hwee; (eds.). *Remapping World Cinema*. London: Wallflower, 2006.

Goethe, Johann von. *Conversações com Eckermann*. Lisboa: Vega, 1990.

Grob, Norbert. 'Life sneaks out of stories': Until the End of the World. In: Cook, Roger; Gemünden, Gerd (eds.). *The Cinema of Wim Wenders*. Detroit: Wayne State University Press, 1997.

Guillén, Claudio. *The Challenge of Comparative Literature*. Cambridge: Harvard University Press, 1993.

Hardt, Michael; Negri, Toni. *Império*. 6th ed. Rio de Janeiro: Record, 2004.

Malcomson, Scott. The varieties of cosmopolitan experience. In: Robbins, Bruce; Cheah, Pheng (eds.). *Cosmopolitics*. Minneapolis: University of Minnesota Press, 1998.

Moretti, Franco. Conjectures on World Literature. In: Prendergast, Christopher (ed.). *Debating World Literature*. London: Verso, 2004.

Nagib, Lúcia. Towards a positive definition of world cinema. In: Dennison, Stephanie; Lim, Song Hwee (eds.). *Remapping World Cinema*. London: Wallflower, 2006.

Parry, Benita. The Contradictions of Cultural Studies. *Transition*, S.l., no. 53, 1991.

Prysthon, Ângela. *Cosmopolitismos Periféricos*. Recife: Bagaço, 2002.

Ribeiro, Gustavo Lins. *Postimperialismo*. Barcelona: Gedisa, 2003.

Robbins, Bruce. Actually existing cosmopolitanism. In: Robbins, Bruce; Cheah, Pheng (eds.). *Cosmopolitics*. Minneapolis: University of Minnesota Press, 1998a.

Robbins, Bruce. Comparative cosmopolitanisms. In: Robbins, Bruce; Cheah, Pheng (eds.). *Cosmopolitics*. Minneapolis: University of Minnesota Press, 1998b.

Roberts, Martin. Baraka: the World Cinema and Global Culture Industry. *Cinema Journal*, S.l., vol. 37, no. 3, pp. 62–82, primavera 1998.

Santiago, Silviano. O cosmopolitismo do pobre. In: *O cosmopoltismo do pobre*. Belo Horizonte, Ed. UFMG: 2004. pp. 45–63.

Santiago, Silviano. Destino: Globalização. ATALHO: Nacionalismo. RECURSO: Cordialidade, *Caderno de Culturais*, Campo Grande, vol. 1, no. 1, pp. 129–134, April 2009.

Wenders, Wim. *On Film: Essays and Conversations*. London: Faber & Faber, 2001.

33

The Strategy of Digital Modernism
Young-hae Chang Heavy Industries'
Dakota *(2008)*

Jessica Pressman

Jessica Pressman entered the new field of digital media studies with her 2007 dissertation at UCLA on relations between modernist poetics and contemporary media, and then joined Yale University's Department of English as their first hire in digital studies, before a subsequent return to California. She works on the relations between literary and artistic experimentalism in the twentieth and twenty-first centuries, with particular attention to new media. These relations reshape the practice of reading and challenge aesthetic assumptions in a world where paper is less and less the dominant form for literary production and circulation. She has co-edited a special issue of *Digital Humanities Quarterly* on "The Literary" (2012) and, together with leading scholar of literature and science N. Katherine Hayles, *Making, Critique: A New Paradigm for the Humanities* (2013). Pressman's essay "The Strategy of Digital Modernism" analyzes the transformations of modernist aesthetics in the Internet narratives of the Korean/American digital collective Young-hae Chang Heavy Industries. Combining text, music, and close reading of modernist literature, Young-hae Chang Heavy Industries both challenges and reinforces the modernist literary canon and its intensive modes of reading, suggesting a need to rethink our concept of literature in a post-postmodern world.

Young-hae Chang Heavy Industries is the name of the collaborative duo, Young-hae Chang and Marc Voge, responsible for some of the most innovative electronic literature online. Their work is programmed in Flash to produce a sophisticated, minimalist aesthetic. Sleek black text in Monaco font – capitalized and

Jessica Pressman, "The Strategy of Digital Modernism: Young-hae Chang Heavy Industries' *Dakota*" (2008). In *Modern Fiction Studies* 54:2 (2008), 302–326. Copyright © for the Purdue Research Foundation by the Johns Hopkins University Press.

World Literature in Theory, First Edition. Edited by David Damrosch.
© 2014 John Wiley & Sons, Ltd. Published 2014 by John Wiley & Sons, Ltd.

unornamented – flashes against a stark white background in speeding synchronization to jazz music. Individual words and phrases pulse out from center screen to take possession of the white space before they are replaced by more text. Young-hae Chang Heavy Industries (YHCHI) refuse to say much about their work – "we can't and won't help readers to 'locate' us" – and revel in a guise of anonymity that they see as constitutive of the medium in which they work: "Distance, homelessness, anonymity, and insignificance are all part of the Internet literary voice, and we welcome them." But in interviews and artist statements, YHCHI repeat the claim that their acclaimed *Dakota* (2002) "is based on a close reading of Ezra Pound's *Cantos* part I and part II" ("Distance").[1] This pronouncement is both a declaration and an invitation: a declaration of alignment with a canonical work of literary modernism and an invitation to read *Dakota* through Pound's first and second cantos. This essay addresses both aspects of YHCHI's statement: I read it as an assertion of literary lineage linking the digital work to a tradition laden with cultural capital in order to analyze how this connection serves *Dakota* and our reading of it. YHCHI's statement expresses a consciously crafted attempt to provide a specific framework through which to approach *Dakota*, a context whose academic and canonical connections are particularly intriguing because *Dakota* exists on the popular and accessible mass media technology of the moment – the Internet. As we will see, *Dakota* exploits this apparent contradiction to promote multiple levels of address and signification in order to defy categorization as high or low, modern or postmodern art. YHCHI demand a cultural repositioning of these critical concepts as literature enters the post-postmodern period and electronic literature, I argue, adopts a strategy of digital modernism.

Dakota is exemplary of what I call "digital modernism," a strategy that adapts literary modernism as a means for challenging the status quo of electronic literature and our assumptions about it. "Digital modernism" is an identifiable organizing principle for a subset of electronic literature that shares a common, conscious modus operandi: these works use central aspects of modernism to highlight their literariness, authorize their experiments, and situate electronic literature at the center of a contemporary digital culture that privileges images, navigation, and interactivity over narrative, reading, and textuality. YHCHI is exemplary of such efforts because their work pursues a minimalist aesthetic that presents a conscious resistance to the central characteristics and expectations of mainstream electronic literature. Works like *Dakota* resist the alignment of electronic literature with hypertext, evade reader-controlled interactivity, and favor the foregrounding text and typography, narrative complexity, and an aesthetic of difficulty. Young-hae Chang, of YHCHI, identifies her simple aesthetic style as an explicit act of defiance: "In my work there is no interactivity; no graphics or graphic design; no photos; no banners; no millions-of-colors; no playful fonts; no pyrotechnics. I have a special dislike for interactivity" ("*Dakota* Description"). It is not simply a "dislike for interactivity" that motivates YHCHI's electronic literature and their desire to connect *Dakota* to modernism. YHCHI see the current state of electronic literature as one in which literature is "not taken very seriously" ("Distance").[2] To rectify this fact, they align their digital literature with a work in a literary canon that is taken very seriously.[3] They appropriate a seminal work from the modernist canon as fodder for their rebellion against mainstream electronic literature; *The Cantos* serve to purchase cultural capital through association and help acquire serious reception for the digital work.[4]

YHCHI identify Pound as their modernist persona, adopting his practice of using personae – literally masks through which to speak to a new age about and through its new literature. Attaching their work to a central figure – or the central figure, for, as T.S. Eliot claims, Pound "is more responsible for the XXth Century revolution in poetry than is any other individual" (xi)[5] – YHCHI induce critical reconsideration of both digital literature and of modernism. As we will see, *Dakota*'s adaptation is both an ironic and an earnest attempt to "MAKE IT NEW" by rearticulating the past. Its text reads as both a simple story about a youthful road trip, complete with colloquial language and allusions to mass culture, but also as a faithful retelling of Pound's first two cantos, the first of which is itself an adaptation of book 11 of Homer's *Odyssey*. YHCHI pursue the modernist practice of renovating an ancient past as inspiration for modern literature, employed by Pound in the opening to his *Cantos*. The result is that *Dakota* not only rereads cantos I and II but repositions them in a contemporary, digital milieu and demands reassessment of "the XXth Century revolution in poetry" that Eliot identifies and whose impact is visible in contemporary electronic literature.

Like all of YHCHI's works, *Dakota* begins with a cinematic countdown that harkens back to the early days of film, the period of literary modernism and its sibling mass media.[6] When the numbers appear onscreen, they are synchronized to the blaring beat of Art Blakey's solo drums in *Dakota*'s soundtrack, "Tobi Ilu." The selection of jazz furthers the connection to modernism, as jazz is the musical and historical counterpart of literary modernism,[7] and also to Pound himself who perceived an intimate connection between poetry and music.[8] The audio visual performance of numbers, text, and drums sets a slow, steady beat that establishes a solid rhythm for the narrative. The beginning of *Dakota* is relatively easy to read, but as the work continues (it runs nearly six minutes), Blakey's drums quicken and the narrative flashes at heightened speeds. *Dakota* does not allow its reader to control the work's pace: there is no button to stop, pause, or slow the text. Instead, as the cinematic countdown introduces, *Dakota*'s flashing performance produces an experience closer to viewing film than reading literature. Even so, YHCHI's authorial claim asserts a connection between *Dakota* and high modernism rather than cinema or the more contemporary popular culture associated with digital media and online art. As Chang states, "My Web art tries to express the essence of the Internet: information. Strip away the interactivity, the graphics, the design, the photos, the banners, the colors, the fonts and the rest, and what's left? The text" ("Web Art"). Focusing on *Dakota*'s text is hard to do because the flashing speed thwarts such efforts, but, as I will show, this difficulty further aligns the work with literary modernism's aesthetic practices and principles. Framed by YHCHI's authorial claim, *Dakota* promotes two seemingly opposed reading strategies: it prompts the reader to sit back and passively consume streams of flashing text but also incites the critical reader to reread the work, transcribe the words, and compare its content to Pound's modernist epic.

Dakota's content calls for a reading strategy of careful and comparative close reading to connect it to Pound's *Cantos*, but its formal presentation challenges such attempts. This paradox is made even more intriguing because *Dakota*'s narrative seems to have no immediate relation to the beginning of *The Cantos*; it is only through closer reading that intertextual connections emerge. Close reading as we know it, a practice of slow examination focused on the text and tensions its language produces, is something that *Dakota*'s performance elides. Its text flashes so fast that it is often impossible to read, let alone close read. This is, I argue, part of YHCHI's digital modernism: the difficulty of following the authors' claim by close reading *Dakota*'s close reading of cantos I and II is a strategic attempt to promote awareness of the distinctively different, digital nature of the work and the types of reading practices it necessitates. Katherine Hayles reminds us that digital textuality is not composed of durable, stable marks inscribed on the page but rather what she labels as constantly refreshed "flickering signifiers."[9] *Dakota* enacts this constitutive fact of digital information; it refuses to remain still onscreen, provoking an awareness of the effects its flickering or flashing has on the way we read. This ambition is evident in the typographical decision to substitute the zero sign for the letter "O." The aesthetic choice permeates YHCHI's oeuvre and visually highlights the digital nature of the text by showing its screenic content to be thoroughly interwoven with the numerical base of binary code that penetrates and enables it flashing performance. This is one way in which *Dakota* calls attention to its digitalness even as it remediates print modernism.

Jay David Bolter and Richard Grusin use the term "remediation" to describe the way that media coevolve in relation to one another or "refashion themselves to answer the challenges of new media" (15); I use "remediation" to describe an aesthetic strategy through which YHCHI refashion their work in relation to the poetics of another period, that is to say, modernism. YHCHI's remediation of modernism starts with their software selection. The authors build all of their digital works in the popular authoring tool Flash by Macromedia, a program for producing animations. Flash is marketed as "the industry's most advanced authoring environment for creating interactive websites, digital experiences and mobile content" (Adobe). YHCHI employ this software extolled for enabling "mobile content" – meaning that Flash makes it easy to adapt and interact with content across various media forms and technologies – to create an aesthetic of difficulty through an experience of visual illegibility. Although YHCHI's works are textual animations, they do not utilize the platform's trademark functions: seamless animations of moving, multimedia images and interactive effects. Instead they employ Flash to pursue a retro-aesthetic that focuses on text and typography through a performance of cinematic, textual montage. Flash is part of a family of animation software or 3D modeling programs that uses a timeline-and-scene cinematic paradigm. The authoring tool employs the metaphor and methodology of film to remediate this analog medium into the creation of web-based animations. Its interface depicts a timeline of cells that collectively comprise the "movie." But this act of backward-remediation only serves to facilitate the ease of its use, for Flash is technically noncinematic. The authorware distinguishes itself from bitmap-based programs like Director that create images through the composition of discrete, cell-like pixels because Flash is a vector-based tool. In other words, the comparison between film and Flash stops at its mediating metaphors: Flash uses the metaphor of film as an approachable interface for the creation of digital animations, but these movies are not based on the serial replacement of the photogram. YHCHI use this vector-based software against its will to highlight the role of the nonexistent frame in their textual montages. In so doing, they use Flash in a fashioned act of resistance to counter enthusiasm for the latest and newest through a retro-aesthetic that resituates our readings of electronic literature in a literary tradition extending back to modernism and its mass media. Examining *Dakota* as both an adaptation and a remediation of Pound's first two cantos identifies the media-specific ways in which this digital work challenges traditional reading practices and, in particular, our assumptions about what it means to close read.

Close Reading *Dakota* Close Reading Cantos I and II

Both Pound's *Cantos* and YHCHI's *Dakota* begin with a classic journey: Odysseus's visit to the Underworld during his journey back to Ithaca and a teenage cross-country road trip. The first line of canto I begins midsentence and midaction as Odysseus's ship enters the Underworld. The reader joins the action through a conjunctive fragment in the first line: "And then went down to the ship, / Set keel to breakers, forth on the godly sea, and / We set up mast and sail on that swart ship" (*Cantos* 3). *Dakota* also begins midsentence and midaction, with the shock of obscenity in large, capitalized letters: "FUCKING". The black letters sit at the center before being swallowed up into the white screen. The action continues with words and phrases flashing consecutively, replacing the previous text and following the action of Pound's canto: "WALTZED—ØUT—TØ THE CAR—PUT THE KEY IN—THE IGNITIØN—READY TØ HIT THE RØAD."[10] The sun is out, the car is packed, and beers are in the trunk: "THE SUN—HIGH ABØVE—PØURING—DØWN ØN—ØUR HEADS." A group of friends head out "CRØSS CØUNTRY—- - - -." *Dakota*'s lucid, linear presentation follows the opening canto as Odysseus's ship pierces the boundaries of the Underworld: "Came we then to the bounds of deepest water / ... / Nor with stars stretched, nor looking back from heaven / Swartest night stretched over wretched men there" (3). While Odysseus continues into the depths of the Underworld, *Dakota*'s characters enter an American Underworld haunted by ghosts. Signs for "BLACKFØØT RESERVATIØN" and "BADLAND, SIØUX FALLS" flash quickly onscreen, and an oppressive tone creeps into the music. The characters have consumed too much alcohol and penetrated territory marked only by a "DEAD MØTEL" and an impenetrable darkness that "NØT A STARRY NIGHT—NØR A LØW FLYING JET-LINER—CØULD PIERCE." The earlier atmosphere of youthful frivolity dissolves as the text begins to flash faster, mirroring the act of reading signs from a moving car. The screen becomes a physical space to be read like South Dakota's stark landscape, and a parallel is invoked not only between *Dakota* and the first canto, but also between the readers of both texts who struggle to make textual fragments cohere. As *Dakota*'s youthful road trip enters the Badlands, the land lending its name to the work's title, the happy but hapless characters intrude into the realm of the Dead as the narrative continues to follow the plot of book 11 of the *Odyssey* on which Pound's first canto is based.

Whereas Pound's alterations to his source material are mostly formal – remaking the ancient epic into a decisively modern poem – YHCHI alter the content in such dramatic ways that the literary parallels are visible only to the reader willing to carefully compare the texts and tease out the intertextual allusions. In this digital remix,[11] the characters start drinking, pounding beers until the word "BEER" covers the screen and shakes for a few seconds while the screen flickers between white and black. Then, a visual reprieve: "(BURP.)" In the midst of the joys of drinking, smoking, talking about sex, and insulting each other's mothers, anxiety seeps in. The "WHØØPIN'—N'—HØLLERIN'" from the beginning of the road trip shifts to "FEELING—LIKE—HELL." "BEER" becomes "BEER—IN—ØNE—HAND—BØURBON—IN—THE—ØTHER." Violence erupts in recollections of an accident and a dead friend: a guy from the old gang was "SHØT—DEAD," and the narrator "DIDN'T—EVEN—GØ—TØ—HIS—FUNERAL." The narrative describing cruising under a "HØT SUN" transitions into tragedy with deepened drumbeats. All of this follows the canto, wherein Odysseus, while in the Underworld, encounters dead soldiers, friends from war: "Men many, mauled with bronze lance heads, / Battle spoil, bearing yet dreory arms, / These many crowded about me; with shouting" (4). The dead men are bloody reminders of the wars that shaped Western civilization. Similarly, *Dakota*'s narrator stands in a dark American landscape riddled with a bloody history of battles to "win" the West and "civilize" its native peoples. In the land of the Dead, Odysseus is visited by Elpenor, "our friend Elpenor, / Unburied, cast on the wide earth, / Limbs that we left in the house of Circe, / Unwept, unwrapped in sepulchre, since toils urged other" (4). *Dakota*'s narrator also encounters a forgotten ghost from his own past. The shade of Elie (hear "Elpenor") appears, "ALL BLØØDY" like the last time the narrator saw him. Elie speaks in a series of quick frames: "I—DIDN'T—EVEN—HAVE—THE—GUN—BUT—I—TØØK—THE—BULLET." Like Elpenor, who suffers "Ill fate" and begs of Odysseus, "'O King, I bid remember me" (4), Elie also fears being forgotten: "NØBØDY—LIKE—ME—AND—ALREADY—FØRGØTTEN." He attests, "NØW—I'M—IN—HELL." Then, faithfully following Pound's (and Homer's) text wherein Elpenor's visit is followed by the appearance of Odysseus's mother – "And Anticlea came, whom I beat off" (4) – so too, in *Dakota*, is the text describing abject Elie replaced onscreen by, "THEN—MY—MØM—SHØWED—UP—BUT—I—TØLD—HER—TØ—LAY—ØFF." *Dakota*'s plot carefully overlays book 11 of the *Odyssey* and Pound's revision of it, and the comparisons are extensive and ripe. However, *Dakota* does not easily divest itself of these connections. It is through careful close reading and rereading that the palimpsestic layers emerge.

Reading this way illuminates the decisive transformations in *Dakota*'s contemporary remaking of the modernist text. Consider, for example, the shift in the identity of Tiresias, the seer Odysseus travels to the Underworld to see. In

Dakota's adaptation Tiresias is reinvented into a twentieth-century cultural icon: Elvis. The name, displayed in oversized letters, throbs hypnotically at the center of the screen, occupying more screen time than any other word in *Dakota*. It is a sentence in and of itself. Just as Odysseus gives Tiresias a bloody elixir to drink to elicit his instructions on how to return to Ithaca, *Dakota*'s protagonist saves his last swig of beer for "ELVIS." Elvis appears "HØLDING—HIS—GUITAR," just as Tiresias holds his sceptre. He is still "The King," not yet the bloated figure of wasted youth whose humanness tarnished the icon. This is the young Elvis, "ELVIS—ØF—MEMPHIS," and the distinction is important to *Dakota*'s narrator who is himself conscious of "GETTING—ØLD—FAST" and obsessed with the being one of the "LØST—SØULS—ØF—LØST—YØUTH." The insistent figuration of the young Elvis, whose metamorphosis the reader (now in the role as seer) foresees, personifies the narrative's sense of wastedness: a wasted landscape (full of "TUMBLE- / WEED TRASH"), occupied by wasted (drunken) characters, cursing their wasted futures ("SMASHED—BØTTLE—AFTER—BØTTLE,—BRØWN—GLASS—ØN—ASPHALT.—THREW UP,—CURSED—FATE"). The sense of being wasted is furthered by the presentation of the text, which speeds by in a steady stream and wastes the reader's opportunity to catch all the words. *Dakota* depicts this wastedness not as a symptom of that which has been completely destroyed, but rather, as in T.S. Eliot's *The Waste Land* (on which Pound's editorial contributions earned him the dedication *il miglior fabbro*), as the ashes from which new literature, phoenix-like, arises.

The transformation of Tiresias into Elvis and, indeed, the entire adaptation of the Homeric journey into an American road trip, is a playful and poignant adaptation that begs the question: is *Dakota* parody or pastiche?[12] *Dakota* presents itself as high art and mass media, remediation and retro-chic, and it revels in these convergences. The single words and phrases – written in simple, colloquial language – are digested easily, but they are also layered with allusions that ask to be deeply mined. The clichéd scenes of male bonding and Americana can be read as simple stereotypes or complex critiques of the globalization of consumer culture. *Dakota* provides for and provokes multiple forms of address, and YHCHI revel in the confusion their work presents: "some see it as poetry, others as pornography" (Email, May 7). Evidence of the challenge *Dakota* poses to traditional aesthetic categorization is apparent in the various types of venues and exhibitions that have displayed the work. Aside from its availability (for free) on YHCHI's website, *Dakota* has been exhibited as visual art at the Whitney Museum in New York, as part of film series at the Getty Museum in Los Angeles, and as literature in the *Iowa Review Web* and *Poems that go.com*.[13] YHCHI position their art at the cusp of high and low culture where it straddles the boundaries between modernism and postmodernism just as it challenges generic distinctions between literature and film, prose and poetry. After all, *Dakota* is both prose and poetry. Its linear narrative is a flashing performance set to music that produces a poetic rhythm; its onscreen presentation of single words, phrases, and multiple lines of text create line breaks and enjambment while also presenting a linear narrative. *Dakota* can also be considered cinema by virtue of the fact that it is built in Flash. Yet, YHCHI resist such medium-based designations: "At first, we didn't realize we were creating an animation. But it seems that by certain new-media-art definition of things, when you use Flash you're doing animation" ("*Dakota* Description"). Expressing their distrust of easy categorizations, YHCHI are aligned with Pound, who viewed genre distinctions as "rubber-bag categories" that academics use to "limit their reference and interest" ("How" 16).[14] Part of YHCHI's strategy is to disturb the ability to limit *Dakota* – to unsettle the hinge on which rests the door dividing literature from film, reading from viewing, modernism from contemporary, digital literature.

Locating *Dakota*

After Elvis's appearance, *Dakota* quickly transitions from a linear narrative that follows Pound's first canto to something decisively different. The text shifts from canto I to canto II and moves towards an aesthetic more akin to postmodernism or, more appropriately, post-postmodernism than modernism. Blakey's drum solo is pierced by voices, applause, and other sounds of liveness.[15] The work turns toward self-reflexive performativity. The text reaches heightened speeds, and the story of a teenage road trip frays into fragmentation. The screen flashes "WHAT THE?" The audience begins to cheer, and its chant is folded into Blakey's drumming. Blakey is now playing not only on the narrator's car radio but also in a live studio, and this performance is captured in a media recording to which the reader listens and in a photograph that the narrator describes: Blakey "WØRE A / WHITE SHIRT—WITH / RØLLED UP / SLEEVES—AND A TIE / THRØUGH- / ØUT." These quick, ekphrastic phrases flash while voices shout out in response to Blakey's jam session, seeming to propel his improvisation. Even in the midst of this mediatized performance, ties to Pound's *Cantos* remain visible. Pound's second canto begins "Hang it all, Robert Browning, / There can be but the one 'Sordello'" (6). In *Dakota*'s second half, the address to Browning is supplanted by one to Blakey: "GØDDAMMITT, / ART BLAKEY" and continues, "IT MAKES / YØU THE /—ØNLY ART / BLAKEY."[16] And then, in this eruption of simulated liveness enabled by real-time media, the reflexive shift: the narrator and the reader both listen to Blakey's performance "NØT IN DETRØIT—ØR IN A / RECØRDING / STUDIØ—IN NEW / JERSEY, BUT— RIGHT—HERE!" Speed complicates the last monosyllabic word: "HERE!" is followed by, "I—MEAN—HØNESTLY,—IN PALPAN—/ DØNG!" Palpan-Dong is a street in Seoul, South Korea, the home of YHCHI. The sequence opens up *Dakota* to narrative interpretations not previously apparent: is the narrator located in Seoul and listening to Blakey while fantasizing about an American road trip?

Identifying the journey as a mental one of cultural "passing" might explain the references to clichéd Americana – besides Elvis and Marilyn Monroe, beer and the Badlands, the narrator and his buddies "ATE—SØME—HAM—AND—CHEESE— SANDWICHES" – but such a reading simply swaps one subject identity (American) with another (Korean) in a replacement that does not allow for the cumulative construction and complexity of *Dakota*'s layered aesthetic. Indeed, although the text supplies support for locating the narrator in Seoul, the details are stereotypical Orientalist tropes that balance out the American ones: for example, "WHILE IN / THE STREET / BELØW" the narrator catches glimpses of "SØUSED / EXECUTIVES—FRØM / KANGNAM" and "GISEINGS—(KØREAN / GEISHAS)— WHØM THE /EXECUTIVES—PAY A LØT / TØ LAUGH—AT THEIR / EVERY— LAME / JØKE." An earlier narrative detail further complicates the conclusion that the narrator is watching Korean executives from a window by hinting at another way to locate the speaker. The following lines are dumped into a sentence as a narrative aside and are nearly eclipsed by the speed at which they appear: "LIKE AT A / BARBECUE—BACK IN—SIØUX FALLS,—WE DUMPED—ØUT—GARBAGE— AND BRØKE—BØTTLES." The text describes a time when the narrator was in South Dakota, a fact that complicates the identity, and particularly the racial identity, of the narrator: is he Native American, living on the "BLACKFØØT / RESERVATIØN" rather than just driving by it? *Dakota* refuses to divulge clear answers, leaving the narrator's identity and location ambiguous because "RIGHT—HERE!" where the narrator hears Blakey play, cannot be confined to either South Dakota or Seoul, for "HERE" also refers to the computer on which the Blakey and *Dakota* play.

In the age of computers, when discrete media forms such as music and photographs are subsumed into a digital format, "HERE" means that Blakey's recording and the digital work for which it provides the beat is actually happening "RIGHT— HERE!" on the reader's networked computer. *Dakota* performs in real-time through a series of interactions across programming and binary code, authoring software and hardware. Thus, wherever the reading machine is, that is where the work is happening and where Blakey's recording is playing. As the narrative nears its end, *Dakota* abandons any sense of a linear narrative and the lyrical voice presenting it. The individual speaker becomes multiple, "WE—BLARE—THE—TUNES—TØ— RØUSE—NØ—ØNE—BUT—ØURSELVES," and *Dakota* moves away from the modernist model of an individual, alienated consciousness to a post-postmodern or posthuman model in which identity is distributed across and informed by network technologies.[17] Its protagonist is neither American nor South Korean but constituted by both places and both cultures simultaneously through the networked computer. In *Dakota*'s digital present, "RIGHT—HERE!", identity is constructed through media technologies. This is true for the narrator and also for his gods. *Dakota* supplants Aphrodite, at the end of Pound's first canto, with the screen goddess "MARILYN," whose domain is not the heavens but celluloid: "YØU ØWNED / THE—SILVER / SCREEN—CLØTHED / ØR NAKED,—… ØR / STANDING / ØVER—AN AIR- / SHAFT / GRATE,—MAKING / LØVE—TØ THE / CAMERA—IN TECH- / NICØLØR- -." The theme of metamorphosis that concludes Pound's second canto is transformed from the biological mutation of men into porpoises into a transcoding through media technologies. "MARILYN" is constituted by the camera, just as Blakey plays through recorded "liveness" and is made visible because of an image captured in a photograph. Media also construct and enable the narrator's consciousness in constitutive ways. Regardless of whether the narrator actually drives across the Badlands or fantasizes about doing so from Seoul, the journey that *Dakota* describes is one that crosses cultural, ethnic, and geographic spaces in a manner that is indicative of and enabled by the technology through which *Dakota* operates. YHCHI adapt the Homeric quest to depict a hero trained as a web surfer rather than warrior, whose contemporary consciousness is shaped by global, transnational economics and digital technology.

This technocultural, mediatized moment also affects *Dakota*'s reader and the reading practice used to approach the Flash animation. With the climax of the final drum roll, *Dakota* twists into a reflexive loop to address the reader for the first time and include her in the digitally-induced location of "RIGHT—HERE!" In an imagistic style of which Pound would be proud, *Dakota* concludes with words flashing faster than ever before, pushing towards illegibility. The reader's engagement with the text is brought into question: "BLACK—SAUCE—THAT—CAN'T—BE—NAMED—NØR—IDENTIFIED—WHEN—TASTED—JUST—MIXED—INTØ—THE—NØØDLES—WITH—DISPØSABLE—CHØP-STICKS—THEN—WØLFED—DØWN—WITH—YØUR—HEAD—TILTED—TØ—THE—LEFT—IF—YØU'RE—A—RIGHTY" (emphasis added). As the reader struggles to absorb the text being hurled at her, she is implicated in the act of consuming the work. She is figured as literally eating a foreign substance speedily without identifying the food she ingests. The scene of consumption depicts the reader ingesting streams of noodles just as she absorbs flashing text streaming through the bandwidth of her computer. Interspersed in this final sputter of speeding text, the screen flickers with a gray background; the detail is a quick reference to the loading sequence at the beginning of *Dakota*. Critic John Zuern reads the return of the gray screens as an intertextual reference that, appropriately for *Dakota*, conveys multiple levels of meaning: it loops back to the opening moments of *Dakota* and to its proclaimed source material but also serves as an "invocation by the reader's browser and its entry into the data-stream." The barely noticeable, flashing gray screens situate *Dakota* in relation to its primary source material and its subject matter: Pound's first cantos, and, moreover, the networked computer and its user/reader. Whereas the opening undulation of flashing gray served to veil the material fact that the Flash work needed time to load, the gray screens at the end are purely aesthetic. Their purpose is not only intertextual but also metaphoric: rather than load the work, they load the reader into the work. *Dakota* identifies the reader as participating in the convergence of "HERE"-ness and real-time-ness that is not only part of the narrative content but also part of its network processing. While *Dakota*'s narrator "wolfed down" images of Elvis and Marilyn Monroe, the reader "WØLFED—DØWN" the flashing text. All of this happens "RIGHT—HERE!" where Blakey plays on "YØUR" computer, before which the reader sits far back in her chair struggling to absorb *Dakota*'s large font flashing onscreen. In its final flashing moments, *Dakota* reminds the reader that digital literature is a performance happening across codes and platforms in the moment of interaction and that she is part of this process. Mark B. Hansen argues digital art depends on the reader's body for emergence because the digital "'image' has itself become a process and, as such, has become irreducibly bound up with the activity of the body" (10). As *Dakota* shows, the digital image plays out on the reader's body in a symbiotic performance. *Dakota* flashes onscreen and over the reader's eyes, consuming the reader's unblinking attention as the reader consumes the work.

The final lines of *Dakota*'s text address not only the reader but the kind of reading experience she has practiced for 5:56 minutes: is this active or passive reading? Is it reading or viewing? With its last screens, *Dakota*, which its authors ally with high modernism, is now depicted as fast food that the reader consumes. This begs the question: should *Dakota* be aligned with lean, mean modernism or mass culture's fast food? To answer this question, we return to YHCHI's claim – that *Dakota* is based on a close reading of Pound's first two cantos – ready to recognize it as a framing device and a strategy of digital modernism.

Reading Against the Grain of YHCHI's Claim

For a reader who does not transcribe the text or choose to compare it to Pound's cantos I and II, *Dakota*'s blaring manifesto visual style, jazz soundtrack, and narrative ethos might invoke a very different literary lineage than the one claimed by its authors. In particular, its narrative about a youthful road trip across the United States resonates with Jack Kerouac's *On the Road* (1957). *Dakota* recounts such Kerouacian subject matter as male friendship, drunken hallucinations, and sexual exploits. The work presents the tone of beatness that John Clellon Holmes describes in his manifesto "This is the Beat Generation": "A man is beat whenever he goes for broke and wagers the sum of his resources on a single number."[18] *Dakota*'s protagonist wagers his resources on a road trip that will take him away from his own demons, but this effort leaves the narrator and his buddies "FEELING—LIKE—HELL,—SØRRY / FOR—ØURSELVES." The beat of this beaten tone is laid down by Blakey's drums, a recording whose date, 1962, is contemporaneous with the period of the Beats and Hard Bop rather than Pound and modernist jazz. In the second half of the work, when the soundtrack registers the sounds of a live audience, the music unleashes further connections to the characteristically oral and improvised performativity of Beat poetry.

The road trip narratives of *Dakota* and *On the Road* share a tone of hypermasculinity and its failure. The shocking profanity that opens *Dakota* and is sprinkled throughout its text expresses dissatisfaction with the constraints of gendered stereotypes and their expectations. For example, when the narrator fantasizes about Marilyn Monroe, the text registers an overt showmanship of sexual desire, one that expresses a forced and performative masculinity: the screen flashes "NØRMA—JEAN,—EXCUSE MY / FRENCH—WHAT A / PIECE / ØF ASS." Instead of sexual potency, however, the narrator recalls that he "FAILED TO SHØØT—A BIG WAD." Similarly, Elie laments not only his premature death and being forgotten, but that he "NEVER / EVEN—GØT / LAID—JUST—A—HAND—JØB—BUT—A—GØØD—ØNE." The presentation of Elie's lament distinguishes his admission that he never got laid from his claim about the value of his single sexual experience. The first part, "NEVER / EVEN—GØT / LAID," presents enjambment on screen, denoting connection between the words that is supported by the fact that the first screen is replaced by the second at a leisurely speed and in a shared beat. In contrast, the text that follows sputters out single words at a time at heightened speeds. The animation of textual ejaculation undercuts the hyperness of the language, revealing it to be hype. Throughout *Dakota* flashing text is used to complicate moments of macho bravado through montage-like layers. For example, "I CRIED" rests on screen, emotive despair presented as a visual sigh that settles onscreen for a moment-ary reprieve. Consecutive screens confuse this initial sense of self-expression and release. "I CRIED" is followed by "TØ THE GUYS" and then, faster, "TØ GET SMASHED." The speeding, textual montage of these phrases generates a variety of meanings: is the narrator crying or yelling, expressing vulnerability or evading it through drunkenness? Is this a moment of male bonding and connection or its refusal? Later, another important narrative moment from the protagonist's memory is similarly obscured and opened to interpretations. "GANG" is followed by "BANG," and the juxtaposition provokes disturbing and unanswered questions about the violent event: does it describe an onomatopoetic shooting or a group rape? These instances depict the doubleness that is constitutive of the definition of "Beat," the energetic beat that propels the poetry and the voice of discontent that the beat-down tone registers. Additionally, the layering of words onscreen depicts a layering of possible meanings produced through a layering of literary influences, from modernism through the Beats and beyond.

Rather than aligning their work with Sal Paradise's bohemian wanderings, however, YHCHI assert a connection to Odysseus's journey back to Ithaca through Pound's recasting of the classical epic into modernist poetry. YHCHI use *The Cantos* similarly to how Pound uses Homer's *Odyssey*: to lay claim to an ancient cultural past as scaffolding to support a contemporary literary moment and recu-perate the relevance of literature in it. For YHCHI, this past is not located in the literature of ancient Greece or the songs of medieval Provençal troubadours but in the writings of the first electric age, the modernist period. As Stephen Kern shows in *The Culture of Time and Space 1880–1918*, this was a period during which emerged contemporary concepts of time, space, speed, and technological media-tion. Kern traces a shift in cultural consciousness prompted by new technologies of communication and speed that emerged along with new artistic methods of representing these changes. Media theorist Friedrich Kittler also identifies the modernist period as a moment of decisive shift in his media-based paradigm of history, wherein the "discourse network" of the 1800s shifted from a model of "continuous connection" to the 1900s mode of the discontinuous and discrete (389).[19] Similarly, Lev Manovich locates this period as the origin of digital media and art, due, in particular, to innovations in cinema and montage. YHCHI return to a past that, although not ancient, is the origin of their aesthetic and techno-logical present. In so doing, they follow Pound, who writes, "A return to origins invigorates" ("Tradition" 92).

The purpose of YHCHI's return to a modernist origin is to invigorate the current state of electronic literature. They articulate a connection with literary modernism in spite of, and indeed because of, *Dakota*'s more obvious connections to Kerouac and postmodernism. YHCHI's authorial claim encourages readers not only to approach *Dakota* in relation to Pound's adaptation of classical antiquity but also to examine the reasons this pursuit is relevant in both modernism and digital modernism. Carroll Terrell offers an explanation for the reason Pound's modernist epic opens with the particular scene from Homer's ancient text, and the interpretation elucidates YHCHI's similar selection of *The Cantos* as its source of inspiration. Terrell identifies the reference to Ithaca in Pound's first canto as a counter-balance to Troy, the city that Odysseus helped to destroy: "The epic 'nostos' ['return journey'] of *The Cantos* is thus polarized between the destruction and the rediscovery of civilization and sovereignty" (2). Pound employs this epic situation of historical tension as a metaphoric parallel to his own cultural moment, recuperating it as a means of producing such influential, lasting literature as Homer's *Odyssey*.[20] A similar moment motivates YHCHI and is expressed in their balanced relationship to Pound and Kerouac. *Dakota* is poised at a balance of "destruction" and "rediscovery" in relation to its literary past and present. Instead of the cataclysmic end of print that many prophesied electronic literature would induce, *Dakota* exposes how digital literature can follow modernism to rediscover a canonical past through contemporary media and reclaim an investment in the power and potential of literature.

Close Reading

Dakota is supposedly based on a close reading, but close reading is something that the work strives to subvert.[21] *Dakota* uses speed to produce difficulty through illegibility, and in this pursuit, it follows its source material; for, *The Cantos* are also famously resistant to interpretation. Donald Davie writes, "Pound seems to have had before him, as one main objective, the baffling and defeating of commentators and exegetes" (229). Pound's famous line from canto CXVI, "I cannot make it cohere," has become a tagline of sorts for the experience of reading *The Cantos* (and other works of high modernist literature), and it is a mantra that YHCHI take up. Just as Pound claims that "the work of art which is most 'worth-while' is the work which would need a hundred works of any other kind of art to explain it" (*Gaudier-Brzeska* 84), so too do YHCHI state, "We present our work the way we do to make it indeed more difficult" (Email, May 2). As is particularly and painfully obvious to *Dakota*'s dry-eyed and unblinking reader, speed is used as a technical tool to enhance the work's difficulty. The use of difficulty as an aesthetic strategy bonds *Dakota* to modernism and the kind of reading practices its literature fostered. John Guillory explains that the canonization of modernism by the New Critics depended on the difficulty of these texts, so that "difficulty itself was positively valued in New Critical practice, that it was a form of cultural capital" (168). Leonard Diepeveen identifies difficulty as "a litmus test" not only for the work but also for the reader, a test through which "one could predict both a given reader's response to modernism by his or her reaction to difficulty, and a writer's place in the canon by the difficulty of his or her work" (xi). The difficulty of these modernist texts promoted the professionalization of readers who could produce explications of these texts through the structured methodology of close reading.[22] The New Critical method has rightly been critiqued for its insular focus on the text as an isolated object and the conservative politics endemic to such a perspective. In arguing that YHCHI promote close reading, I am not claiming that this international, multi-ethnic partnership created by an American and a South Korean, whose work exists at the margins of traditional literary culture and often explicitly engages with issues of contemporary politics and race, should be read in the vein of New Criticism as it developed in the 1930s and 1940s.[23] Yet, I am arguing that YHCHI's claim that *Dakota* is based on a close reading focuses attention on their text and its intertextuality (to Pound's cantos I and II) rather than on other possible elements of the work such as its Flash design, programming code, music, or other media-based effects. That is why, to reproduce a quote used earlier in this essay, Young-hae Chang articulates her artistic mission as an attempt to illuminate the role of text in digital art: "Strip away the interactivity, the graphics, the design, the photos, the banners, the colors, the fonts and the rest, and what's left? The text" ("Web Art"). However, *Dakota*'s text cannot be "strip[ped] away" from its design, font, animation, and music; it is a multimodal performance and because it is programmed in Flash, its source code remains inaccessible to the reader (its narrative text cannot be easily cut and pasted into a Word document). Additionally, the work depends on the physical (hardware) and data-based (software and code) entities that make it run; its literary aesthetic is determined by the configurations of the reader's computer and her Internet connection. This means that the close reading practices of the modernist New Critics must be fundamentally renovated in order to approach digital works like *Dakota*.

YHCHI's *Dakota* both promotes and complicates the practice of close reading that has been passed down from modernism through postmodernism and poststructuralism, and it does so in order to focus critical attention on this central literary activity as it evolves into the digital realm. Such works insist on the importance of the text but also demand attention to the medium-specific materiality of the performance. Digital literature demands a close reading practice that incorporates not only the external cultural and historical influences affecting the text (for example the politics, historical perspective, or embodiedness of the reader and/or author), but also the media-specific aspects (for example the specificities of Flash as an authoring tool and the significance of the work's distribution online rather than on CD-Rom). YHCHI's statement that *Dakota* is "based on a close reading" demands that we read *Dakota* in relation to *The Cantos* and at the same time reflexively reassess our own close reading practices. YHCHI's claim thus poses a challenge to investigate the relationship between the texts in question and presents an opportunity to consider the efficacy of applying the print-based standard of literary criticism, close reading, to electronic literature.

A subtle piece of support for this argument is provided in *Dakota*'s final seconds. As the text races toward its ending, it finally drops the name of its modernist persona in a collage of fragments that flash at nearly illegible speeds: "FUCK—YØU,—ELLMANN,—THAT'S / RIGHT,—RICHARD—ELLMANN—NØRTØN,—NEW YØRK—1973,—ØN—PØUND." Pound is named in an affront on Richard Ellmann, the literary scholar and famous biographer of James Joyce, who, along with Robert O'Clair, edited the *Norton Anthology of Modern Poetry* (1973), which contained Pound's canto I and II. The identification of and attack on the editor of *Dakota's* source material continues YHCHI's adaptation of Pound's canto I. The first canto nears its end by invoking the medieval mediator who translated Homer into the text that Pound adapts: "Lie quiet Divus. I mean, that is Andreas Divus, / In officina Wecheli, 1538, out of Homer" (5). YHCHI's invective against Ellmann also raises questions about the acts of excerpting, explaining, and close reading, all of which Ellmann does in his introduction and explanatory footnotes to cantos I and II in the *Norton*.[24] Ellmann's first footnote to canto I asserts the following: "For Pound, Odysseus is the type of enterprising, imaginative man, and this voyage represents in some sense a symbol or analogy of the poet's own voyage into the darker aspects of his civilization or the buried places of the mind" (357). Ellmann's explanation of what Odysseus represents is precisely the type of reading practice that *Dakota's* speeding text evades: clear equations and analogies between text and meaning, type or symbol and their representation. *Dakota's* defamation of the modernist scholar is a final act of paradoxical doubleness that both invites and refutes close reading. *Dakota* demands to be read by such critics as Ellmann, readers who will pursue connections between the digital and modernist texts, but it also warns against readings that derive simple correspondences and explanations such as Ellmann's New Critical explanation of canto I. This final detail and dig at Ellmann prompts readers who recognize his name (and thus possess a certain knowledge of literary criticism and a modernist cultural cachet) to closely read the text and consider why Ellmann might represent an outmoded and flawed reading practice. Close reading *Dakota* illuminates how this central critical technique of literary study is being pushed by electronic literature to evolve, along with the literature it reads, in medium-specific ways.[25]

"So that:"

The first canto concludes with the phrase "So that:" (5). The fragment does not lead into the second canto, which begins with a new narrator and narrative situation, but rather gestures to future additions and responses. The colon characterizes both the act of rupture and the promise of continuation, a challenge to which *Dakota* rises. The end of the second canto similarly concludes with "And … " (10; ellipses original). "And" is the first word of each preceding line in the last stanza; its repetition creates a cycle of repetition that concludes canto II with the same conjunctive word followed by an ellipsis, a grammatical mark signifying potential amendment and continuation. Instead of a colon or ellipsis, *Dakota's* last word is followed by a period, but that is not the end of its programming. The work is programmed to reload and replay; after the last words dissolve on the white screen, *Dakota* begins again.

This programming detail follows the end of Pound's first two cantos by providing a promise of continuation, but it also identifies *Dakota* as a self-contained and separate file from the hyperlinked network on which it is housed. This assertion of autonomy aligns *Dakota* with the New Critical view of the poem as an autonomous object and with Adorno's characterization of modernist art.[26] Yet, as I have argued, its digital and web-based nature also challenges such claims. *Dakota*'s final programming detail instead presents an affiliation with Michael Fried's later version of Adorno's idea in which the artwork achieves autonomy by rejecting its "objecthood" and accepting a "self-imposed imperative that it defeat or suspend its own objecthood" (153). *Dakota* defeats its status as a digital "object" by refusing interactivity and rejecting instrumentality down to its very last moments. In a final gesture of autonomy and alignment with a modernist aesthetic, *Dakota* reloads and begins again, looping back to remediate Pound's first two cantos and to "MAKE IT NEW" in new media.

Notes

1   In addition to being selected for exhibition at such galleries as the Whitney and the Getty, *Dakota* has been exhibited in numerous online galleries. It was also won Honorable Mention at the 2000 *SFMOMA Webby Prize for Excellence in Online Art*.

2   Interestingly, the tagline for the first and primary publisher of electronic hypertexts, Eastgate Systems in Waltham, Massachusetts, is "serious hypertext."

3   *The Cantos* is one of the least read and least taught of modernist works, but this fact does not diminish its consideration as a central modernist text of high cultural capital. Indeed, the authority it evinces without even being read might paradoxically support and testify to its canonical status. To see this argument at work as it is applied to Joyce's *Ulysses*, see Lawrence Rainey's "Consuming Investments: Joyce's *Ulysses*," chapter 2 in *Institutions of Modernism*.

4   Mark McGurl explains that "one of the strongest definitions one can advance of the so-called modernist novel … is rather simple, but also powerfully, that it is the novel is conceived of as 'art,' and thus as a bearer of cultural capital" (29).

5   Hugh Kenner, as the title of this classic work *The Pound Era* expresses, associates Pound with the modernist era. In *The Dance of the Intellect*, Marjorie Perloff identifies and traces a schism in modernist scholarship based on the identification of either Ezra Pound or Wallace Stevens as the central figure of literary modernism.

6   John Zuern notices a connection to Pound even before this cinematic countdown. While the work is loading, the screen flashes through a gray spectrum before becoming white, and Zuern reads this short sequence as a visual reference that "connects intertextually to Pound as Pound's own dawn-image connects to Homer and other classical writers" while also "contain[ing] another allusion – to the 'loading sequences' that introduce any number of Flash productions currently on the Internet."

7   Alfred Appel, Jr. argues for an interdisciplinary reading of modernism that reads the classic jazz of Louis Armstrong, Duke Ellington, Billie Holliday, Jack Teagarden, and Charlie Parker as part of the modernist movement (1).

8   The first of the three kinds of poetry Pound identifies is "melopoeia" "wherein words are charged, over and above their plain meaning, with some musical property, which directs the bearing or trend of that meaning" ("How" 172). In "A Retrospect," Pound provides

the following advice to poets: "behave as a musician, a good musician, when dealing with that phase of your art which has exact parallels in music" (6). In "The Tradition" he explains his appreciation of Homer and the Provençal troubadours: "both in Greece and in Provence the poetry attained its highest rhythmic and metrical brilliance at times when the arts of verse and music were most closely knit together" (91). Pound worked as a music critic in London, and he supposedly envisioned *The Cantos* as following the musical structure of a fugue. See Murray R. Schafer's *Ezra Pound and Music*.

9   See chapter two, "Virtual Bodies and Flickering Signifiers" in *How We Became Posthuman*.

10   It is impossible to transcribe *Dakota* into print. For the sake of differentiating between consecutively flashing screens and line-breaks contained on a single screen, I use the conventional backslash (/) to denote a line-break and thick dashes (—) to designate the flashing replacement of text between screens. Since there are no URLs or lexia titles, there is no apparent way to denote screens or frames with the work other than to note that *Dakota* is located on YHCHI's website at www.yhchang.com.

11   Lev Manovich identifies digital art and the culture it reflects as operating through the metaphor and practice of "the remix." He sees that "electronic art from its very beginning was based on a new principle: *modification of an already existing signal*" (126), so that "authentic creation has been replaced by selection from a menu" (124); he thus identifies the DJ as the paradigmatic figure of the contemporary artist (135). The concept of remixing is certainly related to YHCHI's relationship to modernism, but, whereas Manovich reads (and celebrates) the remix as constitutive of the digital medium (and of its postmodern culture), I see YHCHI using their remixes or remediations to counter such media-based assumptions. This distinction typifies the greater difference between how Manovich and I read the relationship between modernism and digital art. Manovich focuses on the visual arts and cinema, rather than literature, to argue that avant-garde techniques of collage and montage have become the operating principles of digital computing. He writes, "One general effect of the digital revolution is that avant-garde aesthetic strategies came to be embedded in the commands and interface metaphors of computer software. In short, the avant-garde became *materialized* in a computer" (xxxi; emphasis added). Where Manovich sees modernism as "materialized" into new media, I examine the conscious adaptation of modernist techniques as formal practice and strategic alignment. Rather than a media-determined effect of digital art-making, I see literary modernism serving particular digital writers as a means for rebelling against such expectations and generalizations. See my dissertation, *Digital Modernism: Making it New in New Media*.

12   Fredric Jameson identifies pastiche – "the imitation of a peculiar or unique, idiosyncratic style" as "blank parody" (17) and the "cannibalization of all styles of the past" (18) – as a constitutive characteristic of postmodernism.

13   *Dakota* was shown at "The American Effect" (2003) exhibit at the Whitney Museum and "Video and Media Art by Contemporary Artists" (2004) at the Getty Museum.

14   Pound shows that the difference between prose and poetry is one of degree: "The language of prose is much less highly charged, that is perhaps the only availing distinction between prose and poesy" ("How" 26). He writes, "verse-writing can or could no longer be clearly understood without the study of prose-writing" (30).

15   For a discussion of the technologized mediation of "liveness," see Auslander.

16   A parallel between Art Blakey and Ezra Pound might also be pursued in light of the fact that both served as not only as innovators in their respective arts but also as mentor

figures to younger artists. G. Pascal Zachary explains: "By the time of Blakey's death in 1990, a tour with the peripatetic Messengers was viewed as a sort of pre-requisite for up-and-coming jazz musicians. A quick way to be taken seriously by critics, record producers and audiences was to pass through Blakey's free-form university." An anonymous reader for *Modern Fiction Studies* adds to this that Blakey's "free-form university" might resonate with Pound's "Ezuversity."

17 See *How We Became Posthuman*, wherein N. Katherine Hayles shows how "a historically specific construction called *the human is giving way to a different construction called the posthuman*" (2), a conception of the human that "configures human being so that it can be seamlessly articulated with intelligent machines" and "implies a distributed cognition located in disparate parts" (3).

18 Holmes explains that being "beat" expresses a connection to the wasted spirit of the Lost Generation, the flipside of modernism that the Beats consciously adapted in a similar way to YHCHI's own adaptation. Indeed, in that modernist form of literary assertion, the manifesto, the Beat poets solidify their connection to and difference from literary modernism. As Holmes writes, "unlike the Lost Generation, which was occupied with the loss of faith, the Beat Generation is becoming more and more occupied with the need for it."

19 Friedrich Kittler defines a "discourse network" as "the network of technologies and institutions that allow a given culture to select, store, and produce relevant data" (369). Kittler locates a decisive shift in discourse networks around this period, wherein the "continuous connection of writing and/or the individual was of such importance in 1800" (83) but was replaced by the discourse network of 1900 in which "discourse is produced by RANDOM GENERATORS" (206).

20 In *ABC of Reading*, Pound writes of the *Odyssey*: "The news in the Odyssey is still news. Odysseus is still 'very human'" (44).

21 Indeed, critical analysis of certain fast-moving passages is extremely challenging for a critic attempting to transcribe and interpret the content of the work. For their assistance, I want to thank Julia H. Lee and Yun Woo.

22 For more on the creation of the relationship between modernism and their relationship to professional readers, see Strychacz, Guillory, and Graff.

23 For examples of YHCHI's decidedly more political works, see "Operation Nukorea," "Cunnilingus in North Korea," or "Samsung."

24 Ellmann actually shares editorial duties with Robert O'Clair, but YHCHI cast him as the editor- translator figure, a contemporary renovation of Divus. An anonymous reader for *Modern Fiction Studies* suggests an interesting interpretation of YHCHI's outburst against Ellmann, "FUCK—YØU,—ELLMANN": the line might be read as an allusion to Pound's anti-Semitism. Read in this manner, the line lashing out at Ellmann is an adaptation of Pound's own verbal attacks against Jews in his later cantos. This reading adds another layer to YHCHI's adaptation and the depth of their knowledge about Pound, but it does not discount my reading of Ellmann as a subject of critique due to his New Critical approach to explaining *The Cantos*. The line from *Dakota*, when read in its entirety, specifically identifies Ellmann not only as an individual (or a Jewish individual), but as a critic writing "ØN—PØUND" in the "NØRTØN,—NEW YØRK—1973."

25 Close reading has recently become a vital topic in literary studies focused on electronic literature. The current issue of the online journal *Dichtung-Digital* (edited by Alice Bell and Astrid Ensslin) engages new approaches to close reading works of digital literature;

Roberto Simanowski of Brown University hosted a conference in Fall 2007 dedicated to rethinking close reading of digital literature and art; and a recent collection of essays, *Close Reading New Media* (edited by Jan Van Looy and Jan Baetens) applies a New Critical approach, however, often at the expense of a learned history of New Historicism.

26 See *Aesthetic Theory*, especially the sections titled "Situation" and "Society."

Works Cited

Adobe Flash Homepage. 10 March 2005. www.macromedia.com/soft-ware/flash/flashpro/?promoid=BINT.

Adorno, Theodor. *Aesthetic Theory*. Trans. and Eds. Gretel Adorno and Rolf Tiedemann. Minneapolis: University of Minnesota Press, 1970.

Appel, Alfred Jr. *Jazz Modernism: From Ellington and Armstrong to Matisse and Joyce*. New York: Knopf, 2002.

Auslander, Philip. *Liveness: Performance in a Mediatized Culture*. New York: Routledge, 1999.

Bell, Alice and Astrid Ensslin, eds. *Dichtung-Digital*. 37 (2007) 8 May 2008 http://www.dichtung-digital.com.

Bolter, Jay David and Richard Grusin. *Remediation: Understanding New Media*. Cambridge: Massachusetts Institute of Technology Press, 1999.

Chang, Young-hae. "Web Art" for *Threads of the Woven Maze: Web Exhibition for the Open Space of the International Women's University*. 2000. Pat Binder, Curator. 5 July 2007. http://www.universes-in-universe.de/woven-maze/chang.

Chang, Young-hae, and Marc Voge [Young-hae Chang Heavy Industries]. *Dakota*. 2002. 5 July 2007. www.yhchang.com.

Chang, Young-hae, and Marc Voge. "*Dakota* Description" for "On the Web" (2001–2002). *PS1 Contemporary Art Center*. Anthony Huberman, Curator. 5 July 2007. http://www.ps1.org/cut/animations/web/chang.html.

Chang, Young-hae, and Marc Voge. "'Distance, Homelessness, Anonymity, and Insignificance': An Interview with Young-Hae Chang Heavy Industries." By Thom Swiss. (2002). *Iowa Review Web*. June 2005. http://www.uiowa.edu/~iareview/tirweb/feature/younghae/interview.html.

Chang, Young-hae, and Marc Voge. Email to the author. 2 May 2004.

Chang, Young-hae, and Marc Voge. Email to the author. 7 May 2004.

Davie, Donald. *Ezra Pound*. Chicago: University of Chicago Press, 1982.

Diepeveen, Leonard. *The Difficulties of Modernism*. New York: Routledge, 2003.

Eastgate. Homepage. 12 May 2008 http://www.eastgate.com.

Eliot, T.S. "Introduction." *The Literary Essays of Ezra Pound*. Ed. T.S. Eliot. London: Faber, 1954.

Ellmann, Richard and Robert O'Clair. Footnote 5 to canto I of Ezra Pound's *The Cantos*. *The Norton Anthology of Modern Poetry*. Eds. Richard Ellmann and Robert O'Clair. New York: Norton, 1973.

Fried, Michael. *Art and Objecthood: Essays and Reviews*. Chicago: University of Chicago Press, 1988.

Graff, Gerald. *Professing Literature: An Institutional History*. Chicago: University of Chicago Press, 1987.

Guillory, John. *Cultural Capital: The Problem of Literary Canon Formation*. Chicago: University of Chicago Press, 1993.

Hansen, Mark B. *New Philosophy for New Media*. Cambridge: Massachusetts Institute of Technology Press, 2004.

Hayles, N. Katherine. *How We Became Posthuman: Virtual Bodies in Cybernetics, Literature, and Informatics*. Chicago: University of Chicago Press, 1999.

Holmes, John Clellon. "This Is the Beat Generation." *New York Times Magazine* 16 November 1952. *Literary Kicks: Opinions, Observations, and Research*. Caryn Thurman. 8 May 2008. http://www.litkicks.com/Texts/ThisIsBeatGen.html.

Jameson, Fredric. *Postmodernism: Or, The Cultural Logic of Late Capitalism*. Durham: Duke University Press, 1991.

Kenner, Hugh. *The Pound Era*. Berkeley: University of California Press, 1971.

Kittler, Friedrich. *Discourse Networks 1800/1900*. Trans. Michael Metteer with Chris Cullens. Stanford: Stanford University Press, 1990.

Manovich, Lev. *The Language of New Media*. Cambridge: Massachusetts Institute of Technology Press, 2001.

McGurl, Mark. *The Novel Art: Elevations of American Fiction after Henry James*. Princeton: Princeton UP, 2001.

Perloff, Marjorie. *The Dance of the Intellect: Studies in the Poetry of the Pound Tradition*. Cambridge: Cambridge University Press, 1985.

Pound, Ezra. *ABC of Reading*. New York: New Directions, 1934.

Pound, Ezra. *The Cantos of Ezra Pound. 1934*. New York: New Directions, 1996.

Pound, Ezra. *Gaudier-Brzeska: A Memoir Including the Published Writings of the Sculptor and a Selection from His Letters*. 1916. New York: New Directions, 1961.

Pound, Ezra. "How to Read." *Literary Essays of Ezra Pound*. 15–40.

Pound, Ezra. *The Literary Essays of Ezra Pound*. Ed. T.S. Eliot. London: Faber, 1954.

Pound, Ezra. "A Retrospect." *The Literary Essays of Ezra Pound*. 3–14.

Pound, Ezra. "The Tradition." *The Literary Essays of Ezra Pound*. 91–93.

Pressman, Jessica. *Digital Modernism: Making it New in New Media*. Diss. UCLA, 2007.

Rainey, Lawrence. *Institutions of Modernism: Literary Elites and Public Culture*. New Haven: Yale University Press, 1998.

Schafer, Murray R. *Ezra Pound and Music*. New York: New Directions, 1977.

Strychacz, Thomas. *Modernism, Mass Culture, and Professionalism*. Cambridge: Cambridge University Press, 1993.

Terrell, Carroll T. *A Companion to the Cantos of Ezra Pound*. Berkeley: University of California Press, 1980.

Van Looy, Jan and Jan Baetens, eds. *Close Reading New Media: Analyzing Electronic Literature*. Leuven: Leuven University Press, 2003.

Zachary, G. Pascal. "Successful Mission for Influential Drummer." 3 July 2007. http://www.duke.edu/~aks2/jazz/bio.htm.

Zuern, John. "Matter of Time: Toward a Materialist Semiotics of Web Animation." *Dichtung-Digital*. Feb. 2003. March 2006. http://www.brown.edu/Research/dichtung-digital/2003/issue/1/zuern/index.htm.

Epilogue
The Changing Concept
of World Literature

Zhang Longxi

Most discussions of world literature mention, at some point or other, the German term "*Weltliteratur*" and trace the origin of the concept to Johann Wolfgang von Goethe. Though Goethe was not the first to use that term in German, given his great reputation and influence on the European cultural scene in the late eighteenth and the early nineteenth centuries, as John Pizer remarks, "it is Goethe to whom credit must be given for creating the paradigm that became a significant, widely debated element in critical and pedagogical literary discourse."[1] Pizer helpfully situates Goethe's concept in its historical context, in which Germany was not politically unified and all European nations, after the divisive Napoleonic Wars, were badly in need of mutual understanding and peaceful coexistence. In some sense, that was a situation not so very different from our world today, in which globalizing tendencies in economics, communication, and scientific and technological development coexist with many communities' intensifying grasp on ethnic or national identities, even the resurgence of a tenacious tribalism.

Theoretically speaking, the tension between two opposite forces has always resided in *Weltliteratur* as a concept, which stands poised between the local and the global, national specificities and cosmopolitan claims to literary universality. With regard to Goethe's own understanding, some have questioned whether his

Zhang Longxi is Chair Professor of Comparative Literature and Translation at City University of Hong Kong. He is a foreign member of the Royal Swedish Academy of Letters, History and Antiquities, a member of the executive councils of the International Comparative Literature Association and the Institute for World Literature, and an Advisory Editor of *New Literary History*. His books include *The Tao and the Logos: Literary Hermeneutics, East and West* (1992), *Allegoresis: Reading Canonical Literature East and West* (2005), *Unexpected Affinities: Reading across Cultures* (2007), and *An Introduction to Comparative Literature* (2009, in Chinese).

World Literature in Theory, First Edition. Edited by David Damrosch.
© 2014 John Wiley & Sons, Ltd. Published 2014 by John Wiley & Sons, Ltd.

idea of *Weltliteratur* was actually limited to European literature only, or whether his cosmopolitan concept was contradictory to his emphasis on the important role Germans should play in its formation. To tip the balance of Goethe's concept to the side of German nationalism or Eurocentrism, however, not only ignores Goethe's own positive take on *Weltliteratur*, but is simply anachronistic and wrong. First of all, for Goethe, what was German was not national, but fragmented and divergent, tied together only by a shared language; and second, what was national was not opposed to what he thought to be universal. "It is evident that the best poets and writers of all nations have for some time been concentrating their efforts on universal human concerns," wrote Goethe in 1828 when commenting on Thomas Carlyle's *German Romance*, but "we increasingly see a writer's national and individual characteristics illuminated from within by these universal concerns."[2] In a letter to Count Stolberg, dated June 11, 1827, Goethe clearly stated that "Poetry is cosmopolitan, and the more interesting the more it shows its nationality."[3]

Interestingly, as Pizer shows in the essay included in this volume, it takes a critic from Africa, the Moroccan-born Germanist Fawzi Boubia, to recognize this and "establish the genuinely global dimensions of Goethe's Weltliteratur postulations and foreground their seminal and precocious embrace of alterity in the hermeneutic dialogue among the world's literatures" (p. 28 above). In fact, almost 30 years ago, Claudio Guillén already said as much when he urged us to "remember that Goethe started from the existence of some national literatures – thus making possible a dialogue between the local and the universal, between the one and the many, a dialogue that from that day to this has continued to breathe life into the best comparative studies."[4] Earlier still, René Etiemble argued, in 1974, that Goethe's elevation "of *Weltliteratur* implicitly condemns German nationalism and, with it, all nationalism" (p. 87 above). The suspicion of Eurocentrism reveals a sensibility of our own time, but to Goethe's mind, the either/or dichotomy between the local and the global, or the national and the universal, would probably be quite alien. Great works of literature always take root in particular linguistic, cultural, and national traditions, but they are at the same time capable of transcending the limitations of the local and the parochial to reach readers beyond the boundaries of their provenance, either in original forms or in successful translations.

More importantly, it was in his conversation with Johann Peter Eckermann that Goethe first developed his idea of Weltliteratur in the context of reflecting on poetic production in Asia, and in considering that China in particular enjoyed a flourishing literary culture when Europeans "were still living in the woods" (p. 19 above). Indeed, it was in talking about his reading of a Chinese novel in translation that Goethe made the famous announcement that "poetry is the universal possession of mankind. ... National literature is now rather an unmeaning term; the epoch of World-literature is at hand, and every one must strive to hasten its approach" (pp. 19–20). It is true that Goethe argued for returning to the ancient Greeks for patterns of European literature, but his concept of *Weltliteratur* did open up to non-Western literatures, and *that* constitutes the paradigmatic sense which renders Goethe's concept more relevant to our time than to his own.

As Richard Meyer argued in 1900, Goethe's concept was "future-oriented," a concept that "had just dawned" in his time.[5] It is in our time, when literary scholars everywhere have a much stronger sense of the global connectedness of nations and peoples, a much greater need to open one's eyes beyond the tunnel vision of one's own group or community, and a much greater readiness to embrace alterity beyond one's linguistic and cultural comfort zones, that Goethe's concept of *Weltliteratur* may have found a better condition than ever before to make a real impact on the ways we think globally about literature, culture, tradition, and ultimately about the world in which we live.

Goethe talked about *Weltliteratur* in the 1820s, and the term was picked up again by Karl Marx and Friedrich Engels in the *Communist Manifesto* of 1848, where, in describing the global tendencies propelled by the fast growth of world capitalism, they saw world literature as a cultural phenomenon inevitably superseding national literatures. If Goethe's vision was a humanistic one, Marx conceptualized world literature as part of a global tendency closely related to economic and political developments at the time. Goethe's and Marx's concepts of world literature have been understood differently by different scholars. "That phrase 'world literature,' and the vision that the creation of such a thing was desirable," says Aijid Ahmad, "Marx had taken from his favorite poet, Goethe," even though Marx "associated the creation of 'world literature' not with the self-activity of a high-minded intelligentsia or as a mode of exchange among the principal classicisms, which is more or less what Goethe had in mind, but as an objective process inherent in other kinds of globalisation where modes of cultural exchange follow closely upon patterns of political economy."[6] In Mads Rosendahl Thomsen's understanding, however, Goethe's notion of world literature was an "idealistic vision of the symphony of the masterpieces from different nations," while Marx's concept was a "more cynical vision of global distribution of books as commodities."[7]

Goethe and Marx surely conceived of *Weltliteratur* differently, but given Marx's conviction that history is an evolutionary process of progress, a Hegelian kind of development from a lower to a higher form, his remarks on capitalism and the bourgeois production of world literature are not as negative as some contemporary commentators would have us to believe. For Marx, it was only to the extent that capitalism was to be superseded by a yet higher stage of social and historical development – socialism and communism – that capitalism was negative, but negative in the Hegelian sense of *Aufhebung*, that is, negating the limitations of capitalism but preserving all it would have achieved as a necessary stage of human history and social progress. For Marx, capitalism in its own right was better than the feudalist medieval society and definitely higher than the Asiatic mode of production, the agrarian societies in China and in Asia at large, which in his view represented a more primitive stage of social development. So when Marx declared the demise of national literatures, he was very much in agreement with Goethe in looking at *Weltliteratur* as a new and progressive phenomenon: "National one-sidedness and narrow-mindedness become more and more impossible, and from the numerous national and local literatures there arises a world literature."[8]

This famous statement from the *Communist Manifesto* is not at all a negative evaluation. On the contrary, Marx and Engels saw the globalizing tendency of world capitalism as a necessary prerequisite condition for the socialist revolution, and hence the slogan, repeated later by all political publications in the Soviet Union and the other socialist countries: "Workers of all countries, unite!" The working class, in their understanding, was a global force of revolution, not bounded by national affiliations. The socialist movement was an international one, and the Communist International was based on that global idea. So in that sense, Marx's idea was not an antidote to Goethe's, though he understood world literature as the cultural aspect of the mode of production under global capitalism, rather than as the humanistic appreciation of the major works of the world's different literary and cultural traditions.

Since Goethe's time, the concept of world literature has always been a somewhat flexible and changing idea, not a rigid fixation on a set of canonical works. The various selections in this volume reflect the many changes and different understandings, and a number of questions become central to our rethinking of world literature at the present time. First, the scope or coverage of world literature must be significantly large. The importance of such cultural cartography is already prominent in Goethe's concept, for it was Persian poetry and a Chinese novel he read in translation that brought *Weltliteratur* to its global dimension. As a discipline, comparative literature also started out as an effort to break away from the constraints of national literatures and their attendant monolingual limitations, but in practice it remained largely a European operation. Franco Moretti puts it bluntly: "comparative literature has not lived up" to *Weltliteratur* as Goethe and Marx had in mind. "It's been a much more modest intellectual enterprise, fundamentally limited to Western Europe, and mostly revolving around the river Rhine (German philologists working on French literature)" (p. 160 above). That was why Etiemble wanted to revisit Goethe's *Weltliteratur* as an alternative to comparative literature despite the latter's cosmopolitan intention and emphasis on polyglottism. "The time is over when the Hungarian savant Hugo von Meltzl, a disciple of Goethe and advocate of *Weltliteratur*, could still propose a *Dekaglottismus* as the languages of civilization: German, English, Spanish, Dutch, Hungarian, Icelandic, Italian, Portuguese, Swedish and French – to which he added Latin," says Etiemble, because outside these European languages, literatures in Sanskrit, Chinese, Japanese, Indian, Persian, and Arabic had produced masterpieces "when most of the literatures of the *Dekaglottismus* either did not exist, or were still in their infancy" (p. 88, above).[9]

Etiemble commented on a number of German and French anthologies and bibliographies of world literature and found them woefully ignorant of major works of non-Western literatures. Most of those early anthologies, as Sarah Lawall has observed, were predicated on the Darwinian theories of social and cultural evolution and "saw themselves as illustrating the rise of civilization to its current apogee in Western culture and transmitting the moral lessons of that rise."[10] The influential *Norton Anthology of World Masterpieces* did not include more non-Western works until it came out in an "expanded" edition in 1995.

Things have since changed dramatically, and the rise of world literature can be seen as coeval with changes in social, economic, and political spheres in an increasingly globalized world. By now we may assume that the "world" in world literature has to be truly global or, to borrow a term recently made popular, it should be planetary, in a geographical sense. That is to say, when discussing world literature, the sampling of literary works must cross over not only languages and cultures, but also regions and continents, beyond Eurocentrism or any other ethnocentrism.

The mere expansion of coverage, the conglomeration of different literatures, however, does not make a meaningful concept of world literature. The sheer quantity of works available makes it impossible for anyone to read even a small portion of the world's literatures, so world literature as a concept has to be a theoretical construct, rather than a mere juxtaposition of literatures as textual materials. As Moretti argues, simply reading "more" is not enough. "It has to be different. The *categories* have to be different." The solution he proposes is "distant reading," which "allows you to focus on units that are much smaller or much larger than the text: devices, themes, tropes – or genres and systems" (p. 160, above). Many have responded to Moretti's theoretical model, but few have pointed out the similarity between the strategy of "distant reading" and Northrop Frye's archetypal criticism, which treats literature as a total structure or system rather than individual works randomly amalgamated together. Moretti's model, however, has a different political underpinning than Frye's. Drawing on Immanuel Wallerstein's "world-systems" theory and Fredric Jameson's "law of literary evolution," Moretti argues that the modern novel develops from European centers of metropolitan culture to non-European peripheries, "as a compromise between a western formal influence (usually French or English) and local materials" (p. 163). Despite its remarkable explanatory power, the center–periphery model and, for that matter, the world-systems theory on which it depends fail to recognize the resilience of local traditions that constitute crucial internal contexts, not just "local materials," for the development of the novel in the peripheries. In other words, the tension between the local and the global in the concept of world literature cannot be resolved by ignoring the local dimension, though as a *modern* form of literature, the novel in the peripheries is indeed under a heavy Western influence. In the case of the Chinese novel, for example, influential movers of the May Fourth new culture movement in the early twentieth century, radical iconoclastic figures like Lu Xun and Hu Shih, also looked to China's past in addition to the West. Lu Xun wrote one of the earliest histories of the classical Chinese novel, and Hu Shih advocated the re-examination of China's classical tradition and revolutionized the study of the great eighteenth-century Chinese novel *Hong Lou Meng* (*Dream of the Red Chamber*, also known as *The Story of the Stone*), which remains a major influence on most modern Chinese writers.

Focusing on the modern form does create problems with implications not only of a historical but also of a theoretical nature. This is particularly evident in the case of Pascale Casanova's idea of the "world republic of letters." Describing the formation of the world's literary space "as the product of a historical process," she maintains that

> it appeared in Europe in the 16th century, France and England forming its oldest regions. It was consolidated and enlarged into central and eastern Europe during the 18th and especially the 19th centuries, propelled by Herderian national theory. It expanded throughout the 20ᵗʰ century, notably through the still-ongoing decolonization process: manifestos proclaiming the right to literary existence or independence continue to appear, often linked to movements for national self-determination. (p. 195, above)

Such an account of the history of world literature is unabashedly Eurocentric and modernist, closely mapping on the European expansion in the colonialist era and the subsequent decolonization in the mid-twentieth century, but completely oblivious of the Hellenistic and Roman world and ignorant of the formation of literary constellations outside Europe, such as the Persian and the Ottoman empires, or the East Asian region with the Chinese written language and culture playing a pivotal role in premodern times. Casanova's Paris-centered model, as Alexander Beecroft remarks, "cannot account for the full range of literary production across all cultures and times. … Forms of literary circulation which predate French literary culture, or which exist outside it today, have no real place in Casanova's world-system" (p. 182, above). Aamir Mufti also criticizes Casanova for missing the "philological revolution" in Oriental studies, when "non-Western textual traditions made their first entry *as literature*, sacred and secular, into the international literary space that had emerged in early modern times in Europe" (p. 315, above). Because of such blind spots, Mufti continues, Casanova fails to see non-Western literatures in world literary space until the middle of the twentieth century, as a result of decolonization, when "such figures as Kateb Yacine, V.S. Naipaul, and Salman Rushdie and the psychology of *assimilation* into metropolitan languages and cultures typify the non-Western writer" (p. 315). The formation of Casanova's world literary space thus looks like a process of radiation of European influence, and more specifically Parisian influence, onto the rest of the world, but it is important to realize that though Paris may have been the capital of the Western republic of letters at a certain period of time, such a mapping of world literary space is neither historically accurate nor theoretically productive. It may even smack of a kind of cultural narcissism known to be particularly strong in certain French intellectual circles.

The debate on the manifesto "*Pour une littérature-monde en français*" is noteworthy in this regard, as it reveals the complex relationships of the French language and literature with colonialism and decolonization. Signed by 44 writers, mostly originating from outside France, and published in *Le Monde* on March 16, 2007, the manifesto announced "the end of 'francophone' literature. And the birth of a world literature in French" (p. 272, above). It is an effort to destabilize the center and peripheries and calls for the equality of all writers writing in French, whether hexagonal or francophone. "With the center placed on an equal plane with other centers," the signatories conclude in an idealistic vein, "we're witnessing the birth of a new constellation, in which language freed from its exclusive pact with the nation, free from every other power hereafter but the powers of poetry and the imaginary, will have no other frontiers but those of the spirit" (pp. 274–275). As his response to the manifesto shows, the soon-to-be French President, Nicolas Sarkozy, considers that francophonie is alive and well, a testimony to the influence of the French language from the center to the peripheries – a direct reversal of the direction celebrated in the manifesto itself. Yet Françoise Lionnet points out an irony in the fact that the manifesto, signed in Paris to destabilize the center in the very center itself, "reinforces by the same token the city's role as a site of cultural prestige that can grant distinction and visibility to writers in accordance to the regulatory principles of literary modernity with their well-established systems of coveted awards" (p. 297, above).

Perhaps there is a yet deeper irony concerning another tension, briefly revealed in Sarkozy's defense of the francophone, namely, the rivalry between French and English as lingua franca for world literature. This seems to be an issue too embarrassingly sensitive to be discussed in much of the debate on the manifesto of *littérature-monde français*, but it leads toward what Casanova holds as the "primary characteristic of this world literary space," namely, "hierarchy and inequality" (p. 200). Casanova's sober-minded, realpolitik view of the world literary space has the virtue of presenting the modern and contemporary world in a clear picture, not obscured by a sentimental moralism. "The unequal distribution of literary resources is fundamental to the structure of the entire world literary space, organized as it is around two opposing poles" (p. 201). For Casanova, the two poles are European metropolitan centers and non-European peripheries, but even within European centers, the distribution of cultural and symbolic capitals is likewise unequal, particularly between English and French as they compete for linguistic prestige. In a world that is increasingly globalized and also increasingly diversified, English has long evolved beyond England into a language widely used in social, economical, cultural, and all other aspects of contemporary life, and journals like *World Englishes* are published to discuss the legitimacy of diverse usages. The French language, in contrast, still retains its traditional prestige and centrality yet to be drastically diversified, and therefore the *littérature-monde* movement, as Dutton remarks, may be moving to "a new model that is potentially just as fraught with risk as francophonie" (p. 283). The question is: Is a world literature in French a real alternative to the center–periphery dichotomy with its dubious colonial implications?

The importance of translation as an affirmative force and not merely an unhappy necessity is certainly something new in the concept of world literature. In opening up to translations, world literature differs from comparative literature with its traditional requirement of near-native proficiency in French, German, and Latin. Traditional elite comparative literature programs, as David Damrosch observes, "had a real distaste for translation" (p. 366 above). Thomas Greene in his 1975 ACLA "Report on Standards" considered "the association of comparative literature with literatures in translation" as "the most disturbing" sign of the slackening of disciplinary rigor and standards. "Greene's critique hit home," says Damrosch. "No self-respecting program in his day could wish to be seen as the educational equivalent of the food court in 'the Mall of America'" (p. 368). Perhaps by pure serendipity, "the food court of a mall" is precisely the metaphor Stephen Owen used in his critique of "world poetry," which flattens out regional differences and offers different cuisines as national types, as representatives of food (or literature) that lack "distinct histories and distinct values" (p. 252, above). As a Sinologist and specialist of classical Chinese poetry, Owen's critique a dozen years ago of the modern Chinese poet Bei Dao, who once wrote about democracy and oppression, proved to be misplaced and controversial, for he accused the Chinese poet of "using one's victimization for self-interest: in this case, to sell oneself abroad by what an international audience, hungry for political virtue, which is always in short supply, finds touching."[11] But when oppression and the struggle for democracy form part of the "distinct histories and distinct values" for the modern Chinese, Owen has no legitimate reason to dismiss these as inadmissible in modern Chinese poetry. In the essay included in this volume, however, he raises a pressing question of the world literature "food court" and his worry about a non-Western poet writing for an international audience – which in practical terms means a European and American audience – under the "pressure for linguistic fungibility" (p. 250). The question concerns both the authenticity of literary works, particularly lyric poetry, deeply rooted in a particular language and a national tradition, and the ways in which these works may be understood beyond their historical and cultural contexts.

In a way, Owen's skepticism of poetry in translation may be related to what Gayatri Spivak emphasizes as "singularity," that is, the need to "regionalize" a poet like Tagore in order to understand him in his specific linguistic and cultural background (p. 374, above). Spivak would certainly abhor the food court model of literary representation, and she is skeptical that students with special linguistic knowledge or cultural background in a multicultural class could speak of different literatures with any greater credibility than food court dishes could adequately represent different kinds of the world's cuisines. "Thinking of any international student as an authority on globality because of his/her identity is like thinking all Americans abroad are experts on Melville," says Spivak in a rare moment of absolute clarity out of her typically dense and difficult theoretical discourse (p. 373). But world literature is not taken hostage by translation or national literature specialists, and the idea is not to depend on translation with no knowledge of foreign languages. In his response to Spivak, Damrosch proposes "a *sliding scale* of language study" as a solution, that is, "a near-native grasp of one language" plus "a range of competence in several others" (p. 368).

The important step here is again to cross over the divide between European centers and non-European peripheries, and to acquire languages that are different not within one group, European, Asian, African, and so on, but across linguistic groups. As world literature covers more than the usual ground in linguistic and cultural diversity beyond individual capacities, translation becomes necessary and extremely important, and the often debated issue of translatability brings the question of translation to a much deeper level than the usual kind of translation studies. As Susan Bassnett acknowledges, new and exciting ideas about translation are not coming from translation studies as such: "where we must turn today for the most innovative thinking about translation is to scholars who see themselves as comparatists, as postcolonialists, as world literature people" (p. 239, above). The tension in the concept of world literature between the local and the global, the national and the universal, differences and affinities, pushes the discussion of translation to a level of conceptualization that involves fundamental issues of thinking and communication across vast linguistic and cultural boundaries, issues of the possibility and practice of cross-cultural understanding and communication. In that sense, world literature engages translation in much more complicated theoretical discussions than ever before.

From Goethe and Marx to Casanova, Moretti, and Damrosch, the concept of world literature has been theorized mostly in the context of Western literary studies. Today, in world literature's tendency to go beyond Eurocentrism and any other ethnocentrism, the question necessarily arises: Is world literature to expand not only its coverage or reading materials to a global dimension, but also its critical and theoretical horizon to embrace the entire world, beyond the great East–West divide? Revathi Krishnaswamy raised that question against "a widespread assumption that theory is the product of a uniquely Western philosophical tradition. From this perspective, the non-West may be a source of exotic cultural production but cannot be a site of theory" (p. 135, above). She proposes the notion of "world literary knowledges" that "aims to go beyond inducting a few token non-Western greats into theory's hall of fame; rather, it asks us radically to re-vision the question of what counts as theory in the first place" (p. 136). Drawing on India's rich literary and critical traditions not only of Sanskrit poetics, but also of Tamil/Dravidian linguistics and poetics, the popular multilingual *bhakti* or devotional literatures, and Dalit literatures of the lower castes, Krishnaswamy provides three examples of how literary knowledge may emerge to deal with theoretical questions in different ways and different formulations. It is in this connection that we may appreciate the different notions of world literature presented by Tagore and Zheng Zhenduo, the more recent contributions by Karen Thornber on East Asian literary relations, or Ronit Ricci on literary networks in the Arabic world. In considering world literature in theory, we need to build a level playing field where the West meets the East as equal contributors, and the poetics of world literature should be a set of questions that inquire into the nature of language and expression, meaning and understanding, interpretation and aesthetic values, the origin of poetry and literature, the relationship between art and nature, and so on and so forth. The ways in which these questions get asked and answered are surely different in different literary traditions, but it is such basic questions and their answers that make up what literary theory is in world literature, with valuable insights richly elucidated by different examples and critical formulations.

Thus theory has the tendency to travel, to move from one place to another so that linkages and comparisons can be made in "contrapuntal juxtaposition" of literary creations and cultural practices. Edward Said's classic essay on "Traveling Theory" has long pointed out the geopolitics in the transformations of literary theories in a globalized world that no longer conforms to the simple structure of European metropolitan centers and non-European peripheries. When theoretical concepts travel to a new cultural and political environment, Said argues, they will necessarily encounter resistance as "an inevitable part of acceptance."[12] Mechanical application of a theoretical notion in a new environment is thus always infertile; only adaptation and accommodation will bear fruits that are nurtured by the rich soil in which it has taken root. In that sense, world literature will never be the same everywhere it is studied. As Lawall observes with regard to world literature anthologies, "it is unlikely that any global perspective can be truly decentered, providing equal representation and a neutral framework."[13] That is to say, world literature in practice is always localized, with different works selected for study and critical comment, different issues addressed in different cultural and theoretical perspectives and with different interests.

World literature is thus always a concept that changes in response to local needs and contexts. At the same time, the competitiveness and highly selective nature of works that achieve a secure place within world literature yield a relatively stable set of canonical works from the world's different literary traditions. In that sense, world literature is also a productive way back to literature itself, a way to counter the moving away from literature in much of the discourse of literary theory and cultural studies in recent decades. The conceptual openness or flexibility of world literature, and the dynamic mix of new entries from previously neglected regions along with the ongoing relative stability of major literary works, constitute the strength and vitality of world literature as an exciting field with new possibilities for literary studies, and that may be the secret of the undeniable ascendance and success of world literature in our world today.

Notes

1   John Pizer, "Johann Wolfgang von Goethe: Origins and Relevance of *Weltliteratur*," in Theo D'haen, David Damrosch, and Djelal Kadir, eds., *The Routledge Companion to World Literature* (London: Routledge, 2012), 3–11 (3).

2   Johann Wolfgang von Goethe, *Essays on Art and Literature*, ed. John Gearey, trans. Ellen von Nardroff and Ernest H. Nardroff (Princeton: Princeton University Press, 1994), 207.

3   Goethe, *Essays on Art and Literature*, 208.

4   Claudio Guillén, *The Challenge of Comparative Literature*, trans. Cola Franzen (Cambridge, MA: Harvard University Press, 1993 [1985]), 39–40.

5   Monika Schmitz-Emans, "Richard Meyer's Concept of World Literature," trans. Mark Schmitt, in Theo D'haen, David Damrosch, and Djelal Kadir, eds., *The Routledge Companion to World Literature* (London: Routledge, 2012), 49–61 (50).

6   Aijad Ahmad, "*The Communist Manifesto* and 'World Literature.'" *Social Scientist* 29:7–8 (Jul.–Aug. 2000), 3–30 (13).

7 Mads Rosendahl Thomsen, *Mapping World Literature: International Canonization and Transnational Literatures* (New York: Continuum, 2008), 13.

8 Karl Marx and Friedrich Engels, *The Communist Manifesto* (New York: The Seabury Press, 1967), 136–137.

9 It is only fair to point out, however, that Meltzl was well aware of the problem of focusing purely on European literature, as he criticized August Koberstein for tracing the aubade to Wolfram von Eschenbach without knowing "the fact that Lieder of this type were sung eighteen centuries ago in China (as those contained in the *Shih Ching*) and are frequently found among the folksongs of modern peoples, for instance, the Hungarians" (p. 37, above).

10 Sarah Lawall, "The West and the Rest: Frames for World Literature," in David Damrosch, ed., *Teaching World Literature* (New York: MLA, 2009), 17–33 (21).

11 Stephen Owen, "The Anxiety of Global Influence: What Is World Poetry?" *New Republic* (Nov. 19, 1990), 28–32 (29).

12 Edward Said, *The World, the Text, and the Critic* (Cambridge, MA: Harvard University Press, 1983), 227.

13 Lawall, "The West and the Rest," 29.

Index

Abe Kobo, 391
Abou Nouwas, 92
Abrams, Meyer Howard, 320
Abrams, Robert E., 431
Achebe, Chinua, 141, 171, 308
Adorno, Theodor, 219, 508
Aeschylus, 20–21, 366
Agamben, Giorgio, 350
Ahmad, Aijaz, 136, 406–407, 412–415
Ahmad, Dohra, 307
Ai Qing, 91
Al Farabi, 92
Al Ghazali, 92
al Ma'arri, 92
al-Hakim, Tawfiq, 89, 92
al-Hallaj, Mansur, 93, 95
al-Tabarī, 443
Alberti, Rafael, 90
Albrow, Martin, 24
Aleichem, Sholem, 82
Almeida, Guilherme da, 401
Ambedkar, B.R., 148–149
Anand, Mulk Raj, 90
Anderson, Benedict, 163, 213–214
Andrade, Mario de, 402
Andreyev, Leonid, 62
Antoine, André, 197

Anzaldúa, Gloria, 141, 308
Apollinaire, Guillaume, 89
Appadurai, Arjun, 210, 350, 417, 424, 433, 485
Appiah, Kwame Anthony, 485
Apter, Emily, 9, 138, 172, 176, 230, 345
Apuleius, 3, 6
Arac, Jonathan, 172, 175–176, 355
Araki Toru, 91
Aravamudan, Srinivas, 324
Archer, William, 201
Aristotle, 92, 140, 144, 350, 359, 360
Asad, Talal, 352
Ascasubi, 392–393
Atar, Nabil, 142
Ato Quayson, 163, 348
Attia Naboul Naga, 92
Auerbach, Erich, 175–176, 294, 318, 348, 364
Augustine, 93, 307
Austin, J.L., 360
Averroës, 92, 350
Avicenna, 92
Avila, Teresa of, 95
Azad, Muhammad Husain, 334

Ba Jin, 469–470
Bach, Johann Sebastian, 374–375, 378
Bachelard, Gaston, 89

World Literature in Theory, First Edition. Edited by David Damrosch.
© 2014 John Wiley & Sons, Ltd. Published 2014 by John Wiley & Sons, Ltd.

Bachmann-Medick, Doris, 240
Badiou, Alain, 356–360
Baker, Mona, 240
Bakhtin, Mikhail, 30, 32–33
Balibar, Etienne, 310, 348, 358, 432
Balmer, Josephine, 243, 244
Balzac, Honoré de, 379
Banchs, Enrique, 394
Bandeira, Manuel, 402
Barbery, Muriel, 275
Barbusse, Henri, 62
Basavanna, 147
Basch, Linda, 426
Bassnett, Susan, 8, 136, 138–139, 234, 238, 240, 242, 521
Bastide, Roger, 400–403
Basu, Anustup, 324
Basu, Ramram, 330
Baucom, Ian, 135–136
Baudelaire, Charles, 297, 301, 484
Baudrillard, Jean, 427
Bauman, Zygmunt, 308
Bayly, Susan, 441, 452
Bazin, Hervé, 89
Beauvoir, Simone de, 303
Becker, Alton, 445
Beckett, Samuel, 192–193, 203, 205, 356
Bédier, Joseph, 88
Beecroft, Alexander, 7–8, 180, 184, 518
Beethoven, Ludwig van, 378
Beg Suroor, Rajab Ali, 334
Bei Dao, 249–250, 256, 258, 520
Belaval, Yvon, 89
Bellos, David, 355–356
Bellow, Saul, 423
Ben Arabi, 92
Ben Brahim, Mest'fa, 88
Ben Jelloun, Tahar, 275, 282, 285, 303
Benet, Juan, 198
Benjamin, Walter, 8, 350–351, 353, 383, 385–386
Bennett, Louise, 308
Bensmaïa, Réda, 283
Béranger, Pierre Jean de, 4, 16, 19, 86, 503
Berczik, Árpád, 86, 93
Berg, Leo, 59
Berger, John, 131
Bergerac, Cyrano de, 92

Bernabé, Jean, 297
Bernanos, 400
Bernheimer, Charles, 136, 405
Berryman, John, 418
Berthet, Alice, 90
Bertin, Antoine de, 301
Bhabha, Homi, 29–33, 135, 141, 239, 348, 484–485
Bielsa, Esperança, 241
bin Salām, Abdullah, 441
Bion, 45
Biswas, Moinak, 382
Blake, William, 92
Blakey, Art, 495, 500–503
Bloch, Ernst, 488
Bloch, Marc, 111, 161
Block, Haskell, 366–367, 371
Bloom, Harold, 420
Boas, Franz, 315
Bobzin, Hartmut, 443
Boethius, 243
Boileau, Nicolas, 303, 309
Boisserée, Sulpiz, 26
Boleyn, Ann, 91
Bolter, Jay David, 496
Borer, Alain, 275
Borges, Jorge Luis, 9, 90, 131, 201, 241, 391–392
Börne, Ludwig, 25
Bosteels, Bruno, 358
Boubia, Fawzi, 28, 514
Bourdieu, Pierre, 8, 192, 199, 209, 211, 215–218, 230, 298–299, 349
Bourne, Randolphe, 422
Bouvier, Nicolas, 274
Bradley, Milton, 384
Bradstreet, Anne, 418
Bramen, Carrie, 422
Brandes, Georg, 59
Brassai, Samuel, 35, 36
Braudel, Fernand, 110, 161, 180–181, 188, 192, 199–200, 202
Brecht, Bertolt, 356
Breton, André, 297, 302
Brieux, Eugène, 90, 91
Brink, André, 408
Brival, Roland, 275
Brodzki, Bella, 235–236, 244

Brokaw, Tom, 430
Browning, Robert, 500
Brückner, Martin, 419
Buford, Bill, 408
Bunyan, John, 410
Burke, Edmund, 321, 323
Bush, George W., 424, 427, 429
Butler, Judith, 287–288, 352
Byrne, David, 482
Byron, George Gordon, 92

Caillois, Roger, 201, 400
Calderón, Pedro, 20
Caldwell, Robert, 141
Callaway, Henry, 409
Calvino, Italo, 391
Camões, Luis de, 38
Campo, Estanislao del, 392–393
Candido, Antonio, 197, 403
Cao Yu, 91
Cardinal, Marie, 303
Carelli, Mario, 401
Carey, William, 330–331
Carl August, Duke, 25
Carlyle, Thomas, 86, 514
Carter, Jimmy, 417, 424
Carvalhal, Tania, 9, 398
Casanova, Pascale, 181–188, 192, 296–297,
    314–315, 348–349, 517–521, and *passim*
Casper, S.E., 213
Cassin, Barbara, 345, 347–360
Cassirer, Ernst, 200
Cather, Willa, 422
Cavafy, Constantin, 90–91
Cavalli-Sforza, Luigi Luca, 165
Celestin, Roger, 288
Céline, Louis-Ferdinand, 285
Cellini, Benvenuto, 93
Cendrars, Blaise, 400, 402
Cervantes, Miguel de, 38, 175–176, 380
Césaire, Aimé, 273, 285, 299, 302
Chafetz, Hope, 430
Chah, Nader, 320
Chakladar, Arnab, 406
Chamoiseau, Patrick, 226, 297, 303
Chandler, Raymond, 272
Chang, Young-hae, 10, 493–495, 506

Chapman, Michael, 10, 405
Chartier, R., 213
Chateaubriand, François-René de, 301
Chatterjee, Partha, 154, 324, 326
Chatterji, Suniti Kumar, 330
Chattopadhyay, Bankimchandra, 325–326,
    342
Chatwin, Bruce, 273
Chaucer, Geoffrey, 397
Cheah, Pheng, 348, 484–485
Chen, Peng-hsiang, 140
Cheng, François, 304
Cherbuliez, Victor, 90
Chevrel, Yves, 349
Chikamatsu Monzaemon, 92
Chomsky, Noam, 129–131, 194
Chow, Rey, 136, 138, 141
Chowdhury, Jayasree Roy, 382
Chrupala, G., 215
Cicero, 241
Cioran, Emil, 203
Cixous, Hélène, 303
Claudel, Paul, 400, 402
Clifford, James, 486
Clinton, Bill, 424–426
Coetzee, J.M., 408
Cohen, Bernard, 100
Cohen, Margaret, 160
Cohn, Bernard S., 141
Colebrook, Henry Thomas, 322, 325
Colenso, William, 409
Coleridge, Samuel Taylor, 82
Colie, Rosalie, 371
Collini, Stefan, 198
Condé, Maryse, 275, 277, 295, 302
Condillac, Étienne Bonnot de, 315
Confiant, Raphaël, 297
Confucius, 1, 85, 95
Conley, Tom, 286
Connolly, Cyril, 95
Conrad, Joseph, 76, 203
Conrad, N.I., 88
Constant, Benjamin, 93
Cooper, James Fenimore, 431
Cooppan, Vilashini, 135
Corcoran, Patrick, 303–304
Corneille, Pierre, 92

Coser, L.A., 219
Coste, Didier, 374
Coupland, Douglas, 427
Coutinho, Afrânio, 403
Couto, Mia, 410
Crane, Diana, 210
Culler, Jonathan, 134–135
Curtius, Ernst Robert, 364

Daeninckx, Didier, 275
Dai, Sijie, 275, 304
Dai, Wangshu, 90
Dalmolin, Eliane, 288
Damrosch, David, 135, 319, 346, 348, 363–388, 461, 481–482, 519–521
Dante Alighieri, 61, 186, 384
Darío, Rubén, 204–205
Darwin, Charles, 42, 165
Das, Balaram, 52
Das, Sisir Kumar, 139
David, Jérôme, 349
Davie, Donald, 505
Dazai Osamu, 465–468
De Lille, Jacques, 16
de Man, Paul, 364, 374
De Swaan, A., 210
Debray, Régis, 400
Defoe, Daniel, 163
Deleuze, Gilles, 10, 201, 416, 423, 431, 433
Denilson, Lopes, 10, 480
Denis, Claire, 484
Denning, Michael, 425
Dennison, Stephanie, 482
Depestre, René, 299
Derozio, Henry Louis Vivien, 326, 327
Derrida, Jacques, 9, 347, 352–353, 363, 372–373, 386
Des Rosiers, Joël, 294
Desani, G.V., 406
Detienne, Marcel, 7, 99–100, 353
Devi, Ananda, 275, 295
Devi, Mahasweta, 364
Devy, G.N., 142, 145–146, 330
Dewey, John, 422
D'haen, Theo, 379
Dharwadker, Vinay, 316
Diaz, Junot, 308

Dickens, Charles, 81
Dickinson, Emily, 418
Diebes, Joe, 374–375, 378
Diepeveen, Leonard, 505
Dimock, Wai Chee, 135, 348
Diouf, Abdou, 283, 305–307
Dirkx, Paul, 288
Dirlik, Arif, 406–407
d'Istria, Dora, 40
Djebar, Assia, 277, 295, 299
Dommartin, Solveig, 487
Donzelot, Jacques, 128
Dos Passos, John, 423
Dostoevsky, Fyodor, 176
Doumic, René, 90
Doyle, Roddy, 308
Drabinski, John, 373
Dreiser, Theodore, 422
Drieu La Rochelle, Pierre, 400
Drummond, William Henry, 401
Du Bellay, Joachim, 186
Du Bois, W.E.B., 140, 377
Du Fu, 254
Ducharme, Réjean, 274
Dudden, Alexis, 471
Dugrand, Alain, 275
Dumézil, Georges, 101
Durand, Gilbert, 401, 404
Durand, P., 213
During, Simon, 346
Durkheim, Émile, 111
Dutton, Jacqueline, 9, 279, 519

Eagleton, Terry, 141
Eckermann, Johann Peter, 1, 5, 15, 25, 30, 32, 86, 160, 180, 319, 349, 379, 514
Eco, Umberto, 241, 403
El Moutannabi, 92
Eliot, T.S., 495, 499
Elliott, Emory, 140
Ellmann, Richard, 507
Emerson, Ralph Waldo, 419–421, 425
Engels, Friedrich, 3, 5, 6, 160, 268, 319, 335, 355, 515–516
English, James, 299
Engonopoulos, Nikos, 91
Eschenbach, Wolfram von, 37

Estaunié, Édouard, 90–91
Etiemble, René, 7, 85–86, 142, 514, 516
Euripides, 20–21, 108
Even-Zohar, Itamar, 161–164, 174–175, 213, 237–238
Evin, Ahmet O., 163

Fanon, Franz, 141, 408
Farinelli, Arturo, 94
Faruqi, Shamsur Rahman, 331
Faulkner, William, 197, 391
Ferguson, Niall, 429, 433
Feuillet, Octave, 90
Fichte, Gottlieb, 31, 119
Finley, M.I., 110
Finney, Gail, 28
Fish, Stanley, 302
Fisher, Philip, 422
Fokkema, Douwe, 403
Fontane, Theodor, 94
Ford, Henry, 423, 426
Forsdick, Charles, 286
Forster, E.M., 134, 412
Foster, Georg, 321
Foucault, Michel, 128–131, 194
Frank, Andre Gunder, 182
Freedman, Ralph, 371
Frenz, Horst, 142
Frenzel, Elizabeth, 91
Freud, Sigmund, 357
Fricke, Ron, 483
Fried, Michael, 508
Frieden, Ken, 163
Friederich, Werner, 364–368
Friedman, Thomas, 379
Frost, Robert, 422
Frye, Northrop, 116, 517
Fucilla, Joseph, 172
Fuentes, Carlos, 204, 273, 400
Fujino, Genkurō, 468
Furet, François, 111
Futabatei, Shimei, 164, 170

Gabriel, Peter, 482
Gandhi, 324, 381, 413
Ganne, V., 211
Gao Xingjian, 2, 256, 263
Garcia Lorca, Federico, 90

García Márquez, Gabriel, 159, 198, 391
Garcilaso de la Vega, 393
Gasperetti, David, 163
Gaudier-Brzeska, Henri, 505
Genet, Jean, 316, 374, 378
Gentzler, Edwin, 238, 240, 403
Géraldy, Paul, 93
Gervinus, Georg Gottfried, 36
Ghosh, Amitav, 406
Ghosh, Sri Aurobindo, 145
Giamatti, A. Bartlett, 380
Gibbon, Edward, 395
Gibran, Kahlil, 381
Gibson, William, 427
Gide, André, 201, 391
Gikandi, Simon, 348
Gilchrist, John, 330–331
Giles, Paul, 10, 416
Giong Lim, 489
Glissant, Edouard, 198, 275, 287, 294–295, 347
Godbout, Jacques, 275, 282–285
Goethe, Johann Wolfgang von, 3–6, 15–16, 22–38, 86–95, and *passim*
Goldmann, Lucien, 121–127
Goodman, Nelson, 351
Gordimer, Nadine, 408–409
Gorky, Maxim, 61, 87
Goscilo, Helena, 163
Gournay, B., 214
Gowthaman, Raj, 148–149
Grace, Patricia, 308
Graff, Gerald, 117, 403
Gramsci, Antonio, 131, 287, 317, 376, 381
Greene, Roland, 172
Greene, Thomas, 367–370, 519–520
Grégoire, Abbé, 287
Grenier, Jean, 95
Grierson, G.A., 323
Grimm, Jacob, 4
Grimm, Wilhelm, 4
Grob, Norbert, 488
Groves, J.D., 213
Grusin, Richard, 496
Guattari, Félix, 10, 201, 416, 423, 431, 433
Guha, Ranajit, 321, 341
Guillén, Claudio, 481, 514
Guillory, John, 505

Güiraldes, Ricardo, 395
Gunder Frank, Andre, 182
Guo Moruo, 469–470
Guyot, Arnold, 420–421

Habermas, Jürgen, 432
Hacking, Ian, 129
Hafiz, 15–16, 29, 92, 267, 319–320, 325–326, 370–372
Hagège, Claude, 295
Halhed, Nathaniel Brassey, 322
Hamacher, Werner, 351
Hamann, J.G., 351, 361
Hammett, Dashiell, 272
Handel, Georg Friedrich, 419
Hankiss, M., 87
Hannerz, Ulf, 210
Hansen, Mark, 502
Hardt, Michael, 381, 425, 482
Hardy, Thomas, 243
Harîri, 44
Harman, Graham, 359
Harrison, S.J., 243
Hart, George, 146
Hartley, Hal, 484
Hartman, Geoffrey, 117, 371
Harvey, Bruce, 419
Harvey, David, 212, 417, 424, 433
Hastings, Warren, 321–323, 330
Haykal, Husayn, 170
Hayles, N. Katherine, 493, 496
Hedayat, Sadegh, 91
Hegel, G.W.F., 92, 95, 119
Heidegger, Martin, 92, 269, 350, 356
Heilbron, J., 210, 226
Heine, Heinrich, 23
Held, D., 214
Heller-Roazen, Daniel, 350–352
Herder, J.G. von, 4, 187, 315, 321, 349
Herman of Dalmatia, 443
Hermans, Theo, 238
Hernández, José, 392
Hernández, Miguel, 90
Herodotus, 264, 266–269
Herzog, Werner, 484
Hesiod, 108
Hesse, Hermann, 88–89, 95, 391
Hitler, Adolf, 356

Ho Chi Minh, 1, 10
Hobbes, Thomas, 93
Hoffmeister, Gerhart, 172
Hogan, Patrick, 135, 141–142
Holmes, John Clellon, 503
Homer, 43, 59, 61, 243, 393, 495, 498, 504–507
Honwana, Luis Bernado, 410
Horkheimer, Max, 219, 383
Horta, Paulo, 371
Hou Zhe, 89, 91
Howells, William Dean, 422
Hu Shih, 6, 517
Huang Ren, 6
Hughes, Langston, 140–141
Hughes, Ted, 242–243
Hume, David, 92
Huntington, Samuel, 379
Hurston, Zora Neale, 140, 308
Hurt, Thomas, 486
Husayn Haykal, 170
Hussein, Taha, 85, 89, 92–93, 201
Husserl, Edmund, 92
Huston, Nancy, 275, 289, 304
Hölderlin, J.C.F., 90

Ibáñez, Blasco, 90
Ibn al-Salām, 442–443
Ibn Baṭṭūta, 440, 449
Ibn Hazm, 92
Ibn Hisham, 443
Ibn Khaldoun, 89, 93
Ibn Rouchid [Ibn Rushd], 92
Ibn Sina [Avicenna], 92, 346
Ibnu Salam, Serat Suluk Samud, 442, 445, 447, 455
Ibsen, Henrik, 197, 201, 205
Icukākku, Ceyku Mutali, 444
Idagal, Ilango, 93
Iglesias Santos, Montserrat, 161
Ihara Saikaku, 90, 93
Ilango Idagal, 93
Iñarritu, Alejandro González, 484
Inshallah Khan Insha, 331–332
Ionesco, Eugène, 299–301
Iqbal, Muhammad, 90, 325–326, 336
Irele, Abiola, 163
Irigaray, Luce, 147, 303

Iser, Wolfgang, 405, 407
Ishiguro, Kazuo, 273, 348
Ishikawa Tatsuzō, 471, 472
Isocrates, 108
Iweala, Uzodinma, 308

Jackson, Andrew, 430
Jahn, Friedrich Ludwig, 23
James, Henry, 194, 379
James, William, 420, 422
Jameson, Fredric, 128, 162–164, 166, 417, 517
Jarmusch, Jim, 484
Jauss, Hans Robert, 403
Jean Paul, 90
Jeanpierre, Laurent, 349
Jefferson, Thomas, 432
Jencks, Christopher, 368
Jennar, R.M., 214
Jia Zhang-Ke, 484, 488, 489
Jiang Guangci, 470
Jin Dong Liang, 490
Jippensha Ikku, 90, 93
Jirmounsky, M.M., 88
Johnson, Barbara, 347
Johnson, Lyndon, 374
Jones, William, 141, 320–326, 328, 330–331, 338, 377
Jonson, Ben, 126
Josserand, Pierre, 91
Joyce, James, 92, 196–197, 205, 507
Judy, R.A., 346
Jungmann, Joseph, 239
Jussawalla, Feroza, 406

Kabir, 93, 95
Kadir, Djelal, 8, 136, 264, 345, 379
Kafka, Franz, 193, 199–202, 205, 391
Kaiser, Gerhard, 30
Kalafatides, L., 214
Kalidasa, 15, 319, 321
Kalijaga, Sunan, 453
Kant, Immanuel, 92, 95, 119, 360, 373, 376, 381
Kaplan, Caren, 424
Karatani Kojin, 142, 162–164
Kashnabish, Ashmita, 147
Katz, Jerrold, 356
Kaurismäki, Aki, 484

Kawabata Yasunari, 466–467
Kazantzakis, Nikos, 91
Keaton, Buster, 490
Kemal, Namik, 163
Kenkô, 90
Kennedy, William, 172
Kern, Stephen, 504
Kerouac, Jack, 503, 505
Keshub Chander Sen, 325
Kesteloot, Lilian, 305
Khasnabish, Ashmita, 142
Kilito, Abdelfattah, 347, 350, 352
Kim Chiha, 474
Kim Ilsŏng, 470
Kinzer, Stephen, 227
Kipling, Rudyard, 55, 71, 134, 327, 395, 397
Kittler, Friedrich, 504
Klein, Joe, 425
Klengel, Susanne, 400–401
Koberstein, August, 37
Kohō Banri, 465–466
Kontje, Todd, 25
Korolenko, Vladimir, 62
Kouo, Mojo, 89, 91
Kourouma, Ahmadou, 300–301
Krasicki, Ignacy, 163
Kraus, Werner, 89
Krioukov, Fyodor Dmitrievich, 93
Kripalani, Krishna, 139
Kripke, Saul, 351
Krishnaswamy, Revathi, 7, 134, 521
Kristal, Efrain, 172–174, 241
Kristeva, Julia, 303
Kristof, Nicholas, 386
Kropotkin, Peter, 59
Krytsi, Maria-Venetia, 242
Ksetrayya, 147
Kudus, Sunan, 453
Kumar, Amitava, 135–136
Kwahulé, Koffi, 275

Labro, Philippe, 284
Lacan, Jacques, 147, 307, 357, 360
Lachmann, Karl, 37
Laclau, Ernest, 287
Laclavetine, Jean-Marie, 275
Laferrière, Dany, 275
Lal, Lalluji, 330

Lalande, André, 360
Lamartine, Alphonse de, 92, 301
Lamming, George, 303
Landrin, François Xavier, 349
Lao Tse, 91
Lapouge, Gilles, 275
Larbaud, Valéry, 196, 399–400
Lawall, Sarah, 32, 516, 522
Laxness, Haldor, 90
Layaz, Michel, 275, 287
Lê, Linda, 299
Le Bris, Michel, 271–312 *passim*
Le Clézio, J.-M.G., 271, 275, 279, 285, 295, 301, 400
Le Men, Yvon, 275
Leavis, F.R., 124, 142
Lefevere, André, 236, 238–240
Leibniz, G.W. von, 92
Lenclud, Gérard, 106–107
Lenin, Vladimir Ilyich, 470
Lentricchia, Frank, 116, 128
León-Portilla, Miguel, 380
Léonard, Nicolas Germain, 301
Lévi-Strauss, Claude, 99, 400
Levin, Harry, 367–370
Levitt, Peggy, 427
Lévy, Bernard-Henri, 284
Lewisohn, Ludwig, 59
Lezra, Jacques, 347
Li Kui, 64
Li Sao, 93
Li Zehou, 142
Lim, Song Hwee, 482
Limbale, Sharankumar, 148–150
Lincoln, Abraham, 1, 10, 421
Lind, Jennifer, 471
Lionnet, Françoise, 9, 138, 293, 519
Littell, Jonathan, 304
Liu E, 91
Liu Musha, 472, 477
Lobo-Antunes, António, 198
Longinus, 140
Longley, Michael, 243
Lopes, Denilson, 10, 480
Lord, Albert, 147, 184
Lotter, Matthew, 418
L'Ouverture, Toussaint, 277
Lu Xun, 6, 89, 91, 465–471, 474, 517

Lu Zhishen, 64
Luce, Henry, 423
Lucretius, 45
Lugné-Poe, A.M., 197
Lugones, Leopoldo, 392
Lukács, Georg, 118–127, 175–176, 348
Luther, Martin, 352
Lutz, Tom, 422
Lyotard, Jean-François, 357–358

Maalouf, Amin, 275, 303
Mabanckou, Alain, 275, 277, 282, 284–285, 288–289, 295
Macaulay, Thomas Babington, 237–239
Machado de Assis, J.M., 403
Macpherson, James, 329
Macura, Joaquim Maria, 239
Magdâni, 44
Mahfouz, Naguib, 336
Mahmood, Saba, 352
Mahmud of Gasna, 25
Majumdar, Margaret, 289
Makine, Andreï, 304
Malcomson, Scott, 484–485
Malinowski, Bronislaw, 315
Malkani, Gautam, 308
Malouf, Amin, 303
Manchette, Jean-Patrick, 272
Manero Sorolla, Pilar, 172
Manet, Eduardo, 299
Manley, Michael, 425
Mann, Thomas, 90
Manovich, Lev, 504
Manto, Saadat Hasan, 337
Manzoni, Alessandro, 20
Mao Dun, 90–91
Mao Zedong, 259
Maran, René, 163, 299
Marcus, Greil, 348, 361
Marker, Chris, 484
Martin, H.J., 213
Martí-López, Elisa, 163
Maruyama, Noboru, 471
Marx, Groucho, 359
Marx, Karl, 5–6, 160–161, 515–516, and *passim*
Masagão, Marcelo, 484, 490
Matar, Nabil, 142
Mattelart, A., 214, 230

Matthisson, Friedrich von, 19
Maunick, Edouard, 299
Mayakovski, Vladimir, 490
Mbembe, Achille, 277, 348
McKay, Claude, 308
Medawar, Peter, 163
Meltzl, Hugo von, 5, 9, 35–36, 88, 516
Melville, Henry, 373, 520
Mendele [S.Y. Abramovitsh], 79–82
Mendelssohn Bartholdy, Felix, 315
Merleau-Ponty, Maurice, 121
Mertens, Wim, 490
Metternich, Clemens von, 23, 31
Meyer, Richard M., 94, 515
Meyerbeer, Giacomo, 17
Michaux, Henri, 400
Mignolo, Walter, 143, 348
Milhaud, Darius, 400
Mill, John Stuart, 170
Miller, Arthur, 90, 380
Miller, Henry, 89–90
Milliet, Sergio, 401
Milo, D., 213
Milton, John, 254
Minckwitz, Johannes, 37
Minder, M., 91
Miner, Earl, 142
Minon, M., 211
Mir Amman, 330
Mir Sher Ali Afsos, 330
Mitre, Bartolomé, 393
Miyoshi, Masao, 162–163
Mo Yan, 471–474
Moebius [Möbius], A.F., 273
Mohammed, 395
Moï, Anna, 275, 282, 289
Molière, 92, 360
Mollier, J.-Y., 212
Monius, Anne E., 454
Monroe, Marilyn, 500–503
Montaigne, Michel de, 95, 419
Montesquieu, C.-L. de Secondat, Baron de, 93, 266
Moore, Marion, 89
Moosa, Matti, 163
Moreau, Jeanne, 486
Moretti, Franco, 7–8, 135–136, 159–160, 187–190, 339–346, and *passim*

Mori Ogai, 91
Morse, Jedediah, 419
Moschus, 45
Moulton, Richard G., 59–61, 65–66
Mudimbe-Boyi, Elisabeth, 300
Mufti, Aamir, 9, 313–314, 349, 518
Mukařovský, Jan, 86
Mukherjee, Alok, 139, 149, 163, 170
Mukherjee, Meenakshi, 162
Müller, Johann von, 90
Müller, Max, 325
Murakami Haruki, 462
Murasaki Shikibu, 90
Murphy, David, 286
Musset, Alfred de, 92

Naboul Naga, Attia, 92
Nagib, Lúcia, 483
Nagy, Gregory, 184
Naipaul, V.S., 315, 518
Najjar, Alexandre, 306
Nakano, Shigeharu, 91
Nakata Shōei, 465, 467, 469
Narasimhaiah, C.D., 142, 145
Narayan, R.K., 406, 414
Narayanaravku, Velcheru, 146
Nath, Jayasree, 382
Navarrete, Igancio, 172
Negri, Antonio, 381, 425, 482
Nehru, Jawaharlal, 321, 381, 414
Neruda, Pablo, 400
Ngũgĩ wa Thiong'o, 141, 171–172
Nguyen Du, 90
Nieoupokoyeva, 87
Nietzsche, Friedrich, 90, 92, 376
Nikolau, Paschalis, 242
Nimrod, 275, 289
Nixon, Richard, 424
Noailles, Anna de, 93
Nogueira Galvão, Walnice, 400
Novalis, 321, 358
N'Sondé, Wilfried, 275
Ntsikana, Chief Sicana, 407

Obiechina, Emmanuel, 163
O'Clair, Robert, 507
Ōe Kenzaburō, 472
Ohmann, Richard, 117

Okakura Kakuzo, 90
Okri, Ben, 273, 304
Omprakash Valmiki, 148
Ondaatje, Michael, 226, 273
Orlando, Francesco, 175
Orner, Esther, 275
Orsenna, Erik, 275
Orsini, Francesca, 172
Ortega, Julio, 171
Ottinger, Ulrike, 484
Ou Xilin, 471, 472
Ovid, 244
Owen, Stephen, 8, 249, 520

Pamuk, Orhan, 2, 346
Pandit, Lalita, 141–142
Parameswaran, Uma, 406
Paré, François, 295
Parker, Gabrielle, 286, 288
Parla, Jale, 163, 172, 175
Parmenides, 359, 360
Parny, Evariste, 301
Parry, Benita, 485
Parry, Milman, 184
Pascal, Blaise, 87, 121–122
Patell, Cyrus, 418
Patil, Sharad, 148
Paton, Alan, 410
Paulhan, Jean, 90
Paz, Octavio, 90, 196, 400

Peeters, Benoît, 275
Péguy, Charles, 277
Péladan, Joséphin, 90, 93
Pennington, Brian, 324
Perec, Georges, 356
Peretz, I.L., 76, 81–83
Perón, Juan, 9, 391
Perse, Saint-John, 273
Peters, Arno, 91
Petrarch, Francis, 172, 301
Petrovich, Rastko, 90
Pevear, Richard, 354–355
Phule, Mahatma, 149
Piault, F., 212
Pijper, Guillaume Frederic, 444
Pilinsky, Janos, 242
Pineau, Gisèle, 275

Pinsker, Lev, 79
Pinsky, Robert, 428
Pirotte, Jean-Claude, 275, 311
Pizer, John, 5, 22, 513–514
Plato, 92, 108, 186, 356–358, 359, 397, 419
Plotinus, 92
Poe, Edgar Allan, 391, 418
Polet, Grégoire, 275
Pollock, Sheldon, 185–187, 330, 439,
    448–450, 454
Polo, Marco, 440
Popa, I., 216
Poulantzas, Nicos, 129, 130
Pound, Ezra, 10, 203, 494–508
Pratt, Hugo, 273
Pratt, Mary Louise, 348, 462–463
Premchand, 89
Prendergast, Christopher, 172, 176, 346, 350
Presley, Elvis, 499–500, 502
Pressman, Jessica, 10, 493
Pringle, Thomas, 407
Prokosch, Frederick, 89
Proust, Marcel, 89, 285
Prysthon, Ângela, 485
Pushkin, Alexander, 90, 301
Pym, Anthony, 215, 240

Queneau, Raymond, 88–89, 91–92

Rabelais, François, 93
Racine, Jean, 121–122, 394
Radcliffe-Brown, A.R., 110
Raharimanana, Jean-Luc V., 275, 282–283, 287
Rahimi, Afiq, 304
Rai, Alok, 331
Ramakrishnan, E.B., 381–382
Ramanujan, Attipate Krishnaswami, 145–146
Rambaud, Patrick, 275
Rand, Richard, 372
Rannie, David W., 64
Rassam, Hormuzd, 379–380
Ravel, Maurice, 301
Ravitsh, Melekh, 71
Ray, Amit, 324
Raychaudhuri, Tapan, 324
Raynal, Patrick, 275, 285
Reagan, Ronald, 424, 428
Reclus, Onésime, 282–283, 287, 295

Regev, M., 210
Reggio, Godfrey, 483
Reinhard, Kenneth, 357
Rembrandt van Rijn, 374, 378
Reyes, Alfonso, 400
Reynaud, B., 212
Ribeiro, Gustavo Lins, 485
Ricci, Ronit, 10, 437
Rich, Adrienne, 418
Richards, I.A., 124
Richardson, Samuel, 19
Ricoeur, Paul, 417–418, 432
Riesman, David, 368
Rimbaud, Arthur, 85, 95
Rivas, Pierre, 399
Rivkin, Borekh, 71–72
Rizal, José, 163–164
Robbe-Grillet, Alain, 297
Robbins, Bruce, 348, 485
Roberts, Martin, 483-4
Rojas, Ricardo, 392–393
Rosello, Mireille, 283, 286, 288
Rostropovich, Mstislav, 375
Rouaud, Jean, 271, 275, 279–287, 296, 306
Rouet, F., 212, 218
Rousseau, Jean-Jacques, 301, 315
Roy, Arundhati, 304
Rüdiger, Vogler, 486
Rumsfeld, Donald, 380
Rushdie, Salman, 237, 239, 273, 304, 306, 315, 336–338, 406–407, 412–414, 518

Saadi, 92
Sack, Robert David, 431
Sadaqatullah of Kayalpattinam, 440
Sagan, Françoise, 93
Said, Edward W., 114–115, 140–143, 313–323, and *passim*
Sainte-Beuve, Charles Augustin, 82, 301
Saintsbury, George, 59
Salhi, Kamal, 286
Sall, Amadou Lamine, 305
Santiago, Silviano, 485
Sapiro, Gisèle, 8, 209–210, 349
Sarkozy, Nicolas, 9, 271, 276, 285, 519
Saro-Wiwa, Ken, 308
Sarruf, Yaqub, 170

Sartre, Jean Paul, 92
Sassoon, Donald, 173
Saussy, Haun, 139, 142, 348
Scherr, Johannes, 37
Schiffrin, André, 212, 219
Schiller, Friedrich, 38, 86, 90, 377, 381
Schlegel, August Wilhelm, 321–322
Schmidt, Johannes, 165
Schopenhauer, Arthur, 35, 38, 92
Schulze, Hagen, 23
Schwab, Raymond, 320–321
Schwarz, Roberto, 161–165, 170, 175
Scott, Walter, 21, 170, 176, 201
Sebbar, Leïla, 299
Seferis, George, 91
Sei Shonagon, 90
Seidman, Naomi, 352
Sen, Amartya, 381, 412
Sen, Keshub Chander, 325
Senghor, Léopold Sédar, 277, 289
Serry, Hervé, 223, 225
Seth, Vikram, 406, 414
Seyhan, Azade, 32
Shakespeare, William, 20, 40, 59, 62, 66, 89, 92, 243, 254, 321, 394, 397
Shaw, George Bernard, 197, 201, 397
Shcherbakova, Allá, 490
Shehzad, Nadeem, 382, 383
Shelley, Percy Bysshe, 92, 142, 145
Shen, Zemin, 63
Shiga Naoya, 91
Shih, Shu-mei, 141, 293, 300
Sholem, Aleichem, 82
Sholokhov, Mikhail, 93
Shu Wu, 261, 262
Shukla, Ramchandra, 334
Shuʿayb, ʿAlim, 452
Sikelianos, Angelos, 91
Silko, Leslie Marmon, 430
Simon, Paul, 482
Simon, Sherry, 239
Sivathamby, K., 145
Smith, George, 380, 379
Smith, Linda Tuhiwai, 143, 157
Smith, Neil, 423, 425
Smith, Wilbur, 408
Soja, Edward, 428

Sollers, Philippe, 284
Sollors, Werner, 348
Sommer, Doris, 163
Sophocles, 20–21
Soret, M., 16
Sorolla Manero, Pilar, 172
Soseki, Natsume, 91
Soyinka, Wole, 372
Spemann, Adolf, 89–90
Spencer, Herbert, 42
Spillers, Hortense, 428
Spingarn, Joel Elias, 59
Spitzer, Susan, 356
Spivak, Gayatri Chakravorty, 9, 135–136, 141, 347–348, 363, 520
Stalin, Joseph, 83, 87
Steel, Flora Annie, 134
Stein, Gertrude, 203
Stein, Rolf A., 88, 91
Steinecke, Hartmut, 31
Stendhal, 166
Stevens, Wallace, 264, 420
Sting [Gordon Sumner], 482
Stolberg, Count, 514
Strindberg, August, 203
Subercaseaux, Bernardo, 403
Sugiya Yoshito, 473
Suidas, 44
Sukehiro Hirakawa, 364
Suleri, Sara, 323
Šulgi of Ur, King, 3
Sun Tzu, 95
Surel, Yves, 218
Suroor, Rajab Ali Beg, 334
Svit, Brina, 275
Swift, Jonathan, 397
Sydow, Max von, 487
Symons, Arthur, 59

Tadié, Jean-Yves, 301
Tagore, Rabindranath, 6, 47, 59, 90, 321, 325, 374, 377, 379, 381–382, 386, 414, 520–521
Taine, Hippolyte, 59, 82
Takeuchi Yoshimi, 470
Tanizaki Junichiro, 91
Tashi Dawa, 2

Tasso, Torquato, 26, 267
Taylor, Edward, 418
Taymour, Mahmoud, 92
Teng, Teresa, 260
Tennyson, Alfred, 55
Terrell, Carroll, 505
Tétu, Michel, 286
Thatcher, Margaret, 425
Theocritus, 45
Thiers, Adolphe, 354
Thompson, Edward Palmer, 128
Thompson, John B., 218
Thomsen, Mads Rosendahl, 515
Thoreau, Henry David, 431
Thornber, Karen Laura, 10, 460
Thorsteinsson, Steingrimur, 40
Thrasymachus, 358
Tirado Bramen, Carrie, 422
Todorov, Tzvetan, 112
Toledo, Camille de, 306–307
Tolstoy, Leo, 354–355
Tomlinson, J., 210
Torabully, Khal, 300–301
Torre, Guillermo de, 87
Toschi, Luca, 163
Tötösy de Zepetnek, Steven, 136
Toukaram, 95
Toury, Gideon, 230, 240
Trivedi, Harish, 157, 239–240, 414–415
Trouillot, Lyonel, 275, 287
Trumpener, Katie, 348
Twain, Mark, 308, 395
Tymoczko, Maria, 237–238
Tzara, Tristan, 298

Ueda Akinari, 90
Ueda Bin, 91
umkaSetemba, Lydia, 409
Updike, John, 429–430

Vallaeys, Anne, 275
Valmiki, Omprakash, 148, 150
Vargas Llosa, Mario, 198
Vautrin, Jean, 275
Veblen, Thorstein, 396
Velter, André, 275
Venuti, Lawrence, 210, 240

Vergil, 45
Victor, Gary, 275, 289
Vieira, José Luandino, 410
Vigne, Éric, 219
Vincent, J., 213
Vincent-Munnia, Nathalie, 301
Viswanathan, Gauri, 142, 296, 348
Vivekananda, Swami, 325
Voge, Marc, 493
Vogler, Rüdiger, 486
Volokhonsky, Larissa, 354

Waberi, Abdourahman, 275, 282, 295, 299
Wacquant, Loïc J.D., 230
Wajdi, Mouawad, 275
Walcott, Derek, 226
Wali, Umar, 452
Walkowitz, Rebecca, 348
Wallerstein, Immanuel, 7, 159, 161,
    180–185, 189, 199, 209–210, 213, 289,
    345, 428, 517
Wallia, C.J.S., 406–407
Walsh, William, 412
Wang Chong, 89, 93, 95, 163
Warring, Edward, 330
Watanabe Kazuo, 91
Weber, Max, 160
Weber, Samuel, 347
Wellek, René, 27, 29, 142, 364, 371
Wellesley, Richard,
    1st Marquess Wellesley, 330
Wells, H.G., 67
Wenders, Wim, 484, 486, 488–490
West, Cornel, 422
Whitman, Walt, 419
Wilfert, Blaise, 349
Wilkins, Charles, 322, 324–325
Williams, Melissa, 374
Williams, Raymond, 124–127, 377

Williams, Tennessee, 366
Williams, William Carlos, 422
Wilson, H.H., 141
Winkin, Yves, 213
Wittgenstein, Ludwig, 351, 358
Wolff, Mark, 296
Wolton, Dominique, 281
Wood, Michael, 347
Woodmansee, Martha, 27
Woolf, Virginia, 391
Wordsworth, William, 82, 243, 254

Xenophon, 267

Yacine, Kateb, 198, 285, 315, 518
Yang Kwei-fei, 91
Yang Zhaoquan, 470
Yeats, William Butler, 47
Yi-qun Wang, 490
Yokota-Murakami, Takayuki, 140, 157
Yoshida, Tomio, 473
Yu Jian, 258, 262
Yu Lik-wai, 489
Yu, Pauline, 140

Zaman, Muhammad Qasim, 449
Zangwill, Israel, 422
Zeami, 90–93
Zhang Longxi, 10, 140, 142, 513
Zhao, Henry Y.H., 163–164, 170, 175
Zheng Yi, 474
Zheng Zhenduo, 6, 58–59, 521
Zhitlovsky, Khaim, 79
Zhong Qing'an, 471–472
Zhou Zuoren, 64
Zhu Tianxin, 465–468, 472
Zhuangzi, 89, 95
Žižek, Slavoj, 287–288
Zuern, John, 502